Buy
Wholesale
By
Mail
1998

BUY WHOLESALE BY MAIL 1998

BY THE PRINT PROJECT
AND THE ENLIGHTENED SHOPPER®

Lowell Miller, Executive Producer
Prudence McCullough, Executive Editor

HarperPerennial
A Division of HarperCollins*Publishers*

HarperCollins books may be purchased for educational, business, or sales promotional use. For information please write to: Special Markets Department, HarperCollins Publishers, Inc., 10 East 53rd Street, New York, NY 10022.

FIRST HARPERPERENNIAL EDITION
ISSN 1049-0116
ISBN 0-06-273438-5
97 98 99 ✦/RRD 4 3 2 1

CONTENTS

USING THIS BOOK

Buy Wholesale By Mail 1998 is written to help consumers get good values when buying by mail—or phone, fax, or modem. In this book, "wholesale" denotes the savings required as one of the qualifications for a listing—30% or more on list or comparable retail on some of a firm's products or services. Some of the firms will sell to crafters, small businesses, and others on a wholesale basis. Those firms are denoted with a star in the icon line in their listings. For details, see "Buying at Wholesale," page 602.

There are other icons that will help you get the most from the information, so before sending for a catalog or placing an order, please read the key to the symbols in "The Listing Code" (from page xi). For more detailed information on mail-order shopping, see "The Complete Guide to Buying by Mail," beginning on page 597.

Following is a guide to several of this book's features that will help you make the best use of the material.

"FIND IT FAST"

This list, right after the introduction and before the listings (in most of the chapters), is an at-a-glance guide to different types of products offered by firms listed in that section. For example, if you're looking for companies selling contact lenses and eyeglasses, check the "Find it Fast" roster in the "Medicine and Science" chapter instead of reading through all of the listings. "Find it Fast" supplements the Product Index and the "See Also" section (see below) at the end of each chapter.

"SEE ALSO"

Each firm is listed in the chapter that best reflects its business focus, and *cross-referenced* in the "See Also" sections at the end of other chapters, as appropriate. For example, Gohn Bros. is listed in the "Clothing" chapter because that's its strong suit. Because Gohn also sells horse blankets, you'll find it cited in the "See Also" section at the end of the

"Animal Supplies" chapter. See "Find It Fast," above, for another aid to locating what you need.

PATIENCE

Since companies are constantly revising their catalogs and printing new ones, please allow *six to eight weeks* for delivery, unless the listing indicates potential for a longer delay. If the catalog doesn't arrive within the designated period, write or call the company. Please remember that some products, such as flower bulbs and highly perishable foods, can be ordered only at certain times of the year, and catalogs may be mailed during shipping season only.

PRICE QUOTES

Some firms don't issue catalogs at all. Most of these operate under a price-quote system: You tell them the exact make and model number of the item you want, and they give you the price and shipping cost. Price quotes are given by mail, phone, and fax. Businesses that operate this way are clearly indicated in the listings. (Be sure to check the "Special Factors" notes at the end of each listing as well as the core information.) Price-quote firms often have the lowest prices on such goods as appliances, audio and TV components, and furniture; they usually sell well below both the standard manufacturers' suggested list prices and the less-formal minimum prices that some manufacturers try to enforce. Before writing or calling for a price quote or making a purchase in this way, remember to read the "Price Quotes" section of "The Complete Guide to Buying by Mail."

MINIMUM ORDERS

In a few cases, the best buys are available from firms that require a minimum order in dollars or goods. Minimum requirements are usually flexible, and most firms will accept orders below the minimum, although an extra "handling fee" is often imposed. If you want something that's a real bargain, you may have friends who'll want it as well.

BEFORE SENDING MONEY

If you're unsure of any company, or want to double-check a firm before placing a large order, contact the Better Business Bureau nearest the company. You can locate it by phone, through directory assistance (the firm's area code–555–1212), or by looking it up in the current list of member Bureaus, available free by sending *a stamped, self-addressed envelope* to Council of Better Business Bureaus, 4200 Wilson Blvd., Suite 800, Arlington, VA 22203. If you call, you may be given a report over the phone, or you may be asked to write instead.

A CAVEAT

Buy Wholesale By Mail 1998 is compiled as a resource for consumers, to help you to find good values available by mail. *Never* order goods directly from this book, even if prices are given in the listing. *Always* contact the company first to get a catalog or a current price quote, and follow specific ordering and payment instructions. *Don't request extra discounts or wholesale prices, unless the listing states they are available. Attempting to bargain with these firms makes the vendors quite unhappy.* All of the information in this book is based on research and fact-checking as of press time, and is subject to change.

Enjoy *Buy Wholesale By Mail 1998,* and please report on your experiences with these firms—see "Feedback," page 635, for address information.

THE LISTING CODE

Some of the information in the listings is presented in a simple, coded form at the head of each entry, formatted as follows:

1. Company name, mailing address, and phone numbers, including 800, fax, e-mail, and TDD lines
2. **Catalog:** Form of literature (catalog, brochure, flyer, leaflet, price list, etc.); the price, followed by "refundable" or "deductible" if you can redeem the cost by placing an order; SASE: send a long (business-sized), self-addressed envelope with a first-class stamp (unless more postage is requested); "Information": price quote or information is given over the phone and/or by letter (when there is no catalog)
3. **Pay:** methods of payment accepted for orders (catalog fees should be paid by check or money order unless the listing states otherwise), listed in order of frequency accepted:
   - check: personal check
   - MO: bank or postal money order
   - MC: MasterCard credit card
   - V: VISA credit card
   - AE: American Express credit card
   - CB: Carte Blanche credit card
   - DC: Diners Club credit card
   - Discover: Discover credit card
   - NOVUS: NOVUS credit card
   - JCB: JCB credit card
   - BRAVO: BRAVO credit card
4. **Sells:** general type of goods/services sold
5. **Store:** location(s), hours, and/or phone number(s) of the firm's retail site or other outlets, if applicable
6. **E-mail:** e-mail address
7. **Online:** URL (http) address on the Internet or through an online provider, if applicable

❧ THE MAPLE LEAF

This symbol means the firm will ship goods to Canada. Canadian shoppers should check current import restrictions and tariffs before placing an order, and request shipping charges or an estimate before finalizing the order. *Please note:* U.S. firms generally request payment for goods *and* catalogs in U.S. funds, and may stipulate that payment be drawn on a U.S. bank, or paid via postal money order.

🏴 THE FLAG

A small "Old Glory" on the symbol line means the firm will ship goods to APO and FPO (U.S. military) addresses. For more information, see "Shipments Abroad," page 614.

⊕ THE WORLD

A small globe on the symbol line means the firm has stated that it will ship goods worldwide. Readers ordering from or having goods delivered abroad should read the listing before sending for a catalog; check with local authorities to make sure products can be imported, what restrictions may apply, and what tariffs may be charged. For more information, see "Shipments Abroad," page 614.

¡Si! SPANISH SPOKEN HERE

This icon means that the firm has Spanish-speaking sales representatives on staff. Before calling a company so indicated, read the listing and the "Special Factors" notes, since the person's availability may be limited to certain hours or days.

ℂ THE TDD SYMBOL

This symbol indicates that the firm can communicate with a TDD (telecommunication device for the deaf. In most cases, the firm uses a separate phone line for the equipment; sometimes, it's combined with a fax line. Read the listing, and if a separate phone line or other information isn't noted, send for the catalog.

★ THE "WHOLESALE" STAR

Firms so marked will sell at wholesale rates to *qualified individuals or other firms*. To sell to you at genuine wholesale, most firms require proof that you're running a company—a business card, letterhead, resale number, or all three—and may impose different minimum orders and sell under terms different from those that apply to retail purchases. Please note that, unless specified, all information in these listings applies to consumer transactions only. For more information, see "Buying at Wholesale," page 602.

THE "INTERNET ONLY" SYMBOL

Firms so marked *do not publish a catalog* and *do not give price quotes over the phone*. They require you to use their websites to access product information and initiate orders. (Note that none requires you to *complete* an order online.) The symbol indicates that you *must* have Internet access to do business with the company. Please note that the addresses and phone numbers of such firms are provided solely as references for readers who've placed orders, and to show that the company does have a physical location. *Do not call or write to request catalogs, literature, or prices.*

THE COMPLETE GUIDE TO BUYING BY MAIL

This primer on mail-order shopping, which begins on page 597, can help you with questions on everything from sending for catalogs to interpreting warranties. If a problem arises with a mail-order transaction, look here for help in resolving it. You'll find additional consumer information in the chapter introductions.

Buy
Wholesale
By
Mail
1998

ANIMAL SUPPLIES

Livestock and pet supplies and equipment,
veterinary instruments and biologicals,
live-animal referrals, and services

Owning a pet, especially a cat or a dog, has been shown to be beneficial for people suffering from a range of maladies. Having one may help prolong your life, lower your blood pressure and cholesterol levels, and reduce the incidence of backaches, headaches, and colds you suffer. Pets are now widely used in programs for nursing-home patients, hospitalized children, and psychiatric patients.

If you're thinking about getting a pet, make sure you're picking the best companion for your needs and lifestyle. "The Veterinarian's Way of Selecting a Proper Pet" asks a series of questions to help you define your criteria for the ideal animal. The brochure is available upon request; send a long, stamped, self-addressed envelope with your letter to the American Veterinary Medical Association, Suite 100, 1931 N. Meacham Rd., Schaumburg, IL 60173–4360. Once you've decided on the kind of animal you want, don't rush to the pet store: Seek out pet shelters and animal orphanages, where you can spare an animal a questionable fate *and* save money. Even purebreds can be acquired inexpensively, when a "purebred rescue" group takes in an animal no longer wanted by its owner and holds it for adoption. If your local animal shelter doesn't have information on groups that perform this service, write to Project Breed Inc., 18707 Curry Powder Lane, Germantown, MD 20874 (include a long, stamped, self-addressed envelope). If the dog of your dreams happens to be a greyhound, you may be able to adopt a former racetrack star. For information on the greyhound rescue group nearest you, write to the National Greyhound

Adoption Network, c/o Palo Alto Humane Society, P.O. Box 60715, Palo Alto, CA 94306.

Most of us are unaware of the long-term price of ownership: The typical cat or dog will cost you an average of $9,000 to $12,000 over its lifetime. Much of this expense is food and vet bills, but a portion is the other pet necessities—leashes, toys, carriers, grooming tools and supplies, beds, etc. Fortunately, there's now an alternative to buying pet products from the grocery store, pet boutique, or from the vet-pet superstores. Based on the successful office and home-improvement models, they offer varying savings on food, grooming products, cages, supplies, and a wide range of pet needs. Petco, Petstuff, and PETsMART are the major contenders, and if there's one near you, check the prices on food and litter against the discounts a local pet store may give on case purchases, and see if they'll deliver. The companies listed here won't give you great deals on heavy cans of food and bags of litter—the cost of shipping usually offsets the savings. But check the prices of collars and leashes, cages and carriers, feeding dishes and devices, grooming tools, beds, and medications. These firms carry products for a wide range of animals—from hamsters and ferrets to horses and barnyard animals—and all can save you money.

Mastering the basics of pet care can also save you considerable sums in a variety of ways—in salon costs, the price of obedience school, and sometimes even on vet fees. Hundreds of books and periodicals are available—on breeding, nutrition, training and behavior, grooming, and other aspects of pet care, for every type of animal. The easiest way to get acquainted with what's available is to consult a catalog of current publications. If you own a canine or feline, you'll appreciate the "Dog & Cat Book Catalog" from Direct Book Service. The current issue is 48 pages of books on care, breeds, pet travel, selection, kennel and cattery management, and many other topics, with a special emphasis on dog training, for professionals and pet owners. Standard reference works and encyclopedias are also listed. For a copy of the catalog, call 800–776–2665 or 509–663–9115, e-mail dgctbook@cascade.net, or write to Direct Book Service, P.O. Box 2778, Wenatchee, WA 98807–2778; the website is http://www.dogandcatbooks.com/.

Bird lovers will find helpful videos, CDs, and a full range of supplies at The Bird House. See the website for information (http://www.acmepet.com/birdhous/) or, for a copy of the catalog, e-mail birdhous@bright.net, call 800–992–2473, or write to The Bird House, Inc., 4256 Center Rd., Brunswick, OH 44212. And you can help your vet gain access to help with bird problems, through the Avian Referral Service. Your vet should write to AAHA, Avian Referral Service, P.O. Box 15899, Denver, CO 80215, for more information.

Horse fans have a wonderful resource in The Book Stable, a catalog of books, magazines, and videos on all aspects of horse ownership. The Book Stable offers nearly 40 magazine titles alone (and initiates and renews subscriptions), as well as hundreds of books and videos on every aspect of horse ownership and care. You can see the current offerings listed on the website (http://www.bookstable.com/) or send for the catalog (free, or $2.50 if sent outside the U.S.): e-mail bookmaster@bookstable.com, call 800–274–2665, or write to The Book Stable, Dept. WBMC, 5326 Tomahawk Trail, Fort Wayne, IN 46804, for a copy.

Several of the firms listed in this chapter retain veterinarians who can answer questions on products and use, but usually won't give specific medical advice. If your pet is ailing, consult a vet, and *always* seek professional guidance if you plan to administer any vaccines or medications yourself. To safeguard your pet's well-being, make sure you have the number of a local 24-hour service that handles medical emergencies posted near the phone, and become familiar with symptoms and the first-aid measures you may have to take in order to transport the animal to the clinic.

FIND IT FAST

BIRDS • **Kennel Vet, KV Vet, Omaha Vaccine, Pet Warehouse, R.C. Steele, That Fish Place, Tomahawk Live Trap, United Pharmacal**
FISH • **Daleco, Jeffers, Pet Warehouse, That Fish Place**
HORSES • **Dairy Association, Discount Master Animal Care, Jeffers, Kennel Vet, KV Vet, State Line Tack, United Pharmacal, Valley Vet Supply**
LIVESTOCK • **Dairy Association, Jeffers, KV Vet, Omaha Vaccine, Valley Vet Supply**
PETS (DOGS AND CATS) • **Discount Master Animal Care, Drs. Foster & Smith, Dog's Outfitter, Jeffers, Kennel Vet, KV Vet, Pet Warehouse, R.C. Steele, Valley Vet Supply**
REPTILES AND SMALL ANIMALS • **Dog's Outfitter, Jeffers, KV Vet, Pet Warehouse, That Fish Place, United Pharmacal**
TRAPS • **Tomahawk Live Trap**
VET, KENNEL, AND GROOMER • **Discount Master Animal Care, Drs. Foster & Smith, Dog's Outfitter, J-B Wholesale, Kennel Vet, KV Vet, Omaha Vaccine, R.C. Steele, United Pharmacal, Valley Vet Supply**

THE BIRD HOUSE

4256 CENTER RD.
BRUNSWICK, OH 44212
800–992–2473
330–225–7682

Catalog: free
Pay: check, MO, MC, V, AE, Discover
Sells: bird cages, toys, food, videos, etc.
Store: mail order only
E-mail: birdhous@acmepet.com
Online: http://www.acmepet.com/birdhous

Whether your feathered friend hails from the pet department at Woolworth or a more pedigreed perch, it requires food, amusements, and a cage. The Bird House offers these and more, at prices that average 30% off list.

The 18-page catalog shows cages that run up to 3 square feet, in three colors. Skirts, "mess catchers," water bottles, seed cups, Acrobird playgrounds and ladders, and perch upgrades—manzanita branches and wire rope "bird bouncers"—are available. You can warm the cage area with full-spectrum Chromalux bulbs—the full line is carried. The Bird House also sells both food (Quiko, seed, pellets, powder, hand-feeding formula) and treats, which run from "Madagascar Delight" to "mega millet." The bribe material may come in handy if you invest in one of the Teach Your Bird to Talk cassettes or videos. When lessons are over, reward your bird with some nonverbal fun—like a basketball game, ring toss, or skateboard (instructions are included). The catalog descriptions are quite brief, but you can get more information on the website. In addition to bird supplies, The Bird House can get pet products for your dog, cat, or small animal; inquire for information.

Special Factors: Satisfaction is guaranteed; returns are accepted for exchange, refund, or credit; C.O.D. orders are accepted.

DAIRY ASSOCIATION CO., INC.

DEPT. WBMC

P.O. BOX 145

LYNDONVILLE, VT

05851–0145

802–626–3610

FAX: 802–626–3433

Brochure and Price List: free
Pay: check or MO
Sells: livestock treatments and leather balm
Store: mail order only

Dairy Association Co., Inc. is known to generations of herd farmers for Bag Balm, an unguent formulated to soothe the chapped, sunburned udders of cows. It's also recommended by horse trainers for cracked heels, galls, cuts, hobble burns, and other ailments, and is "great as a sweat" as well. Bag Balm can be used on sheep, goats, dogs, and cats, and is touted as a softener for weather-beaten, chapped hands. A 10-ounce can is $5.55 here; a 4½-pound pail costs just over $37. (A 1-ounce size, great for travel, is also offered.) Green Mt. Horse Products, a division of Dairy Association, produces Hoof Softener—made of petrolatum, lanolin, and vegetable oils, it helps keep hoofs pliable and sound ($4.65 per pint). Tackmaster—a one-step, all-around conditioner, cleaner, and preservative for leather—is cheaper than similar products. Dairy Association has been in business since 1889, and provides product literature free on request.

Canadian readers, please note: Contact Dr. A.D. Daniels Co. Ltd., N. Rock Island, Quebec, for prices and ordering information.

Special Factors: Phone orders are accepted for C.O.D. payment.

DALECO MASTER BREEDER PRODUCTS

3556 N. 400 EAST
WARSAW, IN 46580–7999
800–987–1120
219–268–6300
FAX: 219–268–6302

Catalog: free (see text)
Pay: check, MO, MC, V, Discover
Sells: tropical fish supplies and aquarium specialties
Store: mail order only
E-mail: Daleco@kconline.com

Daleco, in business since 1966, publishes a 120-page catalog/reference book that's packed with information useful to owners of fresh- and salt-water fish. Daleco discounts tank filters, aquarium heaters, lights, chillers, air and water pumps, foods, water test kits, UV water sterilizers, water conditioners, reef trickle filter systems, and related goods. The brands include Aquanetics, Aquarium Products, Aquarium Systems, Eugene Danner, Dupla, Ebo-Jager, Energy Savers, Hagen, Hawaiian Marine, Hikari, Jungle Laboratories, Kordon, Little Giant, Lustar, Mardel, Marineland, Perfecto, Sanders, Tetra, Vortex, and WISA. The catalog is useful to both incidental and serious hobbyists, and Daleco's staff is knowledgeable and helpful.

International readers, please note: the manual costs $10 (in U.S. funds) via airmail.

Special Factors: Shipping included on orders over $50 sent via UPS in the contiguous U.S.; C.O.D. orders are accepted; authorized returns are accepted.

DISCOUNT MASTER ANIMAL CARE

ONE MAPLEWOOD DR.
HAZLETON, PA 18201
800–346–0749
FAX: 717–384–2500

Catalog: free
Pay: check, MO, MC, V, Discover
Sells: dog, cat, ferret, and small-animal supplies
Store: same address; open first Friday (10–6) and Saturday (10–4) of each month

Discount Master Animal Care specializes in dog and cat health supplies, sold at highly competitive prices through the 72-page catalog, which includes helpful information on health care and vaccinating procedures, and includes products for both cats and dogs. You'll find grooming tools, a range of cages, feeding devices, training aids, leashes and leads, and related goods here, at prices up to 50% below list. Vet supplies—such as vaccines, biologicals, and medications—are also available. Discount Master Animal Care offers the latest innovations in pet products, such as airline-approved cages in designer colors, timer-operated feeding dishes that keep two meals fresh, natural and biodegradable cleaners and disinfectants, pet car seats and harnesses, and hot-oil skin treatments for dogs and cats. But it's also a good place to save on pet beds and cartons of rawhide bones—and pet-theme gifts and crafts kits.

Special Factors: Satisfaction is guaranteed; returns are accepted for exchange, refund, or credit.

DRS. FOSTER & SMITH INC.

2253 AIR PARK RD.
P.O. BOX 100
RHINELANDER, WI
54501–0100
800–826–7206
FAX: 800–776–8872

Catalog: free
Pay: check, MO, MC, V, AE, Discover
Sells: dog and cat supplies
Store: mail order only

As "The Company Owned and Operated by Practicing Veterinarians," Doctors Foster & Smith (the actual people) provide owners of cats and dogs with quality products for health, nutrition, and fun.

The color catalog shows beds and mats, cat perches and scratching posts, nutritional supplements and biologicals, grooming tools and products, lots of toys and rawhide bones and treats, leashes and collars (including a "no-pull humane anti-tug system" that won't choke your dog, and a cat muzzle), feeding dishes, cages and carriers, and much more. The catalog is clearly written, with complete product descriptions and helpful sidebars on topics of interest (the role of ash in the diet, heat strokes, how the doctors selected their rawhide bones, how to measure pets for collars, traveling with your pet, etc.). Doctors Foster & Smith also sells books, videos, and training audiotapes, and if that's not enough, on Tuesdays and Thursdays you can speak to a staff vet on general pet issues and health care. The special vet hotline number is in the current issue of the catalog.

Special Factors: Satisfaction is guaranteed; returns are accepted.

THE DOG'S OUTFITTER

DEPT. WBMC
I MAPLEWOOD DR.
HAZLETON, PA 18201
800–367–3647
717–384–5555
FAX: 717–384–2500

Catalog: free
Pay: check, MO, MC, V, AE, Discover
Sells: vet, kennel, groomer, and pet supplies
Store: mail order only

Although The Dog's Outfitter catalog is geared to professionals, it has one of the best selections of products for pet owners around. The firm has been in business since 1969, and is exclusive in name only—the 104-page catalog is full of things for cats, and there's even a section devoted to the needs of ferrets. The Dog's Outfitter offers a full range of pet products, including grooming tools, shampoo, flea and tick collars and insecticides, cages, gates and doors, training aids, feeding and watering equipment, nutritional supplements, collars and leads, pet beds, carriers, toys and bones, and even books and gifts. The brands include Andis, Bio-Groom, 8–1, Farnum, General Cage, Gimborn, Hava-hart, Lambert Kay, Oster, Penn Plex, Resco, Ring 5, Speedy, André Tis-serand (shears), Twinco, and Zodiac.

Pet owners should appreciate the molting combs for dogs and cats, no-tears pet shampoo, herbal flea collars, pet doors made to fit screen doors, the selection of yard scoops, feeding bowls and crocks, "small animal" nurser kits, reflective collars and leads, dog parkas, bulk rawhide bones, and toys in boxes of 50. There are gifts, pet jewelry (for owners), note cards, and books (Arco, Howell, T.F.H.); grooming videos from Oster, and Animal Academy training tapes. The Dog's Outfitter has its own ware-house, does not drop ship, and pays for shipping on most items.

Canadian and APO/FPO readers, please note: Shipments are not made to Canada or APO/FPO addresses.

Special Factors: Satisfaction is guaranteed; shipping is not charged on most items; authorized returns of new and unused goods are accepted within 10 days for exchange, refund, or credit; minimum order is $75; C.O.D. orders are accepted on shipments within the U.S. only.

J-B WHOLESALE PET SUPPLIES, INC.

**5 RARITAN RD., DEPT. WB
OAKLAND, NJ 07436
201–405–1111
FAX: 201–405–1706**

Catalog: free
Pay: check, MO, MC, V, AE, Discover
Sells: vet, kennel, and pet supplies
Store: 289 Wagaraw Rd., Hawthorne, NJ,
and 347 Ramapo Valley Rd., Oakland, NJ;
Monday to Wednesday 9–6, Thursday and
Friday 9–8, Saturday 10–5, Sunday 11–4
E-mail: jbpet@intac.com
Online: http://www.jbpet.com

J-B Wholesale Pet Supplies, in business since 1981, stocks "over 8,500 different items for showing, grooming, training, breeding," and other animal-related functions. J-B is staffed by professional animal handlers who've kennel-tested all of the products the company sells.

The 72-page catalog features a wide range of goods for cats and dogs, with the emphasis on canines: remedies for common health problems, vitamins and nutritional supplements, repellents and deodorizers, shampoos and grooming products, beds and mats, flea and tick control products, cages, kennels, pet doors, grooming tables and dryers, leashes and leads, feeding devices, rawhide bones, and plush and rubber toys. Every major manufacturer is represented, and J-B's own line of grooming aids— shampoo and coat conditioners and tints—is also featured. Send for the catalog, or call for prices and availability on specific name-brand items.

Special Factors: Satisfaction is guaranteed; C.O.D. orders are accepted; returns are accepted within seven days for exchange, refund, or credit; minimum order is $25.

JEFFERS VET SUPPLY

P.O. BOX 100
DOTHAN, AL 36302-0100
800-JEFFERS
FAX: 334-793-5179

Catalog: free
Pay: check, MO, MC, V, Discover
Sells: animal health supplies
Store: 353 West Inez Rd., Dothan, AL; also
Old Airport Rd., West Plains, MO; every day
6 a.m.–10 p.m., both locations

 ¡Si!

Jeffers Vet Supply, in business since 1976, publishes a 160-page quarterly catalog of supplies for livestock farmers and anyone who keeps a horse, as well as goods for cats, dogs, fish, and even rabbits, iguanas, and ferrets. Livestock farmers who raise cattle (including dairy), swine, sheep, goats, and poultry should see the catalog for antibiotics and sulfa drugs, biologicals, wormers, milking equipment, incubators, and other necessities. The horse catalog is devoted to equine supplies—biologicals and nutritional supplements, wormers, grooming tools and products, farrier supplies, stable equipment, and tack—including several pages of saddles. Equine videotapes by Al Dunning and John Lyons are also available. The separate pet catalog includes goods for dogs and cats—everything from the newest flea and tick products to collars, cages, clippers, toys, and grooming and feeding supplies are available.

Special Factors: Satisfaction is guaranteed; quantity discounts are available; returns are accepted for exchange, refund, or credit; C.O.D. orders are accepted.

KENNEL VET CORP.

DEPT. WBMC
P.O. BOX 4092
FARMINGDALE, NY
  11735-0793
800-782-0627
FAX: 516-694-3751
FAX: 302-875-1310

Catalog: $1 (see text)
Pay: check, MO, MC, V, AE, Discover
Sells: vet, kennel, cattery, and pet supplies
Store: mail order only

   ★

If you own or raise dogs or cats, you'll find Kennel Vet's compact, 70-page catalog great reading. This firm is price-competitive on products for horses, as well as house pets, and has been family-owned and run since 1971.

Kennel Vet offers vaccines and biologicals, remedies for common health problems, vitamins and nutritional supplements, repellents and deodorizers, and other professional products. Kennel Vet also sells droppings digesters, shampoos and grooming products, flea and tick control products, cages/crates, pet doors, dog and cat beds, grooming tables, dryers, collars, leads, feeding devices, rawhide bones and rubber toys, and other goods. The brands represented include Adams, Allerderm, Defend, Doskocil (carriers), DVM, Evsco, Gem-Line, General Cage, Gimborn-Redi, Goodwinol, Johnson, Lambert Kay, Lawrence (brushes), Mid-West, Oster, Pet Tabs, Pfizer, Ring 5, Safari, Sulfodene, Vet-Kem, and others. The book and video department offers veterinary manuals, books on dog breeds, and a selection on cats, birds, and horses—all at a discount.

Special Factors: Authorized returns are accepted; shipping is not charged on orders of $75 or more (with some exceptions—see the catalog); vaccines and biologicals are sent where ordinances permit.

KV VET SUPPLY CO., INC.

P.O. BOX 245
DAVID CITY, NE 68632
800–423–8211
402–367–6047
FAX: 800–269–0093

Catalog: free
Pay: check, MO, MC, V, AE, Discover
Sells: vet and pet supplies and equipment
Store: South Hwy. 92 and 15, David City, NE; Monday to Friday 8–5, Saturday 9–12 CT

Reader-recommended KV Vet Supply Co. was founded in 1979 to provide pet owners with veterinary supplies, and the firm has since added equine and livestock needs. KV publishes a 208-page catalog with over 4,000 different products for animal health care, grooming, training, working, showing, and other equipment to serve the needs of all of your animals—dogs, cats, horses, cattle, hogs, sheep, goats, llamas, ferrets, birds, and rabbits—at wholesale prices. You'll find vaccines, nutritional supplements, insecticides, wormers, antibiotics, topicals, shampoos, prescription drugs, tack, books and videos, and much more. Some of the firms represented include Fort Dodge, Veterinarian's Best, Happy Jack, Lambert Kay, Doskocil, Midwest Cages, Oster, Farnam,

Vetri-Science, Les Vogt, Professional Choice, Courbette, Big Horn, and American Saddlery. KV Vet Supply has nearly 40,000 square feet of inventory, so most items can be shipped immediately. The firm has a "dedicated staff of over 60 employees," who "understand the needs of animal owners"—and prices up to 70% below list!

Special Factors: Shipping is included (except on "FOB" items); minimum order is $40; C.O.D. orders are accepted.

OMAHA VACCINE COMPANY, INC.

P.O. BOX 7228
3030 L ST.
OMAHA, NE 68107
800–367–4444
402–731–9600
FAX: 800–242–9447
FAX: 402–731–9829

Catalog: free
Pay: check, MO, MC, V, Discover
Sells: dog, cat, bird, horse, and livestock supplies
Store: same address; order hours Monday to Friday 7–10, Saturday 8–8, Sunday 9–6; other locations in Sioux Falls, SD; Lincoln, NE; Independence and Kansas City, MO; and Rochester, MN

Omaha Vaccine Company was established in 1965 to serve the needs of livestock producers, breeders, and veterinarians. Since then, the firm has expanded to include equine and companion animals. Omaha's three specialty catalogs feature vaccines, antibiotics, topical treatments, surgical instruments, grooming tools, dewormers, carriers, leads, collars, saddles, tack, blankets, and pet apparel. Prescription products are available (the original prescription, written by the attending veterinarian, must be mailed to Omaha with the accompanying order and payment). Omaha Vaccine is dedicated to providing whatever you need for the health of your livestock, horse, or pet, and veterinary consultation services can be arranged. You can use the 800 number to request "Best Care Pet Catalog," "First Place Equine Catalog," or "Professional Livestock Producer Catalog." Whether you're looking for flea treatments for your dog or opening a llama farm, you'll appreciate Omaha's 20,000 products and wholesale pricing.

Special Factors: Some pharmaceutical products are available by prescription only (shipment is subject to local ordinances).

PET WAREHOUSE

DEPT. BMC 98
915 TRUMBULL ST.
XENIA, OH 45385
800–443–1160
937–374–9800
FAX: 800–513–1913
FAX: 937–374–2524

Catalogs: free (see text)
Pay: check, MO, MC, V, AE, Discover
Sells: pet supplies
Store: mail order only
E-mail: petwhse@erinet.com
Online: http://www.petwhse.com

The polished color catalogs from Pet Warehouse are among the best around for the typical pet owner, who probably doesn't need a wall-sized aquarium, but wants good prices on basics and neat pet stuff. The firm has been in business since 1986, and sells supplies for cats, dogs, birds, fish, small animals, reptiles, and ponds. The inventory has been split into five catalogs—one for fish, the second for dogs and cats, the third for small animals and reptiles, the fourth for birds, and the fifth for ponds; please specify which one you want when you call or write.

Whether you have a freshwater or marine aquarium, or even a pond, Pet Warehouse can supply you with filters, air pumps, heaters, feeders, lighting, maintenance equipment and water conditioners, tank decorations and plants, fish medication, food, and other fish goods—but no tanks. The brands include Aquarium Pharmaceuticals, Eheim, Hagen, Marineland, Perfecto, Rainbow Lifeguard, and Tetra, among others. Bird owners can choose from Hagen and Prevue Hendryx cages, Acrobird perches and play structures, cage accessories and bird toys, nests, feeders, bird food from Fiesta, Kaytee, LaFeber's, and other firms, and dietary supplements and medication. For dogs and cats, there are beds, collars and leashes, Regal kibbles, feeding devices, grooming supplies and implements, flea and tick repellents, nutritional supplements, cages and carriers, pet doors, litter boxes and scoopers, toys, and novelty items. And the reptile/small animal catalog shows rabbit hutches, supplies that run from lizard litter to hamster dragsters, and a range of other products. If you want to read up on pet care or breeds, Pet Warehouse can provide Barrons and T.F.H. titles on a wide range of topics, and manuals on caring for your reptile, snake, amphibian, invertebrate, or bird—as well as Puff or Spot.

Canadian readers, please note: Trade restrictions prohibit shipment of certain brands.

Special Factors: Specify catalog desired (aquatic, reptile/small animal, dog and cat, bird, or pond); price quote by phone or letter.

STATE LINE TACK, INC.

RTE. 125, DEPT. HS013
P.O. BOX 1217
PLAISTOW, NH
  03865–0428
800–228–9208
603–382–6008 (STORE)
FAX: 603–382–8471

Catalog: free
Pay: check, MO, MC, V, Discover
Sells: saddles and tack, grooming supplies, medicine, apparel, etc.
Store: Rte. 121 Plaistow, NH; Monday to Saturday 9–6, Thursday and Friday 9–9, Sunday 10–6

¡Sí!

State Line Tack covers the needs of horse and rider with comprehensive catalogs of saddles, tack, stable supplies, rider apparel, grooming needs, medicines, and much more. State Line's regular prices are discounted up to 25% routinely, and the coupon fliers further the savings to 40% plus. State Line publishes a "Western" catalog with clothing and tack for Western riders, a separate catalog for hunt-seat riders, and the National Bridle Shop catalog for saddle-seat riders. When you request the catalog, state your riding preference—pleasure, roping, show, cutting, barrel racing, jumping, dressage, or eventing.

Special Factors: Satisfaction is guaranteed; returns are accepted.

R.C. STEELE CO.

DEPT. WC
P.O. BOX 910
1989 TRANSIT WAY
BROCKPORT, NY
  14420–0910
800–872–3773
FAX: 716–637–8902
TDD: 800–468–8776

Catalog: free
Pay: check, MO, MC, V
Sells: cat, dog, bird, and aquarium supplies
Store: 1989 Transit Way, Brockport, NY; Monday to Friday 9–8:30, Saturday 9–6, Sunday 11–6

R.C. Steele Co. was founded in 1959 and is the wholesale division of Sporting Dog Specialties, well known as a source for products for both companion and hunting dogs. R.C. Steele's prices are excellent—sometimes as much as 50% less than comparable retail—and the only drawback is the $50 minimum order. The 72-page color catalog features products and equipment for canines—cages, pet doors, insecticides, feeding equipment, droppings composters, training dummies and jumps, leashes and leads, grooming supplies and tools, and manuals. There are great buys on rawhide bones, which are sold in case lots at a fraction of full retail, and all types of pet beds, at about half the going rate. The catalog features an extensive list of books and tapes from the American Kennel Club (breed shows), Arco, Denlinger, Doral, Howell, Oster, T.F.H., and Volhard (obedience). There are sections devoted to cats, birds, and 32 pages of aquarium supplies. Customers receive supplemental price lists with new offerings—books, videos, bird supplies, cages, toys, parts, and accessories.

Special Factors: C.O.D. orders are accepted; authorized returns are accepted; minimum order is $50.

THAT FISH PLACE/
THAT PET PLACE

**237 CENTERVILLE RD.
LANCASTER, PA 17603
800–733–3829**

Catalog: free
Pay: check, MO, MC, V, AE, Discover
Sells: supplies for aquariums, reptiles, birds, dogs, cats, and ponds
Store: same address; Monday to Saturday 10–9, Sunday 11–6
Online: http://www.thatpetplace.com

That Fish Place/That Pet Place has been serving the needs of fish and pet owners since 1973, and stocks supplies for aquariums, ponds, dogs, cats, birds, reptiles, and other small animals. The 96-page color Fish Catalog is packed with everything from filters to ornaments and plastic plants, and includes information and tips on maintaining a healthy aquarium. The 96-page Dog & Cat Catalog can save you money on all the basics, including rawhide amusements for the dog and catnip playthings for the feline, as well as grooming supplies, leashes, beds, and much more. Bird lovers will find hundreds of items in the 32-page Bird Book, including all of the top lines of premium bird food, toys, cages, health supplies, and more. Also offered but not available for review: the Reptiles and Small Animals Catalog, and the Pond Catalog. The good pricing and quantity discounts can yield savings of up to 70%, and That Fish Place has a "meet or beat" policy on the advertised prices of other mail-order sellers.

Please note: Request the Dog & Cat, Fish, Bird, Reptile & Small Animal, or Pond Catalog when you call or write—and be sure to mention WBMC.

Special Factors: Authorized, unused returns are accepted (a 15% restocking fee may be charged).

TOMAHAWK LIVE TRAP COMPANY

P.O. BOX 323-WBMC
TOMAHAWK, WI 54487
800–27-A-TRAP
715–453–3550
FAX: 715–453–4326

Catalog: free (see text)
Pay: check, MO, MC, V, Discover
Sells: humane animal traps and equipment
Store: Tomahawk, WI; Monday to Friday 8–5; also Coburn Company, Whitewater, WI; and Plow & Hearth, Madison, VA
E-mail: Trapem@livetrap.com

Tomahawk's box traps are used by people all over the world, by state and federal conservation departments, dog wardens, universities, and others who want to catch a critter without injury to the animal.

Tomahawk, which was established in 1930, manufactures traps in over 80 different sizes and models, for everything from mice to large dogs, as well as fish and turtles, birds, beavers, grackles, raccoons, skunks, bobcats, jackrabbits, and cats. There are rigid and collapsible styles, transfer cages, station wagon and carrying cages, several with sliding doors (for shipping animals), and special sizes can be made to order. Tomahawk also manufactures animal control poles in several sizes, "repeating" (multiple-catch) rodent traps, cat graspers, snake tongs, leather protection gloves, baits, nets, and beaver traps.

If you wish to receive literature on Tomahawk traps, send a long, self-addressed, stamped envelope for the free brochure and price list. Or you can order the comprehensive, 56-page book, "Trapped the Humane Way"; it includes tips on trapping animals, a list of common foods that can be used to lure over 20 species, and trap dimensions and specifications. The book is $3.95 (regularly $4.95) if you identify yourself as a WBMC reader when you order.

Special Factors: Quantity discounts of 50% are available on orders of six or more of the same trap.

UNITED PHARMACAL COMPANY, INC.

DEPT. WBM98

P.O. BOX 969

ST. JOSEPH, MO

64502–0969

800–254–8726

FAX: 816–233–9696

Catalog: free

Pay: check, MO, MC, V, AE, Discover

Sells: supplies for dogs, cats, horses, birds, and small animals

Store: 3705 Pear St., St. Joseph, MO; Monday to Friday 7:30–6, Saturday 7:30–5

E-mail: upco2@aol.com

Online: http://www.upco.com

United Pharmacal Company, better known as UPCO, offers thousands of products for dogs, cats, birds, and horses in a 192-page catalog that runs from hayracks to catnip-filled fur fish. UPCO's veterinary line includes antibiotics, wormers, medical instruments, nutritional supplements, skin treatments, insecticides, grooming aids, and related goods. Horse owners should check the dozen pages of medications and supplements, farrier supplies, and tack. Dog and cat owners will appreciate the savings on leashes and leads, collars, feeders, books, toys, feeding dishes and stations, pet doors, and other goods. Professional groomers should note the selection of grooming products for show dogs. UPCO also has a selection of bird cages and supplies and products for hamsters, gerbils, guinea pigs, ferrets, and rabbits. The manufacturers include Absorbine, Borden, Dubl Duck, Farnam, Happy Jack, Lambert Kay, Nylabone, Oster, St. Aubrey, and Zema, to note a few. And UPCO offers hundreds of books and manuals that cover the care and breeding of a wide range of animals.

Canadian readers, please note: Payment must be made in U.S. funds, and vaccines are not shipped to Canada.

Special Factors: Quantity discounts are available; C.O.D. orders are accepted; returns are accepted within 20 days; minimum order is $10; C.O.D. orders are accepted.

VALLEY VET SUPPLY

EAST HWY. 36
P.O. BOX 504
MARYSVILLE, KS
  66508–0504
800–360–4838
913–562–5106
FAX: 800–446–5597

Catalog: free
Pay: check, MO, MC, V, AE, Discover, NOVUS
Sells: vet and pet supplies for dogs and cats
Store: mail order only

Valley Vet's color catalog offers the latest goodies for dogs and cats—from vegetarian dog bones to state-of-the-art litter-box solutions. You'll find 68 to 84 pages of toys and other playthings, feeding equipment, beds and mats, flea and tick products, grooming tools and preparations, training equipment, barriers and cages, leashes, collars, nutritional supplements, vaccines, and related products, from well-known manufacturers. Both books and videos are offered, on everything from obedience and health care to vacationing with your animal companion. Dogs and cats are the featured players, but the review catalog included a page of supplements and drugs for birds and fish as well. Prices are competitive—the review catalog showed a "cat couch" offered at under $30 that's sold in local pet boutiques for $55. Most items are discounted about 25% from list or regular retail, including the "human" gifts—mugs, T-shirts, key rings, etc.

Please note: Vaccines and other medications are sold by prescription only to pet owners, or to licensed veterinarians.

Special Factors: Satisfaction is guaranteed; returns (except special orders, vaccines, books, and videos) are accepted for exchange, refund, or credit; minimum order is $50.

SEE ALSO

Cabela's Inc. • *dog beds; hunting-dog training equipment* • **SPORTS**
Defender Industries, Inc. • *pet life preservers* • **AUTO**
Gohn Bros. Mfg. Co. • *horse blankets* • **CLOTHING**
Herter's • *hunting-dog specialties* • **SPORTS**
Mellinger's Inc. • *live pest controls, fly traps, bird feeders, etc.* • **FARM**
Sharp Bros. Seed Co. • *forage and fodder seed* • **FARM**
Weston Bowl Mill • *bird feeders and bird calls* • **GENERAL MERCHANDISE**

APPLIANCES, AUDIO, TV, AND VIDEO

Major, small, and personal-care appliances;
sewing machines and vacuum cleaners;
audio components and personal stereo; TV
and video equipment

The companies listed here offer the full range of electronic devices, including white goods (washers, dryers, refrigerators, and ranges), brown goods (TVs, air conditioners, etc.), small kitchen and personal-care appliances, pocket calculators, phones and phone machines (auto-dialers, answerers, line switchers, etc.), sewing machines, vacuum cleaners, and floor machines. Some also sell blank audiotapes and videotapes, luggage, cameras, typewriters, computers, pens, and video games. Thanks to stiff price competition across the country, discounts often run from 15% to 40%—more on extremely popular brands, and less on high-end audio and video components.

Price is important, but it's just one purchase consideration. One of the best product information resources is *Consumer Reports,* which features monthly reviews of name-brand goods and services; it's supplemented by the annual *Buying Guide,* which summarizes scores of the reviews. In addition to dispassionate assessments of product performance and guides to features, the reviews often include both suggested list and "benchmark" retail selling prices. *Consumer Reports* also publishes news on product recalls, deceptive selling practices, health issues, money management, and related consumer interests. The corporate parent, Consumers Union, also publishes books that treat current concerns in depth: chemotherapy, choosing baby products, mutual funds, home maintenance, income taxes, etc. The "Consumer Reports New Car Price

Service" and "Used Car Price Service" are available, as are individual reports, which can be sent by fax. See the "Auto" introduction for more on the car-buying data services. For information on the other services and subscription rates, see the current issue or write to Consumers Union, 256 Washington St., Mount Vernon, NY 10553.

Most appliance and electronics manufacturers will send brochures on specific models upon request. You can often find the manufacturer's address on product packaging, and the consumer contacts and addresses of hundreds of major corporations are listed in *Consumer's Resource Handbook,* which is available from the Consumer Information Center (see the listing in "Books").

Since even small appliances and lightbulbs can consume large amounts of energy over time, determining how much power you're using when you flip the switch will help you figure out wise use of the appliances you own—and help you make energy-efficient purchases in the future. To compute the hourly cost of an appliance, find its *wattage* and divide that figure by 1,000 to find the *kilowattage,* which you can multiply by the price of a *kilowatt hour* (kWh) charged by your utility company. (The wattage of an appliance can usually be found in the same place as its model and serial number, or can be obtained from the manufacturer.) For example, a 600-watt vacuum cleaner has a kilo-wattage of 0.6 (600 divided by 1,000). Run in New York City, where the price per kilowatt hour is 14.204¢, the operating cost per hour is 8.52¢. If you have cheaper rates at night, reserve as much high-consumption use (ironing, running the dishwasher and dryer, self-cleaning the oven) for evening hours.

In addition to price and energy consumption, try to find out as much as possible about a product's repair record before you buy. *Consumer Reports* surveys repair shops periodically, and reveals which brands seem to be turning up most frequently. Unfortunately, models in the same line can vary widely in performance, so undifferentiated reviews of brands may not accurately predict how an individual model will behave. You can conduct your own interviews, too, asking your local appliance repair center about lemons and troublesome brands. And don't overlook your friends, who are probably happy to share both their horror stories and the triumphs of their best buys.

The next best thing to keeping something out of the shop is having it repaired under warranty. The electronics boom of the mid-1980s helped to popularize service contracts (erroneously termed "extended warranties"), which kick in when the manufacturers' warranties expire. Extended warranties are often pushed on big-ticket items at the point of sale on in-store purchases, but they're also sold by mail-order vendors. (Some credit-card companies provide similar protections, free of charge, for products purchased with their cards. Check the fine print of your card's policy instead of assuming that it provides comprehensive coverage.) Extended warranties are honored by the seller, not the manufacturer, at the seller's repair center. Are they worth the money? According to one analyst who examined the warranties, service contracts, and repair records of color TVs, air conditioners, refrigerators, washers, and ranges in the course of a National Science Foundation/MIT study, the answer is no. In many cases, the *probable* repair bill is lower than the cost of the service contract. But if you've had a post-warranty appliance breakdown, you may feel that a contract is worthwhile insurance. If you decide to buy one, get answers to these questions:

1. Does the service contract duplicate the manufacturer's warranty coverage?

2. Does the service contract cover parts and labor?

3. Is the company selling the contract stable, and is its service department reputable? (Contact the local Better Business Bureau for information on its record.)

4. Could you troubleshoot or repair the appliance yourself? Contact the manufacturer (many have 800 lines staffed by technicians who can provide advice on making repairs) or your local repair center before taking in a malfunctioning product—it may be something you could fix at home.

5. What's your *own* history of appliance and electronics failure? If machines seem to enjoy long and healthy lives in your care, you may not need the insurance.

Good maintenance and care will help extend a product's performance. VCRs, which appear susceptible to breakdown, will work better longer if you keep the heads clean, ease wear and tear by using a rewinder, and follow the manufacturers' use and care instructions carefully. Audio components also reward good treatment, and you'll find a battery of cleaning solutions and devices for LPs and CDs available from Lyle Cartridges and several other firms in this chapter.

If you run into trouble with a *major appliance* and can't get it resolved, you may be able to get help from the Major Appliance Consumer Action Panel (MACAP). MACAP, which is sponsored by Association of Home Appliance Manufacturers (AHAM), can request action from a manufacturer and make recommendations for resolution of the complaint. (The panel's advice is not binding, but it resolves over 80% of the cases it handles.) You can turn to MACAP with problems about dishwashers, ranges, microwave ovens, washers, dryers, refrigerators, freezers, garbage disposals, trash compactors, air conditioners, water heaters, and dehumidifiers. If your complaint concerns one of these appliances, and your attempts to get the problem resolved with the seller and the manufacturer have been futile, write to Major Appliance Consumer Action Panel, 20 N. Wacker Dr., Chicago, IL 60606. Your letter should include the manufacturer's name, model number of the appliance, and date purchased, as well as *copies* of relevant receipts and correspondence. (Call 800–621–0477 for more information.)

For listings of additional firms selling appliances and electronics, see "General Merchandise," "Office and Business" (including the "Computing" subchapter), and "Tools." For recorded audiotapes and videotapes, see the "Recordings" section of "Books."

FIND IT FAST

APPLIANCE PARTS • **AVAC**
APPLIANCES • **Beach Sales, Bernie's, Cole's, Dial-a-Brand, Discount Appliance Centers, EBA, LVT, Percy's**
AUDIO • **Audio Concepts, Beach Sales, Bernie's, CAM, Crutchfield, EBA, J & R, Lyle Cartridges, S & S Sound City, Wholesale Tape**
OFFICE MACHINES AND PHONES • **Crutchfield, EBA, J & R, LVT, Percy's, S & S Sound City**
SEWING MACHINES • **Discount Appliance Centers, EBA, LVT, Sew Vac City, Sewin' in Vermont, Sewing Machine Super Store, Suburban Sew 'N Sweep**
TV AND VIDEO • **Beach Sales, Bernie's, CAM, Cole's, Crutchfield, Dial-a-Brand, EBA, J & R, LVT, S & S Sound City, Westcoast Discount**
VACUUM CLEANERS • **AAA-All Factory, ABC Vacuum Cleaner, AVAC, Bernie's, Discount Appliance Centers, EBA, LVT, Sew Vac City**

AAA-ALL FACTORY VACUUM CLEANERS

1230 N. 3RD
ABILENE, TX 79601
915–677–1311
FAX: 915–677–9309

Catalog: $2, refundable
Pay: check, MO, MC, V, Discover
Sells: vacuum cleaners, floor shampooers and polishers
Store: same address; Monday to Friday 8:30–5
E-mail: aaavacs@aol.com

You can save on some of the best names in the cleaning business at AAA-All Factory Vacuum Cleaners, which has been in business since 1975 and offers discounts of up to 50% on list prices. Canister, upright, convertible, and mini vacuum models are available, from Bissell, Dirt Devil, Eureka, Hoover, Oreck, Panasonic, Royal, Sanitaire, Sanyo, Sharp, Tri-Star, and other names. Both home and commercial lines of vacuum cleaners, floor buffers, and rug shampooers are stocked, and AAA-All Factory also sells reconditioned Kirby and Rainbow machines, and supplies and accessories for a range of floor machines. Since you'll receive just a couple of offset sheets for the $2 fee—and there isn't much product information given—call to discuss your needs or for a price quote.

Canadian readers, please note: Only U.S. funds are accepted.

Special Factors: Satisfaction is guaranteed; layaway plan is available; returns are accepted within 10 days; C.O.D. orders are accepted.

ABC VACUUM CLEANER WAREHOUSE

6720 BURNET RD., WM98
AUSTIN, TX 78757
512–459–7643
FAX: 512–451–2352

Catalog: free
Pay: check, MO, MC, V, AE, Discover
Sells: vacuum cleaners
Store: same address; Monday to Friday 9–6, Saturday 9–5
E-mail: discount@abcvacuum.com
Online: http://www.abcvacuum.com

ABC purchases from suppliers who are overstocked or going out of business, and passes the savings—up to 50% on the suggested retail or usual selling price—on to you. ABC has been in business since 1977, and sells machines by Electra Pure, Fantom, Filter Queen, Kirby, Miele, Optima, Oreck, Panasonic, Riccar, Royal, Sanitaire, Sanyo, Sharp, Simplicity, Thermax, and Tri-Star. The Rainbow, by Rexair, is sold at a discount, as well as all of its accessories and parts. (Rebuilt Rainbows are sold at lower prices.) Built-in (central) cleaning systems are also available. See the price list for bags, filters, and accessories and attachments for selected models. ABC also offers repair services by mail—call for information if you're having trouble getting your machine repaired locally.

Canadian readers, please note: Shipments are not made to Canada.

Special Factors: Satisfaction is guaranteed; returns are accepted within 30 days for exchange, refund, or credit; C.O.D. orders are accepted.

AUDIO CONCEPTS, INC.

DEPT. WBMC
901 S. 4TH ST.
LA CROSSE, WI 54601
608–784–4570
FAX: 608–784–6367

Brochure: free
Pay: check, MO, MC, V
Sells: ACI speakers
Store: mail order only
E-mail: 74652.3400@compuserve.com
Online: http://www.audioc.com

If you'd like to assemble a good audio system but don't think you can afford it, here's one way to save on the thing that seems to cost the most—the speakers. Audio Concepts, Inc. (ACI) has been manufacturing and selling speakers factory-direct since 1977, and suggests that you can save up to 40% over the cost of comparable speakers. ACI's models are sold in pairs and individually, and a home theater package is available. ACI sells everything from satellites to three-ways, in-wall speakers to subwoofers, center channels to rear speakers. The cabinets, made with furniture-grade wood veneers, are offered in a number of finishes. Prices begin at $149 per pair for wall speakers and run to around $3,000 for Sapphire III's and Titan subwoofers. The website and brochure show the speakers and a range of accessories—stands, cables, wall brackets, etc.

Special Factors: Satisfaction is guaranteed; authorized returns in new condition sent in the original packaging are accepted within 15 days for exchange, refund, or credit.

AVAC CORPORATION

666 UNIVERSITY AVE.
ST. PAUL, MN 55104–4896
800–328–9430
612–222–0763
FAX: 612–224–2674

Brochure: see text
Pay: check, MO, MC, V, AE, Discover
Sells: vacuum cleaners, related parts, and supplies
Store: 1300 Ridgedale Dr., Minnetonka; 6405 Lyndale Ave., Richfield; and 1441 University Ave., St. Paul, MN
E-mail: Bojacker@aol.com

AVAC Corporation, formerly known as Midamerica, sells the full line of household and commercial vacuum cleaners by Sharp Electronics. AVAC also sells the Hayden Central Vacuum Cleaning System, for do-it-your-selfers, as well as the parts and supplies needed to keep models of most major brands functioning.

Special Factors: Quantity discounts are available; minimum order is $25.

BEACH SALES INC.

80 VFW PKWY.
REVERE, MA 02151
800–562–9020
617–284–0130
FAX: 617–284–9823

Information: price quote
Pay: check, MO, MC, V
Sells: major appliances, audio and video components, scanners, film, etc.
Store: same address

Beach Sales offers "The best brands at wholesale prices," discounts of up to 50% on everything from watch batteries to major appliances. This firm has been serving the greater Boston area since 1947, and offers the same savings to customers nationwide. There is no catalog, but you can call, fax, or write with the manufacturer's name and model number for a quote on audio and video components, fax machines, major appliances, police scanners and related electronics, and even things like snow blowers, from Bose, General Electric, Hewlett-Packard, Infinity, Maytag, Mitsubishi, Polaroid, Whirlpool, and scores of other manufacturers. Beach Sales also has great buys on film and tape (audio and video)— inquire about quantity prices.

Special Factors: Price quote by phone, fax, or letter; returns in original packaging are accepted for exchange, refund, or credit.

BERNIE'S DISCOUNT CENTER, INC.

821 SIXTH AVE., D–8
NEW YORK, NY
  10001–6305
212–564–8758, 8582, 9431
FAX: 212–564–3894

Catalog: $1, refundable (see text)
Pay: check, MO, MC, V, AE (see text)
Sells: appliances, TV and audio components, office machines
Store: same address; Monday to Friday 9:30–6, Saturday (except July and August) 11–4

🍁 (see text) 🇺🇸 ¡Si!

Bernie's has been in business since 1947, and sells "pluggables"—everything from electric brooms to fax machines—at 10% to 15% above dealers' cost, or an average of 30% off list. The catalog is available for $1 (refundable with a purchase), but it shows just a smattering of the stock at Bernie's, and you're better off calling for a price quote. One of the city's best sources for discounted electronics and appliances, Bernie's tries to carry the top-rated goods listed in popular buying guides, and Bernie's does not handle gray-market goods.

Bernie's sells electronics (audio, TV, and video equipment) by Aiwa, AT&T, Brother, Fisher, JVC, Mitsubishi, Panasonic, Quasar, RCA, Sharp, Sony, Toshiba, and Zenith. White goods *(shipped in the New York City area only)* are available from Amana, Caloric, Frigidaire, General Electric, Jenn-Air, Magic Chef, Maytag, KitchenAid, Whirlpool, White-Westinghouse, and other manufacturers. Bernie's is one of the best sources in the metropolitan area for air conditioners (Airtemp, Carrier, Emerson, Friedrich, General Electric, Gibson, Panasonic, etc.), fans by Duracraft and Lakewood, heaters by Duracraft and Pelonis, and air cleaners and ionizers by Bionaire and Envirocare. Bernie's carries Bionaire and Duracraft humidifiers, and a full line of filters and wicks for both brands. Small and personal-care appliances from Black & Decker, Braun, Brita, Clairol, Eureka, Hamilton Beach, Hitachi, Hoover, Interplak, KitchenAid, Krups, Norelco, Oster, Panasonic, Presto, Remington, Sunbeam, Teledyne (Water Pik and Instapure), Toastmaster, Wearever, West Bend, and other brands are available as well.

Please note: Purchases charged to American Express/Optima cards are shipped to billing addresses only, and MasterCard and VISA are accepted for *in-store* purchases only.

Canadian readers, please note: Orders are shipped to Canada via UPS only.

Special Factors: Store is closed Saturdays in July and August.

CAM AUDIO, INC.

**MISSIONARY TAPE &
EQUIPMENT SUPPLY
2210 EXECUTIVE DR.
GARLAND, TX 75041
800–527–3458
972–271–0006
FAX: 972–271–1555**

Catalog: free
Pay: check, MO, MC, V, Discover
Sells: audio and video components, blanks, services, etc.
Store: same address; Monday to Friday 8:30–5
Online: http://www.camaudio.com

CAM Audio, in business for nearly 30 years, was recommended by a reader for excellent service and prices on audio and video products. The audio line includes tapes, labels, albums, and storage units; in video, you'll find cameras, decks and monitors, and a full line of blank videotape. The sound equipment includes microphones, speakers, mixers, and amps. Available brands include Ampex, Anchor Audio, Apollo, Ashley, Bogen, Crown, Draper, Electro-Voice, Elmo, JVC, Kodak, Marantz, Maxell, Motorola, Panasonic, Phonic, Sanyo, Sharp, Shure, Sony, TDK, Teac, Telex, 3M, University Sound, Ultimate Support, and Videonics. See the catalog for current offerings, and if you're pricing anything in the audio or video line from the firms mentioned here, you can call or write with the model number for a price quote. CAM is also a leading supplier of discount-priced church equipment, through its Missionary Tape division.

Special Factors: Price quote by phone or letter.

COLE'S APPLIANCE & FURNITURE CO.

**4026 LINCOLN AVE.
CHICAGO, IL 60618–3097
773–525–1797**

Information: see text
Pay: check, MO, MC, V, Discover
Sells: appliances and home furnishings
Store: same address; Monday and Thursday 9:30–9, Tuesday, Friday, and Saturday 9:30–5:30 (closed Wednesdays and Sundays)

Cole's, founded in 1957, sells electronics (TV and video), appliances, and home furnishings and bedding at discounts of up to 50%. If you're pricing something from Amana, ASKO, Caloric, Dacor, General Electric,

Gibson, Hitachi, Hotpoint, Insinkerator, Jenn-Air, KitchenAid, Magic Chef, Maytag, Panasonic, Pioneer, Premier, Speed Queen, Sub-Zero, Thermador, Viking, Whirlpool, Wolf, Zenith, or any other major manufacturer, call Cole's for a price quote. Deliveries are made by Cole's in the greater Chicago area, and via UPS elsewhere.

Special Factors: Price quote by phone or letter.

CRUTCHFIELD CORPORATION

I CRUTCHFIELD PARK,
DEPT. WH
CHARLOTTESVILLE, VA
22906–6020
800–955–9009
FAX: 804–973–1862
TDD: 800–388–9753

Catalog: free (see text)
Pay: check, MO, MC, V, AE, Carte Blanche, Discover, Crutchfield charge card
Sells: audio and video components, home theater, car stereos, telephones and pagers, and digital satellite systems
Store: Rio Hill Shopping Center, Charlottesville, and Market Square East Shopping Center, Harrisonburg, VA
E-mail: webmaster@crutchfield.com
Online: http://www.crutchfield.com

Crutchfield publishes an informative, 100-plus-page catalog of home and car stereo components, home theater and digital satellite systems, video equipment, telephones, and car alarms. The catalog is loaded with buying tips and product specifications on featured goods, which are priced from 10% to 55% below list. Good prices are just one of the pluses here—you may find the Crutchfield catalog more helpful when you're comparing product features than the articles in industry magazines. And Crutchfield backs everything it sells with a guarantee of satisfaction, and the staff can provide extensive support: Installation walk-throughs over the phone, custom installation kits and wiring harnesses for car stereos, and informative consumer service manuals are among the available benefits. Crutchfield, which was established in 1974, is a factory-authorized repair station for most of the brands it sells, and does not sell gray-market goods.

Crutchfield's car stereo components line, which includes equipment for pickup trucks and hatchbacks, features goods by Alphasonik, Blaupunkt, Cerwin-Vega, Clarion, Denon, Infinity, JBL, Jensen, JVC, Kenwood, Kicker, MTX, Pioneer, Polk Audio, Profile, Pyle, Sanyo, Sony, Soundstream, and Ultimate. Crutchfield also sells radar detectors by BEL and Whistler, as well as dozens of types of car antennas, and Crimestopper alarm systems to protect your investment.

The home audio portion of the catalog includes pages of features, comparisons of current models of receivers, CD players, cassette decks, speakers, and shelf systems, and shows digital satellite systems and accessories, portable and personal audio, home theater systems, remote controls, CD cabinets, and other accessories. The brands include Advent, Bose, Carver, Cerwin-Vega, Harman–Kardon, Infinity, JVC, Kenwood, NHT, Pioneer, Polk Audio, Sony, and Yamaha. You'll also find camcorders, laser disc players, and TVs and VCRs from JVC, Pioneer, RCA, and Sony offered here.

Please note: The catalog is free to readers of this book, but be sure to identify yourself as a WBMC reader when you request your copy.

Special Factors: Satisfaction is guaranteed; returns are accepted within 30 days.

DIAL-A-BRAND, INC.

57 S. MAIN ST.
FREEPORT, NY 11520
516–378–9694
FAX: 516–867–3447

Information: price quote
Pay: check, MO, MC, V, Discover
Sells: appliances, TVs, and video equipment
Store: same address; Monday to Friday 9–6, Saturday 9–12

¡Si! ★

Dial-a-Brand, which was founded in 1967, has earned the kudos of institutions and individuals with its wide range of appliances and popular electronics. Dial-a-Brand offers discounts averaging 30%, and does not sell gray-market goods. Call or write for prices on air conditioners, TVs, video equipment, microwave ovens, and large appliances. Dial-a-Brand ships chiefly within the New York/New Jersey/Connecticut area, but deliveries (via UPS) are made nationwide. Freight charges may offset savings on outsized or heavy items shipped long distances, so be sure to get a firm quote or estimate before you place your order. Please note: You *must* call with the manufacturer's name and model number to receive a price quote.

Special Factors: Returns are accepted for exchange if goods are defective, or damaged in transit; minimum order is $99.

DISCOUNT APPLIANCE CENTERS

8426 20TH AVE., SUITE 100
ADELPHIA, MD 20783
301–559–8932
FAX: 301–559–1335

Information: price quote
Pay: check, MO, MC, V, AE
Sells: vacuum cleaners and sewing machines
Store: mail order only

Discount Appliance Centers sells sewing machines and vacuum cleaners, and accessories and supplies for both, at good discounts. The firm has been in business since 1964, and doesn't have a catalog—you must *write* for prices and availability information, since quotes are given over the phone as staff time permits. Inquire by model name and number about vacuum cleaners by Airway, Electrolux, Eureka, Filter Queen, Hoover, Kirby, Mastercraft, Oreck, Panasonic, Royal, Sanitaire, Sharp, or Tri-Star. The sewing machines include models by Bernina, Elna, Juki, Necchi, New Home, Pfaff, Riccar, Singer, and Viking. If you're trying to find vacuum cleaner bags, belts, or attachments, note the model and product you need, and write for a price quote. Include a stamped, self-addressed business envelope with your inquiry.

Special Factors: Price quote by letter only with SASE; minimum order is $49.

EBA WHOLESALE

2361 NOSTRAND AVE.
BROOKLYN, NY 11210
800–380–2378
718–252–3400
FAX: 718–253–6002

Flyer: free
Pay: check, MO, MC, V, Discover
Sells: appliances, audio, video, mattresses, etc.
Store: same address; Monday to Friday 9–8, Saturday 9–6, Sunday 10–5

Bargains abound at this Brooklyn discount house, which has been in business since 1970 and sets prices based on its cost plus 5% to 10%—the savings run from 10% to 40% on list or suggested selling prices. EBA Wholesale offers everything from Maytag washers and Amana refrigerators to AT&T phones and mattresses; the lines include Aiwa, Brother, Caloric, Eureka, General Electric, Hotpoint, Jenn-Air, KitchenAid, Magic Chef,

Panasonic, RCA, Sanyo, Sharp, Sony, Toshiba, Whirlpool, White-Westinghouse, and Zenith, among others. EBA's flyer features some of the current specials; you can order from it, or call for a price quote on other models.

Special Factors: Satisfaction is guaranteed; price quote by phone, fax, or letter.

J & R MUSIC WORLD

DEPT. WL098

59–50 QUEENS-MIDTOWN

EXPRESSWAY

MASPETH, NY 11378

ORDERS: 800–221–8180

CUSTOMER SERVICE:

800–426–6027

718–417–3737

212–238–9000

FAX: 718–628–3168

Catalog: free
Pay: check, MO, MC, V, AE, Discover
Sells: audio, video, computers, music, small appliances, etc.
Store: Park Row, New York, NY; Monday to Saturday 9–6:30, Sunday 10–6

J & R enjoys top billing among New York City electronics and computer discounters for its depth of saving and selection, especially in the audio, video, and computer departments. You can call for the 200-page catalog, or to get price quotes on current lines of TVs, VCRs and video equipment, audio components and equipment, computers and peripherals, phones, fax machines, radar detectors, cameras, and personal appliances. J & R also sells tapes, CDs, and software, as well as exercise equipment, vacuum cleaners and microwave ovens, and even pens and watches. All major brand names, from Advent to Yamaha, are represented here, and everything sold by J & R is guaranteed to be brand new and factory fresh.

Special Factors: Satisfaction is guaranteed; online with Bloomberg.

LVT PRICE QUOTE HOTLINE, INC.

BOX 444-W98
COMMACK, NY
11725-0444
516-234-8884
FAX: 516-234-8808

Brochure: free
Pay: cashier's check or MO
Sells: major appliances, TVs, vacuum cleaners, electronics, office machines, etc.
Store: (phone hours) Monday to Saturday 9–6
E-mail: calllvt@aol.com
Online: AOL: CALL LVT

LVT, established in 1976, gives you instant access to over 4,000 products from over 70 manufacturers, at savings of up to 30% on suggested list or full retail prices. The brochure includes a roster of available brands, and price quotes are given on individual items. LVT does not sell gray-market goods. For information, read LVT's brochure for the sales and shipping policies, then call with the manufacturer's name and exact model number for a price quote on major appliances, bread-making machines, microwave ovens, air conditioners, vacuum cleaners, washers and dryers, TVs, video equipment, phones and phone machines, calculators, typewriters, scanners, radar detectors, copiers, fax machines, and word processors.

The brands available include Admiral, Airtemp, Aiwa, Amana, AT&T, Bearcat, Bel-Tronics, Bogen, Bosch, Broan, Brother, Canon, Carrier, Casio, Cobra, Eagle, Emerson, Eureka, Fedders, Franke, Friedrich, Frigidaire, Frostman, General Electric, Gaggenau, Hewlett-Packard, Hitachi, Hoover, Hotpoint, Jenn-Air, JVC, Kelvinator, Magic Chef, Maxon, Maytag, Modern Chef, Monroe, Mont Blanc, Murata, Olivetti, Olympus, Pacific, Panasonic, Phone-Mate, Pioneer, Quasar, Rangaire, RCA, Rolodex, Roper, Samsung, Sanyo, Scotsman, Sharp, Smith-Corona, Sony, Southwestern Bell, Sub-Zero, Summit, Tappan, Technics, Texas Instruments, Thermador, Toshiba, Toyatomi, Uniden, V-Tech, Victor, Whirlpool, Whistler, White-Westinghouse, Wolf, Woods, and Zenith— see the brands list for others.

Special Factors: Shipping (UPS), handling, and insurance charges are included in quotes; all sales are final; all goods are sold with manufacturers' warranties; minimum order is $50; C.O.D. orders are accepted on local deliveries.

LYLE CARTRIDGES

DEPT. WBMC
115 SO. CORONA AVE.
VALLEY STREAM, NY 11582
800–221–0906
516–599–1112
FAX: 516–599–2027

Catalog: free with long, self-addressed, stamped envelope
Pay: check, MO, MC, V, AE, Discover
Sells: phono cartridges, replacement styli, and accessories
Store: same address; Monday to Friday 9–5, Saturday 10–1 (Oct. to May)
E-mail: lylemax@aol.com

Lyle Cartridges has been in business since 1952 and is a great source for the cartridges and replacement styli (factory original) that bring your music to life. If you're sticking by your LPs despite CDs, you'll really appreciate this reliable, well-informed source. As the proprietors put it, "We specialize in phono-related products, and have the largest stock of 78 RPM replacement styli in the country. As LPs have become harder to find, so too have our products and services."

Lyle sells phono cartridges and replacement styli by Audioquest, Audio-Technica, Bang & Olufsen, Dynavector, Grado/Signature, Ortofon, Pickering, Shure, Stanton, and Sumiko. Record-care products by Discwasher, LAST, and VPI are stocked. Lyle also sells Grado headphones, and VPI turntables. This is the first source to consult if you have to replace arm parts, since you may be able to save on both labor and material costs—parts prices are up to 60% less than list or comparable retail.

Special Factors: Authorized returns are accepted; defective goods are replaced; minimum order is $15, $25 with credit cards.

PERCY'S, INC.

GOLD STAR BLVD.
WORCESTER, MA 01605
800–922–8194
FAX: 508–797–5578

Information: price quote (no catalog)
Pay: MO, MC, V, Discover
Sells: large appliances, home and car audio,
TV components, video, computers, etc.
Store: same address; Monday to Friday 10–9,
Saturday 10–6
E-mail: alanl@percys.com
Online: http://www.percys.com

Percy's has been selling appliances since 1926, at prices up to 40% below list. Percy's sells no gray-market goods. Call, write, or e-mail for a price quote on washers, dryers, dishwashers, refrigerators, freezers, ranges, microwave ovens, TVs, video equipment and tapes, audio components, computers, satellite dishes, radar detectors, dehumidifiers, air conditioners, disposals, trash compactors, and other appliances. The brands available at Percy's include Aiwa, Amana, Asko, Bosch, Bose, Caloric, Canon, Compaq, Denon, Eureka, Frigidaire, General Electric, Hitachi, Hewlett-Packard, Hotpoint, IBM, Jenn-Air, JVC, KitchenAid, Magic Chef, Maytag, Mitsubishi, Onkyo, Panasonic, Pioneer, Quasar, Samsung, Sharp, Sony, Sub-Zero, Thermador, Toshiba, Viking, Whirlpool, White-Westinghouse, and Zenith. Please note that Percy's *does not sell small appliances,* and *does not publish a catalog.*

Special Factors: Price quote by e-mail, fax, or phone.

S & S SOUND CITY

58 W. 45TH ST.,
DEPT. WBMC
NEW YORK, NY
10036–4280
800–326–1677
(OUTSIDE NY)
212–575–0210
FAX: 212–221–7907

Information: price quote
Pay: check, MO, MC, V, AE, DC, Discover
Sells: audio and video, home-office products, air conditioners
Store: same address; Monday to Friday 8:30–7, Saturday 9–6

S & S Sound City has been in business since 1975, selling TVs and video equipment, audio components, radios, telephones, microwave ovens, air conditioners, DDS, Internet-access TV, DVD, and closed-circuit TV systems. The inventory includes goods from Air Temp, Carrier, Denon, Friedrich, General Electric, Harman Kardon, JBL, JVC, Mitsubishi, Motorola, Onkyo, Panasonic, ProScan, Quasar, RCA, Sharp, Sony, Southwestern Bell, and Technics. Call or write for a price quote.

Special Factors: Returns are accepted within seven days; special orders are accepted.

SEW VAC CITY

DEPT. WBMC
1667 TEXAS AVE.
COLLEGE STATION, TX
77840
800–338–5672
FAX: 409–696–9262

Brochure: $3 (see text)
Pay: MO, MC, V, Discover
Sells: sewing machines, sergers, and vacuum cleaners
Store: same address; Monday and Thursday 9–8; Tuesday, Wednesday, Friday, and Saturday 9–5; also Pittsburg Sewing Machine Warehouse, 602 N. Broadway, Pittsburg, KS; Sewing Machine Warehouse, Willowbrook Ct., 17776 Tomball Pkwy., Houston; and Sew Vac City, Town West Center, Waco, TX

Sew Vac City, in business since 1976, sells sewing machines, sergers, and vacuum cleaners. Call for a price quote on sewing machines by

Singer, White, and other manufacturers, or Oreck, Panasonic, Sharp, and other vacuum cleaners. All of the machines sold here are new, and layaways are accepted—inquire for information.

Special Factors: Layaway plan is available; minimum order is $30; C.O.D. orders are accepted.

SEWIN' IN VERMONT

84 CONCORD AVE.
ST. JOHNSBURY, VT
05819–2095
800–451–5124
802–748–3803
FAX: 802–748–2165

Brochure: free
Pay: check, MO, MC, V, Discover
Sells: sewing machines and accessories
Store: same address; Monday to Friday 9:30–5, Saturday 9:30–1

If you're shopping for sewing or embroidery supplies or a sewing machine or serger, call Sewin' in Vermont. The firm carries several of the best brands, including Jaguar, New Home, and Singer. Professional-quality irons and presses by Rowenta, Singer, and Sussman are also carried. The brochure lists selected models, as well as sewing aids—from thread and pins and needles to pressing hams—and Singer dress forms, Johnson ruffling machines, sewing-machine attachments, cabinets and carrying cases, sewing-room furniture, supplies, books, videos, and more.

Sewin' in Vermont has been in business since 1960 (by mail since 1978), and the sales staff can help you choose the right equipment for your needs; call the 800 number for information and price quotes.

Special Factors: Price quote by phone or letter; C.O.D. orders are accepted.

SEWING MACHINE SUPER STORE

DEPT. WBMC

9789 FLORIDA BLVD.

BATON ROUGE, LA 70815

800–739–7374

504–923–1285

FAX: 800–866–1261

FAX: 504–923–1261

Price List: free

Pay: check, MO, MC, V, AE, Discover

Sells: sewing machines, sergers, embroidery, knitting equipment, and accessories

Store: same address; Monday to Friday 9–6 CT

E-mail: sewserg@aol.com

Online: http://www.allbrands.com

Sewing Machine Super Store, which also does business as All Brands, offers deep stock on a range of home and industrial sewing machines, sergers, embroidery, and knitting machines. The brands include Bernina, Brother, Elna, Horn, Jaguar, Johnson, Juki, National, Necchi, Melco, New Home, Parsons, Passap, Pfaff, Riccar, Simplicity, Singer, Viking, and White, among others. The firm has been in business since 1976, and offers an extensive selection of sewing tools as well as machines—Schmetz needles in bulk, Consew electric rotary cutters and Gingher shears, sewing cabinets, irons by Rowenta, Singer, and Sussman, presses, dress forms and design software, and even weaving equipment by Schacht. In addition to new machines, Sewing Machine Super Store sometimes has refurbished, reboxed, and demonstrator models available for sale—see the website for more information. Goods are shipped both from inventory, and drop-shipped from manufacturers and distribution points across the U.S. and in Canada. Service and repairs are available on all brands of sewing machines, sergers, and embroidery and knitting machines, and many of the models sold here are sold with instructional videos. Workbooks may be available on selected models as well—inquire. You can send for the closely printed price list, which includes a sample of what's available; visit the website, which has a complete product list and sales terms; or call for a price on any model made by the manufacturers represented. If you need more information, contact the firm—Sewing Machine Super Store will mail or fax manufacturers' brochures to you.

Special Factors: Layaway plan is available; authorized returns are accepted (a 15% restocking fee may be charged); C.O.D. orders are accepted for delivery within the 48 contiguous United States.

SUBURBAN SEW 'N SWEEP, INC.

━━━━━━━━━

8814 OGDEN AVE.
BROOKFIELD, IL 60513
800–642–4056
708–485–2834
FAX: 708–387–0500

Information: inquire
Pay: check, MO, MC, V, AE, Discover
Sells: sewing machines and vacuum cleaners
Store: same address; Monday to Saturday
9–5

 ★

Suburban Sew 'N Sweep has been selling sewing machines since 1975, and although a brochure is available, you can call for a price quote on sewing and overlock machines by New Home, Singer, White, and other top brands. Discounts vary, but run up to 50% and Suburban Sew 'N Sweep is an authorized dealer for several major sewing machine manufacturers.

Special Factors: Price quote by phone; C.O.D. orders are accepted.

WESTCOAST DISCOUNT VIDEO

━━━━━━━━━

5201 EASTERN AVE.
BALTIMORE, MD 21224
410–633–0508
410–633–8171
FAX: 410–633–7888

Information Package: free
Pay: check, MO, MC, V, AE, Discover
Sells: camcorders and accessories
Store: Monday to Friday 9–6, Wednesday
and Saturday 9–1, ET

Westcoast Discount Video is a specialty firm that sells camcorders, attachments, and accessories—for both 8mm and VHS formats. Discounts run up to 35% on models by Canon, General Electric, Hitachi, JVC, Panasonic, Quasar, RCA, Sharp, and Sony. This is also a good source for auxiliary lenses and filters, lighting equipment, power packs, rewinders, microphones, tripods, and other equipment. The information package includes specs on "the most popular camcorders" and a price sheet listing the available models. It's nice to know that everything Westcoast Discount Video sells is sent in factory-sealed cartons with the full U.S. manufacturer's warranty.

Special Factors: Price quote by phone; shipping is not charged on orders over $75; C.O.D. orders are accepted.

WHOLESALE TAPE AND SUPPLY COMPANY

P.O. BOX 8277,

   DEPT. WBM

CHATTANOOGA, TN

   37414

800–251–7228

423–894–9427

FAX: 423–894–7281

Catalog: free
Pay: check, MO, MC, V, AE, Discover
Sells: audio and video, duplicating services, CD replication, blank tapes, etc.
Store: 2841 Hickory Valley Rd., Chattanooga, TN
E-mail: wts@wts-tape.com
Online: http://www.wts-tape.com/

Wholesale Tape, which has been selling audiovisual supplies and services worldwide since 1977, publishes a catalog featuring blank audio- and videocassettes, AV accessories, high-speed audio duplicating equipment, and duplication services for CD, audio, and video. Wholesale Tape produces audiotapes for professional duplication; different types of cassettes are available in clear, white, and black shells (housing) and standard tape lengths (12 to 122 minutes); custom tape lengths and colors can be provided. Wholesale Tape also sells audio- and videotape from Ampex, Fuji, and Maxell.

If you need an audiotape or videotape copied or distributed but don't have the necessary equipment, consider Wholesale Tape's duplicating and fulfillment services. Custom labels and shell imprinting can be produced, and cassette boxes, albums, shipping envelopes, and storage units are also sold.

Special Factors: Satisfaction is guaranteed; quantity discounts are offered; C.O.D. orders are accepted; minimum order is $30.

SEE ALSO

Atlanta Thread & Supply • commercial sewing machines, sergers, and irons • **CRAFTS: TEXTILE ARTS**
B & H Photo-Video • pro-audio and video equipment • **CAMERAS**
CISCO • garbage disposals, spas, whirlpools, etc. • **HOME: IMPROVEMENT**

The Cleaning Center • vacuum cleaners, replacement bags • **HOME: IMPROVEMENT**

Defender Industries, Inc. • marine electronics • **AUTO**

E & B Marine Supply, Inc. • marine electronics • **AUTO**

Ewald-Clark • video cameras • **CAMERAS**

Goldberg's Marine Distributors • marine electronics • **AUTO**

Kaplan Bros. Blue Flame Corp. • commercial restaurant appliances • **HOME: KITCHEN**

Main Lamp/Lamp Warehouse • lamps and ceiling fans • **HOME: LIGHTING**

Peerless Restaurant Supplies • commercial restaurant fixtures, appliances, and supplies • **HOME: KITCHEN**

Solo Slide Fasteners, Inc. • professional pressing and sewing equipment • **CRAFTS: TEXTILE ARTS**

Thread Discount Sales • sergers, overlock machines, etc. • **CRAFTS: TEXTILE ARTS**

West Marine • marine electronics • **AUTO**

ART, ANTIQUES, AND COLLECTIBLES

Fine art, limited editions, antiques,
and collectibles

The firms listed here offer an eclectic selection of the rare and unusual, from Victoriana to fruit crate labels. Although buying from "dealer" sources means you're usually getting the piece at a lower price than you'd pay at retail, don't buy with the expectation of reselling at a profit unless you're sure of what you're doing. Make sure you're buying from firms that have liberal return policies.

Getting to know the market is one of the pleasures of collecting, and there are hundreds of reference books available to give you the necessary grounding. The guides to prevailing market prices for antiques and collectibles are especially helpful in determining whether you're over-paying—or getting a real buy. Ralph and Terry Kovel have been publishing price indexes and collectors' guides for decades, and are best known for the annual *Kovels' Antiques and Collectibles Price List*. The Kovels also help you get the best price on what you buy—or sell—with *Kovels' Guide to Selling, Buying and Fixing Your Antiques and Collectibles* (both titles from Crown). And you can hear from them through their monthly newsletter, *Kovels on Antiques and Collectibles*. Write to Kovels on Antiques, P.O. Box 420347, Palm Coast, FL 32142–0347, for current rates.

There's no substitute for old-fashioned legwork when it comes to learning about your field of interest. Visit flea markets, antique shops, art galleries, museums, and auction previews, and don't just look—*ask questions*. Dealers enjoy an appreciative customer, and will usually share valuable tips on what to look for if you demonstrate interest in their wares.

A collection of any merit usually requires the protection of archival quality materials. University Products, Inc. (in the "Small Business" section of "Office") is an excellent source for display binders, albums, boxes, and restoration materials for art works, books, manuscripts, photographs, textiles, posters, and postcards. The firm's archival products catalog includes goods for mounting, display, and storage, and a number of reference works to help do it right, including Jill Snyder's *Caring for Your Art: A Guide for Artists, Collectors, Galleries, and Art Institutions*. See *Kovels' Antiques and Collectibles Price List* for other resources.

FIND IT FAST

FRUIT CRATE LABELS • **Original Paper Collectibles**
MILITARIA • **John W. Poling**
NOSTALGIC ITEMS (REPRODUCTION) • **Desperate Enterprises**
PHONES • **Phoneco**
POSTERS • **Cinema City, Miscellaneous Man**

CINEMA CITY

P.O. BOX 1012-W
MUSKEGON, MI 49443
616–739–8303
FAX: 616–733–7234

Catalog: $3, refundable
Pay: check, MO, MC, V, Discover
Sells: movie posters and ephemera
Store: mail order only
E-mail: info@cinema-city.com

Movie posters circa 1975 and later are the specialty at Cinema City, which has been selling to collectors and dealers since 1976. Thousands of movies are listed in the 64-page catalog, from *A Bridge Too Far* ($15 for a set of 12 stills) to *Ziggy Stardust* (27" by 41" poster, $25). Press kits, scripts, and lobby cards are available for some of the titles. The catalog is arranged alphabetically by movie title and includes a glossary of terms and guide to the poster sizes. Cinema City adds to its gigantic inventory with each new movie release, and once you're on the mailing list, you'll receive periodic updates—including offerings of autographed posters and photos. Cinema City also handles materials for foreign films and limited-release items. You can send inquiries about these, as well as queries about films made before 1975—include a self-addressed, stamped envelope for a reply.

Canadian readers, please note: Only U.S. funds are accepted.

Special Factors: Posters are sent rolled if Cinema City received them "flat"; folded materials are stiffened to minimize damage and shipped that way.

DESPERATE ENTER-PRISES, INC.

DEPT. WBMC
620 E. SMITH RD., #E–8
MEDINA, OH 44256
800–732–4859
FAX: 330–725–0150

Catalog: free
Pay: check, MO, MC, V, AE, Discover
Sells: tin ad and poster reproductions, nostalgic light-switch plates
Store: mail order only
E-mail: tinsigns@apk.net
Online: http://www.desperate.com

Desperate Enterprises takes its name from an observation made by Thoreau, not from the nature of its industry. The firm began business in 1987, selling two reproductions of tin advertising signs, which has expanded to a line of over 680 different images. Desperate Enterprises uses two production processes—four-color photolithography and silkscreen printing—to approximate the detail and depth of color in the originals.

Most of the examples shown in the 64-page color catalog are from the late 1800s through the 1950s, chiefly endorsements by famous people, ads for gas and oil companies, seeds and vegetables, drinks, baseball-related advertising, food, ammunition, fishing, tobacco, transportation, highway, liquor, postage stamps, and African-American images. You can find Lucille Ball boosting Royal Crown Cola, a number of images from Remington, wonderful Art Deco ads, images for Cracker Jack, Jell-O, Heinz pickles, Grape-Nuts cereal, Sunbeam bread, and Dewar's, among others. The ads, which average 11" by 16", begin at $12 and go down to about $4 each, depending on how many you buy. Miniatures of 112 of the ads are offered as refrigerator magnets ($14 to about $8 per set of six). Real vintage soda-bottle caps are also available as refrigerator magnets. Sepia-toned photo assortments in broad categories (movies and westerns, sports, motorcycle, etc.) are sold for $54 per hundred, and 20" by 30" posters, light-switch plates in 67 images, and T-shirts are also available. Desperate Enterprises is constantly adding products and images, and is a great resource for gifts.

Special Factors: Satisfaction is guaranteed; C.O.D. orders are accepted.

MISCELLANEOUS MAN

P.O. BOX 1776-W8
NEW FREEDOM, PA 17349
717–235–4766
FAX: 717–235–2853

Catalog: $5
Pay: check, MO, MC, V
Sells: rare and vintage posters and labels
Store: mail order only

George Theofiles, ephemerologist extraordinaire, is the moving force behind Miscellaneous Man. He founded his firm in 1970, trading in vintage posters, handbills, graphics, labels, brochures, and other memorabilia, all of which are original—he sells no reproductions or reprints.

Each Miscellaneous Man catalog offers an average of about a thousand items, including posters, theater and movie publicity materials, collections of colorful product labels, and broadsides. Posters are the strong suit, representing everything from aviation to weaponry: patriotic themes (including both World Wars, other conflicts, and related topics), sports of all sorts, wines and spirits, food advertising, labor, publishing, fashion, African-Americana, the performing arts, and travel, among other subjects. Some of the posters are offered mounted on linen or conservation paper, and Mr. Theofiles can provide references for other firms that can mount your poster after purchase (proper backing helps to preserve the poster, and doesn't detract from its value). Collections of unused broom handle labels, luggage stickers, cigar box labels, and other ephemera have appeared in previous catalogs. The catalog entries note size and condition, and photos of many items are included; larger shots of individual items may be purchased for $2.

Miscellaneous Man's prices are usually at least 30% below the going rate, and regular customers receive sale catalogs with further reductions. If you're in the market for a vintage poster, call Miscellaneous Man before you buy elsewhere. Although his prices are sometimes comparable (especially on scarce or rare posters), Miscellaneous Man can and has charged 30% to 75% less than New York City sources—and his selection is invariably better.

Special Factors: Layaways are accepted; returns are accepted within three days; minimum order is $50 with credit cards.

ORIGINAL PAPER COLLECTIBLES

700-W CLIPPER GAP RD.
AUBURN, CA 95603

Brochure, Sample Label: free with *long*, self-addressed, stamped envelope (see text)
Pay: check or MO
Sells: original, vintage labels
Store: mail order only

   ¡Si!

William Wauters began his business in 1970, when fruit crate labels were among the hot collectibles in antique and curio shops nationwide. Original Paper Collectibles has thrived over the years, attesting to the enduring appeal of the label designs. At this writing, Mr. Wauters offers labels originally intended for brooms, soda pop, canned fruits and vegetables, and produce—apples, pears, lettuce, oranges, asparagus, lemons, and other fruits and vegetables. Collectors of African-Americana will find a selection of 10 labels depicting black characters.

The collections offer the best per-label prices, and Mr. Wauters says that dealers routinely double his prices when they resell. The price list describes the most popular collection of fruit crate labels that include orange, apple, asparagus, lemon, pear, lettuce, cherry, grape, and carrot varieties—150 for $25, postpaid. (A vintage poster gallery in New York City charges that much for a *single* label.) Sliding discounts of 10% to 35% are given on orders of $100, $250, and $500. If you're searching for a specific label, you may find it among the listings of individual labels, which are grouped by size and type. If you're looking for something out of the ordinary to cover the walls, ask here—the labels can be used as wall treatments. One Detroit pizza parlor even used them in a decoupage treatment on the tabletops!

Please note: Payment for orders should be made to William Wauters, *not* Original Paper Collectibles, and requests for catalogs *must* include the long, stamped, self-addressed envelope.

Canadian and non-U.S.-based readers, please note: Send a self-addressed envelope with an International Reply Coupon, available at your local post office (do not include a stamp, unless it's U.S. postage).

Special Factors: Satisfaction is guaranteed; price quote by letter with SASE; quantity discounts are available.

PHONECO, INC.

■■■■■■■

DEPT. WBMC
P.O. BOX 70
GALESVILLE, WI 54630
608–582–4124
FAX: 608–582–4593

Catalog: $3
Pay: check, MO, MC, V, AE, Discover
Sells: vintage telephones and accessories
Store: same address; Monday to Friday 9–5
E-mail: phonecoinc@aol.com

Communicate through the instruments of the pre-digital age—literally—with a vintage telephone from Phoneco. This firm has been repairing and restoring old phones since 1971, and sells both refurbished models and hard-to-find components through a 28-page catalog. The current edition begins with the 1893 "Eiffel" and candlestick phones that date from World War I, and shows scores more—Kellogg's 1937 Redbar desk model, the Art Deco Stromberg Carlson, Trimline and Princess phones, the award-winning Ericofone from Ericsson, the original Mickey Mouse phone, genuine wooden "country-junction" models, baroque phones from France, and transparent Touch-Tones from the 70s are just a few.

Most of the phones are fully operational, but if you can repair the old ones, you can save by buying "as-is" models and refurbishing them yourself. Here Phoneco can help as well, with a great selection of cords (including the old cloth-covered style), magnetos and ringer boxes, dials and touch pads, receiver parts, line jacks and adapters, and even the decals and brass nameplates that identified the originals. Phone posters, original GTE Communications Handbooks, and books on collecting and repairing old phones are also available, as well as old key-phones, cable, substations, and even old oak phone booths.

Price checks on two of the models in Phoneco's catalog revealed savings of 38% (on the Ericofone) and over 50% (on a Bakelite Oslo phone), compared to a local phone boutique. The terms of the sales policy are given in the catalog ($3), but if you have a specific vintage phone or part in mind, you can call or write to inquire about availability and prices.

Special Factors: Price quote by phone or letter; authorized returns are accepted within 30 days for exchange, refund, or credit.

JOHN W. POLING: MILITARY & POLITICAL COLLECTIBLES

Catalog: $2 each (see text)
Pay: check or MO
Sells: military and political collectibles
Store: mail order only

DEPT. WBMC
5998 SOUTH RIDGEVIEW RD.
ANDERSON, IN 46013
765–778–2714

Wars, political slugfests, governmental chicanery—apart from anything else, they all leave a trail of souvenirs in their wake. John Poling sells both political memorabilia, chiefly campaign buttons, and an extensive collection of militaria from the U.S. and abroad—all at very low prices.

The review catalog of political collectibles opened with a group of Indiana election buttons and concluded with a page of Desert Storm support pins. Most of the items dated from the 1960s to the current era, although a William Jennings Bryan glass paperweight, dating from his turn-of-the-century presidential election bids, was also listed. Mr. Poling is strong on Alaska political and pinback buttons and related memorabilia. Buttons begin at under $1, and even an unused donkey's-head liquor decanter made by Regal China for the Democratic Party in the mid-1950s is just $15.

Mr. Poling's forte is militaria—58 pages of clothing, accessories, headgear, insignias and emblems, patches, field equipment, and much more, including an extensive listing of used books, some rare, and a range of printed material (magazines, manuals, broadsides, and newspapers). This is a collector's gold mine—among the helmets and liners alone there are specimens from the French, British, East German, South African, Spanish, and Italian armies, as well as several branches of the U.S. armed forces. A sample of stock from the current catalog includes Swiss Alpine Corps caps, Soviet Lenin portrait pins, World War II U.S. mess kits, unused dog tags and chains, East German suspenders, U.S. tropical combat coats (jungle jackets), and Iraqi headgear. Both the political collectibles and militaria catalogs also include several pages of "civilian" collectibles—movie posters, Olympic games and World's Fair memorabilia, tourist brochures, and extremely miscellaneous items—everything from a smattering of Fiesta Ware to a Packard hubcap can turn up here.

Like the items listed in the "political" catalog, the military collectibles are very well priced. Mr. Poling allows you to review your purchases for 10 days, and accepts returns (in the same condition sent) for a full refund, not including shipping. Please note that each catalog costs $2, payable in U.S. funds. All items are "guaranteed to be genuine" and described accurately; some reproductions were listed in the review catalog, but they were clearly marked as such.

Special Factors: Satisfaction is guaranteed; returns are accepted within 10 days for exchange or refund.

SEE ALSO

Barrons • *Goebel and Royal Doulton collectibles* • **HOME: TABLE SETTINGS**
Beverly Bremer Silver Shop • *heirloom and estate silver pieces* • **HOME: TABLE SETTINGS**
Editions • *first editions and rare books* • **BOOKS**
Elderly Instruments • *vintage fretted instruments* • **MUSIC**
Fountain Pen Hospital • *rare and vintage fountain pens, repair services, supplies, etc.* • **OFFICE**
Mandolin Brothers, Ltd. • *vintage fretted instruments* • **MUSIC**
Record-Rama Sound Archives • *vintage LPs and 45s* • **BOOKS: RECORDINGS**
Rogers & Rosenthal, Inc. • *figurines and collectibles* • **HOME: TABLE SETTINGS**
The Scholar's Bookshelf • *remaindered university-press art books* • **BOOKS**
The Silver Queen Inc. • *estate silver* • **HOME: TABLE SETTINGS**
Strand Book Store, Inc. • *books on the fine and applied arts* • **BOOKS**
University Products, Inc. • *archival-quality collection storage, mounting, and display materials* • **OFFICE: SMALL BUSINESS**

ART MATERIALS

Materials, tools, equipment, and supplies for the fine and applied arts

You don't *have* to starve to be an artist, but the cost of good tools and supplies almost guarantees it—unless you buy them discount. Small art stores seldom knock off more than 10% on list prices, except on quantity purchases. But mail-order discounters routinely offer savings of at least twice that. The firms listed here sell supplies and materials for fine arts and some crafts: pigments, paper, brushes, canvas, frames, stretchers, pads, studio furniture, vehicles and solvents, silkscreening supplies, carving tools, and much more.

Since different materials can have a profound effect on the quality and direction of your work, familiarize yourself with what's on the market through catalogs and artists' magazines. The catalog from Daniel Smith, listed in this chapter, provides a wealth of information. For a comprehensive assessment of the properties and uses of almost every medium available today, see *The Artists' Handbook of Materials and Techniques* (Viking Press), which can be found in libraries and is available from several firms in this chapter.

Concern about the safety of art materials has led to the Art Materials Labeling Act of 1988, and Congress has also asked the Consumer Products Safety Commission to create standards for the art materials industry, and banned the use of hazardous materials by children in the sixth grade or younger. This is important legislation, since the list of substances found in widely used materials has included toluene, asbestos, chloroform, xylene, n-hexane, carbolic acid, trichlorethylene, and benzene, to note just a few. Even with reformulation and warnings, art materials can still pose some hazards. Good studio protocol can minimize much of the exposure:

1. Select the least toxic and hazardous products available.

2. If your work creates dust or fumes, use a quality, OSHA-approved respirator suitable to the task—there are masks to filter organic vapors, ammonia, asbestos, toxic dusts, mists and fumes, and paint spray.

3. Use other protective gear as applicable: gloves to reduce the absorption of chemicals through the skin, earplugs to protect against hearing damage from loud machinery, and safety goggles to avoid eye damage from accidents.

4. A good window-exhaust system is essential to reducing inhaled vapors. Create a real airflow when working with fume-producing materials—the breeze from an open window isn't enough.

5. Keep children and animals out of the work place since chemicals reach higher levels of concentration in their systems.

6. Don't eat, drink, or smoke in the work area, or before cleaning up.

7. Keep appropriate safety equipment on hand to deal with emergencies: an eyewash station if caustics are being used, a first-aid kit, a fire extinguisher if combustible materials are present, etc.

8. Ask your school board to make sure the least toxic and hazardous products are used in the classroom.

For further reading, consult the information on toxicity in *The Artists' Handbook of Materials and Techniques*, referenced above. Michael McCann's *The Hazards in Working with All Art and Craft Materials and the Precautions Every Artist and Photographer Should Take* (Lyons & Burford, 1993), is the definitive book for artist, student, and parent. *Health Hazards Manual for Artists* (Lyons & Burford, 1994), a smaller book by Mr. McCann, includes specifics on materials commonly used by children. Both are sold by Ceramic Supply of New York & New Jersey (listed in this chapter), and online (at this writing) from Book Stacks (http://www.books.com/).

For firms that sell art-related products, see "Crafts and Hobbies" and "General Merchandise."

FIND IT FAST

CERAMICS AND POTTERY • **Ceramic Supply**
CHILDREN'S AND EDUCATIONAL ART SUPPLIES • **Texas Art**
FINE ARTS • **Art Express, Cheap Joe's, Italian Art Store, Jerry's Artarama, Napa Valley, Ott's, Pearl Paint, Daniel Smith, Texas Art, Utrecht**
FRAMES • **American Frame, Frame Fit, Graphik Dimensions, Daniel Smith, Stu-Art, Utrecht**
GRAPHIC DESIGN • **A.I. Friedman, Texas Art, Utrecht**
MAILING TUBES • **Yazoo**
PAPER AND PRINTMAKING • **Daniel Smith**
SILKSCREENING • **Ott's, Texas Art**

AMERICAN FRAME CORPORATION

400 TOMAHAWK DR.
MAUMEE, OH 43537–1695
800–537–0944
FAX: 800–893–3898

Catalog: free
Pay: check, MO, MC, V, AE, Discover
Sells: preassembled and sectional frames
and supplies
Store: same address; Monday to Friday
9–4:30
E-mail: info@americanframe.com

American Frame, in business since 1973, sells assembled *wood* frames—a great way to get the look of a custom framing job, at do-it-yourself prices—as well as *metal* sectional frames in a wonderful selection of colors. American Frame's prices are 35% to 50% lower than those charged by other art-supply firms.

The 36-page catalog features frame sections in basswood, maple, poplar, oak, and cherry, in a variety of stains and treatments, many of which are gilded. Each wood frame includes spring clips to hold the mounted artwork securely in place, hangers, and wall protectors. (Assembly requires screwing the spring clips and hangers—the joints are preassembled.) The metal frames are offered in dozens of colors and a choice of 12 profiles, to accommodate ordinary flat work and extra-deep canvases.

Bainbridge board—acid-free mat, perfect-mount, and foam core—is sold in groups of 10 or more sheets, depending on the item. The mat board is offered in over 100 colors in the 32" by 40" size or cut to order; foam core and perfect-mount boards are cut to order in dimensions up to 24" by 30". Rolls of polyester film are available, as well as acid-free acrylic picture "glass" (cut to order in dimensions up to 24" by 30").

Special Factors: Measure carefully before ordering; phone hours are 8:30 a.m. to 6 p.m. ET.

ART EXPRESS

DEPT. C
P.O. BOX 21662
COLUMBIA, SC 29212
800–535–5908
FAX: 803–750–1492

Catalog: $3.50
Pay: check, MO, MC, V, AE, Discover
Sells: art supplies and equipment
Store: mail order only

Art Express publishes an 80-page catalog featuring a well-chosen selection of art tools and equipment at discounts averaging 40%. The inventory includes papers and board, canvas, brushes, mediums and solvents, pens, portfolios, paint (including casein), Art Bin artists' cases, folding stools, art racks, inks, pastels, pencils, airbrushing equipment, easels by Anco, Best, Julian, Stanrite, and Trident; light boxes, Logan mat cutters, and Artograph and Seerite opaque projectors. Among the other names represented are Arches, Berol, Bienfang, Blockx, Canson, Da Vinci, Fabriano, Fredrix, Golden, Grumbacher, Holbein, Isabey, Lana, Liquitex, Luma, Raphaæl, Rembrandt, Rives, Bob Ross, Rowney, Schmincke, Sennelier, Shiva, Speedball, Strathmore, Studio RTA, Talens, and Winsor & Newton. Several pages list available books and videotapes on art technique, history, and related topics. If you don't see what you're looking for, write or fax Art Express with product information—the item might be in stock.

Special Factors: Quantity discounts are available; institutional accounts are available; minimum order is $25 on stock paper.

CERAMIC SUPPLY OF NEW YORK & NEW JERSEY, INC.

7 RTE. 46 W.
LODI, NJ 07644
201–340–3005
FAX: 201–340–0089

Catalog: $4
Pay: check, MO, MC, V
Sells: sculpture, pottery, glazing, and crafts supplies and equipment
Store: same address; Monday to Friday 9–5, Thursday 9–9
E-mail: ceramicnynj@aol.com

   ¡Si!

Ceramic Supply of New York & New Jersey serves both of its name states with free delivery (in many areas) on orders of $125 or more. The company has been doing business since 1981, and offers good values on glazes, brushes, and a wide range of lightweight ceramics supplies that can be shipped worldwide at nominal expense. The 212-page catalog devotes most of its space to ceramics supplies and equipment: gas and electric kilns (including some that run on household current), raku and fiber kilns, glazes, resists, mediums, brushes, airbrushing tools, slip-casting equipment, potters' wheels, armatures, grinders, and related goods. The manufacturers include Alpine, Amaco, Brent, Kemper, Kimple, North Star, Shimpo, and Skutt, among others. The catalog includes color charts of glazes, underglazes, and other finishes by Duncan and Mayco, bisque dinnerware and assorted pieces, and dozens of types of clay, from white Grolleg porcelain to water-based to "economy" clay made of odds and ends of other clays. And there are lots of other modeling materials—Sculpey, plasters, and wax—as well.

Even if you're not a potter or sculptor, the catalog may interest you for the music box parts and movements in scores of tunes, lights and accessories for ceramic Christmas trees, hard-to-find lamp parts, clock movements and parts, jewelry findings, studio furniture, or safety equipment. Don't overlook the reference section, which features books on sculpture, ceramics, art hazards, and related topics, and videotapes and filmstrips.

Special Factors: Returns are accepted within 10 days (a restocking fee may be charged).

CHEAP JOE'S ART STUFF

████████████

374 INDUSTRIAL PARK RD.
BOONE, NC 28607
800–227–2788
704–262–0793
FAX: 800–257–0874
FAX: 704–262–0795

Catalog: free
Pay: check, MO, MC, V, Discover
Sells: art supplies and equipment
Store: Boone Drug Co., 617 E. King St., Boone, NC

There's a real Joe here at Cheap Joe's, the driving force behind the 88-page, full-color catalog that's full of tips on how to make the most of your tools and materials. Cheap Joe's dream of keeping his company small may be confounded by his great prices—savings of 30% are routine, and quantity pricing deepens the discounts to 60% on at least a few items.

The catalog features papers by Arches, Bockingford, Canson, Fabriano, Lana, and Waterford, paint from Da Vinci, Daler Rowney, Holbein, Rembrandt, Sennelier, and Winsor & Newton, paintbrushes from Robert Simmons and Winsor & Newton, as well as Cheap Joe's own line. You'll also find easels, shrink-wrap systems, Logan mat cutters, adhesives, foam core, Artograph projection equipment, Fredrix canvas, print racks, and books and videotapes on painting and art theory. Cheap Joe set up shop in 1986, and he wants to keep his company from getting too big so he can stay in touch with his artist customers. He's a serious watercolorist, and welcomes your questions and suggestions about materials and equipment.

Special Factors: Satisfaction is guaranteed; shipping is not charged on brushes; institutional accounts are available.

FRAME FIT CO.

DEPT. WBMC
P.O. BOX 8926
PHILADELPHIA, PA 19135
800–523–3693
215–332–0683
FAX: 800–344–7010

Brochure and Price List: free
Pay: check, MO, MC, V
Sells: aluminum, wood, and composite sectional frames
Store: mail order only
E-mail: framefit@netaxs.com
Online: http://www.netaxs.com/~framefit

Frame Fit sells aluminum, wood, and composite sectional frames and hardware. The aluminum frames are offered in four profiles, for both stretched canvas and other works of art. The colors include anodized metallics in polished and satin finishes, and 22 enamels (the canvas profile is available in eight metallics only). Stock sizes run from 4" to 40", but larger sizes are available; any frame can be cut to a fractional measurement, so they can be made as small as you like. All of the sections are sold in pairs, and include corner assembly hardware (springs, screw hangers, and picture wire are sold separately). Wood sectional frames are available in four profiles and six different wood finishes. The Evolutions line of picture frames are available in 38 different styles; although they resemble wood frames, they're made of composite plastic.

Frame Fit has been in business since 1977, and the firm's prices beat those of *discounted* frames sold elsewhere by 20% and more. If you can use 50 pairs of the same color, size, and profile, you can save from 15% to 25% more, depending on the color you choose. And if your order totals $300 plus, shipping is free (except on bulk chop goods).

Special Factors: Shipping is not charged on orders over $300 sent within the continental United States; C.O.D. orders are accepted.

A.I. FRIEDMAN

DEPT. WBMC
44 W. 18TH ST.
NEW YORK, NY 10011
212–337–8600
FAX: 212–929–7320

Catalog: $5 (see text)
Pay: check, MO, MC, V, AE
Sells: graphic arts supplies and tools
Store: same address; Monday to Friday 9–6; also 431 Boston Post Rd., Port Chester, NY; open daily

 ¡Si! ★

If you're a professional graphic designer or artist, you'll want to add A.I. Friedman to your short list of suppliers. The firm, which has been in business since 1929, serves the creative community with the best in tools and equipment. You can send $5 for the well-organized loose-leaf catalog, but it's free to design professionals requesting it on letterhead.

The catalog itself is an object lesson in good design, making it easy to find what you want amid the equipment for computer graphics, presentation materials, studio furniture, drawing instruments, markers, paint, brushes, paper and board, airbrushing supplies, audiovisual equipment, frames, and reference books. Friedman offers goods not found in every art supply catalog: light boxes, dry-mounting presses, the *complete* Pantone line, precision drawing and drafting tools, a large selection of templates, and complete photostat systems. Among the manufacturers represented are Agfa, Apple, Bainbridge, Canson, Chartpak, D'Arches, Dr. Ph. Martin's, Grumbacher, Hewlett-Packard, Iris, Iwata, Koh-I-Noor, Letraset, Liquitex, Luxo (lamps), Mayline, Mont Blanc, Osmiroid, Paasche, Pelikan, Staedler-Mars, Strathmore, 3M, Tektronix, and Winsor & Newton. The catalog prices are not discounted, but if your order totals $50 or more, discounts of 20% to 40% are given. (Some items aren't discounted, including the Agfa products.) Call or write for a quote on specific items.

Special Factors: Price quote by phone or letter; institutional accounts are available; minimum order is $50 (see text).

GRAPHIK DIMENSIONS LTD.

2103 BRENTWOOD ST.
HIGH POINT, NC 27263
800–221–0262
910–887–3700
FAX: 910–887–3773

Catalog: free
Pay: check, MO, MC, V, Discover
Sells: sectional and custom-made frames and accessories
Store: same address

You can get the frame you want with frame sections from Graphik Dimensions—or you can have it custom-made by the firm's expert crafters. Graphik Dimensions is run by an artist and photographer who have firsthand experience in selecting the right frame for the piece, and finding the best price. Their 36-page color catalog offers the "classic" metal sectional frames often sold in art supply stores, in both standard depths, for use with glass, and "canvas" depth, for oil paintings, in metallics and enamels. The selection also includes wooden gallery frames in plain, gilded, embossed, rustic, and natural finishes. Graphik Dimensions' custom line features wood moldings, some of which include linen liners at no extra charge. If the prospect of putting a frame together seems overwhelming, there's help: Graphik Dimensions also sells preassembled and custom-made assembled frames in several different styles, and offers custom-cut mats.

Framing kits are available in your choice of wood frames, and include the glass (or acrylic), backing board, retainer clips, hanging screws, and wire—no tools necessary. Before you order a frame, order the sample set of corners. These are actual pieces of the frame that show color, depth, and corner joinery style. The cost of the sample sets ($5 to $30, depending on the line) is repaid in the trouble you save if the frame wasn't right for the work. (Individual pieces of framing are available free on request.) And all wood frames come with hangers, retainer clips, and wire.

Special Factors: Satisfaction is guaranteed; quantity discounts are available; authorized returns (except custom frames) are accepted (a 15% restocking fee may be charged); C.O.D. orders are accepted.

THE ITALIAN ART STORE

84 MAPLE AVE.
MORRISTOWN, NJ 07960
800–643–6440
201–644–2717
FAX: 201–644–5074

Catalog: free
Pay: check, MO, MC, V, Discover
Sells: fine art supplies
Store: same address; Monday to Friday 9–5

The Italian Art Store began business paying homage to the epicenter of the Renaissance, selling *only* Italian art supplies. Raphael watercolor brushes, Maimeri Restoration Colors, Fabriano papers, and Sennelier pastels—all among the finest of their type—are offered. The Italian Art Store has since expanded the selection, with oils from Blockx, Old Holland, and Schmincke, Golden acrylics, Fredrix canvas, Holbein, Rowney, and Winsor & Newton watercolors and mediums, Rembrandt and Aquarelle pencils, Schmincke gouache, Classico paints, Isabey brushes, and easels by Julian and Mabef. The Italian Art Store's own line includes pigments, brushes, canvas, and easels. Discounts average 50% on list prices, but specials and closeouts run up to 75% off.

Special Factors: Unused goods in their original wrapping are accepted within 45 days for exchange, refund, or credit.

JERRY'S ARTARAMA, INC.

DEPT. WBMC
P.O. BOX 58638
RALEIGH, NC 27658
919–878–6782
FAX: 919–873–9565

Catalog: $2
Pay: check, MO, MC, V, AE, Discover
Sells: art supplies, picture frames, etc.
Store: 1109 New Britain Ave., West Hartford, CT (860–232–0073); 248–12 Union Tpk., Bellerose, NY (718–343–0777), and Southtown Plaza, 3333 West Henrietta Rd., Rochester, NY (716–424–6600); and 270 S. Federal Hwy. (U.S. 1), Deerfield Beach, FL (954–427–6264)
E-mail: uartist@aol.com
Online: http://www.jerryscatalog.com

Jerry's Artarama, in business since 1968, publishes a 144-page compendium of materials, tools, and equipment for commercial and fine arts that includes both basics and specialty goods that are seldom discounted elsewhere.

The catalog offers pigments, brushes, vehicles and solvents, airbrushes and compressors, studio furniture, lighting, visual equipment, canvas and framing supplies, papers, and other goods, and features an extensive section supplies for oil, watercolor, and acrylic painting. Jerry's also sells supplies for drawing, graphic arts, drafting, calligraphy, printmaking, sumi-e, airbrushing, fabric painting, marbleizing, and professional framing. There are some "generic" brands, but most are familiar names: Alvin, Badger, Blockx, Conté, Deka, D'Arches, Fabriano, Fredrix, Grumbacher, Holbein, Isabey, Iwata, Koh-I-Noor, Langnickel, Mayline, Paasche, Bob Ross, Robert Simmons, Stabilo, Strathmore, Winsor & Newton, and X-Acto are among the many represented. Don't miss the dozen pages of publications, including technique manuals, color guides, and workshop videotapes—all of which are discounted.

Special Factors: Satisfaction is unconditionally guaranteed; color charts and product specifications are available on request; quantity discounts are available; minimum order is $20, $50 with phone orders.

NAPA VALLEY ART STORE

1041 LINCOLN AVE.
NAPA, CA 94558–4913
800–648–6696
707–257–1810
FAX: 707–257–1111

Catalog: free
Pay: check, MO, MC, V
Sells: fine-arts supplies and equipment
Store: same address; Monday to Friday 7–4 PT; closed 12–1, closed weekends

Napa Valley Art Store sells fine-arts supplies at discount prices, and you can see the 50-page catalog for the current offerings, or call the store with your needs. Napa Valley stocks products by Altos (mat cutters), Arches, Canson, Fredrix, Grumbacher, Isabey, Julian, Liquitex, Prismacolor, Rembrandt, Sennelier, and Winsor & Newton, among others—and everything from paint and canvas to easels and instructional videos are available. See the catalog for the current specials and quantity prices.

Special Factors: Minimum shipping fee is $6.95; shipments made to the 50 United States only; returns are accepted within 45 days for exchange, refund, or credit; minimum order is $25.

OTT'S DISCOUNT ART SUPPLY

DEPT. WBMC
102 HUNGATE DR.
GREENVILLE, NC
27858–8045
800–356–3289
919–756–9565
FAX: 919–756–2397

Catalog: free
Pay: check, MO, MC, V
Sells: art, graphics, and crafts supplies
Store: mail order only
Online: http://www.otts.com/

Painters, sculptors, and artists of all types can get great prices on all of their needs from Ott's, a family-run firm that also serves schools and institutions. The 64-page catalog runs from Academy watercolors to Zec Quick Dryer from Grumbacher. The brands include Amaco (clay and kilns), Amsterdam, Arches, Aztek, Badger, Bemis-Jason, Berol, Bienfang, Canson, Crayola, Dixon, Faber Castell, General Pencil, Grumbacher, Hunt, Koh-I-Noor, Liquitex, Loew-Cornell, Morilla, Paasche, Prang, Rembrandt, Bob Ross, Sakura, Strathmore, Tara-Fredrix, Van Gogh, Winsor & Newton, and X-Acto, among others. You'll find oils and tempera paints, acrylics, watercolors, pastels, stretchers, canvas, pencils and charcoal, paper, airbrush and silkscreening equipment, easels, projection equipment, craft paints, clay and kilns, styrofoam, candle-making and wood-burning supplies, adhesives, craft knives and brushes, and more. There's a good selection of instructional materials, including guides from North Light Books, and great rainy-day projects like the Deluxe Volcano and Solar System Kits. Ott's has been in business since 1972, and will special-order items not in the catalog.

Special Factors: Satisfaction is guaranteed; returns are accepted within 30 days for exchange, refund, or credit; institutional orders are accepted; orders under $30 are charged shipping, handling, and a small-order fee.

PEARL PAINT CO., INC.

DEPT. WBM
308 CANAL ST.
NEW YORK, NY
10013–2572
800–221–6845
212–431–7932
FAX: 212–274–8290

Catalog: $1
Pay: check, MO, MC, V, AE, Discover
Sells: art, craft, and graphics supplies, studio furniture, etc.
Store: same address; also 42 Lispenard St., New York, NY (architectural furniture showroom); open daily; also San Francisco, CA; Altamonte Springs, Ft. Lauderdale, South Miami, and Tampa, FL; Atlanta, GA; Chicago, IL; Cambridge, MA; Rockville, MD; Cherry Hill, Paramus, and Woodbridge, NJ; East Meadow, NY; Houston, TX; and Alexandria, VA
Online: http://www.pearlpaint.com

Gotham artists have been flocking to Pearl Paint since 1933 for good prices on fine paints, tools, and supplies, and since then Pearl has opened stores in nine other states as well (locations are listed in the catalog). Since the 144-page catalog represents a fraction of the available stock (fine art materials), call, fax, or write if you're looking for something that's not listed. In addition to tools and supplies for the fine arts,

Pearl sells materials and equipment for all kinds of crafts: pigments, brushes, stretchers, papers, canvas, manuals, studio furniture, children's supplies, and much more. The brands include Bainbridge, Canson-Talens, Caran D'Ache, Deka, DeVilbiss, Fabriano, Grumbacher, Holbein, Iwata, Koh-I-Noor, Lascaux, Letraset, Liquitex, Paasche, Pantone, Pebeo, Pelikan, Raphaël, Sculpture House, Sennelier, Robert Simmons, Staedtler, and Winsor & Newton, among others. Pearl also stocks fine writing instruments, house paint, frames and framing supplies, and gilding and faux finishing supplies.

Special Factors: Quantity discounts are available; weekly specials are run on selected items; minimum order is $50.

DANIEL SMITH

P.O. BOX 84268
SEATTLE, WA 98124–5568
800–426–6740 (U.S. AND
   CANADA)
206–223–9599
FAX: 800–238–4065

Catalog: free
Pay: check, MO, MC, V, AE
Sells: fine-arts supplies and equipment
Store: 4150 First Ave. South, Seattle, WA;
Monday, Tuesday, Thursday, Friday, Saturday
9–6, Wednesday 9–8, Sunday 10–6

Daniel Smith's catalogs are designed by artists, for artists, and are appreciated as much for their book reviews, technical discussions, and visual appeal as for their offerings. Daniel Smith has been recommended by artists impressed by the company's line of materials and responsive service department; the firm features competitive pricing and regular sales.

The annual Reference Catalog presents an extensive collection of paper from Arches, Canson, Fabriano, Lana, Magnani, Rising, Strathmore, and other makers, for watercolors, printmaking, drawing, bookmaking, and other applications. This catalog also features uncommon specialty papers, including banana paper from the Philippines, Mexican bark paper, genuine papyrus, and Japanese "fantasy" paper embedded with maple leaves.

Daniel Smith has been manufacturing etching inks and artists' paints for more than 18 years, and features the Daniel Smith Original Oils, Autograph Series Oils, and the newly created Daniel Smith Extra-Fine line of artists' watercolors—paints notable for their quality, rich formulation, and unique color range—including luminescent and metallic colors. Daniel Smith sells acrylics, oils, watercolors, egg tempera, and gouache from such companies as Golden, Lascaux, Rowney, Schmincke, Talens, and Winsor & Newton. The brush line covers all painting media, and includes Daniel Smith's own line, as well as brushes from Isabey, Strathmore, and Winsor & Newton. Canvas, Nielsen sectional metal frames, wood frames, airbrush equipment, solvents, pastels, colored pencils, calligraphy pens, printmaking materials, and other tools and supplies are available, rounded out by a fine collection of studio furniture, portfolios, easels, and reference books.

Canadian readers, please note: Only U.S. funds are accepted.

Special Factors: Satisfaction is guaranteed; authorized returns are accepted for exchange, refund, or credit; minimum order of paper is 10 sheets.

STU-ART

2045 GRAND AVE.,
DEPT. WBMC
BALDWIN, NY 11510–2999
516–546–5151
FAX: 516–377–3512

Catalog and Samples: free
Pay: check, MO, MC, V, Discover
Sells: mats, frames, and framing supplies
Store: same address; Monday to Saturday 9–5

Stu-Art sells sectional frames and framing materials—everything you'll need to do a professional job. The firm has been supplying galleries and institutions since 1970, and it offers the best materials, a range of sizes, and savings of up to 50% on list prices.

Nielsen metal frames are offered in nine profiles, for flat, stretched canvas and dimensional art (deep) mounting, in a stunning array of brushed metallic finishes, soft pastels, and deep decorator colors. Sectional wood frames are also available, in different profiles and a variety of finishes. Acid-free single and double mats are sold in rectangles and ovals. The catalog includes precise specifications of the frames, and samples of the mats. Stu-Art also sells nonglare and clear plastic (which can be used in place of picture glass), and shrink film and dispensers. If you have to get work framed, see the catalog before handing it over to a professional—you may decide you can do the job yourself.

Special Factors: Shipping is not charged on UPS-delivered orders over $300 net; authorized returns are accepted (a restocking fee may be charged); minimum order is $15 on sectional frames, $25 on other goods.

TEXAS ART SUPPLY

2001 MONTROSE BLVD.
HOUSTON, TX 77006
800–888–9278
713–526–5221
FAX: 713–526–4062

Print Catalog: $3
CD-ROM Catalog: $2.50
Pay: check, MO, MC, V, AE, Discover
Sells: fine arts, graphics, and craft supplies
Store: same address; also 2237 South Voss
and 1507 Baybrook Mall Dr., Houston, TX
E-mail: info@texasart.com
Online: http://www.texasart.com

Texas Art Supply, which marks half a century in business this year, packs the 400-plus pages of its catalog with a wide range of products for fine arts, graphics and design, ceramics, and other crafts. The brands include the trusted standards—Berol, Bienfang, Chartpak, Conte, Crescent, D'Arches, Duncan, Grumbacher, Koh-I-Noor, Liquitex, NuPastel, Pantone, Paragon, Robert Simmons, Speedball, Strathmore, Winsor & Newton, and X-Acto, among many others. Basics for silkscreening, airbrushing, block printing, scratch art, clay and stone sculpture, stenciling, fabric painting and batiking, and other crafts are also available, as well as products with broad appeal: lettering and sign supplies, glue guns and refills, bronzing powders and metal leaf, projectors, office supplies, lamp parts, music-box works, cotton "blanks," crayons, and educational supplies and teaching aids are all offered.

The price list shows the list and discounted prices, and the terms of sale are stated clearly in the catalog, in English and Spanish. The catalog costs $3 ($2.50 for the CD-ROM version), and you can also call directly for a quote. Note that Texas Art Supply lists only a portion of the stock in the catalog anyway, so if you don't see what you want, ask.

Special Factors: Price quote by phone or letter; quantity discounts are available; shipping is included on orders over $100 sent to the 48 contiguous United States; authorized returns are accepted in original, unopened packaging within 30 days for exchange, refund, or credit.

UTRECHT ART AND DRAFTING SUPPLY

33 35TH ST.
BROOKLYN, NY 11232
800–223–9132
718–768–2525
FAX: 718–499–8815

Catalog: free
Pay: check, MO, MC, V
Sells: art supplies
Store: 111 Fourth Ave., Brooklyn, NY; Monday to Saturday 9–6; also Berkeley and San Francisco, CA; Washington, DC; Chicago, IL; Boston, MA; Detroit, MI; and Philadelphia, PA (numbers listed in catalog)

  ¡Si!

Utrecht has been selling supplies and equipment for painting, sculpture, and printmaking since 1949, and manufactures some of the best-priced oil and acrylic paints on the market. The 48-page catalog describes the manufacturing process and quality controls used to produce Utrecht's paint, and features Utrecht acrylics, oils, watercolors, gesso, and other mediums and solvents. The firm also sells a full line of professional artists' materials and equipment, including canvas, stretchers, frames, pads, paper, brushes, books, easels, flat files, taborets, pencils, drafting tools, and much more. In addition to the Utrecht label, goods by Arches, Bainbridge, Bienfang, Canson, Chartpak, Claessens, D'Arches, Deka, Eberhard Faber, Grumbacher, Koh-I-Noor, Kolinsky, Liquitex, Niji, Pentel, Rembrandt, Speedball, Strathmore, Vermeer, Winsor & Newton, and other manufacturers are available. Utrecht's prices are competitive, and the best buys are on the house brand and quantity purchases.

Special Factors: Institutional accounts are available; quantity discounts are available; minimum order is $40.

YAZOO MILLS, INC.

305 COMMERCE ST.
P.O. BOX 369
NEW OXFORD, PA 17350
800–242–5216
717–624–8993
FAX: 717–624–4420

Catalog: free
Pay: check, MO, MC, V, AE, Discover
Sells: shipping tubes
Store: mail and phone orders

Yazoo Mills takes its name from the Mississippi town where it was founded in 1902, but since moving to Pennsylvania in 1936, Yazoo has run the plant from New Oxford. The firm manufactures paper tubes for shipping and industry—carpet "cores," cable reels, fax paper tubes, even heavy blast casings for the mining industry—Yazoo makes them all. Yazoo also offers shipping tubes in the sizes most popular among artists: lengths from 12" to 85", in diameters of 2" to 12" (the larger sizes are "heavy duty" or "extra heavy duty"). The tubes are sold by the case—48 in a carton of 2" by 12" tubes, to one of the 12" by 85"—with plastic plug inserts for the ends. The prices, which include shipping, are so low that even if all you need are two mid-sized tubes, it's probably worth buying from Yazoo—they're priced up to 80% below art-supply houses!

The tubes can be used for storage as well as shipping art and other objects; note that they're made of recycled paperboard, and may be made in acid-free stock. Yazoo does much of its manufacturing to job specifications, and can give you quotes on custom sizes or colors.

Special Factors: Shipping is not charged; minimum order is one carton of stock tubes; C.O.D. orders are accepted.

SEE ALSO

Dharma Trading Co. • *tools and materials for fabric painting and dyeing* • **CRAFTS: TEXTILE ARTS**
Fidelity Products Co. • *drafting and graphic arts supplies* • **OFFICE**
Gramma's Graphics,Inc. • *paper and fabric imaging materials and supplies* • **CRAFTS**
Hacker Art Books, Inc. • *books on the fine and applied arts* • **BOOKS**
Lighthouse Colorprint • *full-color postcards and brochures* • **OFFICE**
Plexi-Craft Quality Products Corp. • *acrylic display pedestals* • **HOME: FURNISHINGS**

The Potters Shop Inc. • *books on pottery and ceramics* • **BOOKS**

Print's Graphic Design Book Store • *books and manuals on the graphic arts* • **BOOKS**

Thai Silks • *silk fabrics for fabric painting* • **CRAFTS: TEXTILE ARTS**

Utex Trading Enterprises • *silk fabric for fabric painting* • **CRAFTS: TEXTILE ARTS**

AUTO, MARINE, AND AVIATION EQUIPMENT

Parts, supplies, maintenance products,

and services

You'll find a range of parts and supplies for cars, motorcycles, RVs, trucks, and vans in this chapter—mufflers, shocks, tires, batteries, and much more. Some companies stock products for vintage cars, and one offers products for the "general pilot." You can buy salvaged parts through several of the firms listed here, priced as much as 70% less than the same parts if new. You can also buy cars, trucks, and vans, through services offered by American Auto Brokers (listed in this chapter), and on the Internet, through such services as Auto-By-Tel (http://www.auto-bytel.com/) and Microsoft's CarPoint (http://carpoint.msn.com/). Here are some additional information sources to help you make the best selection when buying a car:

1. *Consumer Reports* publishes reliable vehicle ratings each year and offers price comparisons and reliability ratings of new and used cars. The "Consumer Reports Auto Price Service" provides a computer print-out showing both list price and dealer's cost for the model you specify, information on rebates and recommended options, and guidelines for negotiating the lowest possible price. At this writing, one report costs $12, and additional reports ordered at the same time are $10 each. See the current *Consumer Reports* for information. The "Consumer Reports Used Car Price Service" gives current prices, in your region, on models as far back as 1988. To get a price, you answer questions about a specific model—condition, mileage, year, number of cylinders, major options, etc.—to which the computer adds other facts, and calculates a price. The service is terrific for someone who wants to negotiate a bet-

ter deal on a used car, or set a price when they sell. See the current issue of *Consumer Reports* for the 900 number and per-minute charges (Touch-Tone required).

2. Another benchmark pricing service, *IntelliChoice,* provides two types of reports: "Just the Facts," which gives you data on *one* car, for all models within that line—factory and dealer prices, taxes and sur-charges, nationwide rebate programs, standard and available options, etc. The "Arm-Chair Compare" report ($19.95) compares two different models in a line; you provide IntelliChoice with a list of all the options and finishes you want on *each* model. Call IntelliChoice at 800–227–2665 for current rates and to order a report (have the car infor-mation ready when you call).

3. *Consumer Reports Cars: The Essential Guide,* is a CD-ROM that includes buying guidelines, safety information, maintenance tips, and a roundup of cars made in the past 10 years, with comprehensive specs—a worthy addition to your CD-ROM library if you're shopping for a new car, priced right at under $20. (Make sure you're getting this year's edi-tion of the CD, and that your computer is equipped to handle it—since future editions may alter configuration requirements, they aren't listed here, so check the specs before buying.) See the latest edition of *Con-sumer Reports* for information.

4. More car-buying tips and traps are detailed in W. James Bragg's *In the Driver's Seat: The New Car Negotiating Bible* (Random House), and Burke Leon's *The Insider's Guide to Buying a New or Used Car* (Better-way Books, 800–289–0963).

5. *The Car Book,* by Jack Gillis (HarperCollins), rates current domestic and imported models on crash-test performance, as well as fuel econ-omy, preventive-maintenance costs, repair costs, and insurance rates. This annual also includes valuable information on evaluating warranties, service contracts, insurance, tires, children's car seats, and used cars. A comprehensive, easy-to-understand "Complaint" chapter can help you to resolve difficulties, and the "Checklist" will help you ask the right questions while shopping. *The Car Book* is available in bookstores or from The Center for Auto Safety, 2001 S St., NW, Suite 410, Washington, DC 20009. (Send a long, self-addressed, stamped envelope for the pub-lications list and ordering information.)

6. *The National Highway Administration Auto Safety Hotline* can help you check safety factors when you're shopping for a new or used car. In addition to crash test reports and guidelines to buying a safer car, the Hotline has recall information on autos and related products, such as infants' car seats. And you can *report* safety problems here, too. Call 800–424–9393 for more information, or visit the website at http://www.nhtsa.dot.gov/

7. The Better Business Bureau publishes guides to buying cars and tires, as well as other consumer goods. Send a self-addressed, stamped envelope to the Council of Better Business Bureaus, Inc., 4200 Wilson Blvd., Suite 800, Arlington, VA 22203, Attn.: Publications Dept., and request the list of available brochures and ordering information. The Bureau also administers the BBB AUTO LINE, a program to resolve disputes between individual consumers and auto manufacturers over perceived manufacturing defects. Thirty manufacturers are involved, on a national or state-by-state basis, at this writing. Note that the AUTO LINE does *not* handle complaints about auto dealers, repair services, or insurers—just manufacturers. For more information, call 800–955–5100, or see the website at http://www.bbb.org/complaints/BBBautoLine.html

You can save hundreds or even thousands of dollars when buying your car, only to squander as much thanks to bad driving habits. The following tips will conserve funds and fuel, keeping your wallet fatter and the air cleaner:

1. Drive at 55 mph or less, whenever possible. You'll go about 20% farther on the same tank than you do when traveling at 70 mph.

2. Don't burn fuel you don't have to: If the car will be idling for more than a minute, turn it off instead; use the air-conditioning only when you really need it; and keep the car free of excess weight.

3. Have the wheels aligned at least once a year, and switch to radials, which maximize mileage.

4. Check your tire pressure monthly, using a gauge (the old pencil style is inexpensive and reliable, and stows easily in the glove compartment). If you're driving on under-inflated tires, you're using more gas than necessary—as much as 2% of your bill at the pump could be waste. Take the reading when the tires are cold, using guidelines provided by the car manufacturer.

5. Follow other care instructions outlined in your car manual, including scheduling tune-ups and changing oil and filters.

Preventive maintenance notwithstanding, your car will need some kind of repair eventually. Mark Eskeldon, a car mechanic himself, tells all in *What Auto Mechanics Don't Want You to Know* ($14.95 postpaid from Upper Access Books; 800–528–8634). It will help you identify good repair shops and to recognize deceptive trade practices. Last, the monthly *Nutz & Boltz* provides regular reading on a wide range of automotive topics; write to Box 123, Butler, MD 21023, for current subscription information.

Fear of getting stranded far from home with a disabled car leads many drivers to join auto clubs. Service and survival are great benefits, but most of the organizations provide far more than emergency towing. The best-known club, the American Automobile Association (AAA), boasts about 30 million members among its affiliates and offers a wide range of membership benefits. The AAA of New York, for example, provides travel-planning services, discounts on lodging and car rentals, fee-free travelers' checks, special services for travel abroad, personal accident insurance, assistance in solving license problems, home-equity loans, discount eyeglass prescriptions, a newsletter, and other benefits. The package of services varies from affiliate to affiliate; to find the AAA club nearest you, call 800–222–4357. Other clubs worth contacting for rates and services are Amoco Motor Club (800–782–7887) and Exxon Travel Club (800–833–9966).

If you find you're stuck with a lemon, you have help—consumer advocates uncovered the auto industry's "secret warranties" several years ago, and Consumer Reports Books has produced the guide to making them work for you: *Get Your Car Fixed Free,* by Mort Schultz. For other sources of assistance *after* you've worked your way through the service manager, dealer, and the manufacturer (check your sales agreement and warranty for procedures), first, contact The Center for Auto Safety, 2001 S St. NW, Washington, DC 20009; the staff can often suggest agencies you can contact. If you exhaust other remedies, you may proceed to *mediation:* car manufacturers have arrangements with groups that mediate and arbitrate consumer disputes. For the name of the group handling problems with your car's manufacturer, call the National Automobile Dealers Association, Autocap, at 703–821–7000. The names of many of the mediators, as well as government agencies, are listed in *The Consumers Resource Handbook,* available free of charge from the Consumer Information Center (see the listing in "Books" for more information).

If your interest is boating, you already know about the expenses—insurance, dock fees, upkeep, and new equipment. You can save 30% *routinely* on the cost of maintenance products, gear, and electronics by buying from the marine suppliers listed here, who sell every type of coating, tool, and device you'll need to keep your vessel afloat. You'll find exhaustive selections of electronics, hardware, and instruments, as well as galley accoutrements and foul-weather clothing. Even landlubbers should see these catalogs for the well-designed slickers and oiled sweaters. And the reference sections of the biggest catalogs have a full range of books and videos on boat maintenance and other marine topics.

If you're a private pilot who'd like to save on some of the gear and electronics you need while flying high, see the listings of Aircraft Spruce and San-Val, aviation discounters. Like the marine suppliers, these firms also sell goods of interest to those on terra firma, at savings of up to 50%. For great leads on good buys in used aircraft, try *Trade-A-Plane,* a tabloid packed with ads for planes and aviation equipment. For current rates, write to Trade-A-Plane, P.O. Box 509, Crossville, TN 38557–9909.

FIND IT FAST

AVIATION • **Aircraft Spruce, San-Val**
BOATING SUPPLIES AND EQUIPMENT • **Defender, E & B, Goldbergs',**
M & E Marine, West Marine
CAR PARTS AND ACCESSORIES • **Car Racks Direct, Cherry Auto, Clark's**
Corvair, IMPCO, Mill Supply, WorldWide Auto
CARS, TRUCKS, JEEPS • **American Automobile Brokers**
FARM EQUIPMENT PARTS • **Central Michigan**
MOTORCYCLE PARTS • **Capital Cycle**
RACING EQUIPMENT • **Racer Wholesale**
RV • **RV Direct**
TIRES • **Discount Tire, Tire Rack**

AIRCRAFT SPRUCE & SPECIALTY CO.

P.O. BOX 424
201 W. TRUSLOW AVE.
FULLERTON, CA 92632
714–870–7551
FAX: 714–871–7289

Catalog: $5, refundable (see text)
Pay: check, MO, MC, V, AE, Discover
Sells: small aircraft and pilot equipment
Store: 201 W. Truslow Ave., Fullerton, and Aircraft Spruce Avionics, 7000 Merrill Ave., Chino, CA; Monday to Friday 6–6, Saturday 7–3:30
Online: http://www.aircraftspruce.com

Aircraft Spruce & Specialty Co. has been selling aircraft parts and equipment since 1965 and is the source to call for aircraft plywood, flight seats, tubing and sheeting, cable, wire, circuit breakers, AN-MS hardware, headsets, and all kinds of avionics. The brands represented include Arnav, Bendix/King, B.F. Goodrich, Champion, David Clark, Flybuddy, ICOM, Magellan, Pelican, Randolph, S-Tec, Sony, Telex, Terra, TKM, Trimble, and Whelen (lighting), among others. In addition to an exhaustive inventory of supplies, equipment, and electronics for plane and pilot, there are neat things for the nonflyer: Dahon folding bicycles, propeller wall clocks, and a ceiling fan that's an authentic replica of the P–40 Warhawk World War II fighter, complete with shark mouth. Savings are comparable to those offered by other major aircraft supply discounters, and the firm has a "lowest price" policy. Call for a quote if you know what you want, or send $5 for the 456-page catalog ($20 for overseas orders, U.S. funds only); it's refundable with a $50 purchase.

Special Factors: Satisfaction is guaranteed.

AMERICAN AUTO-MOBILE BROKERS, INC.

24001 SOUTHFIELD RD., SUITE 110
SOUTHFIELD, MI 48075
248–569–5900
FAX: 248–569–2022

Information: see text
Pay: check or MO (see text)
Sells: new vehicles
Store: same address; Monday to Friday 10–6

✆ (see text)

If you're buying a new vehicle, American Automobile Brokers offers you an alternative to the showroom experience. The firm, in business since 1972, brokers the sale: Prices include dealer prep, all factory rebates, and delivery directly from the factory to a dealership near you by train or truck (for domestic vehicles), and savings depend on the prices in your area.

If you're looking for a domestic make, you can buy vehicles by General Motors, Ford/Lincoln-Mercury, and Chrysler/Jeep/Eagle. The foreign models include Acura, BMW, Honda, Jaguar, Mazda, Mercedes, Mitsubishi, Nissan, Porsche, SAAB, and Toyota, among others. (American Automobile Brokers doesn't sell imports to residents of California.) To get a quote, call or write with complete details about the vehicle and options desired, or send a self-addressed, stamped envelope for American Automobile Brokers' price-quote form. You get *one free quote;* extra quotes cost $5 each. *Send a self-addressed, stamped envelope both when requesting the form and when sending it back for the quote.* You can shop your local dealers, then get a quote here and see what you'll save by buying through American Automobile Brokers.

TDD callers: American Automobile Brokers has worked with operators who assisted incoming calls on TDD equipment, and has successfully completed transactions—but the firm doesn't have its own TDD.

Special Factors: Price quote by phone, letter, or American Automobile Brokers quote form *with SASE*; checks and money orders are accepted for deposit only, balance payable by certified check, cashier's check, or wire transfer.

CAPITAL CYCLE CORPORATION/CAPITAL EUROSPORT

21580 BEAUMEADE CIRCLE, #170
ASHBURN, VA 20147-6010
800–642–5100
703–729–7900
FAX: 703–729–7908

Catalog: free
Pay: check, MO, MC, V, AE, Discover
Sells: BMW and European after-market motorcycle parts and accessories
Store: 21580 Beaumeade Circle, #170, Ashburn, VA; Monday to Friday 8:30–6, Saturday 9–5
E-mail: capeuro@erols.com

Capital Cycle is the nation's definitive source for replacement parts for BMW motorcycles, with an inventory of over 10,000 genuine, original part lines, priced up to 65% below what dealers generally charge. The firm has been in business since 1972, and handles component repairs by mail.

Capital's stock includes genuine BMW motorcycle parts manufactured from 1955 through the current year. The 54-page catalog includes only a fraction of the enormous inventory, including engine parts and electronics, carburetors, fuel tanks, mufflers, pipes, clutches, gears, steering bearings, shocks, springs, handlebars, mirrors, brakes, tires, rims, forks, fenders, fairings, locks and keys, paint, seats, switches and relays, tachometers, voltmeters, lights, tools, and decals. Parts books and factory repair manuals for BMW cycles are offered, as well as original BMW tools. Capital Cycle's European division, Capital Eurosport, offers premium after-market parts and accessories from top manufacturers in Europe. Items include luggage, panniers, gloves, covers, and exhausts, among others.

Canadian readers, please note: Only U.S. funds are accepted.

Special Factors: Authorized returns are accepted within 30 days (a 15% restocking fee may be charged).

CAR RACKS DIRECT

**80 DANBURY RD.
WILTON, CT 06897
800–722–5734
FAX: 203–761–0812**

Catalog: free
Pay: check, MO, MC, V, AE
Sells: vehicle racks
Store: 82 Danbury Rd., Wilton, CT; Monday to Friday 10–6
Online: http://www.outdoorsports.com

Car Racks Direct sells just that—Thule and Yakima car racks, to secure bicycles, kayaks, canoes, skis, surfboards, and less playful items like lumber and furniture. In addition to basic racks, Car Racks Direct carries security cables, locks, straps, crossbars, fairings, brackets, and even cases and boxes engineered to fit the racking systems. Discounts vary on individual items, generally running from 12% to 18% off suggested retail—not deep, but better than paying list. Car Racks Direct has been in business since 1987, and will give you a price quote over the phone, or send you the Thule and Yakima catalogs on request. The Thule catalog includes guidelines for care and maintenance of the racks and accessories, and terms of the limited warranty.

Special Factors: Price quote by phone or letter; authorized returns are accepted.

CENTRAL MICHIGAN TRACTOR & PARTS

**2713 N. U.S. 27
ST. JOHNS, MI 48879
517–224–6802
FAX: 517–224–6682**

Catalog: free
Pay: check, MO, MC, V
Sells: used, new, and rebuilt parts for tractors, combines, and construction equipment
Store: mail order only

Central Michigan can save you up to 50% on parts for tractors and combines. The company stocks new, used, reconditioned, and rebuilt parts, all of which are backed by a 30-day guarantee. The 220-page catalog gives you access to everything from starters to cylinder blocks for machines made by almost every major manufacturer—Allis, Case, Chalmers, John Deere, Massey Ferguson, Ford, International, Moline, White/Oliver, and others. The rebuilt parts are overhauled completely, so they should function as well and for as long as new ones. Central Michigan, one of 13 firms that make up the "Parts Express Network," maintains customers' want lists for parts not in stock. Call between 8 and 5:30, Monday to Friday, or 8 and 3:00 on Saturdays for information.

Special Factors: Price quote by phone or letter; C.O.D. orders are accepted.

CHERRY AUTO PARTS

5650 N. DETROIT AVE.
TOLEDO, OH 43612
419–476–7222
FAX: 419–470–6388

Information: price quote
Pay: check, MO, MC, V
Sells: used and rebuilt imported-car parts
Store: same address; Monday to Friday 8:30–5, Saturday 8:30–12; also 25425 John Rd., Madison Heights, MI (Detroit area); Monday to Friday 8:30–5

Why pay top dollar for new car parts if you can get perfectly good ones, used, for up to 70% less? Cherry Auto Parts, "The Midwest's Leading Imported Car Dismantler," can supply you with used and rebuilt imported-car components at sizable savings. Cherry Auto has over 45 years of experience in the business, and keeps rebuilt cylinder heads, engines, starters, steering gears, alternators, drive axles, turbos, and other vital parts on hand. If you drive an Acura, Alfa Romeo, Audi, BMW, Chrysler Import (Champ, Colt, Conquest, Raider Vista), Nissan, Eagle, GEO, Honda, Isuzu, Jaguar, Mazda, Mercedes, Merkur, MG, Mitsubishi, Peugeot, Porsche, Renault, SAAB, Spectrum, Sprint, Subaru, Toyota, Triumph, Volkswagen, Volvo, or other imported car, you may save up to 70% on your parts bills by getting them here. Cherry can access two nationwide computerized parts-locating networks to trace hard-to-find parts.

Please note: There is no retail brochure or literature.

Special Factors: Price quote by phone (preferred) or letter; "All parts are guaranteed in stock at the time of quotation, guaranteed to be the correct part, and in good condition as described"; minimum order is $20.

CLARK'S CORVAIR PARTS, INC.

DEPT. WBMC
RTE. 2, 400 MOHAWK TRAIL
SHELBURNE FALLS, MA 01370
413–625–9776
FAX: 413–625–8498

Catalog: $5
Pay: check, MO, MC, V, Discover
Sells: Corvair parts
Store: mail order only
E-mail: clarks@corvair.com
Online: http://www.corvair.com

Clark's, in business since 1973, is an indispensable source for the Corvair owner since it stocks parts available nowhere else. Clark's can save you up to 40% on original and replacement General Motors parts, reproductions, and goods by Champion, Chevrolet, Clevite, Delco, Gabriel, Loctite, Michigan Bearings, Moog, Permatex, Sealed Power, TRW, and hundreds of other suppliers. The exhaustive inventory includes brakes, cables, lights, air filters, body parts and panels, carburetor and engine parts, gauges, gas tanks, manuals, pistons, points, seals, rims, specialty tools, paint, reproduction upholstery, trim, carpets, and many other parts and supplies. Every other year, Clark's Corvair Parts publishes an inventory of over 10,000 new Corvair parts in an indexed, 400-page catalog, supplemented by a second, 120-page catalog of used car parts, NOS parts, and high-performance parts—all for $5 to U.S. addresses. If you're looking for a specific part, you can call for a quote—but the catalogs are valuable reference tools and well worth the $5 to any do-it-yourself Corvair owner.

Special Factors: Price quote by phone or letter; returns are accepted; C.O.D. orders are accepted; minimum order is $10.

DEFENDER INDUSTRIES, INC.

42 GREAT NECK RD.
WATERFORD, CT 06385
860–701–3400
FAX (U.S. AND CANADA):
800–654–1616

Catalog: free (see text)
Pay: check, MO, MC, V, Discover
Sells: marine supplies, gear, equipment, and clothing
Store: same address; also The Marine Discount Supermarket, 321 Main St., New Rochelle, NY; Monday to Friday 9–5:45, Thursday 9–8:45, Saturday 9–4:45 (call 914–632–2318 for hours, October–February)
E-mail: info@defenderus.com
Online: http://www.defenderus.com

Defender has been selling marine hardware and equipment since 1938, and backs its claim of "the largest selection in the USA at the very lowest prices" with a 400-plus-page catalog that runs from anchors to zippers. It features page after page of boat maintenance supplies, resins and coatings, winches, windlasses, cordage, communications devices, foul-weather gear, books, tools and hardware, optics, galley fittings, navigation equipment, and electronics. You'll find sailboat hardware from Harken, Schaefer, and Lewmar, Evinrude, Nissan, and Ronstan outboard engines, and lines of marine electronics from Apelco, Autohelm, Humminbird, ICOM, Impulse, Lowrance, Micrologic, Motorola, Navico, Northstar, and Raytheon. Also available: Shakespeare antennae, Pioneer and Sony radios, optics from Fujinon, Minolta, Nikon, and Steiner, inflatable boats and life rafts by Avon, Zodiac, and over a dozen other lines; Henri Lloyd, Musto, and Douglas Gill boating wear, Sebago and Timberland shoes, Force 10 cookers, and Hurricane boat tops and covers—among other items. Defender also sells computers and peripherals by Apple, Compaq, IBM, Toshiba, and other makers. In addition to equipment, Defender is a national leader in boat-building supplies: fiberglass, xynole, epoxy and polyester resins, and other boat construction and maintenance materials are stocked in depth. Defender also offers a range of custom services, such as life raft repacking and repair, rigging services, and canvas goods to order (seat covers, pool covers, car covers, etc.).

Defender's wholesale affiliate, Atlantic Main Corp., specializes in small boat marine hardware and safety gear. Atlantic Main is also the U.S. agent for Blake heads, Taylor heaters, Dynous and Force 4 inflatable boats, and Ibberson yachting knives, XM Yachting inflatables, and safety gear. For details, contact Atlantic Main at 42 Great Neck Rd., Waterford, CT 06385.

Overseas customers, please note: Defender will send the catalog for the cost of postage—write to request the catalog, and you'll receive a quote. The firm has customer sales representatives who speak French, German, Spanish, Dutch, Cantonese, and Portuguese.

Special Factors: Price quote by phone, fax, or letter; returns are accepted within 20 days (a restocking fee may be charged); minimum order is $25.

DISCOUNT TIRE DIRECT

7333 E. HELM DR.
SCOTTSDALE, AZ 85260
800–739–8999
602–443–4341
FAX: 602–483–9230

Information: price quote
Pay: check, MO, MC, V, AE, Discover
Sells: tires, wheels, and suspension
Store: mail order only; phone hours Monday to Friday 8–9, Saturday 9–3 ET
E-mail: direct@tires.com
Online: http://www.tires.com/

 ¡Si!

Discount Tire Direct entered the mail-order arena several years ago, and is now a major direct marketer of tires—all-season, high-performance, snow, and light truck. The manufacturers represented include Continental, Dunlop, B.F. Goodrich, Goodyear, Michelin, Nitto, Pirelli, and Yokohama. You'll find wheels here by Antera, Concord, Dial, Enkei, Konig, Momo, TSW, and other makers. You can call, write, or e-mail for a price quote on specific models, or see the website—it was under construction at this writing, but already has a helpful FAQ on selecting tires and maintaining wheels. Discount Tire Direct also runs ads in major auto magazines, which will show you the latest specials.

Special Factors: Satisfaction is guaranteed; returns are accepted within 30 days for exchange, refund, or credit.

E & B MARINE SUPPLY, INC.

DEPT. WBMC
201 MEADOW RD.
EDISON, NJ 08818
800–533–5007
FAX: 908–819–9222

Catalog: free
Pay: check, MO, MC, V, AE, Discover
Sells: marine supplies, gear, and equipment
Store: 64 outlets in AL, CT, FL, GA, IL, MA, MD, MI, MS, NC, NH, NJ, NY, OH, PA, SC, VA, and WI (locations are listed in the catalog)

E & B Marine, founded in 1946, has a lowest-price policy that assures you great savings on a full range of products for power boating and sailing, boat maintenance and repair, safety, communications, and navigation. The brands include Apelco, Aqua Meter, Boatlife, Bow t' Stern, Chelsea, Eagle, Humminbird, Icom, Igloo, Interlux, Kidde, Micrologic, Pettit, Raytheon, Ritchie, SeaFit, SeaRanger, Standard, and Stearns, among others. Water skis and Bombard inflatables are stocked, as well as boating apparel and sportswear. New products are featured in every catalog, and many items are useful on land as well—clothing, safety equipment, and hardware. Savings vary, but are typically 10% to 25%, and up to 60% on sale items and specials.

Special Factors: Authorized returns are accepted; minimum order is $15, $25 on phone orders.

FREEPORT MARINE SUPPLY CO., INC.

47 WEST MERRICK RD.
FREEPORT, NY 11520
516–379–2610
FAX: 516–379–2909

Catalog: free
Pay: check, MO, MC, V, AE, DC, Discover
Sells: boating and marine supplies and equipment
Store: same address; Monday to Saturday 8:30–6 (Friday til 9 April to Labor Day, Sunday 9–3 April to July 4)

Freeport Marine has been in business, owned by the same family, since 1939, and publishes a 264-page catalog of marine hardware, maintenance products, and electronics for sailboats and powerboats. The stock includes epoxies and finishes, rope, anchors, windlasses, buoys, horns, seacocks, winches, VHF radios, global positioning systems, navigation instruments, safety equipment, radar, marine optics, inflatable boats, and a complete line of marine hardware. Among the manufacturers represented are Apelco, Avon, Barr, Garelick, Icom, Interlux, ITT Night Vision, Jabsco, Magellan, Marinco, Perko, Raritan, Raytheon, Sitex, Standard, Stearns, Steiner, and Teleflex. Savings run up to 60%, and if you don't see what you're looking for, call and ask.

Special Factors: Satisfaction is guaranteed; minimum order is $25 with credit cards.

GOLDBERGS' MARINE DISTRIBUTORS

DEPT. WBMC
201 MEADOW RD.
EDISON, NJ 08818
800–262–8464
FAX: 908–819–9222

Catalog: free
Pay: check, MO, MC, V, AE, Discover
Sells: marine supplies, gear, and equipment
Store: 12 W. 37th St., New York, NY

Goldbergs' has been a marine supplier since 1946, and offers thousands of products at discounts of up to 60%, and even better savings in the sales catalogs. Goldbergs' sells everything from anchors to zinc collars, including rope, bilge pumps, fishing tackle, rigging, knives, lifeboats, life preservers, navigation equipment, boat covers, winches, and even kitchen (galley) sinks. The brands are the best in boating—SeaRanger electronics, Taylor Made buoys, PowerWinch windlasses and winches, motors, and Stearns life preservers are but a few. The emphasis is on pleasure-boat equipment, but much of the sailing apparel—heavy sweaters, sunglasses, boots, Sperry boating shoes, and slickers—has landlubber appeal. A selection of stylish galley gear, teak bulkhead racks, and other yacht accessories rounds out the catalog.

Special Factors: Authorized returns are accepted (policy is stated in the catalog); minimum order is $10.

IMPCO, INC.

DEPT. WBMC

5300 GLENMONT DR.

HOUSTON, TX

  77081–2002

800–243–1220

713–661–0900

FAX: 800–243–8893

Catalog: free

Pay: check, MO, MC, V, AE, Discover

Sells: OEM Mercedes-Benz auto parts, 1977 to current year

Store: same address; Monday to Friday 8–7, Saturday 9–2

E-mail: mbz-help@impco.com

Online: http://www.impco.com

IMPCO has been in business since 1984 and sells first-quality, original equipment parts through several catalogs for different Mercedes-Benz models. Whether you're overhauling your engine, or just want to replace the wiper blades, IMPCO provides everything from front fender moldings to trunk seals, as well as electrical parts and supplies, bulbs, cooling and heating system components, upholstery materials, filters, brake parts, suspension and drive-line parts, exhaust systems, window switches, accessories, tools, and Owner's Workshop manuals. If you're overhauling your engine, check out IMPCO's engine rebuilding kits. IMPCO also sells Lexol leather cleaner and conditioner, and fuel and engine additives by Lubro Moly. IMPCO's unlimited, transferable two-year warranty on all parts is reportedly an industry exclusive, and should give you peace of mind. If you're looking for a part or Mercedes-Benz product that's not listed, or have any questions, just call the toll-free tech line at 800–243–4662.

Special Factors: Satisfaction is guaranteed; authorized, unused returns (except tools and manuals) are accepted within 30 days for exchange, refund, or credit; C.O.D. orders are accepted.

M & E MARINE SUPPLY COMPANY, INC.

P.O. BOX 601
CAMDEN, NJ 08101–0601
800–541–6501
FAX: 609–757–9175

Catalog: free
Pay: check, MO, MC, V, AE, Discover
Sells: boating supplies and equipment
Store: Glasgow, DE; and Collingswood, Northfield, and Trenton, NJ
E-mail: memarine@k2nesoft.com
Online: http://www.k2nesoft.com/memarine

M & E has been serving boaters since 1946 with good prices on everything needed to set sail and stay afloat. The 330-page catalog gives you access to over 30,000 products from anchors to zippers, from well-known manufacturers like Apelco, Barient, Garmin, Harken, Magellan, Maxxima, Schaefer, Si-Tex, Tasco, and Weems & Plath. If you have a boat or enjoy sailing, you'll appreciate the savings, which average 25% but can reach 80%. A recent sale catalog included navigation equipment, lighting, pumps, electronics, safety equipment, hull repair compounds and finishes, ladders, rope, inflatables (dinghies), horns, bells, and other equipment and supplies. There are lots of products useful on land, like the Sperry Top-Siders, teak boat accessories, acrylic glassware, watches, fishing equipment, and flags. Both list and M & E's discount prices are given, and everything is covered by the blanket guarantee of satisfaction.

Special Factors: Satisfaction is guaranteed; returns are accepted within 30 days for exchange, refund, or credit; C.O.D. orders are accepted from established customers.

MILL SUPPLY, INC.

DEPT. WBMC
19801 MILES RD.
CLEVELAND, OH 44128
800–888–5072
216–518–5072
FAX: 216–518–2700

Catalog: $4 ($8 outside the U.S.)
Pay: check, MO, MC, V, Discover
Sells: automotive restoration parts and supplies
Store: same address; Monday to Friday 8–5
E-mail: msinfo@millsupply.com
Online: http://www.millsupply.com

Whether you're a car buff or you own a body shop, you'll want Mill Supply's 192-page catalog on your shelf. Mill Supply has been selling car parts since 1944, and specializes in replacement panels and supplies for collision and rust repairs for American and foreign vehicles. The index runs from Alfa Romeo to Volvo, with all the hardware, tools, finishes, and other shop equipment you need to do installations. You have to have the know-how to do certain types of jobs, but even driveway mechanics can install rubber mud flaps and replacement side mirrors, or use the professional brushes and car-washing equipment.

Readers outside the U.S. please note: The catalog costs $8, payable in U.S. funds; orders from Canada should be paid by postal money order only.

Special Factors: Quantity discounts are available; authorized returns are accepted (a 10% restocking fee is charged) within 60 days for exchange, refund, or credit.

RACER WHOLESALE

DEPT. WBM
1020 SUN VALLEY DR.
ROSWELL, GA 30076
770–998–7777
FAX: 770–993–4417

Catalog: free
Pay: check, MO, MC, V, Discover
Sells: auto racing safety equipment
Store: same address; Monday to Friday 9–6

Racer Wholesale has been serving the serious amateur and professional auto-racing markets since 1985, offering safety equipment and accessories at savings of up to 70% on list prices. The 96-page catalog shows professional driving suits from AutoPro, Bell, Pyrotect, Racequip, Simpson, and other manufacturers, as well as gloves, boots, helmets, belts, harnesses, window nets, arm restraints, Cobra and Ultrashield racing seats, fire extinguishers, and other safety products. Auto equipment is also available, including K & N filters and accessories, Supertrapp mufflers, Oberg filters and heavy-duty oil, coolers, Aeroquip hoses and connections, fueling accessories, canopies, towing equipment, Wink wide-view mirrors, battery cutoff switches, rod ends, and related goods. Racer Wholesale has a policy of "guaranteed lowest prices"—see the catalog for details.

Special Factors: Authorized, unused returns (except special orders) are accepted within 15 days for exchange, refund, or credit (a restocking fee may be charged); C.O.D. orders are accepted.

RV DIRECT

DEPT. 24633

P.O. BOX 1499

BURNSVILLE, MN

   55337–0499

800–438–5480

FAX: 612–894–0083

Catalog: free
Pay: check, MO, MC, V, AE, Discover
Sells: RV equipment and accessories
Store: mail order only
Online: http://www.northern-online.com

Make the most of the time you spend in your RV or camper with the right furnishings, equipment, and accessories. RV Direct dedicates 56 color pages to answering your needs, with everything from air-conditioning units to water pumps, hoses, and water-delivery equipment. There's an extensive selection of covers and tarps, awnings and screen rooms for sun and bug protection, steps and mounts, chairs and tables, lighting, galley gear, outdoor cooking equipment, heating units, plumbing and sanitation equipment, pressure-washing equipment, air compressors, RV storage units, directional electronics, generators and power supplies, trailer accessories, towing gear, jacks, chocks, ramps, levels, and much more. Prices are competitive, but just one "value" price is given in the catalog, so shop around to be sure you're getting the best deal. If you find a lower price in a national ad, send RV a copy—"we'll meet or beat it."

   Special Factors: Authorized returns are accepted within 30 days for exchange, refund, or credit.

SAN-VAL DISCOUNT, INC.

7444 VALJEAN AVE.
VAN NUYS, CA 91406
800–423–3281
IN CA: 800–924–9658
CUSTOMER SERVICE:
   818–786–8274
FAX: 818–786–9072

Information: price quote
Pay: check, MO, MC, V, AE, Discover
Sells: aircraft parts and pilot supplies
Store: same address; Monday to Friday
7:30–6, Saturday 8–5

San-Val guarantees "lowest prices" on a huge inventory of parts, supplies, and electronics for small aircraft and pilots. Call for a price quote on headsets, gyros, magnetos, scanners, compasses, batteries, fuel pumps, or anything else you need for your craft. Flight cases, kneeboards, flight seats, training aids, textbooks and study manuals, log books, charts, and other pilot gear is sold as well. Shipping is not charged on certain items, and San-Val is committed to your satisfaction; ask for terms of the sales and return policy before ordering.

Special Factors: Satisfaction is guaranteed; authorized returns of defective items are accepted (subject to restocking fee) within 30 days for exchange, refund, or credit; minimum order is $10; C.O.D. orders are accepted on some items.

THE TIRE RACK

771 WEST CHIPPEWA AVE.
SOUTH BEND, IN
   46614–3729
800–428–8355
219–287–2345
FAX: 219–236–7707

Catalog: free
Pay: check, MO, MC, V, AE, Discover,
NOVUS
Sells: tires, wheels, and packages
Store: same address; Monday to Friday 9–4,
Saturday 9–3
E-mail: sales@tirerack.com
Online: http://www.tirerack.com/

   ¡Sí!

The Tire Rack moved its sales focus to the mail-order market nearly 15 years ago, and has found it the ideal way to deliver the best values in the latest models to customers around the world. The staff are serious driving enthusiasts who test the new models as they arrive on the market, and are able to provide informed advice about the best tire for your climate, driving style and conditions, and budget.

The tires available include lines by Bridgestone, Continental, Dunlop, Firestone, General, B.F. Goodrich, Goodyear, Hoosier, Michelin, Pirelli, Sumitomo, and Yokohama. The Tire Rack's specialty is performance tires, but the firm also carries all the others—including models for sport-utility vehicles, minivans, light trucks, and pickups. If you're shopping for wheels, you can call for pricing on models by BBS (including Moda), Borbet, Fittipaldi, Gara (light truck), Kosei, Manaray Sport, Mille Miglia, MSW, O.Z. Italy, ProCast, Sportline, TR Motorsport, and Zagato; tuner wheels for BMW, Mercedes, and Porsche models are available from AKT, AMG, Breyton, Carlsson, and Lorinser. And if you're in the market for both, you've come to the right place: The Tire Rack assures you that "When you purchase tires and wheels together, they will be expertly mounted and balanced, packaged with all necessary accessories and will be delivered to you ready to install on your car or light truck." An instruction manual is included with each package.

You can call or write for the catalog, or visit the website, which is very well organized and includes a lot of information on selecting tires and wheels. You'll find the online map helpful if you want to pay the firm a visit—if you're in the South Bend area, you can have The Tire Rack install your purchase while you're there. And if you can't make it to Indiana, ask your sales rep to consult the company database of over 800 recommended installation experts nationwide for the one nearest you.

Special Factors: Satisfaction is guaranteed; phone hours are Monday to Friday 8–8, Saturday 9–4 ET; returns are accepted within 30 days for exchange, refund, or credit.

WAG-AERO GROUP OF AIRCRAFT SERVICES

DEPT. WBM98

P.O. BOX 181

LYONS, WI 53148–0181

800–558–6868

414–763–9586

FAX: 414–763–7595

Catalog: free

Pay: check, MO, MC, V, Discover

Sells: aircraft parts, supplies, and aviation accessories

Store: 1216 North Rd., Lyons, WI; Monday to Friday 8:30–4:30

Wag-Aero is so attuned to the needs of small-aircraft pilots that the catalog includes directions for "fly-in" customers! The firm has been in business for over 35 years, and carries everything from spark plugs and propellers to aircraft decals, aviators' jackets, and manuals. The 148-page catalog features a full range of piloting instruments, windshields, radios, lighting, spinners, engine mounts, wheels, and much more, by some major names—Aeronca, Cessna, Grumman, etc. And there are many value-priced products sold under Wag-Aero's own label. Specials and sale items show up in the seasonal tabloid catalogs as well. Whether you're a dedicated pilot maintaining an aircraft or just dream of taking to the wild blue yonder, you'll find much of interest here.

Special Factors: Satisfaction is guaranteed; authorized returns are accepted within 90 days for exchange, refund, or credit; C.O.D. orders are accepted.

WEST MARINE

500 WESTRIDGE DR.
WATSONVILLE, CA 95076
800–538–0775
WHOLESALE, U.S.:
  800–621–6885
408–728–2700
FAX: 408–728–4360

Catalog: $4.50, $10 outside the U.S.
Pay: check, MO, MC, V, AE, Discover
Sells: marine supplies and equipment
Store: 66 outlets nationwide
Online: http://www.gsn.com

West Marine (also known as "Port Supply") publishes a mammoth color compendium of marine electronics, hardware, and maintenance products for sailboats and powerboats, as well as related goods, such as foul-weather clothing and plumbing supplies. (The catalog costs $4.50 plus tax if shipped within the U.S., and $10 outside—refundable with purchase.) The comprehensive selection of gear and materials includes epoxies and finishes, rope, anchors, windlasses, buoys, horns, seacocks, winches, VHF radios, global positioning systems, navigation instruments, safety equipment, hardware, kerosene lamps, marine optics, inflatable boats, and a complete line of galley gear. There are scores of manufacturers represented, including Apelco, Barient, Harken, Interphase, Lewmar, Magellan, Marinco, Navico, Patagonia, Ritchie, Schaefer, Stearns, Steiner, Taylor Made, and Weems & Plath, as well as the firm's private label. West Marine also offers rope-splicing services at "a reasonable fee." Savings run up to 50%, and West Marine has over 18,000 items in stock, so call and ask if you don't see what you're looking for.

Spanish-speaking readers, please note: West Marine has operators who speak Spanish on *some,* but not *all,* shifts.

Special Factors: Satisfaction is guaranteed; special orders are accepted.

WORLDWIDE AUTO PARTS

RTE. 38

MAPLE SHADE, NJ 08052

800–500–PART

Information: price quote
Pay: check, MO, MC, V, Discover
Sells: OEM car parts (see text)
Store: mail order only; phone hours Monday to Thursday 8–7, Friday 8–5, Saturday 8–4 ET
E-mail: sales@wwparts.com
Online: http://www.wwparts.com/

Finding genuine factory car parts isn't difficult, it's *paying* for them that's painful. Enter WorldWide Auto Parts. The firm began life in 1962 as MSO Parts, offering discounts on OEM goods for Honda, Acura, and Mazda models. Now doing business as WorldWide, the company has access to nearly two million parts for both foreign and domestic vehicles.

WorldWide can help you beat local dealer prices on parts on foreign cars made after 1980 by Acura, BMW, Honda, Mazda, Nissan, and Toyota; the domestic models include Buick, Cadillac, Chevrolet, Chrysler, Dodge, Ford, GMC, Lincoln, Mercury, Oldsmobile, Plymouth, and Pontiac. You can call or e-mail to ask about availability and prices, or visit the website and search the online database. Even if you're not shopping right now, it's worth a stop for the Tech Tips and the nice collection of car-related links.

Special Factors: Satisfaction is guaranteed; returns are accepted within 30 days for exchange, refund, or credit.

SEE ALSO

Arctic Sheepskin Outlet • *sheepskin cover steering wheel and seat covers* • **CLOTHING**
Bart's Watersports • *boat mounts and hardware for water-skiing equipment* • **SPORTS**
Bennett Brothers, Inc. • *infants' car seats* • **GENERAL MERCHANDISE**
Cabela's Inc. • *boat seats, covers, electronics, etc.* • **SPORTS**
Camelot Enterprises • *automotive tools* • **TOOLS**
Campmor • *inflatable boats* • **SPORTS**
Crutchfield Corporation • *auto audio and security devices* • **APPLIANCES**
Herter's • *ATV accessories* • **SPORTS**
The House • *sailboard car racks* • **SPORTS**

The Kennel Vet Corp. • *dog seat belts* • **ANIMAL**

LVT Price Quote Hotline, Inc. • *radar detectors, scanners, etc.* • **APPLI-ANCES**

Manufacturer's Supply • *parts for motorcycles, snowmobiles, ATVs, etc.* • **TOOLS**

Mardiron Optics • *marine optics* • **CAMERAS**

Northern Hydraulics, Inc. • *wheels and parts for ATVs, minibikes, etc.; auto tools* • **TOOLS**

Overton's Sports Center, Inc. • *marine equipment and electronics* • **SPORTS**

Percy's, Inc. • *radar detectors* • **APPLIANCES**

Red Hill Corporation • *auto-body refinishing products* • **TOOLS**

R.C. Steele Co. • *life preservers and auto safety harnesses for pets* • **ANIMAL**

BOOKS AND PERIODICALS

Print publications and educational materials

The firms in this chapter can save you hundreds of dollars a year on your own reading and entertainment buys, as well the titles on your gift lists. Many of them also sell videos and CDs, but companies that specialize in magnetic/vinyl media (except software) are listed in "Recordings," immediately following this section. Looking for stationery, cards, and gift wrapping and ribbon? They're offered by a few of the booksellers, but see "Cards, Stationery, Labels, and Check-Printing Services," the section following "General Merchandise," for the specialists.

The handling and storage of books and printed matter is of special concern to collectors, whose investments can become degraded if improper techniques or materials are used. University Products (listed in the "Small Business" section of "Office") offers a wide range of conservation supplies, including acid-free book-jacket covers, manuscript cases and folders, rare-book boxes, record sleeves, interleaving sheets, and archival-quality repair materials. The quantity discounts make taking care of your whole library much more affordable.

The "See Also" listings at the end of this chapter are especially helpful if you're looking for a how-to or self-help publication in a specific field. You'll find gardening guides among the firms in "Farm and Garden," cookbooks offered by firms selling gourmet ingredients, books on color theory sold by art-supply houses, and so on. Many of the firms listed throughout this book also offer videotapes, and some offer CDs. For software and CD-ROM titles, see the "Computing" section of "Office."

FIND IT FAST

ALTERNATIVE CULTURE• **Essential Media**
ART AND CRAFTS • **Barnes & Noble, Dover, Hacker, Hamilton, Potters**

Shop, Print's Graphic Design, Purchase for Less, Woodworkers' Discount

AUDIO AND VIDEO MEDIA • *Astronomical Society, Bargain Book Warehouse, Barnes & Noble, Daedalus, Dover, Potters Shop, Print's Graphic Design, Scholar's Bookshelf, Woodworkers' Discount*

ASTRONOMY • *Astronomical Society*

CARDS AND STATIONERY • *Dover*

CHILDREN'S • *Barnes & Noble, Daedalus, Dover*

COOKBOOKS • *Barnes & Noble, Daedalus, Editions, Hamilton, Jessica's Biscuit*

GOVERNMENT PUBLICATIONS • *Consumer Information Center, Superintendent of Documents*

MAGAZINE SUBSCRIPTIONS • *American Family, Below Wholesale, Delta, Publishers Clearing House*

PAPERBACKS • *Hamilton, Olde Methuen*

RELIGIOUS • *Christian Book Distributors*

REMAINDERED BOOKS • *Bargain Book Warehouse, Barnes & Noble, Daedalus, Hamilton, Scholar's Bookshelf, Strand*

UNIVERSITY PRESSES • *Daedalus, Hamilton, Scholar's Bookshelf*

USED BOOKS • *Editions, Olde Methuen, Strand, Tartan*

AMAZON.COM BOOKS

549 S. DAWSON

P.O. BOX 80387

SEATTLE, WA 98108–0387

800–201–7575 (NOT FOR ORDERS)

206–346–2992

FAX: 206–346–2950

Information: on website

Pay: check, MO, MC, V, AE, Discover

Sells: books

Store: Internet only; phone hours Monday to Friday 8–7 PT

E-mail: info@amazon.com

Online: http://www.amazon.com

Amazon.com Books is one of the preeminent Internet-based booksellers. Amazon aims to make every book in print available, at discounts that run from 10% on paperbacks and hardcovers to 40% on the "Amazon.com 500". And because "we sell the books we love at even higher discount levels, often 20%, 30%, and 40% off," if you're in sync with the Amazon editors, you're well rewarded. (Check the choices for the "Amazon.com Journal" feature and the Editors' Favorites to see how well your tastes jibe.) But many customers simply arrive at the site with their own book lists in hand, or search the 2.5 million-plus-title database for books on a particular topic. Title, author, publisher, publication date, ISBN, and cover type are noted, and synopses or brief reviews are included for many titles.

Orders may be completed entirely online, or up to the entry of credit-card data. At that point, you may call Amazon with your credit-card information, or fax it in, or you may mail a check or money order (which will slow the processing of the transaction). The website includes an excellent FAQ and extensive customer-service information, but if you have additional questions, you can reach Amazon staff by phone or e-mail for answers.

Special Factors: Satisfaction is guaranteed; returns are accepted within 15 days for exchange, refund, or credit.

AMERICAN FAMILY PUBLISHERS

Information: inquire
Pay: check or MO
Sells: magazine subscriptions
Store: mail order only

P.O. BOX 62000
TAMPA, FL 33662–2000
800–237–2400

American Family Publishers is a magazine clearinghouse that offers subscriptions to dozens of popular periodicals at rates that are usually much better than those offered by the publishers themselves. In addition to savings, every time you order you'll be entered into the current sweepstakes, which doesn't happen when you buy your magazines at the newsstand. A typical American Family mailing includes offers for *Travel America, Windows, People, Golf Digest, TV Guide, Parents, Dolls, Horticulture, Taste of Home, Field & Stream*, and other popular publications. Periodically, American Family features books and other products—*The Columbia University Complete Home Medical Guide*, Rodale's home-improvement series, cookbooks, and other popular reference works have appeared in past mailings, all offered on the installment plan that allows you to spread payments over four months.

Special Factors: Satisfaction is guaranteed; inquire for information.

THE ASTRONOMICAL SOCIETY OF THE PACIFIC

**390 ASHTON AVE.
SAN FRANCISCO, CA
94112
800–335–2624
415–337–1100
FAX: 415–337–5205**

Catalog: free
Pay: check, MO, MC, V, Discover
Sells: astronomy resources and gifts
Store: mail order only
E-mail: catalog@aspsky.org
Online: http://www.aspsky.org/

The Astronomical Society of the Pacific (ASP) is a nonprofit organization that was founded in 1889 to support astronomical research and improve the public's appreciation of science, especially astronomy. To further this end, ASP publishes a variety of materials: videotapes, books, charts and maps of the heavens, slides, observing tools, software, CD-ROMS, educational items, and astronomy-related gifts. The 32-page color catalog features an intriguing collection that includes the latest images from the Hubble Space Telescope, Carl Sagan's award-winning *Cosmos* series, the *Starship Earth* 16" celestial globe, and a comprehensive collection of star atlases and maps. There are breathtaking posters of the planets, a moon phase calendar for the whole year, astronomical CD-ROMs, computer programs that simulate travel through the galaxy, and a number of slide sets covering nebulas and galaxies, the solar system, images from the Hubble, and Space Shuttle views of Earth.

ASP's prices are reasonable but don't seem particularly low ($29.95 for videotapes and $8.95 for posters), until you check the catalogs of supplies for educators selling similar publications. There are school sources charging an astonishing $300-plus for a *single* videotape. So even if you're not in the market for ASP's publications yourself, let your school board or PTA know about this source. Proceeds are used to advance the Society's education programs.

Canadian readers, please note: Only U.S. funds are accepted.

Please note: Wholesale discounts, based on volume, are given to organizations and companies.

Special Factors: Satisfaction is guaranteed; returns in "as-new" condition are accepted for exchange, refund, or credit; institutional accounts are available.

BARGAIN BOOK WAREHOUSE

SODA CREEK PRESS

P.O. BOX 8515

UKIAH, CA 95482–8515

800–301–7567

707–463–1351

FAX: 800–949–4946

FAX: 707–463–2072

Catalog: free

Pay: check, MO, MC, V, AE, Discover

Sells: clearance and publishers' overstock

Store: mail order only

E-mail: scp@sodacreekpress.com

Online: http://www.sodacreekpress.com

The "Bargain Book Warehouse" catalog from Soda Creek Press brings you 116 pages of current and out-of-print titles in a number of categories—history and biography, romance, fantasy and science fiction, and horror and mystery. The last category is especially strong here—you'll find "proper British mysteries," historical intrigues, detective stories, and espionage. The romances run from Regencies (and romantic suspense) to love stories in contemporary settings: Barbara Cartland to Danielle Steel. The horror titles include some gothics, and you'll also find a number of stories for children.

The copy summarizes the plotlines of each title, and both the publisher's and Soda Creek's discount prices are given. And the discounts are great—you can find books by James Clavell, originally $27.50, for under $10, a collection of *five* Rex Stout mysteries for $12.99, and children's books for as little as $2.49. Soda Creek Press also offers the "Book Lover's Surprise Package," with four books of the firm's choosing for as little as $6.99. Visit the website, and you can find "Internet Specials" with even greater savings—and search the online catalog for the titles of your choice. The generous returns policy makes this a "can't go wrong" resource for your recreational reading.

Special Factors: Satisfaction is guaranteed; returns are accepted for exchange, refund, or credit.

BARNES & NOBLE BOOKSTORES, INC.

126 FIFTH AVE., DEPT. 861F
NEW YORK, NY 10011
201–767–7079

Catalog: free
Pay: check, MO, MC, V, AE
Sells: books, tapes, CDs, gifts, etc.
Store: same address; other locations in AZ, CA, CO, CT, FL, IL, MA, MD, MI, MN, NC, NH, NJ, NV, and OH

Barnes & Noble, founded in 1873, considers itself "America's #1 book sale catalog," with prices up to 80% off published rates. The typical Barnes & Noble catalog is 48 to 72 pages of best-sellers, reference works, publishers' overstock, and the firm's own reprints, as well as audiotapes, CDs, videotapes, calendars, and other gifts. The areas of interest include history, mystery, the arts, science, literature, film, medicine, satire, juvenilia, current fiction, linguistics, religion, reference, crafts, and photography. The audiotapes and CDs usually include classical music, jazz, drama, and language tapes, and the videotapes run from BBC comedies to travel guides. Stunning art books, calendars, lighted globes, beechwood bookshelves, book embossers, statuary, cassette cases and cabinets, and book lights have all appeared in past catalogs.

Canadian and APO/FPO readers, please note: Inquire for shipping charges, and allow extra time for order processing.

Special Factors: Satisfaction is guaranteed; returns are accepted; minimum order is $15 with credit cards.

BELOW WHOLESALE MAGAZINES, INC.

1909 PROSPERITY ST., DEPT. WBM
RENO, NV 89502
800–800–0062
FAX: 702–785–7509

Price List: free
Pay: check, MO, MC, V, AE, Discover
Sells: magazine subscriptions
Store: mail order only
E-mail: MagSub@aol.com

Below Wholesale Magazines lives up to its billing with access to over 1,000 magazines at prices that beat the magazine subscription clearinghouses. The brochure runs from *Accent on Living* to *Zillions,* and prices are up to 80% below newsstand rates (and often 15% to 30% less than the "best" prices you see elsewhere). Below Wholesale Magazines requires a business card for the best rates on about two dozen popular titles, as well as a trade name or business identification for select publications. There are hundreds of titles available that aren't listed in the brochure, so call if you don't see yours mentioned. You can also extend or renew current subscriptions through Below Wholesale Magazines, which has been supplying waiting room subscriptions since 1984, and selling to the public since 1988. The brochure states terms of the sales policy, and usually includes coupons and special offers for extra savings.

Canadian readers, please note: Only U.S. funds are accepted.

Special Factors: Satisfaction is guaranteed; gift service is available; allow 12 weeks for first issue to arrive.

BOOK STACKS UNLIMITED, INC.

████████

1621 EUCLID AVE.,
  SUITE 724
CLEVELAND, OH 44115
800–266–5909 (NOT FOR
  ORDERS)
216–694–5747
FAX: 216–696–0386

Information: on website
Pay: MC, V, AE, Discover
Sells: books
Store: Internet only
E-mail: see website
Online: http://www.books.com

Book Stacks Unlimited, Inc., is, in the company's own words, "an online bookstore and readers' conference system accessible via the Internet or modem from anywhere in the world." Book Stacks lists about half a million titles in its easy-to-use database, and includes the title, author, publisher, date of publication, ISBN, and often a summary or review in each listing. Many titles are discounted from 15% to 30%, and when you buy at Book Stacks, you also earn "Bookmarks"—points that can be redeemed for free books.

Book Stacks operates exclusively on the Internet, and requires you to initiate your order online. You can stop at the point at which you'd otherwise submit credit-card information, and either call or fax it to Book

Stacks to complete the transaction. The order form has been set up to facilitate both styles, and there's plenty of information in the "help" section to answer any questions you might have, and e-mail addresses of company contacts if you stump the FAQ.

Special Factors: Satisfaction is guaranteed; resalable returns are accepted within 30 days for exchange, refund, or credit.

CHRISTIAN BOOK DISTRIBUTORS, INC.

P.O. BOX 7000
PEABODY, MA 01961–7000
508–977–5000
FAX: 508–977–5010

Catalog: free
Pay: check, MO, MC, V, Discover
Sells: Christian-oriented books, videotapes, software, gifts, etc.
Store: mail order only

"Why pay retail?" asks the cover of the catalog from Christian Book Distributors, which is followed by 48 pages of reasons that you don't have to. CBD represents a broad cross-section of mainstream Christian interests, addressing topics as diverse as church history and theology and diet and health. The review catalog included a number of series, including the Anchor, Apostolic Fathers, Interpretation, Tyndale, Black's, Kittel, and other Bible commentaries; Greek and Hebrew grammars and lexicons; and collections of Spurgeon's sermons and the works of John Wesley, among others. The catalog also features devotional classics from John Bunyan, C.S. Lewis, and others; software for Bible study; church newsletter clip-art and biblical atlases on CD-ROM; games for the whole family; videos; and many pages of guides on using Christian values to live better—to build character and improve marriages and family relationships.

Most of the prices in the catalog are discounted about 25% to 30%, but sale titles are marked up to 75% off original published prices. And you can glean extra savings through CBD's "club" membership, which includes a bimonthly newsletter with special offers, clearance items, and other goodies among its benefits. Membership can be ordered through the catalog; it costs $5 per year to U.S. addresses (including all states and APO/FPO), and $8 to customers in other countries. CBD also offers a number of specialty catalogs, including Academic, Bible, Family, Fiction, Gifts, Homeschooling, Music, and Resources & Studies for Small Groups; request individual titles by name.

Please note: Returns are not accepted, but items that are damaged in shipment, defective, or are incorrectly shipped are replaced, and return postage is reimbursed.

Special Factors: Note restrictions on returns; specialty catalogs available through the main catalog (see order form).

CONSUMER INFORMATION CENTER

P.O. BOX 100

PUEBLO, CO 81009

Catalog: free
Pay: check, MO, MC, V
Sells: consumer publications
Store: over 1,300 Federal Depository Libraries nationwide (see text)
BBS: 202–208–7679
Online: http://www.pueblo.gsa.gov

 ¡Si!

The government's Consumer Information Center was established in 1970 "to help federal agencies promote and distribute useful consumer information." Many of the pamphlets and manuals in the Center's 16-page quarterly catalog are free, like the *U.S. Government TDD Directory*. The topics include careers and education, child care, federal benefits and laws, food handling and nutrition, health, home building and buying, energy conservation, appliances and electronics, home improvement and safety, travel, hobbies, and money management. You can subscribe to *FDA Consumer* through the Consumer Information Center's catalog, and order pamphlets that help you to learn about ultrasound, find out about Social Security, get tips on buying a mobile home, and obtain government records under the Freedom of Information Act, among other things.

You can also request the *Consumer's Resource Handbook*, a guide to effective complaint procedures, from the Department of Consumer Affairs (it's available in its entirety on the website as well). The *Handbook* lists the best sources of help if you have a problem as a consumer: contact names, addresses, and phone numbers of customer relations departments of hundreds of major corporations, Better Business Bureau offices worldwide, trade associations, consumer protection offices, and federal agencies—all at the best possible price: free.

If you'd like to see the literature before buying, you can visit one of the over 1,300 Federal Depository Libraries around the country; they don't do *sales*, but they have copies of nearly every Federal Government publication (in print or microfilm) that's designated for use by the general public. Your local library should be able to help you locate one, or you can write to Federal Depository Library Program, Office of the Public Printer, Washington, DC 20401. To locate a U.S. Government Bookstore, see the listing for "Superintendent of Documents" in this chapter.

Please note: A Spanish-language catalog of dozens of federal consumer guides in Spanish is also available.

Special Factors: A handling fee is charged on all orders.

DAEDALUS BOOKS, INC.

P.O. BOX 9132 (WBM)
HYATTSVILLE, MD
  20781–0932
800–395–2665
FAX: 800–866–5578

Catalog: free
Pay: check, MO, MC, V, AE, Discover
Sells: literary publications, CDs
Store: mail order only
Online: http://www.daedalus-books.com

Daedalus, founded in 1980, offers fine books from trade publishers and university presses at 50% to 90% off publishers' prices. These remainders have been culled from thousands to appeal to literary readers looking for culture on the cheap. Daedalus isn't *just* remainders, though—about half the catalog is devoted to current titles that are discounted about 25%. And the witty, clearheaded descriptions of each book are reading pleasures in themselves. The categories include literature and general interest, visual and performing arts, philosophy, history, feminism, politics, children's books, travel, cookery, and the social sciences. A gift certificate from Daedalus, presented with the latest edition of the catalog, should delight a reader with wide-ranging interests.

Audiophiles have something to celebrate with the latest offering from Daedalus—the music catalog. Here are 48 pages of classical, jazz, and esoteric recordings on CD, including Library of Congress Great Performances, Deutsche Grammophon "Originals" series, nominees for best-of-year by *Gramophone* magazine, and hard-to-find European imports.

Canadian and international readers, please note: Payment must be made by credit card, a money order drawn in U.S. funds, or a check drawn on a U.S. bank.

Special Factors: Institutional accounts are available; returns are accepted within 30 days.

DELTA PUBLISHING GROUP/MAGAZINE WAREHOUSE

1243 48TH ST.
BROOKLYN, NY 11219
800-SEND-LIST
718–972–0900
FAX: 718–972–4695

Catalog: free
Pay: check, MO, MC, V, AE, Discover
Sells: magazine subscriptions
Store: mail order only
E-mail: sswimer@mail.idt.net

 ★

Delta Publishing Group, aka Magazine Warehouse, is the subscription wholesaler we've all been looking for, with over 800 titles at the absolute lowest prices anywhere. It's *shocking* to see magazine after magazine here at prices that beat the ones offered by the sweepstakes operations by 40% or so. You don't get the chance at $10 million and you can't split the payments over three or four months, but at these prices and with a selection that runs from *A & E Monthly* to *Zoo Books,* you won't miss the perks.

Delta/Magazine Warehouse, founded in 1991, is a major supplier of wholesale subscriptions to corporation and doctors' offices, and extends similar "courtesy" rates to readers of this book. The firm offers many of the titles in subscriptions of up to three years, so you can lock in the rate of a favorite. (All of the terms are for *full* years.) Delta offers free tracking service on subscriptions bought from other sources, so you can have your renewals picked up seamlessly. And check the price list you receive for specials—bonus subscriptions and free magazine racks have been offered in the past.

Please note that a score of titles require a "trade" address that includes a business name, and a handful ask for a business card or letterhead; the magazines will be mailed to that address only. Be sure to mention WBMC when you call (800-SEND-LIST) or write for the price list.

Special Factors: Lowest subscription rates are guaranteed.

DOVER PUBLICATIONS, INC.

DEPT. MC
31 EAST 2ND ST.
MINEOLA, NY 11501–3582
516–294–7000

Catalog: free
Pay: check or MO
Sells: Dover publications
Store: same address; Monday to Friday 8–4; also 180 Varick St., 9th Floor, New York, NY; Monday to Friday 9–4:30

Many of the firms listed in this book sell selections of Dover books, but if you deal with the publisher directly you can buy any in-print Dover publication. In over half a century of publishing, Dover has built a reputation for books as notable for their quality construction as they are for their content. Dover's catalogs feature paperbacks on crafts and hobbies, Americana, mathematics and physics, American Indian arts, architecture, cooking, games, travel, music, and many other topics. Dover's "Pictorial Archives," featuring designs and graphics, typography, banners and scrolls, borders, etc., and the "Clip-Art Series" are copyright-free art that can be used in newsletters, ads, menus, and the like. Dover's postcard sets run from NASA shots to Tiffany windows, and there are stickers, coloring books, posters, and even gift wrap. Dover publishes facsimiles and reprints of rare and valuable texts, "Listen & Learn" language tapes, as well as birdsong tapes and musical scores by Scriabin, Liszt, Scott Joplin, Couperin, Ravel, Bizet, Brahms, and other greats. The prices are easily up to 50% less than those charged for comparable publications, and there are children's books and literary classics for just $1.

Canadian readers, please note: The shipping surcharge on orders sent to Canada is 20%.

Special Factors: Satisfaction is guaranteed; returns are accepted within 10 days for refund.

EDITIONS

DESK WM
BOICEVILLE, NY 12412
914–657–7000
FAX: 914–657–8849

Catalog: $2
Pay: check, MO, MC, V, Discover
Sells: old, used, and rare books
Store: 2740 Rte. 28, Ashokan, NY; daily 10–5
E-mail: nleditions@aol.com
Online: http://www.nleditions.com

Editions is a great source for used and out-of-print books, which are often priced 30% to 50% less here than elsewhere. Editions has been selling by mail since 1948, and operates a sprawling store that's stocked with a separate book inventory—55,000 at last count—worth a stop if you're in the area.

The 64-page monthly catalogs include *partial* listings from a range of categories. For example, the January catalog may list poetry titles from Eliot to Neruda, and February's issue will run from Powys to Wyse. Each catalog lists about 10,000 titles, most priced under $20, from categories that include fiction, literature, history, the social sciences, natural history, travel, folklore, the law, women, soldiers and war, the Irish, Americana, British history, theater, philosophy and religion, food, labor, espionage, sports, antiques, gardening, animals, publishing, and Judaica. And it's always interesting to see what ends up in the "Miscellaneous Subjects & Nonsense" section. The original hardcover titles, in fine condition, are often cheaper here than the paperback editions. Collectors and researchers may wish to see the catalogs for the first editions and books from the Heritage Press and Lakeside Press, as well as the occasional listings of regimental histories, genealogies, and books on local history. Note that the entire stock may be perused on the Editions website.

Special Factors: Inquiries by letter, fax, or e-mail only; returns are accepted within three days.

ESSENTIAL MEDIA

P.O. BOX 661245
LOS ANGELES, CA
  90066–1245
310–574–1554
FAX: 310–574–3060

Catalog: $2
Pay: check, MO, MC, V
Sells: "alternative media" books, recordings, etc.
Store: mail order only
E-mail: media@cyberjava.com
Online: http://www.essentialmedia.com

Essential Media is the catalog equivalent of an extremely independent bookstore, run by caring iconoclasts who discount just about everything they sell. The firm fulfills its mission of "providing a guide to some of the most significant works of postmodern, alternative, and fringe culture" with a catalog and website showcasing hundreds of well-chosen books, videos, and CDs. Essential Media offers the classics of counter-culture—*The Whole Earth Catalog,* Re/Search journals, the collected observations of Loompanics and *Utne Reader,* the best of the Beats (Burroughs, Ginsberg, Bukowski, et al.), diverse comics (Fritz the Cat, Mad, Feiffer, Art Spiegelman), and the literary theory of Foucault and Chomsky, to cite a few. The connoisseur of underground media will appreciate the more obscure treasures, from the secrets of Schwa and the primary documents of The Church of the Sub-Genius to *Memoirs of a Sword Swallower,* Annie Sprinkle's playing cards, and Guy Debord's *Society of the Spectacle.* Performance art, "transgressive" fiction, conspiracies, feminism, punk, anarchy, 'zines, and culture—cocktail, cyber, club, ambient, and gay—are some of the other categories celebrated here. The $2 catalog fee will bring you 36-plus pages of books, recordings, and ephemera, and regular mailings listing the monthly specials—or you can check EM's scintillating website for the regular stock, sale items, and new additions to the repertoire.

Special Factors: Satisfaction is guaranteed; returns in original, resalable condition are accepted within 30 days for exchange, refund, or credit.

HACKER ART BOOKS, INC.

45 W. 57TH ST.
NEW YORK, NY
10019–3485
212–688–7600
FAX: 212–754–2554

Catalog: free
Pay: check, MO, MC, V
Sells: books on the fine and applied arts and related topics
Store: same address; phone hours Monday to Saturday 9:30–6, ET
Online: http://www.hackerartbooks.com

Seymour Hacker, an avid art scholar and publisher, opened his store in Greenwich Village in 1947. Hacker offered the same kinds of titles then that form the core of the current collection—books on the fine and applied arts, architecture, archaeology, and related works. Today, both the store and the 64-page catalog reflect the same informed scrutiny and exacting standards. Each title includes a concise summary of the text, page count and number of illustrations or color plates, size, year and place of publication, and the price. Hacker is listed here because so many of the books are impressively discounted—a typical title that was published at $37.50 sells here for $12.95.

Past catalogs have included a group of books on ancient Chinese bronzes, monographs on new findings in prehistoric art, books on Mondrian, Alice Neel, art forgeries, a study of the rhinoceros in art, social critiques of twentieth-century architecture, and a Basquiat retrospective, to cite random examples. Each catalog offers hundreds of titles, some of which are already out of print. The store is believed to have the largest inventory of art books in the world, and should be part of every collector's visit to New York City.

Please note: The minimum shipping charge on international orders is $10; the *maximum* shipping charge on orders sent within the U.S. is $20, at this writing.

Special Factors: Institutional accounts are available.

EDWARD R. HAMILTON, BOOKSELLER

**DEPT. 5166
FALLS VILLAGE, CT
06031–5005**

Catalog: free
Pay: check or MO
Sells: new, closeout, and remaindered books
Store: mail order only

Hamilton's monthly catalog lists *thousands* of bargain books in every conceivable category, at savings that average 30% to 80% off the publishers' prices. The tabloid catalog appeals to the bargain-hunting bookworm who likes to explore old bookstores—it's the literary equivalent of shelves and stacks of volumes—art, humor, poetry, fiction, literature, photography, self-help, reference, business, crafts, psychology, history, film, science, cooking, sports, and biography are all featured. Hamilton's offerings are all new—current best-sellers from *The New York Times* lists are offered at 30% off published prices, as well as remainders, closeouts, and publishers' overstock. Past best-sellers show up here frequently, as well as imports and other books no other remainder source seems to have. Hamilton was founded in 1968 and has proven a personal favorite; orders are shipped promptly, and refund checks for out-of-stock titles often arrive before the order itself!

Special Factors: Satisfaction is guaranteed; returns are accepted; prepaid institutional orders are accepted; shipments to U.S. addresses only.

JESSICA'S BISCUIT

**THE COOKBOOK PEOPLE
P.O. BOX 301
NEWTONVILLE, MA 02160
800–878–4264
617–965–0530
FAX: 617–527–0113**

Catalog: free
Pay: check, MO, MC, V, AE, Discover
Sells: cookbooks and food and wine reference
Store: mail order only
Online: http://www.jessicas.com

Jessica's Biscuit sweetens its luscious catalog with sale books—scores of them are scattered throughout the 72 color pages of over 800 books on cooking, food service, and domestic arts. Jessica's Biscuit is the preeminent catalog for in-print specialty cookbooks and updates on the culinary commandments of the taste dictators. Even the newest cookbooks are often sold at a discount, while catalogs featuring titles "on super sale" appear several times a year. In addition to national cuisines, Jessica's Biscuit offers books with recipes for vegetarian, macrobiotic, microwave, diabetic, gluten-free, low-salt, sugar-free, low-cholesterol, wheat-free, fiber-rich, kosher, and low-cost dishes. There are regional books for everything from soul food to Amish fare, as well as volumes devoted to herbs, muffins, tofu, pizza, biscuits, corn, mushrooms, barbecuing, cheesecake, beans, children's food, chili, garlic, and potatoes. Related topics include professional food service, canning and preserving, outfitting a working kitchen, buffets, wines, and entertaining in style, among others. Savings on the sale titles average 45% and run as high as 80%. If you don't see what you're looking for in the catalog, call; Jessica's Biscuit has thousands of other titles in the warehouse.

Special Factors: Satisfaction is guaranteed; returns are accepted.

OLDE METHUEN BOOKSHOPPE

250 BROADWAY

P.O. BOX 545

METHUEN, MA 01844

508–682–9972

FAX: 603–891–0606

Catalog: $5
Pay: check, MO, MC, V, AE, Discover
Sells: used paperbacks
Store: same address; Monday, Friday, and Saturday 10–5, Tuesday and Wednesday 10–1, Thursday 10–6
Online: http://www.alcasoft.com/booknews

If you like popular fiction but balk at paying $8 for a slim paperback, Olde Methuen Bookshoppe has the answer. This firm's affiliate, Book News, publishes a catalog of used paperbacks in all categories—fiction, children's stories, mysteries and suspense, science fiction, romances, fantasy, and various nonfiction works.

Special Factors: Quantity discounts are available; returns of shipping-damaged, defective, or incorrectly shipped books are accepted for replacement; institutional orders are accepted; minimum order is $15 with credit cards.

THE POTTERS SHOP INC.

31 THORPE RD.
NEEDHAM HEIGHTS, MA
02194
617–449–7687
FAX: 617–449–9098

Catalog: free
Pay: check, MO, MC, V, Discover
Sells: books and videotapes on ceramics and pottery, ceramics tools
Store: same address; Monday to Thursday 9:30–5:30, Friday 9:30–1:30; also by appointment
E-mail: sbranfpots@aol.com

The Potters Shop, established in 1977, sells books and videotapes on ceramics and pottery at discounts of at least 15%, and as much as 75% on sale titles. The brochure lists hundreds of books and tapes, many of them obscure or hard-to-find imports. You'll find works on pottery technique, historical surveys, profiles of individual potters, ceramics of the East, health and business for the potter, and even a selection of books for children. Among the videotapes (all VHS) are workshops on raku, form, and technique, and The Potters Shop also sells bamboo and Dolan tools. The firm will search for books, maintains want lists, and buys used books on pottery and related topics. If you find yourself in Needham Heights, stop in at the shop. The books are there, as well as a pottery school and workshop, where you can both see member potters at their craft, and buy their work.

Wholesale customers, please note: "You must operate a bona fide retail establishment and be buying our products for resale to qualify for our program." The minimum wholesale order is five titles, and the discount is 30%. Request complete terms and price lists on company letterhead.

Special Factors: Price quote by phone, e-mail, or letter.

PRINT'S GRAPHIC DESIGN BOOK STORE

━━━━━

3200 TOWER OAKS BLVD.
ROCKVILLE, MD
20852–4216
301–770–2900
FAX: 301–984–3203

Catalog: free
Pay: check, MO, MC, V, AE
Sells: books on the graphic arts
Store: mail order only
E-mail: PrintCirc@aol.com
Online: http://www.printmag.com

Print Magazine, which serves the graphic-design community, has run a mail-order bookstore since 1962, offering well-chosen manuals, color charts, and other aids and reference materials on a range of design-related topics. All of the books are discounted, typically 20%, but some are tagged at 30% and 50% below their published prices. The 16-page color catalog offers annuals, desktop publishing and computer graphics, working with color on computer, advertising, graphic design, corporate logos and trademarks, type and typography, design and layout, illustration, color, and Pantone color manuals and fanfold color guides. You can also subscribe to *Print Magazine* through the catalog.

Canadian readers, please note: Only U.S. funds are accepted.

Special Factors: Satisfaction is guaranteed; undamaged returns are accepted within 15 days for exchange, refund, or credit; institutional accounts are available.

PUBLISHERS CLEARING HOUSE

━━━━━

101 WINNERS CIRCLE
PORT WASHINGTON, NY
11050
800–645–9242
516–883–5432

Information: inquire
Pay: check or MO
Sells: magazine subscriptions, books, gifts, etc.
Store: mail order only

Publishers Clearing House primarily acts as an agent for magazine publishers, offering subscriptions to popular and special-interest magazines at savings of up to 50% on regular rates. PCH guarantees lowest-to-the-public prices, and mailings usually feature over 100 periodicals, including such popular titles as *House Beautiful, Reader's Digest, Consumer Reports, Organic Gardening, Changing Times, Money, TV Guide, Time,* and *People,* as well as more obscure special-interest publications. The mailings usually include bonuses, premiums, and sweepstakes, and you can spread payments for your magazines over four months.

Special Factors: Satisfaction is guaranteed; inquire for information; installment plan is available.

PURCHASE FOR LESS

P.O. BOX 363 WBM
PHILO, CA 95466–0363

Catalog: $2
Pay: check or MO
Sells: new books on sewing and quilting
Store: mail order only

Home sewers, and more particularly quilters, will appreciate the collection of pattern books, historical surveys, general reference works, and related titles sold through the 20-page catalog from Purchase for Less. The company's name is based on its other distinguishing feature—discounts that average 33% on publishers' prices. Each book sold here is chosen for its value to the craftsperson who's looking for new designs, techniques, and fresh interpretations of the classics. There are dozens of books on quilting, general sewing and serging techniques, fitting clothing, sewing for the home, creating wearable art, sewing fashion accessories, and related topics. Whether you're just mastering the basics or are highly experienced in sewing and design, you'll find something of interest here.

Special Factors: Satisfaction is guaranteed.

THE SCHOLAR'S BOOKSHELF

110 MELRICH RD.

CRANBURY, NJ 08512

609–395–6933

FAX: 609–395–0755

Catalog: free
Pay: check, MO, MC, V
Sells: scholarly and university press books
Store: mail order only
E-mail: books@scholarsbookshelf.com
Online: http://www2.scholarsbookshelf.com/scholars/

University presses still produce highbrow texts for scholars, but many are of interest—and accessible—to nonprofessionals as well. These books sometimes suffer the same fate as their commercial counterparts—remaindering. The Scholar's Bookshelf, in business since 1974, turns publishing misfortune into intellectual excitement 18 times a year with a wide variety of university press and scholarly imprint remainders, and a selection of videos. The books are sold at an average of 30% below published prices, although savings can run up to 75%.

The 80-page general sale catalog is packed with concise descriptions of volumes on literature and drama, music, the Civil War, architecture and urban planning, archaeology, art history (ancient to modern), photography, world history and politics, psychology, philosophy, religion, Judaica, and the sciences. Past issues have included Jane's reference works on military ships and aircraft, Page Smith's eight-volume history of the United States, the *Atlas of Medieval Europe,* and other illuminated manuscripts (reproductions) and special editions. History is the strong suit at The Scholar's Bookshelf, and throughout the year the firm produces separate catalogs devoted to world history and militaria, as well as collections of fine art books, and literature.

Special Factors: Returns are accepted within 30 days for exchange, refund, or credit; minimum order is $10, $15 with credit cards.

STOREY COMMUNI-CATIONS, INC.

SCHOOLHOUSE RD.
P.O. BOX 445
POWNAL, VT 05261
800–441–5700
FAX: 413–664–4066

Catalog: free
Pay: check, MO, MC, V, AE, Discover
Sells: Country Wisdom Bulletins and books
Store: mail order only
E-mail: storey@storey.com
Online: http://www.storey.com

Storey features "books for country living," guides to gardening, cooking, preserving, raising animals, nature appreciation, homesteading, and related topics. Storey can help you learn all about hive management, composting, organic pest control in the garden, home-brewing beer, raising your own flock of ducks, and outwitting squirrels. The 56-page catalog features the Country Wisdom Bulletins, a collection of over 110 manuals that include "all the how-to information you need to easily master dozens of country living skills in 30 minutes or less." The titles illustrate the possibilities of self-reliance: "Building a Solar-Headed Pit Greenhouse," "Drought Gardening," and "Creating a Wildflower Meadow" are examples. The Bulletins are a good buy even at $2.95 each (they're often sold for as little as $1.50), especially for the person who needs to know the basics, but doesn't have to become an authority on the topic. And even if you're the consummate urbanite, you may find some of the Bulletins of interest, as well as other items—cookbooks, houseplant guides, and crafting manuals.

Canadian readers, please note: Only U.S. funds are accepted.

Special Factors: Satisfaction is guaranteed; returns are accepted within one year for exchange, refund, or credit.

STRAND BOOK STORE, INC.

**828 BROADWAY
NEW YORK, NY
10003–4805
212–473–1452
FAX: 212–473–2591**

Catalog: free
Pay: check, MO, MC, V, AE, Discover
Sells: new, used, remaindered, and rare books
Store: main store, same address; Monday to Saturday 9:30–9:30, Sunday 11–9:30; also Strand Book Annex, 95 Fulton St., New York, NY (212–732–6070); Monday to Friday 8:30–8, Saturday and Sunday 11–8
E-mail: strand@strandbooks.com

The Strand Book Store is the largest used book store in the world. Legendary in stature, the Strand boasts over 2.5 million volumes on eight miles of shelves. Founded in 1929, Strand publishes a number of catalogs of used, rare, and discounted reviewers' copies at 50% off list price. In addition, a huge selection of quality remainders is available.

Call, write, or fax for any of these free catalogs: the "Specials" catalog, published several times a year, lists thousands of works. This catalog includes books on art, architecture, philosophy, critique and commentary, biographies, literature, politics, food, drama, and other fields of interest. The "Review" catalog, available to institutional accounts, lists new releases at 50% off the publishers' prices. (Request this catalog on your institution's letterhead.) And, in the tradition of British used booksellers, Strand can supply books by the foot for decorators, TV studios, and hotels.

You have to visit the store to do justice to the Strand; if you do, don't miss the Rare Books Department, which has first, fine, and scarce editions, as well as signed and inscribed books.

Special Factors: Satisfaction is guaranteed; want lists are maintained; appraisals are available; libraries are bought; returns are accepted.

SUPERINTENDENT OF DOCUMENTS

INFORMATION CATALOG
U.S. GOVERNMENT
  PRINTING OFFICE
P.O. BOX 371954
PITTSBURGH, PA 15250
202–512–1800
FAX: 202–512–2250

Catalog: free
Pay: check, MO, MC, V, Discover, NOVUS
Sells: Federal government publications
Store: U.S. Government bookstores in AL,
CA, CO, DC, FL, GA, IL, MA, MD, MI, MO,
NY, OH, OR, PA, TX, WA, and WI (see the
catalog for locations)
Online: http://www.access.gpo.gov/su_docs

Did you know there's an "Office of Government Ethics"—or that it produces a CD-ROM every six months on new, ethics-related legislation? This is just one of the offerings in the current catalog from the Superintendent of Documents. You may find *Riparian Forest Buffers* a more credible read, or *Information Technologies for the Control of Money Laundering*. These are among the hits from the Superintendent of Documents, whose 28-page catalog offers everything from *To See the Unseen*, a "history of planetary radar astronomy," to the 434-page *NIOSH Pocket Guide to Chemical Hazards*. None of the books or pamphlets is free, but many cost under $10 and are real treasure troves of useful information. (Quantity discounts of 25% on orders of 100 of the same title—with some exceptions—are available.) Subscriptions to consumer magazines published by the government can be ordered through the catalog, and there are calendars and a number of posters of American artists' work as well as space shots and maps.

Special Factors: Quantity discounts are available; authorized returns due to Government error are accepted within six months for exchange or credit; institutional accounts are available.

TARTAN BOOK SALES

500 ARCH ST., DEPT. 5N
WILLIAMSPORT, PA 17705
800–233–8467, EXT. 508
FAX: 800–999–6799

Catalog and Brochure: free
Pay: check, MO, MC, V
Sells: used books
Store: same address (Brodart Outlet Bookstore); Monday to Wednesday 11–5, Thursday and Friday 10–6, Saturday 10–4
E-mail: sechrist@brodart.com
Online: http://www.brodart.com

Tartan Book Sales, a direct-mail division of Brodart Co., sells recent hardcover titles, including best-sellers, at discounts of up to 75% on the published prices. All of Tartan's books have seen limited circulation in libraries across the country and are inspected prior to shipping.

Hardcover titles by such popular authors as John Grisham, Stephen King, Tom Clancy, Danielle Steele, Dick Francis, and Patricia Cornwell are listed in the current catalog, which also features biographies, books on business and finance, crime, sports and entertainment, health and self-help, politics, current affairs, mysteries, romance novels, books in large print, and much more. Tartan has been in business since 1960 and offers an excellent opportunity for readers to buy hardcover popular reading at paperback prices. As the company puts it, "Tartan books make good reading cents."

If you're purchasing for resale or for an institution, see the catalog for sales terms, and contact Tartan for pricing.

Special Factors: Quantity discounts are available; institutional and retail accounts are available.

WOODWORKERS' DISCOUNT BOOKS

735 SUNRISE CIRCLE
WOODLAND PARK, CO
  80863
800–378–4060
719–686–0756
FAX: 719–686–0757

Catalog: free
Pay: check, MO, MC, V, AE
Sells: woodworking books, videos, and plans
Store: mail order only
E-mail: orders@discount-books.com
Online: http://www.discount-books.com

Why fool around with novelty company names when you can say it all in "Woodworkers' Discount Books"? The 64 well-annotated pages of this catalog list everything from basic wood-identification primers to David Pye's *The Nature and Aesthetics of Design*. There are several pages devoted to furniture making and cabinetry (including plans), joinery and veneering, carving and turning, miniatures and toys, making boxes, tool techniques, wood finishing, and more, including projects to test your skills. The *Fine Woodworking* videos are available, as well as text classics like Mowat's *A Treatise on Stairbuilding and Handrailing*. Check here for books and videos from *Fine Homebuilding*, including the series of practical single-topic manuals that cover everything from roofing to flooring.

The prices are discounted up to 20% (more on specials offered on the website), but the strength of this catalog is the selection—these books have been chosen by experts for serious woodworkers—and the excellent summaries of each title. Call or write for the catalog, or visit the website—the catalog is available online and for download.

Special Factors: Satisfaction is guaranteed; returns (except nondefective videos) are accepted in new condition within 30 days for exchange, refund, or credit; shipping is included on deliveries of three or more items within the 48 contiguous United States.

Recordings

Audiotapes, LPs, CDs, videotapes, and films

Whether you want to hear original bluegrass, listen to the gurus of the self-actualization movement, or see a John Wayne favorite anytime you feel like it, you've reached the right place. The firms listed here specialize in recordings—chiefly audiotapes, CDs, and videotapes, and there are some that sell vinyl, some digital audiotape (DAT). The savings vary with the offerings, and often compare fairly to record megastores and the big discount chains. Use both kinds of sources—store and catalog—to maximize selection and savings.

If you tape movies or dupe the occasional cassette, you need blank tapes. The choices are confusing—Types I, II, or III, chrome or high bias, high grade vs. ultra, standard or extended play—the labels themselves don't make the differences clear. For help in figuring out what tape best suits your purposes (and which one was judged best of the batch), see the clarifying November 1994 (video) and January 1993 (audio) articles in *Consumer Reports*. J & R and Wholesale Tape, both listed in "Appliances," have good prices on both blank audio- and videotapes, but you'll save even more by being picky about what you tape in the first place. That's much easier done with a good movie reference at hand. *VideoHound's Golden Movie Retriever* is one such book, with film reviews, cross indexes (including one for laser disk and CD-I recordings), and distributor listings packing over 1,600 pages. It tells you what's in release (so you know what you *have* to record if you want a copy), and you'll avoid critical embarrassments, like recording the wrong version of *A Star Is Born*. To see whether the *VideoHound* (or any review resource) is right for you, look up several movies you know well, and see whether you agree with the descriptions and evaluations. If they don't, look for others more suited to your tastes.

For more firms that offer recordings, see the companies in the preceding section, "Books."

DEEJAY EQUIPMENT • **Upstairs Records**
RECORDS, TAPES, CDs • **Adventures in Cassettes, Audio House, Berkshire, Collector's Choice, Harvard Square, Record-Rama, Upstairs Records**
VIDEOTAPES • **Adventures in Cassettes, Critics' Choice, Fusion Video, Harvard Square**

ADVENTURES IN CASSETTES

A DIVISION OF METACOM, INC.

DEPT. WO98

5353 NATHAN LANE

PLYMOUTH, MN 55442

800–328–0108

FAX: 612–553–0424

Catalog: free
Pay: check, MO, MC, V, AE, Discover
Sells: audiotapes and CDs
Store: mail order only
E-mail: AIC4Radio@aol.com

Adventures in Cassettes offers hundreds of audiotapes featuring vintage radio classics, including such comedy greats as Amos and Andy, Abbott and Costello, Baby Snooks, The Great Gildersleeve, The Bickersons, Fibber McGee and Molly, Burns and Allen, Jack Benny, Fred Allen, and Our Miss Brooks. If mysteries, thrillers, and adventure are more your line, see the selection of Sherlock Holmes, Arch Oboler's "Lights Out Everybody," Sam Spade, Bold Venture, The Green Hornet, Dimension-X, and other favorites. And the Western classics are here as well—*Hopalong Cassidy, Gunsmoke,* the *Lone Ranger, Have Gun Will Travel,* and *Tales of the Texas Rangers.*

Special Factors: Satisfaction is guaranteed; returns are accepted within 30 days for exchange, refund, or credit.

AUDIO HOUSE

P.O. BOX 531-G
GRAND BLANC, MI
   48439–0531
810–695–3415
FAX: 810–695–1753

Catalog: $3, refundable (see text)
Pay: check, MO, MC, V, AE, DC, Discover
Sells: used CDs
Store: mail order only
E-mail: ahcd@tir.com
Online: http://amsquare.com/ahcd

Audio House has been brokering used CDs to individuals since 1983 and provides you with a great market and great prices—whether you're buying or selling. Audio House publishes a master catalog of CD listings every two months, and releases a 10-page supplement in the off months. A sample costs $3 (refundable with purchase), and a year's subscription is $10 ($12 to Canada—but it's a free download from the website). A recent edition opened with 10,000 Maniacs and ended with Zamfir's "The World's Most Beautiful Melodies," offering something for everyone. Audio House makes its stock of 15,000 titles available through the catalog only—there is no membership fee. A number of the selections are on obscure labels, and locating them here at an average of about $8, guaranteed to play like new, is an audiophile's dream. If you want to cull your own collection, see the catalog for details on selling your used CDs to Audio House.

Wholesale buyers, please note: Contact Audio House for details on resale terms and pricing.

Canadian readers, please note: Only U.S. funds are accepted, or payment should be made by credit card.

Special Factors: Satisfaction is guaranteed; returns are accepted within 30 days for exchange, refund, or credit; phone hours Monday to Friday 10–6.

BERKSHIRE RECORD OUTLET, INC.

RR 1, RTE. 102 PLEASANT ST.
LEE, MA 01238–9804
413–243–4080
FAX: 413–243–4340

Catalog: $5 (paid by check or credit card)
Pay: check, MO, MC, V
Sells: classical recordings
Store: same address; Saturday 10–5:30
Online: http://www.Berkshirerecoutlet.com

If you're an LP holdout who loves classical music, Berkshire is your source: 220 pages of thousands of classical overstocked and remaindered recordings—LPs, tapes, and compact discs—at savings of 33%-plus on the release prices. The catalog is organized alphabetically by label—from Abbey to Xenophone—and by price within those groupings. Each entry is coded to indicate whether the recording is offered in stereo, mono, quadraphonic, or reprocessed stereo mode (or in digital or analog CD), and the country of origin is noted if the recording is an import. Berkshire has been in business since 1974, and a gold mine for lovers of classical music, but note that sound tracks, ethnic music, folk songs, and poetry readings also appear. Several pages of remaindered books on classical music and musicians round out the collection.

Japanese customers, please note: The website includes a Japanese-language version.

Special Factors: Minimum order is $15, inclusive of shipping.

COLLECTOR'S CHOICE MUSIC

P.O. BOX 838
ITASCA, IL 60143–0838
800–494–2211
FAX: 630–775–3355
TDD: 800–272–2900

Catalog: free
Pay: check, MO, MC, V, AE, Discover, NOVUS
Sells: CDs and cassettes
Store: mail order only; customer service phone hours Monday to Friday 8–8, Saturday 9–5 CT
E-mail: gordona@ccmusic.com

Collector's Choice Music brings the same good pricing and product selection to audio possibilities that its parent firm, Critic's Choice Video, brings to the small screen. The firm's 96-page catalog is heavy on AM favorites—something you expect from "America's Pop Music Library"— but you'll also find folk, jazz, classical, Big Band, and even movie and TV show theme and background music. Barbershop quartets, Jo Stafford, disco, the Monkees, Xavier Cugat, and gospel—you'll find it all here. And if you *don't* see what you're looking for among the 2,500 titles in the catalog, call and ask. The firm's database of artists and albums will probably yield your desiderata, if it's in print. (You can also access the database yourself as the Music Search Line, or search the Old Radio Search Line for radio programs—see the catalog for details.) Prices on tapes begin at $4, CDs at $7.50, and the 10 pages of "Budget Cuts" give you scores of choices of tapes at three for $12.

Please note: TDD service is available Monday to Friday 7–7, Saturday 9–5 CT.

Special Factors: Satisfaction is guaranteed; returns are accepted within 30 days for exchange, refund, or credit; orders must be paid in U.S. funds.

CRITICS' CHOICE VIDEO

DEPT. 70061
P.O. BOX 749
ITASCA, IL 60143–0749
800–367–7765
FAX: 630–775–3355
TDD: 800–272–2900

Catalog: $3
Pay: check, MO, MC, V, AE, Discover
Sells: videotapes and digital video discs (DVD)
Store: mail order only
E-mail: Vcatalog@ccvideo.com

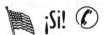 ¡Sí! Ⓒ

You don't go to every movie that's released, so why weed through listings of every video in existence just to find what you want? Critics' Choice Video turns something burdensome to your benefit, with a 100-page catalog of over 2,100 titles, culled from tens of thousands. Critics' Choice Video has developed a good mix of hits, cult favorites, and lesser-known gems, in the categories of movie classics, musicals, drama, foreign films, comedy, family films, action/adventures, great performances, suspense, science fiction, and westerns. Most of the movies cost under $20, and overstock and sale titles are priced under $10.

Critics' Choice also offers titles on digital video disc as well as VHS video, and provides a "Video Search Line" to locate any of 70,000 movies currently available, including titles in Spanish.

Special Factors: Satisfaction is guaranteed; returns are accepted within 30 days for exchange, refund, or credit; Spanish-speaking representatives/TDD service available Monday to Friday 7–7, CST.

FUSION VIDEO

17311 FUSION WAY
COUNTRY CLUB HILLS, IL
60478
800–959–0061
FAX: 800–822–4010

Catalog: $2, $3 outside the U.S.
Pay: check, MO, MC, V, Discover, AE
Sells: videotapes and gifts
Store: mail order only

Fusion Video's new catalog, "The Discount Collection," offers 48 pages of video titles in every category, priced from under $10 each. Music, drama, British comedy, TV shows, self-improvement, travel, sports, and science fiction are represented. The current issue offers everything from the Three Stooges to *The Martian Chronicles,* including a number of collections (the Civil War, *Black Adder,* the Beatles), popular movies old and new, great vintage TV series (*The Honeymooners, Gunsmoke),* dozens of travel tapes from Rand McNally, and instructional videos on everything from yoga to dog training. The catalog also features theme collectibles—Speed Racer mugs, James Bond neckties, and *Star Trek* boxer shorts among them. The giftware isn't discounted, but you might not be able to resist.

Special Factors: Satisfaction is guaranteed; returns are accepted for exchange, refund, or credit.

HARVARD SQUARE RECORDS, INC.

P.O. BOX 381975-W8
CAMBRIDGE, MA 02238
617–868–3385
FAX: 617–547–2838

Catalog: $2–$5 (see text)
Pay: check, MO, MC, V
Sells: out-of-print LPs, audiotapes, and videotapes
Store: mail order only
E-mail: hsrecord@user1.channel1.com
Online: http://www.lpnow.com/

Harvard Square has been doing business since 1985 selling sealed, current-issue and out-of-print LPs, and offers a large selection of imports and cutouts. (Cutouts are discontinued records, equivalent to remaindered books; they're often so marked by notching or cutting out a small piece of the corner of the jacket, or cover—hence the name.) Harvard Square's current catalog runs from the A House to Zydeco Ranch, and many of the LPs cost just $4 to $6. Compilations are listed separately, along with EPs (12" singles), soundtracks, original cast albums, picture LPs, and a handful of videos. Separate catalogs feature comparatively extensive inventories of audiotapes, imported and cutout, current and out-of-print.

Because of the volume of the listings, Harvard Square divides them into separate 56-page catalogs. When you send your catalog fee ($2 to the U.S., $3 to Canada, $5 to international addresses), specify LPs or audiotapes (cassettes), and you'll receive the appropriate catalog. Please note that stock cannot be held, so order promptly; if the item is sold out, you'll receive a refund check or a merchandise credit—you can indicate which you'd prefer on the order form.

Special Factors: Returns of defective (unplayable) goods are accepted within 14 days for replacement or merchandise credit; minimum order is $30 with credit cards only.

RECORD-RAMA SOUND ARCHIVES

4981 MCKNIGHT RD.
PITTSBURGH, PA
15237-3407
412-367-7330 (SEE TEXT)
FAX: 412-367-7388

Information: price quote
Pay: check, MO, MC, V, AE, Discover
Sells: vintage 45s, LPs, and CDs
Store: same address; Tuesday to Saturday 10–6, closed Sunday and Monday
E-mail: recordrama@city-net.com
Online: http://www.musicmaster.com

When word reached the Library of Congress that a retired paper goods salesman was claiming to have the country's largest known collection of 45s, a curator was sent over to check it out. Sure enough: Record-Rama Sound Archives, which shares a building with the local Post Office, holds the record with 1.5 *million* oldies on 45s, plus a million LPs. Paul C. Mawhinney's collection began with his youthful purchase of Frankie Lane's "Jezebel," and an obsession was born.

Mr. Mawhinney isn't sitting on this national treasure; he's created the *MusicMaster: The 45 RPM Singles Directory,* the ultimate reference on 45s produced from 1948 to 1996. The *MusicMaster,* organized by artist and title, is now the most-used reference in the New York Public Library, and a must-have for any library or serious collector. Record-Rama offers the MusicMaster Database, and other directories—the *CD–5 Singles Directory* and *The 45 RPM Christmas Singles Directory,* both by artist/title. (Call for current directory prices.) Mr. Mawhinney's CD collection currently numbers over 300,000, and he's amassed a large selection of CD-ROMs as well. If you're looking for a title, he probably has it—just call and ask, or use his WORLDSEARCH LP and CD locating service. Maintenance products for LPs and CDs are available, as well as over 10,000 phonograph needles and other supplies for DJs.

Please note: "Just mention Wholesale-by-Mail and get an additional 10% discount on any record and any single disk CD (multiple discs and boxed sets are excluded)."

Special Factors: Calls are not accepted on the weekends; phone quotes are limited to two requests per call.

UPSTAIRS RECORDS, INC.

DEPT. WBM
140 58TH ST., SUITE 6W
BROOKLYN, NY
11220-2521
800–487–7824
718–567–3333
FAX: 718–567–2310

Catalog: free
Pay: check, MO, MC, V, AE, Discover
Sells: DJ equipment, sound, lighting, and recordings
Store: same address; Monday to Thursday 9–7, Friday 9–5, Sunday 10–5, closed Saturdays
E-mail: sales@upstairsrecords.com
Online: http://www.upstairsrecords.com

 ¡Sí!

Whether you're just looking for a classic copy of *Boogie Down Productions* on wax, or are buying the lighting and equipment for a club, Upstairs Records is your source. This Brooklyn-based music emporium specializes in DJ equipment, club gear, and hip hop music, much of which is produced by small independent labels—hard to find at all in some parts of the country, and rarely at savings of up to 35% (see the catalog for the "low price guarantee"). Upstairs Records offers a fax service that notifies subscribers to new 12" releases, and the "Vinyl Record Pool," a standing-order service for new releases in "rap, R & B, hip hop, club/dance, techno, and reggae." (Current terms and order forms for these services can be found in the catalog.) "Breakbeats" are listed in the main catalog, and a separate catalog of cassettes and CDs is planned.

Upstairs Records has everything to turn you into a mixing, sampling, scratching fool—or at least that's what the neighbors will think. Turn here for discount prices on CD players, turntables, "scratchmaster" and full-size mixers, digital samplers, voltage regulators and effects boxes, echo chambers and beat counters, cassette players, signal processors, DJ consoles, digital sound boxes, amps, MIDI keyboard controllers, speakers, mics, cables, slipmats (for turntables), turntable cartridges, and other club equipment—foggers, strobe lights, mirror balls, bubble machines, and more. The brands include Akai, AKG, Alesis, American DJ, BBE, Boss, Bullfrog, Carver, DBX, Denon, Digitech, DOD, E-MU, Furman, Gemini, GLI, Lineartech, LyteQuest, Martin, MTX, Numark, Odyssey, Ortofon, Pioneer, QSC, Rane, Roland, Shure, Soundtech, Stanton, Tascam, Technics, and Vestax, among others. See the catalog for specials and complete details on the sales policy, and if you have Internet access, check the website—the entire catalog is posted there, with photos, descriptions, and prices, and a list of current releases. Upstairs Records can also help you design a sound system for your restaurant, club, or bar—just fax the blueprints with your sound and lighting ideas.

Special Factors: Authorized returns are accepted within 30 days with some limitations and restrictions; see the catalog for sales terms and price protection policy.

SEE ALSO

The William Alden Company • woodworking reference texts • **TOOLS**
American Musical Supply • books, manuals, and videos on rock and roll technique • **MUSIC**
The American Stationery Co., Inc. • custom-printed stationery, wedding invitations • **GENERAL: CARDS**
Art Express • art-related books, manuals, and videotapes • **ART MATERIALS**
Sam Ash Music Corp. • sheet music • **MUSIC**
Atlanta Thread & Supply • books and manuals on sewing and serging techniques • **CRAFTS: TEXTILE ARTS**
Bailey's, Inc. • books on logging, chain-saw use and maintenance, etc. • **TOOLS**
Baron/Barclay Bridge Supplies • books, cards, and teaching aids for bridge • **TOYS**
B & H Photo-Video • books and videos on all aspects of photography • **CAMERAS**
BFK Sports • books, magazines, and videos on kiting and kite building • **SPORTS**
Bike Nashbar • manuals on bicycle repair • **SPORTS**
The Bird House • tapes, videos, and CDs on bird breeds, training, etc. • **ANIMAL**
Bosom Buddies • books on breastfeeding and maternity topics • **CLOTHING: MOTHER AND CHILD**
Bruce Medical Supply • books on vitamins, health care, and medical topics • **MEDICINE: SPECIAL NEEDS**
Butterbrooke Farm Seed Co-Op • booklets on gardening topics • **FARM**
Campmor • field guides, survival and outdoor guides • **SPORTS**
The Caning Shop • books on seat weaving, upholstery, basketry • **CRAFTS**
Capital Cycle Corporation • factory-repair manuals for BMW cycles • **AUTO**
Caprilands Herb Farm • books on herbs and gardening, making wreaths, and cooking • **FARM**
Ceramic Supply of New York & New Jersey, Inc. • art-related manuals and books on crafts • **ART MATERIALS**
Cheap Joe's Art Stuff • art-related books, manuals, and videotapes • **ART MATERIALS**

Cheap Shot, Inc. • reloading manuals • **SPORTS**

Cherry Tree Toys, Inc. • manuals on wood projects and toy making • **CRAFTS: WOODCRAFT**

ChuckWagon Outfitters • cookbooks and videos on Dutch-oven cooking, camp cooking, etc. • **HOME: KITCHEN**

Clark's Corvair Parts, Inc. • Corvair manuals • **AUTO**

The Cleaning Center • books and videos on cleaning • **HOME: IMPROVEMENT**

The CMC Company • cookbooks on Mexican, Asia, Mid-East and other cuisines • **FOOD: BEVERAGES AND FLAVORINGS**

Cutlery Shoppe • books and videos on knife use and collecting • **SPORTS**

Daleco Master Breeder Products • books on fish and saltwater fish care and breeding • **ANIMAL**

Deer Shack • deer-hunting books and videos • **SPORTS**

Defender Industries, Inc. • manuals and videotapes on boating topics • **AUTO**

Dharma Trading Co. • books on textile dyeing, painting, batiking, etc. • **CRAFTS: TEXTILE ARTS**

Discount Master Animal Care • veterinary handbooks • **ANIMAL**

The Dog's Outfitter • books and videotapes on dogs, cats, horses, etc. • **ANIMAL**

EduCALC Corporation • computer books and programs • **OFFICE: COMPUTING**

Elderly Instruments • folk, rock, and esoteric recordings, songbooks, history, and manuals • **MUSIC**

Fedco Seeds Inc. • books on seed-saving, cultivation, varieties, organic farming, etc. • **FARM**

The Fiber Studio • books on knitting, spinning, dyeing, and weaving • **CRAFTS: TEXTILE ARTS**

Frank's Cane and Rush Supply • books on basketry, seat weaving, upholstery, etc. • **CRAFTS**

A.I. Friedman • art-related books, manuals, and videotapes • **ART MATERIALS**

Giardinelli Band Instrument Co., Inc. • records and books on music • **MUSIC**

Gohn Bros. Mfg. Co. • Amish and country cookbooks, quilting books • **CLOTHING**

Goldbergs' Marine Distributors • manuals and videotapes on boating topics • **AUTO**

Golfsmith International, Inc. • texts on golf-club making and repair, golfing, etc. • **SPORTS**

Great Northern Weaving • books on shirring, rug weaving, and rug braiding • **CRAFTS: TEXTILE ARTS**

H & R Company • reference books on computing and technical topics • **TOOLS**

Herter's • *hunting-related books and videos* • **SPORTS**

The House • *windsurfing books and videotapes* • **SPORTS**

IMPCO, Inc. • *Mercedes-Benz car maintenance manuals* • **AUTO**

Jerry's Artarama, Inc. • *art-related books, manuals, and videotapes* • **ART MATERIALS**

Johnny's Selected Seeds Inc. • *books on seed-starting, cultivation, etc.* • **FARM**

The Kennel Vet Corp. • *manuals, books, and videos on dogs, cats, and horses* • **ANIMAL**

E.C. Kraus Wine & Beermaking Supplies • *books on wine- and beer-making* • **FOOD: BEVERAGES AND FLAVORINGS**

KV Vet Supply Co, Inc.. • *manuals, books, and videos on dogs, cats, small animals, and horses* • **ANIMAL**

Lone Star Percussion • *books on drumming and percussion recordings* • **MUSIC**

M & E Marine Supply Company, Inc. • *books and manuals on boating* • **AUTO**

Mandolin Brothers, Ltd. • *music books, audiotapes, videotapes, and sheet music* • **MUSIC**

Mass. Army & Navy Store • *survival manuals and outdoor guides* • **CLOTHING**

Mellinger's Inc. • *books on gardening, farming, landscaping, food preservation, etc.* • **FARM**

Metropolitan Music Co. • *manuals and plans for making and repairing stringed instruments* • **MUSIC**

Micro-Mark • *books and videos on modeling (cars, ships, railroading), dollhouse building, workshop basics, etc.* • **TOOLS**

Model Expo, Inc. • *books on ship models, naval history, maritime topics* • **CRAFTS**

Mueller Sporting Goods, Inc. • *books and videos on billiards, pool, and darts* • **SPORTS**

Musician's Friend • *books and videos on music technique and theory* • **MUSIC**

National Educational Music Co. • *music software* • **MUSIC**

New England Cheesemaking Supply Company, Inc. • *publications on making cheese* • **HOME: KITCHEN**

Newark Dressmaker Supply, Inc. • *patterns, books, and guides on needlework and other crafts* • **CRAFTS: TEXTILE ARTS**

Orion Telescopes & Binoculars • *star charts and manuals on astronomy* • **CAMERAS**

Overton's Sports Center, Inc. • *windsurfing books and videotapes* • **SPORTS**

Patti Music Company • *sheet music* • **MUSIC**

Pet Warehouse • *books and manuals on dogs, cats, birds, and fish* • **ANIMAL**

John W. Poling: Military & Political Collectibles • *used and hard-to-find* books and printed matter on military and political topics • **ART & ANTIQUES**

Porter's Camera Store, Inc. • books and videos on photography • **CAMERAS**

Professional Cutlery Direct • commercial cookbooks • **HOME: KITCHEN**

Rafal Spice Company • cookbooks • **FOOD: BEVERAGES AND FLAVOR-INGS**

Retired Persons Services, Inc. • health-care manuals • **MEDICINE**

Scope City Inc. • star charts, books, manuals • **CAMERAS**

Sewing Machine Super Store® • instructional workbooks on operating sewing, embroidery, and knitting machines, etc. • **APPLIANCES**

Shar Products Company • sheet music, classical music videotapes, and audio cassettes • **MUSIC**

Solar Cine Products, Inc. • books on photography • **CAMERAS**

R.C. Steele Co. • AKC dog show videotapes, manuals for pet professionals • **ANIMAL**

Sultan's Delight • cookbooks featuring Middle Eastern and Greek cuisine • **FOOD**

That Fish Place/That Pet Place • books on aquariums, fish, and related topics • **ANIMAL**

Think Ink • guides to Print GOCCO printers • **CRAFTS**

Tool Crib of the North • shop manuals, woodworking guides, and videos • **TOOLS**

Tools on Sale™ • woodworking and construction books, manuals, and videos • **TOOLS**

Turner Greenhouses • books on gardening • **FARM**

United Pharmacal Company, Inc. • manuals and tapes on animal training and breeds • **ANIMAL**

University Products, Inc. • preservation supplies for book collections, references (books and videos) on archival conservation • **OFFICE: SMALL BUSINESS**

Wag-Aero Group of Aircraft Services • aviation manuals • **AUTO**

Walnut Acres Organic Farms • natural foods and vegetarian cookbooks • **FOOD**

Warner-Crivellaro Stained Glass Supplies, Inc. • books and manuals on stained glass • **CRAFTS**

Weinkrantz Musical Supply Co., Inc. • student music books and cassettes • **MUSIC**

West Manor Music • small selection of music manuals • **MUSIC**

Wholesale Tool Co., Inc. • shop manuals • **TOOLS**

The Winfield Collection. • woodcraft how-to books and patterns • **CRAFTS: WOODCRAFT**

World Wide Aquatics • books on swimming, aquatic fitness, and triathloning • **SPORTS**

CAMERAS, PHOTOGRAPHIC AND DARKROOM EQUIPMENT, OPTICS, FILM, AND SERVICES

Equipment, supplies, and services

In the highly competitive camera market, even major electronics outlets with small camera departments can usually offer good discounts on list price. In addition to cameras, bulbs, and film, large camera houses carry video equipment, lighting equipment, screens, film editors, splicers, batteries, projection tables, lenses, filters, adapters, cases, darkroom outfits and chemicals, and custom photofinishing services—at discounts averaging 40%. Even if you don't need custom work done, you can have your film processed, enlargements made, slides duplicated, and other services done by a discount mail-order lab for half the price often charged by a drugstore or retail outlet.

Take care of your pictures: Keep them out of "magnetic" photo albums, which are made with polyvinyl-film that gives off vinyl chloride gas, and cardboard pages that exude peroxide vapors. Both can cause deterioration of slides and prints. (Photographs should be kept in temperate, relatively dry areas, out of light as much as possible.) To preserve your pictures, use archival-quality materials—acid-free albums and storage boxes, Mylar sheet protectors, "safe" slide sheets, etc. These and other conservation materials are available from University Products, listed in the "Small Business" section of "Office."

THE GRAY MARKET AND OTHER CONCERNS

Some years ago, the camera and electronics industries were plagued with problems caused by gray-market goods—products intended for sale in other countries. The goods are usually imported outside manufacturer-approved distribution channels, without authorization of the U.S. trademark owner. Gray-market goods are usually less expensive than their "authorized" counterparts, and although they may be just as good, they may be produced under different quality-control standards, contain ingredients not approved for use in the United States, or have a warranty that is not honored in the United States.

Gray-marketers who sell goods not intended for the U.S. market are not knowingly listed in this edition of WBMC. But because companies can change selling policies, if you want to be sure a firm is an authorized distributor of a product, call the manufacturer. Ask the mail-order company whether the warranty is honored by the service centers of the U.S. *manufacturer,* and make your purchase by credit card, which gives you certain protections under the Fair Credit Billing Act. See page 635 for more information.

Gray-market activity has abated, but another form has become prevalent—"diversions" of goods from the authorized path, often by a wholesaler or mass merchant. In this case, the product was intended for the domestic market, but not for the store in which it's sold. Often, the consumer benefits, as when major department stores buy enormous inventory (to get the lowest possible price), and resell the surplus "out the back door" to other stores and discounters. If it's a product that should be used at the direction of a professional, the manufacturer may assume no liability for poor performance unless the product is sold by an authorized dealer. This may not matter much when the product is shampoo, but it does if it's a carburetor.

Before you buy, whether it's from a local store or mail-order firm, you might want to heed the advice of the owner of a buying service, who knows all the "tricks" used by the vendors. He urges you to take the time to contact the manufacturer about the model you've chosen (most manufacturers have toll-free lines, or websites), and find out what the manufacturer includes with the camera—case, lens, cap, strap, manual, coupons, etc. He suggests that, when you're examining the camera, you check the markings on the lenses to make sure the original hasn't been swapped for a lesser model. As he puts it, "You have to do the legwork, or you won't get the best deal, and you can be ripped off. The bad businesses shouldn't be there, but they are."

FIND IT FAST

BINOCULARS • *Mardiron, Orion, Scope City*
CAMERAS • *B & H, Ewald-Clark, Porter's, Solar Cine*

ABC PHOTO & IMAGING SERVICES, INC.

**9016 PRINCE WILLIAM ST.,
  DEPT. WBMC
MANASSAS, VA 22110
703–369–1906
FAX: 703–631–8064**

Catalog: $3, refundable
Save: up to 30%
Pay: check, MO, MC, V, AE
Sells: film processing
Store: same address; Monday to Friday 9–6, Saturday 8–2

 ¡Si!

ABC Photo & Imaging, whose parent firm has been in business since 1945, is a full-service professional and commercial mail-order lab that offers film and slide processing, negative duplication and slide copying, prints, and photographic packages (portraits and weddings) at competitive prices. Formerly known as Skyline Color Lab, ABC's 28-page catalog lists the available services and prices, includes directions for cropping, and features a helpful glossary of terms like "internegative," "dodging," and "push/pull processing." ABC will process your color or black-and-white film (roll or sheet), produce contact sheets, make prints and enlargements (from 3½" by 5" to 48" by 144"), and create murals and photographic displays (from 40" square to 48" by 96"; larger sizes are available on a custom basis). Custom services are offered, including "push" processing to compensate for underexposed film, glass mounts for slides, slide remounting, duplicate negatives and negatives made from slides or transparencies (internegatives), a choice of finishes for enlargements (canvas, pebble, matte, or luster), dry mounting of prints (on art board, foam core, or "gator" foam), mounting on canvas panels or canvas stretchers, and printing for backlit display. ABC has also put together a "relative's special" perfect for sending to friends and family—as well as wedding album packages. Complete details of the firm's sales policy and guarantees are given in the catalog.

Special Factors: Liability for damaged or lost film is limited to replacement with unexposed film; minimum order is $25; C.O.D. orders are accepted (for delivery within the 48 contiguous United States).

B & H PHOTO-VIDEO

119 W. 17TH ST.
NEW YORK, NY 10011
800–947–9950
212–444–6600
FAX: 800–947–7008
FAX: 212–242–1400

Catalog: free
Pay: check, MO, MC, V, AE, Discover
Sells: photography and imaging equipment, video and pro-audio equipment, and supplies
Store: same address; Monday and Tuesday 9–6, Wednesday and Thursday 9–7:15, Friday 9–1, Sunday 10–4:45, closed Saturday
E-mail: see website
Online: http://www.bhphotovideo.com

B & H has been serving New York City photographers for over two decades with the latest in professional equipment, accessories, and supplies, all at discount prices. Over the years, the company has expanded its product line and now carries a range of pro-audio, video, and digital imaging (computer) components. The inventory is extensive—80,000 products and counting, with over 100 manufacturers represented in the video department *alone*. To see what's currently available, you can send for the monthly "flyer," a 72-page catalog sampling all the departments, or see the regular multi-page ads in *Popular Photography* and other industry magazines. B & H also plans to publish "The Professional Photo SourceBook," to complement the edition for the video pro that's now in its second edition. And you can find a wealth of information on the B & H website, including one of the best collection of photography-related links around.

Special Factors: Satisfaction is guaranteed; authorized returns are accepted for exchange, refund, or credit (see catalog or website for stipulations); C.O.D. orders are accepted.

CLARK COLOR LABS

P.O. BOX 96300
WASHINGTON, DC 20090
301–595–5300

Mailers: free
Pay: check or MO
Sells: film-processing and enlargement services
Store: mail order only

Clark Color Labs is a prominent mail-order film processor that develops 110, 126, 127, 620, disc, 35 mm, and single-use cameras, as well as slides and movies. You can also order reprints and enlargements (wallet size to 20" by 30") from negatives and slides, have copy negatives made from prints (color and black-and-white), and buy fresh film (Agfa and Kodak). Clark Color Labs uses the Colorwatch system, which means the paper, chemicals, and quality-control standards are all from Kodak. Clark's prices are much lower than those charged by minilabs, averaging 15¢ for one processed print compared to 40¢ for the same print from a typical minilab. Clark Color Lab has a dozen locations around the country to expedite your order, issues credit for unprintable negatives, and will give you a refund or credit if you're not completely satisfied with your pictures.

Special Factors: Returns are accepted for exchange, refund, or credit.

EWALD-CLARK

17 W. CHURCH AVE.
ROANOKE, VA 24011
540–342–1829
FAX: 540–345–9943

Information: price quote only
Pay: MO, MC, V, AE, Discover
Sells: cameras, darkroom equipment, optics, services, and repairs
Store: same address; Monday to Friday 8:30–5:30; also Bedford, Blacksburg, Roanoke, and Salem, VA

Ewald-Clark is a full-service photography center that's been in business since 1949, but *does not publish a catalog*—call or write for a price quote on specific models. In addition to cameras (including digital models), lenses, camera accessories, darkroom equipment, and finishing services, Ewald-Clark sells binoculars, all at discounts of 2% to 40%, or an average of 30% off list prices.

Among the available brands are Amphoto, Beseler, Bogen, Bronica, Canon, Fuji, Gitzo, Gossen, Gralab, Ilford, Kodak, Logan, LowePro, Mamiya, Minolta, Nikon, Novatron, Pelican, Pentax, Polaroid, Quantum, Ricoh, Samyang, Tamrac, Tamron, Tiffen, Varta, and Vivitar. You can also inquire for rate and specifications on custom photofinishing services.

Please note: Shipments to non-U.S. destinations are subject to hazardous materials regulations.

Special Factors: Price quote by phone or letter with SASE.

MARDIRON OPTICS

THE BINOCULAR PLACE
4 SPARTAN CIRCLE,
 DEPT. WBMC
STONEHAM, MA 02180
617–938–8339

Brochures and Price Lists: 2 first-class stamps
Pay: check or MO
Sells: binoculars, telescopes, microscopes, opera glasses, night vision optics, etc.
Store: mail order only

Mardiron, in business since 1983, sells binoculars, spotting scopes, astronomical telescopes, rifle scopes, microscopes, night-vision binoculars and scopes, range finders, theater glasses, global positioning sensors, cameras, and camcorders—at savings of up to 45% on list prices. Mardiron features goods from Bausch & Lomb, Burris, Bushnell, Canon, Celestron, Copitar, Fujinon, Kowa, Leica, Leupold, Nikon, Parks, Pentax, Redfield, Sigma, Swift, Tasco, Vivitar, Weaver, and the Steiner military, hunting, and fully integrated compass marine binoculars. Mardiron also offers Brunton binoculars, which were developed especially for eyeglasses-wearers, as well as camcorders by Minolta, and cameras by Bronica, Gossen, Konica, Mamiya, Minox, Motormarine, Olympus, Ricoh, Rokunar, and other firms. To receive catalogs, brochures, and price lists, send two first-class stamps, and mention the brand that's of particular interest to you.

Special Factors: Price quote by phone; shipping is not charged on deliveries within the 48 contiguous United States.

MYSTIC COLOR LAB

MASON'S ISLAND RD.
P.O. BOX 144
MYSTIC, CT 06355–9987
800–367–6061
860–536–4291
FAX: 860–536–6418

Mailers: free
Pay: check, MO, MC, V, AE, Discover
Sells: film-processing and enlargement services
Factory Store: same address; Monday to Friday 9:30–5:30
Online: http://www.mysticcolorlab.com/

Mail-order film labs abound, but Mystic is one that's gotten good marks in quality comparisons with other labs. Mystic has been in business since 1969, and offers free shipping in postpaid mailers with no handling charges. Mystic Color Lab's prices on processing film, for one set of standard-size prints, are up to 30% below those of other mail-order labs—and considerably less than the one-hour minilabs. But the firm does its best to come close to the minilab turnaround time, by pledging to get your processed film and prints in the mail to you within 24 hours of receipt.

Mystic develops 110, 35 mm color print, and slide film, along with one-time-use cameras. The firm makes enlargements (up to 20" by 30" posters), and offers the hour film at great prices—a three-pack of 24-exposure, 200 ASA film is only $7.95 at this writing. If you're looking for great ways to enjoy your photos, Mystic offers a variety of options, from photo mugs and mouse pads to photo greeting cards and calendars. Cameras and albums are also available. Call for the latest catalog and film mailers, or order through the website.

Special Factors: Shipping is not charged.

ORION TELESCOPES & BINOCULARS

DEPT. WBM
P.O. BOX 1815
SANTA CRUZ, CA
**   95061–1815**
408–763–7000
FAX: 408–763–7017

Catalog: free
Pay: check, MO, MC, V, Discover
Sells: telescopes, binoculars, and accessories
Store: 89 Hangar Way, Watsonville, CA (408–763–7000); also 10555 S. De Anza Blvd., Cupertino, CA (408–255–8770), and 3609 Buchanan St., San Francisco, CA (415–913–9966)
E-mail: sales@oriontel.com
Online: http://www.oriontel.com

  (see text)

Orion brings you stellar savings on top-quality telescopes and accessories through an informative, 100-page color catalog that includes sidebars on telescope selection and sky watching, as well as complete product descriptions. (The website also has extensive information on evaluating and selecting telescopes, binoculars, and other optics.) Orion has been in business since 1975 and stocks astronomical and terrestrial telescopes by Celestron, Orion, TeleVue, and others. If you visit Orion's Telescope Center stores, you'll also find goods by Bausch & Lomb, Bushnell, Fujinon, Nikon, Pentax, Swarovski, Swift, and Zeiss. Camera adapters, filters, lenses, optical tubes, tripods, eyepieces, star charts, books, and other accessories are available. Orion is known for its comprehensive selection of binoculars for astronomy, sightseeing, and other outdoor uses, as well as spotting scopes for sport and nature enthusiasts.

Please note: Orion ships only to the United States and Canada.

Special Factors: Satisfaction is guaranteed; price quote by phone or letter for institutional orders.

OWL PHOTO CORP.

701 E. MAIN ST.
WEATHERFORD, OK 73096
405–772–3353
FAX: 405–772–5804

Mailers: free
Pay: check, MO, MC, V
Sells: film processing and reprinting services
Store: same address; Monday to Friday 7:30–5, Saturday 9–1

Owl Photo has been in business since 1934, and offers reasonably priced film processing services by mail, and will send you self-mailers on request. Owl will develop your color and black-and-white film at prices that are competitive with discount drug store processing, and you can also order reprints and fresh film—a price list comes with the mailer. Disc, 110, 120, 126, 127, 135, 616 color (C–41), and 620 film is processed, and reprint sizes run up to 11" by 14". Owl uses Kodak paper and chemicals, and guarantees your satisfaction or your processing costs and postage will be refunded.

Special Factors: Satisfaction is guaranteed; returns are accepted for refund or credit.

PORTER'S CAMERA STORE, INC.

P.O. BOX 628
CEDAR FALLS, IA 50613
800–553–2001
319–268–0104
FAX: 319–277–5254

Catalog: free (see text)
Pay: check, MO, MC, V, Discover
Sells: photographic and darkroom equipment and supplies
Store: 323 Viking Rd., Cedar Falls, IA; Monday to Saturday 9:30–5:30
Online: http://www.porters.com

Porter's has been selling photographic and darkroom equipment since 1914, and publishes a 128-page tabloid catalog packed with an enormous range of photographic products, at prices up to 67% below list. Both amateurs and professionals will appreciate the buys on cameras and lenses, filters, darkroom equipment, film, bags and cases, batteries, studio equipment, chemicals, paper, and much more. The brands run from Agfa to Vivitar, the sales policy is clearly detailed in the catalog, and Porter's has deputized one of its staff to answer your questions about equipment. A separate, 40-page video catalog is also available. If you're in Cedar Falls, drop by the warehouse outlet store where you'll find everything tagged at catalog prices—a welcome departure from the two-tier policies prevailing at most discount stores.

Canadian readers, please note: The catalog costs $3 in *Canadian funds,* but orders must be paid in U.S. funds. The catalog describes purchasing procedures and includes a shipping rate chart.

Please note: The catalog costs $10 in U.S. funds if sent to an address without a U.S. or Canadian postal code.

Special Factors: Price quote by phone or letter; authorized returns are accepted; institutional accounts are available; orders are shipped worldwide, subject to a $100 minimum order.

SCOPE CITY INC.

**730 EASY ST.
SIMI VALLEY, CA 93065
805–522–6646
FAX: 805–582–0292**

Price List: free
Pay: check, MO, MC, V, Discover
Sells: telescopes, binoculars, microscopes, and other optics
Store: same address; Monday to Friday 9–6, Saturday 10–6; also Costa Mesa, San Diego, and Sherman Oaks, CA; Monday to Friday 10–7

Scope City has been selling telescopes, binoculars, spotting scopes, and other optics since 1977. Telescopes and accessories by Bushnell, Celestron, Edmund Scientific, Meade, Parks, Questar, and TeleVue are available, as well as field and specialty binoculars and scopes by Bausch & Lomb, Dr. Optics, Fujinon, JMI, Kowa, Leica, Minolta, Parks, Steiner, Swarovski, Swift, Zeiss, and other manufacturers. Scope City also offers lenses, eyepieces, adapters, mirrors, star charts, manuals, and other reference tools, and telescope-building components. Most of the prices are discounted, and savings of up to 45% are possible on selected items. If you know the model you want, you can call for a price quote, or request the free price list.

Special Factors: Satisfaction is guaranteed; returns are accepted within 15 days for exchange, refund, or credit; minimum order is $25.

SKRUDLAND PHOTO

**5311 FLEMING CT.
AUSTIN, TX 78744
512–444–0958**

Catalog: free
Pay: check or MO
Sells: film processing and reprinting services
Store: mail order only

Skrudland Photo has performed well in tests of mail-order film processors, and offers low prices—as little as $2 a roll—for color film processing (with one set of prints, glossy or matte). In addition to developing 110, 126, Disc, and 35 mm film, Skrudland can make prints and enlargements from your negatives, and develop your slides and super-8 movies. The film mailers (available on request) include prices and the standard liability disclaimer used by most mail-order film processors.

Special Factors: Satisfaction is guaranteed; returns are accepted for credit.

SOLAR CINE PRODUCTS, INC.

**4247 SOUTH KEDZIE AVE.
CHICAGO, IL 60632
800–621–8796
312–254–8310
FAX: 312–254–4124**

Catalog: free
Pay: check, MO, MC, V, AE, DC, Discover
Sells: photo equipment, supplies, and services
Store: same address; Monday to Friday 8:30–5, Saturday 9–1

 ¡Si!

Solar Cine's 24-page catalog gives a sample of the thousands of items carried by the company—a full range of photographic equipment and accessories from a large number of manufacturers. Solar Cine has been supplying professionals and serious amateurs since 1937, and stocks a full range of still and movie equipment, including videotapes and video batteries. Range Finder cameras, lenses, studio lights, light meters, tripods, and darkroom materials are available from Canon, Kalt/Brandess, Kodak, Pentax, Polaroid, and Vivitar, among others. Scores of books on photography for beginners and professionals are available, as well as electronics and processing services (movies, slides, reprints, and prints). The services are described in the catalog; for more information on cameras and equipment, call or write for a price quote.

Special Factors: Returns (except defective goods) are subject to a restocking fee.

SEE ALSO

Beach Sales Inc. • *camera film and videotape* • **APPLIANCES**

Berry Scuba Co. • *underwater cameras* • **SPORTS**

Cabela's Inc. • *binoculars and spotting scopes* • **SPORTS**

Central Skindivers • *underwater cameras* • **SPORTS**

Defender Industries, Inc. • *binoculars and marine optics* • **AUTO**

Herter's • *hunting optics and binoculars* • **SPORTS**

The Sportsman's Guide, Inc. • *hunting optics and binoculars* • **SPORTS**

20th Century Plastics, Inc. • *photo storage sheets and albums* • **OFFICE**

University Products, Inc. • *archival-quality storage materials for photographs, slides, film, negatives, microfiche, etc.* • **OFFICE: SMALL BUSINESS**

Wiley Outdoor Sports, Inc. • *binoculars, spotting scopes, etc.* • **SPORTS**

CLOTHING, FURS, AND ACCESSORIES

Clothing, furs, and accessories for men, women, and children

The firms listed here sell a wide range of clothing for men, women, and children—Amish clothing from Indiana, lingerie from New York City's Lower East Side, executive suiting, custom-made deerskin coats and jackets, and much more—at good savings.

Finding discount sources for bridal attire isn't easy (see Discount Bridal Service in this chapter), and anyone facing the challenge of planning a wedding today will find *Bridal Bargains: Secrets to Throwing a Fantastic Wedding on a Realistic Budget* an absolute necessity. Written by the intrepid Alan and Denise Fields, the book describes the mechanics of the entire industry, and gives the best strategies for everything from booking the site, buying the dress, ordering food and flowers, hiring the photographer, and covering all of the details—without getting burned. The Fields are so confident that you'll benefit from their research that they offer a complete refund on the cost of the book if it doesn't save you at least $500 on your wedding expenses. To order a copy, call 800–888–0385, or write to Windsor Peak Press, 1223 Peakview Circle, Suite 7000, Boulder, CO 80302.

Clothing that's made in the United States must bear labels that provide specific information on cleaning and care. The Federal Trade Commission has compiled "What's New About Care Labels," a booklet defining the terms used in the labeling that answers a number of typical consumer questions. For a copy, request it by title from the Federal Trade Commission, Public Reference Office, Washington, DC 20580. If you want to make the best of what you own, you'll appreciate *Taking Care of Clothes,* by Mablen Jones (St. Martin's Press, 1982). It can help you evaluate clothing before purchase, and gives tips on stain removal, laundering, dry cleaning, ironing and pressing, storage, and caring for leather, fur, and other special materials. You can also get it from the horse's mouth: The Neighborhood Cleaners' Association (NCA) publishes the "Consumer Guide to Clothing Care," a brochure of tips on the care and cleaning of different fabrics and trims. Send a long, self-addressed, stamped envelope to NCA, 252 W. 29th St., New York, NY 10001, for the pamphlet.

Last, your very best deals on clothing are usually found in *stores,* where very limited inventory, drastic markdowns, closeouts, and irregulars—all of which pose fulfillment problems if sold by mail—can be snatched up at big savings. Thrift shops are another resource prized by people who must build a wardrobe on a shoestring. Thrift shops are also one of the best places to learn about clothing's quality points, since they tell the story of how the fabric, weave, tailoring, and style have performed over the years. The better you train your eye to identify the kind of wool that pills, the soft sheen of good silk, collars that have survived fads, and countless other clothing details, the better you'll be at imagining how something in a catalog actually looks, and will wear.

FIND IT FAST

BRIDAL ATTIRE • **Discount Bridal Service**
DANCEWEAR • **Dance Distributors**
HATS • **Manny's Millinery**
MEN'S CLOTHING • **Jos. A. Bank, Bridgewater, Huntington, Mass. Army, Quinn's Shirt Shop**
SHEEPSKIN, DEERSKIN, AND FUR • **Arctic Sheepskin, Deerskin Place**
SPORTSWEAR • **No Nonsense Direct, One Hanes Place, Sport Europa, Sportswear Clearinghouse**
UNDERWEAR AND HOSIERY • **Asiatic Hosiery, Chock, National Wholesale, No Nonsense Direct, One Hanes Place**
UNIFORMS • **Mass. Army, Tafford, Uniform Connection**
WOMEN'S CLOTHING • **Jos. A. Bank, Bridgewater, Chadwick's, Lady Grace, No Nonsense Direct, One Hanes Place, Ultimate Outlet, Willow Ridge**
WORK CLOTHING • **Cahall's, Gohn, Todd, WearGuard**

ARCTIC SHEEPSKIN OUTLET

565 CO. RD. T, BOX WB
HAMMOND, WI 54015
800–428–9276
715–796–2292
FAX: 715–796–2295

Brochure: $2, refundable
Pay: check, MO, MC, V, Discover
Sells: sheepskin clothing and accessories
Store: 30 miles east of St. Paul on I–94 at the Hammond exit; also 3015 E. Hamilton Ave., Eau Claire, WI; Monday to Thursday 8–8, Friday 8–5, Saturday 9–5

Arctic Sheepskin Outlet was founded in 1980 by the energetic Joseph Bacon, who's been quite successful with mail-order skylights and insulated glass panels (see the listing of Arctic Glass & Window Outlet in the "Improvement and Maintenance" section of "Home"). His Arctic Sheepskin Outlet features sheepskin favorites—slippers, mittens, hats, car seat covers, rugs, etc.—from the largest sheepskin tannery in the world. Savings vary from item to item; rubber-soled sheepskin moccasins sell here and elsewhere at $49.95, but the car seat covers are buys at $39 (two for $75), as are mittens for $16.95, kids' slippers for under $15, and deep-pile sheepskin rugs from $59.95—about a third less than the going rate. There are also hats with earflaps, sheepskin headbands, steering wheel covers, and bicycle seat covers. All purchases are covered by Arctic's "money-back guarantee," and you can call for the current specials.

Special Factors: Satisfaction is guaranteed; returns are accepted for exchange, refund, or credit; minimum order is $10.

ASIATIC HOSIERY CO.

P.O. BOX 31
LITTLE FALLS, NJ
07424–0031
201–872–2111
FAX: 201–872–2114

Catalog: $2, $4 to non-U.S. addresses, refundable with first order
Pay: check or MO
Sells: hosiery for men, women, and children
Store: mail order only
E-mail: sock1@ix.netcom.com
Online: http://pw2.netcom.com/~sock1/Asiatic.html

If you're willing to buy a dozen of the same color, size, and style of hosiery, Asiatic Hosiery will reward you with amazing savings on a full selection of socks, panty hose, and other legwear for the whole family.

The prices range from women's sheer knee-highs at $4 per dozen ($6, queen), to pantyhose from under 84¢ a pair to $1.67 for a sheer support style in seven colors and sizes to 2X. A *gross* of nylon "shoe try-ons," which can be used as footlets, cost just $6. In addition, Asiatic Hosiery sells opaque tights, knee-high and over-the-knee socks, anklets, slouch socks, and athletic socks for both women and girls, and dress and athletic socks for men and boys.

The eight-page catalog from Asiatic has no pictures or color charts, so you have to correlate the descriptions to products you're familiar with. There are no brand names, so order on the generous side (if you're a D in premium pantyhose, take a Q or 1X here). Some color selections will include "assortments," which will be the company's choice. You're really buying at wholesale here, so place a small order to begin with to make sure you'll be happy.

Special Factors: Minimum order is one dozen of a style or color.

JOS. A. BANK CLOTHIERS, INC.

■■■■■■■■

500 HANOVER PIKE,
   DEPT. WBMC
HAMPSTEAD, MD 21074
800–285-BANK
FAX: 410–239–5911

Catalog: $1
Pay: check, MO, MC, V, AE
Sells: men's and women's career clothing and sportswear
Store: 50 stores in 29 states (locations are listed in the catalog)

Bank's business is executive suiting, which it serves with separate catalogs for men and women. Fine tailoring details and prices up to 30% below comparable goods—but not "discount"—distinguish the company's offerings. The men's catalog features suits, jackets, pants, shirts, ties, accessories, weekend separates, and underwear. The suits are handsomely executed in fine wool worsteds, in pin and chalkline stripes, glen plaids, and herringbones. Chesterfield and cashmere topcoats, tuxedos and formal wear, blazers, tweed jackets, and complementing pants and shirts are among the standards, and swatches are available for the suits and sports coats. Braces, silk ties, shoes, and pajamas are sold as well.

The offerings in the women's catalog include fine business ensembles in the "relaxed traditional" style—softly colored suits, coatdresses, and

Chanel-style jackets are a few examples from past catalogs. Some of the women's clothing is offered in petites and talls, as well as regular sizes. Scarves, belts, jewelry, bags, and coordinated weekend separates are also available. Bank's garments often compare well to similar garments sold elsewhere for more, but note that Bank is recommended more for quality and selection than for prices, and *do not ask for discounts.*

Special Factors: Satisfaction is guaranteed; returns are accepted for exchange, refund, or credit.

BRIDGEWATER

BOX 1600
BROCKTON, MA
02403–1600
800–525–4420
508–583–7200
FAX: 800–448–5767
TDD: 800–978–8798

Catalog: free
Pay: check, MO, MC, V, AE, Discover
Sells: women's clothing and accessories
Store: mail order only

Bridgewater is a new catalog from Chadwick's of Boston (also listed in this chapter). It's "a classic collection for men and women," and differs from the regular Chadwick's catalog in the styles—which are more conservative—and the inclusion of a line of clothing for men. Bridgewater offers women perfect choices for the office and professional settings—linen blazers, unadorned white cotton shirts, linen skirts in two lengths, a silk jacket dress, and other wardrobe basics. The men's section opens with a silk/wool blend blazer, and includes sports shirts, gabardine trousers, and a great selection of polo shirts, twill pants, and other pieces that are well suited to after-work and weekend activities. The brands, pricing, and policies are identical to those of the parent company.

Special Factors: Satisfaction is guaranteed; returns are accepted for exchange, refund, or credit.

CAHALL'S WORK WEAR

**P.O. BOX 450-WM
MOUNT ORAB, OH 45154
937–444–2094**

Information: price quote
Pay: check, MO, MC, V, Discover
Sells: working clothing and footwear
Store: Cahall's Work Wear Store; 112 S. High St., Mount Orab, OH; Monday to Saturday 9–6

The Cahall family opened its department store in 1946, and took the leap into mail order nearly 30 years later with heavy-duty apparel and footwear. Cahall's can supply your favorites—jeans, shirts, jackets, and overalls—at savings of up to 30% on suggested list or retail prices. Popular lines from Carhartt, Hanes, Key, Levi's, OshKosh, Wolverine, and other well-known manufacturers are available. Cahall's also offers an excellent selection of work shoes and boots for men and women from Carolina, Danner, LaCrosse, Wolverine, and other names, in hard-to-find sizes. Hush Puppies and Rocky Boot sport boots are also stocked, as well as heavy-duty socks, work gloves, bandannas, T-shirts, hats, and even nail aprons. Call or write with the manufacturer's name, style code, size, and color for availability and prices.

Special Factors: Satisfaction is guaranteed; returns are accepted for exchange, refund, or credit.

CHADWICK'S OF BOSTON, LTD.

**BOX 1600
BROCKTON, MA
02403–1600
800–525–4420
FAX: 800–448–5767
TDD: 800–978–8798**

Catalog: free
Pay: check, MO, MC, V, AE, Discover
Sells: women's clothing and accessories
Store: mail order only

Chadwick's publishes "The Original Off-Price Fashion Catalog," full of pretty, professional outfits for office, great dresses for evenings and special occasions, weekend and casual separates, and shoes and accessories. Chadwick's has been in business since 1983, and features labels like Ellen Ashley, Averroe, Harvé Bernard, Pierre Cardin, Herman Geist,

J.G. Hook, Carol Horn, Mootsies Tootsies, Giorgio Sant' Angelo, and Savannah. The styles run from kicky to classic, the sizing from 2P to 26W (although not in every item). The catalog descriptions include care information, and skirt length and pant inseams. Pricing is terrific—many office-worthy dresses are priced at under $50, and just about every edition of the catalog features a seasonable blazer or jacket in a great choice of colors, at a special price—$39 for linen, merino for $49, cashmere blend for $79—with blouses or sweaters to match. And the catalogs often offer no-strings deferred billing, which can give your budget another assist.

Special Factors: Satisfaction is guaranteed; returns are accepted for exchange or refund.

CHOCK CATALOG CORP.

74 ORCHARD ST., DEPT. WBMC

NEW YORK, NY

10002–4594

212–473–1929

FAX: 212–473–6273

Catalog: $2, $5 outside the U.S.
Pay: check, MO, MC, V, Discover, JCB
Sells: hosiery, underwear, sleepwear, and infants' layettes
Store: same address; Sunday to Thursday 9:30–5:30, Friday 9–1
E-mail: chock1@juno.com

 ¡Si!

Chock, known to generations of New Yorkers as Louis Chock, is a family operation that's been selling unmentionables since 1921. Chock's 66-page catalog is packed with good values on name-brand underthings for men, women, children, and infants. The women's department features underpants by Carter's, Hanes Her Way, Jockey for Her, Lollipop, and Vanity Fair; hosiery by Berkshire, Hanes, Calvin Klein, Mayer, and PrimaSport; well-priced dusters, smocks, aprons, slips, pajamas, and nightgowns. (For those with special needs, there are two pages of dusters, nightgowns, and slips that snap up the back.) Men are offered underwear by BVD, Chock's private label, Duofold, Hanes, Jockey, Calvin Klein, Manshape, and Munsingwear; socks by Burlington, Chock's own line, Doré Doré, Thorlo, and Wigwam; and pajamas and robes from Knothe, Munsingwear, and Oscar de la Renta. Men's sizes run up to XXXL (58 to 60).

Chock's has a good choice of basics for babies and children, running from cloth diapers and complete layettes by Carters and Gerber, creepers and sleepers, underwear and sleepwear for boys and girls by Carters and Hanes, socks by Buster Brown and Tic-Tac-Toe, to toys by Montgomery Schoolhouse, bathing accessories, sheets, blankets, and more.

Chock's catalogs usually offer well-priced accessories that make great gifts—typically gloves and Totes umbrellas. How wonderful to find a choice of Caswell-Massey soaps and creams, at nifty discounts of about 25%!

Special Factors: Satisfaction is guaranteed; unopened returns with manufacturer's packaging intact are accepted within 30 days.

DANCE DISTRIBUTORS

DEPT. WBMC
P.O. BOX 11440
HARRISBURG, PA 17108
800–333–2623
FAX: 717–234–1465

Catalog: free
Pay: check, MO, MC, V, AE, Discover
Sells: dance wear and accessories
Store: mail order only
E-mail: DanceDstr@aol.com

Both aspiring amateurs and professional dancers can trim at least 25% from the cost of their next pair of toe shoes, leotards, or tights by buying from Dance Distributors. The 26-page catalog lists shoes for ballet, pointe, jazz, tap, modern, and folk dance. Dance Distributors also offers a complete line of bodywear for men, women, and children, including leotards, dance skirts, tights, trunks, and warmups. The manufacturers include Baryshnikov, Bloch, Body Wrappers, Capezio, Chacott, Freed, Grishko, Harmonie, Mirella, Prima Soft, Sade, and Sansha, and Dance Distributors also sells its own line of leotards, tights, and legwarmers. Prices are generally 25% below list, but sale offerings can double the discounts. Special orders are accepted on items not listed in the catalog (no returns). The catalog has helpful size conversion charts for street shoes to dance styles, and for Continental sizing to inches.

Special Factors: Satisfaction is guaranteed; price quote by phone or letter; returns (except special orders) are accepted within 30 days for exchange, refund, or credit.

THE DEERSKIN PLACE

283 AKRON RD.
EPHRATA, PA 17522
717–733–7624

Catalog: $1, refundable (see text)
Pay: check, MO, MC, V
Sells: deerskin clothing and accessories
Store: same address; Monday to Saturday
9–9, Sunday (January-December) 12–5

The Deerskin Place, in business since 1969, features clothing and accessories made of deerskin, cowhide, and sheepskin, at prices up to 50% less than those charged elsewhere for comparable goods. Among the offerings are fingertip-length shearling jackets for about $400, fringed buckskin-suede jackets for under $200, bomber and motorcycle jackets, and sporty deerskin handbags for about $70. The Deerskin Place offers moccasins and casual shoes, knee-high suede boots, and crepe-soled slip-ons for men and women (from $17), deerskin wallets, clutches, coin purses, and keycases (from about $6), mittens and gloves for the whole family, beaded belts (under $6), and many other accessories.

Special Factors: Satisfaction is guaranteed; inquire before ordering if unsure of color, size, etc.; returns are accepted; C.O.D. orders are accepted.

DISCOUNT BRIDAL SERVICE, INC.

14415 NORTH 73RD ST.,
   SUITE 115
SCOTTSDALE, AZ 85260
800–874–8794
FAX: 602–998–3092

Information: call for referral (see text)
Pay: check, MO, MC, V
Sells: women's bridal attire
Store: see text

How would you like to carve 20% to 40% off one of the biggest single expenses of your wedding—The Dress? Discount Bridal Service (DBS), a network of hundreds of authorized bridal dealers across the United States and Japan, can refer you to the representative nearest you. You'll work with her directly, ordering your gown at savings that average 20% to 40%, and you can also order the dresses and accessories for the bridesmaids, mother of the bride, the flower girl, and others, at similar savings. There's no catalog—simply choose the gown of your dreams from the advertising and editorial in *Bride's, Modern Bride, For the Bride, Elegant Bride, Bridal Guide, Wedding Day Magazine*—or any other source showing current bridal styles. All of the merchandise is first-quality—no seconds or copies are sold. DBS deals with the same manufacturers and resources as do conventional bridal retailers. You'll be responsible for alterations (if they're needed), and if you don't know a good seamstress who specializes in bridal fittings, the DBS rep can give you local references. In addition to savings hundreds of dollars on the gown (and possibly thousands if you outfit the bridal party through DBS), the rep can accommodate you with invitations, accessory items, tuxedos, and many other bridal-related services.

DBS can perform miracles for your wedding budget, but it can't change time: It's still going to take at least 10 weeks, or as many as six months, from the time your order is submitted to when you receive your gown. (The differences depend on the manufacturer and the complexity of the dress; your rep will tell you the time frame for your choice.) And note that you'll have to prepay the entire cost of the gown when you place the order. Even with savings, that requires confidence in your rep, but DBS couldn't have survived in this highly competitive business since 1985 unless it had a great reputation and thoroughly reliable salespeople.

Special Factors: Consult with your DBS rep for terms of the sales policy; many accept credit cards.

GOHN BROS. MFG. CO.

▬▬▬▬▬▬▬

105 S. MAIN
P.O. BOX 111
MIDDLEBURY, IN
   46540–0111
219–825–2400

Catalog: $1
Pay: check or MO
Sells: general merchandise and Amish specialties
Store: same address; Monday to Saturday 8–5:30

While other firms add fax machines and websites, Gohn Bros. remains firmly rooted in a world where bonnet board and work coats were stock items in the general store. Gohn has been in business since 1904, and sells practical goods at prices up to 40% below comparable retail.

Home sewers appreciate Gohn for yard goods staples and notions, such as the all-cotton Sanforized blue denim ($5.98), muslin (as low as $1.39), cotton oxford shirting ($2.98), quilting thread ($1.29), cotton percale and quilting prints, pillow tubing, all-cotton sheeting, tailor's canvas, haircloth, mosquito netting, Coats & Clark embroidery floss (25¢ per skein), and wool overcoating (under $13 per yard, in navy, black, and "Confederate gray").

At least half of Gohn's closely printed 12-page stock lists are devoted to work-tailored, sturdy Amish clothing, including men's cotton chambray work shirts ($16.98), cotton denim broadfall pants ($17.98), men's underwear, rubber galoshes and footwear by LaCrosse and Tingley, work gloves, felt hats, and handkerchiefs. Much of the clothing is available in large sizes, and many of the items in the men's department are also offered in boys' sizes. If you're assembling a layette, see the catalog for good buys on the basics—diapers, receiving blankets, sleepers, pacifiers, baby pants, and other goods by Curity and Gerber. Nursing bras are available, and women's underwear and hosiery are offered at low prices. And the "book and game" department has some interesting Amish and Mennonite titles.

Special Factors: Satisfaction is guaranteed; C.O.D. orders are accepted.

HUNTINGTON CLOTHIERS

1285 ALUM CREEK DR.
COLUMBUS, OH
43209–2797
800–848–6203
614–252–4422
FAX: 614–252–3855
FAX OUTSIDE U.S.:
800–848–0644

Catalog: free (U.S.), $3 (international)
Pay: check, MO, MC, V, AE, DC, Discover, JCB, NOVUS
Sells: traditional menswear
Store: same address; Monday to Friday 10–6, Saturday 10–5
E-mail: 71154.2355@compuserve.com
Online: http://www.hclothiers.com

The 56-page catalog from Huntington Clothiers illustrates all the basics of a conservative wardrobe, at prices that are competitive with those of old-line haberdashers; some items cost up to twice as much elsewhere.

Huntington's own line of shirts are offered in Oxford cloth, pima cotton solids, Sea Island cotton, Egyptian cotton broadcloth, and cotton/poly blends. (Monogramming is available for $5.) Huntington also sells neckwear—foulards, regimental stripes, patterns, and "conversationals." Cotton polo shirts are shown as well as cotton and wool sweaters, belts, suspenders, underwear, and even shoes and cuff links. Huntington has been in business since 1978, and its catalogs feature color photos, a departure from the old hand-drawn color illustrations that were one of the catalog's trademarks.

Special Factors: Satisfaction is guaranteed; returns (except monogrammed goods) are accepted for exchange, refund, or credit.

LADY GRACE STORES, INC.

DEPT. 74
P.O. BOX 128
MALDEN, MA 02148
800–922–0504
617–322–1721
FAX: 617–321–8476

Catalog: free, $2 outside the U.S.
Pay: check, MO, MC, V, Discover
Sells: women's intimate apparel
Store: 14 stores in MA, ME, and NH (see catalog for locations)
Online: http://www.ladygrace.com

The Lady Grace catalog offers women's intimate apparel and is especially strong in large and hard-to-find sizes. You'll find bras, bodyshapers, girdles, control briefs, slips, panties, and post-breast-surgery needs from top makers such as Bali, Carnival, Flexees, Goddess, Edith Lances (minimizers), Olga, Playtex, Smoothie, Subtract, Vanity Fair, and Warners, among others. Lady Grace also sells a wide assortment of sleepwear, loungewear, and swimwear from top sources. You'll also find a good selection of nursing bras, maternity items, and other specialty accessories. Bra sizes run to 54 and bra cups run to "J." Bottoms come up to 9X. If you have a hard time finding quality intimate apparel in your size, you'll appreciate this collection. Lady Grace has been "serving the needs of America's women" since 1937.

Special Factors: Satisfaction is guaranteed; price quote by phone; returns of resalable goods are accepted within 30 days for exchange, refund, or credit.

MANNY'S MILLINERY SUPPLY CENTER

26 W. 38TH ST.
NEW YORK, NY 10018
212–840–2235, 840–2236
FAX: 212–944–0178

Catalog: $3
Pay: check, MO, MC, V, AE
Sells: hats, millinery supplies, gloves, bridal trimmings
Store: same address; Monday to Friday 9:30–5:30, Saturday 10–4:30

Manny's is nestled among the shops in New York City's "trimmings" district, which has more sequins, tassels, and decorative add-ons per square foot than a Las Vegas floor show. Manny's offers some of that glitter, but the company's specialty is women's hats, millinery supplies, and bridal accessories.

About half of Manny's 68-page catalog is devoted to hats, many of which are trimmed. Hundreds of styles are shown, in parisial, milanette, genuine Milan straw, felt, and fabric. Scores of "frames," or fabric-covered hat forms, are offered. The satin frames are suitable for bridal outfits, and the buckram frames provide a base for limitless flights of fancy. Stunning bridal headpieces, which can be used to decorate the hats and headpieces, are shown in the catalog, as well as satin and velvet gloves and edged veils. In addition, Manny's offers over a dozen jeweled or beaded hat pins, pearl and sequin trims, bugle-bead appliqués and trims, fringe, fabric flowers, rhinestone buttons, and even feathers— loose and in boas. Professional millinery supplies and equipment are available, including horsehair braid, hat stretchers, display heads and racks, hat boxes and travel cases, netting, and cleaning products. Savings vary from item to item, but average 33% below regular retail.

Please note: If you're buying hats only, the minimum order is three; if you buy one or two hats, you must also buy $15 in assorted items (frames, trims, etc.); if you're buying assorted items only, the minimum order is $25.

Special Factors: Price quote by phone; minimum order on certain items (see text).

MASS. ARMY & NAVY STORE

DEPT. WBMC
15 FORDHAM RD.
BOSTON, MA 02134
800–343–7749
617–783–1250
FAX: 617–254–6607

Catalog: free
Pay: check, MO, MC, V, AE, Discover
Sells: government surplus apparel and accessories
Store: 895 Boylston St., Boston; Monday to Friday 9:30—8, Saturday 12–8, Sunday 12–6; also 1436 Massachusetts Ave., Cambridge, MA; Monday to Saturday 10–9, Sunday 12–8

 ¡Si!

Mass. Army & Navy offers both reproduction and genuine government surplus, presented as a fashion statement. The 64-page color catalog features camouflage clothing, French and Spanish army raincoats, U.S. and European battle dress uniforms, field and flight jackets, East German guards' boots, U.S. Air Force sunglasses, survival manuals, Yukon hats, and similar surplus. Mass. Army & Navy also offers casual footwear, bandannas, gloves, Levi's jeans, Dockers, bomber jackets, peacoats, knapsacks, sleeping bags, air mattresses, backpacks, duffel bags, tents, mess kits, security products, and insignias and patches, among other useful items. This is a great resource for surplus chic, or the place to turn when you want a gas mask (East German) or WWII-issue grenade (defused, three styles)—they're all here, too.

Special Factors: Satisfaction is guaranteed; returns are accepted for exchange, refund, or credit.

NATIONAL WHOLESALE CO., INC.

---

400 NATIONAL BLVD.,
   DEPT. WK
LEXINGTON, NC 27294
910–249–0211
FAX: 910–249–9326

Catalog: free
Pay: check, MO, MC, V, AE, Discover
Sells: women's hosiery, underwear, and apparel
Store: mail order only

Founded in 1952, National Wholesale publishes a 96-page catalog that features hosiery, underwear, nightwear, career clothing, and separates.

The hosiery runs from a range of panty hose (control-top, light and full support, nonrun, and standard) in sizes to fit heights to six feet and hips to 60") to stockings, thigh-highs, knee-highs, footlets, and socks. In addition to hosiery, National Wholesale sells bras, girdles, and body shapers by Bestform®, Exquisite Form®, Flexees®, Glamorise®, Playtex®, and Vanity Fair®, slips by Figurfit® and Shadowline®, nightgowns and pajamas, cotton-knit vests, briefs, long-leg underpants, thermal underwear, pants liners, slippers, and dickeys. A "special needs" section offers mastectomy bras and incontinence panties. And half the catalog is devoted to a nice selection of dresses, blouses, skirts, sweaters, coats, and jackets that are perfect wardrobe staples, and well priced—suit jackets at under $50 and denim skirts for $25.95 are two examples.

Special Factors: Satisfaction is guaranteed; returns are accepted.

NO NONSENSE DIRECT

P.O. BOX 26095
GREENSBORO, NC
27420–6095
800–677–5995
FAX: 910–275–9329

Catalog: free
Pay: check, MO, MC, V, AE, Discover
Sells: hosiery
Store: mail order only

¡Si!

If you wear "No nonsense," Burlington, or Easy Spirit legwear, you can save up to 60% on the price of your favorite styles through No Nonsense Direct. This mail-order factory outlet of Kayser Roth has been delivering great buys on panty hose and socks and other items since 1985. You'll save the most on 12 pairs or more of "Practically Perfect" No nonsense, Burlington, and Easy Spirit panty hose, including Sheer & Silky, Control Top, Light Support, Regular, Custom Full Figure, A Touch of Silk, and other lines. The "Practically Perfect" goods have "minor, virtually undetectable imperfections that do not affect looks or wear," and are covered by the No Nonsense Direct guarantee of satisfaction. In addition to saving you money, you get a full choice of sizes and colors when you buy from the catalog—and that means that unless you're under 4' 11", 85 lb., or over 6', 280 lb., you should find a good fit.

Please note: Most items are sold in minimum quantities of three.

Special Factors: Satisfaction is guaranteed; quantity discounts are available; returns are accepted for exchange, refund, or credit.

ONE HANES PLACE CATALOG

Catalog: free
Pay: check, MO, MC, V, Discover
Sells: first-quality and "slightly imperfect" women's hosiery and underwear
Store: mail order only

P.O. BOX 748
RURAL HALL, NC
  27098–0748
800–300–2600
FAX: 800–545–5613
TDD: 800–816–4833

The 84-page color catalog from One Hanes Place brings you savings of up to 60% on your favorite panty hose, activewear, and lingerie from Bali, Hanes, Isotoner, L'eggs, Playtex, and Underalls. (This is the mercifully renamed "L'eggs Hanes Bali Playtex Outlet Catalog," after all.) The best buys are on the "slightly imperfect" irregulars, and the whole range of L'eggs is available, as well as Hanes hosiery, Bali and Playtex foundation garments and slips, and Hanes socks, underwear, T-shirts, and sweats for the whole family. See the detailed sizing guide in the catalog to be sure of the best fit.

Special Factors: Satisfaction is guaranteed; "slightly imperfect" goods are clearly identified; returns are accepted; TDD service is available Monday to Friday, 8 a.m. to midnight.

QUINN'S SHIRT SHOP

Price List: see text
Pay: check or MO
Sells: Arrow shirts
Store: 245 W. Main St., Dudley, MA; Monday to Saturday 10–5

RTE. 12
P.O. BOX 131
N. GROSVENORDALE, CT
  06255
508–943–7183

Quinn's, a factory outlet for the Arrow Shirt company, offers slightly irregular shirts at up to 60% below the price of first-quality goods. The firm has been in business since 1956, and will send you a price list for $2 and a stamped, self-addressed envelope (the $2 charge is refundable with your first order). You can also call or write for a price quote on your favorite Arrow shirt (Bradstreet, Dover B.D., Kent Collection, Fairfield, etc.—you must have the style name or line). Quinn's carries in regular, big, and tall sizes, 14½" to 20" neck, 32" to 38" sleeve. When you order, note whether you want short sleeves or long, and specify the length if long. The shirts may be exchanged if the flaws are too apparent.

Special Factors: Satisfaction is guaranteed; price quote by phone or letter with SASE; returns are accepted for exchange; minimum is four shirts per order; only C.O.D. orders are accepted.

SPORT EUROPA

7871 NW 15TH ST.
MIAMI, FL 33126
800–695–7000
305–477–5520
FAX: 305–477–1699

Catalog: free
Pay: check, MO, MC, V, AE, Discover
Sells: workout, beach, and leisurewear
Store: mail order only; phone hours Monday to Friday 9:30–5 ET

If you've been paying your dues at the gym and fitness center and have the body to prove it, you've earned Sport Europa. This catalog of clothing for men and women includes workout wear, warmups, bathing suits and outfits for poolside, and even party dresses and separates, in styles designed for maximum asset exposure. (Where other catalogs have sizing charts, Sport Europa has a visual guide to the difference between standard and Brazilian thongs—both men's and women's.) If you're less blessed than the models, who are truly fine specimens, you can still find much to love and wear here—loose warm-up pants in great prints and colors, T-shirts, running tights and pullovers, jackets, footwear, and gloves. The prices are terrific—up to 70% on some items on the clearance pages, and an average 25% off the rest of the goods. Whether you have the body for these clothes or are still working toward it, you'll appreciate the look for less.

Special Factors: Satisfaction is guaranteed; unused returns are accepted within 30 days for exchange, refund, or credit.

SPORTSWEAR CLEARINGHOUSE

P.O. BOX 317746–08
CINCINNATI, OH
45231–7746
513–522–3511

Brochure: free with SASE
Pay: check, MO, MC, V, Discover
Sells: printed sportswear overruns
Store: mail order only

Forget about dayglo cycling shorts and $200 court shoes—you won't find these at Sportswear Clearinghouse. The fare is sportswear basics—T-shirts in sizes from youth XS to adult XXXL, golf shirts, sweatshirts, shorts, night shirts, and hats, already printed or embroidered with corporate or institutional logos. If you succumb to the brochure, you can wind up wearing a T-shirt printed for the American Embassy at Sanaa, Yemen, Notre Dame running shorts, and a hat emblazoned with an advertising message from a local welding shop. The Clearinghouse, which has been in business since 1976, also offers T-shirts bearing the names of courses, sports themes, and slogans in foreign languages. Prices are hard to beat; T-shirts and shorts cost a few dollars each, and hats and visors are priced under $2 apiece. Most of these items are sold at retail in lots of three or more, and the Clearinghouse selects the colors, logos, and slogans. First-quality undecorated athletic socks and baseball hats embroidered with the replica logos of major league baseball teams and other pro sports, as well as colleges of your choice, are also available.

Special Factors: Satisfaction is guaranteed; unused returns are accepted within 30 days for exchange, refund, or credit; C.O.D. orders are accepted (UPS delivery only).

TAFFORD MANUFACTURING, INC.

104 PARK DR.
P.O. BOX 1001
MONTGOMERYVILLE, PA
  18936
800–283–0065
215–643–9666
FAX: 215–643–4922

Catalog: free
Pay: check, MO, MC, V, AE, Discover
Sells: nurses' uniforms, shoes, and accessories
Store: same address

Compared to the average catalog of uniforms for health-care professionals, Tafford has the best fashion buys for the dollar around. The firm manufactures its own uniforms, which means you beat at least one markup, and the size selection is great—from XS petite to 3X tall for women, and XS to 6X for men. The 64-page color catalog shows mostly women's clothing, although there are two pages of men's separates in blues and white. Some of the women's outfits are quite chic, and there are uniforms to suit every figure type, including maternity styles. The catalog also shows cardigans, jackets, shoes, emblem pins, and nursing equipment—stethoscopes, blood pressure kits, scissors, otoscopes, etc. Both the retail and the discount prices of the clothing are given, so you see how much you're saving—usually 20% or 30% on the regular retail. Consult your colleagues before ordering, because if you buy as part of a group, Tafford also offers special services such as swatches and samples, volume discounts, and custom embroidery and logo silkscreening.

Special Factors: Satisfaction is guaranteed; unworn, undamaged, unwashed returns are accepted within 30 days for exchange, refund, or credit.

TODD UNIFORM, INC.

3668 SOUTH GEYER RD.
ST. LOUIS, MO 63127-1244
800-458-3402
FAX: 800-231-8633

Catalog: free
Pay: check, MO, MC, V, AE, Discover
Sells: work clothing and uniforms
Store: Service Centers in St. Louis, MO, and Louisville, KY; Monday to Friday 8–5; also Outlet Store, Ripley, TN; Monday to Saturday 9–5:30

Todd has been manufacturing and selling uniforms and work apparel since 1881, and offers factory-direct prices—up to 30% below the competition. The clothing runs from the classic work shirt for men and women, which is offered in a range of colors, to jumpsuits, pants, jeans, jackets, T-shirts, polo shirts, aprons, rainwear, and caps. Your logo or slogan can be embroidered on the garments or on emblems, and the order form is designed to make it easy to specify even complicated orders.

Special Factors: Satisfaction is guaranteed; minimum order requirements apply to custom work; institutional accounts are available.

THE ULTIMATE OUTLET

A SPIEGEL COMPANY
P.O. BOX 182557
COLUMBUS, OH
43218-2557
800-332-6000
FAX: 800-422-6697

Catalog: $2
Pay: check, MO, MC, V, AE, Optima, FCNB PREFERRED Charge
Sells: clothing, housewares, etc.
Store: Spiegel Ultimate Outlet Stores in CO, FL, GA, IL, IN, MI, MN, MO, NV, OH, PA, TX, and VA

 ¡Si!

The Ultimate Outlet from Spiegel offers consumers solid values on name-brand fashion apparel and home furnishings. With an emphasis on women's fashions and home textiles, The Ultimate Outlet stands out by offering a high level of style and quality at competitive prices.

Please note: Deliveries to Alaska, Hawaii, and APO/FPO addresses are made by the postal service (Priority Mail or Parcel Airlift), *not* UPS.

Special Factors: Satisfaction is guaranteed; returns are accepted for refund or credit.

UNIFORM CONNECTION

Catalog: free
Pay: check, MO, MC, V, Discover
Sells: uniforms for healthcare workers
Store: mail order only

DEPT. WBM
P.O. BOX 1104
WINSTON-SALEM, NC
  27102–1104
800–326–3261
FAX: 910–722–1960

You can't do anything about the long hours you're assigned as a nurse, hospital tech, or healthcare professional, but you *can* look good and stay comfortable to the end of your shift. Uniform Connection lets you do it for less, offering 56 pages of colorful scrub jackets, pants, overalls, cardigans, and more, from Barco, Cherokee, Landau, White Cross, and White Swan. Most of the styles are for women, although there are lab coats and unisex scrubs for men as well. You'll also find nursing shoes from Birkenstock (both white and colors), Cherokee (Rockers), Dansko and Haflinger clogs, and Dr. Scholl's Oxfords and slip-ons. The sizing scale is generous, running from XS to 5X on some items, and to $13\frac{1}{2}$ (women's) in selected shoe models. The prices are "guaranteed lowest" (see the catalog for details), and shipping is free at this writing on orders over $150.

Special Factors: Satisfaction is guaranteed; returns are accepted within 30 days for exchange, refund, or credit.

WEARGUARD CORP.

Catalog: free
Pay: check, MO, MC, V, AE, Discover
Sells: work clothing, outerwear, and accessories
Store: mail order only

LONGWATER DR.
NORWELL, MA 02061
800–388–3300
617–871–4100
FAX: 800–436–3132

WearGuard, which was founded in 1952, supplies more than a million U.S. companies and consumers with work clothing and outerwear, at prices up to 30% below comparable retail. The 60-page color catalogs show jackets and parkas, work shirts, heavy-duty pants, T-shirts, knit shirts, jeans, gloves, baseball caps, thermal underwear, rainwear, and coveralls. In addition to WearGuard's own label, WearGuard's footwear includes Timberland and Wolverine boots and work shoes. A few jackets and boots are offered in women's styles.

WearGuard's Custom Logo department provides designs on jackets, knit shirts, T-shirts, and work shirts; stock logos and lettering are also available. The screen printing and direct embroidery are done "in house," which means WearGuard should be able to get your custom job to you faster.

Special Factors: Satisfaction is guaranteed; returns are accepted.

WILLOW RIDGE

■■■■■■■

421 LANDMARK DR.
WILMINGTON, NC 28410
800–388–8555
FAX: 910–343–6859
TDD: 800–945–1118

Catalog: free
Pay: check, MO, MC, V, AE, Discover
Sells: business and casual women's wear
Store: mail order only

Finally—a source for attractive business and casual wear for misses *and* petites—at cash-conserving prices. Willow Ridge does it with great jackets, shirts, pants, sweaters, dresses, suits, and other pieces, in 4 to 16 in petites, and 6 to 20 (with some 4s) in misses' sizing; women's and talls are also available. The Willow Ridge look is classy but not stuffy, strong on good, flattering color choices and washable fabrics. The prices will please your budget, with linen-weave pants at under $25, pretty summer dresses for under $36, poly shells for $10, and linen-blend jackets for under $30. The sizing guide in every catalog helps ensure a proper fit (be sure to double-check your measurements against it), and everything is covered by an assurance of satisfaction.

Special Factors: Satisfaction is guaranteed; returns are accepted for exchange, refund, or credit.

SEE ALSO

Bailey's, Inc. • *outdoor apparel and footwear* • **TOOLS**
Bart's Watersports • *water-skiing vests, T-shirts, swim trunks, and wet suits* •
SPORTS

Bike Nashbar • bicycling and sports apparel, and sunglasses • **SPORTS**

Bowhunters Warehouse, Inc. • camouflage clothing • **SPORTS**

Bruce Medical Supply • dressing aids for the disabled, stoma scarves, incontinence products • **MEDICINE: SPECIAL NEEDS**

The Button Shop • replacement zippers for jeans, garment shoulder pads • **CRAFTS: TEXTILE ARTS**

Cabela's Inc. • hunting and fishing wear, outdoor clothing and footwear • **SPORTS**

Campmor • outdoor clothing and accessories • **SPORTS**

Clothcrafters, Inc. • aprons, garment bags, and tote bags • **GENERAL MERCHANDISE**

Defender Industries, Inc. • foul-weather wear • **AUTO**

Dharma Trading Co. • cotton clothing and silk scarves for fabric painting, etc. • **CRAFTS: TEXTILE ARTS**

E & B Marine Supply, Inc. • foul-weather wear • **AUTO**

Gettinger Feather Corp. • feather marabous and boas, loose feathers • **CRAFTS**

Goldbergs' Marine Distributors • foul-weather wear • **AUTO**

Golfsmith International, Inc. • golf clothing and footwear • **SPORTS**

The House • windsurfing apparel • **SPORTS**

Leather Unlimited Corp. • sheepskin mittens, hats, and bags • **LUGGAGE**

M & E Marine Supply Company, Inc. • foul-weather wear • **AUTO**

Marshall Domestics • Dickies work clothing, men's underwear, institutional clothing (scrubs, food-service clothing, lab coats, etc.) • **GENERAL MERCHANDISE**

Mueller Sporting Goods, Inc. • T-shirts and polo shirts with billiards and darts themes • **SPORTS**

Nelson Marketing • imprinted polo shirts, sweatshirts, hats, etc. • **OFFICE: SMALL BUSINESS**

New England Leather Accessories, Inc. • leather handbags and accessories • **LUGGAGE**

Northern Hydraulics, Inc. • work clothing and rugged footwear • **TOOLS**

Omaha Vaccine Company, Inc. • Wells Lamont work gloves, Red Ball boots • **ANIMAL**

Overton's Sports Center, Inc. • boating and windsurfing apparel • **SPORTS**

Performance Bicycle Shop • cycling clothing, footwear, and helmets • **SPORTS**

Pet Warehouse • dog costumes • **ANIMAL**

John W. Poling: Military & Political Collectibles • vintage collectible military clothing, accessories, and insignia • **ART & ANTIQUES**

Racer Wholesale • auto racing suits and accessories • **AUTO**

Retired Persons Services, Inc. • support hosiery, slippers, socks, etc. • **MEDICINE**

Ruvel & Company, Inc. • *government surplus clothing and outdoor wear* • **TOOLS**

Senior's Needs, Inc. • *adaptive clothing and extra-large men's and women's underwear* • **MEDICINE: SPECIAL NEEDS**

Sierra Trading Post • *outdoor clothing and accessories* • **SPORTS**

Solo Slide Fasteners, Inc. • *clothing care and cleaning products* • **CRAFTS: TEXTILE ARTS**

Sunglasses U.S.A., Inc. • *sunglasses* • **HEALTH**

Support Plus • *support hosiery, comfort-styled shoes, therapeutic apparel* • **MEDICINE: SPECIAL NEEDS**

Thai Silks • *silk ties, scarves, handkerchiefs, lingerie, and blouses* • **CRAFTS: TEXTILE ARTS**

Tool Crib of the North • *work clothing* • **TOOLS**

Utex Trading Enterprises • *silk scarves and ties* • **CRAFTS: TEXTILE ARTS**

Wag-Aero Group of Aircraft Services • *aviator clothing and headwear* • **AUTO**

West Marine • *foul-weather wear* • **AUTO**

Wiley Outdoor Sports, Inc. • *hunting (camouflage) clothing and accessories* • **SPORTS**

Footwear

Shoes, boots, and slippers for men, women, and children

These firms offer everything from arctic boots to moccasins to nurses' shoes, at savings of up to 40%. But there's still the problem of fit, unless you're ordering more of the same model you've worn before. Here are some tips to improve the odds, and to make returns—if necessary—as easy as possible:

1. Have your feet measured at least once a year, and order your true size. (Feet continue to grow and change as you age.)
2. Buy from firms with liberal return policies, preferably an unconditional guarantee of satisfaction with a 30-day return period.
3. Buy styles and shapes that you know fit your foot.
4. If the shoes you're buying are also available in a local store, try on a pair before ordering them.
5. When the shoes arrive, unwrap them carefully and save the packaging.
6. Try them on in the late afternoon, when your feet have swollen slightly.
7. Walk around in a carpeted area to avoid scratching the soles.
8. Leave the shoes on for at least half an hour, checking for rubbing and pinching after 20 minutes.
9. If they fit, consider ordering a second pair *now,* while they're still in stock.
10. If the shoes don't fit, return them according to the firm's instructions, indicating whether you want another size or a refund or credit.

A brochure with fitting guidelines and information on foot problems is available from the American Orthopedic Foot and Ankle Society.

Send a long, stamped, self-addressed envelope to AOFAS, 701 16th Ave., Seattle, WA 98122; request the "shoe fit/foot problems" brochure.

Good maintenance is critical in preserving the looks and longevity of your shoes and boots. Some of the firms listed in "Luggage" sell leather-care products, as do a number of companies listed in the "See Also" listings of that chapter. If your shoes and boots need professional help and you don't have a good repair service nearby, contact the Houston Shoe Hospital, 5215 Kirby Dr., Houston, TX 77098; 713–528–6268. This firm overhauls worn footwear, and handles mail-order repairs.

GENE'S SHOES DISCOUNT CATALOG

DEPT. WBM98
126 N. MAIN ST.
ST. CHARLES, MO 63301
314–946–0804
FAX: 314–946–0804

Catalog: $1
Pay: check, MO, MC, V, Discover
Sells: dress, casual, and athletic shoes
Store: same address; Monday to Saturday 9–5:30

Gene's Discount "specialty size" catalog offers women's footwear by Easy Spirit, New Balance, Selby, and Soft Spots. Men's footwear from Florsheim, Hush Puppies, New Balance, and other manufacturers is available. The shoes are discounted about 20%, but savings run to over 30% on some styles. And you're in luck if you're hard to fit; Gene's offers the women's shoes in AAAA to EEE widths, sizes 3 to 13, and the men's in 2A to 5E widths, from size 5 to 18.

Please note: The prices in the catalog are good on mail orders only, not on in-store purchases.

Special Factors: Satisfaction is guaranteed; unworn, salable returns are accepted within 30 days for exchange, refund, or credit.

JUSTIN DISCOUNT BOOTS & COWBOY OUTFITTERS

P.O. BOX 67
JUSTIN, TX 76247
800–677-BOOT
FAX: 817–648-3282

Catalog: free
Pay: check, MO, MC, V
Sells: Western boots and clothing
Store: 101 W. Hwy. 156, Justin, TX; Monday to Saturday 9–6

This firm, although not owned by the Justin Boot Co., sells a number of the Justin boot lines in men's and women's styles. The footwear choices shown in the 56-page color catalog run from work boots and "ropers," comparatively plain, thick-soled boots with Western vamps that rise to mid-calf (about $90), to artful creations in exotic skins—ostrich, shark, lizard, and bull hide. "Lace-r" lace-up models are also offered. The catalog shows dozens of women's styles, including lizard Western boots, and "fashion" ropers in a range of colors. Children can get their Justin Juniors in red, navy, brown, and other colors, for under $60 a pair. Coordinating belts are available. Justin Discount Boots, in business since 1978, also sells Stetson Western hats, German silver buckles and belt tips, leather-care products, Wrangler shirts and jeans for men, women, and boys, and Comfy and Tempco goosedown jackets.

Special Factors: Satisfaction is guaranteed; unworn, unscuffed, unaltered returns are accepted for exchange, refund, or credit; C.O.D. orders are accepted.

KNAPP SHOES INC.

ONE KNAPP CENTRE
BROCKTON, MA 02401
800–869-9955, EXT. 258
FAX: 508–583-7578

Catalog: free
Pay: check, MO, MC, V, AE, Discover
Sells: work shoes for men and women
Store: 26 locations in CA, GA, IL, MA, ME, MI, NC, NJ, NY, OH, and PA; locations are given in the catalog

 ¡Si!

Knapp has been keeping America in shoes since 1921, and although only a few discounts top 30% (most are between 18% and 25%), there are shoes in the Knapp catalog that aren't easy to find at any savings.

The 32-page color catalog shows work shoes and boots (including steel toe and slip-resistant safety styles) for men by Baffin Boots, Florsheim, Knapp, and Red Label; dress shoes and loafers; and even slippers. Women can choose from athletic-style service shoes, wedge-sole Oxfords, low-heel pumps, loafers, and slip-ons, all of which are priced under $50 a pair at this writing. If you live near one of the 26 Knapp stores, drop by and try them on; otherwise, anything you buy by mail that doesn't fit can be returned, unworn, for an exchange or refund.

Special Factors: Satisfaction is guaranteed; returns of unworn or defective shoes are accepted for exchange, refund, or credit.

SEE ALSO

Jos. A. Bank Clothiers, Inc. • men's shoes • **CLOTHING**
Bike Nashbar • bicycling footwear • **SPORTS**
Cabela's Inc. • hunting and fishing wear, outdoor clothing and footwear • **SPORTS**
Cahall's Work Wear • rugged footwear for men and women • **CLOTHING**
Campmor • outdoor footwear • **SPORTS**
Dance Distributors • professional footwear for classic and jazz dance, gymnastics, etc. • **CLOTHING**
The Deerskin Place • suede boots, moccasins, etc. • **CLOTHING**
Defender Industries, Inc. • boating shoes • **AUTO**
Gohn Bros. Mfg. Co. • work shoes and boots for men and women • **CLOTHING**
Goldbergs' Marine Distributors • boating shoes • **AUTO**
Golf Haus • golf shoes • **SPORTS**
Golfsmith International, Inc. • golf clothing and footwear • **SPORTS**
Holabird Sports • shoes for sports activities • **SPORTS**
Huntington Clothiers • small selection of men's shoes • **CLOTHING**
M & E Marine Supply Company, Inc. • boating shoes • **AUTO**
National Wholesale Co., Inc. • small selection of women's footwear • **CLOTHING**
Northern Hydraulics, Inc. • rugged footwear • **TOOLS**
Omaha Vaccine Company, Inc. • Red Ball boots • **ANIMAL**
Performance Bicycle Shop • cycling clothing, footwear, and helmets • **SPORTS**
Sierra Trading Post • outdoor shoes • **SPORTS**
Support Plus • support hosiery, comfort-styled footwear, therapeutic apparel • **MEDICINE: SPECIAL NEEDS**
Tafford Manufacturing, Inc. • nurses' shoes • **CLOTHING**
Uniform Connection • nurses' shoes • **CLOTHING**
Wiley Outdoor Sports, Inc. • hunting and outdoor footwear • **SPORTS**

Mother and Child

Clothing and accessories for babies, children, and expectant and nursing mothers; and related goods

The firms in this section sell clothing for babies, children, and expectant and nursing mothers—all at savings of up to 60%. In addition, a number of the firms listed elsewhere in this book sell similar products. Chock Catalog Corp. ("Clothing") features Carter's receiving blankets and crib sets, Curity diapers, and underwear and nightwear for newborn through toddler sizes. Gohn Bros. ("Clothing") sells Curity diapers and Gerber bibs, baby sleepers, waterproof pants, and shirts. Campmor ("Sports") offers baby buntings, Snuglis, and a diaper-changer backpack for the intrepid parent.

One of the best all-around sources for discount baby supplies and buying strategies is *Baby Bargains: Secrets to Saving 20% to 50% on Baby Furniture, Equipment, Clothes, Toys, Maternity Wear and Much, Much More!* by Denise and Alan Fields (Windsor Peak Press, 1997), who wrote an equally valuable guide to saving money on wedding expenses (see the introduction to "Clothing"). In the format of their earlier opus, *Baby Bargains* describes the market for baby-related products, covers some of the issues, like breastfeeding and paper vs. cloth diapers, and gives source after source for information and products. The Fields guarantee that you'll save $250 on the cost of your baby expenses, or they'll refund the cost of the book. Call 800–888–0385 to order, or see the introduction to "Clothing" for the mailing address.

The Consumer Information Center and Superintendent of Documents ("Books") offer publications devoted to baby-care advice and related information—usually free, or at a small cost. For other tips on buying baby goods, see the *Guide to Baby Products* and other books from Consumers Union in the current issue of *Consumer Reports*. See "Toys" for playthings and games, the "Computing" section of "Office" for entertainment software, and "Books" for literature for and about children.

FIND IT FAST

DIAPERS AND COVERS • **After the Stork, As A Little Child, Baby Bunz, Natural Baby, Snugglebundle**
NURSING CLOTHING • **After the Stork, Bosom Buddies, Natural Baby, Snugglebundle**
CHILDREN'S CLOTHING • **After the Stork, As A Little Child, Baby Bunz, Baby Clothes Wholesale, Basic Brilliance, Natural Baby, Rubens & Marble, Snugglebundle**
TOYS • **After the Stork, Baby Bunz, Natural Baby**

AFTER THE STORK

**4321 FULCRUM WAY NE
RIO RANCHO, NM
87124–8445
800–333–5437
505–867–7000
FAX: 505–867–7101**

Catalog: free
Pay: check, MO, MC, V, AE, Discover
Sells: children's clothing
Store: 4411 San Mateo, Albuquerque, NM;
Monday to Saturday 10–8, Sunday 12–5

Real clothes for real kids from birth to 12 years old are sold at After the Stork, where cotton is king and prices are a friendly 25% to 40% below comparable retail. The 48-page color catalogs show playwear and sleepwear in snappy prints and kicky colors, so your kids can look hip without breaking your budget. The company has been price-shopped by pros who've found that you can assemble outfits that look like the upmarket Swedish brand, for less than half the cost. After the Stork has lots of T-shirts, sweats, long johns, pull-on pants, coveralls, dresses, rompers, and outerwear, as well as shoes, socks, sneakers, slippers, tights, underwear, and a choice bear or two. Check the size chart before you order—note that After the Stork sizes its clothing after shrinkage, so you don't have to order large—unless you're stockpiling against growth spurts.

Wholesale customers, request information on company letterhead; write to the attention of Kathy Thomas.

Special Factors: Satisfaction is guaranteed; returns are accepted.

AS A LITTLE CHILD, INC.

DEPT. W
10701 W. 80TH AVE.
ARVADA, CO 80005
303–456–1880

Catalog: free
Pay: check or MO
Sells: diaper covers and diapers
Store: mail order only

As A Little Child celebrates children as one of life's great blessings, making baby's health and happiness its first order of business with a selection of environmentally positive diapering products that are kind to family budgets. The featured item is the Wabby, the only diaper cover made with Gore-Tex fabric, so it's both waterproof and "breathable." Since air can flow through the cover, baby's bottom stays cooler, which helps to prevent diaper rash. Wabbies are constructed to last, wash and dry quickly, and have newly designed closures that are strong and durable. The covers are offered in white, colors, and prints, sized from newborn to XL; they work well with Wabby diapers, which team all-cotton flannel with terry cloth for comfort and absorbency. Washcloths and miniwipes are also available.

Special Factors: Quantity discounts are available.

BABY BUNZ & CO.

P.O. BOX 113-WB98
LYNDEN, WA 98264–0113

Catalog: $1
Pay: check, MO, MC, V
Sells: diapering supplies and layette items
Store: mail and phone orders only

If you use cloth diapers instead of disposables, you may be overwhelmed by all the prefolded diapers and diaper "systems" on the market. One of the most popular diapering duos among the cloth set is a standard or fitted diaper with a natural-fiber cover. Baby Bunz & Co. has been selling the best-known covers, Nikkys, since 1982. Nikkys are made in soft lambswool, waterproof cotton, "breathable" poly, and vinyl-lined cotton, and are available in sizes from newborn to three years (up to 34 pounds). Training and all-night pants are also offered, and they're priced at up to 35% below retail.

The Baby Bunz 20-page color catalog also offers a variety of diaper styles—contour, prefolded, flat, and diaper doublers. The catalog includes guides to folding diapers and how to use Nikkys. Adorable layette wear, colorful cotton playsuits, baby buntings, lambskin and wool booties, pima cotton and Merino wool blankets, and a crib-sized lambskin are also featured. The natural theme is carried on with Aromatherapy for Kids, natural baby shampoo, Weleda baby-care products, bath sponges, and natural bristle baby brushes. You'll also find wooden rattles, natural-fiber soft toys, and an ideal lovey, "First Doll." Many other useful items are available, including a comfortable baby carrier, a "Boppy" baby pillow, and classic storybooks for children up to three years. These and other new additions to the latest Baby Bunz catalog include several guides on rearing healthy and happy children.

Canadian readers, please note: Only U.S. funds are accepted.

Special Factors: Satisfaction is guaranteed; unused returns are accepted within 30 days for replacement, refund, or credit.

BABY CLOTHES WHOLESALE

60 ETHEL RD. WEST
PISCATAWAY, NJ 08854
908–572–9520

Catalog: $1 (see text)
Pay: check, MO, MC, V, AE, Discover
Sells: layettes, baby and children's clothing
Store: mail order only

   ¡Si!

It's a shame to spend lots of money on children's clothing when they grow so quickly, especially when you don't have to: Baby Clothes Wholesale brings you everything from underwear to snowsuits for sizes newborn to seven, at savings of up to 50%. The company's 20-page color catalog features coveralls and rompers, sunsuits, terry sleepers and crawlers, creepers, bibs, receiving blankets, underwear, socks, overalls, party dresses, T-shirts, sweatsuits, turtlenecks, playsuits, cardigans, bonnets and caps, bathing suits, nightwear, vests, and bomber jackets. All of the clothing is first-quality, but some of the layette items (blankets, sheets, bibs, etc.) are irregular, and clearly indicated.

Canadian readers, please note: Only U.S. funds are accepted.

Special Factors: Satisfaction is guaranteed; quantity discounts are available; returns of unworn, unused, unwashed goods are accepted for exchange, refund, or credit.

BASIC BRILLIANCE

P.O. BOX 1719
PORT TOWNSEND, WA
  98368
360–385–3835

Catalog: free
Pay: check, MO, MC, V
Sells: clothing for children and mothers
Store: mail order only
E-mail: basicb@olympus.net

Kids love brightly colored clothing they can really *play* in, and parents want it to last until they grow out of it—without costing a fortune. That's the concept behind Basic Brilliance, where "everything is cotton, garment-dyed, preshrunk, easy to wear and easy to care for." Most of the clothes are sized for 3 to 24 months and 2 to 8 years, and there are some great knockabout clothes for Mom—dresses, T-shirts, and leggings—in sizes S to XL.

Kids have the run of the catalog, in cotton interlock snap rompers ($15), a hooded cardigan in French terry cotton ($16.50), ribbed pants ($10), loose empire-waisted jumper dresses ($16), leggings ($7.50), and lots of other great clothes at great prices. The colors in the current catalog are winners, too: sage, cranberry, periwinkle, purple, butter, and the basics. You can't go wrong with the sizes, since there's a chart in the catalog for kids *and* their mothers, and everything is covered by an unconditional guarantee of satisfaction.

Please note: Only U.S. funds are accepted.

Special Factors: Satisfaction is guaranteed; returns are accepted.

BOSOM BUDDIES

212 BROADWAY,
  DEPT. WBM
P.O. BOX 1250
PORT EWEN, NY 12466
914–338–2038

Catalog: free
Pay: check, MO, MC, V, AE, Discover
Sells: nursing bras and clothing
Store: Wednesday to Friday 11–5, and by appointment

  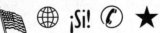

Bosom Buddies was founded in 1983 by a nursing mother who saw a market for "breastfeeding fashions." Nursing bras by Leading Lady and TR Sport are offered, including many all-cotton styles. This is a great source for hard-to-find sizes—Leading Lady bras run up to size 46H, and other lines go up to 46J. Nightgowns and other clothing designed to make nursing easy are sold as well. Bosom Buddies also carries nursing pads and a full line of equipment for expressing and storing breast milk, and a number of helpful books. The 12-page catalog includes a guide to taking your measurements, so you're sure to order the right size. Not every item is discounted, but prices are reasonable, and savings run up to 50% on sale items.

Special Factors: Order sale merchandise promptly, since quantities may be limited.

THE NATURAL BABY CO., INC.

816 SILVIA ST., SUITE
  800B-WBM8
TRENTON, NJ 08628-3299
609-771-9233
FAX: 609-771-9342

Catalog: free
Pay: check, MO, MC, V, Discover
Sells: diapers, baby and children's clothing, nursing clothing, toys, remedies, etc.
Store: Forrestal Village, Princeton, NJ; Monday, Tuesday, Wednesday, Saturday 10–6, Thursday and Friday 10–9, Sunday 12–6

Everything in The Natural Baby Co. catalog has been chosen with an eye to making children comfortable and keeping them healthy, without costing Mom and Dad a bundle. The Natural Baby Co. was established in 1983, and has a policy of supporting home-based businesses—so the quilt you buy here for your own baby may have been made by a mother of nine, and the wood cradles and toys crafted by carpenters "in between pouring out the Cheerios"!

The Natural Baby has built its business on cloth diapers and covers, beginning with the firm's own "Rainbow" diaper, a fitted cloth style (pinless, foldless) made of flannel-lined terry cloth ($29.95 per dozen). If you're on a tight budget, you can get the "Natural Baby Diapers" of bird's-eye, from $15.75 a dozen. Diaper covers from Nikky's and The Natural Baby are available, as well as diaper pads and conventional cloth diapers. Past catalogs have included helpful sidebars on diapering with pinless covers, the cloth vs. disposables debate, and tips on preventing diaper rash.

There's much more for baby: a line of baby clothing from organically grown cotton, baby carriers, and sheepskin rugs and play balls, woolen crib blankets, flannel creepers, and Storkenworks shoes. The catalog offers some clothing for older kids, including long johns, Nikky's substantial underpants (in sizes to fit children up to 110 pounds), socks, sweaters, turtlenecks, and other goods. Mothers are treated to Leading Lady bras, and sportswear and nightwear designed to make nursing easier. Among the offerings are natural and homeopathic remedies for treating everything from cradle cap to poison ivy, as well as a splendid selection of wooden toys, dolls, rattles, balls, cradles, and other safe and nontoxic diversions.

Special Factors: C.O.D. orders are accepted.

RUBENS & MARBLE, INC.

P.O. BOX 14900-A
CHICAGO, IL 60614–0900

Brochure: free with self-addressed, stamped envelope
Pay: check or MO
Sells: infants' clothing and bedding
Store: mail order only

Rubens & Marble has been supplying hospitals with baby clothes since 1890, and sells the same goods to consumers at up to 60% below regular retail prices. The babywear basics include undershirts in sizes from newborn to 36 months, with short, long, and mitten-cuff sleeves; they're offered in snap, tie, and double-breasted slipover styles (many are seconds, with small knitting flaws). First-quality cotton/wool blend and preemie-sized cotton undershirts are available as well. Rubens & Marble also offers fitted bassinet and crib sheets, training and waterproof pants, kimonos, drawstring-bottom baby gowns, and terry bibs.

Special Factors: You *must* send a self-addressed, stamped envelope to receive the price list; seconds are clearly indicated; minimum order is one package (varying number depending on type of item).

SNUGGLEBUNDLE ENTERPRISES

DEPT. WBM

444A NORTH MAIN ST.,
#165

E. LONGMEADOW, MA
01028

413–525–1972

FAX: 413–525–1972 (CALL
FIRST)

Catalog: $1
Pay: check, MO, MC, V
Sells: diapers, covers, children's clothing,
nursing pads, etc.
Store: mail order only
E-mail: Snugbdl@aol.com

The woman who runs this company offers literally dozens of diapering options, from EZ Bottoms classic cotton flannel prefolded, to Diaperap and Kangarap covers. She's even assembled diaper samplers that allow you to test several methods at once, to see which one works best. Diaper soakers, cotton wipes, and other diapering accessories are sold, as well as nursing pads, layette items, crib sheets and blankets, gowns, creepers, bibs, rompers, and more. Natural fibers prevail, and Snugglebundle Enterprises features "green" (organic) cotton in most products. In addition to diapers and layette items, the firm offers a small selection of clothing for kids (newborn to 4T)—brightly colored cotton in sturdy styles for boys and girls.

Special Factors: Satisfaction is guaranteed.

SEE ALSO

Alfax Wholesale Furniture • *institutional nursery and day-care center furniture* • **OFFICE**
Chock Catalog Corp. • *baby clothing and bedding* • **CLOTHING**
Clothcrafters, Inc. • *crib sheets* • **GENERAL MERCHANDISE**
Michael C. Fina Co. • *sterling silver baby gifts* • **HOME: TABLE SETTINGS**
Gohn Bros. Mfg. Co. • *nursing bras, layette and baby goods* • **CLOTHING**
Lady Grace Stores, Inc. • *maternity and nursing underwear* • **CLOTHING**
The Linen Source • *crib and juvenile bedding* • **HOME: LINEN**
One Hanes Place Catalog • *maternity hosiery and underwear* • **CLOTHING**
Wicker Warehouse Inc. • *wicker nursery furniture, doll buggies* • **HOME: FURNISHINGS**

CRAFTS AND HOBBIES

Materials, supplies, tools, and equipment for crafts and hobbies

These firms can provide the materials for nearly any craft—miniatures, stenciling, basketry, clock making, wheat weaving, quilling, decoy painting, jewelry making, and much more. Some of these companies have been in business for generations and specialize in avocations that your local crafts shop may not even know exist. If you have a problem with a material or technique, most can provide assistance by phone. Ordering from a firm usually assures you a place on the mailing list, which means you'll probably receive the sales flyers, with savings of up to 70%. Save your catalogs, both for comparison shopping, and as sources of technical information.

The firms listed in the first part of this chapter are either general crafts suppliers with a very broad selection, or firms specializing in one item or type of goods—hobby models, feathers, parts for stuffed bears, stained glass supplies, bandboxes, etc. For help in locating a particular item, see "Find It Fast," below. If you're looking for a fiber, fabric, or related product, see "Textile Arts," right after this section. And if your interests run to carving, whittling, and bandsaw challenges, see "Woodcraft," following "Textile Arts."

If your craft or hobby involves the use of hazardous materials, find out about safety precautions; see the introduction to "Art Materials" for more information. For additional sources selling wooden toy parts, see the listings in "Tools." For lapidary equipment and findings, see the firms listed in "Jewelry."

FIND IT FAST

BASKETRY AND SEAT REWEAVING • **Caning Shop, Frank's Cane**
DOLL- AND BEAR-MAKING • **Bolek's, CR's Bear and Doll**
FABRIC FLOWERS • **Bolek's**
FEATHERS • **Gettinger**
GENERAL CRAFTS • **Artist's Club, Atlantic Spice, Bailey's Wholesale, Bolek's, Circle Craft, Craft Resources, Think Ink, Vanguard**
GOURD CRAFT • **Caning Shop**
LEATHERWORKING • **Weaver**
METAL DETECTING AND PROSPECTING • **Northwest Treasure Supply**
MODELS • **Model Expo**
POTPOURRI AND WREATHS • **Bolek's**
STAINED GLASS SUPPLIES • **Warner-Crivellaro**
"SUN-PRINTING" SUPPLIES • **Gramma's Graphics**
WOODWORKING PLANS AND SUPPLIES • **Artist's Club**

THE ARTIST'S CLUB

P.O. BOX 8930
VANCOUVER, WA
98668–8930
800–845–6507
FAX: 360–260–8877

Catalog: free
Pay: check, MO, MC, V, AE, Discover, JCB
Sells: craft painting materials and supplies
Store: mail order only

 ¡Si!

The Artist's Club is devoted to artisans whose painting skills are applied to surfaces other than canvas, creating what might be called contemporary folk art. Half of the firm's 88-page color catalog is filled with books on painting flowers, decorating in the Victorian modes, Christmas and other holiday themes, creating clocks, decorating with gardening themes, painting jewelry, angel motifs, working with crackle medium, fabric painting, Americana, and more. Many of the complete project kits employ cute country designs done on wood forms, including eggs, clock blanks (which accept "fit up" clock works), and useful household items—napkin holders, keepsake boxes, step stools, tissue boxes, quilt racks, lap desks, menu boards, etc. Also available are papier-mâché forms and boxes, lovely hand-blown glass Christmas ornaments awaiting decoration, unpainted canvas items, woodenware, and ready-to-paint tinware. The Club also offers a great selection of DecoArt, Delta, and Jo Sonja paints, and brushes by Bette Byrd, Loew Cornell, and

Robert Simmons. Prices are discounted an average of 20% to 35%, and the regular sales catalogs yield greater savings.

Non-U.S. readers, please note: Only U.S. funds are accepted. If you are located in Japan, contact The Artist's Club Japan Call Center at 045–711–6558 for information.

Special Factors: Satisfaction is guaranteed; returns are accepted within 30 days for exchange, refund, or credit.

ATLANTIC SPICE CO.

P.O. BOX 205

NORTH TRURO, MA 02652

800–316–7965

508–487–6100

FAX: 508–487–2550

Catalog with Potpourri Recipes: free

Pay: check, MO, MC, V

Sells: ingredients for potpourri and spices, teas, and herbs

Store: same address; Monday to Friday 9–5, Saturday 10–2

Online: http://www.atlanticspice.com

If potpourri, pomanders, and wreaths are your specialty, Atlantic Spice Co. can supply you with many of the botanicals and fragrance oils you need, at savings of 50% and more. Atlantic Spice also sells culinary herbs and spices (the smallest size is one pound), organic botanicals, and even tea, dehydrated vegetables, seeds for sprouting, baking products (powdered lemon juice, bee pollen, vanilla extract, etc.), and shelled seeds and nuts.

The potpourri ingredients run from whole Jamaican allspice to yellow yarrow flowers, and the botanicals begin with alfalfa and end with yucca powder. Looking for a source for the freeze-dried fruits that are used so extensively in wall decorations and wreaths? They're here— apple slices, artichokes, orange peel and slices, pieces of peach, and pomegranates—as well as whole nutmeg, bay leaves, three-inch chile peppers, cinnamon sticks, pinecones, hibiscus pods, oak moss, rosebuds, and other natural materials. The fragrance oils are offered in 1-ounce bottles, the botanicals in 1- and 5-pound units. Rounding out the map-sized, one-page catalog are related supplies and equipment— sachet bags, potpourri jars, self-seal tea bags—and a number of recipes for jar and simmering potpourri, sachets, and pomanders. There are no illustrations, but the listings are flagged to note items that shouldn't be used in food or drink, and others that are especially well suited for "wreathes, centerpieces, topiaries & garlands." Atlantic's very low prices drop 15% on orders of 25 or more pounds of the same item (based on the 1-pound rate), and shipping is free on orders over $200 (subject to some restrictions).

Special Factors: Satisfaction is guaranteed; quantity discounts are available; minimum order is $30.

BOLEK'S CRAFT SUPPLIES, INC.

330 N. TUSCARAWAS AVE.
P.O. BOX 465
DOVER, OH 44622–0465
800–743–2723
330–364–8878
FAX: 800–649–3735

Catalog: $1.50
Pay: check, MO, MC, V, Discover
Sells: general crafts supplies
Store: same address; Monday to Saturday 9–5

Bolek's is one of those amazing places that stocks 22 sizes of dolls' eyes, aurora borealis beads, carved wooden unicorns, and Bronze Schlappen chicken feathers. It's hard to imagine a craft *not* supplied here—jewelry making, beading, woodworking, ceramics, potpourri and fragrance blending, doll and toy making, Christmas ornaments, macramé, plastic canvas crafts, stenciling, Styrofoam crafts, silk flowers, yarn crafts, and much more. Bolek's, in business since 1977, sells at prices up to 50% below those charged by local crafts supply stores for the same types of items. If you're looking for something you don't see in the 130-page catalog, write to Bolek's with a description or sample, and include a self-addressed, stamped envelope for a reply.

Canadian readers, please note: Only U.S. funds are accepted.

Special Factors: Authorized returns are accepted within 30 days for exchange, refund, or credit (refunds are subject to a 25% restocking fee); shipping is not charged on orders over $40 in the continental United States; C.O.D. orders are *not* accepted.

THE CANING SHOP

926 GILMAN ST., DEPT.
WBM
BERKELEY, CA 94710–1494
800–544–3373
510–527–5010
FAX: 510–527–7718

Catalog: $1, refundable
Pay: check, MO, MC, V, Discover
Sells: seat-reweaving, gourd-crafting, and basketry supplies
Store: same address; Tuesday to Friday 10–6, Saturday 10–2
E-mail: wbm@caning.com
Online: http://www.caning.com

   ¡Si!

The Caning Shop stocks the materials, tools, and instructions you'll need to restore your woven-seat chairs—or weave a basket from scratch. The firm was established in 1969 by Jim Widess, one of the authors of *The Caner's Handbook*. His more recent interest in gourds, an ancient craft, has culminated in *The Complete Book of Gourd Craft* (coauthored with Ginger Summit). Other texts are available, as well as a line of gourd-related tools and supplies.

The 40-page catalog shows 15 kinds of prewoven cane webbing, which is used in modern and mass-produced seating. For older chairs, The Caning Shop offers hanks of cane in a full range of sizes, including binder cane, and also sells Danish seat cord, rawhide lacing, fiber rush, Hong Kong grass (sea grass), ash splint, Shaker tape, whole reed (for wicker), wicker braid, rattan, pressed fiber (imitation leather) seats, and tools. Basket makers should look here for kits, materials, hoops, and handles. And there are 20 pages of books and videos on both subjects. If you live in or near Berkeley, check the schedule of classes—"Pine Needle Basketry," "Gourd Masks," and "Miniature Rustic Furniture" are typical of the fascinating topics.

Canadian readers, please note: Payment for the catalog and goods orders must be in U.S. funds.

Special Factors: Satisfaction is guaranteed; C.O.D. orders are accepted.

CIRCLE CRAFT SUPPLY

DEPT. WBMC
P.O. BOX 3000
DOVER, FL 33527–3000
813–659–0992
FAX: 813–659–0017

Catalog: $1
Pay: check, MO, MC, V, Discover
Sells: general crafts supplies
Store: 13295 U.S. Hwy. 92, Dover, FL; Monday to Saturday 9–5

   ¡Si!

The 96-page catalog from Circle Craft Supply lists everything, from "abaca shapes" to zip-lock bags, that you'll need to indulge in any of scores of arts, crafts, and hobbies. Circle Craft was founded in 1982, and sells at discounts that average 30%, and reach 40% on some items. There are tools and materials here for a wide range of crafts and pastimes—beading, jewelry making, basketry, flower making, quick-count plastic canvas crafts, doll making, lamp making, clock making, Christmas ornaments, macramé, chenille crafts, and much more.

Special Factors: Authorized returns are accepted within 10 days; C.O.D. orders are accepted.

CRAFT RESOURCES, INC.

BOX 828
FAIRFIELD, CT 06430–0828
203–259–4473

Catalog: $1
Pay: check, MO, MC, V
Sells: crafts kits for education, rehab use, etc.
Store: mail order only

Craft Resources, founded in 1972, specializes in crafts projects in kit form and offers "the largest selection of latch-hook kits available for schools, hospitals, and other institutions." The 16-page color catalog shows kits for projects in latch hooking, stamped and counted cross-stitch, embroidery, crewel, wood crafts, rubber stamp art, and cut-and-copy clip art. The kits range from very basic designs for the beginner to more complex patterns, but a patient novice should be able to tackle any of these projects, with reasonable to impressive results. Craft Resources also sells yarn, embroidery floss, needlepoint and embroidery tools, knitting needles and crochet hooks, and embroidery hoops and frames. Therapists and instructors will find great values, and the kits provide an ideal way for the rest of us to "try out" a craft without investing much money.

Special Factors: Satisfaction is guaranteed; unused returns are accepted within 60 days; minimum order is $20 with credit cards.

CR'S BEAR AND DOLL SUPPLY CATALOG

BOX 8-WM81
LELAND, IA 50453
515–567–3652
FAX: 515–567–3071

Catalog: $2 (see text)
Pay: check, MO, MC, V, Discover
Sells: doll- and bear-making supplies
Store: 109 5th Ave., Leland, IA; Monday to Friday 8:30–3:30 CT

Never considered trying your hand at making a doll or Teddy bear? Then you haven't seen the catalog from CR's Bear and Doll Supply, also known as CR's Crafts. It's 136 pages of patterns, kits, parts, and the related miscellany that go into making some of the most adorable, collector-quality dolls and furry friends you'll find anywhere. If you don't fall in love with Tyler, Brewster Bear, or Cotton Tail, you're made of pretty stern stuff.

CR's Crafts sells everything you need to make any of hundreds of delightful creatures, including the fabric and fur, bodies and limbs, heads and faces, voice boxes and squeakers, armatures, wigs and hair, teeth, eyelashes, stuffing, music boxes, stands, books and manuals, and much more. Prices are competitive with other toy-making supply catalogs, and *very* low compared to finished products purchased elsewhere. CR's is also a good place to pick up parts and materials for repairing damaged dolls and stuffed toys, and a source for well-priced clothing, accessories, and furnishings for dolls and toys. CR's Crafts has been in business since 1981, and if you're in Leland during showroom hours, you're invited to drop in and see the stock of 4,000-plus items in person.

Please note: The catalog for consumers costs $2 if sent within the U.S., $4 if sent to Canada, $7 if sent elsewhere outside the U.S.; the wholesale catalog costs $5 (U.S. funds only).

Special Factors: Orders shipped outside the contiguous 48 United States are sent via U.S. Parcel Post.

FRANK'S CANE AND RUSH SUPPLY

DEPT. WBMC

7252 HEIL AVE.

HUNTINGTON BEACH, CA

  92647

714–847–0707

FAX: 714–843–5645

Catalog: free
Pay: check, MO, MC, V, AE, Discover
Sells: seat-reweaving supplies, furniture, kits, books, etc.
Store: 7252 Heil Ave., Huntington Beach, CA; Monday to Friday 8–5

Frank's has been in business since 1975, and the firm's comprehensive 40-page catalog of seat replacement materials includes over a dozen weaves of cane webbing as well as strand and binding cane, spline, fiber and wire-fiber rush, fiber wicker, Danish cord, oak and ash splints, round and flat reed, and fiber and real reed braid (often used as trim on wicker furniture). Frank's also sells rattan, basketry materials, raffia, sea grass, "tissue flex" (for rag coil baskets), wood hoops and handles, brass hardware, upholstery tools and supplies, dowels and woodcrafts parts, and spindles and finials. Prices are competitive on these goods, and there are some bargains—Frank's sells the same decorative upholstery nails that cost $5.25 per hundred locally, for just $3.25. Bamboo is also available, in sizes from ½" to 6" in diameter. The catalog also has six pages of books on seat reweaving, woodworking, basketry, and upholstery.

The furniture kits include hardwood Shaker-style arm and side chairs, rocking chairs, and stools. Prices are reasonable: $12.95 for a stool kit, $34.50 for a child's ladder-back chair kit, and $73 for an adult's chair. (The furniture comes with enough fiber rush or flat fiber—your choice—to complete the seat.)

Special Factors: Minimum order is $10 with credit cards; C.O.D. orders are accepted.

GETTINGER FEATHER CORP.

16 W. 36TH ST.
NEW YORK, NY 10018
212–695–9470
FAX: 212–695–9471

Price List and Samples: $2
Pay: check or MO
Sells: feathers
Store: same address (8th floor); Monday to Thursday 8:30–5:30, Friday 8:30–3

Gettinger has been serving New York City's milliners and craftspeople since 1915 with a marvelous stock of exotic and common feathers. Even if you're not a creative type, you can add cachet to a tired hat with a few ostrich plumes, and Gettinger's feather boas are a dashing alternative to furs for gala occasions.

Pheasant, guinea hen, turkey, duck, goose, rooster, and peacock feathers are available here, loose or sewn (lined up in continuous rows of even length), by the ounce or the pound, beginning at $5 (loose) and $8 (sewn) per ounce. Pheasant tail feathers, 6" to 8" long, cost $13 per hundred; yard-long peacock feathers are priced at $25 per hundred; and pheasant hides cost $9 and up per skin. Feather boas are available, sold in two-yard pieces, as well as ostrich and marabou fans. And if you're reviving old feather pillows, you may be interested in the bedding feathers, which cost $10 to $45 per pound, depending on the quality (minimum 5 pounds).

Special Factors: Minimum order is $20.

GRAMMA'S GRAPHICS, INC.

DEPT. TWBM-P8
20 BIRLING GAP
FAIRPORT, NY 14450–3916
716–223–4832, 4309
FAX: 716–223–4789

Brochure: $1 and long, stamped, self-addressed envelope (see text)
Pay: check or MO
Sells: Blueprint cloth-imaging materials and Sun Print diazo paper
Store: mail order only
E-mail: 70671.321@compuserve.com
Online: http://www.computer-connection.net/~donnelly

Can't draw, paint, or appliqué? You can still create original designs with Sun Prints, which "blueprint" an image on prepared fabric, creating a photographic representation in shades of blue (which can be toned to brown, charcoal, tan, amethyst, or green). The fabric must be untreated, 100% cotton or natural fiber, since the imaging solution will bead up and roll off synthetics, sizing, or resin. Gramma's Graphics sells all of the ingredients, from the imaging solution to the fabric, as well as instructions for creating the prints, assembling a pillow, and making an heirloom portrait quilt. The brochure suggests a number of subjects for projects—family portraits, wedding invitations, certificates and degrees, photographs—and other applications, including banners, dolls, place mats, tote bags, etc.

Gramma's Graphics also sells the Sun Silhouette dry-process paper "sun"-printing materials, in a notecard kit with 12 cards and envelopes, and the economical "classroom" kit, which has five times the amount of paper (although no envelopes), but costs less than $1 more at this writing. The paper is offered in blue, brown, or black, and all of the kits and components are unconditionally guaranteed. For the last word in Gramma-approved activities with the little ones, see her book, *Grandloving: Making Memories with Your Grandchildren*. It's packed with ideas for low-cost fun, as well as guides to favorite children's books, good programming, and other helpful resources.

Overseas readers, please note: The catalog costs $3 if sent outside the U.S.

Wholesale buyers, please note: The minimum order for wholesale pricing is 24 kits.

Special Factors: Satisfaction is guaranteed; quantity discounts are available.

MODEL EXPO, INC.

P.O. BOX 229140
HOLLYWOOD, FL 33020
800–222–3876
954–925–7650
FAX: 800–742–7171

Catalog: $1
Pay: check, MO, MC, V, AE
Sells: ship, plane, and car model kits and supplies, and electric trains
Store: 3850 N. 29th Terrace, Hollywood, FL
Online: http://www.modelexpoinc.com

 ¡Si!

If you've never considered building a model ship, you probably haven't seen Model Expo's catalog of models, parts, tools, and books. It's 92 pages of full-color photos of beautiful historical ship models, from transport vessels of ancient Egypt to Jacques Costeau's *Calypso*. In addition to the firm's own models (by its manufacturing arm, Model Ship-ways), the catalog shows lines from Amati, Constructo, Corel, Heller (plastic), Mamoli, and Mantua. Each of the featured models is described fully and rated according to difficulty (entry level, intermediate, or advanced). Well over half of the catalog is devoted to books (on model making, ship design and development, maritime history, naval aviation, and military topics), as well as historic and modern fittings, display cases and pedestals, shipwrights' tools, and hand and power tools. Both novice and experienced modelers will find much to interest them, and for those just taking up the hobby, Model Expo's guarantee will be reas-suring: If you should break or lose a part during construction, Model Expo will replace it, free of charge!

Special Factors: Satisfaction is guaranteed; returns (except partially built kits) are accepted within 30 days for exchange, refund, or credit.

NORTHWEST TREASURE SUPPLY

DEPT. E52

P.O. BOX 52802

BELLEVUE, WA 98015–2802

206–881–7340

FAX: 206–883–6730

Catalog: free
Pay: check, MO, MC, V, AE, Discover
Sells: metal detectors and prospecting tools
Store: 3096 125th Ave., NE, Bellevue, WA;
by appointment only
E-mail: nwts@treasurenet.com
Online: http://www.treasurenet.com

Whether you're a beachcomber who wants a little help, or a dedicated prospector setting up a dredging operation, Northwest Treasure Supply can equip your venture. "Detectorists" can start with an inexpensive model and add the "beginner's kit" of headphones, coil cover, trash-and-treasure bag, and a trowel, all for under $200. Recover enough coins to justify the cost, and you can upgrade. Prospectors can choose from scores of metal detectors by Fisher, Garrett, Keene, Minelab, ProMack, Tesoro, and White's, and headphones by Cal-Rad, DepthMaster, and Koss. Once you've found the ore, you'll need recovery tools—knives, trowels, shovels, picks, scoops, etc.—and bags, sifters, and pans, as well as the tools and chemicals to test for the presence of gold and silver. Sluice boxes are sold, and Northwest Treasure Supply can work with you to determine the right dredging equipment for your needs. The firm offers over a dozen instructional videotapes on prospecting and metal detecting, and a long list of books on *where* to find old mines and stakes, hidden treasure, and even water. The people who run Northwest Treasure have been in the business since 1985, and can answer most questions on treasure hunting and panning. The website includes a full catalog, with pictures, of all of Northwest Treasure's products.

Special Factors: Price quote by phone or letter; C.O.D. orders are accepted.

THINK INK

7526 OLYMPIC VIEW DR.,
SUITE E-W
EDMONDS, WA
98026–5555
425–778–1935
FAX: 425–776–2997

Catalog: $2, refundable with first order
Pay: check, MO, MC, V, Discover
Sells: thermography/embossing powders, Gocco printers, supplies, etc.
Store: same address; Monday to Friday 9:30–5:30

Think Ink features Print GOCCO's printing press silkscreen devices and embossing powders, which provide crafters with a great way to get custom prints inexpensively. Use clip-art designs, or if you can draw, GOCCOs will enable you to custom-color and print flyers, bulletins, cards, tote bags, T-shirts, and nearly anything else made of paper, fabric, wood, or leather. There are two Print GOCCO presses, the B6 model (with a 3⁹/₁₆" by 5⁹/₁₆" print area) for $99, and the B5 (with a 5¹⁵/₁₆" by 8¹¹/₁₆" print area) for $360. Both models work by creating a master of your design that can be inked like a silkscreen and printed.

The Gocco Printer inks are offered in a wide range of colors and types, including 40 cc tubes of textile ink, metallics, fluorescents, pastels, pearlescents, and basics, as well as enamel inks for nonporous surfaces. One application of the ink yields 80 to 100 prints. If you send $2 (refundable with purchase), Think Ink will send you Gocco-printed samples, a price list, and a brochure on the Print GOCCO printers. Rubber-stamp artists should check the prices they're currently paying for embossing powders. Think Ink's powders do the same job, but are sold at bulk discount prices—as much as 60% to 70%, compared to the prices charged by rubber-stamp supply firms. The selection of 115 powders includes many unique powders: Midnight Stars, Rose Ruby, Silver Surf, and Metallic Medley, among others.

Wholesale customers, please note: Send a copy of your business license to receive the wholesale terms and pricing.

Special Factors: C.O.D. orders are accepted.

TOM THUMB WORKSHOPS

14100 LANKFORD
HIGHWAY
P.O. BOX 357-WBMC
MAPPSVILLE, VA 23407
757–824–3507
FAX: 757–824–4465

Price List: free with a long, stamped, self-addressed envelope
Pay: check, MO, MC, V
Sells: potpourri, spices, herbs, oils, etc.
Store: same address (Rte. 13); Monday to Friday 9–5

Although they're both called potpourri, there's a world of difference between an artificially scented pile of dried things and dyed wood shavings, and a blend of flowers, herbs, spices, essential oils, and natural fixatives. Tom Thumb sells the ingredients and directions for making the real thing, from premixed blends like "Blackberry Royal" and "Yuletide," to a list of hundreds of herbs, spices, dried flowers, cones, and pods. The eight-page price list also shows a range of botanicals perfect for wreaths and arrangements—artemisia, eucalyptus, dried pomegranates, wheat, and lotus pods among them. Dozens of essential oils and blends are available in ⅛ ounce vials for $3.25, and the blended potpourri costs $6.95 for four ounces, or $19.95 per pound. These prices are 20% to 45% below those charged elsewhere for "house blends" of potpourri, and you can deduct 25% from the cost of the goods (with some exceptions) if your order is over $100. Tom Thumb, in business since 1975, also sells materials and equipment for drying flowers, as well as pressed flowers, spice jars and other containers, and the bookshelf includes a number of guides to aromatherapy, perfumery, and making wreaths, candles, and soap.

Wholesale buyers, please request the *bulk price list* and include a long, stamped, self-addressed envelope.

Special Factors: Satisfaction is guaranteed; returns are accepted within 30 days; minimum order is $15, $30 with credit cards.

VANGUARD CRAFTS, INC.

DEPT. WMC
P.O. BOX 340170
BROOKLYN, NY
11234–0003
718–377–5188
FAX: 718–692–0056

Catalog: $1, refundable
Pay: check, MO, MC, V, Discover
Sells: crafts, kits, and materials
Store: 1081 E. 48th St., Brooklyn, NY; Monday to Friday 10–6, Saturday 10–5

Vanguard has been selling fun since 1959 through a 68-page color catalog of crafts kits and projects. Vanguard is geared to educators and others buying for classroom use, but it's a great source for rainy-day project materials at home.

You'll find kits and supplies for hundreds of crafts, including shrink art, foil pictures, grapevine wreaths, mosaic tiling, basic woodworking crafts, suncatchers, Styrofoam crafts, leatherworking, fabric flowers, decoupage, copper enameling, pom-pom crafts, stenciling, string art, crafts-sticks projects, Indian crafts, clothespin dolls, calligraphy, and other diversions. Vanguard also features a line of kits inspired by the "spirit of the Southwest"—Santa Fe picture frames, "Pueblo" pottery, concho accessories, bead looms, kachina dolls, and more. Basic art supplies and tools—adhesives, scissors, paper, paint, pastels, hammers, craft knives, etc.—are also available. The prices are *very* reasonable, and the large selection makes it easy to meet the $25 minimum order.

Special Factors: Minimum order is $25.

WARNER-CRIVELLARO STAINED GLASS SUPPLIES, INC.

**1855 WEAVERSVILLE RD.
ALLENTOWN, PA 18103
800–523–4242
610–264–1100
IN SPANISH: 800–523–4245
FAX: 610–264–1010**

Catalog: $2 (see text)
Pay: check, MO, MC, V, AE, Discover
Sells: stained-glass tools and supplies
Store: same address; Monday to Saturday 9–5 ET
E-mail: warnerc@fast.net
Online: http://www.warner-criv.com

Warner-Crivellaro serves the old art of stained glass with an 80-page catalog of glass sheets (Wissmach, Kokomo, Spectrum, Youghiogheny, and other types), bevels, glass cutting tools and machines, grinders, foil and foiling equipment, strips and spools of lead came, soldering tools and irons, patinas, flux, etching acid, finishing compound, cutting oil, and several pages of books and manuals. If you're new to the craft, see the starter kits, which begin at under $46 and include everything you need to begin a project. Once you've mastered a suncatcher or one of the beautiful bevel ornaments, you may be ready to tackle a lampshade.

Warner-Crivellaro also publishes a 200-plus-page catalog (free with your first $50 order) of materials and supplies for more complex projects. But even the general catalog ($2) includes nearly four dozen lamp bases, most with a bronze-look or antique brass finish. The bases are fully wired and harped, and begin at under $9 for minis. Since reproduction lamps made in these styles usually fetch much more when they're sold in stores, consider saving by buying the base here and the shade elsewhere. The catalog shows other lamp and shade parts, including harps, vase caps, spiders, brass channel and bead edging, and two pages of solid bronze reproduction Tiffany lamp bases, which run from $140 to $775. Even the red oak frames sold here, which are designed to encase stained glass panels, can be employed by nonartisans to frame and finish other works of a similar thickness.

Please note: Orders sent to Alaska, Canada, and overseas must be paid in U.S. dollars or by credit card.

Special Factors: Authorized returns are accepted; minimum order is $25; C.O.D. orders are accepted.

WEAVER LEATHER, INC.

P.O. BOX 68
MT. HOPE, OH 44660
800–932–8371
330–674–7548
FAX: 800–693–2837
FAX: 330–674–0330

Catalog: free
Pay: check, MO, MC, V
Sells: leather and leatherworking and saddlery supplies, parts, and tools
Store: mail order only; phone hours Monday to Friday 7:30–7 ET

Weaver Leather is a supplier to professional leatherworkers and saddlery shops, but if you can meet the $50 minimum order, you can buy here too—and take advantage of Weaver's great stock, selection, and prices.

The 109-page color catalog opens with a range of leather—strap and tooling, chrome-tanned top grain, suede chap splits, skirting, shearling, and latigo. If you make or repair saddles or harnesses, you'll appreciate the English bridle leather, bridle sides, harness leather, and rawhide. Patent leather is also available. There are quantity price breaks at five and ten sides. The catalog includes a visual guide and helpful facts on selecting leather and minimizing waste. You'll find a range of leatherworking tools and equipment here, many made by Weaver, from hand tools for cutting and stamping to heavy equipment for production work (Adler sewing machines and shoe-repair equipment, strap cutters, riveters, edge finishers, etc.). Thread, glue, dye, oil, conditioner, and cleaners are also offered, both Fiebing's and Weaver's own line.

Half of the catalog is devoted to saddlery and harness making. Here are wooden and rawhide stirrups, harness and saddle hardware (bits, chain, buckles, snaps, loops, harness and saddle ornaments), and leather and nylon billets and cinch straps. If you'd like to learn to repair or build saddles, you'll find help in *Saddlemaking: Lessons in Construction, Repair, and Evaluation,* a 110-minute video that takes you through creation and finishing of a saddle.

The pricing here is competitive on single items, but even better if you can buy in quantity. Weaver makes it easy to save, too, by allowing you to mix and match leather, hardware, and stirrups to meet the minimums. Some products are offered in case lots, and these count toward the volume discounts as well.

Special Factors: Satisfaction is guaranteed; authorized returns are accepted for exchange, refund, or credit; minimum order is $50 ($15 service charge for orders below minimum); C.O.D. orders are accepted.

SEE ALSO

The Astronomical Society of the Pacific • materials on astronomy topics • **BOOKS**

Baron/Barclay Bridge Supplies • teaching and playing supplies for bridge • **TOYS**

BFK Sports • kite-building materials • **SPORTS**

C & T Bridge Supplies • bridge supplies • **TOYS**

Caprilands Herb Farm • potpourri ingredients, pomanders, essential oils, etc. • **FARM**

Ceramic Supply of New York & New Jersey, Inc. • ceramics and sculpting materials, music box parts • **ART MATERIALS**

Daleco Master Breeder Products • tropical and freshwater fish supplies and equipment • **ANIMAL**

Eloxite Corporation • jewelry findings, lapidary equipment, and clock-making supplies • **JEWELRY**

Golfsmith International, Inc. • supplies for making golf clubs, including stains, finishes, etc. • **SPORTS**

Hong Kong Lapidaries, Inc. • scarabs, inlaid intaglios, beads, and other crafts materials • **JEWELRY**

House of Onyx, Inc. • semiprecious and precious gems, cabochons • **JEWELRY**

Johnny's Selected Seeds Inc. • herb-drying bags, flower-drying supplies, dehydrators, etc. • **FARM**

Leather Unlimited Corp. • leather, dyes, kits, etc. • **LUGGAGE**

M.C. Limited Fine Leathers • steer hides • **HOME: DECOR**

Original Paper Collectibles • vintage fruit crate labels • **ART & ANTIQUES**

The Potters Shop Inc. • books on pottery and ceramics • **BOOKS**

San Francisco Herb Co. • dried flowers, potpourri ingredients, potpourri recipes, etc. • **FOOD: BEVERAGES AND FLAVORINGS**

Sewing Machine Super Store® • sewing machines, sergers, sewing equipment, instructional workbooks, dressmaker forms, weaving equipment, etc. • **APPLIANCES**

Storey' Communications, Inc. • books and manuals on country crafts • **BOOKS**

Texas Art Supply • wide range of arts and crafts supplies and equipment • **ART MATERIALS**

That Fish Place/That Pet Place • aquarium supplies and equipment • **ANIMAL**

Triner Scale • pocket scale • **OFFICE**

University Products, Inc. • archival-quality collection storage, mounting, and display materials • **OFFICE: SMALL BUSINESS**

Weston Bowl Mill • unfinished wooden boxes, spool holders, etc. • **GENERAL MERCHANDISE**

Textile Arts

Sewing and needlework of all kinds, and other crafts using textiles

Sewing it yourself—clothing, home accessories, and crafts—can not only save you money, but if you're skilled you'll get a custom job, with the fabric and details *you* want. The sources here can help you find the right tools and materials for your clothing project; see the listings in "Home: Decor" for decorator fabrics.

If you do needlework and use DMC floss, you'll want the DMC Embroidery Floss Card in your files. This reference includes samples of each DMC floss color and a guide to which colors are available in pearl cotton in sizes 3, 5, and 8. (Most discount sources carry DMC floss, but not all offer color guides.) The American Needlewoman sells the DMC Floss Card; request the free catalog from The American Needlewoman, P.O. Box 6472-WBMC, Fort Worth, TX 76115.

For more firms selling fabric, notions, and sewing-crafts supplies, see the preceding listings in "Crafts and Hobbies."

FIND IT FAST

FUN FUR • **Monterey**
NOTIONS AND SEWING TOOLS • **Button Shop, Clotilde, A. Feibusch, Home-Sew, Newark Dressmaker, Solo Slide, Taylor's, Thread Discount Sales**
TEXTILE ARTS, YARN, FABRIC • **Atlanta Thread, Connecting Threads, Dharma Trading, Fashion Fabrics Club, Fiber Studio, Global Village, Great Northern Weaving, Natural Fiber Fabrics, Oppenheim's, Smiley's Yarn, Thai Silks, Utex, Webs**

ATLANTA THREAD & SUPPLY

695 RED OAK RD., DEPT. WBMC 98
STOCKBRIDGE, GA 30281
800–847–1001
770–389–9115
FAX: 800–298–0403,
770–389–9202

Catalog: $1
Pay: check, MO, MC, V, AE, Discover
Sells: sewing tools, notions, and pressing equipment
Store: mail order only

Atlanta Thread, a division of a major distributor of sewing equipment, has been doing business since 1948, and boasts the lowest prices around on Gingher shears, Gosling drapery tapes, Kirsch drapery hardware, YKK zippers, and many other goods. This is a great source for quality supplies and equipment—coned thread, zippers and parts, custom tailoring linings and pads, buttons, Singer's sewing guides and professional tailoring manuals, cords, crinoline stiffening bands, fringe, hook-and-loop tape, professional pressing equipment—tables and boards, irons by Hi-Steam/Naomoto, Rheem, Rowenta, and Sussman—and commercial-quality sewing machines, sergers, and parts. The 64-page catalog is illustrated, but if you need more information on a product, call and ask.

Special Factors: Satisfaction is guaranteed; returns are accepted within 30 days for exchange, refund, or credit; C.O.D. orders are accepted.

BUFFALO BATT & FELT CORP.

DEPT. WBMC
3307 WALDEN AVE.
DEPEW, NY 14043
716–683–4100, EXT. 130
FAX: 716–683–8928

Brochure and Samples: $1, refundable
Pay: check, MO, MC, V
Sells: fiberfill, quilt batts, and pillow inserts
Store: mail order only

Buffalo Batt's "Super Fluff" polyester stuffing is so springy and resilient, the snowy-white samples nearly bounce out of the brochure. The firm has been in business since 1913, and sells this craft and upholstery stuffing by the case at savings of 40% or more on regular retail prices.

Super Fluff is manufactured in rolls 27" wide by 20 yards long and is the ideal filler for upholstery and crafts in which support and a down-like feel are desired. In addition to having high loft and nonallergenic properties, Super Fluff is machine washable and dryable, mildew-resistant, and easy to sew. Buffalo Batt also sells Super Fluff in 12-ounce and 2-pound bags, bulk rolls, pillow inserts (from 14" square to 30" square, 12" by 16" and 14" by 18" rectangles, and neckrolls), and both "traditional" and 2-inch-thick "comforter-style" quilt batts. Ultra Fluff, a slick, premium fiberfill that gives a softer hand, was recently introduced; it's also available in 10-ounce bags and in bulk. Another new product, "thermobonded" quilt batt, is soft, dense, and flame-retardant; it's available on 20-yard rolls. Buffalo Batt also sells "Soft Heart" Quallofil pillow inserts, in sizes from 14" to 26" square, as well as the popular rectangles, and in bulk rolls.

The only negative is the minimum order of any two cases, which may be more than most single projects require. But it's a manageable amount for a home-based crafts business, quilting circle, cooperative, or for a major decorating project—or store the surplus for future use, or share with crafty friends!

Please note: Orders are shipped via UPS within the continental United States only.

Special Factors: Quantity discounts are available; minimum order is any two cases; C.O.D. orders are accepted.

THE BUTTON SHOP

P.O. BOX 1065-HM
OAK PARK, IL 60304
708–795–1234
FAX: 708–795–1234

Catalog: free
Pay: check, MO, MC, V
Sells: buttons and sewing supplies
Store: 7023 Roosevelt Rd., Berwyn, IL; Monday to Friday 9–4, Saturday 10–2

The Button Shop, founded in 1900, stocks closures of all kinds, as well as trims, sewing machine parts, scissors, and other sewing tools and notions at savings of up to 50% on list prices or regular retail. Several pages of the 18-page catalog are devoted to buttons—anonymous white shirt buttons, clear waistband buttons, tiny buttons for doll clothes, classic four-hole coat and suit buttons, gilt heraldic buttons for blazers, designs for dressy clothing, Navy peacoat buttons, braided leather buttons for tweeds, and dozens of others, including baseball gloves and other novelty designs for children's clothing. If you want to custom-cover buttons with your own fabric, you'll find Maxant and Prym kits, as well as make-your-own fabric belt and buckle materials, gripper snaps and grommet sets, hooks and eyes of all types, zippers (including odd sizes to 108"), and Velcro by the inch and by the yard. The Button Shop sells all kinds of rickrack, bias tape, cording, white and black elastic (from ⅛" to 3"), replacement jacket cuffs, elbow patches, trouser pockets, shoulder pads, and other notions and supplies. Thread in cotton, cotton-covered polyester, and polyester is offered; the brands include Dritz, Fiskars, Gingher, Molnycke, Oncore, Prym, Singer, Talon, Wiss, and Wrights.

The Button Shop's comparatively deep inventory of sewing machine supplies and parts includes needles, presser feet, bobbins, bobbin cases, needle plates, motors, foot controls, light bulbs, and belts. The catalog descriptions are brief, and line drawings are the only illustrations. If you're not sure an item is the right one and need more information, call or write before ordering. You may also send a fabric swatch for the best color match if you're buying trim, thread, or buttons, and The Button Shop custom-makes zippers in lengths up to 120".

Special Factors: Returns are accepted within 30 days for exchange, refund, or credit; minimum order is $5, $10 with credit cards; C.O.D. orders are accepted.

CLOTILDE, INC.

**B3000
LOUISIANA, MO
63353–3000
800–772–2891
FAX: 800–863–3191**

Catalog: free
Pay: check, MO, MC, V, Discover
Sells: sewing and quilting notions, books, patterns, machine accessories, etc.
Store: mail order only
E-mail: clotilde@clotilde.com
Online: http://www.clotilde.com

Clotilde has been providing sewers with notions since 1971, and presents current offerings in a well-organized, 100-page color catalog. Clotilde's extensive collection of sewing tools and machine attachments (for both electronic and computerized models) makes it a great source for every home sewer.

Clotilde sells a broad range of sewing aids and equipment: ironing hams and boards, sewing and work tables, pattern design supplies, serging notions, scissors and cutters, quilting supplies, appliqué notions, and a large number of books, videos, and patterns. Everything is discounted 20% from regular retail, and throughout the catalog you'll find specials with further reductions. Clotilde has so many problem-solvers and gadgets to make the difficult easy—like turning narrow fabric tubes, making even knife pleats, and cutting perfect circles—you'll want to have the catalog before you begin your next big project.

Wholesale buyers, please note: You must resell Clotilde's products to qualify for wholesale terms (40% to 50% off); minimum order is $100, no minimum quantities.

Special Factors: Satisfaction is guaranteed.

CONNECTING THREADS

P.O. BOX 8940
VANCOUVER, WA
98668–8940
800–574–6454
FAX: 360–260–8877

Catalog: free
Pay: check, MO, MC, V, AE, Discover, JCB
Sells: quilting patterns, materials, and supplies
Store: mail order only

Connecting Threads answers the needs of "the busy quilter" with 64 pages of pattern and reference books, fabrics and batts, project plans, cutting and sewing tools, stencils, and equipment. If you haven't worked on a quilt in years, you may be surprised by the complexity and sophistication of the designs: Seminole patchwork, Amish miniatures, Sashiko (Japanese quilting), "photo" keepsake quilts, reverse appliqué, and Jewish quilting may be new to you. In addition to books, Connecting Threads offers EZ International's WaterFall and ColorBars ombré cottons, stencils for both hand and machine quilting (top-stitching through the batt), and lots of other tools and sewing helpers. There are also books on related crafts—fabric painting, ribbon work, dolls, fabric ornaments, and "art" clothing. Savings average 25%, and both retail and discount prices are listed.

Special Factors: Satisfaction is guaranteed; returns are accepted for exchange, refund, or credit.

DHARMA TRADING CO.

P.O. BOX 150916
SAN RAFAEL, CA
94915–0916
415–456–7657
FAX: 415–456–8747

Catalog: free
Pay: check, MO, MC, V, Discover
Sells: textile craft supplies and clothing "blanks"
Store: 1604 Fourth St., San Rafael, CA; Monday to Saturday 10–6
E-mail: catalog@dharmatrading.com
Online: http://www.dharmatrading.com

The "whole earth" movement may have peaked in 1969, the year this firm was founded, but Dharma Trading has survived—and prospered.

The firm sells tools and materials for the textile arts—dyes, paints, resists, fabrics, and clothing "blanks"—and declares, "We are the source for the tie-dye dyes used by most tie-dyers." The informative, 112-page catalog provides helpful tips on the features of the dyes and paints, application techniques and suggested fabrics, and even metric conversion charts and a shrinkage "estimator." Prices are good, running up to 50% off list or comparable retail.

Coloring agents by Deka, Dupont, Jacquard, Jones Tones, Pebeo, Peintex, Procion, Sennelier (Tinfix Design), Setacolor, Versatex, and other firms are offered, as well as color remover, soda ash, urea, Synthrapol, gutta serti, and other resists. The tools include bottles and droppers for dye mixing and application, textile pens, tjantings, brushes (flat, foam, sumi), and steamers for setting dyes. Nearly half of Dharma Trading's catalog is devoted to silk and cotton clothing blanks—everything from cotton jester hats and silk earring blanks to cotton skirts, jackets, sweats, and more are shown in the current catalog. A list of cotton, rayon, and silk fabrics that have yielded good results with dyeing and painting is included in the catalog; samples (silk or cotton/rayon) are available for 25¢ each. Selected books dealing with fabric design, painting, screening, direct dyeing, batiking, tie-dyeing, and other techniques are also sold.

Special Factors: Quantity discounts are available; institutional accounts are available; C.O.D. orders are accepted.

FASHION FABRICS CLUB

10490 BAUR BLVD.
ST. LOUIS, MO 63132
800–468–0602
FAX: 314–993–5802

Membership: $10 (see text)
Pay: check, MO, MC, V
Sells: dress fabric
Store: 10512 Baur Blvd., St. Louis, MO; Tuesday to Saturday 10–5, Sunday 12–5

Fashion Fabrics Club speaks to the needs of home sewers who make their own clothing, but don't have the time to comb fabric stores for the perfect selection. Each month, Fashion Fabrics Club sends its members a brochure with over a dozen coordinated fabric swatches, discount coupons, and other offers. The fabrics are chosen to allow you to create coordinated outfits; a recent mailing featured selections from JH Collectibles, Evan Picone, and Leslie Fay, at $3.99 to $9.99 a yard. Care recommendations and "usual" selling prices are noted for each selection.

Write to Fashion Fabrics Club to buy an introductory membership for $4.95; a $5 gift certificate will be included in your first mailing. All purchases are covered by the Club's pledge of satisfaction, and you'll receive discount coupons (including one for a $5 rebate on your first purchase) with each order you place, entitling you to savings on future orders.

Please note: Membership is available only to individuals living in the United States or its possessions.

Special Factors: Satisfaction is guaranteed; returns are accepted for exchange, refund, or credit; minimum order is $5; shipping and handling is $5.95 per order.

A. FEIBUSCH CORPORATION

27 ALLEN ST.
NEW YORK, NY 10002
212–226–3964
FAX: 212–226–5844

Information: price quote
Pay: check or MO
Sells: zippers, thread, notions, and garment supplies
Store: same address; Monday to Friday 9:30–5, Sunday 10–5

Feibusch has been helping New Yorkers zip up since 1941, handling requests from the mundane to the exotic. Zippers of every conceivable size, color, and type are sold here—from minuscule dolls' zippers to heavy-duty closures for tents, luggage, and similar applications. If your requirements aren't met by the existing stock, Feibusch can have your zipper made to order. Talon and YKK zippers are available, and Feibusch also carries all-cotton and polyester thread in a full range of colors. There is no catalog, so *write* with your requirements. Describe what you're looking for or send a sample, specifying length desired, nylon or metal teeth, open or closed end, and other details. Enclose a scrap of fabric, if possible, to assure a good color match. Be sure to include a self-addressed, stamped envelope with your correspondence if you want to receive a reply. If you'd prefer to call with general information questions, note that Feibusch has salespeople who speak Chinese, French, and German, as well as Spanish!

Special Factors: Price quote by letter.

THE FIBER STUDIO

DEPT. WBMC
9 FOSTER HILL RD.
P.O. BOX 637
HENNIKER, NH 03242
603–428–7830

Book and Equipment Catalog: $1 (see text)
Pay: check, MO, MC, V
Sells: knitting, spinning, and weaving equipment and supplies, doll hair fiber, skins, etc.
Store: 9 Foster Hill Rd., Henniker, NH; Tuesday to Saturday 10–4, Sunday by chance
E-mail: fiberstudio@conknet.com
Online: http://www.conknet.com/fiberstudio

The Fiber Studio has been serving the needs of knitters, spinners, weavers, and doll makers since 1975 with a well-chosen line of tools and supplies, and great prices on yarn. The catalog lists looms, spinning equipment, and accessories by Ashford, Glimarkra, Harrisville Design, Leclerc, Louet, Norwood, and Schacht. The prices on these aren't discounted, but shipping is included on some models (see "Special Factors," below). Natural dyes, mordants, and a good selection of spinning fibers—from mohair tops to silk roving—are offered at competitive prices. (The sample card of current spinning fibers costs $4.) And scores of texts on knitting, spinning, and weaving are available.

The bargains here are on yarns, which are sold in two ways: through the stock shown in the yarn sample set ($5), and through the yarn closeouts. The stock yarns include rug wools, natural yarns, Superwash wool, Norwegian wool, cotton, silk, Shetland wool, mercerized cotton, and more, priced up to 35% less at The Fiber Studio than at other sources. Quantity discounts on these yarns run from 10% on orders over $100 to 20% on orders over $200. If you can get to Henniker, you have a treat: the shop offers an extensive selection of beads from around the world, made of semiprecious stones, wood, bone, glass, horn, clay, and other materials, as well as unusual findings. The Fiber Studio also sells Tibetan lambskins, of special interest to doll makers. These items aren't listed in the catalog, but you can make inquiries and order by phone.

Canadian readers, please note: Only U.S. funds are accepted.

Special Factors: Specify the *spinning fibers* ($4) or *yarns* ($5) sample set; shipping is not charged on most models of Harrisville Design, Leclerc, and Schacht looms; quantity discounts are available; minimum order is $15 with credit cards; C.O.D. orders are accepted.

GLOBAL VILLAGE IMPORTS

3439 NE SANDY BLVD.,
#263-W
PORTLAND, OR
97232-1959
503-236-9245
FAX: 503-233-0827

Brochure and Swatches: see text
Pay: check or MO
Sells: Guatemalan ikat fabrics
Store: mail order only
E-mail: sales@globalfabric.com
Online: http://www.globalfabric.com/~gvi/

Ikat is a type of weaving that uses tie-dyed warp threads to create striated designs that blend into overall patterns, which may be as subtle as Zen or as colorfully riotous as a Mardi Gras parade. (Double ikats, in which both warp and weft threads are so dyed, represent a further refinement of the art.) Global Village has been selling handwoven Guatemalan ikats since 1988, and will send you an information packet and swatches of what's currently available for the sample fee of $5 ($7 for international inquiries), refundable with purchase. Most of the fabrics are 36" wide, are woven by hand on large looms, and run from $10 to $25 per yard; the double ikats, hard to find at any price, are woven by the roll especially for Global Village. Upholstery-weight cottons, embroidered-look and brocade designs, and double ikats shot through with Lurex threads are also available. Brightly colored tapes and trims, ½" to 2¼" wide, are also available. Quilters can take advantage of the "Quilter's Grabbag"—a generous pack of odds and ends, for $25 postpaid (note color preferences and minimum sizes needed, if applicable). The prices at Global Village are nearly 50% below the rates prevailing in New York City specialty shops. Fabric designers should take note of the company's custom weaving services, and wholesale inquiries are welcomed.

Special Factors: Minimum order is 1 yard; quantity discounts are available; C.O.D. orders are accepted.

GREAT NORTHERN WEAVING

451 EAST D AVE.

P.O. BOX 462

KALAMAZOO, MI

49004–0462

616–341–9752

FAX: 616–341–9525

Catalog and Samples: $2.50, refundable
Pay: check, MO, MC, V
Sells: rug-making supplies and tools
Store: same address; Monday to Friday 9–4, Saturday 10–1

The homey crafts of braiding, crocheting, and weaving rugs are served at Great Northern Weaving, which has been in business since 1985, and prices most items competitively—rags and filler cost up to 50% less here than elsewhere.

The 12-page catalog lists tools and materials for rug weaving and rug braiding. Braid-Aids, Braidkins, Braid-Klamps, Fraser rag cutters, reed and heddle hooks, shuttles, and warping tools are all available. The materials include coned cotton warp (8–4 ply) in over two dozen colors, and the same gauge cotton/poly warp in colors and "natural"; all-cotton rug filler in 15 shades, 16-ply rug roping, new cotton "rags" on rolls, color loopers, and loopers in bulk. Great Northern Weaving is introducing a two-harness folding rug loom, designed by Kessineck Looms. You don't have to commit to full-scale rug weaving, though—see the "palmloom," small frame looms and pot-holder looms, and even "inch worm kits," recommended as child pleasers. Reference books are also available.

Canadian readers, please note: Payment must be made in U.S. funds.

Special Factors: Handling fee on orders under $40; C.O.D. orders are accepted.

HOME-SEW

DEPT. WM8

P.O. BOX 4099

BETHLEHEM, PA

   18018–0099

610–867–3833

FAX: 610–867–9717

Catalog: 50¢
Pay: check, MO, MC, V, Discover
Sells: sewing and crafts supplies and notions
Store: mail order only

Home-Sew, which has been in business since 1960, offers savings of up to 70% on assorted laces and trims, as well as a wide range of sewing and crafts supplies. Home-Sew's 32-page catalog is well organized and easy to use, with clear photographs of the trims and notions.

In addition to scores of laces (Cluny, Venice, nylon, poly, eyelet, etc.), Home-Sew offers elastic, satin and velvet ribbon, rickrack, tape, and appliqués. Specialty thread—for general sewing, overlock machines, carpets, and quilting—is available on cones and on spools. There are zippers, snaps, hooks and eyes, buttons, Velcro dots, belts and buckles, pins, needles, and scissors, as well as floss, adhesives, Styrofoam wreaths, spangles, beads, animal and doll parts, interfacings, and related items. If you're making your own curtains or slipcovers, check the prices on shirring and pleater tape, tasseled and moss fringe, cording, and related goods. Home-Sew makes it easy to see the trims before you buy—just join the Sample Club (50¢, order through the catalog), and you'll receive three mailings of lace, trim, ribbon, and elastics samples per year.

Wholesale customers, deduct 25% on all orders over $100.

Special Factors: Satisfaction is guaranteed; returns are accepted for exchange, refund, or credit; quantity discounts are available; shipping is not charged on orders over $50 that are paid by check or money order.

MONTEREY, INC.

**1725 E. DELAVAN
JANESVILLE, WI 53547
800–432–9959
608–754–8309
FAX: 608–754–3750**

Price List: free with SASE (see text)
Pay: check, MO, MC, V
Sells: fake-fur fabric
Store: 1725 E. Delavan Dr., Janesville, WI;
Monday to Friday 8–4:30; Saturday 8–12
noon (April to Sept.), 8–4:30 (Oct. to March)

Monterey, Inc. has been manufacturing deep-pile fur fabrics for a quarter of a century, and sells them at prices up to 50% below the usual retail. The brochure describes the fiber content of the different "fun" furs and lists the available colors, pile height, and ounces per yard. In addition to basic plush, "kurl," and shag, you'll find patterns and colors simulating the pelts of bear, seal, calf, tiger, and cheetah. Prices are given per cut yard, per yard on the roll (there are 15 to 20 yards per roll), and for quantity orders. Cut yards run from between about $11 and $19 per yard, and prices drop from there. You can buy the fabric in remnants (the Mill will choose the fur type) for $4.50 a pound, or $4.00 per pound by the carton (35 to 40 pounds). Stuffing for craft projects is available as well, at 85¢ a pound and up.

Please note: A set of samples is offered for $5 ($10 to addresses in Canada), a worthwhile investment unless you're buying only remnants.

Special Factors: Minimum yardage order is 1 yard; minimum order is $25, $100 on orders shipped C.O.D.

NATURAL FIBER FABRICS DIRECT

**10490 BAUR BLVD.
ST. LOUIS, MO 63132
800–468–0602
FAX: 314–993–5804**

Membership: $10 (see text)
Pay: check, MO, MC, V
Sells: natural-fiber fabrics
Store: 10512 Baur Blvd., St. Louis, MO;
Tuesday to Saturday 10–5, Sunday 12–5

A year's membership in Natural Fiber Fabrics Direct usually costs $10, but an introductory membership is available for $4.95, and includes a $5 gift certificate with your first mailing. You'll receive regular collections of about two dozen fabric swatches, with prices and fiber information.

The cottons, silks, linens, woolens, and blends are dress and suit weight, and the prices are often 50% below those charged elsewhere for fabrics of similar quality. The mailings are sent about a season early, which gives you plenty of time to select a pattern and complete your clothing. The choices range from novelty knits and prints for playwear to dressy wovens for business clothing. You may recognize some of the fabrics, since they're also used in the workrooms of Campus Outfitters, Leslie Fay, Dan River, Schwartz Leibman, Spring Mills, and other makers. As an added service to members, Natural Fiber Fabrics matches most of the materials to Gutermann threads, which you can order with the fabric. And rebate coupons are issued for 5% of the value of fabric purchases (except clearance selections), further enhancing the values.

Please note: Membership is available only to individuals living in the United States or its possessions.

Special Factors: Satisfaction is guaranteed; uncut returns are accepted for exchange, refund, or credit; minimum order is $5; shipping and handling costs $5.95 per order.

NEWARK DRESS-MAKER SUPPLY, INC.

6473 RUCH RD.
DEPT. WMJ
P.O. BOX 20730
LEHIGH VALLEY, PA
    18002–0730
610–837–7500
FAX: 610–837–9115

Catalog: free
Pay: check, MO, MC, V, Discover
Sells: sewing notions, crafts, and needlework supplies
Store: mail order only

Searching for specialty patterns, smocking guides, bear joints, alphabet beads, silk thread, or toy squeakers? Such requests are routine at Newark Dressmaker Supply, which offers trims, appliqués, scissors, piping, ribbon (including wire-edged), lace, braid, twill, zippers, sewing gadgets, bridal supplies, knitting supplies, name tapes and woven labels, interfacing, buttons, thread, floss, bias tape, rhinestones, wreath-decorating materials, supplies for making dolls and stuffed bears, fabric, upholstery materials, books and manuals, and much more. Among the brands of goods stocked here, you'll find Coats & Clark's, Dritz, Pellon, Plaid, Sta-Flex, and Talon. "Sew Little" patterns for infants' and children's clothing are stocked, as well as doll patterns to fit Barbie dolls, dolls from the American Girl Doll Collection, and the 18" Goetz dolls.

Newark Dressmaker has been in business since 1950 and is a great mail-order source for home sewers, since it offers a huge array of notions and other supplies, from glass-headed pins to yard goods, through the 60-page catalog. The prices are very competitive—up to 50% below regular retail on some items—and that doesn't count the 10% discount you get if your order totals $50 or more.

Wholesale customers, request the wholesale order form with the catalog; the minimum order is $125, and no specials, bonuses, or other offers apply to wholesale sales.

Canadian readers, please note: Only U.S. funds are accepted.

Special Factors: Satisfaction is guaranteed.

OPPENHEIM'S

BOX 29
NORTH MANCHESTER, IN
  46962–0029
800–277–9807
219–982–6848
FAX: 219–982–6557

Catalog: free
Pay: check, MO, MC, V, Discover
Sells: yard goods, notions, crafts materials
Store: mail order only

The venerable Oppenheim's has been in business since 1875, and publishes a 64-page newsprint catalog of all kinds of crafts staples and specials. The firm's strength is fabrics, sold in cutaways, remnants, and by-the-yard cuts. The catalog includes collection of calico, broadcloth, rib knits, Pendleton woolens, fun fur, denim, and other fabrics, in remnants and cutaways (sold by the lot or the pound). The yard goods will appeal to anyone looking for great prices on fabrics for crafts, plain clothing, and home decorating: shirting, sheeting, chambray, flannel, pillow ticking, cheesecloth, Onasburg, Pacific silver cloth, terry cloth, Rembrandt rug canvas and needlepoint canvas, bridal fabrics, velvet, rip-stop nylon, and stretch fabric for exercise wear are all offered in the lists of "staple" fabrics. Some of the fabrics are irregular; Oppenheim's will send you swatches (include a SASE with your request), and returns are accepted.

The catalog also includes an extensive roundup of notions—laces, ribbon, facings, cording, buckles, hook-and-loop tape, and more.

Sewing tools, from seam rippers to sleeve boards, are featured, and there are lots of pillow tops and stuffed toy kits, appliqués, and preprinted quilt tops, pillow forms, and panels. If you're long on ideas and imagination but short on funds, Oppenheim's will be a welcome addition to your list of sources.

Special Factors: Satisfaction is guaranteed; returns (exceptions noted in catalog) are accepted within 10 days for exchange, refund, or credit.

SMILEY'S YARNS

DEPT. W
92–06 JAMAICA AVE.
WOODHAVEN, NY 11421
MAIL ORDER:
  718–847–2185
STORE: 718–849–9873

Brochure: free with SASE
Pay: check or MO
Sells: yarn for hand knitting and crocheting
Store: same address; Monday, Tuesday, Thursday, Friday, and Saturday 10–5:30
Online: http://www.stitching.com/smileysyarns/

Smiley's, where "Yarn Bargains Are Our Business," has been selling first-quality yarns at a discount since 1935. Each month, Smiley's offers a different "Yarn of the Month" selection at discounts from 30% to as much as 80% off list prices. Among the manufacturers represented are Bernat, Emu, Grignasco, Hayfield, Lion Brand, Patons, Phildar, Pingouin, Plymouth, Reynolds, Schachenmayr, Schaffhauser, Unger, and Wendy. You can call or write for a price quote on goods by these firms, or inquire about knitting and crocheting yarns by other manufacturers—they may be available. For samples of the current "Yarn of the Month" offering, send a long, stamped, self-addressed envelope. Requests without envelopes can't be honored.

Wholesale customers, inquire for terms.

Special Factors: Price quote by phone or letter with SASE; quantity discounts are available; store is closed Wednesday and Sunday.

SOLO SLIDE FASTENERS, INC.

8 SPRING BROOK RD.,
DEPT. WB
P.O. BOX 378
FOXBOROUGH, MA 02035
800-343-9670
FAX: 800-547-4775

Catalog: free
Pay: check, MO, MC, V, AE, Discover
Sells: dressmaking and dry-cleaning equipment and sewing supplies
Store: mail or phone order only
E-mail: solozip@tiac.com

Solo Slide is a family-run business that's been supplying dressmakers, dry cleaners, tailors, and other clothing-care professionals with tools and equipment since 1954. Among the offerings in the firm's 66-page catalog are a number of items found in the "hard-to-find" sections of notions catalogs, at prices as much as 50% less.

Solo offers an extensive selection of zippers by Talon and YKK, zipper parts (slides and stops), straight pins in several sizes, snaps, hooks and eyes, machine and hand needles, buttons (dress, suit, metal, leather, etc.), thread on cones and spools, knit collars and cuffs for jackets, shoulder pads, elbow patches, belting, elastic, and other notions. Fine-quality linings, including Milium and Bemberg, are stocked, as well as pocket material. There are scissors in the most useful models from Gingher, Marks, and Wiss, pressing boards for sleeves and other specialty tasks, Qualitex pressing pads and other hams and rolls, and professional irons, pressers, and steamers by Cissell, Hi-Steam/Namoto, Rowenta, Panasonic, Spartan, and Sussman. The catalog also shows commercial/industrial sewing machines (blind stitch and lockstitch) and overlock machines by Consew, Juki, Singer, and Tacsew. And don't miss the stain removers (including one for Magic Marker) that can save you trips to the dry cleaner.

Please note: Solo Slide has Korean-speaking sales reps on staff.

Special Factors: Authorized, unused returns (except custom-ordered or cut goods) are accepted within 30 days for credit; minimum order is $30; C.O.D. orders are accepted.

TAYLOR'S CUTAWAYS AND STUFF

Brochure: $1 (see text)
Pay: check, MO, MC, V
Sells: cutaways and patterns
Store: mail order only

DEPT. WBMC–98
2802 E. WASHINGTON ST.
URBANA, IL 61802–4699

"Cutaways" are what's left when the pieces of a garment are cut from material. These scraps, sometimes running to a yard long, are perfect for doll clothing, piecework, quilting, and other crafts. Taylor's Cutaways, in business since 1977, offers bundles of polyesters, cottons, blends, calicos, and other assortments, as well as silk, satin, velvet, velour, felt, and fake fur cutaways. The brochure (available for $1, or from the fax-back service by calling 703–904–7770) lists a wide variety of patterns and project designs for such items as draft stoppers, puppets, dolls, Teddy bears, pigs, ducks, and other animals. (Teddy bears seem to be a specialty; there are precut Teddies, mini sachet Teddies, velvet Teddies, Teddies made of cotton flannel, and Teddy bear adoption certificates sold in packs of 15.) Crocheting patterns for toys and novelties, iron-on transfer patterns, button and trim assortments, and toy eyes and joints are available.

The completely unskilled will appreciate Taylor's for the potpourri, already blended and scented, and "Potpourri Magic" fixative, essential oils, and satin squares for making sachets. Prices of these and most of the other goods average 50% below comparable retail, and savings can reach as high as 75%. This seems an especially good source for anyone who makes sachets and potpourris, dolls, toys, pieced quilts, and bazaar items.

On the practical side, Taylor's sells "tea baglets," little fiber bags you fill with the tea of your choice and heat-seal with a household iron. (This is a great way to take a favorite loose tea with you when you travel.)

Wholesale customers, request the catalog on business letterhead or with your business card; minimum order is $20.

Special Factors: Quantity discounts are available.

THAI SILKS

252 STATE ST.
LOS ALTOS, CA 94022
415–948–8611
FAX: 415–948–3426

Brochure: free
Pay: check, MO, MC, V, AE
Sells: silk fabric, scarves, lingerie, etc.
Store: same address; Monday to Saturday
9–5:30

Beautiful, comfortable silk is also affordable at Thai Silks, where the home sewer, decorator, and artist can save up to 50% on yardage and piece goods (compared to average retail prices). The large selection includes sueded silk, jacquard weaves, crepe de chine, bouclé, pongee, China silk, silk satin, raw silk noil, silk rayon velvet, tapestry brocade, silk taffeta, prints, Dupioni silk, and upholstery weights. A complete set of samples is available for $20. Hemmed white and colored silk scarves and neckties for painting and batiking, Chinese embroidered handker-chiefs, silk lingerie, kimonos, boxer shorts, pajamas, camisoles, and ted-dies are also available.

If you're a serious sewer or textile artist, consider joining Thai Silk's "Silk Fabric Club." For $20 a year, you'll receive four swatched mailings of new silks, and samples of closeouts. Thai Silks has been in business since 1964, and can answer your questions about fabric suitability for dyeing and specific uses.

Wholesale customers, the minimum order is 15 to 17 yards (if fabric); $100 in goods. Request the "wholesale" price list.

Special Factors: Satisfaction is guaranteed; samples are available (details are given in the brochure); authorized returns are accepted; minimum order is ½ yard of fabric; C.O.D. orders are accepted.

THREAD DISCOUNT SALES

10222 PARAMOUNT BLVD., DEPT. W
DOWNEY, CA 90241
310–928–4029
FAX: 310–928–1064

Price Sheets: free with long, stamped, self-addressed envelope
Pay: check, MO, MC, V, AE, Discover
Sells: coned thread, sewing machines, and sergers
Store: same address; Monday to Saturday, 10–6

This firm sells machines and supplies for the serious sewer—sewing machines, sergers, overlock machines, and "coned" thread—at savings of up to 50% on list prices. Thread Discount Sales, in business since 1962, offers a batch of photocopied sheets as its catalog; they feature White and Singer sewing and overlock machines at an average 50% discount on list or original prices.

Among the coned thread available is all-purpose polyester thread, 6,000 yards of overlock at under $3 a cone in black and white ($3.49 in any of the 200 colors), and "super rayon" embroidery thread in 500-yard cones, in 500 colors, for $1.99. Most of the thread is offered in a full range of colors, which are listed by name and number (color charts are available for $1.50). In addition, Thread Discount Sales carries novelty metallics in a variety of colors, two sizes of nylon filament thread for "invisible" work, and "wooly" nylon in 200 colors at $2.99, regularly $5.99.

Please note: A shipping surcharge is imposed on orders sent to Alaska, Hawaii, Puerto Rico, and Canada.

Special Factors: Minimum order is 6 cones of thread (on thread orders; colors may be mixed).

UTEX TRADING ENTERPRISES

826 PINE AVE.
NIAGARA FALLS, NY 14301
716–282–4887
FAX: 716–282–8211

Price List: free with SASE
Pay: check, MO, MC, V, AE
Sells: imported silk fabric
Store: same address; by appointment only

Utex was established in 1980 and offers textile artists, decorators, designers, and home sewers something special—over 200 weights, weaves, and widths of silk. The enormous inventory includes silk shantung, pongee, taffeta, tussah, crepe de chine, brocade, twill, habotai, peau de soie, lamé, and suiting. Most of the fabrics are 100% silk, and the price list includes a guide that recommends appropriate fabrics for specific purposes. Unprinted scarves and ties, silk thread, floss, yarns, and fine brushes and dyes for hand-painting are also stocked.

Canadian readers, please note: Utex's Canadian address is 111 Peter St., Suite 212, Toronto, Ontario, M5V 2H1; the phone number is 416–596–7565.

Special Factors: Volume discounts are available; C.O.D. orders are accepted.

WEBS

DEPT. WBMC
P.O. BOX 147
NORTHAMPTON, MA
  01061–0147
413–584–2225
FAX: 413–584–1603

Price Lists and Samples: $2 (see text)
Pay: check, MO, MC, V, Discover
Sells: yarns and spinning and weaving equipment and books
Store: Service Center Rd. (half a mile off I–91), Northampton, MA; Monday to Saturday 10–5:30
E-mail: webs@yarn.com
Online: http://wwww.yarn.com

Knitters and weavers of all types—production, hand, and machine—will find inspiration in the yarns from Webs, which has been selling natural-fiber yarn for up to 80% below the original prices since 1974. Webs' mailings offer conventional and novelty yarns of cotton, wool, linen, silk, rayon, and blends, sold in bags, coned, wound off, sometimes in balls, and in packs. (The packs come in assortments of 25, 50, and 100 pounds, at outstandingly low prices.)

Each set of samples is folded into a descriptive price sheet, which notes special considerations concerning supply, suitability for knitting or weaving, gauge, length per unit (e.g., yards per ball, cone, or pound), and prices and minimums. There are usually great buys, like mohair in choice colors, ribbon yarn in several hues, fine-quality cotton yarns in different weights and fashion colors, and novelty yarns. The stock features Webs' own private label yarns, including mohair, rayon chenille, cottons, wools, silks, and linens, in solid and variegated colors, as well as mill-ends, discontinued lines, and yarn overstock from such names as Berroco, Brunswick, Classic Elite, Knitting Fever, Phildar, Plymouth, and Reynolds. Savings can be boosted with an extra 20% discount if your yarn order totals $60 or more, or 25% on orders over $120. (Take note of the exceptions, marked "no further discount" or "NFD" in the price sheets.) Looms, spinning wheels, and drum carders are available at nondiscounted prices, although shipping is free on these items (which can be worth $25 to even $100, depending on where you live and the weight of the article).

Please note: State your craft—hand knitter, machine knitter, or weaver—when sending $2 for the price list and samples.

Special Factors: Shipping is not charged on looms, spinning wheels, or drum carders; quantity discounts are available; authorized returns are accepted within 30 days (a 15% restocking fee may be charged); minimum order is $20 with credit cards.

SEE ALSO

Campmor • *tent zippers, Eureka yard goods, grommet kits, etc.* • **SPORTS**
Gohn Bros. Mfg. Co. • *sewing and quilting notions and supplies* • **CLOTHING**
Gramma's Graphics, Inc. • *cloth-imaging supplies and materials* • **CRAFTS**
Hancock's of Paducah • *quilters' fabrics, sampling club, notions, materials, etc.* • **HOME: DECOR**
Homespun Fabrics & Draperies • *ultra-wide cotton homespun, curtain sheers, and tow cloth* • **HOME: DECOR**
Manny's Millinery Supply Center • *millinery supplies, bridal supplies, etc.* • **CLOTHING**
Purchase for Less • *quilting and sewing books* • **BOOKS**
Sew Vac City • *sewing machines and sergers* • **APPLIANCES**
Sewin' in Vermont • *sewing machines and accessories* • **APPLIANCES**
Sewing Machine Super Store® • *sewing machines, sergers, sewing equipment, instructional workbooks, dressmaker forms, weaving equipment, etc.* • **APPLIANCES**
Shama Imports, Inc. • *crewel-embroidered fabric* • **HOME: DECOR**
Suburban Sew 'N Sweep, Inc. • *sewing machines and sergers* • **APPLIANCES**

Woodcraft

Wood, tools, parts, plans, etc.
for woodworking

The ancient pleasures of working with wood—whittling, woodburning, marquetry, toy making, carving—all are honored by the firms listed here. If you enjoy making whirligigs or yard ornaments, duck decoys, wooden toy trains, or just refinishing furniture, you'll find the plans, patterns, reference works, toy parts, tools, hardware, stains, and finishes you need, at good to great prices. Related products, such as lamp parts, seat materials, clockworks, drawer organizers, and music boxes, are sold by some of the firms. For listings of other companies that sell woodworking supplies and materials, see the listings in the main section of "Crafts" and "Tools."

CHERRY TREE TOYS, INC.

408 S. JEFFERSON ST.
P.O. BOX 369
BELMONT, OH 43718
614–484–4363
FAX: 614–484–4388

Catalog: $1
Pay: check, MO, MC, V, Discover
Sells: woodworking and crafts supplies
Store: I–70, Exit 208, Belmont, OH; Monday to Saturday 9–5, Sunday 11–5

Cherry Tree Toys sells kits for delightful playthings, clocks, and door harps, as well as scores of wooden parts for your own designs. The company was founded in 1981 and prices its goods up to 50% below what toy and gift shops charge for similar items. The 68-page color catalog shows kits for dozens of whirligigs, musical banks, decorative clocks (depicting motifs ranging from trains to football helmets), door harps, wooden wagons and sleds, pull toys, miniatures, dollhouses, and "Wild West" wagons. Clock movements and markers, music boxes, and hundreds of wooden parts—wheels, spindles, smokestacks, beads, knobs, pulls, pegs, etc.—are offered as well. Cherry Tree sells plans, kits, and books on making toys, banks, dollhouses, whirligigs, clocks, and door harps, in addition to the supplies you'll need to finish the projects. See the collection of brass stencils in a range of holiday motifs, and the blank stencil sheets, Dover cut-and-use stencil sets, rubber stamps, paintbrushes and tole paint, and sets of gift tags, cards, and envelopes. If you're able, visit the factory outlet store in Belmont, where you'll find discontinued catalog items and seconds.

Special Factors: Satisfaction is guaranteed; returns are accepted within 30 days for exchange, refund, or credit; C.O.D. orders are accepted ($4.50 surcharge).

MEISEL HARDWARE SPECIALTIES

━━━━━━━━━━

P.O. BOX 70-MW

MOUND, MN 55364–0070

800–441–9870

FAX: 612–471–8579

Catalog: $2
Pay: check, MO, MC, V, Discover
Sells: hardware, woodcrafts parts and plans
Store: 4310 Shoreline Dr., Spring Park, MN; Monday to Friday 9–6, Saturday 9–3

Woodworkers, toy makers, and creative souls should appreciate Meisel's 84-page color catalog of plans and project ingredients. Meisel has been in business since 1977, and prices routine items like lamp harps, wood screws, and foam brushes up to 40% below the going rate.

The catalog features woodworking plans for over 1,100 projects, including indoor and outdoor furniture, yard ornaments, silhouettes, toys, lamps, whirligigs, birdhouses, useful things for the home, kitchen projects, and dollhouses. In addition to project plans for woodworking, there are parts and supplies for many projects, including 13 sizes of wooden wheels, Shaker pegs, dowels, plastic eyes, turned spindles, finials, wood furniture knobs, cork sheets, clock movements and parts, music boxes, and picture-hanging hardware. Meisel also sells brass hardware, sandpaper, glues, stains, acrylic paints, and other finishing touches. The catalog is a good source for fix-up materials as well—screw-hole buttons and furniture knobs, magnetic cabinet catches, and furniture glides are all available.

Special Factors: Satisfaction is guaranteed; minimum order is $15 with credit cards; returns are accepted for exchange, refund, or credit.

TURNCRAFT CLOCKS, INC.

P.O. BOX 100—WBM
MOUND, MN 55364–0100
800–544–1711
FAX: 612–471–8579

Catalog: $2
Pay: check, MO, MC, V, Discover
Sells: clock plans and movements
Store: 4310 Shoreline Dr., Spring Park, MN;
Monday to Friday 8–5

Clock makers and woodworkers will enjoy Turncraft's full-color, 32-page catalog of clock plans, movements, and hardware components. Turncraft is celebrating nearly a quarter of a century of supplying home hobbyists with materials at savings of up to 30%.

You'll find over 150 clock projects in the catalog, as well as clock dials, time rings, bezels, mini-quartz movements, pendulum movements, chime and strike movements, clock hands, knobs and hinges, hangers, latches, brass decorations, weight shells, and quartz fit-ups. Paint and stains, glue, drill bits, plywood, walnut letters, numbers, and symbols are offered, making this a good source for both clock makers and woodworkers.

Special Factors: Satisfaction is guaranteed; minimum order is $15 with credit cards.

VAN DYKE SUPPLY COMPANY

Catalog: $1
Pay: check, MO, MC, V
Sells: restoration supplies and tools
Store: mail order only

DEPT. 80027
P.O. BOX 278
WOONSOCKET, SD 57385
605–796–4425
FAX: 605–796–4085

The "Restorers" catalog from Van Dyke's is 272 pages packed with the odd and innumerable things that a furniture doctor might need: moldings, veneering tools and adhesives, fiber and leather replacement seats, upholstery tools, a huge range of decorative wooden carvings and handles, and brass house and furniture hardware. Here are isinglass sheets (mica) for the woodstove door window, bentwood chair components, an extensive selection of replacement chair and table legs, and carousel horse eyes. Van Dyke's also sells Aladdin oil lamps and a wide selection of other lamps, bases, shades, and other components.

Van Dyke's offers discounts of 2% on prepaid orders of $25 or more, to 10% on orders over $1,000, and bulk pricing beyond that. But even without those discounts, the prices here are lower than those found in hardware stores and crafts shops for several of the same products, and the selection is unbeatable.

Special Factors: Satisfaction is guaranteed; returns of salable goods are accepted within 30 days.

THE WINFIELD COLLECTION

Catalog: $2
Pay: check, MO, MC, V, Discover
Sells: full-size woodcraft patterns and supplies
Store: same address; Monday to Friday 8–6, Saturday 9–3

112 E. ELLEN ST.
FENTON, MI 48430–2197
800–946–3435
FAX: 810–629–7784

The Winfield Collection is home to hundreds of full-size plans for a range of woodcraft projects: yard signs and "swingers," yard "shadows"

(silhouettes), animal figures, bird houses and feeders, whirligigs, mail-boxes, door toppers, mantelpiece decorations, and even simple furniture scaled for dolls and children, including a cradle. Every 64-page color catalog features a seasonal theme—Easter, St. Patrick's Day, Valentine's Day, patriotic motifs, Halloween, Thanksgiving, and Christmas are strong—and there are always lots of plans with cute animals and country motifs. The Winfield Collection also sells the supplies for the job, including Olson scroll saw blades, hinges and other hardware, transfer and graphite paper, glue and sealers, and Delta acrylic craft paint and paintbrushes. Wooden parts, including balls, eggs, wheels, hearts, candle cups, finials, knobs, Shaker pegs, and buttons, are also shown. And help is available from the how-to books, which cover everything from scroll saw basics to painting techniques.

The plans are well priced, and you can save up to 50% more with selections from the sale pages, and with Winfield's collections. If you're a true woodcraft enthusiast, consider joining the Winfield Pattern Club. Every three months, you'll receive a set of 100 new patterns, on approval. They're yours to keep for about $12 at this writing, plus shipping (about $14 in Canada).

Readers outside the U.S., please note: All orders must be paid in U.S. funds.

Special Factors: Satisfaction is guaranteed; unused returns are accepted within 30 days for exchange, refund, or credit; minimum phone or fax order is $25.

WOODWORKER'S SUPPLY, INC.

5604 ALAMEDA PL. NE
ALBUQUERQUE, NM
  87113
505–821–0500
FAX: 505–821–7331

Catalog: $2
Pay: check, MO, MC, V, Discover
Sells: woodworking tools and equipment
Store: same address; Monday to Friday 8–5:30, Saturday 9–1; also 1125 Jay Ln., Graham, NC; and 1108 N. Glenn Rd., Casper, WY

Woodworker's Supply publishes a 156-page, color catalog of woodworking tools and hardware, priced up to 30% below comparable goods sold elsewhere. The company has been in business since 1972, selling basics—from abrasives to rolling table shapers—as well as a number of hard-to-find items. Typical offerings include drills (including cordless models), power screwdrivers, routers, saws (circular, jig, orbital, table, band, etc.), sanders (finish, belt, orbital, etc.), laminate trimmers, heat guns, biscuit joiners, power planes, grinders, jointers, drill presses, shapers, and other tools. The manufacturers represented include Bosch, Delta, Freud, Gerstner, Glit, Jorgensen, Porter-Cable, Ryobi, Sioux, Skil, and Woodtek, among others. Drawer slides by Alfit, Delta, and Knape & Vogt are carried, as well as Hettich hinges, coated-wire fixtures for custom kitchen cabinets, furniture and cabinet levelers, cassette storage tracks, halogen canister lights, wood project parts, veneers, butcher block, locks and latches, glue scrapers and injectors, steel wool-backed sheets for finish sanders, Preserve nontoxic wood finish, and Haas knock-down joint fasteners. The line of wood-finishing supplies includes restoration products and finishes by Behlen, Franklin, Moser's, Old Village, Watco, and other firms. Like the best of such catalogs, Woodworker's Supply can give you as many ideas for new projects as it provides solutions to old woodworking problems.

Special Factors: Satisfaction is guaranteed; returns are accepted; minimum order is $5 ($25 to Canada).

SEE ALSO

Metropolitan Music Co. • *violin wood, stain, varnish, tools, etc.* • **MUSIC**
Woodworkers' Discount Books • *books and videos on woodworking and related topics* • **BOOKS**
Woodworker's Hardware • *cabinetry hardware, knobs, etc.* • **TOOLS**

FARM AND GARDEN

Seeds, bulbs, live plants, supplies, tools, and equipment

The earliest mail-order catalog in this country is believed to have been a seed list, and if you're one of the nearly 70 million Americans who gardens, you probably use catalogs extensively to plan your garden. So you know that the mails (or UPS truck) can bring you a fantastic selection of bulbs, plants, flowers, herbs, and other growing things, as well as tools and equipment—often at considerable savings, compared to farm and garden centers. Choosing what to grow depends on what you want—an apple orchard, a little alyssum edging the walkways, a crop of asparagus, a windbreak at the property line—all require completely different kinds of resources. And they yield different benefits, from aesthetic (flowers) to nutritional (vegetables) to financial (market crops, property enhancement, etc.). Before you buy a single seed, make sure what you're planting is suitable for your climate or home environment. In addition to evaluating the light and drainage, test the soil. One of the best-known names in soil tests is LaMotte, which has been manufacturing soil test kits, reagents, and apparatus for analyzing water and air, as well as soil, for over 65 years. The best home gardener kit costs about $35, and a simplified version that tests just pH levels is available for about $10. The "LaMotte Soil Handbook" that comes with the kit includes a definition of soil nutrients and a "pH preference guide" for over 600 plants, shrubs, and trees. LaMotte's kits can be found in many garden-supply catalogs.

After you decide what you're going to do with your land or growing space, hit the books—horticultural literature is rich with masterworks on every aspect of the "whats" to grow and the "hows" of doing it. Hugh Johnson's *The Principles of Gardening* (Simon & Schuster, 1979), answers the "whys," giving you a grounding in the concepts and history that inform good garden planning. A bookshelf of the classics must also include Norman Taylor's *The Garden Dictionary* (updated as *The Encyclopedia of Gardening,* multi-volume) and *Taylor's Master Guide to Gardening* (Houghton Mifflin, 1994), all highly regarded references. *America's Garden Book* (New York Botanical Garden, Scribner's) and Rodale's *The Encyclopedia of Organic Gardening* are others prized for information and inspiration.

The business of preserving old plant varieties is the focus of *The Heirloom Gardener* (Sierra Club Books, 1984), by Carolyn Jabs. This wonderful guide to "living heirlooms"—endangered, rare, and nearly extinct fruit and vegetable varieties—includes a brief history of the business of seeds, information on "seed savers" and seed exchanges, finding lost varieties, capsule histories of some select heirloom varieties, seed research resources, tips on harvesting seeds, and other useful information. For information on this book and other titles, request the publications list from Sierra Club Mail-Order Service, 730 Polk St., San Francisco, CA 94109.

Kent Whealy's *Garden Seed Inventory* is something of a bible for vegetable seed savers. This book lists varieties alphabetically, describes each (height, appearance, variations, days to maturity), indicates which seed companies offer it, and also shows *how many* firms have offered that variety over the past few years—usually a declining number. The mandate is clear to seed savers: Buy, cultivate, and save those varieties! For price and ordering information on the current edition of the *Garden Seed Inventory,* send a request for the publication list with a long, self-addressed, stamped envelope to Seed Savers Exchange, RR 3, Box 239, Decorah, IA 52101.

If you need farm machinery, see the listing of Central Michigan Tractor & Parts in "Auto." In addition to the Department of Agriculture publications, university cooperative extensions also disseminate technical information of use to farmers and production growers. Among those in the "Small Farms Series," published by the Northeast Regional Agricultural Engineering Service, the 34-page *Used Farm Equipment: Assessing Quality, Safety, and Economics* is a clear and well-illustrated overview of points to consider before making such a purchase. Write to Northeast Regional Agricultural Engineering Service, Cornell University, 152 Riley-Robb Hall, Ithaca, NY 14853 for a list of current publications and prices.

The U.S. government operates an information clearinghouse staffed by agricultural pros who can advise you on technical matters, including how to go organic ("sustainable agriculture" is part of the agency's mandate). Please try other sources, including your local extension agent, before calling; if you can't get help or adequate information, call ATTRA

(Appropriate Technology Transfer for Rural Areas), at 800–346–9140, Monday to Friday, 8:30–4:30 CST.

In addition to the books mentioned here, don't overlook the helpful consumer guides and how-to manuals published by HP Books, Ortho, and Sunset. If you're building your own greenhouse or cold frames, see Arctic Glass & Window Outlet ("Home: Improvement") for thermopane panels. Other garden-related products are sold by some of the companies listed in "Tools." And see the companies listed in the "Find It Fast" section of the "Home: Furnishings" chapter for lawn and patio furniture.

FIND IT FAST

BULBS, SEEDS, PLANTS • **Breck's, Burrells, Butterbrooke, Caprilands, Carino, Dutch Gardens, Fedco, Gurney's, Johnnys, Le Jardin, Mellinger's, J.E. Miller, Pinetree Garden, Rohrers, Scheepers, Seymour's, Sharp Bros., R.H. Shumway, Twilley, Van Bourgondien, Van Dyck's, Van Engelen**
DAYLILIES • **Daylily Discounters**
GREENHOUSES AND SUPPLIES • **Bob's Superstrong, Mellinger's, Turner**
GROUND COVER • **Gurney's, Prentiss Court**
PLANT MARKERS • **EON Industries**
ROSES • **Gurney's, Jackson & Perkins, Nor'East**
STRAWBERRIES • **Brittingham**

BOB'S SUPERSTRONG GREENHOUSE PLASTIC

BOX 42-WM
NECHE, ND 58265
204–327–5540

Brochure: $1 or two first-class stamps
Pay: check or MO
Sells: greenhouse plastic and fastening systems, and pond liners
Store: same address; by appointment

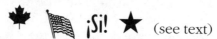 ¡Si! ★ (see text)

Bob Davis and his wife, Margaret Smith-Davis, are resourceful gardeners who experimented with different materials while trying to create an inexpensive greenhouse and discovered that woven polyethylene makes an ideal greenhouse skin, even in harsh climes. Their experiences with the material were so successful that they decided to market it themselves. In 1979, they founded Bob's Superstrong Greenhouse Plastic (also known as Northern Greenhouse Sales), which has become a great source for other resourceful gardeners who want to design their own greenhouses. The Davises offer "superstrong" woven poly and two anchoring systems. One is "Cinchstrap," a bright-white, flat, flexible poly strapping material that can be used for permanent anchoring, abrasion reduction in installation, and as a replacement for wood lathing in greenhouse assembly. The other, "Poly-Fastener," is a channel-system anchor that uses a flat spline to secure the poly. Prices for the woven poly run from 16¢ to 25¢ per square foot, depending on the quantity ordered; the standard width is 10 feet, but Bob can heat-seal additional widths together to create a wider swath. The Poly-Fastener runs between 53¢ and 58¢ a linear foot in 300' and 100' rolls (or $1 per foot for cut pieces), and the Cinchstrap costs 11¢ a linear foot on 100' rolls.

The 32-page catalog also includes several pages devoted to money-saving ideas and problem-solving tips from other customers. The poly applications aren't limited to greenhouses: solar collectors, vapor barriers, storm windows, pool covers, and tent floors are other possibilities. The current issue of the catalog announces the debut of a collective newsletter, "Greenhouse Buddies," which is actively soliciting input from serious greenhouse gardeners. For more information and a copy of the catalog, send $1 or two first-class stamps. Call if you have questions, but please note the phone hours, below.

Canadian readers, please note: Write to Box 1450WM, Altona, Manitoba R0G 0B0, for literature.

Special Factors: Calls are taken daily between 6 a.m. and 8 p.m., CST; minimum order is $1; C.O.D. orders are accepted.

BRECK'S DUTCH BULBS

▬▬▬▬▬▬▬

DEPT. CA9524A6

U.S. RESERVATION
   CENTER

6523 N. GALENA RD.

PEORIA, IL 61632

309–691–4616

FAX: 309–691–2632

Catalog: free
Pay: check, MO, MC, V, AE, Discover
Sells: Dutch flower bulbs
Store: mail order only

Breck's has been "serving American gardeners since 1818" with a fine selection of flower bulbs, imported directly from Holland. The 52-page catalog is bursting with tulips, crocuses, daffodils, hyacinths, irises, jonquils, anemones, and wind flowers. Blooming period, height, color and markings, petal formation, and scent are all described in the text. Each order is shipped with the Breck's "Dutch Bulb Handbook," which covers naturalizing, planting, indoor growing, bulb care, and related topics. Discounts of up to 50% are offered on orders placed by July 31 for fall delivery and planting, and there are special savings on "samplers" and bulb collections.

Special Factors: Satisfaction is guaranteed; early-order discounts are available; returns are accepted for exchange, replacement, or refund.

BRITTINGHAM PLANT FARMS, INC.

DEPT. WBM8
P.O. BOX 2538
SALISBURY, MD 21802
410–749–5153
FAX: 800–749–5148

Catalog: free
Pay: check, MO, MC, V
Sells: berry plants
Store: Rte. 346 and Phillip Morris Dr., Salisbury, MD; Monday to Friday 8–4:30, Saturday 8:30–12

Brittingham, a family business established in 1945, specializes in berries. The firm's 32-page color catalog is packed with cultivation tips and handling guidelines, and details on Brittingham's participation in Maryland's strawberry certification program. (The strict standards assure you virus-free strawberry plants.) Strawberries dominate the offerings, with over two dozen varieties in the current catalog, for early through late yields. Prices begin at $10 for 25 plants, and top at $81 per thousand for 25,000 plants (you may mix up to four varieties; new and patented varieties cost more). In addition to strawberries, Brittingham sells blackberries, raspberries, grapes, blueberries, asparagus, and rhubarb; quantity pricing also applies to these offerings.

Please note: Plants are not shipped to AK, CA, HI, NM, Canada, Mexico, or outside the continental United States.

Special Factors: Satisfaction is guaranteed; replacements, refunds, or credits are offered within a specified date (see catalog); minimum orders vary, depending on the item; C.O.D. orders are accepted.

D.V. BURRELL SEED GROWERS CO.

**P.O. BOX 150—WBMC
ROCKY FORD, CO 81067
719–254–3318
FAX: 719–254–3319**

Catalog: free
Pay: check, MO, MC, V
Sells: flower and vegetable seed, growing supplies
Store: 405 North Main, Rocky Ford, CO; Monday to Friday 8–5

The home gardener who muses on the possibilities of turning a hobby into an income-producer should know about D.V. Burrell Seed Growers Co., which has been serving commercial growers and florists since 1900. Burrell also offers the home gardener modestly priced seed packets, but the professional grower will appreciate the quarter and half ounces and pounds—with price breaks at 1, 5, 25, 50, and 100 pounds. (You can combine orders with friends and neighbors to consolidate shipping costs on the larger sizes.)

Burrell's understands its mission: "No seedsman can hope to survive the critical judgment of the trade unless his product consistently delivers satisfaction." The varieties are chosen for a combination of marketability (appearance, disease resistance, longevity, and durability), and sensory pleasure. Burrell's treats some of its seeds, but you can request untreated. The catalog include cultivation tips and typical yields for hundreds of varieties of vegetables and melons, from Mary Washington asparagus to Crimson Sweet watermelon. A few herbs—basil, chives, sweet marjoram, sage, etc.—are offered, as well as nearly 20 pages of flowers, including alyssum, asters, candytuft, digitalis, the "world's finest hybrid" petunias, sweet William, viola Johnny jump-up, wildflower seed blends (in dry and moist mixtures for different climates and soil types), and zinnias. Burrell's also sells a mechanical seeder, heater cables for out-of-season cultivation, weeders, sprayers, insecticides, peat pellet starter pots, 42" greenhouse "umbrellas" for under $17 each, and other cultivation tools, and several books helpful to the small commercial grower.

Customers outside the United States, please note: Catalogs cost $5 (in U.S. funds) and orders must be paid by postal money order or checks (drawn on U.S. banks) in U.S. currency.

Special Factors: Shipping is included on certain items; quantity discounts are available; institutional accounts are available; minimum order is $7.50, handling is $1 per order.

BUTTERBROOKE FARM SEED CO-OP

78 BARRY RD.
OXFORD, CT 06478–1529
203–888–2000

Price List: free with long, self-addressed, stamped envelope
Pay: check or MO
Sells: seeds
Store: mail order only

"Only pure, open-pollinated seeds will produce plants from which you can save seeds for planting another year." So says the straightforward price list from Butterbrooke Farm Seed Co-Op, where becoming "seed self-reliant" is one of several gardening objectives. Butterbrooke's members include organic farmers and seed savers, and the co-op has been in business since 1978. For just $15 per year, co-op members receive a 33% seed order discount, the quarterly Farm newsletter, *Germinations,* advisory services, the opportunity to buy rare or heirloom seeds, and other benefits. This is no-frills gardening at its sensible best, from the selection of scores of seeds (a well-rounded kitchen-garden full) to the Farm's own "Home Garden Collection" for first-time planters—a group of vegetable favorites. The packets are measured to reduce waste: the standard size (65¢) will plant one to two 20-foot rows, and the large size ($1.50), three to four times that. All of the seeds are fresh, and they've been selected for short growing seasons. Butterbrooke also offers booklets on related topics—mulching, making compost, saving seeds—at nominal sums. You don't have to be a co-op member to buy from Butterbrooke, but the price of membership is low and the advice service alone should justify the expense.

Special Factors: C.O.D. orders are accepted.

CAPRILANDS HERB FARM

534 SILVER ST.
COVENTRY, CT 06238
860–742–7244

Brochure: free
Pay: check, MO, MC, V, NOVUS
Sells: live herbs and gifts
Store: same address; daily 9–5 except holidays

Caprilands offers live and dried culinary and medicinal herbs and a potpourri of herbaceous gifts, seasonings, and rite materials. The Farm is run by Mrs. Simmons, a herbalist of 60 years' standing, who provides a legendary luncheon program for visitors to her 18th-century farmhouse. (Reservations are essential; details on the program are given in the brochure.) In the years since its founding in 1929, Caprilands has become a respected source among collectors of hard-to-find herbs and those who dabble in "natural magic." Over 300 kinds of standard culinary herbs and less common plants are available, including Egyptian onions, rue, wormwood, mugwort, monardas, artemisia, santolinas, germander, lamb's ears, nepetas, ajuga, chamomile, woodruff, and many varieties of thyme ($2 to $3 per plant). Scented geraniums, roses, and flowers are also offered. (The plants are available at the Farm only, not by mail.) Packets of seeds for herbs and herbal flowers are available by mail for $1.25 each. Mrs. Simmons' own guides to the cultivation and use of herbs, including one of the bibles of herbal horticulture—*Herb Gardening in Five Seasons*—are sold through the brochure.

Caprilands offers a marvelous array of related goods: bronze sundials, wooden "good luck crows" for the garden, kitchen witches and costumed collectors' dolls, pomanders and sachet pillows, spice necklaces, wreaths, herbal hot pads, stoneware, note paper and calendars, and much more. Amid this olfactory plenty are two other great buys—rose petals and buds and lavender flowers for $12 per pound, compared to $15 and $22 in other catalogs; essential oils are also sold.

Wholesale customers, books *alone* are sold at wholesale, with a minimum order of 6 or 12 of the same title, discounted 10% to 40%.

Special Factors: Certain goods listed in the catalog are available only at the Farm.

CARINO NURSERIES

DEPT. WBMC
P.O. BOX 538
INDIANA, PA 15701
800–223–7075
412–463–3350
FAX: 412–463–3050

Catalog: free
Pay: check, MO, MC, V, Discover
Sells: evergreen seedlings and transplants
Store: mail order and nursery pickup only

Carino Nurseries has been supplying Christmas tree farmers, nursery owners, and other planters with evergreen seedlings since 1945, and its prices and selection are excellent—savings of 60% are routine. The 36-

page color catalog lists varieties of pine (Scotch, white, Mugho, Ponderosa, Japanese black, American red, and Austrian), fir (Douglas, Balsam, Canaan, Fraser, and Concolor), spruce (Colorado blue, white, Englemann, Black Hills, Norwegian, and Serbian), and white birch, dogwood, olive, black walnut, Chinese chestnut, Canadian hemlock, arborvitae, and other deciduous shrubs and trees.

Each entry in the 32-page color catalog includes a description of the variety, age, and approximate height of the plants, and the number of years spent in original and transplant beds. There are specials on 10-plant collections, but most of the seedlings are sold in lots of 100 at prices up to 65% below those of other nurseries. If you're buying 500 or more, Carino's prices drop 50%. Recommendations on selecting, planting, and shearing (for later harvest as Christmas trees) are given, and the shipping methods and schedule policies are detailed in the catalog as well.

Special Factors: Shipments are made by UPS; minimum order is 10 or 100 plants (see text).

DAYLILY DISCOUNTERS INTERNATIONAL

Catalog: $2
Pay: check, MO, MC, V, AE, Discover
Sells: daylilies
Store: mail order only

RTE. 2, BOX 24
ALACHUA, FL 32615
904–462–1539
FAX: 904–462–5111

If you think that there are three kinds of daylilies—orange, yellow, and pink-and-white—Daylily Discounters will enlighten you. Between the voluminous text and the color photos, the firm's catalog covers 94 pages and includes details on the plant anatomy (including bracts and scopes), cultivation and disposal, and the hundreds of flowers themselves, from Agape Love to Yellow Lollipop. Companion perennials are available, as well as soil enrichers, plant tags, and reference books. If you're not familiar with daylilies, you'll find them quite varied in color, markings, and formation; many bear a resemblance to orchids, but they're much less tricky to cultivate. Daylilies are less expensive, and more modestly priced yet at Daylily Discounters. And once you're on the mailing list, watch for flyers on clearance sales, with further savings of up to 50%.

Non-U.S. readers, please note: Before ordering, obtain import permits (if required), as indicated in the catalog.

Special Factors: Quantity discounts are available; minimum order is $25.

DUTCH GARDENS, INC.

Catalog: free
Pay: check, MO, MC, V, AE
Sells: Dutch flower bulbs and perennials
Store: mail order only

████████████

DEPT. WMC8
P.O. BOX 200
ADELPHIA, NJ 07710
800–818–3861
FAX: 908–780–7720

Dutch Gardens publishes one of the most beautiful bulb catalogs around—over 200 varieties shown in breathtaking flower "head shots" that approximate perfection. Dutch Gardens has been in business since 1961, and its prices on flower bulbs are solidly below other mail-order firms and garden supply houses—30% less on average, and up to 50% on some bulbs and collections.

The fall planting catalog offers tulip, hyacinth, daffodil, narcissus, crocus, anemone, iris, snowdrop, allium, amaryllis, and other flower bulbs. The tulip selection alone includes single, double, fringed, parrot, lily, and peony types. The spring planting catalog showcases a dazzling array of lilies, begonias, dahlias, gladioli, peonies, tuberoses, anemones, freesia, hostas, and other flowers; and onions and shallots (for planting) are also available. Each Dutch Gardens catalog lists the size of the bulbs and the common and botanical names, height, planting zones, blooming period, and appropriate growing situations of each variety. A zone chart, guide to planting depth and bulb grouping, sun requirements, hints on naturalizing, rock gardening, terrace planting, indoor growing, and forcing are included.

Special Factors: Bulbs are guaranteed to bloom (conditions are stated in the catalog); bulb bonuses are available on quantity orders.

EON INDUSTRIES

DEPT. WBM
107 W. MAPLE
P.O. BOX 11
LIBERTY CENTER, OH
  43532
419–533–4961

Brochure: free
Pay: check or MO
Sells: plant markers
Store: mail order only

EON Industries specializes in a useful garden item: metal plant markers. EON has been manufacturing markers since 1936, and currently offers four styles in several sizes, at prices that begin at under $20 (plus shipping) for 100 10" Rose markers and run up to $29 per hundred (plus shipping) for the 20" Nursery style. There are two styles of Mini Marker for about $15 and $16 per hundred—these are ideal for miniature roses, rock gardens, or wherever an understated marker is appropriate. (Volume pricing is available on large orders—inquire.) The markers create the impression of serious horticultural doings when staked among even common specimens, which is why upmarket garden catalogs carry them—at nearly twice the price!

Wholesale buyers, please send your inquiry on wholesale pricing on company letterhead, or fax to 419–533–6015.

Special Factors: Satisfaction is guaranteed; minimum order is 25 markers at retail, 100 markers at wholesale.

FEDCO SEEDS INC.

P.O. BOX 520-WBM
WATERVILLE, ME
  04903–0520
207–873–7333

Catalog: $1 (see text)
Pay: check or MO
Sells: seeds, trees, seed-starting and cultivation tools, etc.
Store: warehouse open in season

At first glance, Fedco's charming lists of bulbs and trees and the tabloid seed and supply catalogs, illustrated with engravings of fruits and vegetables and densely printed descriptions, give one the impression that this is an old family firm. The perception is only furthered by the modest prices, which are 20% to 70% below those charged by the competition. Fedco was actually founded in 1978, beginning as a seed cooperative, adding trees and bulbs in 1984, seed potatoes the next year, and taking over a project begun by the Maine Organic Farmers and Gardeners Association in 1988. Fedco runs as a cooperative, sharing profits with employees *and* customers—in markups forgone. The catalog includes every conceivable detail—the names of each department head, order deadlines, shipment schedules, a volume discount schedule, back-order policy, a précis on the origins of seeds, a description of the process of developing varieties, and even a list of *other* seed suppliers!

And then there are the seeds themselves, from over 30 kinds of beans and other vegetables, greens, and roots and tubers to a nice group of culinary and medicinal herbs, to annuals, perennials, ornamental grasses, and gourds. The "big" catalog also features a bookshelf with a worthy collection of titles that run from natural lawn care to farming philosophy. There are trees listed in the separate catalog of that name, chiefly hardy varieties of fruit and nut trees, small fruits and berries, and things like rhubarb, asparagus, and cranberries. If you're looking for conifers, dogwood, ginkgos, burning bush, lilac, roses, or honeysuckle, there's all here. Books and tools—including Felco pruners and tree saws—are also sold, and the catalog is annotated with a roster or recommended horticultural organizations, and a bibliography. If bulb planting is on your list, see the fall bulb list, or the "Trees" catalog for the spring list—vernal classics like irises, daffodils, tulips, et al.—and shallots, lilies, summer bulbs, forcing varieties, and pips or live plant slips and hardy perennials.

Last, the general catalog offers over three dozen varieties of seed potatoes, listed with the name, skin and flesh color, shape, and scab resistance. Seed for soil-*building* grasses and legumes—buckwheat, sorghum, soybeans, Japanese millet, and others—is also available. The remainder features tools, seed-starting supplies, mulches, garden-care supplies, soil amendments, fertilizers, pest control (including a bat-attracting house), and more books. You get a year of mailings for the $1 fee, which is usually $2, so be sure to mention WBMC when you order.

The warehouse is open for pickups on certain days in spring; see the catalog for details.

Wholesale and quantity buyers, please contact Fedco directly for pricing and terms.

Canadian readers, please note: Only seeds are shipped outside the United States (no live plants), and payment is required in U.S. dollars.

Special Factors: Satisfaction is guaranteed; handling is included on orders over $50; quantity discounts are available.

GURNEY'S SEED & NURSERY CO.

110 CAPITAL ST.
YANKTON, SD 57079
605–665–1671
FAX: 605–665–9718

Catalog: free
Pay: check, MO, MC, V, Discover
Sells:general garden and nursery stock, gardening toos and supplies, etc.
Store: same address; Monday to Friday 8–5:30, Saturday 8–5 (extended hours March 15 to June 15)

The oversized, 64-page color catalog from Gurney's is a welcome arrival in the dead of winter, with its promise of great spring planting at great prices. The catalog shows annuals and perennials, roses, vegetables, berries, fruit and nut trees, landscape trees, shrubbery, ground cover, grasses, and even houseplants. You'll also find all the equipment and supplies you'll need, from "seed-starting helpers" to pest control to the kitchen equipment you'll need to make the most of your edible harvest—dehydrators, steamers, canning tools, etc. Quantity pricing is offered on *everything,* and the catalog is peppered with special offers that translate into real bargains. Gurney's also provides a great deal of gardening information, including "How to Choose" sidebars, a zone chart, a vegetable seed-planting chart, a key to tree shapes and mature heights, and a guide to planting windbreaks and shrubs. If you're new to gardening and easily overwhelmed, this catalog can give you a manageable amount of information and help you get started at a very reasonable cost.

Special Factors: Satisfaction is guaranteed; returns are accepted for exchange, refund, or credit; seeds, plants, and nursery stock are guaranteed 1 year from shipping date.

JACKSON & PERKINS

I ROSE LANE, DEPT. 83B
MEDFORD, OR 97501
800–854–6200
FAX: 800–242–0329
TDD: 800–348–3222

Catalog: free
Pay: check, MO, MC, V, AE, Discover
Sells: roses, bulbs, perennials, gifts, etc.
Store: mail order only

¡Si! Ⓒ

The subject is roses at Jackson & Perkins, which has been supplying gardeners nationwide since 1872. The horticultural classic absorbs three-fourths of the 60-page catalog—from miniatures and patio roses to classic hybrid teas, floribundas, and grandifloras. Jackson & Perkins is prominent in variety development, and has taken a number of "rose of the year" awards from All-American Rose Selections, an independent organization that ranks entries on how well they grow in diverse settings (they're tested in gardens all over the country).

Unlike many other catalogs, Jackson & Perkins notes the type of fragrance and the bud shapes of the roses, as well as plant height range, blossom size, number of petals, color, variety, patent notes, awards, and other data. In addition to a stunning collection of hybrid tea roses, Jackson & Perkins sells classic and striated floribundas, grandifloras, hedge roses, tree roses, patio roses (2" to 4" tall), and climbers. There are roses selected for their fragrance, exhibition roses, varieties from Germany and Denmark, David Austin's English roses, bush roses, and miniatures. And there are collections of favorites of each type, which are offered at extra savings.

Jackson & Perkins also sells daylilies and hybrid lilies, "garden classics"—hydrangeas, phlox, wisteria, lavender, astilbes, etc.—and begonias, ranunculus, and more. The catalog is peppered throughout with sundials, books, bronze garden plaques, trellises, and cast stone sculptures. And "The Basics," a guide to planting and enjoying your roses, is included with every order. Follow the planting directions, and you should enjoy show-worthy blooms—your gardening success is guaranteed!

Special Factors: Satisfaction is guaranteed; returns are accepted for exchange, refund, or credit.

JOHNNY'S SELECTED SEEDS INC.

RR 1, BOX 2580
ALBION, ME 04910
207–437–4301
207–437–9294
FAX: 800–437–4290
Catalog: free

Pay: check, MO, MC, V, AE, Discover
Sells: seeds, roots, tubers, seed cultivation supplies
Store: Monday to Saturday 8:30–5; phone hours June to Dec.: Monday to Friday 8:30–5; Jan. to May: Monday to Friday 8–7, Saturday 8–5
E-mail: homegarden@johnnyseeds.com
Online: http://www.johnnyseeds.com

 ¡Si!

Johnny's Selected Seeds received a high recommendation from a reader who appreciates the firm's clear catalog, low shipping fees, and the impressive germination rate of the seeds. It was a pleasure to discover that Johnny's packets were priced consistently lower than those from firms selling the same varieties. Johnny's holds an open house each summer at the farm in Albion, Maine, where trials are run and stock is raised. (The store is open year-round, and workshops are held seasonally.)

The 136-page color catalog shows photos of the farm, the staff, and the stock—anticipated yields from the seeds for vegetables, flowers, and culinary and medicinal herb seeds. The descriptions include seed counts on the mini-packets, and you can calculate the counts on larger amount. There are price breaks at fractions of an ounce and pound, and on 1, 5, 25, 50, and 100 pounds (the last for corn). The catalog, half of which is devoted to vegetable seeds, opens with Alpine strawberries and ends with zinnias. Everlastings, vines and trailing flowers, a variety of farm seed (legumes and grasses), seed-starting supplies and equipment, pest control, hand tools, garden carts, watering equipment, food mills and dehydrators, flower-drying materials, and books are also sold, and everything has been chosen to make the most of your time and money. Johnny's, in business since 1971, also offers one of the most generous guarantees of satisfaction in the industry, marking it as a genuinely consumer-friendly company.

Special Factors: Satisfaction is guaranteed; shipping is included on orders over $100 within the 48 contiguous United States; quantity/volume discounts are available; returns are accepted for exchange, refund, or credit.

LE JARDIN DU GOURMET

P.O. BOX 75-WC

ST. JOHNSBURY CENTER,

VT 05863

802–748–1446

FAX: 802–748–9592

Catalog: 50¢

Pay: check, MO, MC, V, AE, DC, Discover

Sells: seeds, plants, and gourmet foods

Store: mail order only

E-mail: flowers.herbs@kingcon.com

Online: http://www.kingcon.com/AGLJDG/

   (see text)

If you like to cook, and if you have even a small patch of land on which you can grow things, you'll appreciate Le Jardin du Gourmet. Founded by a transplanted New York City chef who developed a business from growing his own shallots, Le Jardin is now run by his daughter and her husband. They share an appreciation for fine food—chestnut spread, chutney, fancy mustards, and Pompadour herbal teas are a few of the catalog offerings. The prices of some of these food items are very good, but the firm is listed here for one of the last great mail-order buys—the 25¢ seed packet.

Le Jardin du Gourmet sells seeds for hundreds of herbs, vegetables, peas, beans, and even some flowers: angelica, bok choi, pennyroyal, milk thistle, kohlrabi, dwarf corn, French endive, mache, salsify, German "beer garden" radishes, African pumpkins, Vidalia onions, fava beans, and forget-me-nots are all here. The 16-page catalog has a few line drawings and horticultural tips, as well as a recipe for scotched chestnut-bacon appetizers and a guide to making popcorn-on-the-cob in a microwave oven. If you're a novice gardener, invest a few quarters and test a number of "sample" packs of seeds, or play it safe with the live herbs and perennials also available from Le Jardin. The plants are sold in 2¼" pots, and suggestions for herb use and growth conditions are given in the catalog. Don't overlook the books on herbs and preserving food (canning, pickling, etc.), and good prices on plain and decorated balsam wreaths, roping, and small cut trees at Christmastime.

Canadian readers, please note: Only U.S. funds are accepted, and plants and bulbs are *not* shipped to Canada.

Special Factors: Minimum order is $15 with credit cards.

MELLINGER'S INC.

DEPT. WBMC
WEST SOUTH RANGE RD.
NORTH LIMA, OH
  44452–9731
330–549–9861
FAX: 330–549–3716

Catalog: free
Pay: check, MO, MC, V, Discover
Sells: seeds, bulbs, live plants, and home and garden supplies
Store: same address; Monday to Saturday 8:30–5 (June 16 to April); 8–6 (April to June 15)

Mellinger's publishes "the garden catalog for year-round country living," 104 pages of seeds, bulbs, live plants, reference books, greenhouses, garden supplies, and tools. Mellinger's, in business since 1927, has outstandingly low prices on some items, and nominal savings on others. The offerings include flower seeds and bulbs, potted trees and shrubs, shade tree and evergreen seedlings, herb plants, fruit trees, vegetable seeds and vines, tropical plants, and seeds for rare and unusual plants. Everything you'll need for successful cultivation is available, from seed flats to greenhouses. You'll find insect and animal repellents, plant fertilizers, soil additives, pruning and grafting tools, spades, cultivators, hoes, seeders, watering systems, cold frames, starter pots, planters and flower boxes, and related goods. In addition to chemical fungicides and insecticides, Mellinger's sells ladybugs, praying mantis egg cases, and other "natural" predators and beneficial parasites. Bird feeders and seed are also stocked.

Mellinger's stocks poly-skin greenhouses in small and commercial sizes, polyethylene (by the foot), and ventilation equipment, heaters, and thermostats. Books on topics from plant propagation and insect control to herbs and cooking are also available. The catalog includes a guide to hardiness zones, and a statement of the terms of the warranty covering plant orders.

Special Factors: Plants are warrantied for 13 months (see the catalog for terms); authorized returns are accepted (a 10% restocking fee may be charged); $1 service fee on credit card orders under $10.

J.E. MILLER NURSERIES, INC.

DEPT. WBM 5060 WEST LAKE RD.
CANANDAIGUA, NY 14424
800–836–9630
716–396–2647
FAX: 716–396–2154

Catalog: free
Pay: check, MO, MC, V, AE, Discover
Sells: plants, shrubs, trees, and nursery stock
Store: same address; Monday to Friday 8–4:30 (daily during the spring)
Online: http://www.millernurseries.com

Miller's spring and fall catalogs offer a full range of plants, seeds, bulbs, shrubs, and trees, at savings of up to 50%, compared to prices charged at garden centers. Miller Nurseries has been in business since 1936, and features a fall selection that includes russet apple, golden plum, grapes (including seedless varieties), red raspberry, blueberry, cherry, strawberry, and dozens of other fruit and nut trees, plants, and vines. Shade trees are offered, including poplar, locust, maple, and ash; and there are ornamental grasses and plants for the vegetable garden and some common flower bulbs as well. Garden supplies and equipment, including pruners, animal repellent, soil additives, wheelbarrows, mulch sheeting, etc., are also offered. The 60-page catalog includes horticultural tips, and each order is sent with Miller's 32-page planting guide. This firm has gotten rave reviews from several readers of this book, who've praised Miller's service and prices.

Please note: Orders are shipped to U.S. addresses only (not APO/FPO).

Special Factors: Trees and shrubs are sent as plants, guaranteed to grow; minimum order is $10 with credit cards.

NOR'EAST MINIATURE ROSES, INC.

P.O. BOX 307-WB
ROWLEY, MA 01969
508–948–7964
FAX: 508–948–5487

Catalog: free
Pay: check, MO, MC, V
Sells: miniature roses
Store: 58 Hammond St., Rowley, MA; also
955 West Phillips St., Ontario, CA; Monday
to Friday 8–4, both locations

Nor'East publishes a 32-page catalog of its specialty, miniature roses, which are priced at $5.25 each, compared to over $7 for the same varieties sold elsewhere. (Nor'East doesn't tack on a per-plant handling fee, as do some of its competitors.) Dozens of types of miniature bush roses are available, including micro-minis (4" to 8" tall at maturity), climbers, and tree roses (miniatures budded to understocks). The varieties are grouped by colors, which include reds, pinks, yellows, oranges, apricots, whites, mauves, and blends. Among the fancifully named specimens are old favorites and new entries: Good Morning America, Cupcake, Party Girl, Scentsational, and Ice Queen, to name a few. The catalog descriptions include height of the mature plant, blooming pattern and coloring, scent, suitable growth situations, and other information.

Nor'East offers quantity discounts and specially priced bonuses for large orders. "We pick 'em" collections are also offered—prices drop if you let the firm make the selection. Nor'East offers other collections, including easy-to-cultivate choices, fragrant types, and a beginners' kit that includes pots and potting mix. Planting and care directions are sent with each order. And a selection of small vases, Ortho's *Guide to Enjoying Roses,* and gifts are available.

Special Factors: Returns of plants that fail to perform are accepted within 90 days for replacement.

PINETREE GARDEN SEEDS

P.O. BOX 300
NEW GLOUCESTER, ME
04260
207–926–3400
FAX: 888–52–SEEDS
FAX: 207–926–3886

Catalog: free
Pay: check, MO, MC, V, AE, Discover
Sells: seeds, bulbs, plants, garden equipment, and books
Store: mail order only
E-mail: superseeds@worldnet.att.net
Online: http://www.superseeds.com

Pinetree Garden Seeds was established in 1979 to provide home gardeners with seeds in small packets, suitable for backyard gardens or horticultural experiments. The firm has far exceeded this mandate, with a 152-page catalog packed with well-chosen kitchen gadgets, gardening tools and supplies, books and other useful goods. But Pinetree's strength is the stock that built the business—over 800 varieties of vegetable and flower seeds, just a handful of which are treated. Of special interest are the "vegetable favorites from around the world," including radicchio, fava beans, snow peas, entsai, epazotes, and chiles. You'll also find plants and tubers for shallots, asparagus, berries, and potatoes. The flower section features seeds, tubers, and bulbs for annuals, perennials, everlastings, and wildflowers.

The tools and equipment run from kitchen and canning helps to hand tools. Fertilizers, Havahart traps, netting, and related goods are offered. Over 30 pages of the catalog are devoted to books, including a number of gardening literature classics, cookbooks, garden planners, and many other well-priced titles. Prices are quite competitive, and even the seed packets are backed by Pinetree's ironclad guarantee of satisfaction.

Canadian and non-U.S. readers, please note: The catalog costs U.S. $1.50 if sent to a non-U.S. address.

Special Factors: Satisfaction is guaranteed; returns are accepted for exchange, refund, or credit.

PRENTISS COURT GROUND COVERS

Brochure: $1
Pay: check, MO, MC, V
Sells: live ground-cover plants
Store: mail order only

DEPT. WBM

P.O. BOX 8662

GREENVILLE, SC

29604–8662

864–277–4037

FAX: 864–299–5015

Prentiss Court, in business since 1978, offers a wide range of plants at up to 50% below nursery prices, and gives spacing and planting guides in the brochure. The current crop includes varieties of Cotoneaster, crown vetch, daylilies, Euonymus fortunei, fig vine, Hedera canariensis and helix, honeysuckle, hosta, jasmine, hypericum, Ophiopogon japonicus, Pachysandra terminalis, Parthenocissus, Trumpet creeper, and Vinca major and minor. In English, there are over 70 kinds of plants, including many types of ivy and flowering and berry-bearing ground cover. The plants are sold bare-root and/or potted, at prices that run from 41¢ for "Green Muscari," a liriope, to $5.70 for a large-blossomed hosta; most are under $1.

Ground cover provides an attractive, labor-efficient alternative to a conventional lawn—which may have to be "limed, aerated, re-seeded, fertilized, weed-treated, mowed, and raked," to quote the admittedly partisan but accurate president of Prentiss Court. Ground cover, on the other hand, should be mulched, not fertilized, and it seems to discourage weeds and pests all by itself. Follow the soil and light guidelines when selecting and planting, and you should be able to enjoy lush, low-maintenance grounds *without* chemical intervention.

Special Factors: Minimum order is 50 plants of the same variety.

P.L. ROHRER & BRO., INC.

P.O. BOX 250
SMOKETOWN, PA 17576
717-299-2571
FAX: 717-299-5347

Catalog: free
Pay: check, MO, MC, V, Discover
Sells: flower and vegetable seeds, gardening supplies, lawn seed, forage, crop seed, etc.
Store: 2472 Old Philadelphia Pike, Smoketown, PA; call or see the catalog for directions and hours

Pennsylvania's Lancaster County boasts some of the best farmland in this country. For the past 75 years, Rohrer's has been supplying the farmers who work it with corn, soybeans, pasture mixture, legumes, grazing and haying mixtures, and other grasses and crop seed. You'll find several pages of this stock in the catalog, as well as herbicides, insecticides, fungicides, and soil enrichment. But most of the 56-page catalog is devoted to home gardening needs, with a good selection of perennials and annuals, vegetables, legumes, herbs (seed), potatoes (seed), berries, and bulbs. There's also a good roundup of tools and supplies, including seed-starting supplies, watering equipment, and both organic/natural and conventional insect and fungus control. Houseplant treatments by Dragon, Jobe's, Peter's Professional, and Stern's are also offered. And Rohrer's sells both lawn seed blends and treatments.

In addition to the company's magnanimous commitment to your happiness—"Every Seed You Buy Must Satisfy You—or Your Money Back" —Rohrer's prices are much, much lower than those of several other firms selling the same varieties of seed, in the same amount. "Autumn Beauty" sunflower seed are under $2 a half ounce here, $3 elsewhere. Bachelor's Buttons run $3.25 an ounce at Rohrer's, but $6 for three-quarters of an ounce from another firm. A packet of Walla Walla Sweet onion seed is 99¢ here, $1.80 in another catalog, and so on. You won't find a lot of color in the catalog, but if you know your varieties and the prices others are charging, you won't miss the pictures.

Special Factors: Satisfaction is guaranteed (see the catalog for terms of warranty); returns are accepted for exchange, refund, or credit.

JOHN SCHEEPERS, INC.

DEPT. WBM
23 TULIP DR.
BANTAM, CT 06750
860–567–0838
FAX: 860–567–5323

Catalog: free
Pay: check, MO, MC, V
Sells: Dutch flower bulbs
Store: mail order only

John Scheepers has been in business since 1910, serving gardeners with premium, exhibition-quality Dutch bulbs of cultivated stock, at very good prices. Scheepers is affiliated with Van Engelen, which offers wholesale pricing on large orders (see that listing if you buy in 100-bulb lots). Scheepers' own prices are lower than market price, but the bulbs themselves—and the plants and blossoms—are significantly bigger.

The 64-page color catalog from Scheepers is heavy on tulips and narcissi: early-flowering Fosterianas, tulips from Asia Minor, trumpet narcissi, peony-like tulips, Giant Darwins, parrot tulips, and more. Like Van Engelen, Scheepers has a good selection of crocus, allium, fritillaria, iris, lilies, and other spring flower bulbs, as well as a number for shady, woodsy areas, and for holiday forcing. Bulb food, gifts, and books are available, and cultivating instructions are packed with each order. Most of the bulbs are sold in lots of 10, and the per-bulb price drops the more you order. The sales policy is similar to Van Engelen's, except the minimum order is just $25.

Wholesale customers, please call or write about placing large orders.

Special Factors: Quantity discounts are available; minimum order is $25 per address.

SEYMOUR'S SELECTED SEEDS

**P.O. BOX 1346
SUSSEX, VA 23884–0346
803–663–3084
FAX: 888-SEYMOUR**

Catalog: free
Pay: check, MO, MC, V, Discover
Sells: "English garden" flower seeds
Store: mail order only

  (see text)

"Lady Sarah Seymour" opens the catalog with a letter to her "American Gardening Friends," detailing her efforts to bring the blooms of the classic English country garden to the yards of the United States. She explains that the key to success is variety; that "Americans rightfully appreciate the sparkling jewels of impish impatiens or the billowing sails of bouncing petunias, but very few indeed have experienced the grace and charm of climbing asarinas or the sinister beauty of devilish nemophilas. . . "

What follows is over 80 pages of the kinds of flowers that create the English country look: convolvulus, geraniums, alyssum, papaver, lavender, pansies, lobelia, nasturtium, tropaeolum, sweet peas, lathyrus (the Matucana is said to be the original sweet pea, dating back to 1699), viola, portulaca, primrose, hollyhocks, and many others. The catalog descriptions include the common names of the varieties, origins, general sowing and care tips, mature height, bloom size, and other details. (You'll have to find garden layout suggestions and hardiness zone information from other sources, however.) Germination rates are estimated as 60% to 80%, and the data includes the seed count. The packets themselves are reasonably priced, and savings are considerable if you're buying quantity (750 to 4,000 seeds); there are "Early Bird" offers of bonus packets (terms are subject to change). Seymour's promises a replacement, refund, or credit if you're not completely satisfied with what you buy.

Overseas customers, please note: Seymour's ships *only seeds* outside the U.S.

Special Factors: Satisfaction is guaranteed; shipping is included; quantity discounts are available.

SHARP BROS. SEED CO.

396 SW DAVIS ST.-LADUE
CLINTON, MO 64735-9058
800-451-3779
FAX: 816-885-8647

Catalog: $1, refundable
Pay: check, MO, MC, V
Sells: grasses, legumes, and wildflowers
Store: mail order only

Sharp Bros. sells the fruit of the plains, specializing in bluegrass and other native grasses and prairie wildflowers. The firm's "Catalog of Grasses, Legumes, Lawn Grasses, and Field Seeds" lists warm-season grasses by common name, with complete data on habit, color, preferred soil type, exposure, and other characteristics, and as many cold-season grasses. Some of the grasses are suited to forage, others erosion control and general ground cover; among the favorites at Sharp are Big Bluestem, Little Bluestem, Indian Grass, Switchgrass, and wildflower mixes native to the Midwest and Great Plains.

Sharp Bros. also sells legumes and certified field crops—soybeans, wheat, oats, barley, etc., and markets everything under the Buffalo Brand label. You have to be familiar with the grasses to best use the catalog, but Sharp serves all kinds of buyers—"backyard gardeners," farmers, ranchers, conservation agencies, and prairie restoration groups, among others.

Special Factors: Quantity discounts are available; minimum order is 1 ounce of seed.

R.H. SHUMWAY SEEDSMAN

P.O. BOX 1-WBMC
GRANITEVILLE, SC 29829
803-663-9771
FAX: 888-437-2733

Catalog: free
Pay: check, MO, MC, V, Discover
Sells: seeds, bulbs, and nursery stock
Store: Graniteville, SC; Monday to Friday 8:30-4 (open Saturday 8:30-1 in spring season only)

 (see text)

"Good Seeds Cheap" declares the cover of R.H. Shumway's catalog, which is full of old-fashioned *engravings* of flowers, fruits, and vegetables—there's not a photograph in sight. Shumway has been "The Pioneer American Seedsman" since 1870, and is notable for the number of old, open-pollinated seeds it carries, as well as new varieties.

The 64-page catalog features spring flower bulbs, many pages of berries, vines, beans, vegetable seeds, corn, onions, squash, tomatoes, and Shumway specialties—lawn grasses, grasses for pasturage and hay, millet and other "forage" seed, sorghums, Sudan grasses, clover, legumes, and alfalfa. Another specialty catalog, "Totally Tomatoes," offers over 400 varieties of tomato and pepper seeds, together with all of the supplies you'll need to grow America's favorite crop, at savings of 30% to 40%.

Shumway offers over a dozen types of ornamental gourds—dishcloth gourds, small spoon, birdhouse, dipper, bottle, and more. Herb seeds are available, for both culinary and ornamental plants—angelica, coriander, shiso, burnet, pyrethrum, upland cress, and cardoon, as well as the spice rack standards. Market gardeners and other small commercial growers should check Shumway's wholesale prices on bulk seed orders, or get together with gardener friends and combine orders to take advantage of the bulk pricing. Special offers and bonuses are sprinkled liberally throughout the catalog, which also offers a selection of well-priced garden helpers.

Wholesale customers, the 136-page "HPS" catalog offers wholesale prices on flower and vegetable seeds to greenhouse growers and nursery operators. (Request this catalog by name on company letterhead.)

Overseas customers, please note: Seymour's ships *only seeds* outside the U.S.

Special Factors: Satisfaction is guaranteed; quantity discounts are available; returns are accepted within 90 days for exchange or replacement; C.O.D. orders are accepted; minimum order is $15 with credit cards.

TURNER GREEN-HOUSES

DEPT. 131
P.O. BOX 1260
GOLDSBORO, NC
  27533-1260
800-672-4770
FAX: 919-736-4550

Catalog: free
Pay: check, MO, MC, V
Sells: greenhouses and accessories
Store: mail order only
Online: http://www.turnergreenhouses.com

Turner Equipment Company was founded in 1939, and has been producing greenhouses since 1957. Turner currently offers three basic series with a choice of options, or a total of 46 models. Prices average 25% less than the competition, and similar greenhouses in other catalogs sell for 35% more.

The three series include a 7-foot-wide lean-to, and two freestanding lines, 8 and 14 feet wide. Each greenhouse comes equipped with a ventilating system and aluminum storm door, and can be expanded lengthwise in four-foot increments. You can choose from a 6-mil polyethylene cover or fiberglass (warrantied for 10 years). Turner also sells electric and gas heaters, exhaust fans and air circulators, cooling units, greenhouse benches, thermometers, misters, and sprayers. In addition, the 20-page color catalog features well-chosen books on composting, organic gardening, greenhouse growing, herb cultivation, and related topics.

Special Factors: Satisfaction is guaranteed; authorized returns in original condition are accepted within 30 days for refund or credit (less freight); minimum order is $10.

OTIS S. TWILLEY SEED CO., INC.

DEPT. 161
P.O. BOX 65
TREVOSE, PA 19053–0065
215–639–8800
FAX: 215–245–1949

Catalog: free
Pay: check, MO, MC, V
Sells: seeds and small-grower supplies
Store: mail order only

The Otis S. Twilley Seed Co., better known as Twilley's, is dedicated to the needs of "roadside, u-pick, and bedding plant growers" with 98 pages of vegetable, melon, and flower seeds and commercial grower supplies. The catalog descriptions include a per-ounce seed count, description of the mature plant, market attributes, and notes on tolerance to common ailments. The catalog also tells you the number of plants you can expect per packet, days to germination, plants or seeds per foot, row, or acre, and other data vital to calculating how much seed you'll need. Varieties especially suitable for bedding, shipping, roadside sales, "self-picking" operations, and cut-flower production are noted with codes and symbols. And Twilley's has compiled a guide to which varieties do best—or are undergoing trials—in your state or area (including Alaska, Canada, and Hawaii). Both commercial growers and home gardeners will appreciate the cultivation supplies and equipment, pest control products, and growing and marketing tips and suggestions. Warranty information, conditions of sale, "grower" (volume) discounts, handling charges (waived on orders over $100), and other policy details are given on the order form and in the catalog, and repay close reading.

Please note: Most of the seed is treated, and Twilley's is unable to provide untreated seed as of this writing.

Special Factors: Quantity discounts are available; authorized returns are accepted (a 20% restocking fee is charged); institutional accounts are available; minimum order is $25 with credit cards and C.O.D. orders.

VAN BOURGONDIEN BROS.

P.O. BOX 1000
BABYLON, NY 11702
800–622–9997
516–669–3500
FAX: 516–669–1228

Catalog: free
Pay: check, MO, MC, V, AE, Discover
Sells: flower bulbs and perennials
Store: mail order only
E-mail: retail@dutchbulbs.com
Online: http://www.dutchbulbs.com

¡Si!

The 68-page spring and fall catalogs from Van Bourgondien offer a wealth of growing things for home, lawn, and garden at up to 40% less than other suppliers. Van Bourgondien was founded in 1919, and offers early-order discounts, bonuses, and specials on collections.

Both of the catalogs feature hosta and hybrid lilies, ground covers, and a wide range of flowers. Past fall issues have shown tulip, daffodil, hyacinth, iris, crocus, narcissus, anemone, allium, fritillaria, and other bulbs. Geraniums, delphiniums, shasta daisies, tiger lilies, lavender, flowering houseplants, foxtails, black-eyed Susans, native ferns, and other greenery and flowers are usually offered. If you can't wait for the thaw, you can buy prepotted lilies of the valley, Aztec lily, paperwhites, amaryllis varieties, and crocus bulbs, all of which can be forced. The spring catalogs feature begonias, gladiolus, dahlias, caladiums, perennials, hostas, ferns, cannas, ground cover, and similar goods. Bulb planters and plant supplements are offered as well, and orders are shipped to the 48 contiguous United States.

Special Factors: Goods are guaranteed to be "as described" and to be delivered in perfect condition; quantity discounts are available.

VAN DYCK'S FLOWER FARMS, INC.

Catalog: free
Pay: check, MO, MC, V, AE, Discover
Sells: Dutch flower bulbs
Store: mail order only

P.O. BOX 430
BRIGHTWATERS, NY
11718–0430
800–248–2852
FAX: 516–669–3518

¡Sí!

Van Dyck's not only offers "wholesale Dutch bulbs," but also makes ordering a snap: Everything is sold in a "pack," whether it's one amaryllis or 35 mixed Iris Beauty bulbs. This firm goes back generations in Holland, and has been doing business in the United States since 1990.

The Van Dyck's catalog features irises and other favorites—tulips, daffodils, crocuses, narcissi, hyacinths, alliums, fritillaria, ranunculus, and snowdrops. Anemones, crown imperials, daylilies, and other later-blooming flowers are offered. All of Van Dyck's bulbs are commercially cultivated, and the 100-page color catalog includes a hardiness guide and cultivation tips to help maximize the success of your plantings. The pricing structure rewards big buys, and the proprietors recommend combining orders with friends and gardening co-ops to get the best discounts.

Special Factors: Satisfaction is guaranteed; quantity discounts are available; returns of bulbs are accepted for replacement; minimum order is 5 packs or $25.

VAN ENGELEN INC.

Catalog: free
Pay: check, MO, MC, V
Sells: flower bulbs
Store: mail order only

DEPT. WBM
23 TULIP DR.
BANTAM, CT 06750
860–567–8734
FAX: 860–567–5323

Van Engelen, in business since 1971, is the wholesale affiliate of John Scheepers, another vendor of Dutch flower bulbs. Scheepers serves the needs of gardeners buying fewer than 50 of the same bulb at the same time, but Van Engelen sells most bulbs in lots of 50 or 100, and requires a $50 minimum order. If you can meet the minimum, you'll have the choice of over 550 different varieties of tulip, narcissus, crocus, daffodil, anemone, allium, freesia, iris, fritillaria, hyacinth, amaryllis, and lilies, all of which are shown in the 32-page catalog. In addition to buying bulbs à la carte, you can choose from several collections that are priced below listed wholesale. Each has from 215 to 525 bulbs, and if you like the selection of varieties and colors, they're a real buy.

Special Factors: Quantity discounts are available; minimum order is $50.

SEE ALSO

Arctic Glass & Window Outlet • *glass panels for cold frames, greenhouses* • **HOME: IMPROVEMENT**

Central Michigan Tractor & Parts • *used and rebuilt parts for tractors and combines* • **AUTO**

Clothcrafters, Inc. • *knee pads, gardening aprons, porous plastic sheeting* • **GENERAL MERCHANDISE**

Dairy Association Co., Inc. • *livestock liniment* • **ANIMAL**

Daleco Master Breeder Products • *kits for yard ponds* • **ANIMAL**

Manufacturer's Supply • *replacement parts for lawn mowers, rototillers, trimmers, tractors, etc.* • **TOOLS**

Micro-Mark • *kits for models of old buildings and wooden ships* • **TOOLS**

Northern Hydraulics, Inc. • *trimmers, tractors, lawnmower parts, garden carts, log stackers, lawn sweepers, etc.* • **TOOLS**

Red Hill Mushrooms • *mushroom-growing kits* • **FOOD**

Storey Communications, Inc. • *books and manuals on farm and garden topics, homesteading, etc.* • **BOOKS**

That Fish Place/That Pet Place • *live aquarium plants* • **ANIMAL**

Zip Power Parts, Inc. • *lawn mower parts* • **TOOLS**

FOOD AND DRINK

Foods, beverages, and condiments

Sales of mail-order food now exceed $2 billion annually, reflecting an increase in the demand for good foods not available locally, and hard-to-find cooking ingredients. The dominant mail-order foodstuffs are cheese, fruit, and nuts, as well as preserves and condiments, coffee, tea, and seasonings. The listings here are representative: You'll find caviar and Italian truffles, Mexican and Lebanese foods, giant pistachio nuts, Vermont maple syrup, and more from the firms listed here—at savings that run to 80%. Consider them when making out gift lists—packets of rare herbs, a tin of trail mix, a crate of sunny grapefruit in the dead of winter—even modest gifts can delight. If you want to maximize your savings, choose a popular food like pecans or dried fruit, buy it in bulk, and repackage it yourself in gift tins. Or try your hand at making herb-infused vinegars and oils. The firms listed here sell the ingredients for all of these and more; please note that the specialists in coffee, tea, herbs, and spices are listed in the next section, "Beverages and Flavorings."

If you'd like to improve your diet and cut food costs, a food co-op may be the answer. If you don't have one nearby, send a long, stamped, self-addressed envelope to Co-Op Directory Services, 919 21st Ave. South, Minneapolis, MN 55404. You'll receive a list of food co-ops across the country, and the contact information for local wholesalers who can advise you on setting up your own co-op. (The *National Green Pages* from Co-Op America has some of this information; see the description in the introduction of "General.")

Even if you can't manage a natural, whole-foods diet, you can save money just by eating better. One researcher who studied the effects of a diet with no more than 30% of the calories derived from fat (the government-approved level) found that it was *cheaper* to eat leaner, by an average of about $275 per year, per person. Great to know, but how do you get there? In the early 1990s, the FDA recast its dietary guidelines, throwing out the famous "four food groups" for the better-balanced "pyramid." The U.S. Department of Agriculture (USDA) has prepared a helpful, 30-page brochure, "The Food Guide Pyramid" (HG–252); request it by name and number form the U.S. Department of Agriculture, Human Nutrition Information Service, 6505 Belcrest Rd., Hyattsville, MD 20782 (include a long, stamped, self-addressed envelope). As simple as the pyramid seems, changes in the government's food labeling regulations are not. Some of the best ongoing sources of information that sort food facts from fallacies are newsletters: *Nutrition Action Healthletter*, published by the Center for Science in the Public Interest (CSPI), broke the stories about the high-fat content of Chinese and Mexican restaurant food. It's a fearless champion of truth in advertising, which is what you'd expect of a Ralph Nader publication. Subscriptions are currently $24 per 10-issue year; write to CSPI-Circulation, 1875 Connecticut Ave. NW, Suite 300, Washington, DC 20009–5728 for updated information and rates out of the United States. Another helpful newsletter, *Environmental Nutrition,* summarizes abstracts and current food-health controversies and findings, with good, balanced reporting. A 12-issue year is currently $30 from *Environmental Nutrition,* P.O. Box 420451, Palm Coast, FL 32142–0451.

In addition to nutrition, food safety is a big concern among consumers. Warm weather gives rise to "picnic anxiety," and the fall brings "stuffing fears," common concerns about handling troublesome foods properly. Help is just a call or letter away:

1. **The American Dietetic Association** answers questions on all aspects of food safety; 800–366–1655, Monday to Friday 8 a.m. to 8 p.m. CT, for a registered dietitian.

2. **USDA Meat and Poultry Hotline** answers your questions on safe handling of meat and poultry; 800–535–4555, in DC 202–720–3333 (both TDD); Monday to Friday 10 a.m. to 4 p.m., November 1–30 and the weekend before Thanksgiving, 9 a.m. to 5 p.m., Thanksgiving Day 8 a.m. to 2 p.m., all ET.

3. **Butterball,** the turkey company, lays on four dozen food-service professionals to answer your questions on how to handle, cook, carve, and store the big bird. United States and Canada: 800–323–4848; TDD: 800–833–3848; both English and Spanish are spoken. November 1 to the day before Thanksgiving, 9 a.m. to 9 p.m., the day before, 9 a.m. to 7 p.m., Thanksgiving Day, 7 a.m. to 7 p.m.; weekdays after Thanksgiving to Christmas, 9 a.m. to 7 p.m. The website is http://www.butterball.com.

4. **A Quick Guide to Safe Food Handling,** a USDA publication, gives guidelines on food handling and charts of cooking requirements for dif-

ferent meats and egg dishes—plus one that gives the projected shelf life of refrigerated and frozen foods. Send a long, stamped, self-addressed envelope to the USDA at the address given above, with your request for HG–248.

5. **Get Hooked on Seafood Safety,** published by the FDA, covers risks and safety precautions for buying, handling, storing, and preparing fish. A copy can be ordered from the Consumer Information Center, listed in "Books."

6. **The FDA's Seafood Hotline** dispenses answers to your specific questions on fish-related safety issues; call 800–FDA–4010 Monday to Friday 12 p.m. to 4 p.m. ET.

7. When you're ordering food by mail, keep food safety in mind. Don't purchase highly perishable or temperature-sensitive items like chocolate, soft cheese, fruits, vegetables, and uncured meats during the summer, unless you have them shipped by an express service and plan to eat them immediately.

FIND IT FAST

CHEESE • **Gibbsville**
COFFEE AND TEA • **Festive Foods, The Maples**
GOURMET FOODS • **Caviarteria, Festive Foods**
HERBS, SPICES, FLAVORINGS • **Festive Foods**
MAPLE SYRUP • **Palmer's, Elbridge C. Thomas**
MUSHROOMS • **Festive Foods, Jaffe Bros., Red Hill**
NUTS, DRIED FRUITS • **Bates Bros., Durey-Libby, The Maples**
ORGANIC AND NATURAL FOODS • **Deer Valley, Jaffe Bros., Walnut Acres**

BATES BROS. NUT FARM, INC.

15954 WOODS VALLEY RD.
VALLEY CENTER, CA 92082
760–749–3333
FAX: 760–749–9499

Catalog: free
Pay: check, MO, MC, V, Discover
Sells: nuts, dried fruits, and candy
Store: same address; daily 8–5; also Terra Nova Plaza, 358 E. H St., #604, Chula Vista, CA; every day, 10–7:30

Nuts are the featured item at Bates, which was founded in 1971 and grows some of what it sells. Price checks routinely show savings of almost 40% on selected items, compared to the competition. Bates'

eight-page brochure lists the standard almonds, walnuts, peanuts, cashews, pecans, and mixes, as well as macadamia nuts, filberts, pignolias, pumpkin seeds, sunflower seeds, and pistachios. You can buy them raw, roasted and salted, smoked, and saltless. The dried fruits include apricots, raisins, dates, papaya, figs, banana chips, pineapple, and coconut, as well as other sweets. These are the ingredients for trail mix, which Bates also sells ready-made, as well as granola, wheat germ snacks, popcorn, and old-fashioned candy—malted milk balls, English toffee, yogurt pretzels, nut brittle, saltwater taffy, gummy bears and worms, and candy corn, among others. And look here for good prices on glacé fruit: fruitcake mix, cherries, colored pineapple wedges, orange and lemon peel, and citron. Gift packs are available year-round.

Special Factors: C.O.D. orders are accepted.

CAVIARTERIA INC.

DEPT. WBMC
502 PARK AVE.
NEW YORK, NY 10022
800–4-CAVIAR
IN NY 212–759–7410
IN CA 800–287–9773
FAX: 718–482–8985

Catalog: free
Pay: MO, MC, V, AE
Sells: caviar and gourmet foods
Store: same address (store and tasting bar); also 158 S. Beverly Dr., Beverly Hills, CA; Monday to Saturday 9–8, both locations

 ¡Si!

Caviarteria, established in 1950, brings its line of caviar to the world through a 10-page catalog. This family-run business stocks every grade of fresh Caspian Beluga, Oscetra, and Sevruga caviar, plus American sturgeon, whitefish, trout, and salmon caviar. What Caviarteria believes is the "world's most exquisite Caspian Beluga caviar costs $695 for 14 ounces—but is available as "partly broken grains" for half that. Prices begin a bit more affordably at about $18 per ounce for Kamchatka bottom-of-the-barrel vacuum-packed, and run up to $285 for 3½ ounces of "Ultra" Beluga. Price comparisons of Caviarteria's Beluga Malassol to those of another caviar-by-mail firm show you can save as much as 40% here, and even the caviar servers—spoons and bowls—are already priced lower than usual retail.

The catalog lists other gourmet treats: whole sides and "center cut" packages of smoked Scottish salmon, Icelandic gravlax, fresh pâté, foie gras from the U.S. and France, game meats, and other delicacies. If you're in New York City, stop by Caviarteria's tasting bar on Park Avenue for a glass of Champagne, or a caviar sampler with toast points. Caviarteria will send caviar, foie gras, and other delights for next-day delivery *anywhere*.

Special Factors: Satisfaction is guaranteed; minimum order is $25 with credit cards.

DEER VALLEY FARM

R.D. 1, BOX 173
GUILFORD, NY 13780
607-764-8556

Catalog: $1
Pay: check, MO, MC, V
Sells: organic and natural foods
Store: Rte. 37, Guilford, NY; Monday to Friday 8–5; 19B Ford Ave., Oneonta, NY; Monday to Saturday 9:30–5:30, Thursday 9:30–8:30; and 64 Main St., Cortland, NY; Monday to Saturday 9:30–5:30, Thursday 9:30–8:30

Deer Valley Farm, which has been in operation since 1947 and is certified organic by New York State Natural Food Associates, sells a full line of foods—from baked bread and cookies to wheat middlings. Whole grains, flours, cereals, nut butters, crackers, fruits, pasta, herbs and spices, tea, soy milk, preserves, and yeast and other baking ingredients are usually available. You can buy "organically grown" meats here at substantial savings: hamburger, typically priced at $4.50 to $6 per pound in health food stores, costs $3.49 per pound, and the trimmed sirloin is $6.29 a pound; veal, pork, lamb, and even fish are also available. Deer Valley sells raw milk cheese, and the cheddar is only $3.29 to $4.89 per pound, less than some of the supermarket varieties. The only drawback here is the minimum order, $150, necessary to reap savings of 25% to 40% on the prices you'd pay if buying the same goods from your local health food store. But if you get your friends together, you can meet that amount easily with a combined order—just be prepared for an impromptu feast when the cartons arrive!

Special Factors: Deliveries are made by Deer Valley truck in the New York City area (elsewhere by UPS); minimum order is $15, $150 for wholesale prices.

DUREY-LIBBY EDIBLE NUTS, INC.

Catalog: $1
Pay: check or MO
Sells: nuts
Store: mail order only

100 INDUSTRIAL RD.
CARLSTADT, NJ 07072
201–939–2775
FAX: 201–939–0386

Durey-Libby, established in 1950, picks and processes "delicious fresh nuts you don't have to shell out a fortune for." You can't eat fancy tins, stoneware crocks, and rattan baskets, so if you're buying nuts, why not *pay* for nuts—and nothing but. Durey-Libby's no-frills price list features walnuts, pecans, cashews, almonds, macadamia nuts, pistachios, and cocktail mixes, packed in bags and vacuum tins. The prices are up to 50% less than those charged by gourmet shops and many food catalogs. The smallest units are 3-pound cans, which will give you enough for cooking and snacking.

Special Factors: Satisfaction is guaranteed; shipping is not charged on orders within the contiguous United States.

FESTIVE FOODS OF THE ROCKIES

Catalog: $2
Pay: check, MO, MC, V, AE
Sells: baking ingredients, fancy foods, herbs and spices, etc.
Store: mail order only
Online: http://www.delve.com/festive.html

DEPT. WBMC–98
P.O. BOX 49172
COLORADO SPRINGS, CO
  80949–9172
719–594–6768
FAX: 719–522–1672

Festive Foods of the Rockies has been supplying serious home cooks and bakers with fine ingredients since 1984, and offers a number of items not often seen in other fancy foods catalogs. There are 20 pages of temptations, from pure Belgian chocolate to fine dried fruits. Festive Food's per-ounce prices of the bulk-packed herbs are much lower than those charged at the supermarket: 8 ounces of pure vanilla extract cost

$8.25 here, while just *2 ounces* of extract cost $5.39 locally. The 12-ounce pack of Old Bay seasoning is $3.95 here, compared to $3.13 for 6 ounces. Savings on the other goods vary, depending on the item and amount ordered.

Festive Foods offers a wide range of products, including pastry and baking ingredients, chocolate and cocoa, extracts, essential oils of plants and spices, a wide variety of herbs and spices in spice-jar "refill" packs as well as the more economical bulk sizes, seasoning blends, tea (black, green, herbal, and flavored), dried mushrooms (porcini, morels, shiitake, chanterelles), maple syrup, sun-dried tomatoes, flavored vinegars, dried fruits, gourmet beans, rice, and grains. Among notable products are French coffee extract, Tahitian vanilla beans, pine nuts, asafetida powder, horseradish powder, fine sea salt, Chaat Masala, chutneys, and mushroom powder. If you enjoy cooking and eating, stock up—Festive Foods will pay shipping if your order totals $150 or more.

Special Factors: Satisfaction is guaranteed; shipping is not charged on orders over $150; returns are accepted for exchange, refund, or credit.

GIBBSVILLE CHEESE SALES

W–2663 CTH–00
SHEBOYGAN FALLS, WI
53085–2971
414–564–3242
FAX: 414–564–6129

Price List: free
Pay: check or MO
Sells: Wisconsin cheese and summer sausage
Store: same address (5 miles south of Sheboygan Falls on Hwy. 32); Monday to Friday 7:30–5, Saturday 7:30–4

Gibbsville Cheese Sales is a standout even in Wisconsin, the Dairy State, where *everyone* produces cheese. The company's prices are appetizingly low—as little as $2.80 a pound for mild cheddar in 5-pound bulk packaging. Several types of Old Wisconsin summer sausage and beef sticks are also offered, in addition to well-priced gift packages for a variety of budgets and tastes.

Gibbsville has been in business since 1933, and produces the most popular kinds of cheese, including Cheddar (mild, medium, aged, super-sharp white, garlic, and caraway), Monterey Jack (including Jacks flavored with salami, hot pepper, dill, and vegetables), and Colby (including a reduced-fat version). Five pounds of rindless Colby cost $2.80 a pound, and prices of other cheeses are just as reasonable. If you can get to the store in Gibbsville, you can even watch the production process through a viewing window. In addition to the cheeses of its own manufacture, Gibbsville Cheese sells Swiss (baby, medium, aged, and lace), provolone, Muenster, Parmesan, Romano, mozzarella, Gouda, Pine River Cold-Pack Cheese Spreads (including Sharp Cheddar, Swiss Almond, Port Wine, Smoked, etc.), and blue, Limburger, and string cheeses. The price list indicates which cheeses are "lower in fat," and includes several "lite" versions of favorites.

Please note: Shipments are not made during summer months (approximately June to September).

Special Factors: Price quote by letter with SASE.

JAFFE BROS., INC.

P.O. BOX 636-W
VALLEY CENTER, CA
  92082–0636
760–749–1133
FAX: 760–749–1282

Catalog: free
Pay: check, MO, MC, V, Discover
Sells: organically grown food
Store: (warehouse) 28560 Lilac Rd., Valley Center, CA; Sunday to Thursday 8–5, Friday 8–3

Jaffe Bros., established in 1948, sells organically and naturally grown dried fruit, nuts, seeds, beans, grains, nut butters, honey, and many other organically grown items, through the 22-page catalog. Prices average 30% below comparable retail, but there are greater savings on certain items, and quantity discounts are offered on many goods. Jaffe's products are marketed under the Jaybee label, and virtually all of them are grown "organically" (without fumigants or poisonous sprays and with "nonchemical" fertilizers) or "naturally" (similarly treated but not fertilized).

You'll save on wholesome foods here—dried peaches, Black Mission figs, Monukka raisins, papaya, dates of several types, almonds, pine nuts, macadamias, nut butters, brown rice, flours and grains, seeds for eating and sprouting, 15 kinds of peas and beans, unheated honey, coconut, jams, juices, carob powder, salad oil, olives, herb teas, and much more. (Most of the produce is packed in 2-, 5-, 25-, and 50-pound units.) The catalog also lists dehydrated mushrooms, sun-dried tomatoes, canned olives, organic spaghetti sauce, low-salt dill pickles and sauerkraut, organic whole wheat pasta, kosher maple syrup, organic applesauce, and even a biodegradable peppermint-and-castile soap/shampoo.

If you'd like to bestow goodness upon a friend, be sure to see the group of gift assortments—nicely packaged selections of favorites, at reasonable prices.

Wholesale customers, please request the "wholesale" catalog on your company letterhead; minimums (pounds or number of items) apply.

Special Factors: Quantity discounts are available; problems should be reported to Jaffe within 10 days of receipt of goods; warehouse is closed Saturdays; C.O.D. orders are accepted.

THE MAPLES FRUIT FARM, INC.

P.O. BOX 167

CHEWSVILLE, MD 21721

301–733–0777

Catalog: $1

Pay: check, MO, MC, V, Discover

Sells: dried fruit, nuts, coffee, gift baskets, etc.

Store: 13144 Pennsylvania Ave., Hagerstown, MD; Monday to Thursday 9–6, Friday 9–7, Saturday 8–5

The 16-page catalog of dried fruits, nuts, coffee, tea, and sweets from Maples Fruit Farm pictures an early view of the Farm, which has been operated by the same family for 200 years. The prices here are mouthwatering—savings of 25% to 50% were found on selected items. The dried fruits include apricots, dates, pears, peaches, and pineapple. (Fruits prepared with sulphur dioxide are clearly indicated in the catalog.) Raw and roasted (salted and unsalted) nuts are offered, including cashews, almonds, peanuts, pecans, macadamia nuts, filberts, black walnuts, and a number of others, including trail mix. Two pounds of raw pecans from Maples are half as expensive than those from a specialty pecan source, and the roasted macadamia nuts, honey-roasted peanuts, and cashews are all better buys here. Among sweets, Maryland grade-A amber maple syrup costs less than the syrup offered by competitors (who sell Canadian and New York state products). Maples Fruit Farm also sells 38 kinds of gourmet coffee, roasted fresh at the firm's gourmet shop daily.

Reasonably priced gift baskets are available, and if you can stock up or share orders, check the *wholesale* prices on cases. Don't miss the store if you're in the Hagerstown area—drop in to smell the coffee roasting, and sample some of the 5,000 gourmet treats on the shelves.

Please note: The Maples accepts faxes over the regular phone line, but you must call to let them know before transmitting.

Special Factors: Satisfaction is guaranteed; minimum order is $25 (excluding shipping).

PALMER'S MAPLE PRODUCTS

BOX 240 RD
WAITSFIELD, VT
05673–9710
802–496–3696
FAX: 802–496–3696

Brochure and Price List: free with long, stamped, self-addressed envelope
Pay: check, MO, MC, V
Sells: maple syrup, cream, candy, maple jelly
Store: Mehuron's Market and Bisbee's Hardware, Waitsfield, VT

Delbert Palmer has been sugaring since he was 10 years old, and in early spring he heads for the woods to draw the sap that will be transformed into a season's worth of maple syrup. He's still using the sugar house that his great-grandfather built 180 years ago! The Palmers' brochure describes the entire process, including grading and canning.

The Palmers are nice when it comes to the price, which at this writing is $11.40 a quart, compared to $16.95 for the same grade of Vermont syrup sold through another gourmet foods catalog. Even the Palmers' highest per-ounce price, for half pints, is lower by a third than what other mail-order firms are charging. The Palmers sell three grades of syrup—light amber (Fancy), medium amber (A), and dark amber (B)—at the same price. If you like a very delicate flavor, try the Fancy grade; grade B has a strong "mapley" flavor that suits some palates and purposes (cooking and baking) more than the other two grades. Maple cream, maple jelly, and candies may also be available; see the price list for information.

Special Factors: Send long, stamped, self-addressed envelope for brochure and price list.

RED HILL MUSHROOMS

P.O. BOX 4234
GETTYSBURG, PA 17325
800–822–4003
717–337–3038
FAX: 717–337–3936

Price List: free
Pay: check, MO, MC, V
Sells: fresh mushrooms and growing kits
Store: 1540 Biglerville Rd., Gettysburg, PA
E-mail: Redhill@mail.cvn.net

¡Si!

Shiitake and oyster mushrooms enjoyed a great vogue in fashionable food several years ago, and have subsequently found a permanent home in the dishes of many good cooks. Red Hill Mushrooms sells oyster mushrooms, which have a fine, delicate flavor, and the slightly nutty Shiitake, which is crunchy when raw. The price at this writing is competitive—$10 a pound for Shiitake, $8 for oyster mushrooms—and they're offered in 3- and 5-pound boxes. Red Hill is also home to the "Shiitake Log Kit" ($25), a compressed sawdust log enriched with wheat germ and millet and infused with Shiitake spawn. Follow the care directions given in the literature, and you should be rewarded with as many as four crops of Shiitake. When the log ceases to produce, you can crumble it up and use it as mulch in your garden!

Special Factors: Minimum order is $25.

SULTAN'S DELIGHT

P.O. BOX 090302
FORT HAMILTON STA-
   TION
BROOKLYN, NY
   11209–0302
800–852–5046
718–745–2121
FAX: 718–745–2563

Catalog: free with a stamped, self-addressed envelope
Pay: check, MO, MC, V, AE, Discover
Sells: Middle Eastern and Mediterranean foods and gifts
Store: mail order only

Sultan's Delight specializes in authentic Middle Eastern food specialties, sold at excellent prices—up to 50% below comparable goods in gourmet shops. The firm was established in 1980, and offers both raw ingredients and prepared specialties. See the catalog if you're looking for canned tahini, couscous, tabouleh, fig and apricot jams, stuffed grapevine leaves, bulghur, orzo, fava beans, ground sumac, or Turkish figs. You'll also find olives, herbs and spices, jumbo pistachios and other nuts, roasted chick peas, halvah, Turkish delight, marzipan paste, olive oil, Turkish coffee, fruit leather, filo, feta cheese, and other specialties. Cookbooks for Greek, Lebanese, Indian, and Middle Eastern cuisine are available, as well as Turkish coffee pots, inlaid backgammon sets, and other intriguing items.

Special Factors: Minimum order is $20.

ELBRIDGE C. THOMAS & SONS

RTE. 4, BOX 336
CHESTER, VT 05143
802–263–5680

Catalog: $1
Pay: check or MO
Sells: Vermont grade-A maple syrup
Store: by appointment

   ★

Mr. Thomas makes and sells the nectar of New England—pure, grade-A Vermont maple syrup. He's been in business since 1938, and his prices on large sizes are as much as 30% lower than those of his competitors—and even better than those charged for lesser grades. The stock is pure and simple: Vermont maple syrup, grade A, available in half-pint, pint, quart, half-gallon, and gallon tins. (Plastic containers are available upon request.) Maple sugar cakes, which make irresistible gifts, are also offered (by special order only). The brochure includes a number of suggestions for using maple syrup in your favorite foods—maple milk shakes, maple ham, frosting, and baked beans are just a few examples.

Special Factors: Quantity discounts are available; prices are subject to change without notice.

WALNUT ACRES ORGANIC FARMS

DEPT. WBMC000
WALNUT ACRES RD.
PENNS CREEK, PA 17862
800–433–3998
717–837–0601
FAX: 717–837–1146

Catalog: free
Pay: check, MO, MC, V, Discover
Sells: organically grown foods, natural toiletries, cookware, etc.
Store: Penns Creek, PA; Monday to Saturday 9–5, Sunday 12–5
E-mail: walacres@prolog.net
Online: http://walnutacres.com

Walnut Acres Organic Farms has marked 52 years in the organic foods business, and still produces most of its own goods on "500 acres of chemical-free soil" in Pennsylvania. The 56-page color catalog presents the bounty in full, appetizing color: grains, cereals, granola, bread and pancake mixes, flours, seeds and nuts, nut butters, soups, salad dressings, sauces, pasta, dried fruits, juices, honeys, and other goods. Herbs and spices, relishes, dehydrated vegetables, canned fruits, vegetables, and beans, powdered milk, crackers, jams and preserves, cheeses, and baked goods are also offered. Walnut Acres sells cookbooks, nutritional supplements, and some natural toiletries and unguents as well, and a variety of products "friendly to the environment." See the catalog for air and water filters, humidifiers, full-spectrum light bulbs, grain mills, rice cookers, bread machines, and other home and kitchen equipment. The website includes the full range of products, and ordering instructions as well.

Walnut Acres is known for its quality and selection, but savings of 30% to 40% are possible on the dried fruits and nuts, compared to other mail-order sources. Walnut Acres sells its nuts, seeds, grains, cereals, and dried fruits in bulk packages (3 and 5 pounds) at additional savings.

Wholesale customers must be doing business as stores, or selling for resale; request the wholesale catalog on company letterhead. The minimum wholesale order is $250.

Special Factors: Products are guaranteed to be as represented; minimum order for delivery by Walnut Acres truck is $250.

WOOD'S CIDER MILL

RD #2, BOX 477
SPRINGFIELD, VT 05156
802–263–5547

Catalog: free with SASE
Pay: check, MO, MC, V
Sells: cider jelly and syrups
Store (farm): call for appointment

   ¡Si! ★

The Wood family has maintained a farm in Vermont since 1798 and today produces wonderful, cider-based treats for mail-order customers. The prices here are better than reasonable—in fact, Wood's cider jelly can be found selling in other catalogs at prices nearly twice as high as those charged by the Woods themselves! And another firm's cider jelly costs over twice as much for the same amount.

The Cider Mill is best known for its jelly, which is made of evaporated apple cider. From 30 to 50 apples are needed to make the cider that's concentrated in just 1 pound of jelly, but you'll understand why when you taste it on toast or muffins, or try it with pork and other meats as a condiment. Boiled cider is also available; it's a less-concentrated essence that is recommended as a base for a hot drink, as a ham glaze, and as a topping for ice cream and pancakes. For pancakes, however, try the cider syrup, a blend of boiled cider and maple syrup. (It's also outstanding as a basting sauce for Thanksgiving turkeys, and even roast chicken.) Straight maple syrup is also produced on the farm, and look for the Woods' newest—cinnamon cider syrup.

Special Factors: Satisfaction is guaranteed; returns are accepted for exchange or refund; quantity discounts are available; minimum order is four 8-ounce jars.

Beverages and Flavorings

Coffee, tea, infusions and tisanes, herbs, spices, seasonings, and condiments

Herbs, spices, coffee, and tea are mail-order naturals, and all of them are available from the firms listed here. You can save up to 90% on the cost of herbs and spices by buying them from discounters, but that won't help you if you don't know how to use them. Even the smaller savings on coffee and tea won't mean as much if you're not using the best brewing techniques. The following resources are accessible, colorful, and they all include recipes:

The Complete Book of Herbs, by Lesley Bremness, and *The Complete Book of Spices,* by Jill Norman, are guides to identifying, storing, and using herbs and spices. Coffee lovers will appreciate *The Perfect Cup,* by Timothy James Castle, which covers selecting, serving, and tasting the magic bean. *The Afternoon Tea Cookbook,* by tea authority Michael Smith, includes history and great recipes for the proper English interlude. (Try Jessica's Biscuit, in "Books," if you can't find them locally.) Don't overlook the books and tips mentioned in the catalogs, and see the listings in the foregoing section, "Food and Drink," for other firms selling coffee, tea, and seasonings.

FIND IT FAST

COFFEE AND TEA • **CMC, Grandma's Spice Shop, Northwestern Coffee Mills, Old Town Gourmet, Rafal Spice**
HERBS, SPICES, FLAVORINGS • **Bickford, Brew City, CMC, Grandma's Spice Shop, E.C. Kraus, Northwestern Coffee Mills, Old Town Gourmet, Penzeys', Rafal Spice, San Francisco Herb, Spices Etc.**
WINE- AND BEER-MAKING • **Brew City, E.C. Kraus**

BICKFORD FLAVORS

19007 ST. CLAIR AVE.
CLEVELAND, OH
44117–1001
216–531–6006
FAX: 216–531–2006

Price List: free
Pay: check, MO, MC, V
Sells: flavorings
Store: same address; Monday to Friday 9–5

Bickford, established in 1914, makes and sells its own concentrated flavorings, from naturally derived oils, leaving out the usual alcohol and sugar that you'll find in other "pure" essences. Over 100 flavorings are offered, from almond to wintergreen. Vanilla is sold here in white, dark, and regular versions. (The white vanilla won't tint your angel food cake or meringues.) All of Bickford's flavorings are sold in 1-ounce bottles for $2.29, which is competitive pricing, but the good buys are pints ($19.95) and larger sizes. (Vanilla is also sold in bottles of 2, 4, and 8 ounces.) In addition to an unparalleled selection of flavorings, Bickford also sells about 100 exotically flavored oils (ginger, peach, caramel, and sherry oil are all available), food colorings, chlorophyll, and carob syrup.

Special Factors: Flavorings are free of alcohol and sugar.

BREW CITY SUPPLIES, INC.

DEPT. WBMC
P.O. BOX 27729
MILWAUKEE, WI 53227
414–425–8595
FAX: 414–425–3596

Catalog: free
Pay: check, MO, MC, V
Sells: home-brewing equipment
Store: mail order only
E-mail: brewcity@execpc.com
Online: http://www.execpc.com/~brewcity

You can start a *real* microbrewery right in your own kitchen, with the help and guidance of the folks at Brew City. This five-year-old firm is dedicated to the proposition that anyone can brew a batch of beer, and leads you through the process of turning malt, water, yeast, and hops into pilsner in "Nine Easy Steps" and dozens of books and videos.

Brew City offers beginner kits with everything you need to set up operation for under $50, and all of the supplies you'll need: yeast by YeastLab, malt extracts from all over the globe, including Australia (Coopers), Belgium (Brewferm), Britain (John Bull, and Munton Fison), Germany (Ireks-Arkady), Holland (Laaglander), Ireland (Mountmellich), Scotland (Glenbrew), and the United States (Premier). Sugars, yeasts, additives, and pellet hops are sold, as well as soda pop extracts (cola, cream, birch beer, orange, etc.). The 36-page catalog also shows an extensive selection of equipment and tools—grain mills, boilers, fermenters, paddles, bottles, cappers, and keg taps are available. The prices are "guaranteed lowest," and the informative catalog teaches you the role of "wort chillers," "sparging bags," and other strangely named devices.

Special Factors: Satisfaction is guaranteed.

THE CMC COMPANY

P.O. DRAWER 322
AVALON, NJ 08202
609-624-8412
FAX: 609-624-8414

Catalog: $1, refundable with first order
Pay: check, MO, MC, V, AE
Sells: gourmet seasonings and ethnic specialties
Store: mail order only

If you're one of the legion of home cooks who'd love to replicate the great flavors of Mexican and Eastern restaurant cuisine, you've just found the source for the flavorings that make the dishes authentic. CMC has been in business since 1990 with a seasonings line that features Mexican chiles (dried, powdered, canned, etc.), and hot sauces, moles (rojo, verde, poblano, pepian), as well as such specialties as Mexican dried shrimp, chorizos, masa harina, and cooking utensils for Mexican dishes. CMC's Thai food selection includes curry pastes, tamarind paste, trassi (dried shrimp paste), Kaffir lime leaves, jasmine rice, and all of the sauces—fish, mushroom soy, satay, sriracha, etc.—that make Thai food transcendental. Your efforts at inspired Indian food will be improved by tandoori paste and Patak chutneys, black cumin seed, chapati flour, a great selection of individual curry spices, ghee (clarified butter), and the other ingredients sold here. And there are Szechuan spices, Japanese seasonings and ingredients, and Busha Browne's Jamaican Specialties (pukka hot sauce, hot pepper sherry, jerk sauce and seasoning, etc.). Many of the spices and flavorings listed in the 32-page catalog are hard to find elsewhere, and therefore hard to comparison-price, but several products—garam masala, basmati rice, and lemon grass powder, for example—were found to be 10% to 50% less expensive here than at other gourmet sources.

Wholesale customers, please note that discounts are given to resellers and food-service professionals.

Special Factors: Keep the catalog, since it's updated with inserts from printing to printing.

GRANDMA'S SPICE SHOP

Catalog: $1, refundable
Pay: check, MO, MC, V
Sells: herbs, spices, coffee, tea, etc.
Store: mail order only

HC 62
BOX 65-D
UPPER TRACT, WV 26866
304–358–2346
FAX: 304–358–2346

Once upon a time, a real Grandma—rocking chair and all—ran this gourmet emporium. Since its sale several years ago, the firm has expanded the range and depth of the stock to include coffee from Havana, Nougatine coffee (flavored with hazelnut oil), Jasmine tea from Fukien province, beet powder, raspberry leaves, and herbal Worcestershire sauce, among other items. The 26-page inventory includes coffees (regular, flavored, and decaffeinated), loose teas (green, black, flavored, decaffeinated) and rare estate teas, Benchley tea bags, a large herb and spice selection, cocoa, herbal vinegars and honeys, hot sauces, McCutcheon preserves, and fruit-sweetened preserves. Spice racks, mortar and pestle sets, gift baskets, and Melitta travel sets are all available. The herbs and spices afford the best savings, up to 60% if bought in bulk (half or full pounds). Coffee and tea connoisseurs should see the catalog for the unusual and rare varieties (which are not sold at a discount).

Several catalog pages are devoted to potpourri, sachets, and related ingredients—simmering spice blends, cedar moth mixes, bath herbs, pomander rolling mixes, pinecones, dried flowers, potpourri oils, and bath oils (stock scents and custom blends are available). Prices of the smaller sizes are competitive with bath and gift shops; as with the herbs, you'll save the most on the potpourri and ingredients when you buy by the pound.

Please note: Grandma's Spice Shop offers a recorded (audio) version of the catalog, and can supply labels for spices and other purposes in Braille, at no extra charge.

Special Factors: Minimum order is $15.

E.C. KRAUS WINE & BEERMAKING SUPPLIES

P.O. BOX 7850-WC
INDEPENDENCE, MO
  64054
816–254–7448
FAX: 816–254–7051

Catalog: free
Pay: check, MO, MC, V
Sells: wine- and beer-making supplies
Store: 733 S. Northern, Independence, MO;
Monday to Friday 8–5:30, Saturday 9–1

E.C. Kraus, founded in 1967, can help you save up to half of the cost of wine, beer, and liqueurs by producing them yourself. The firm's 24-page illustrated catalog features supplies and equipment for the home vintner and brewer, beginner or experienced: malt and hops, fruit and grape concentrates, yeasts, additives, clarifiers, purifiers and preservatives, fruit acids, acidity indicators, hydrometers, bottle caps, rubber stoppers, corks and corkscrews, barrel spigots and liners, tubing and siphons, steam juicers, fermenters, fruit presses, dried botanicals, and much more. The T. Noirot extracts can be used to create low-priced liqueurs, and there are books and manuals to provide help if you want to learn more. If you're just getting started, you may find the Kraus "Necessities Box"—equipment and supplies for making 5 gallons of wine or 4 gallons of beer—just what you need.

Special Factors: Local ordinances may regulate production of alcoholic beverages.

NORTHWESTERN COFFEE MILLS

MIDDLE RD.
BOX 370
LA POINTE, WI 54850
800–243–5283
715–747–5825
FAX: 715–747–5405

Catalog: free
Pay: check, MO, MC, V, AE
Sells: coffee, tea, herbs, spices, coffee filters, coffee flavors, and syrups
Store: same address and 217 North Broadway, 2nd Floor, Milwaukee, WI; Monday to Friday 10–5:30, Saturday 10–4
E-mail: nwcoftsp@win.bright.net

If coffee is America's drink, Wisconsin may be harboring a national treasure. It's the home of Northwestern Coffee Mills, which set up shop in 1875 in a town better known for a different sort of brew. Northwestern begins with top-quality Arabica, and roasts each type of bean separately to develop its optimum flavor. The "Midwest" Roast is the specialty here; like European roasts, it's lighter than the "West Coast" coffees best characterized by the famous Seattle beanery.

The 12-page catalog describes each of the blends, straights, dark roasts, and decaffeinated coffees, noting relative strength, body, aroma, and flavor. Among the blends are American Breakfast, North Coast Blend (a strong, after-dinner coffee), Mocha Java, a New Orleans chicory blend, and Island Blend, a favorite of local restaurateurs that "stands up well when heated for hours on end." There are fancy straights, including Brazil Santos, Costa Rica Tarrazu, Kenya AA, Colombia Excelso, and Sumatra Lintong. Puerto Rico Yauco Selecto is available, as well as estate-grown Java and Hawaiian Kona, Yemen Mocha (the *real* mocha from Yemen), and other rare straight coffees. Decaf drinkers can choose from water-processed blends and straights. Northwestern Coffee anticipates a good supply of organic beans, which it plans to offer in regular and dark roasts, plain and decaffeinated. Coffee filters for all types of drip and percolator systems are sold, including Chemex, Melitta, and the Wisconsin-made "Natural Brew" unbleached filters. Northwestern also maintains a premium tea department. The catalog describes how tea is grown and processed, tea grading, and the types of teas Northwestern sells—flavored, black, green, oolong, and decaffeinated. The varieties include Ceylon, Indian Assam, Indian Darjeeling, Irish Breakfast, Russian Caravan, Japan Sencha, "China Dragon Well Panfired Leaf," and Orange Spiced tea, among others. Northwestern's prices on single pounds of coffee or four-ounce packages of tea are market-rate, but the firm will sell both to consumers at bulk rates. There are price breaks at 5, 10, and 25 pounds, and since coffee in whole-bean form will keep well for several months in the freezer, it makes sense to order as much as you can store. Northwestern is also introducing a coffee subscription plan to save you money on shipping charges—see the current catalog for details.

Last but not least, Northwestern publishes a separate price list that features herbs, spices, and other flavorings, in supermarket sizes and in bulk. Several capsicums (peppers) are offered, and dried vegetables (garlic granules, horseradish powder, mushrooms, etc.), blended salt-free and salted seasonings, coffee syrups, and natural extracts (vanilla, almond, cocoa, cinnamon, orange, etc.) are also listed.

Special Factors: Satisfaction is guaranteed; quantity discounts are available; returns are accepted within 90 days for exchange, refund, or credit.

THE OLD TOWN GOURMET

1617 SAN PEDRO N.E.
ALBUQUERQUE, NM
87100–0000
505–842–5643

Price List: free with long, stamped, self-addressed envelope
Pay: MO, MC, V
Sells: coffee, tea, chiles, gourmet food, etc.
Store: same address; daily 10:30–5 (except Monday, January–March)

The Old Town Gourmet has been selling New Mexican gourmet specialties at the same location in Albuquerque since 1952. The firm roasts, blends, and flavors its own Arabica coffee beans, and incorporates native nuts in several, including "Southwest Piñon," a three-bean blend with piñon nuts that is the store's most popular blend. The store also stocks a vast assortment of dried New Mexican chiles, which are offered whole or ground, as well as chile-flavored products—jams, jellies, salsas, vinegars, bread and cake mixes, and even chile peanut butter (touted as an excellent marinade for chicken or fish). The Old Town Gourmet also carries flavored teas, and things like cactus jelly and marmalade, chocolate piñon coffee, mabañero salsas (very hot), and dry chile and vegetable mixes for dips; custom gift baskets can be created for a surcharge. For chile connoisseurs and specimen collectors, this firm's specialty in New Mexican varieties offers a special attraction. If you have the opportunity to visit the store, you'll find it in Albuquerque's "old" section, in one of the town's original adobe buildings.

Special Factors: Satisfaction is guaranteed.

PENDERY'S INC.

1221 MANUFACTURING ST.
DALLAS, TX 75207
800–533–1870
214–741–1870
FAX: 214–761–1966

Catalog: $2, $3.50 outside the U.S.
Pay: check, MO, MC, V, AE, Discover
Sells: herbs, spices, and Mexican seasonings; hot sauces and cooking equipment
Store: 304 E. Belknap St., Fort Worth, TX

Pendery's has been spicing up drab dishes since 1870 and can add the authentic touch of real, full-strength chiles to your Tex-Mex cuisine for a fraction of the prices charged by gourmet shops. The firm's 96-page catalog describes the origins of the company and its contributions to the development of Tex-Mex chile seasonings. It's not a coincidence that "those captivating capsicums" occupy several catalog pages and include pods, ground peppers, and blends. Pendery's carries over *200* sauces and salsas. Scores of general and specialty seasonings and flavorings are offered, including fajita seasoning, jalapeño peppers, and spice-rack standards from allspice to white pepper. Among the unusual or hard-to-find ingredients available here are masa harina, Mexican chocolate, annatto, horseradish powder, Worcestershire powder, dehydrated cilantro, corn shucks for tamales and cornhusk dolls, and dried diced tomatoes. The catalog also offers handsome, handblown Mexican glassware, pepper mills, and food-related gifts. Prices of the spices are far lower than those charged by gourmet stores and supermarkets—up to 50% less on some of the specialty seasonings.

Special Factors: C.O.D. orders are accepted.

PENZEYS' SPICE HOUSE

1921 S. WEST AVE.
WAUKESHA, WI 53186
414–574–0277
FAX: 414–574–0278

Catalog: free
Pay: check, MO, MC, V
Sells: spices, herbs, and seasonings
Store: same address; Monday to Friday 9–5,
Saturday 9–3

Penzeys' Spice House is a family-run firm that "grinds and blends our spices weekly to ensure freshness," something no one else in the business seems to be doing. The selection is extraordinary—there are 11 forms and types of cinnamon, for example. Penzeys', established in 1957, prices even 1-ounce sizes of seasonings at below-supermarket rates and offers savings of up to 40% on full pounds.

The informative, 36-page catalog begins with adobo seasoning and ends with vanilla beans. In between, you'll find Brady Street Cheese Sprinkle, Bicentennial "Rub" Seasoning (an early American blend), cassia buds from China, cardamom, chile peppers (rated for heat in Skoval units), tandoori chicken seasoning, fenugreek seeds, mulled wine spices, "Old World Seasoning," pot herbs for soups and stews, Spanish saffron, seasonings for salad dressings and homemade sausages, star anise, taco seasoning, French tarragon, and many other straight seasonings and blends. (Nearly three dozen are offered in salt-free versions, and Penzeys' Spice House also offers a line of soup bases.) The descriptions include provenance, ingredients in the blends, and suggested uses. Recent editions of the catalog have included a number of recipes, including a retinue for Thanksgiving dinner, spicy cheese bread, pan-seared tuna steaks, and sauerbraten.

The Penzeys offer several appealing gift packages, including "Spicy Wedding," "Great Baker's Assortment," "Indian Curries," and a "Spice Replacement" set (when "the love of your life has left you taking all of your spices, maybe your house burned down or was just swept away by a tornado/hurricane"). Zassenhaus pepper mills and inexpensive jars for herb and spice storage are also available.

Special Factors: Satisfaction is guaranteed; price quote by phone or fax; returns are accepted for exchange, refund, or credit.

RAFAL SPICE COMPANY

2521 RUSSELL ST.
DETROIT, MI 48207–2632
313–259–6373
FAX: 313–259–6220

Catalog: free
Pay: check, MO, MC, V, Discover
Sells: coffee, tea, flavorings, cookbooks, etc.
Store: same address; Monday to Saturday
7–4

If you have a weakness for Cajun and Creole dishes, you'll love Rafal Spice, which charges up to 57% less than a New Orleans mail-order firm selling the identical foods. Rafal Spice also sells coffee and tea in a range of blends and flavors, and well-priced herbs and spices, from alfalfa leaves to za'atar powder. Rafal offers a number of very uncommon ingredients, like bladderwrack, devil's claw tuber powder, hawthorn berries, sanicle, skunk cabbage root, and powdered soy sauce.

Among the food and flavorings brands you'll find in the 72-page catalog are Angostura, Bell's, Buckeye, Clancy's, Crystal, Gayelord Hauser, Jamaican Hell, Konriko, Lawry's, Mrs. Dash, Mrs. Wages, Old Bay, Trappey, Wright's, and Zatarain's. Liquid Spice by Dilijan, Lorann flavorings and extracts, food coloring, kitchen tools, spice grinders, labels, storage jars, coffee, filters, tea infusers, and six pages of cookbooks wrap up the catalog. The shipping is computed fairly (on weight and distance), and the catalog even includes a few recipes.

Please note that botanicals not intended for consumption are indicated in the catalog with an asterisk.

Special Factors: Satisfaction is guaranteed; allow three weeks for delivery of order.

SAN FRANCISCO HERB CO.

250 14TH ST., DEPT. WBMC

SAN FRANCISCO, CA 94103

800–227–4530

415–861–7174

FAX: 415–861–4440

Catalog: free
Pay: check, MO, MC, V, Discover
Sells: culinary herbs, teas, spices, and pot-pourri ingredients
Store (wholesale outlet): same address; Monday to Friday 10–4, Saturday 10–2
E-mail: gnarly@sfherb.com
Online: http://www.sfherb.com

 ¡Si! ★

Reader-recommended San Francisco Herb is known for excellent prices and a great selection of herbs, spices, potpourri ingredients, fragrance oils, botanicals, and teas. San Francisco Herb was founded in 1973 and is primarily a wholesaler, but anyone who meets the $30 minimum order can buy here, too.

The culinary herbs and spices range from the routine—allspice, cinnamon, marjoram, tarragon—to such uncommon seasonings as spice blends for Greek foods and cilantro leaf. Among the botanicals are alfalfa leaf, balsam fir needles, chamomile, kelp powder, lavender, orris root, pinecones, rosebuds, pennyroyal, spearmint leaf, and yerba maté. (Some of these can be consumed, and others can't; check with a reliable information source before using botanicals for food use.) Recipes for mulling spice blend, no-salt flavor enhancers, bouquet garni, and garam masala (a spice blend used in Indian cuisine) are all available on request.

The catalog also features dozens of recipes for sachets and simmering and jar potpourris. The "Hollyberry Christmas Jar Potpourri" has a delectable scent and lovely combination of colors, and "Plantation Peach" is delightfully fruity. If you're not experienced in making potpourri, try some of the recipes to become more familiar with blending colors and fragrances.

The spices and botanicals are sold by the pound (most items are available in 4-ounce units), with quantity discounts of 10% on purchases of 5 pounds or more of the same item. San Francisco Herb also sells glass vials and spice jars, flavored teas in bulk, dehydrated vegetables, shelled nuts, sprouting seeds, and such miscellaneous food goods as lemon powder, arrowroot powder, bacon bits, pine nuts, and roasted chicory root.

Special Factors: Satisfaction is guaranteed; volume discounts are available; authorized returns are accepted within 15 days (a 15% restocking fee may be charged); minimum order is $30; C.O.D. orders are accepted.

SPICES, ETC.

P.O. BOX 5266
CHARLOTTESVILLE, VA
22906
800–827–6373
804–293–9410
FAX: 800–827–0145
FAX: 804–293–4655

Catalog: free (see text)
Pay: check, MO, MC, V, Discover
Sells: herbs, spices, tea, etc.
Store: mail order only
E-mail: spices@comet.net
Online: http://www.spicesetc.com

Spices Etc., in business since 1991, offers a wealth of seasonings through a 48-page catalog, including straight bulk-packaged herbs and spices at savings of up to 75%. The spice blends cover a wide culinary range, from celery salt and apple pie seasonings to garam masala, pesto, and exotic specialty blends. Chiles, snack seasonings, dehydrated vegetables, natural seasonings, bulk-packaged teas, hot pepper sauces, mustards, and other edibles are available. There are pages of grinders, mortar-and-pestle sets, spice racks, and empty jars in several sizes. Gift assortments and seasoning collections are also offered.

Please note: The catalog, regularly $2, is free if you mention WBMC.

Special Factors: Spices and seasonings are available in one-gallon quantities.

SEE ALSO

Atlantic Spice Co. • *culinary herbs and spices, blends, teas, etc.* • **CRAFTS**
Cabela's Inc. • *freeze-dried foods, trail packs* • **SPORTS**
Campmor • *dehydrated camping food, beef jerky, etc.* • **SPORTS**
Caprilands Herb Farm • *live and dried herbs, herbal vinegars, and teas* •
FARM
Don Gleason's Campers Supply, Inc. • *freeze-dried food for camping and survival* • **SPORTS**
Le Jardin du Gourmet • *gourmet foods, live herb plants, etc.* • **FARM**

New England Cheesemaking Supply Company, Inc. • *cheese-making supplies and equipment* • **HOME**: **KITCHEN**

The Paper Wholesaler • *catering supplies, restaurant paper goods, disposable tableware* • **TOYS**

Plastic BagMart • *plastic food storage bags* • **OFFICE**: **SMALL BUSINESS**

Sally Distributors, Inc. • *party-packs of candy* • **TOYS**

Storey Communications, Inc. • *cookbooks and manuals on food preservation* • **BOOKS**

Survival Supply Co. • *dehydrated and "survival" food* • **SPORTS**

Taylor's Cutaways and Stuff • *tea "baglets" for making your own tea bags* • **CRAFTS**: **TEXTILE ARTS**

Triner Scale • *pocket scale* • **OFFICE**

U.S. Toy Company, Inc. • *penny candies* • **TOYS**

Weston Bowl Mill • *sugar buckets and butter churns* • **GENERAL MERCHANDISE**

Zabar's & Co., Inc. • *gourmet foods and condiments* • **HOME**: **KITCHEN**

GENERAL MERCHANDISE, BUYING CLUBS, AND GOOD VALUES

Firms and buying clubs offering a wide range of goods and services

Most of the companies listed in this chapter offer such a diverse selection that it might be confusing to put them elsewhere: everything from mosquito netting to potpourri turns up. Go through the listings carefully, since there are some real finds here, and countless answers to the question of what to give for Christmas, birthdays, and other occasions. (See the following section, "Cards, Stationery, Labels, and Check-Printing Services," for firms specializing in those goods.)

The following guides can help you to shop faster, smarter, and better, depending on your needs and habits:

1. The *AT&T Toll-Free 800 Consumer Directory* is a big help in finding 800 numbers quickly; it has over 60,000 listings, from "accountants" to "yarn." The current consumer edition costs $14.99 at this writing (plus shipping, handling, and applicable sales tax), and can be ordered by calling 800–426–8686 between 8 a.m. and 6 p.m. ET. A listing of 120,000 business-to-business numbers is also available from AT&T; inquire for the current price.

2. *The Practical Guide to Practically Everything: Information You Can Really Use* is just that, over 1,000 pages on money, health, education, employment, travel, entertainment, consumer issues, and lots of helpful charts that you can never find when you need them—metric converters, anniversary gift lists, perpetual calendars, time-zone maps, and much more. It's edited by Peter Bernstein and Christopher Ma, two editors at *U.S. News & World Report,* and published by Random House (about $14, updated annually).

3. The *National Green Pages,* from Co-Op America, lists "green" companies—firms that meet the organization's standards for social and environmental responsibility. This 152-page guide runs from "advertising services" to "wood," and includes a list of steps you can take in your own life to help build a sustainable society. The book is one of the benefits of membership in this not-for-profit organization; membership costs $20 for individuals, or $60 for businesses. For an information package, write to Co-Op America, 1612 K St. NW, Suite 600, Washington, DC 20006, or call 202–872–5307, Monday to Friday 9–5.

Finding ways to save on all the things you buy—food, clothing, housing, transportation, education, insurance, vacations, and even luxury goods—is covered in *Cut Your Spending in Half: How to Pay the Lowest Price for Everything,* by the editors of Rodale Press (Rodale Books, 1994). It's a mine of information and ideas that can help you buy smarter and cheaper. Unfortunately, you can surrender all of your gains if you don't know how to handle a problem—whether it's fighting a bad utility bill, returning a defective product, or negotiating a 30-year mortgage. *Getting Unscrewed and Staying That Way* (Klein, Klein and Walsh, 1993) covers the range of remedies you have in curing problems that can crop up in the course of any transaction. And *The Consumer Bible: 1001 Ways to Shop Smart* (Workman Publishing, 1995), by consumer advocate Mark Green, outlines strategies for getting the best buys and will help you avoid problems in the marketplace, whether you're shopping for flu remedies or funeral services. All three of these books would make valuable additions to a consumer reference bookshelf.

FIND IT FAST

CANVAS AND FLANNEL PRODUCTS • **Clothcrafters**
COUNTRY ACCENTS • **Tender Heart**
GIFTS • **Bennett Bros., Grand Finale, Tender Heart**
HOSPITALITY AND FOOD-SERVICE INDUSTRY SUPPLIES • **Marshall Domestics**
OVERSTOCK AND CLOSEOUTS • **Andy's Garage Sale**
SOAP, CLEANING SUPPLIES • **Cal Ben, EDGE Distributing, J & R**
WOODENWARE • **Weston Bowl Mill**

AARP

601 E. ST. NW
WASHINGTON, DC 20049
202–434–2277

Information: inquire
Pay: check, MO, MC, V
Sells: membership (see text)
Store: mail order only

The AARP, or American Association of Retired Persons, is a not-for-profit organization dedicated to improving the lives of older Americans, especially in the areas of finance and health. Membership is open to anyone aged 50 or older, retired or not, at a cost of just $8 a year. Among the benefits are subscriptions to the bimonthly *Modern Maturity* and the monthly *AARP Bulletin,* the opportunity to buy low-cost supplemental health insurance, auto and homeowner insurance, obtain the AARP VISA or MasterCard, the AARP Motoring Plan (affiliated with Amoco Motor Club), publications on health topics, discounts on hotels and car rentals, and access to a pharmacy-by-mail. (See the listing for Retired Persons Services in "Medicine" for more details.)

Special Factors: Inquire for information.

AMERICAN SCIENCE & SURPLUS

3605 HOWARD ST., DEPT.
WBM–98
SKOKIE, IL 60076
847–982–0870
FAX: 800–934–0722

Catalog: free
Pay: check, MO, MC, V, Discover
Sells: industrial, educational, and scientific surplus goods
Store: 5696 Northwest Hwy., Chicago, IL; Rte. 38, East of Kirk Rd., Geneva, IL; and 15138 S. LaGrange Rd., Orland Park, IL; also 6901 W. Oklahoma Ave., Milwaukee, WI
E-mail: jarvis@sciplus.com
Online: http://www.sciplus.com

¡Si!

American Science & Surplus offers a wide variety of surplus wares through witty catalogs that are published about six times a year. The firm has been selling surplus since 1937, and offers that blend of the strange and useful that is catnip to fans of surplus goods: everything from "humongo scissors and son" (a big and a small pair of scissors), to a Baggies-type plastic bag sized to fit a motorcycle. American Science is also cited on several websites devoted to educational materials, as a great source for well-priced tools and supplies for teaching sciences to all grade levels.

Past catalogs have shown small DC motors, staplers, grow-your-own butterfly kits, microscopes, lasers, magnets, pharmaceutical bottles, collections of drive belts, dozens of kinds of tape, whetstones, DPDT switches, pumps, casters, glow-in-the-dark bats, piano hinges, Chinese riffler tools, aircraft drill bits, and magnifying lenses. (Please *don't* expect to find these particular items in the catalogs you receive—these are surplus goods, and stock is limited.) The descriptions, which are droll and explicit, note the original and possible new uses for the products, as well as technical data, when available. Savings on original and if-new prices can reach 95%.

Special Factors: Satisfaction is guaranteed; returns are accepted within 15 days; minimum order is $10 in goods.

ANDY'S GARAGE SALE, INC.

25 MCLELAND RD.
ST. CLOUD, MN
56395–2007
320–654–4624
FAX: 320–654–7565

Information: on website
Pay: check, MO, MC, V, Discover
Sells: manufacturers' overstock, closeouts, etc.
Store: Internet only; customer service phone hours Monday to Friday 8–8 CT
Online: http://www.andysgarage.com

If the gritty experience of flea-market shopping leaves you cold but you love the bargains, now you can have it both ways. Power up the modem and log onto Andy's Garage Sale (affiliated with Fingerhut), where fantastic buys await. Andy, who may be a mythic figure but delivers real goods, pulls together a "Top 20" every week for your budgetary pleasure. It's a well-rounded list with at least one "gotta-have-it," especially at savings of up to 70% on the original selling price. In one week, the "Top 20" list included a 16-piece set of Bake King bakeware for $13, an electric roaster oven, a set of three Wearever sauté pans, an American Camper queen-sized air bed for $24, an Audiovox auto subwoofer, a Nikko radio-controlled racer for $30, packs of four chintz throw pillows ($10) and three standard bed pillows ($13), a gold and diamond pendant, a Magnavox cordless phone, a 15-piece Campbell Hausfeld air tool set for $45, a West Bend coffee maker, and 220-count all-cotton comforter covers for $16. (A test order placed on this last item arrived promptly and was exactly as represented.) If the "Top 20" aren't enough, there's "Andy's Big Deal of the Day," which was an enormous stuffed animal on one occasion, ridiculously priced.

Andy's Garage Sale is an Internet phenomenon—there is no catalog. But Andy makes it easy to order once you've seen what you want. You can do it online, or over the toll-free line, or fax it in, or write it up and mail it in. Andy's online "Fax Gizmo" allows you to enter your choices on a form, print it out, and fax it in, without sending your credit information over the Internet. (If you wish to pay by check or money order, you can mail your order.) The shipping fee is a flat $4.95 per order at this writing, which represents significant savings if you succumb to the pine country storage unit and 6¼ ton jack that appeared in one "Top 20." If you have questions, consult "Ask Andy" on the website, and if you don't see the answer, you're urged to e-mail your query—as well as jokes and your favorite recipes.

Special Factors: Satisfaction is guaranteed; authorized returns are accepted within 30 days for exchange, refund, or credit.

BENNETT BROTHERS, INC.

30 E. ADAMS ST.
CHICAGO, IL 60603
ORDERS: 800–621–2626
312–263–4800
FAX: 312–621–1669

Catalog: free
Pay: check, MO, MC, V, AE, Discover
Sells: jewelry, appliances, electronics, luggage, furnishings, etc.
Store: same address; Monday to Friday 8:15–5 (see the catalog for holiday shopping hours); also 211 Island Rd., Mahwah, NJ: Monday to Saturday 9–5:30
E-mail: bennettbros@worldnet.att.net
Online: http://www.bennettbros.com

At the turn of the century, much of Bennett Brothers' business was in jewelry, gems, and watches. They're still a big part of the company's trade, but Bennett's current offerings, shown in the annual *Blue Book*, also include furnishings, leather goods, electronics, cameras, sporting goods, and toys.

The *Blue Book* is 144 color pages of name-brand goods, of which jewelry comprises over a third of the offerings—wedding and engagement bands, pearls, pins and bracelets, necklaces, and other pieces featuring all kinds of precious and semiprecious gems, as well as charms, lockets, medallions, anniversary jewelry, Masonic rings, and crosses and religious jewelry. The watch department offers models from Armitron, Bulova, Casio, Citizen, Jules Jurgensen, Pulsar, Seiko, and Timex.

Bennett Brothers offers a fine selection of clocks, timepieces, and weather instruments. Silverware and chests, silver giftware, tea sets, pewterware, and fine china are also sold. The catalog shows kitchen cutlery sets, cookware sets, small kitchen appliances, microwave ovens, vacuum cleaners, air cleaners, exercise equipment, sewing machines, personal-care appliances, bed linens, towels, tablecloths, and luggage. The leather goods department includes briefcases and attaché cases and luggage from American Tourister, Monarch, Samsonite, and Winn.

The *Blue Book* also features a large group of personal electronics and office supplies—clock radios, portable cassette players, stereo systems and components, TVs and video equipment, phones and answering machines, cameras, projectors, telescopes, binoculars, pens, globes, cash registers, calculators, typewriters, files, and office furnishings. Home furnishings are also available, including patio furniture. The catalog includes Bachmann trains, Cox radio-controlled planes, playing cards, and board games. There are also exercise machines, golf clubs, basketballs, fishing rods, and croquet sets. Flashlights, chain saws, and other tools round out the offerings.

Bennett's prices are listed next to "suggested retail" prices throughout the book. Price comparisons of several goods substantiated Bennett's guideline prices (suggested retail), and the savings of 30% to 40%. Corporate buyers should contact Bennett Brothers for details on the firm's corporate gift programs, which can provide incentives at price levels from $16 to $1,000.

Special Factors: Authorized returns are accepted within 10 days for exchange or credit.

CAL BEN SOAP COMPANY

DEPT. WBMC
9828 PEARMAIN ST.
OAKLAND, CA 94603
800–340–7091
510–638–7091
FAX: 510–638–7827

Catalog: free
Pay: check, MO, MC, V, AE, Discover
Sells: bath soap, shampoo, dish and laundry soap
Store: mail order only

The Cal Ben Soap Company has been in business for half a century, and employs a curious blend of old-fashioned product and eye-popping futuristic promotional materials. As producers of "Five Star Natural Ecology Pure Soap Products for the Third Planet From the Sun" (no relation to the TV show), Cal Ben emphasizes simple ingredients—white vegetable tallow, cocoa butter oils, natural extracts of almond, citrus, and coconut—and environmental safety concerns. They also deliver a good value: The 3-ounce bar of hand soap is offered in packages of 24, 36, 100, and 150 bars, for as little as an average of 70¢ each. Cal Ben also sells concentrated shampoo, liquid cream soap for hand-washables and dishes, dishwasher concentrate granules, and all-temperature laundry soap, most in graduated sizes at varying savings. Free "Data Bulletins" with guidelines for using the products are available upon request, and everything can be bought in sample sizes. If you like everything Cal Ben makes, consider stocking up with one of the four "Super Star" collections, 65 to 290 pounds of bar soap, shampoo, dishwasher granules, liquid cream soap, and laundry soap. The prices of these packages run from $125 to $395, and they're calculated to last the average family one to five years. Anything that could keep a daily necessity off your shopping list for that long is worth checking into. Mention WBMC when you send for the literature and when you order.

Special Factors: Satisfaction is guaranteed; returns are accepted for exchange, refund, or credit.

CLOTHCRAFTERS, INC.

DEPT. WM98

P.O. BOX 176

ELKHART LAKE, WI 53020

800–876–2009

414–876–2112

FAX: 414–876–2112

Catalog: free

Pay: check, MO, MC, V

Sells: home textiles

Store: mail order only

E-mail: catalog@clothcrafters.com

Online: http://www.clothcrafters.com

This firm, established in 1936, sells "plain vanilla" textile goods of every sort, from cheesecloth by the yard to flannel patches for cleaning guns. The 20-page catalog is packed with inexpensive, useful things: pot holders, chefs' hats, bouquet garni bags (12 for $4), salad greens bags, fabric coffee filters, striped denim place mats, cotton napkins ($12 a dozen), hot pads, aprons, and supermarket produce bags ($9 for 6). Clothcrafters has a great selection of well-priced kitchen tools, including parchment paper, rubber spatulas, spatter lids, radiant heat plates, and other handy utensils.

You'll also find laundry bags, tote bags, flannel shoe bags, woodpile covers and firewood carriers, garment bags, cider-press liners, computer covers, flannel polishing squares, and mosquito netting. The bed and bath department offers cotton duck shower curtains, lightweight cotton terry towels and bath wraps, terry tunics, barbers' capes, flannel sleeping-bag liners, and flannel crib sheets. Textile artists should check this source, since many of these items can be painted, embroidered, dyed, and otherwise embellished.

Gardeners will find the "PlyBan" porous plastic sheeting ideal for protecting newly planted rows from frost and insects ($9 for 4' by 50'). Clothcrafters also sells mosquito-netting helmets, multi-pocketed aprons, and denim knee pads—add an old shirt and dungarees, and you'll be ready to tackle the back forty.

Canadian readers, please note: Only U.S. funds are accepted.

Wholesale customers, please note: Request the wholesale price list on business letterhead.

Special Factors: Satisfaction is guaranteed; returns are accepted for exchange, refund, or credit.

EDGE DISTRIBUTING, INC.

Price List: free
Pay: check, MO, MC, V
Sells: cleaning and personal-care products
Store: mail order only

760 BUSSE HWY.
P.O. BOX 307
PARK RIDGE, IL 60068
800–373–3726
847–696–1623
FAX: 847–696–9284

Competition for supermarket shelf space is fierce these days, so if some of your favorite products aren't *everyone's* favorites, they may be bumped for better sellers. So what do you do when that tried-and-true cleaner, stain remover, or floor wax disappears from your local mart? If it's one of the brands represented by EDGE Distributing, you can buy it by mail—as long as you're willing to order at least a case of it.

EDGE's current 20-page price list includes a range of Lysol products—disinfectant spray, surfactants, glass cleaners, and bathroom products, as well as Easy-Off oven cleaners, Sani-Flush and Bully, Mop & Glo and Beacon, Old English polishes and scratch cover, metal polishes (Noxon, Brasso, Silvo, Oneida), Resolve carpet and upholstery cleaner, Snowy bleach, Woolite, Zout and Mother's Little Miracle laundry products, and Red Devil lye, Rid-X septic system treatment, Gulfwax paraffin, and D-Con rodenticides.

The lists include the product name, size, number per case, and case weight, but you must call for current prices and shipping costs. Depending on prices and availability in your area, you may be able to save a little money here—spot checks on several products showed per-item prices that were 13% to 20% below supermarket rates. (The calculations don't factor coupons, sales tax, or shipping.) EDGE is listed here not for the discounts, but for *availability* of a number of products you may not be able to find locally.

Special Factors: Minimum order is one case.

GRAND FINALE

SUBSCRIPTIONS DEPT.
P.O. BOX 620049
DALLAS, TX 75262–0049
800–955–9595

Catalog: $3, year's subscription, refundable on first purchase
Pay: MC, V, AE, Discover, NOVUS
Sells: upmarket and name-brand goods
Store: mail order only

Your catalog fee brings you a year of "luxury for less," 48-page catalogs of special values, clearance items, and closeouts from well-known mail-order houses. It's possible to save up to 75% on the original selling or list prices through Grand Finale, which has been in business since 1980.

Past catalogs have featured designer clothing, shoes, handbags, hand-embroidered table linens, hand-hooked rugs, Lane occasional furniture, cashmere sweaters, needlepoint pillows, quilts, and Christmas decorations. Almost every catalog offers Limoges bibelots, coasters, designer bed linens, rugs, cookware, flatware, fine china and crystal, and women's clothing. There's usually a sale section in the catalog featuring exceptional bargains; quantities of these items are limited, so order promptly. The quality is consistently high, and Grand Finale provides a gift boxing service ($3) and can forward presents to recipients directly.

Special Factors: Satisfaction is guaranteed; quantities are limited, so order promptly; returns are accepted for exchange, refund, or credit.

J & R SYSTEMS INTERNATIONAL

INDEPENDENT DISTRIBU-
    TOR, FULLER BRUSH
    COMPANY
5117 NW WALDEN DR.
KANSAS CITY, MO 64151
800–8-FULLER
816–741–1042

Catalog: $2
Pay: check, MO, MC, V, Discover
Sells: Fuller Brush products
Store: mail order only

  ★

The Fuller Brush Company was founded in 1906 and built its reputation on honest practice and quality products. In fact, the company's hairbrushes and cleaning tools are so durable that a large part of Fuller's product line now consists of cleaning solutions, polishes, laundry products, and toiletries.

J & R Systems International, an independent distributor of the Fuller Brush Company, sells the line by mail through the Fuller Brush catalog. The 36 pages are strong on general cleaning tools—brooms, mops, carpet sweepers, utility brushes, wax applicators, dusters, squeegees, etc.—as well as special-purpose implements, such as jar brushes, refrigerator coil brushes, grill scrubbers, car dusters, metal-polishing brushes, and bathtub swabs. Fuller makes a cleaning solution, wax, shampoo, deodorizer, or polish for every tool, and the most popular products— laundry detergent, degreaser, germicide, etc.—are offered in larger, money-saving sizes. Several pages of the catalog are devoted to personal-care products, including Fuller's famed boar-bristle hairbrushes, brush-cleaning tools, bath brushes, lint brushes, shampoos, body lotions, foot products, bubble bath, and more.

The Fuller Brush catalog prices are suggested retail, but other companies that sell the same products may mark them up—one catalog of household gadgets featured a number of Fuller Brush items at prices 11% to 26% *higher* than suggested retail. J & R Systems International enhances the savings with regular specials and quantity discounts.

Special Factors: Satisfaction is guaranteed; price quote by phone or letter.

MARSHALL
DOMESTICS

Catalog: free
Pay: check or MO
Sells: institutional and restaurant textiles and supplies
Store: mail order only

P.O. BOX 107
12 FACTORY ST.
WEST WARWICK, RI 02893
800–556–7440
FAX: 401–821–2230

Marshall Domestics was recommended by a reader who was ecstatic about the great buy he'd gotten there on dish towels. He was right: Marshall, in business since 1970, serves restaurants and institutions with competitive prices on everything from those dish towels (heavyweight, under $13 a dozen) to latex exam gloves, and will do business with individuals as well.

Marshall provides the food-service industry with kitchen textiles, chef's coats and toques, shirts and pants for kitchen workers, and table linens and skirting. The hospitality industry shops here for bed and bath linens, pillows, blankets and bedspreads, mattress protectors, shower curtains, and little hotel soaps. The healthcare industry buys latex gloves, patient gowns, bibs, scrub shirts and pants, lab coats, and incontinence products from Marshall. Everyone cleans up with the janitorial supplies—scrub brushes, mops, dusters, disinfectants, deodorizers, laundry detergent, and more. And Marshall also sells the full line of Dickies work clothing, Fruit of the Loom underwear for men and boys, socks, and T-shirts. Prices are very low, but note that some items are sold only by the dozen or in quantity, and special-order items (including some of the table linens) may not be returned. But a sample order for a dozen kitchen bib aprons was delivered quickly, and the aprons were perfect—good, heavyweight cotton, a great value at the price. Marshall has separate flyers for the Dickies clothing, and a line of uniforms and goods for the health care industry, so inquire specifically if you'd like those as well.

Special Factors: Satisfaction is guaranteed; claims are not honored on laundered goods; notify Marshall of discrepancies in your order within 10 days of receipt; volume discounts are available.

TENDER HEART TREASURES, LTD.

10525 "J" ST.
OMAHA, NE 68127–1090
800–443–1367
402–593–1313
FAX: 402–593–1316

Catalog: free
Pay: check, MO, MC, V, AE, Discover
Sells: "country" home decor and gifts
Store: mail order only
Online: http://www.tenderheart.com

Tender Heart Treasures has a staggering collection of "country" home accents and seasonal displays and decorations at prices that are a solid 30% to 50% below retail. The 62-page color catalog features hundreds of gifts, display pieces, and seasonal decorations: bears of all types in costume and the buff, "welcome" signs and hospitality plaques, dolls and figurines, angels, electrified kerosene lamps, bent-wire decorations, baskets, picture frames, birdhouses, doll furniture, planters, wooden apples and other fruit, wreaths, miniatures, and lots more. In addition to terrific prices, Tender Heart Treasures makes ordering a breeze—there's no minimum, and shipping charges are easy to compute to any destination.

Wholesale inquiries should be made to 800–443–1367; a copy of your resale tax certificate will be required with your first order.

Special Factors: Satisfaction is guaranteed; quantity discounts are available; authorized returns are accepted within 30 days for exchange, refund, or credit; C.O.D. orders are accepted.

TERRY'S VILLAGE

DEPT. 826
P.O. BOX 2309
OMAHA, NE 68103–2309
800–200–4400
402–331–5511
FAX: 800–723–9000
TDD (RELAY):
  800–833–7352

Catalog: free
Pay: check, MO, MC, V, AE, Discover
Sells: gifts, home accessories, and crafts
Store: mail order only

What wonderful catalogs arrive from Terry's Village, full of decorative treats to make your home special for the holidays, and mark the seasons throughout the year. The spring edition is full of bunnies celebrating Easter, shown on tin boxes that can be filled with candy, outside their own miniature village, and on banners, wreathes, and soap dishes. Cherub wall and shelf statues, terra-cotta birdbaths, handpainted mushroom finches, muslin dolls, candles, and vegetable-shaped soup crocks describe the range of gifts and accents. The Christmas edition shows angels of every type, Nativity scenes, beautiful collector dolls, grand Santas in gold with fur trim, winter villages (including a porcelain gingerbread version), ornaments, water globes, and even wrapping paper and ribbon assortments. The prices are so low that it sometimes costs more to make a craft item yourself than it does to buy it as a finished product here. For holiday gifts, favors, hostess presents, home decor, and even resale (depending on the prices prevailing in your area), don't buy elsewhere until you've checked the Terry's Village catalog.

Special Factors: Satisfaction is guaranteed; returns are accepted within 30 days for exchange, credit, or refund.

WESTON BOWL MILL

P.O. BOX 218-WBMC
WESTON, VT 05161–0218
802–824–6219
FAX: 802–824–4215

Catalog: $1, $2 outside the U.S.
Pay: check, MO, MC, V, Discover
Sells: woodenware and wooden household items
Store: Main St. (Rte. 100), Weston, VT; daily 9–5

Weston Bowl Mill has been known since 1960 for its wooden salad bowls, but the Mill produces hundreds of other wooden items for use throughout the home. Prices of many of the goods run about 30% below comparable retail, and savings are even better on selected goods. Almost everything is available with and without finish (oil or lacquer). The popular salad bowls, thick curves milled from a solid piece of maple or birch, are offered in sizes from 6" to 20" across. You can save by buying the seconds (when available), but note that sales are final— no returns are accepted on seconds.

Weston sells much more for dining table and kitchen, including birch plates and trays, maple lazy Susans, salt-and-pepper shakers, cheese plates, knife racks, tongs, a great selection of carving and cutting boards, and carbon steel knives. The 14-page catalog offers a wide variety of other home items, including shelves with brackets, towel and tissue holders, spoon racks, pegged coat racks, a large selection of wooden boxes, quilt racks, benches, stools, wooden fruits and vegetables, sugar buckets and churns, and baskets. Weston's bird feeders and whirligigs are well priced; likewise the delightful group of wooden toys—vehicles, tops, puzzles, game boards, cradles, and other classics— that are oil-finished. And the "country store" department includes "magic" massagers, lap boards, door stops and window props, outlet plates, spool holders, bells, yardsticks, and many other useful items.

Special Factors: Minimum order is $5, $20 with credit cards.

SEE ALSO

Baron/Barclay Bridge Supplies • bridge-playing gifts • **TOYS**
Bruce Medical Supply • dining, dressing, bathing, and other aids for the disabled and motor-impaired • **MEDICINE: SPECIAL NEEDS**
Business Technologies • cash registers • **OFFICE**

Caprilands Herb Farm • *herb charts, note cards, potpourri, pomanders, etc.* • **FARM**

Michael C. Fina Co. • *silver and crystal giftware* • **HOME**: **TABLE SETTINGS**

Gohn Bros. Mfg. Co. • *Amish "general store" goods* • **CLOTHING**

Kaye's Holiday • *holiday ornaments* • **TOYS**

Oriental Trading Company, Inc. • *gifts, novelties, etc.* • **TOYS**

Paradise Products, Inc. • *wide variety of party goods* • **TOYS**

Pendery's Inc. • *potpourri ingredients and gifts* • **FOOD**: **BEVERAGES AND FLAVORINGS**

La Piñata • *piñatas* • **TOYS**

Plexi-Craft Quality Products Corp. • *acrylic furniture, accessories, and gifts* • **HOME**: **FURNISHINGS**

Rafal Spice Company • *potpourri ingredients, oils, etc.* • **FOOD**: **BEVERAGES AND FLAVORINGS**

Nat Schwartz & Co., Inc. • *bridal registry for gifts* • **HOME**: **TABLE SETTINGS**

Albert S. Smyth Co., Inc. • *giftware, bridal and gift registry* • **HOME**: **TABLE SETTINGS**

Surplus Center • *tools, electrical components, security equipment* • **TOOLS**

Survival Supply Co. • *"survivalist" gear, books, and food* • **SPORTS**

Think Ink • *inexpensive thermographic color hand printers* • **CRAFTS**

Thurber's • *gifts, collectibles, and Christmas ornaments* • **HOME**: **TABLE SETTINGS**

U.S. Box Corp. • *ribbons, bows, gift wrap, etc.* • **OFFICE**: **SMALL BUSINESS**

U.S. Toy Company, Inc. • *toys, games, and novelties* • **TOYS**

Wag-Aero Group of Aircraft Services • *aviation-related gifts* • **AUTO**

Cards, Stationery, Labels, and Check-Printing Services

Greeting and correspondence cards, personal and business stationery, mailing and novelty labels, related services, and check-printing services

You may remember when cards were something you bought for special occasions and the big three—Mother's Day, Father's Day, and Christmas. You chose between Hallmark and American Greetings and bought them at the local drugstore. That changed in the 70s when small, independent card companies introduced "real" sentiments and "soft touch" cards. The current card market is a $4 billion industry that celebrates every remotely memorable life event and holiday, at prices that have risen from 35¢ and 50¢ to $2 to $3 *each*. If you send cards regularly, you can save considerably by buying from the firms listed here—50% and more on the cost of the same type of cards if bought individually. And when you buy by the box, you have cards whenever you need them.

Card manufacturers usually offer other goods as well—personal stationery, labels, and related goods—luggage tags, printed napkins and party goods, desk organizers, calendars, etc. In addition to the firms listed here, museum shops can supply great designs. Many of them run mail-order specials after Christmas, with special assortments and bonuses that bring per-card prices to under $1 each.

A great way to save money effortlessly is having your checks printed by one of the companies listed here. You can choose from a wide selection of designs and pay well under $15 for the same number of checks that will cost $45 or more if ordered through the bank. The editor has used checks from two of these printers for several years, and has never had a problem with any of them; Current even updated the account data format on one set of checks to conform to the bank's newest protocols, despite having received an old sample check. Send for information from these firms a couple of months *before* you need new checks, and file the brochures with the bank's reorder reminder. When the time arrives, you simply pull the materials, select the design, place the order with one of the check-printing services, and save an easy 50% plus.

FIND IT FAST

CARDS AND STATIONERY • **American Stationery, Current**
LABELS • **Current**
CHECK-PRINTING SERVICES • **Check Store, Checks in the Mail, Image Checks**
WEDDING STATIONERY • **American Stationery, Invitation Hotline**

THE AMERICAN STATIONERY CO., INC.

Catalog: free
Pay: check, MO, MC, V, AE, Discover
Sells: personalized stationery
Store: mail order only

DEPT. W
P.O. BOX 207
PERU, IN 46970
800–822–2577
FAX: 317–472–5901

The American Stationery Co. offers an excellent selection of personalized stationery, at prices up to 45% below those charged by other firms for comparable goods and printing. The company has been in business since 1919, and also produces "The American Wedding Album," a 52-page color catalog with a wide range of wedding invitations and accessories.

The correspondence selections include embossed sheets and notes in four colors, deckle-edged and plain sheets and envelopes in white and pastels, and heavyweight Monarch sheets, business envelopes, and "executive" stationery of heavyweight, chain-laid paper. The styles range from traditional to casual-but-tasteful, for both business and personal correspondence. There are great buys here, including the "Typewriter Box" of 100 printed sheets and the same number of printed envelopes for $25, as well as informals and notes in contemporary and calligraphic typefaces, notepads in spiffy designs, and a choice of ink colors—navy, teal, and gray, as well as the standard range. Stationery for children, personalized memo pads, bill-paying envelopes, bordered postcards, a good selection of gummed and self-sticking return-address labels, desk accessories, and related goods are shown in the 48-page color catalog.

Special Factors: Satisfaction is guaranteed; returns are accepted for replacement or refund.

THE CHECK STORE

790 QUAIL ST.
P.O. BOX 5145
DENVER, CO 80217–5145
800–424–3257

Brochure: free
Pay: check or MO
Sells: check-printing services
Store: mail order only

 ¡Sí!

The Check Store offers over 20 personal check designs, chiefly classic marble-grain and safety backgrounds and soft-focus illustrations—clowns, wildlife, mountain views, puppies, flowers, nature scenes, and Western motifs among them. The standard introductory offer—200 wallet-style checks with single-copy deposit tickets for $4.95—is being offered at this writing, and self-duplicating checks and printer-friendly (continuous-form and laser) designs are available at a higher price. The brochure of business check styles shows general and multipurpose, payroll, itemized invoice, and checks with voucher stubs, in three-to-a-page, continuous-form, and laser printer formats, beginning at $19.95 for 300 nonduplicating checks. Confidentiality of all of your bank data is guaranteed.

Special Factors: Satisfaction is guaranteed; request the "personal" or "business/computer" checks brochure.

CHECKS IN THE MAIL, INC.

5314 NORTH IRWINDALE AVE.
IRWINDALE, CA 91706
800–733–4443

Brochure: free
Pay: check or MO
Sells: check-printing services
Store: mail order only; phone hours Monday to Friday 7–7 CT
Online: http://www.checksinthe-mail.com

  ¡Si!

The designs offered by Checks in the Mail are among the liveliest available from the big check-printing firms. The "Stars and Stripes" check, for example, doesn't confine its flag to the upper-left corner—this banner spans the whole check face. Ageless party girl Betty Boop does a cameo on one, richly colored fish swim across "Ocean Wonder," and a personal favorite, "Ransom," adds a playful touch to every bill payment. There are over four dozen designs for personal checks, offered in wallet and carbonless duplicate styles, and in three-to-a-page desk sets. Business checks are available in a choice of formats and designs, in continuous-feed and laser-printer styles.

Prices begin at $4.95 for 200 wallet-style personal checks (the introductory offer), and run up to $29.95 for a desk set of 300 duplicate checks. The checks are guaranteed to be printed to your bank's standard, and confidentiality of your bank data is assured.

Special Factors: Satisfaction is guaranteed.

CURRENT, INC.

KEYCODE DM24
1005 E. WOODMAN RD.
COLORADO SPRINGS, CO 80941
800–525–7170
719–593–5900

Catalog: free
Pay: check, MO, MC, V, AE, Discover
Sells: stationery, gifts, wrapping paper, cards, etc.
Store: outlets in CA, CO, and OR

Current, in business since 1950, publishes a monthly, 68-page color catalog of stationery, gifts, and household items in appealing designs, many exclusive to Current, ranging from animal and nature scenes to quilt motifs and other Americana. All-occasion and holiday cards are available, as well as notepads, personal cards and stationery, gift wrapping, ribbon, stickers, recipe cards and files, toys, games, organizers, kitchen helps, calendars, memo boards, mugs, and other gifts. Current's "Expressions of Faith" line features Christian-oriented cards, gifts, and products for children. Prices are very reasonable, and discounts are given based on the number of items ordered.

Special Factors: Satisfaction is guaranteed; sliding discounts of 20% and more are offered on orders of eight or more items; returns are accepted.

IMAGE CHECKS, INC.

P.O. BOX 548
LITTLE ROCK, AR
72203–0548
800–562–8768
501–225–5957

Brochure: free
Pay: check or MO
Sells: check-printing services
Store: mail order only, phone hours Monday to Friday 8–4:30 CT

Image Checks has over 40 years of experience printing checks for businesses, and offers a great choice of options in check and record formats. In addition to general disbursement checks, Image Checks sells payroll and voucher versions, in standard (desk) and computer (continuous-form and laser printer) styles. Personal checks are also offered in three formats (single, top-stub, and duplicate), desk and wallet style, in a number of nice designs. Savings vary, depending on the format, options (custom logo or ink color), and amount you're buying, from about 30% to 50%, compared to bank prices.

Special Factors: Phone lines are staffed Monday to Friday 8 a.m. to 4:30 p.m. CT.

INVITATION HOTLINE

68 HAWKINS RD.
MANALAPAN, NJ 07726
800–800–4355, EXT. 921
732–536–9115
FAX: 732–972–4875

Information: price quote
Pay: check, MO, MC, V, AE, Discover
Sells: printed wedding invitations, business and social stationery, favors, holiday cards, etc.
Store: by appointment only; phone hours Monday to Friday 9–5 ET

When you're budgeting your wedding, every chance to save money helps. Invitation Hotline can cut the cost of invitations, reply cards, wedding stationery, favors, programs, and the other printed goods you may need by 25% (save more on volume and multiple orders). Invitation Hotline offers the products you've probably seen in the big books of samples at the local stationery or print shop, and can also provide envelopes laser-printed in calligraphic script at 25% below rates commonly charged by print shops. Nearly two dozen manufacturers and scores of lines are available at this writing, but Invitation Hotline stresses customer service over price and selection as its greatest asset. The proprietors understand everything about the selection process—including your state of mind—and help you work toward the best choice for your tastes, needs, and budget. They can help you to compose the wording on invitations and other printed matter, and are experienced in custom design work and processing foreign-language orders.

Invitation Hotline can also supply other goods that are shown in the stationery books—general invitations, personal and business stationery, business cards, birth announcements, and notices of bar and bat mitzvahs, anniversaries, and other red-letter days. If you don't have access to the sample books, call Invitation Hotline to discuss your needs.

Special Factors: Accuracy is guaranteed; price quote by phone or letter.

SEE ALSO

Dover Publications, Inc. • *cards, labels, graphics, posters, etc.* • **BOOKS**
Moore Business Products • *check-printing services, forms, etc.* • **OFFICE**
Reliable Corp. • *laser-compatible and continuous-form checks* • **OFFICE**
Sally Distributors, Inc. • *cards, gift wrap, gift bags, ribbon, etc.* • **TOYS**

Internet and Online Services

Computer-based information services, communication, and shopping

You can attend an auction, buy stock, do thesis research, communicate with people in New Zealand, learn a new language, play bridge, and do tens of thousands of other things just sitting at your computer, thanks to the complex of technology known as the Internet. The following is a summary of some of what you'll need to go online, and some general information on how it works.

The Internet, or World Wide Web, is a system of live data connections (mainly via phone lines) that ties together countless huge and tiny network "servers"—the command centers of the network—that make up the Internet. The computers communicate with each other via programming that's seen by the computer user as graphics, or hypertext "links." These connections retrieve information—data, images, sounds, etc.— from files on other computers, or servers. The computer does this with the aid of a tool called a "browser."

BROWSERS AND SEARCH ENGINES

The Internet comes alive thanks to the connections created by browsers, software navigators that deliver Internet sites, or pages, with sound, graphics, and full-format text, to computer users around the world. Whether you use an Internet Service Provider (ISP) or an online service like CompuServe or America Online to access the Internet, you'll use a browser to go places. The most popular browsers at this writing are Microsoft's Internet Explorer, better known as "IE," and Netscape's Navigator. IE and Navigator differ in their "interface," or how they look, and in the package of tools, including e-mail and other functions, that are bundled with them or are available as add-ons. The browser you choose is usually a matter of personal preference, and your operating system—if you can, try both to see which works better for your needs.

Browsers are the way you get around, and "search engines" are the way you locate what you want to find. These tools locate sites on the Internet based on topics you supply in a "query." The success of any given search—how closely the search results match your objectives—depends on how the search engine indexes sites on the Internet, and how well you frame your queries. Each search engine has different rules governing how to write, expand, and limit a search. Take the time to read the tips and guidelines on doing "advanced searches" to optimize results. The most popular search engines at this writing are Excite, Yahoo!, Lycos, Infoseek, AltaVista, Magellan, WebCrawler, and HotBot; each browser will include several on its "search" page, along with tips on how to use them. They also have their own web pages (usually http://www.*search-engine-name*.com/), which have more information and extras. Try the different search engines with identical queries to see which ones yield the best results for you.

COMMUNICATION: E-MAIL AND CHAT

E-mail, or electronic mail, is reportedly the most-used application on the Internet. E-mail uses a memorandum format—a blank for the name and e-mail address of the recipient, a "re" spot for the subject of the message, a section for the message text, and features such as carbon copies, file attachments, etc. Options and formats vary with the e-mail program, and the way your message is received is affected by the e-mail program, or "client," used by the recipient. But the procedure is pretty uniform: Type your message, address it, and click the "send" button—that's e-mail at its most basic. E-mail is this powerful and that plain. You can send it to thousands of people at the same time, but most programs don't even allow you to underline or italicize words. These limitations, and other peculiarities of e-mail and other computer-based communications, have given rise to a set of protocols governing how you address, punctuate, and mail or post your messages. If you're new to online communication, you'll probably find guidelines in the help screens and online manuals provided with the e-mail and browsers you use. (You can also search the Internet for guidelines, using "netiquette" as a query term.) E-mail protocol, commonly used contractions, and the language of "emoticons," punctuation symbols arranged to represent facial expressions, are the subject of *Smiley's,* by David W. Sanderson, and *!%@: A Directory of Electronic Mail Addressing & Networks,* by Donnalyn Frey and Rick Adams (both titles from O'Reilly & Associates, 1993).

"Chat" is exactly what it sounds like—discussion, which may be typed or may be spoken, or both. When people refer to chat, they usually mean "real time" communications, not messages that are mailed or posted, and responded to later. Chat is one of the fastest-growing functions on the Internet, and it's available through both major online services, on Internet chat sites, and through independent connections. Most chat services on the Internet are free; some require you to register your e-mail address and a screen name to receive access, and some require you to use their communication software (available as a download). Some programs allow you to type back and forth, send files while talking, post images on electronic white boards, and even have live voice and video transmissions, depending on your computer's equipment and configuration. Some of the most popular free "type" chat and IRC (Internet Relay Chat—live voice) programs at this writing are PowWow, RoChE, mIRC, Pirch, Microsoft's NetMeeting, InterChat, and IBM's IC Phone. For a listing of IRC Clients, try http://www.windows95.com/apps/chat.html and, for general assistance, http://www.irchelp.org/

SECURITY: PROTECTING CHILDREN AND DATA

If your *children* are using the computer, it's vital to take steps to screen the content to which they have access, and to oversee chat and communications. Some services, such as PowWow, have established "kid" versions of their chat areas for children. The online services make "parental controls" available that allow you to block access to adult material and areas. You can also get software that rates pages and blocks access to sites on the Internet at large based on different criteria. Some of the most popular programs are SurfWatch, Net Nanny, daxHOUND (from Net Shepherd), Cyber Patrol, Cybersitter, Safe Surf, The Internet Filter, and Web-Track. However, there is *no substitute* for direct, attentive, parental supervision.

At this writing, there is no assurance that any data on the Net is safe from hackers and "phone phreaks," or people who enjoy invading networks and systems. When you go online, you usually have to set up an account that bills one of your credit cards; to reduce exposure in the really unlikely event someone obtains this data, use a card with a low ($1,000 or lower) line of credit, and *never* use a debit card. Bear in mind, also, that your e-mail communications may be read at many points during transmission—again, this is not likely outside a job environment, but it can happen. Encryption programs, the most popular of which is "PGP" (for "Pretty Good Privacy"), can help to safeguard the content of your letters. If you're posting communications publicly or within online services, be aware that most services have guides to acceptable behavior and speech. If you have questions, the customer service department or the sysop (who plays the role of hall monitor and traffic supervisor) should be able to give you guidance.

REFERENCES

At this point, the best strategy for getting acquainted with the Net is to make your first stop one of the big online services (see below). But if you want to tackle the Net, bravo! Following are several books on how to do it. If one doesn't help, try another, and remember: The rewards for making it easy for millions of people to navigate the Net successfully are so great, that *someone* will come up with the "dream browser." Until then:

GUIDES TO THE INTERNET AND RELATED REFERENCES

1. *The Online User's Encyclopedia:* Bulletin Boards and Beyond, by Bernard Aboba (Addison-Wesley), manages to be big and deep and lots of fun, covering both Mac and Windows Net surfing with lots of graphics and command examples. Extensive bibliographies, reviews of software and books, a guide to cable configuration, and lists of bulletin board sites (BBSs), conferences, online resources, UNIX tips, and a glossary are great extras. Register for the book online and you can download the updates.

2. *The Whole Internet User's Guide and Catalog,* by Ed Krol (O'Reilly & Associates, Inc.), is an excellent, accessible guide that defines the Internet and covers access, file transfers, e-mail, newsgroups, navigating, performing searches, the Web, and troubleshooting problems. The "catalog" of the book lists hundreds of intriguing Net sites, from "aeronautics" (NASA's Langley Research Center) to "zymurgy" (sources for home-brewed beer). A detachable card of basic UNIX commands ends this useful volume.

3. The *Dummies* books, as in "DOS for," "Windows for," and "Modems for," also carries titles on modems, the Internet, and online services. If you like the format, check out the most recent titles.

INTERNET SERVICE PROVIDERS AND ONLINE SERVICES

By using an online service as your Internet Service Provider (ISP), you can access the Internet for less than $10 a month—*if* you can hold your time online to five hours or less. This has proven nearly impossible for many people, which accounts for the popularity of ISPs—firms whose reason for being is to provide access to the Internet. You usually get e-mail services from your ISP, and may have a personal web page thrown in. The going rate for unlimited use is $19.95, but rates vary across the country and by provider, so it pays to shop around. The computer magazines rank the services periodically, and *Consumer Reports* has also evaluated national ISPs. You can also check the reviews published by CNET (http://www.cnet.com), which count customer satisfaction and performance problems (busies, disconnects, diminished connection speed, etc.). To locate an ISP provider in your area, your best source is on the Internet: the List (http://thelist.com), a database of ISPs around the world—nearly 5,000 at this writing. It's searchable by physical locus or area code, and is especially valuable for anyone living in a remote area not widely served by the ISPs.

Online services, such as America Online and CompuServe, are freestanding networks with gateways to the Internet. America Online claims the hearts of its users with chatrooms and exuberant graphics and "fun stuff," while CompuServe appeals to the minds of its users, with business and computer forums and "hard" information services. Microsoft Network and Prodigy are also multi-featured providers. The online services all offer different services, pricing structures, and amenities, and are best evaluated when you're ready to sign on. You can visit their websites (which is not the same as using their services): America Online is at http://www.aol.com/, CompuServe Information Services is at http://world.compuserve.com/, Microsoft Network is at http://www.msn.com/, and Prodigy is at http://www.prodigy.com/.

HEALTH, FITNESS, AND BEAUTY

Cosmetics, perfumes, and toiletries;

vitamins and dietary supplements;

exercise equipment

You can save a solid 30% on many of your cosmetic and beauty needs and still get the same name brands featured in beauty emporiums and department stores when you buy by mail. Products may be in perfectly good but discontinued colors, promotional sizes or packaging, or have some other attribute that distinguishes them from the full-size, full-price product. Another source for savings is Sally Beauty Supply, a network of beauty-supply stores across the country that sell to both consumers and cosmetologists. Find the store nearest you by calling 800–284-SALLY; once you're familiar with the products, you may be able place phone orders instead of shopping in the store. Good discounts on perfumes are somewhat elusive; the savings tend to be closer to 20% off list, and if the discounts are deeper, the scent may be specially packaged, a gray-market product, or counterfeit. You may find a bargain in "copycat" scents, which are produced by Essential Products and other firms. If you like their version, you'll save up to 90% on the cost of the real thing.

Since they're not regulated as drugs by the FDA, supplements are listed here. You can stay informed about the debate about regulation of nutritional supplements, as well as research findings in nutrition and general medical issues, through the health sections of papers and newsweeklies, but you may find more focused coverage in such specialty newsletters as the monthly *University of California at Berkeley Wellness Letter* ($24 per year in the U.S.; to subscribe, write to P.O. Box 420148, Palm Coast, FL 32142, or call 904–445–6414). If you're going to take anything to augment your diet and improve your sense of well-being, be sure to consult your primary-care physician, especially if you're already taking medication or have a health problem. And always tell your doctor about any supplements you're taking prior to surgery.

For more information on nutrition-related health resources, see the introduction to "Food and Drink"; for firms selling related products and pharmaceuticals, see the listings in "Medicine."

FIND IT FAST

EXERCISE EQUIPMENT • **Creative Health**
PERFUME AND BEAUTY PRODUCTS • **Beauty Boutique, Essential Products, Fragrance International, Kettle Care**
SUNGLASSES • **Sunglasses U.S.A.**
VITAMINS • **Freeda, Hillestad, L & H, PIA, Star**

BEAUTY BOUTIQUE

6836 ENGLE RD.
P.O. BOX 94520
CLEVELAND, OH
 44101–4520
216–826–3008

Catalog: free
Pay: check, MO, MC, V, Discover
Sells: cosmetics and treatment products
Store: mail order only

Before you pay top dollar for cosmetics and perfumes, see the 80-page catalog from Beauty Boutique, which can save you as much as 90% on the original or full-size selling prices. You'll find page after page of cosmetics, beauty treatments, perfumes, and accessories, from names like Almay, Elizabeth Arden, Borghese, Chanel, Coty, Giorgio, Halston, Calvin Klein, Lancôme, Estée Lauder, L'Oréal, Monteil, Prince Matchabelli, Oscar de la Renta, Revlon, Stendhal, and Yves St. Laurent. In addition, the catalogs feature skin treatments, beauty tools, jewelry, a small selection of lingerie, home care products and organizers, and other useful items. Prices are genuinely low, and because some products are packaged in promotional sizes, buying here is a great way to try something out without making a full-size investment.

Special Factors: Satisfaction is guaranteed; returns are accepted for exchange, refund, or credit.

CREATIVE HEALTH PRODUCTS

DEPT. WBM
5148 SADDLE RIDGE RD.
PLYMOUTH, MI 48170
313–996–5900
FAX: 313–996–4650

Catalog: $2
Pay: check, MO, MC, V, AE, Discover
Sells: fitness testing equipment, health-monitoring products
Store: mail order only (see text)

Creative Health Products has been selling health, fitness, and exercise equipment since 1976, and carries some of the best product lines available. Savings vary from item to item, but average 30% on list or regular retail prices. The 20-page catalog lists current models of stationary bicycles, ergometers, and stair climbers by Cateye and Monarch. There are heart-rate monitors from Biosig Instruments, Cardio Sport, Nissei, Polar/CIC, and Sensor Dynamics. Fitness measuring equipment, strength and flexibility testers, blood pressure testers, stethoscopes, body-fat calipers, bio-impedance body-fat analyzers, and other measurement tools are available, from American Diagnostic, Baseline, Harpenden, Jamar, Lafayette, Lange, Novel, Omron/Marshall, and Preston. Professional-quality scales from Detecto, Health-O-Meter, Seca, and Tanita are available. A number of books on health and fitness are offered, and the catalog includes guides on buying different types of devices. Please note that this is professional equipment and, even with discounts, the prices are not low. Creative Health welcomes questions about any of the products, and can help you find the best equipment for your needs. Although primarily a mail-order firm, Creative Health welcomes visitors (weekdays, 9–4), so drop by if you're in the area (call first for directions).

Special Factors: Quantity discounts are available; institutional accounts are available; C.O.D. orders are accepted.

ESSENTIAL PRODUCTS CO., INC.

DEPT. WBM
90 WATER ST.
NEW YORK, NY
10005–3587
212–344–4288

Price List and Sample Cards: free with SASE (see text)
Pay: check or MO
Sells: "copycat" fragrances
Store: same address; Monday to Friday 9–6

"We offer our versions of the world's most treasured and expensive ladies' perfumes and men's colognes, selling them at a small fraction of the original prices." Essential was founded in 1895 and markets its interpretations of famous perfumes under the brand name of "Naudet."

Essential Products stocks 50 different copies of such costly perfumes as Beautiful, Coco, Eternity, Giorgio, Joy, L'Air du Temps, Obsession, Opium, Passion, Poison, White Diamonds, and Ysatis, as well as 23 "copycat" colognes for men, from Antaeus to Zizanie. A 1-ounce bottle of perfume is $20 (½ ounce, $11.50), and 4 ounces of any men's cologne cost $11. When you write to Essential Products, please identify yourself as a WBMC reader, which entitles you to five free "scent cards" of Essential's best-selling fragrances. The sample cards give an idea of how closely the Naudet version replicates the original, but you should try the product to evaluate it properly. You must also enclose a long, stamped, self-addressed envelope for the set of samples.

Special Factors: Satisfaction is guaranteed; returns are accepted within 30 days for refund; minimum order is $20.

FRAGRANCE INTERNATIONAL, INC.

398 E. RAYEN AVE.
YOUNGSTOWN, OH 44505
800–877–3341
800–543–3341
330–747–3341
FAX: 330–747–7200

Information: price quote
Pay: check, MO, MC, V, Discover
Sells: men's and women's scent
Store: mail order only

Living well may be the best revenge, but doing it at a discount goes one better. Fragrance International can help you carve an average of 28% to 33% off your next purchase of men's or women's scent, whether you're buying full-strength perfume, eau de parfum, eau de toilette, cologne, after shave, body cream, lotion, dusting powder, or deodorant. Not every scent is offered in every form, but the current list includes hundreds—from Adolfo to Yves Saint Laurent's "Y" for women, and Aramis to Zizanie for men. In addition, a selection of bath salts and shower gels, cosmetic bags, manicure accessories, cosmetic trays, makeup mirrors, and other beauty and bath accessories is available.

Special Factors: Orders under $50 are charged a $5 handling fee.

FREEDA VITAMINS, INC.

36 E. 41ST ST.
NEW YORK, NY
10017–6203
800–777–3737
212–685–4980
FAX: 212–685–7297
TDD: 800–777–3737

Catalog: free
Pay: check, MO, MC, V, AE, Discover
Sells: dietary supplements and prescriptions
Store: Freeda Pharmacy, same address; Monday to Thursday 8:30–6, Friday 8:30–4

 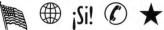

Freeda, a family-run operation, has been manufacturing vitamins and minerals in its own plant since 1928. Freeda is dedicated to providing the purest possible product, and its formulations are free of coal-tar dyes, sulfates, gluten, starch, animal stearates, pesticides, sugar, and artificial flavorings, and are suitable for even the strictest vegetarian or kosher diet—and don't upset sensitive stomachs. The Zimmermans, who run the firm, put an extra tablet in every bottle just to be nice, and their prices represent savings of up to 40% on some of the supplements.

The 36-page catalog lists vitamins, minerals, multivitamins, and nutritional products, which are available in a dizzying choice of combinations and strengths. The vitamin selection includes A and D, B, C, and E; among the minerals are calcium, iron, magnesium, potassium, selenium, and zinc; amino acids, proteins, and other dietary extras are offered. Freeda is listed here not for its megadose formulations, but because of its emphasis on quality production and additive-free goods. It's great to find a source for children's (and adults') vitamins made without sugar, coal-tar dyes, sulfiting agents, animal stearates, sulfates, or artificial flavorings. (Freeda's chewable vitamins are naturally flavored, and there is an unflavored version for children on restricted diets. All of the Freeda vitamins are approved by the Feingold Association.) Needless to say, the Freeda catalog is free of the preposterous claims and misleading information often given by supplement sellers. And wonderful as all of this is, it's still important to check with your health-care professional before taking supplements and to avoid megadoses unless they're specifically recommended.

Special Factors: Courtesy discounts are given to health-care professionals; most major health plans are honored; C.O.D. orders are accepted.

HILLESTAD INTERNATIONAL, INC.

P.O. BOX 1700
178 U.S. HWY. 51 NORTH
WOODRUFF, WI 54568
800–535–7742
715–358–2113
FAX: 715–358–7812

Catalog: $3
Pay: check, MO, MC, V, Discover
Sells: nutritional supplements, toiletries, and cleaning products
Store: same address; Monday to Friday 8–5

 ¡Si!

You can get "factory-direct" prices on the Hillestad lines of vitamins, minerals, and other supplements by ordering from the manufacturer, who's been in business since 1959. Prices here are up to 40% lower than those charged elsewhere for comparable goods.

Hillestad offers a good selection of vitamins and minerals through a comparatively hype-free catalog. There are multivitamin and mineral formulations for adults, chewable versions for children, vitamins A, B-complex, C, and E; a "stress" formula; and chelated iron, bone meal, lecithin, alfalfa, amino acids, protein, and antioxidants. Hillestad also sells a host of herbs, pet vitamins, garlic and parsley, cranberry tablets, vitamin E cream and aloe body lotion, shampoo, and cream rinse. Complete label data on most products are given in the catalog.

Special Factors: Satisfaction is guaranteed; all goods are guaranteed against defects in manufacturing; returns are accepted within 30 days.

KETTLE CARE

DEPT. WBMC
710 TRAP RD.
COLUMBIA FALLS, MT
59912
406–892–3294
FAX: 406–892–3294

Catalog: $1, $2 outside the U.S.
Pay: check, MO, MC, V, Discover
Sells: natural skin-care and bath products
Store: Kembali Imports, Gateway West Mall, Kalispell, MT; Monday to Friday 10–9, Saturday 10–6, Sunday 12–5

Every skin-care empire ever built began with someone at the stove, turning improbable ingredients into the stuff of dreams. That's the business of Kettle Care, where natural products and botanicals are combined to create moisturizers, facial creams, facial scrubs, lotions, balms, and other things to soothe your skin and spirit. The 16-page color catalog features lavender liquid castile-based facial soap, botanically scented massage oils, hand-saving Worker's Creme, natural facial scrubs, lotion for normal-to-oily complexions, Aromatherapy Facial Creme, and pure essential oils. Herbal sleep and dream pillows, bath herbs, and woodsy herbal sachets are part of the "Herbal Pleasures" section. The prices are very reasonable: Kettle Care's Herbal Aid Creme with cocoa butter and almond oil costs $8 for 2 ounces, while Caswell-Massey's Almond Night Cream costs nearly $15 for the same amount. (The offerings here compare favorably to favorite unguents from Weleda and Aubrey Organics, too.) Among the other good buys are quarter ounces of essential and fragrance oils for $5 and jars of naturally flavored lip balm for $2.25. You can buy everything individually, or take advantage of the sample sets and discounted "packs" of four or six of the same kind of item. (Kettle Care offers a 25¢ credit for every container rcturned; many products are available packaged in glass.) The catalog lists the ingredients of most of the products, and includes directions for use. And there's a guide to which skin-care products suit which complexion types, so you can develop your own treatment line and regimen.

Wholesale customers: The wholesale catalog costs $1, the minimum order is $35, and the discounts average 45% to 50% off retail catalog prices.

Special Factors: Satisfaction is guaranteed; retuins are accepted for exchange, refund, or credit.

L & H VITAMINS, INC.

32–33 47TH AVE.
LONG ISLAND CITY, NY
11101
800–221–1152
FAX: 718–361–1437

Catalog: free
Pay: check, MO, MC, V, Discover, NOVUS
Sells: nutritional supplements and self-treatment products
Store: same address
Online: http://www.lhvitamins.com

"Take good care of yourself" means different things to different people, but for many of us, the translation is a good diet, exercise, and nutritional supplements. And when it comes to deciding what to take, the interpretations are even more wide ranging. Enter L & H Vitamins, which offers over 10,000 different items in the closely printed, 84-page catalog. The listings run from amino acids to zinc, and include treatment lines for skin, hair care products, and pet vitamins. The catalog is organized by brand name, and cross-referenced in the "VitaFinder" by category, making it easy to find what you want. L & H represents scores of manufacturers and labels, including American Health, Bach, Doctor's Best, Food Science Laboratories, Futurebiotics, Kyolic, Natrol, Nature's Way, Reviva, Schiff, Synergy Plus, Thompson, Twinlab, and many others. Prices are 20% to 40% below list, a welcome break from the rates charged at health food stores. Do your homework before picking up the catalog, though, because you'll have to find out about the formulations and ingredients of these products elsewhere—catalog space doesn't permit both this enormous selection and a lot of product information.

Special Factors: Satisfaction is guaranteed; returns are accepted within 30 days for exchange, refund, or credit.

PIA DISCOUNT VITAMINS

708 SAW MILL RIVER RD.
ARDSLEY, NY 10502
800–662–8144
914–693–3632
FAX: 914–693–3557

Catalog: free
Pay: check, MO, MC, V, AE, Discover
Sells: supplements, homeopathic remedies, vitamins, herbs, etc.
Store: mail order only
E-mail: PIAvitamins@prodigy.net

There are plenty of companies selling generic lines of vitamins, but the 32-page catalog from PIA offers name-brand vitamins, minerals, and remedies, at a minimum savings of 20% on list. The formulations are not given, but they're easy to locate when you visit your health food store or pharmacy to price shop.

The catalog, which includes a guide to vitamins, minerals, and botanicals, begins with Alacer ascorbates and ends with zinc lozenges, and offers savings on Bach Flower remedies (hard to find at a discount), Boiron, FutureBiotics, Good 'N Natural, Kwai, Kyolic, Medicine from Nature, Nature's Way, Gary Null's products, Schiff, and Twinlab. The name of the product, form (caplet, tablet, etc.), potency, and amount are given, with the retail and discounted prices. If you don't see what you're looking for, call PIA to see whether it can be ordered.

Special Factors: Satisfaction is guaranteed; price quote by phone or letter.

STAR PROFESSIONAL PHARMACEUTICALS

1500 NEW HORIZONS
  BLVD.
AMITYVILLE, NY 11701
800–274–6400
516–957–8371

Catalog: free
Pay: check, MO, MC, V, AE, Discover
Sells: supplements, toiletries, health-care products
Store: mail order only
Online: http://starhomehealth.com

Star Professional Pharmaceutical, the consumer division of a corporation serving the needs of the health care industry, publishes a 56-page catalog that features nutritional supplements, over-the-counter remedies, and a variety of personal-care products. If you don't have access to superstores and discount drugstores, you'll probably appreciate the good buys on generic equivalents of name-brand pain relievers, ointments, cold remedies, foot preparations, shampoos, digestive aids, and skin treatments. Both name-brand vitamin equivalents and Star's own supplements are available. Depending on the item, price comparisons showed savings of 15% to 50% on the prices of comparable or name-brand equivalents.

Special Factors: Satisfaction is guaranteed; returns are accepted within 30 days for exchange, refund, or credit.

SUNGLASSES U.S.A., INC.

469 SUNRISE HWY.
LYNBROOK, NY 11563
800-USA-RAYS
FAX: 516–599–4825

Catalog: free
Pay: check, MO, MC, V, AE, Discover
Sells: Ray-Ban sunglasses
Store: same address; Monday to Friday 10–5:30

Sunglasses U.S.A. sells Ray-Ban sunglasses at 33% to 50% off suggested retail. The catalog includes information on the lens material, color, and protection factors against glare and ultraviolet light. The Ray-Ban lines currently available include Classic Metals, Killer Loop (shields), Traditionals and Premier Traditionals, Wayfarers, Leathers, Tortuga, Cats, and Retrospecs. The price list includes sizing and style numbers, making it easy to be sure you're buying the right model.

Special Factors: Shipping and handling cost a flat $2 per order.

SEE ALSO

Baby Bunz & Co. • *natural bathing toiletries for babies* • **CLOTHING: MOTHER AND CHILD**
Better Health Fitness • *exercise equipment* • **SPORTS**
Cal Ben Soap Company • *natural soap, laundry and bath products, etc.* • **GENERAL MERCHANDISE**
Caprilands Herb Farm • *potpourri ingredients, essential oils, etc.* • **FARM**
Dairy Association Co., Inc. • *Bag Balm liniment* • **ANIMAL**

Deer Valley Farm • *nutritional supplements and natural toiletries* • **FOOD**

Fitness Factory Outlet • *exercise equipment* • **SPORTS**

J & R Systems International • *personal and household cleaning products and tools* • **GENERAL MERCHANDISE**

Jaffe Bros., Inc. • *Jaybee brand soap/shampoo* • **FOOD**

The Natural Baby Co., Inc. • *homeopathic and natural remedies* • **CLOTHING: MOTHER AND CHILD**

Penzeys' Spice House • *salt-free seasonings* • **FOOD: BEVERAGES AND FLAVORINGS**

Retired Persons Services, Inc. • *vitamins, beauty products, shampoo, etc.* • **MEDICINE**

Walnut Acres Organic Farms • *natural toiletries, nutritional supplements* • **FOOD**

— HOME —
Decor

Floor coverings, wall and window treatments, lighting, upholstery materials, tools, and services

The section of the "home" decor chapter immediately following this introduction covers treatments for windows, walls, and furnishings. That's where you'll find firms selling fabric, stock and custom blinds and shades, wallpaper and borders, and drapery hardware and painting accessories. If you're looking for lamp and shade specialists, you'll find them in "Lighting," immediately after this section; for carpeting and floor-covering suppliers, see "Flooring," following that.

Doing your own decorating instead of hiring someone is a time-honored tradition, and there are scores of books on interior design written specifically for consumers, such as *Interior Design on Your Own,* from Consumer Reports Books. *Interior Design,* by John F. Pile (Harry N. Abrams, Inc., 1988), is a sumptuous, oversized guide to classics old and new, that includes design principles and fundamentals. Shelter magazines (*House Beautiful, Metropolitan Home, World of Interiors,* etc.) can be great sources for ideas, but beware the chic totem: Tizio lamps, the Atelier "red and blue" chair, banana plants, overdone windows, and Pirelli floors have all enjoyed endorsement as "timeless" by the design establishment, but have become dated clichés. Focus on styles that *you* find refreshing and beautiful, products with good materials and workmanship that have special appeal to you, and you'll make better buying decisions.

If you haven't already done so, set up decorating files. Create one for each room or project, with the budget, floor plan, measurements, paint chips, swatches, sources, and other reference materials. Before embarking on the project, you might take one designer's advice and shoot a series of "before" pictures, which can help you see the room's strengths and possibilities, as well as its limitations. Even if they don't prove useful when you're designing the room, you'll enjoy seeing the contrast when everything is done!

Until recently, access to the best fabrics, furnishings, and accessories has been limited to design professionals ("to the trade"). Over the last few years, many of these products have become available from discounters and retail decorators. They sell to consumers who've shopped the showrooms and read the shelter magazines and want the best, and are willing to pay for it. Some decorators now offer their buying services (with or without design consultations), enabling consumers to purchase once-unavailable fabrics, accessories, and furnishings, sometimes at a discount.

All of this sounds good—consumers become educated, discounters respond with access to more products, manufacturers sell more goods, small design firms increase their business. Manufacturers take a different view, sometimes threatening to pull their product lines from discounters and nontraditional sellers if their brand or trade names appear in ads—or even in editorial mentions, such as the listings in this book. As a result of this problem (which affects a number of other industries, not just the home furnishings trade), certain brand names may not appear in a merchant's listing, even when that brand is available. If you want to find out whether a firm offers a line that's not mentioned in the listing, you must call or write.

In addition to the firms listed in this section, you'll find companies selling clocks, mirrors, mattresses, lamps, and related goods in the "Furnishings" chapter—see the "Find it Fast" section of that chapter for a thumbnail guide.

FIND IT FAST

DECORATOR FABRIC • **BMI, Dorothy's, Fabric Center, Hancock's, Home Fabric Mills, Homespun Fabrics, Marlene's, Shama, Silk Surplus**
DECORATOR TRIM • **Fabric Center, Hancock's**
WINDOW AND WALL TREATMENTS • **Benington's, BMI, Dorothy's, Hang-It-Now, Harmony, Homespun Fabrics, Robinson's, Wells Interiors**

BENINGTON'S

DEPT. WBMC
1271 MANHEIM PIKE
LANCASTER, PA 17601
800-252-5060
717-299-2381
FAX: 717-299-4889

Catalog: $4 (see text)
Pay: check, MO, MC, V, AE, Discover
Sells: wall coverings, rugs, and carpeting
Store: same address; Monday to Friday
9:30–9, Tuesday and Saturday 9:30–5:30;
seven other outlets in PA and VA
Online: http://www.beni.com

 ¡Si!

Benington's observes that "decorating is exciting when you can get what you want at a price you can afford," and aims to deliver with discounts of up to 83%. The firm incorporates wall coverings, decorator fabrics, and area rugs under one roof, representing the major names in all three industries. Call with the name of the manufacturer, the pattern book name or number, style, color, and amount you'll require, to receive a price quote. Extra-wide commercial wall coverings are also available. Prices average 50% below list, and if you're ordering large quantities, you may receive deeper discounts.

Benington's full-color catalog "of wall coverings, rugs and decorating ideas," which costs $4—refundable with your first order—includes a number of actual wallpaper samples, and plenty of photos showing how the wallpapers and borders look in real installations.

Special Factors: Price quote by phone, fax, or letter; wall coverings (except commercial or institutional orders) are shipped free within the continental United States.

BMI HOME DECORATING

6917 CATALPA CT.
SPRING GROVE, IL 60081
815-675-3703
FAX: 815-675-3603

Information: price quote
Pay: check, MO, MC, V
Sells: decorator fabric, wall coverings, window treatments, etc.
Store: mail order only

BMI Home Decorating can give you access to "almost all fabrics," from names that are "too many to list" but number over 200, including many that are usually limited to the trade. In addition to fabric, BMI offers wall coverings, blinds, and drapery hardware, and can fabricate pillows, bedspreads, and headboards to order. The firm has been in business since 1978, and believes it can offer customers savings averaging 35% on suggested list prices, depending on the item, amount ordered, and other criteria. When you call for a price quote, be sure you know the brand name, style and/or number, book name (for wall coverings), and quantity or amount you require.

Special Factors: Price quote by phone or letter.

DOROTHY'S RUFFLED ORIGINALS, INC.

6721 MARKET ST.
WILMINGTON, NC 28405
910–799–6386
FAX: 910–799–5798

Catalog: free
Pay: check, MO, MC, V, AE, Discover
Sells: decorator fabrics and custom window treatments
Store: same address; also Goldsboro, NC; and Newport News, VA

Dorothy's Ruffled Originals celebrates the swags, poufs, jabots, flounces, and flourishes of fully dressed windows with a large collection of custom- and ready-made draperies, bed linens, table toppers, pillows, shower curtains, canopies—plus all the hardware and rods you need to put things in place.

Dorothy's catalog features full-color showcases of the firm's designs, coordinated in room settings. These creations have a Southern glamour and add a distinctly feminine touch to a room. Dorothy uses a generous six-to-one ratio of yardage to finished ruffle in many of her creations, which produces dense, luxurious gathers—most draperies are only half as voluminous. The catalog includes a guide to the fabrics Dorothy offers, and detailed price and measurement guides.

The prices of the custom work aren't *cheap,* but they're reasonable, compared to local decorating shops. If you can sew, see the good buys on Dorothy's fabric—200 different chintzes, eyelets, moirés, laces, etc.— as well as romantic florals, damask-print solids, stripes and paisleys, "wallpaper" prints on fabric, and more, from about $3 to $11 a yard. Don't miss the hardware section in the back of both catalogs, which has an excellent selection of rods, brackets, finials, supports, sashes, shelves, and other drapery fittings.

Wholesale customers, please note: A tax I.D. number is required, and discounts run up to 20%.

Special Factors: Satisfaction is guaranteed; returns of defective goods are accepted for exchange, refund, or credit; minimum order is 1 yard fabric; C.O.D. orders are accepted.

THE FABRIC CENTER, INC.

███████████

DEPT. WBMC
485 ELECTRIC AVE.
FITCHBURG, MA 01420
508–343–4402
FAX: 508–343–8139

Catalog: $2
Pay: check, MO, MC, V
Sells: interior decorator fabrics
Store: mail order only

  ⊕

The Fabric Center has been in business since 1932, selling fine fabrics for home decorating at savings of up to 50% on suggested list prices. Fabrics for upholstery and window treatments are available, including lines from Robert Allen, American Textile, Paul Barrow, Covington, George Harrington, Kravet, Peachtree, Waverly, and many others. The firm's splendid 164-page color catalog ($2) shows more fabrics than you'd find in many stores—hundreds from a wide range of manufacturers, photographed in room settings and grouped with complementary patterns and colorways. The catalog descriptions include fiber content, width, vertical repeat, and a usage code to help you determine if the material is appropriate for draperies, home accessories, or upholstery. And The Fabric Center's "Sampling Service" allows you to try the fabric in your home before you order. The 3" by 4" samples cost 15¢, the 8" by 10" pieces are 50¢, and 24" by 27" samples cost $3.95 each. (The price of each $3.95 sample can be credited to each $50 in goods ordered.) Don't miss the scores of trim—tassels, bullion fringe, cording, brush fringe, tiebacks, and more—in colors chosen to complement the widest decorative range.

Special Factors: Minimum order is 1 yard.

HANCOCK'S OF PADUCAH

DEPT. WBMC
3841 HINKLEVILLE RD.
PADUCAH, KY 42001
800–845–8723
502–443–4410
FAX: 502–442–2164, 3152

Catalog: $2, refundable (see text)
Pay: check, MO, MC, V, Discover
Sells: decorator fabrics, printed and solid cottons, pillow forms, quilting supplies, etc.
Store: same address; Monday to Friday 9:30–7, Saturday 10–6, Sunday 1–5
E-mail: DsingBear@aol.com
Online: http://www.fabric-world.com

You might not expect "America's Largest Fabric Store" to be found in Paducah, Kentucky, but the folks at Hancock's will enlighten you. They've pulled together a 64-page color catalog of the best-sellers on the retail floor there, hundreds of fabrics that represent the most popular looks in decorating today, from traditional to eclectic design. And they sell them at prices 50% to 70% below suggested retail.

The catalog includes a color shot of the fabric, the name of the design (but not the maker), and the price per yard; width, fiber content, and repeat information are not given consistently. But if you've been going through the shelter magazines and swatch books, you'll recognize much of what you see—except the prices. To be sure, avail yourself of Hancock's sampling service: 12" squares for 75¢, or 2" by 4" cuttings upon request. If you're looking for a good selection of solid colors, see the choice of chintzes, warped sateen, jacquards, and other offerings. In addition, Hancock's sells trim (brush and loop fringe, bullion, cording, tassels, etc.), drapery lining (under $3 a yard at this writing), pillow forms (up to 27" square in polyfil, and 20" square in duck- and goose-down feather, for under $13), fusible backing for roller shades, and heavy felt, and will do custom lamination for under $6 a yard.

Hancock's separate catalog for quilters ($1) is 68 pages of notions, tools and equipment, materials, a variety of quilt batts, thread, and more. You'll find quilters' collections of fabric by Bernartex, Concord, Nancy Crow, Alexander Henry, Hoffman, Debbie Mumm, P & B, South Seas, and VIP; a broad selection of interfacing, basic fabrics (from bridal satin to heavy canvas), and sewing and quilting products by Coats & Clark, Dritz, Gingher, Hobbs, Mundial, Olfa, Schmetz, and June Taylor.

Savings on list average 60% plus, and you can join the Hancock's swatch club for quilting or home fabrics, and receive a batch of snippets of Hancock's newest fabrics every month (see the catalogs for details).

Special Factors: Price quote by phone or letter; all goods are first quality; special orders are accepted.

HANG-IT-NOW WALLPAPER STORES

**304 TRINDALE RD.
ARCHDALE, NC 27263
800–325–9494
910–431–6341
FAX: 910–431–0449**

Information: price quote
Pay: check, MO, MC, V, AE, Discover
Sells: wall coverings and decorator fabrics
Store: same address; also 4620 W. Market St., Greensboro, NC; Monday to Friday 9–6, Saturday 9–3, both locations

Hang-It-Now Wallpaper, established in 1981, sells wall coverings at savings of 30% to 65% on list prices. A limited selection of decorator fabrics is also available, at discounts of up to 40%. All major brands of wall coverings (plus strings, grass cloth, and borders) are offered here, including Color House, Crutchfield, Eisenhart, Fashion, Imperial, Katzenbach and Warren, Carey Lind, Sanitas, Seabrook, Sunworthy, United, Van Luit, Warner, and York, among others. Hang-It-Now specializes in providing wall coverings to retail establishments, and has done numerous installations for furniture retailers and decorators.

Special Factors: Only first-quality goods are sold; shipping is not charged on orders sent within the contiguous 48 United States.

HARMONY SUPPLY INC.

**P.O. BOX 313
MEDFORD, MA 02155
617–395–2600
FAX: 617–396–8218**

Information: price quote
Pay: check, MO, MC, V, Discover
Sells: wall coverings, window treatments, and decorator fabrics
Store: 18 High St., Medford, MA; Monday to Saturday 8–5:30, Thursday 8 a.m.–9 p.m.

Harmony Supply, in business since 1949, can give your home a face-lift at a discount with savings of up to 70% on wallpaper, coordinating fabrics, and window treatments. Harmony carries over 2,500 designs and patterns of wallpaper, grass cloth, and string cloth, including Laura Ashley, Imperial, Katzenbach and Warren, Ralph Lauren, Sunworthy, Van Luit, and many others. Harmony Supply also sells window treatments—made-to-measure mini, micro, and vertical blinds, including wood, and pleated shades and blinds (Duette, Crystal Pleat, Silhouette, etc.) manufactured by Graber, HunterDouglas, Kirsch, LouverDrape, and Verosol. You'll save the most on goods that are currently in stock, but even special orders are discounted up to 70%, and everything Harmony sells is first quality. Call or write for a price quote, since there's no catalog or price list.

Special Factors: Satisfaction is guaranteed; returns (except custom blinds and fabrics) are accepted within 30 days (a 25% restocking fee is charged on special-order goods).

HOME FABRIC MILLS, INC.

882 S. MAIN ST.

P.O. BOX 888

CHESHIRE, CT 06410

203–272–3529

FAX: 203–272–6686

Information: price quote free
Pay: check, MO, MC, V (see text)
Sells: decorator fabrics and custom services
Store: same address; also Rte. 202, Belchertown, MA; and 443 Saratoga Rd., Rte. 50, Scotia, NY; Monday to Wednesday 10–9, Thursday to Saturday 10–5

Home Fabric Mills has been in business since 1968 and is a good source for the home decorator who's unsure of what type of fabric is best for a particular project, or the person who's trying to match a color.

The three Home Fabric Mills stores are stocked with thousands of bolts of upholstery and drapery materials, lining, trims, and workroom supplies from Bloomcraft, Conso, Covington, Graber, Kaufman, Kirsch, Lanscot-Arlen, Waverly, Wolf, and other manufacturers. Only first-quality goods are sold, and Home Fabric Mills will sell in half-yard increments—great to know if you're still deciding on your fabrics. Swatches are also available on request.

Special Factors: Price quote by phone or letter; minimum order is half a yard.

HOMESPUN FABRICS & DRAPERIES

P.O. BOX 4315-WBM

THOUSAND OAKS, CA

91359

FAX: 800–251–0858

Price List and Samples: $2

Pay: check, MO, MC, V

Sells: 10'-wide fabrics, custom-made draperies, etc.

Store: mail order only

E-mail: corporate@homespunfabrics.com

Online: http://www.homespunfabrics.com/~homespunfabrics

 (see text)

Homespun "10-Foot Wide" Fabrics & Draperies has a solution to some of the biggest drapery headaches—bulkiness, sun rot, the expense of dry cleaning, and the hassle of pleater hooks among them. Homespun Fabrics sells all-cotton material that's 10 feet wide, or about 105" to 109" after shrinkage. The fabric includes homespun, hobnail, barley, and monkscloth weaves, in white and natural. The width makes the fabric perfect for "seamless draperies," and even eliminates some of the finishing work. Homespun Fabrics manufactures all styles of draperies (suitable to the fabric), and can also custom-make "Fan Pleat" draperies. These operate on a track system that's hung from the ceiling or mounted on the wall, with a buckram header tape with nylon tabs that engage the track. The drapery folds are 4" or 5" deep, so the stackback (the area covered by the curtain when it's drawn back) that would be 37" deep with conventional pinch-pleat draperies is only 11" deep with the Fan Pleat system. Made in Homespun Fabrics' heavyweight cottons, this system produces handsome, neutral window coverings that give you maximum glass exposure. They have a crisp, tailored appearance that's ideal for modern decor and office settings, and are machine washable and dryable, and guaranteed against sun rot for seven years

In addition to the heavy cottons, Homespun Fabrics offers open-weave casement fabric, wide muslin, and both regular-width and ultra-wide semi-sheers—batiste, voile, and bouclé slub, in lots of colors. Homespun can create the draperies, or you can do it yourself—and you'll find helpful books on home decorating and guides to making fan pleat draperies, slipcovers, bedspreads, table linens, and accessories.

Special Factors: Returns are accepted within 10 days for exchange, refund, or credit; $5 cutting fee on orders of 5 or fewer yards.

MARLENE'S DECORATOR FABRICS

301 BEECH ST., DEPT. 2J
HACKENSACK, NJ 07601
201–843–0844

Flyer: free with stamped, self-addressed envelope
Pay: check, MO, MC, V
Sells: decorator fabrics
Store: mail order only; phone hours Monday to Friday 9:30–6

Marlene's Decorator Fabrics has been selling upholstery, slipcover, and drapery goods since 1946, and can save you up to 60% on the list prices of fabrics by Ametex, Anju, Artmark, Paul Barrow, Berger, Covington, Kasmir, P. Kaufmann, Kravet, Ralph Lauren, Sanderson, Stout, Stroheim & Roman, Waverly/Schumacher, Wesco, and many others. Write or call for a price quote, or send a self-addressed, stamped envelope with a sample if you're not sure of the manufacturer or pattern, or to request a brochure. Specify the yardage needed and whether you're interested in upholstery, drapery, or other decorator fabric.

Special Factors: Minimum order is 10 yards retail, 15 yards wholesale.

M.C. LIMITED FINE LEATHERS

DEPT. WBM
P.O. BOX 17696
WHITEFISH BAY, WI 53217
414–263–5222
FAX: 414–263–5508

Brochure and Price List: free
Pay: check, MO, MC, V
Sells: steer hides and hide pillows
Store: mail order only

Whether your home style is New Western, chromed modern, 90s eclectic, or Neolithic, there's nothing like steer hide to add decorative depth. M.C. Limited offers processed skins in full hides (36 square feet on average, 5' to 6' wide by 7' to 8' long) in eight natural colors and stencilled animal prints for $235. This is nearly 40% below prices by two New York City leather suppliers for comparable skins. M.C. Limited also makes steer hide pillows backed with pigskin suede, which are offered plain or with fringe, tassels, medallions, or other embellishments. Sizes range from 6" by 13" to 24" square, priced from $35 to $175. Custom options—down filling, steerhide backs, special shapes and sizes—are also available. M.C. Limited notes that all of its hides are byproducts of the beef industry, and are not claimed from animals raised primarily for their skins. A special new tanning process is reputed to render the hides "soft and beautiful" as they age, so they won't stiffen, dry out, and lose hair.

Special Factors: Satisfaction is guaranteed; authorized returns (except pillows) are accepted (a percent restocking fee is charged) within 30 days.

ROBINSON'S INTERIORS, INC.

DEPT. 8LY
225 W. SPRING ST.
P.O. BOX 427
TITUSVILLE, PA
16354–0427
800–458–2426
814–827–1893
FAX: 814–827–1693

Catalog: $2
Pay: check, MC, V, AE, Discover
Sells: wallpaper, borders, decorator fabrics, and accessories
Store: same address; also 3506 Liberty Center, Erie; 1720 Wilmington Rd., Rte. 18, New Castle, PA
E-mail: rwallcover@mail.usachoice.net

Robinson's has been in business since 1919, and sells both vinyl-coated and solid vinyl wallpaper, coordinating borders, and fabrics that are suitable for use throughout the home. The 40-page catalog also offers tools and supplies for installation, as well as decorating accents to complement your scheme. Robinson's provides color photographs that show how different designs look when they're installed—a very helpful feature. Free samples of any wall coverings shown in the catalog are available. Prices are competitive—an average of $8.99 for a single roll of wallpaper, and $8.49 for 5 yards of border trim.

Patterns not shown in the catalog are available through Robinson's Custom Order Department at savings of 35% to 60% off book price. See the catalog for details, or call with manufacturer's name, book name, pattern number, price code, and suggested retail price, to receive a quote.

Overseas customers, please note: Robinson's ships orders overseas to APO/FPO addresses and to Japan only.

SHAMA IMPORTS, INC.

DEPT. WBM–98

P.O. BOX 2900

FARMINGTON HILLS, MI

  48333–2900

248–478–7740

Brochure: free

Pay: check, MO, MC, V

Sells: crewel fabrics and home accessories

Store: mail order only

Shama Imports, which began business in 1982, offers good prices on Indian crewel fabrics and home accessories. Crewel is hand-embroidered on hand-loomed cotton, offered here in traditional serpentine flower-and-vine motifs and other distinctive designs, in a range of colors. The eight-page color brochure that shows the patterns also includes decorating suggestions. Background (unembroidered) fabric is also available by the yard, and Shama stocks crewel chair and cushion covers, tote bags, bedspreads, and tablecloths as well. All of the fabric is 52" wide and can be washed by hand or dry-cleaned. Samples are available for $1 each; those showing one-fourth of the complete pattern cost $5 (refundable). The brochure lists the pattern repeats for all of the designs.

Special Factors: Satisfaction is guaranteed; uncut, undamaged returns are accepted within 30 days for refund or credit; C.O.D. orders are accepted.

SILK SURPLUS

DEPT. 55
37–24 24TH ST.
LONG ISLAND CITY, NY
11101
718–361–8500, EXT. 55
FAX: 718–361–8311

Information: price quote
Pay: check, MO, MC, V, AE
Sells: discontinued decorator fabric and trim (see text)
Store: same address; Monday to Saturday 10–5:30, Sunday 12–5; also 235 E. 58th St., New York; 1215 Northern Blvd., Manhasset; and 281 Mamaroneck Ave., White Plains, NY

Silk Surplus is well known to budget-minded New Yorkers who covet luxurious upholstery and drapery fabrics because it's where they can save up to 75% (and sometimes even more) on sumptuous Scalamandré and Boris Kroll closeouts and fabrics from other mills. Silks, cottons, velvets, woolens, chintzes, brocades, damasks, and other weaves and finishes are usually available from Silk Surplus, which opened its doors in 1962. Walk-in customers can select from among the bolts in any of the Silk Surplus shops. But if you're buying by mail, you must know exactly which Scalamandré or Boris Kroll fabric you want, and in which color. If it's there, you're in luck. You may also send the store a fabric sample with a query. This is a great shopping stop on a trip to New York City, but only serious searchers for Scalamandré or Boris Kroll closeout fabrics should contact the store intending to buy by mail. If you're a design professional, you may ask for an additional trade discount.

Special Factors: Price quote by phone or letter with SASE; sample cuttings are free; all sales are final; minimum order is 3 yards.

WELLS INTERIORS INC.

7171 AMADOR PLAZA DR.
DUBLIN, CA 94568
800–547–8982
FAX: 510–829–1374

Catalog: free
Pay: check, MO, MC, V
Sells: window treatments and accessories
Store: same address; Monday to Friday 10–6, Saturday 10–5, Sunday 12–4; 19 other stores in CA and OR (see the catalog for locations)

Wells Interiors has been in business since 1980, guarantees "the lowest prices" on its goods, and will beat any other dealer's price down to cost on a wide range of top brands. Discounts can run up to 85% on retail prices on Levolor's mini-blinds, verticals, wood blinds, and similar styles by other manufacturers, such as Bali, Del Mar, Graber, HunterDouglas, Joanna, LouverDrape, Jenny Lynn, M&B, and Windsor. Kirsch woven woods, pleated shades, decorator roller shades, verticals, and mini-blinds are also available, as well as a line of "value-priced" verticals from Wells.

The catalog includes a guide to the lines currently available, and includes instructions on measuring your windows and installing the blinds. Details of the firm's warranty are given in the catalog as well.

Special Factors: Written confirmation is required on phone orders.

Lighting

Residential indoor and outdoor lighting fixtures, lamp shades, and related goods

The artful use of lighting ranks with color in the success of a room, but it's also one of the biggest design challenges. None of the firms listed here can tell you how to light *your* home, but you'll find the basics in interior design textbooks and decorating manuals, and the books mentioned in the introduction to "Home: Decor," preceding this section. *Lighting Style,* by Kevin McCloud (Ebury Press, 1995), showcases a wide range of possibilities. You'll find another authority in your own observations of lighting that pleases you—whether it's good general illumination, glare-free task lighting for reading or needlework, a combination of the two in a kitchen, subdued but reader-friendly lamps in a bedroom or library, or outdoor lighting that improves security while highlighting the architecture. Note how effects are created, and work with the fixtures you have to try out new ideas—raise or lower the wattage, alter the shading, change the location of the lamp, use tinted bulbs, etc. Study the optimal *placement* and *height* of light fixtures, which have distilled to rules of measurement in interior design textbooks. You can do so much with lamps (floor, table, swag, desk, etc.) and conventional ceiling fixtures (canopy and chandelier), that you might not think of retrofitting high-hats, eyeballs, or other recessed fixtures when you review your home lighting. Consider them when you want to update a track system, increase hallway lighting discreetly, or create a special effect with a spotlight or wall-washer.

The firms listed here sell lighting for the home—lamps, ceiling fixtures, bathroom and kitchen fixtures, patio and walkway lighting, building lanterns, etc.—and related electrical accessories, shades, and replacement parts. Some also sell ceiling fans and attachments. Discounts average about 30% to 40% on name-brand goods, and the firms that manufacture their own fixtures sell at competitive prices.

FIND IT FAST

CEILING FANS • **American Light Source, Golden Valley, Main Lamp**
CRYSTAL CHANDELIERS • **King's Chandelier, Luigi Crystal**
REPLACEMENT PRISMS, HURRICANES, BOBECHES • **King's Chandelier, Luigi Crystal**

AMERICAN LIGHT SOURCE

5211D WEST MARKET ST.,
SUITE 803
GREENSBORO, NC 27409
800–741–0571

Catalog: $5, refundable (see text)
Pay: check, MO, MC, V, AE
Sells: light fixtures and ceiling fans
Store: mail order only

American Light Source has been in business for several years, selling lighting fixtures for every room of the house (and porch and patio, too), at savings of up to 40%. The firm represents over 100 major manufacturers, and sends you a batch of brochures on lighting fixtures, ceiling fans, and accessories for your $5 literature fee. If you know what you want, you can call or write with the manufacturer's name and model number of the piece for a price quote. Please note the minimum order: $150.

Special Factors: Satisfaction is guaranteed; price quote by phone or letter; minimum order is $150.

BRASS LIGHT GALLERY, INC.

DEPT. WBMC
131 S. 1ST ST.
MILWAUKEE, WI 53204
800–243–9595
FAX: 414–271–7755

Catalog: $6, refundable (see text)
Pay: check, MO, MC, V
Sells: lighting fixtures
Store: same address; Monday to Friday 9–5, Saturday 10–4

After you've seen the fixtures from Brass Light Gallery, you'll know why you've held off buying from other sources. Not only are the materials and workmanship here of superior quality, but the designs have that satisfyingly "right" quality that's so often lacking in lighting fixtures. The Goldenrod and Continental Collections showcase classic architectural styles for kitchens, bathrooms, bedrooms, and other interior spaces. The Alabaster Collection offers timeless chandeliers, sconces, and table lamps in natural alabaster, at prices often lower than those charged for the originals from the 20s and 30s—when you can find them, intact and unchipped, in antique stores. The Prismatic Collection features authentic vintage glass pendants (ribbed glass), suitable for kitchen and loft spaces. Most of the fixtures are offered in a choice of metal finishes and/or choices of glass shade color or style, allowing you to customize each fixture to your room's decor.

The Brass Light Gallery's catalog—over 100 pages of lighting, plus technical specifications—has been designed for use by homeowners, interior designers, and architects. (The catalog costs $6, refundable with purchase, but a 12-page color brochure is free on request.) Prices here average 20% below retail, but the fixtures are better quality than those being sold by many of Brass Light Gallery's competitors.

Special Factors: Satisfaction is guaranteed.

GOLDEN VALLEY LIGHTING

274 EASTCHESTER DR.,
  #117A
HIGH POINT, NC 27262
800–735–3377
910–882–7330
FAX: 800–760–6678
FAX: 910–882–2262

Catalog: $2, refundable (see text)
Pay: check, MO, MC, V, Discover
Sells: lighting fixtures and ceiling fans
Store: mail order only
Online: http://www.gvlight.com

Golden Valley, whose parent company was founded in 1926, is run by veterans of the lighting industry who offer savings of up to 50% on lighting fixtures and ceiling fans. You can call to order, or send $2 (refundable with purchase) for Golden Valley's color catalog featuring chandeliers, ceiling fixtures, sconces, bathroom and vanity strip lighting, ceiling fans, and more. Or you can request a price quote. (Call when you've decided what you want, and have the manufacturer's name, model number, color, finish, and any other details at hand.) When you're ready to order, you can make a deposit of 50% of the cost of the fixture, and pay the balance before shipment, or prepay the entire amount and expedite the order. Undecided and need some assistance? Visit Golden Valley's website, where you'll find tips on lighting, selecting fixtures, conserving energy, and making the most of your home lighting.

Special Factors: Price quote by phone or letter with SASE.

KING'S CHANDELIER CO.

DEPT. WBM98

P.O. BOX 667

EDEN, NC 27288–0667

910–623–6188

FAX: 910–627–9935

Catalog: $4, $5 outside the U.S.

Pay: check, MO, MC, V

Sells: Czech, Venetian, and Strass crystal chandeliers

Store: Hwy. 14 (Van Buren Rd.), Eden, NC; Monday to Saturday 10–4:30

E-mail: crystal@vnet.net

Online: http://www.chandelier.com

The Kings have been designing and producing chandeliers since 1935, and offer their designs through their catalog of light fixtures to suit every taste, at prices for all budgets. There are chandeliers, candelabras, and wall sconces in a range of styles: Victorian and many variations on the classic lighting fixture dripping with prisms, pendalogues, faceted balls, and ropes of crystal buttons, as well as the Kings' own magnificent designs made of Strass crystal. Prices begin at about $190 for a small chandelier and go up to $12,500 for the palatial Strass Royal Belvedere. Options include different finishes on the metal parts, hurricane shades or candelabra tapers, and candelabra bulb sockets. Replacement parts for these lighting fixtures are stocked as well.

Since even the 36-page catalog can't show the chandeliers to best advantage, King's will create a videotape of the lighting fixtures that interest you—preferably not more than six models. The VHS tapes are available for $15.

Wholesale buyers, please note: King's Chandelier extends a 15% discount (on regular catalog prices) to designers, decorators, and contractors. Send for the catalog ($4) on company letterhead.

Special Factors: Satisfaction is guaranteed; returns are accepted within five days for refund or credit.

LUIGI CRYSTAL

**7332 FRANKFORD AVE.
PHILADELPHIA, PA 19136
215–338–2978**

Catalog: $2 refundable
Pay: check, MO, MC, V, AE, Discover
Sells: crystal lighting fixtures
Store: same address; Monday to Friday
9–5:30, Saturday 10–4

Luigi Crystal may be located in the land of Main Liners, but its heart belongs to Tara. Luigi has been creating crystal lighting fixtures since 1935, and the prices are surprisingly low—under $200 for a full-sized chandelier, for example. The 44-page catalog shows each candelabra, chandelier, sconce, and hurricane lamp in black-and-white photographs. Many of the styles are formal and ornate, heavily hung with prisms and pendalogues and set in marble or faceted crystal bases. Several lamps feature globe shades, gold cupid bases, "Aurora" crystal prism shades, and even stained glass. At the other end of the spectrum are simple "Williamsburg chimney lamps" for under $50 a pair, and several graceful five-arm chandeliers.

If you're searching for replacement parts for your own fixtures, see the catalog for glass chimneys, bobeches, strung button prisms, drop prisms in several styles (3" to 8" long), and pendalogues. In addition to those models, Luigi's workshops can produce designs to your specifications; call or write to discuss details and prices.

Please note: The minimum order on goods sent outside the United States and Canada is $1,000.

Special Factors: Orders are shipped worldwide ($1,000 minimum order).

MAIN LAMP/LAMP WAREHOUSE

**1073 39TH ST.
BROOKLYN, NY 11219
718–436–8500
FAX: 718–438–6836**

Information: price quote
Pay: check, MO, MC, V, AE, Discover
Sells: lighting fixtures and ceiling fans
Store: same address; Monday, Tuesday, and Friday 9–5:30, Thursday 9–8, Saturday and Sunday 10–5

 ¡Sí! ★

Main Lamp/Lamp Warehouse, established in 1954, is noted for its comprehensive inventory of better-quality lamps, lighting fixtures, and ceiling fans, all sold at everyday discounts of up to 50%. Call, fax, or write for prices on lighting fixtures by Corbett, Framburg, Kichler, Nulco, and World Imports. Fredrick Cooper, Crystal Clear, George Kovacs, Lenox, and Stiffel are among the premium lines available. Ceiling fans by Casablanca, Craftmade, Emerson, and other firms are also stocked.

Please note: There is no catalog.

Special Factors: Price quote by phone or letter with SASE; store is closed Wednesdays; minimum order is $100.

Flooring

Rugs, carpeting, floor coverings, padding, underlays, tiles, flooring, etc.

Large rugs and wall-to-wall carpeting can represent the biggest single expense in redecorating a room. Saving up to 50% on the cost of the rug and padding is easy through the firms listed here. They're based in North Carolina and Dalton, Georgia, close to the carpet mills that turn out millions of miles of broadloom every year.

Before you order wall-to-wall carpeting, make sure you have someone local who can install it. (It's almost impossible for a novice to do a good job, and a poor one leads to shifting, rippling, and uneven wear.) Choice of carpet weave, fiber, and color depend on where it's going, the purpose of the room or area and the anticipated foot traffic, and overall decor. Interior design textbooks (see the introduction of "Home: Decor" for references) usually discuss the difference in fiber and construction, as well as appropriate sites for different types of carpeting. For information on installation, maintenance, and a stain-removal guide, send a long, stamped, self-addressed envelope to The Carpet and Rug Institute, Box 2048, Dalton, GA 30722.

For more firms selling rugs and carpeting, read "See Also" at the end of this section, and those mentioned under "Rugs and Carpeting" in "Find it Fast" in the introduction of "Home: Furnishings."

BEARDEN BROS. CARPET & TEXTILES CORP.

◼︎

DEPT. WBMC

4109 S. DIXIE HWY.

DALTON, GA 30721

800–433–0074

888–BEARDEN

706–277–3265

FAX: 706–277–1754

Catalog: $2 (see text)
Pay: check, MO, MC, V, AE, Discover
Sells: carpeting, rugs, padding, and vinyl flooring
Store: same address; Monday to Friday 8:30–6

Bearden Bros. Carpet & Textiles set up shop in 1989 in Dalton, "Carpet Capital of the World," joining hundreds of other companies in the manufacturing and sales of carpeting and flooring. Bearden sells carpeting and flooring lines from scores of mills, including Aladdin, Beaulieu, Cabin Craft, Citation, Cumberland, Evans and Black, Galaxy, Horizon, Interloom, J.P. Stevens, L.D. Brinkman, Lees, Mohawk, Philadelphia, Salem, Shaw, United Carpet, and World—and that's just a few of the many brands available.

You can call with the manufacturer's name, style name, and color codes, and number of square yards you plan to buy and ask for a price quote, or send a carpet sample if you don't have that information. Bearden Bros. also sells its own line of flooring and carpet products, as well as reproduction Oriental, Victorian, and contemporary designs, braided rugs, border designs, and even brass stair rods. A 32-page catalog of rugs—braided, flat weave, designer, Oriental, etc.—is available for $2 (regularly $4); mention WBMC when you send for it. Bearden Bros. ships carpeting to all 50 states and countries around the world, and offers special discounts to religious institutions and carpet dealers.

Special Factors: Written confirmation of phone orders is required; quantity discounts are available.

CHARLES W. JACOBSEN, INC.

DEPT. WBMC
LEARBURY CENTER
401 N. SALINA ST.
SYRACUSE, NY 13203–1773
315–422–7832
FAX: 315–422–6909

Catalog: free
Pay: check, MO, MC, V
Sells: new and antique Oriental rugs
Store: same address (Learbury Centre); also
268 Broadway, Saratoga Springs, NY; Monday
to Saturday 10–5, Monday and Thursday
10–8

Charles W. Jacobsen, Inc. has over 70 years of experience in the sale of fine Oriental rugs, and publishes a 26-page color portfolio that shows a portion of rugs selected from the 8,000 the firm has in inventory. Rug collectors know Jacobsen for the company's stock and good prices, but both are worth considering if you're buying a rug for your home and want something more than run-of-the-mill.

Jacobsen's stock-in-trade is handwoven carpets, of recent vintage, from India, Pakistan, Turkey, Iran, Afghanistan, China, and other countries (subject to trade restrictions and availability). The sizes vary with the type of rug, but most are available from 2' by 3' to 10' by 14', with some available in sizes to 12' by 20'; many of the designs are also made as runners. If you've been shopping for good, machine-made reproductions of Oriental rugs, you'll be familiar with some of the names: Kashan, Herez, Tabriz, Sarouk, Abadeh, Sarabend, Bijar, Ferraghan, Shirvan, and Bokhara are some of the most commonly known. Even if you think your budget relegates you to no more than a good copy of a handmade rug, check here before you buy. In some cases, Jacobsen's prices on the new rugs—made completely by hand, with wool or silk pile, often with some vegetable dyes (which lend a mellow quality to the rug over time)—are not much higher, and are lower than those charged for comparable examples by other rug merchants.

Buying a one-of-a-kind *anything* by mail can be tricky, but Jacobsen will work with you to get it right. The questionnaire provided with the catalog captures information about your preferences, room requirements, and budget; based on this information, you'll be sent slides of rugs that best suit your needs. When you've settled on a selection, you can have the rug sent on approval to try in the intended setting—the only way to be sure it's the right choice.

Special Factors: Satisfaction is guaranteed.

JOHNSON'S CARPETS

**3510 CORPORATE DR.
DALTON, GA 30721
800–235–1079, EXT. 601
706–277–2775
FAX: 706–277–9835**

Brochure: free
Pay: check, MO, MC, V, AE, Discover
Sells: vinyl and wood flooring, carpeting, area rugs, and padding
Store: same address; Monday to Friday 8–5, Saturday 9–1

Johnson's sells its own line of residential and commercial carpeting, guaranteed against wear and stains just like the national brands. Carpet samples are available, showing the range of colors and the specifications (fiber content, guarantee, etc.) of each style. Johnson's also works with over 40 carpet mills and flooring makers to get good deals on carpet and vinyl and wood lines from a wide range of manufacturers, at prices up to 80% below those charged by department stores and other retail outlets. If you've decided on your floor covering, call or write with the name of the manufacturer, the style name or number, and the square yardage required. Johnson's also creates its own "custom designer" rugs, and can produce patterns to match wallpaper or furnishings—samples are shown in the catalog (available upon request). Padding, adhesives, and tack strips for installation are also available.

A deposit is required when you place your order, and final payment must be made before shipment (common carrier is used). Both residential and commercial carpeting needs are served here—details on the products and sales policy are given in the brochure.

Special Factors: Orders are shipped worldwide.

RARE EARTH HARDWOODS

6778 E. TRAVERSE HWY.
TRAVERSE CITY, MI
  49684–8364
800–968–0074
616–946–0043
FAX: 800–968–0094
FAX: 616–946–6621

Information: inquire
Pay: check, MO, MC, V, Discover
Sells: lumber, hardwood flooring, inlays, etc.
Store: same address; Monday to Friday 8–5,
Saturday 8–12
E-mail: rare.earth@traverse.com
Online: www.rare-earth-hardwoods.com

Rare Earth Hardwoods sells genuine hardwood flooring—not laminate or composition—in woods that run from American Cherry to Zebrawood. Prices are often better than those of other specialty dealers, though you won't beat the cost of a floor-in-a-box. Rare Earth manufactures stair risers, treads, moldings, paneling, and more, and specializes in custom millwork. You can purchase a set of 30 sample pieces of the lumber for $22 (price includes shipping) and experience the colors first-hand. Price lists for the ¾" tongue-and-groove flooring, Brazilian decking, hardwood plywood, and marine lumber and plywood are available upon request.

Special Factors: Price quote by phone, fax, or letter with SASE.

VILLAGE CARPET & INTERIORS

3203 HWY. 70 SE
NEWTON, NC 28658
704–465–6818

Brochure: free
Pay: check or MO
Sells: carpeting and padding
Store: same address; off I–40 near Hickory;
Monday to Friday 8:30–5, Saturday 9–3

Village Carpet & Interiors offers well-known names in carpeting—Aladdin, Beaulieu, Cabin Crafts, Citation, Cumberland, Evans-Black, Galaxy, Mohawk, New Visions, Philadelphia, Queen, Salem, and others, at discounts of up to 40%. Padding and underlays are also available. All of the carpeting is first quality, and shipping is made by common carrier. The only drawback is the minimum order, $500, which might be high if you're doing a small job. If you have difficulty getting style information or calculating the amount you need, just ask—the salespeople deal with these problems regularly.

Special Factors: Satisfaction is guaranteed; quantity discounts are available; minimum order is $500.

WALL RUG & CARPETS

4309 WILEY DAVIS RD.
GREENSBORO, NC 27407
800–877–1955
FAX: 910–292–3601

Information: price quote
Pay: check, MO, MC, V
Sells: rugs
Store: same address (Exit 120, I–85), next to Byerly's Antiques

Wall Rug & Carpets sells first-quality Karastans, at prices up to 40% below Wall's suggested list, as well as designs by Oriental Weavers, 828 Trading Company, and Mastercraft Imports Ltd. Wall has been in business since 1928 and provides dealer warranties on the rugs it sells. Call or write to Wall if you need advice, or when you're ready to order.

Special Factors: Inquire about returns policy.

WAREHOUSE CARPETS, INC.

P.O. BOX 3233
DALTON, GA 30719
800–526–2229
706–226–2229
FAX: 706–278–1008

Brochure: free
Pay: check or MO
Sells: carpeting, vinyl flooring, and padding
Store: Walnut Ave. (Exit 136 off I–75), Dalton, GA; Monday to Friday 8–5

Warehouse Carpets began in 1977 as a carpeting wholesaler, and has since moved into mail order, offering customers savings of as much as 50% on carpeting and floor coverings. Call for a quote if you're shopping for carpeting from Aladdin, Cabin Crafts, Columbus, Coronet, Diamond, Evans & Black, Galaxy, Horizon, Interloom, Mannington, Mohawk, Philadelphia, Queen, Salem, Shaw, Sutton, or World; or vinyl flooring from Armstrong, Congoleum, Mannington, or Tarkett. And if you'd like to save an average of 50% on padding, Warehouse Carpets can provide several types.

Call or write with the names of the manufacturer and style of the carpeting you want. Shipments are made by common carrier.

Special Factors: All goods are first quality; price quote by phone or letter.

SEE ALSO

American Frame Corporation • sectional frames and mats • **ART MATERIALS**

Arctic Sheepskin Outlet • sheepskin rugs • **CLOTHING**

Buffalo Batt & Felt Corp. • throw pillow inserts and upholstery stuffing • **CRAFTS: TEXTILE ARTS**

The Caning Shop • seat-weaving materials, replacement seats, upholstery supplies • **CRAFTS**

The Deerskin Place • sheepskin rugs • **CLOTHING**

Defender Industries, Inc. • teak kitchen and bath accessories • **AUTO**

Designer's HardWareHouse • decorative furniture and house hardware • **HOME: IMPROVEMENT**

Domestications • home accents, window treatments, etc. • **HOME: LINEN**

Eldridge Textile Co. • window treatments • **HOME: LINEN**

Frank's Cane and Rush Supply • seat-reweaving materials, upholstery supplies, etc. • **CRAFTS**

Global Village Imports • upholstery-weight ikat fabrics • **CRAFTS: TEXTILE ARTS**

Goldberg's Marine Distributors • teak kitchen and bath accessories • **AUTO**

Home-Sew • upholstery supplies • **CRAFTS: TEXTILE ARTS**

Leather Unlimited Corp. • sheepskin rugs • **LUGGAGE**

The Linen Source • window treatments, home accents • **HOME: LINEN**

Loftin-Black Furniture Company • mirrors • **HOME: FURNISHINGS**

M & E Marine Supply Company, Inc. • teak boat accessories for kitchen and bath • **AUTO**

Monarch Radiator Enclosures • radiator enclosures • **HOME: IMPROVEMENT**

Mueller Sporting Goods, Inc. • pool-table lights, bar stools, posters, clocks, signs, and other poolroom fixtures • **SPORTS**

Murrow Furniture Galleries, Inc. • lamps • **HOME: FURNISHINGS**

Newark Dressmaker Supply, Inc. • upholstery supplies • **CRAFTS: TEXTILE ARTS**

Quality Furniture Market of Lenoir, Inc. • *lamps, decorator fabrics, etc.* • **HOME: FURNISHINGS**

Sally Distributors, Inc. • *banners and seasonal decorations* • **TOYS**

Shuttercraft, Inc. • *interior and exterior wooden window shutters* • **HOME: IMPROVEMENT**

Stumps • *banners and seasonal decorations* • **TOYS**

Thai Silks • *upholstery-weight silk fabrics* • **CRAFTS: TEXTILE ARTS**

Utex Trading Enterprises • *upholstery-weight silk fabric* • **CRAFTS: TEXTILE ARTS**

Warner-Crivellaro Stained Glass Supplies, Inc. • *lamp bases and parts* • **CRAFTS**

Furnishings

Household furnishings of all types, including outdoor and home office furnishings, and services

You can save as much as 50% on suggested retail by ordering your furniture from North Carolina, the manufacturing center of the industry. The discounters don't take the staggering markups that make furnishings and home accessories prohibitively expensive in department and furniture stores. This doesn't endear them to the furniture manufacturers; in fact, it's becoming common for manufacturers to do everything they can to make it difficult for discounters to sell by mail, by forbidding them to trade outside designated "selling areas" and sometimes prohibiting the firms from having 800 phone lines. (Manufacturers elicit compliance by threatening to refuse to fill the discounters' orders.) This practice has the effect of limiting trade, and raising the prices we all have to pay. To avoid creating problems for the discounters, while giving access to the best buys possible, brand names have been *omitted* from these listings. So while you're reading the listings, bear in mind that most of the firms listed here can supply catalogs, brochures, and swatches, give decorating advice over the phone, and take orders for furniture and accessories from hundreds of manufacturers.

It's smart to use the "in-home delivery service" when a firm offers it, since your furniture will be uncrated exactly where you want it, and if there are damages, you'll see them right away and can contact the company while the shipper is there to find out what to do. In-home delivery is usually made either by the company's own truck, or with a moving-van service that's accustomed to handling furnishings.

To see listings of other firms that sell furnishings and home accents, see "Home: Decor" and "General Merchandise." Some of the companies in this chapter also sell lines of office furniture; see "Office and Business" for a comprehensive selection.

FIND IT FAST

ACRYLIC FURNITURE • **Plexi-Craft**
BEDDING AND MATTRESSES • **Blackwelder's, Carolina Interiors, Murrow, Parkway, Priba, Quality Furniture Market, Southland, Stuckey Brothers**
BRASS BEDS • **Parkway, Priba**
CLOCKS • **Blackwelder's, Parkway, Southland, Stuckey Brothers**
COUNTRY FURNISHINGS • **Eastern Butcher Block, Marion Travis**
DECORATOR FABRIC • **Furniture Patch, Priba**
LAMPS AND LIGHTING • **Blackwelder's, Furniture Patch, Parkway, Priba, Southland, Stuckey Brothers, Wicker Warehouse**
LAWN AND PATIO FURNISHINGS • **Blackwelder's, Loftin-Black, Parkway, Priba, Quality Furniture Market, Southland, Stuckey Brothers, Wicker Warehouse**
MIRRORS • **Furniture Patch, Hunt Galleries, Parkway, Southland, Stuckey Brothers, Wicker Warehouse**
MODERN FURNISHINGS • **Genada Imports**
OFFICE FURNISHINGS • **Blackwelder's, Furniture Patch, Don Lamor, Parkway, Priba, Shaw Furniture, Sobol House, Southland**
RUGS AND CARPETING • **Carolina Interiors, Furniture Patch, Priba, Southland**
TABLE PADS • **Factory Direct Table Pad, Loftin-Black, Parkway**
UNFINISHED FURNITURE • **Marks Sales, Marion Travis**
VICTORIAN REPRODUCTIONS • **Heirloom Reproductions**
WALL TREATMENTS • **Carolina Interiors**
WICKER FURNITURE • **Ellenburg's Furniture, Fran's Wicker, Wicker Warehouse**

BLACKWELDER'S INDUSTRIES, INC.

294 TURNERSBURG HWY.
STATESVILLE, NC
   28677–8241
800–438–0201 (U.S.)
704–872–8921
FAX: 704–872–4491

Catalog and Price List: $17.95, refundable (see text)
Save: up to 50%
Pay: check, MO, MC, V, AE, NOVUS
Sells: home and office furniture and accessories
Store: phone hours Monday to Friday 9:30–5:30
E-mail: blackwelders@homefurnish.com
Online: http://www.homefurnish.com/blackwelders

Blackwelder's Industries, Inc. was founded in 1936 with the aim of giving the customer access to fine furniture at fair prices, with full-service delivery. The firm is well regarded among consumers, and offers an "information worksheet" to help you keep track of price quotes and shopping information. The 175-page color catalog showcases home and office furnishings and other goods from a number of the hundreds of manufacturers represented at Blackwelder's, and the price list helps to give you a sense of the possible savings. The catalog and price list cost $17.95—refundable upon return to Blackwelder's *within 90 days of receipt*—and includes a $30 gift certificate. The catalog selections have been very carefully selected and represent some of the best values available, but you may also call or write for a price quote on specific items or brands. The shopping worksheet, which is available upon request, lists details of the sales policy, delivery costs, and other options; inquire directly if you need information on contract services and quantity prices on large runs. You'll find an online catalog, with selections not shown in the print version, at Blackwelder's website.

International readers, please note: Blackwelder's is experienced in shipping to Japan, the Middle East, and other countries around the world. Fax your inquiries to 704–872–4491.

Special Factors: Satisfaction is guaranteed; price quote by phone, fax, e-mail, or letter; shipments are made by van or common carrier; authorized returns are accepted within 30 days (a 25% restocking fee is charged) for exchange, refund, or credit.

CAROLINA INTERIORS

115 OAK AVE.
KANNAPOLIS, NC 28081
704–933–1888
FAX: 704–938–2990

Brochure: free
Pay: check or MO
Sells: home furnishings and accessories
Store: same address (I–85, Exit 63); Monday to Saturday 9–6; 3 other locations in NC

Carolina Interiors is run by several veterans of the furnishings trade, whose relationships with over 350 manufacturers help assure discounts of 30% to 60%. If you're traveling through North Carolina near Cannon Village, locate the Fieldcrest Cannons factory outlet store, and you'll find Carolina Interiors next door—over 250,000 square feet of furnishings, wall and floor treatments, rugs, and bedding. You can call or write for a price quote if you know what you want, and to request the brochure that lists a number of the available brands and details the sales policy. Carolina Interiors requires a 30% deposit (protected by surety bond) when you place the order, and features in-home delivery in most areas.

Special Factors: Price quote by phone, fax, or letter.

EASTERN BUTCHER BLOCK

25 EAGLE ST.
PROVIDENCE, RI 02908
401–273–6330
FAX: 401–274–1811

Catalog: free
Pay: check, MO, MC, V
Sells: contemporary and casual home furnishings
Store: same address; Monday to Friday 8:30–5:30, Thursday 8:30–8, Saturday 10–5, Sunday 10–5; also Danvers and Orange, CT; Boston, Framingham, Hanover, and Seekonk, MA; and Nashua, NH

Eastern Butcher Block specializes in dining tables and chairs, most with butcher-block tops, in country or contemporary styling. The 24-page catalog shows scores of combinations of tops (extension, drop-leaf, rounded, oblong, etc.) and bases (pedestal, trestle, straight-leg, folding, Shaker-style, turned-leg, with and without drawers, etc.) in maple or red oak. The hardwood chairs run from Breuer reproductions to Windsor-style side chairs. Swivel-seat stools, rockers, children's chairs, and even office styles are offered. Accessories include chopping blocks, hutches and sideboards, microwave carts, accessories, toy chests, snack tables, folding screens, book cases, and end tables.

Prices range from nominal to serious, depending on whether the item is on sale, in the "promotional" group (of lower-grade maple or oak), or incorporates customer options in base style and finish. Eastern Butcher Block manufactures the furniture, and offers eight stains and four paint colors, with the option of an age-sanded "antique" finish. All of the furniture is finished in a durable epoxy and carries a lifetime structural warranty. The butcher block can be ordered as custom-cut countertops, and ordering instructions are given in the literature.

Special Factors: Price quote by phone or letter.

ELLENBURG'S FURNITURE

Catalog: $6.50, refundable
Pay: check, MO, MC, V, Discover
Sells: home furnishings
Store: same address

I–40 STAMEY FARM RD.
P.O. BOX 5638
STATESVILLE, NC 28687
704–873–2900
FAX: 704–873–6002

Ellenburg's Furniture sells some of the country's most popular lines of American-style furniture, from scores of manufacturers, and is a great source for wicker and rattan furnishings as well. The $6.50 catalog fee (refundable with purchase) brings you a sheaf of brochures from different manufacturers, a price list, details on Ellenburg's sales policy, and current specials. A 25% deposit is required when you place your order, and delivery is available from Ellenburg's own van service, a furniture carrier, or common carrier. Ellenburg's has been in business since 1978, and offers savings of 40% to 50% on retail, and up to 75% on sale items and closeouts.

Special Factors: Price quote by phone or letter; returns of damaged and defective goods only are accepted.

FACTORY DIRECT TABLE PAD CO.

1501 W. MARKET ST.
INDIANAPOLIS, IN 46222
800–428–4567
FAX: 317–631–2584

Prices and Samples: $1
Pay: check, MO, MC, V, Discover
Sells: custom-made table pads
Store: mail order only

Factory Direct's spiffy little color brochure states that about half of the cost of a custom-made table pad is the fee paid to the person who measures the table. For $1, Factory Direct Table Pad will send you a guide to doing this yourself, as well as several sample swatches of the table pad top, which can be made in pebble-grain or smooth finish, in plain colors or in wood grain, in different thicknesses. Factory Direct has been in business since 1982, and warrants its table pads for 7, 15, or 20 years. Complete details of the terms of sale are given in the literature.

Special Factors: Authorized returns are accepted within 15 days.

FRAN'S WICKER & RATTAN FURNITURE, INC.

295 RTE. 10E
SUCCASUNNA, NJ 07876
201–584–2230
FAX: 201–584–7446

Catalog: $2
Pay: check, MO, MC, V, AE, Discover
Sells: wicker and rattan furniture and accessories
Store: same address; Monday to Friday 9–5:30, Wednesday and Thursday til 8:30, Saturday 9–6, Sunday 12–5

Fran's Wicker is in its third generation of family management, having grown from a basket importer to one of the best local sources for wicker and rattan furniture. The 58-page color catalog is packed cover to cover with furniture and decorative accessories in natural and painted wicker, and a more limited selection of rattan. If you're looking for a seating and table set for porch or patio, or your living or dining room, you'll find dozens here. The styling runs from Victorian curves to modern shapes. Breakfast sets, bedroom furniture, étagères, rockers, TV carts and entertainment centers, office furniture, trunks, plant stands, bookcases, magazine racks, hampers, mirrors, lamps, and baskets are offered. There are a number of pieces for children, including a bassinet, changing table, chairs and tables, rockers, and toy chests. The catalog details your options in cushion coverings and delivery, and the "lowest price" guarantee.

Special Factors: Satisfaction is guaranteed.

THE FURNITURE PATCH OF CALABASH, INC.

DEPT. WBMC
10283 BEACH DR. SW
P.O. BOX 4970
CALABASH, NC 28467
910–579–2001
FAX: 910–579–2017

Brochure: free
Pay: check or MO
Sells: furniture, lighting, carpeting, accessories
Store: same address; Monday to Saturday 9–5:30

The Furniture Patch of Calabash invites you to spend some time at their showroom when you're in the area visiting Myrtle Beach, but if you can't make the trip, help is available by phone or mail. The Furniture Patch represents several hundred manufacturers of home (indoor and outdoor) and office furnishings, decorator fabric, lighting, mirrors, rugs and carpets, and decorative accessories. The brochure includes a partial listing of some of the best names in home and industrial design, and savings run up to 60%. Details on the sales policy and ordering guidelines are included, and the sales assistants can answer any other questions you may have, and give you quotes on specific items you're pricing. The Furniture Patch has been in business since 1990, and provides in-house (van) delivery to all states in the continental United States.

Special Factors: Price quote by phone, fax, or letter; returns of transit-damaged goods are accepted for repair or replacement.

GENADA IMPORTS

DEPT. W–98
P.O. BOX 204
TEANECK, NJ 07666
201–790–7522
FAX: 201–790–7522

Catalog: $1
Pay: check, MO, MC, V
Sells: Danish, modern, and contemporary furniture
Store: mail order only

Genada has been in business since 1968, selling Danish modern furniture in its most American incarnation: low-slung, teak-finished chairs and couches, with loose-cushion backs and seats of tweed-covered foam. The style has weathered fad and fatigue quite well, and the furniture's basic appeal is only enhanced by its low prices. Armchairs begin at under $100, couches at under $170, and armless divans are priced from $120.

Genada isn't limited to Scandinavian design; the catalog shows reproductions of the Eames chair and other modern classics, folding chairs with woven rope seats and backs, knock-down bookcases and cabinets, butcher block tabletops and bases, convertible foam-block chairs and sofas, gateleg tables with chairs that store in the base, and bentwood chairs. The catalog also features modern chairs by Paoli Chair Co., suitable for home or office, as well as several handsome styles in molded teak, walnut, and rosewood finishes, from about $300 and up. Imported armoires, patio furniture, "country" kitchen furniture, freestanding wall units, computer workstations, desks, VCR carts, and bar stools are all available. If you're shopping for a bridge table with folding hardwood chairs, you'll find several reasonably priced styles here.

Special Factors: Price quote by phone or letter; specify upholstery and finish materials when ordering.

HEIRLOOM REPRODUCTIONS

Catalog: $3, refundable
Pay: check, MO, MC, V
Sells: Victorian and French reproduction furniture, clocks, etc.
Store: same address; Monday to Friday 10–5

1834 W. FIFTH ST., DEPT.
  WBM
MONTGOMERY, AL
  36106–1516
800–288–1513
334–263–3511
FAX: 334–263–3313

If a button-tufted, damask-covered, center-medallion camelback sofa speaks to you, you have a weakness for Victorian decor. But as anyone who's tried to find *good* examples of the style knows, they're hard to come by at a reasonable price. Enter Heirloom Reproductions, where gooseneck rockers, fainting sofas, and bustle chairs are stock-in-trade. The 28-page color catalog and other literature show classic parlor sets—sofas and marble-topped occasional tables—and curio cabinets, entertainment centers, hall trees, armoires, dining room sets, bedroom furniture, folding screens, and other pieces. The copy includes dimensions, some notes on construction features, and prices, which are discounted 40% to 55% from list. You can select the wood finish from several options, and specify fabric—damasks, brocades, prints, tapestries, and velvets—if you're not supplying your own. Heirloom Reproductions also offers a collection of reproduction clocks (regulator, anniversary, Westminster chime, cuckoo, etc.), and collectors' cabinets. If you need help in choosing the best pieces for your decorating scheme, consult the staff designer, who can also give you complete details on fabrics, construction, and the firm's sales policy.

Special Factors: Price quote by phone or letter; swatches are available on request; orders are shipped from the factory by insured truck.

HUNT GALLERIES, INC.

P.O. BOX 2324 WBMC
HICKORY, NC 28603
800–248–3876
704–324–9934
FAX: 704–324–9921

Catalog: $10, refundable (see text)
Pay: check, MO, MC, V
Sells: upholstered furniture
Store: same address; Monday to Friday 10–5

Hunt Galleries, a family business that was founded over half a century ago, manufactures a complete line of handsome upholstered furniture. Hunt's catalog and price list ($10, refundable with purchase) are models of clarity—every piece is shown in color, fully described with complete measurements. Most of the line is seating—sofas, love seats, chaises, chairs, armchairs, sectionals, dining room chairs, tuffets, ottomans, benches, and vanity stools, of traditional design—and there are even several chairs sized for children. Hunt Galleries also offers upholstered headboards, mirrors, and sofa tables.

The price list specifies charges for upholstery in your fabric, as well as options that include fabric lining, casters, swivel rocker mechanisms, seat filling choices (poly foam, down and feather blends, blends with innersprings, and foam with springs), and quilting. And the catalog shows the quality points of the furniture itself—doweled and glued hardwood frames, hand-tied coil springs, deep padding, and careful pattern matching, among others. The terms of sale are detailed in the price list, including the shipping alternatives: truck, inside delivery, and UPS (when possible). If you still have questions, just give the Hunts a call.

Special Factors: Satisfaction is guaranteed.

DON LAMOR INC.

2220 HWY. 70 EAST
BH9 HICKORY FURNI-
   TURE MART
HICKORY, NC 28602
704–324–1776

Information: price quote
Pay: check, MO, MC, V
Sells: home and office furnishings
Store: same address; Monday to Friday 9–6,
Saturday 9–5

Don Lamor lays claim to "North Carolina's largest display of fine home furnishings," and is an authorized dealer for a number of prominent manufacturers. The sales consultants can assist you in selecting the right furnishings for your needs, and require a 50% deposit on your order (the balance is due before the order can be shipped). Furnishings for both home and office, as well as rugs, accessories, and occasional pieces are available.

Special Factors: Price quote by phone or letter.

LOFTIN-BLACK FURNITURE COMPANY

111 SEDGEHILL DR.
THOMASVILLE, NC 27360
800–334–7398
800–745–3876
910–472–6117
FAX: 910–472–2052

Brochure: free
Pay: check, MO, MC, V, Discover
Sells: furnishings, bedding, and accessories
Store: same address; Monday to Friday
8:30–5:30, Saturday 8:30–5; also 214 N. Main
St., High Point, NC (910–883–4711)

Loftin-Black, founded in 1948, delivers selection, service, and savings on fine home, office, and patio furniture and accessories from hundreds of companies, including the top names in furnishings. Check with Loftin-Black before ordering table pads or mattress sets—they're also available, at sizable savings. Loftin-Black is an authorized factory dealer for hundreds of prominent manufacturers, listed in the free brochure. It also includes the terms of sale (a 50% deposit is required when ordering, and the balance is due upon delivery), and shipping options. Loftin-Black will provide in-home delivery and setup, although you can engage a common carrier if you prefer. If you're in the Thomasville area, drop in and see Loftin-Black's 14,000 square feet of furniture on display.

Special Factors: Price quote by phone or letter; in-home delivery is made by Loftin-Black's van service.

MARKS SALES CO., INC.

DEPT. 2G
151–20 88TH ST.
HOWARD BEACH, NY
11414
718–835–9319

Catalog: $2.50/$3.75 (see text)
Pay: check or MO
Sells: unfinished, assembled furniture
Store: mail order only

The Marks Sales catalog is 62 pages of clear photographs of over 100 pieces of reproduction antiques that await your finishing hand. The flavor is Continental—side chairs and armchairs and matching counter and bar stools with graceful legs, rush seats, and cane backs, imposing cane-back "tub" chairs with lion's head-arms, settles with serpentine ladder-backs and carved aprons, Chinese Chippendale styles, bombé chests, and even tables, desks, headboards, and semanieres are among the offerings. Every piece is made in Spain or Italy, carved by hand from beechwood and arrives completely assembled and sanded (these are not kits), ready for paint or stain and finish. Seats are made by hand of rush, cane, or muslin-covered foam. Prices are wholesale, and if you finish your selection yourself (or even have the furniture done professionally), you can create a custom look for 30% to 60% less than you'd pay for the same pieces in local decorator shops. Please note: The catalog costs $2.50 and is sent via bulk mail, which takes up to three weeks to arrive; if you want yours sooner, send a check or money order for $3.75 and request first-class mailing.

International readers, please note: Only U.S. funds are accepted.

Special Factors: Satisfaction is guaranteed; authorized returns are accepted within 20 days for full refund, less cost of freight.

MURROW FURNITURE GALLERIES, INC.

DEPT. WBMC
P.O. BOX 4337
WILMINGTON, NC 28406
910–799–4010
FAX: 910–791–2791

Brochure: free
Pay: check or MO
Sells: home furnishings, bedding, and accessories
Store: 3514 S. College Rd., Wilmington, NC; Monday to Friday 8:30–5:30, Saturday 9–5:30

Murrow Furniture Galleries, founded in 1979, sells furnishings, bedding, and accessories from over 500 manufacturers (listed in the brochure; color brochures showcasing a broad range of styles are also offered). The extensive selection of brands and consistently good savings make this one of the best furniture discounters around. If you're able to visit the store in Wilmington, you'll find five gallery showrooms of 45,000 square feet, with fine furnishings and accessories on display. Delivery options and terms of sale are detailed in the brochure.

Special Factors: Price quote by phone or letter; deposit is required.

PARKWAY FURNITURE GALLERIES

P.O. BOX 2450
BOONE, NC 28607
704–264–3993
FAX: 704–262–3530

Catalog: free
Pay: check or MO
Sells: home and office furnishings, decorative accessories
Store: Hwy. 105 South, Boone, NC; Monday to Saturday 8–5

Parkway Furniture Galleries has published a lovely 18-page color catalog showcasing a sample of the home furnishings, patio furniture, lamps, clocks, mirrors, table pads, bedding, and decorative accents that are available. Parkway has been in business since 1979 and represents over 200 manufacturers, at savings of 40% to 50%. The sales policy is detailed in the brochure, which also lists the manufacturers that are represented. Van line service is available, with in-home setup.

Special Factors: Satisfaction is guaranteed; price quote by phone or letter.

PLEXI-CRAFT QUALITY PRODUCTS CORP.

---

514 W. 24TH ST.,
DEPT. WBMC
NEW YORK, NY
10011–1179
212–924–3244
FAX: 212–924–3508

Catalog: $2
Pay: check, MO, MC, V
Sells: acrylic furnishings and accessories
Store: same address; Monday to Friday
9:30–5
E-mail: plexi@escape.com
Online: http://www.escape.com/~plexi

Plexi-Craft manufactures its own line of premium acrylic goods, and prices them at up to 50% less than what department and specialty stores charge for comparable items. The 16-page catalog shows acrylic furnishings and accessories of all kinds. There are a number of tables—dining, cocktail, Parsons, TV, snack, and side—and the models with separate bases may be ordered with glass instead of acrylic tops. Several rolling bars are available, as well as chairs, pedestals, computer stands, vanities and stools, luggage racks, magazine units, and telephone tables. Desk sets, kitchen organizers and paper towel holders, and bathroom fixtures round out the selection, and there's an anti-static cleaner and a polish formulated for acrylic to keep everything gleaming. Plexi-Craft, founded in 1972, also accepts orders for custom work.

Special Factors: Price quote by phone, fax, or letter on custom work.

PRIBA FURNITURE SALES & INTERIORS, INC.

P.O. BOX 13295
GREENSBORO, NC
27415–3295
910–855–9034
FAX: 910–855–1370

Brochure: free
Pay: check, MO, MC, V, Discover
Sells: furniture, accessories, bedding, carpeting, etc.
Showroom: 210 Stage Coach Trail, Greensboro, NC; Monday to Friday 9–5:30, Saturday 9–5

Priba's 40,000-square-foot showroom is a must-see if you're in the High Point/Greensboro area, but if you're not planning to travel, Priba will bring the furnishings to you. The firm has been in business since 1972, and represents over 300 manufacturers of home furnishings, including bedroom and dining room suites, leather, patio furniture, lamps and accessories, carpeting, decorator fabrics, wall coverings, and mattresses. The choice of manufacturers tends to the upmarket end of the scale, and a number are usually listed as "to the trade only" in decorator magazines. Send for the brochure for details on Priba's sales policy, and call for price quotes or for assistance in making your selection. Savings run up to nearly 50% on list or regular retail, and Priba uses van-line service, so your furniture will be uncrated and set up within your home.

Special Factors: Credit cards are accepted for deposits only; shipping charge is calculated on a minimum weight of 150 pounds.

QUALITY FURNITURE MARKET OF LENOIR, INC.

Information: price quote
Pay: check, MO, MC, V
Sells: furnishings, bedding, and accessories
Store: same address; Monday to Saturday 8:30–5

2034 HICKORY BLVD. SW
LENOIR, NC 28645
704–728–2946
FAX: 704–726–0226

Quality Furniture Market, in business since 1955, takes its name seriously: You're invited to check the firm's ratings with Dun and Bradstreet, the Lyons listing, and the Lenoir Chamber of Commerce (800–737–0782) before you buy. The firm's magnificent selection is offered at prices that are 20% over cost, compared to the usual 110% to 125% markups.

Quality Furniture sells indoor and outdoor furniture, bedding, and home accessories by literally hundreds of firms. The list of brands is given in the brochure, as well as terms of sale and other conditions. Readers have written to say they were very pleased with Quality's prices and the firm's in-home delivery service. If you're traveling near Lenoir, drop by and get lost in the three floors of furniture galleries and display rooms.

Special Factors: Price quote by phone or letter with SASE; all orders must be prepaid before shipment; shipment is made by common carrier or in-home delivery service.

SHAW FURNITURE GALLERIES, INC.

131 W. ACADEMY ST.
RANDLEMAN, NC 27317
910–498–2628
FAX: 910–498–7889

Brochure: free
Pay: check, MO, MC, V
Sells: home and office furnishings
Store: same address; Monday to Friday
9–5:30, Saturday 9–5
E-mail: shaw@northstate.net

The Shaw family has been selling furniture at a discount since 1940 and represents over 300 manufacturers; the large inventory can be seen in Shaw's showroom in Randleman. The brochure includes a partial listing of the available brands, but call Shaw if you're pricing a piece of furniture or an item by a manufacturer not mentioned—it may be available. Shaw's references and the terms of sale are detailed in the brochure.

Special Factors: Price quote by phone or letter with SASE.

SOBOL HOUSE OF FURNISHINGS

141 RICHARDSON BLVD.
P.O. BOX 219
BLACK MOUNTAIN, NC
  28711
704–669–8031
FAX: 704–669–7969

Brochure: free
Pay: check or MO
Sells: home and office furnishings
Store: same address; Monday to Friday
9–6:30, Saturday 9–5:30; Sunday 12–5 (June
to October)

Sobol House has been saving informed consumers on their furniture purchases since 1971, and the firm's low prices have helped build a clientele worldwide over the years. Although Sobol carries contemporary furnishings, the firm's specialty is traditional, 18th century, and country styles, from the most prominent names in the business. Sobol can help you make your selection—with advice and manufacturers' catalogs—and gives price quotes on specific items. Both sidewalk and in-house delivery are available, and details of the sales policy are given in the brochure and order form.

Special Factors: Price quote by phone or letter.

SOUTHLAND FURNITURE GALLERIES

1244 HIGHWAY 17
P.O. BOX 1837
LITTLE RIVER, SC 29566
803–280–9342
FAX: 803–249–4527

Brochure: free
Pay: check or MO
Sells: home furnishings and accessories
Store: same address; Monday to Saturday 9–5:30

The 30,000 square feet of Southland Furniture Galleries is a short jaunt from the attractions of Myrtle Beach, worth a stop between visits to the local beaches and rounds of golf. Southland is run by people who own two other furnishings galleries, and have many years of experience in selling and shipping to customers out of state. In addition to home furnishings, Southland sells lighting, rugs, mirrors, clocks, and bedding by some of the best names in the business. The brochure lists the hundreds of manufacturers represented here, and takes you through the ordering and delivery process. The full-service amenities include a professional interior designer on staff, and in-home delivery with setup. Savings vary depending on the manufacturer and line, but average more than 40% off suggested list.

Special Factors: Sales policy is detailed in the brochure; price quote by phone, fax, or letter.

STUCKEY BROTHERS FURNITURE CO., INC.

RTE. 1, BOX 527
STUCKEY, SC 29554
803–558–2591
FAX: 803–558–9229

Information: price quote
Pay: check or MO
Sells: indoor and outdoor furnishings and accessories
Store: same address; Monday to Friday 9–6, Saturday 9–5

Stuckey is South Carolina's answer to High Point—it sells a full line of furniture and accessories at North Carolina prices and has been doing business by mail since 1946. Furnishings and accessories, including patio and office furnishings, are available from over 300 manufacturers. Lines of clocks, lamps, mirrors, and bedding are offered as well. Request the brochure that details the sales terms and shipping options (van line or common carrier).

Special Factors: Price quote by phone or letter with SASE.

MARION TRAVIS

P.O. BOX 1041
STATESVILLE, NC 28687
704–528–4424
FAX: 704–528–3526

Catalog: $1
Pay: check, MO, MC, V
Sells: country chairs, benches, and tables
Store: 354 S. Eastway Dr., Troutman, NC; Monday to Thursday 8–3:30, Friday 8–12 noon

You can pay hundreds of dollars for an oak pedestal table at your local antique shop, and search every tag sale in the state for a matched set of ladderback chairs. Or you can send $1 to Marion Travis for the catalog that shows these and other furnishings. The 12 pages of black-and-white photographs show country furniture, including a good selection of ladderback chairs with woven cord seats. There are armchair and rocker styles and children's models, beginning at under $25. Plain, slat-seat kitchen chairs and a classic oak kitchen table with utility drawer are shown, as well as a porch swing and Kennedy-style rockers with cane rush backs and seats. The prices cited are for unfinished furniture, but Marion Travis will stain and finish your selection in natural, oak, or walnut for a surcharge. If you're in the vicinity of Troutman, you can receive a 25% discount on most items by going to the store, making a purchase, and taking it with you, unboxed.

Wholesale customers, request the wholesale catalog and price list from Shaver Woodworks, P.O. Box 946, Troutman, NC 28166. The minimum wholesale order is 12 pieces.

Special Factors: Minimum order is 2 pieces of furniture; authorized returns of defective goods are accepted within 30 days.

WICKER WAREHOUSE INC.

195 S. RIVER ST.
HACKENSACK, NJ 07601
800–989–4253
201–342–6709
FAX: 201–342–1495

Catalog: $6, credited to first purchase
Pay: check, MO, MC, V, Discover
Sells: wicker furniture and accessories
Store: same address; Monday to Saturday
10–6, Wednesday til 7
Online: http://www.wickerwarehouse.com

Why comb antique stores and flea markets for vintage wicker furniture when you can find freshly minted versions of the same styles, in pristine condition, at comparable prices? Wicker Warehouse, established in 1978, sells current styles by the top names in the business, including lines treated to withstand the elements—so you don't have to drag everything inside the garage when it starts raining. The 112-page color catalog shows great groupings for sunporch and summer home, and wicker-embellished bedroom furnishings, mirrors, lamps, dining chairs, stools, nursery accoutrements, bathroom accessories, trunks, and even doll buggies. You'll also find teak and wrought-iron furniture, sectionals, recliners, sleepers, dining room furniture, and dinettes. Fabric and finish options are shown as well. The line has been expanded to include sectionals, recliners, sleepers, and dining sets and dinettes. Wicker Warehouse also offers teak and wrought-iron furniture. Prices are 30% to 50% below list, and orders are shipped anywhere within the continental United States.

    Special Factors: Satisfaction is guaranteed; price quote by phone.

SEE ALSO

Alfax Wholesale Furniture • *office and institutional furnishings* • **OFFICE**
Bennett Brothers, Inc. • *small selection of home furnishings* • **GENERAL MERCHANDISE**
BMI Home Decorating • *custom-made headboards* • **HOME: DECOR**
Business & Institutional Furniture Company, Inc. • *office and institutional furniture* • **OFFICE**
Cole's Appliance & Furniture Co. • *home furnishings* • **APPLIANCES**
Coppa Woodworking Inc. • *Adirondack chairs, screen doors* • **HOME: IMPROVEMENT**

Designer Secrets • home furnishings • **HOME**: LINEN

Eldridge Textile Co. • custom-upholstered headboards, ottomans, footstools, etc. • **HOME**: LINEN

The Fabric Center, Inc. • upholstery and decorator fabrics • **HOME**: DECOR

Frank Eastern Co. • office furniture • **OFFICE**

Frank's Cane and Rush Supply • small selection of unfinished furniture • **CRAFTS**

Harmony Supply Inc. • decorator fabrics • **HOME**: DECOR

Home Fabric Mills, Inc. • upholstery and drapery fabrics • **HOME**: DECOR

Marlene's Decorator Fabrics • upholstery and drapery fabric • **HOME**: DECOR

Shama Imports, Inc. • crewel upholstery fabric and cushion covers • **HOME**: DECOR

Silk Surplus • upholstery and drapery fabric • **HOME**: DECOR

Improvement and Maintenance

Hardware, tools, equipment, supplies, and materials

Buying a home may be the largest single investment you'll make during your lifetime, so the rewards for doing your homework before you sign the contract can be significant. Even if you've bought real estate before, go over the basics before you buy again so you're familiar with the basics of contract obligations with agents and buyers, types of mortgages and bridge loans, assessments and inspections, zoning and environmental restrictions, deeds and titles, insurance, and local use regulations.

If you're looking for the ideal community, you can check any number of guides: *The Hundred Best Small Towns in the U.S.* and *Places Rated Almanac* look at statistical indices: The cost of living, housing availability, climate, medical facilities, arts and recreational opportunities, and other criteria are tallied as part of the final recommendations. *Money* magazine also performs regular ratings, based on a number of criteria. Once you've chosen the location, get acquainted: subscribe to the local newspaper, drop in on public hearings on land and water use, attend a couple of community events, and study maps and surveys of the area. Learn as much as possible about the local history (including fires, floods, manufacturing and agriculture, water and sewerage systems, etc.), and plans for future development, tax hikes, and factors that influence the local economy. *Country Bound,* by Marilyn and Tom Ross (Communication Creativity, 1992) gives lots of useful advice on the whole process of evaluation. When you're ready to look for property, you may find *How to Buy a House, Condo, or Co-op,* from Consumer Reports Books, a helpful primer; *Finding & Buying Your Place in the Country,* by Les and Carol Scher, is one of several popular guides to realizing that dream (available from Storey Communications; see the listing in "Books"). *The Home Buyer's Kit* and *The Home Seller's Kit*, by Edith Lank, walk you through both sides of the transactions, with lots of checklists and charts to keep you organized. And *Your New House: The Alert Consumer's Guide to Buying and Building a Quality Home*, by Alan and Denise Fields, focuses on building—258 pages on what puts the "con" in "construction," and how to avoid and solve every problem that can arise. (See the mention of *Bridal Bargains* in the introduction to "Clothing" for ordering information.)

After buying, furnishing, and decorating your house, you have to keep it. That means maintaining it against those ills that befall even the finest homes: roof leaks and ice dams, damp basements, peeling paint, insect infestation, and a hundred other problems. Keeping it clean and in good repair can be a never-ending task, so doing it faster, better, and cheaper is a common goal. Consumers Union publishes several books that can help, including *Year-Round House Care, The Complete Guide to Home Repair and Maintenance, Home Security* (on locks, alarms, etc.), and *How to Clean Practically Everything*. (See the current issue of *Consumer Reports* to order, or check your local bookstore.) Reader's Digest Books publishes *The Family Handyman Helpful Hints: Quick and Easy Solutions, Timesaving Tips, and Tricks of the Trade* (1995), nearly 400 well-organized pages of great ideas for doing everything from setting up a workshop to repairing masonry. Time-Life's current series, "New Home Repair and Improvement," updates the best-selling first edition of the series, which was released in the 70s. You can order a "customized" library of any of the titles—from *Adding On* to *Walls and Ceilings*—that meet your needs from Time-Life, 800–621–7026 (Monday to Friday 9 a.m.–9 p.m. ET), or look for volumes at your library or local bookstore.

For sources selling related goods, see the listings in "Home: Decor" and "Tools."

FIND IT FAST

ARCHITECTURAL DETAILS • **Oregon Wooden Screen Door, Shuttercraft**
CLEANING SUPPLIES AND TOOLS • **Cleaning Center**
INSULATED GLASS PANELS • **Arctic Glass**
PLUMBING FIXTURES • **Baths from the Past, CISCO, Faucet Outlet**
RADIATOR ENCLOSURES • **ARSCO, Monarch**
SCREEN DOORS AND WINDOWS • **Coppa Woodworking**

ARCTIC GLASS & WINDOW OUTLET

DEPT. WB
565 COUNTY RD. T
HAMMOND, WI 54015
800–428–9276
715–796–2292
FAX: 715–796–2295

Catalog: $4, refundable
Pay: MO, MC, V, Discover
Sells: exterior doors, windows, skylights, glass panels
Store: I–94 at Hammond Exit, 35 miles east of St. Paul, MN; also 1232 W. Clairemont Ave., Eau Claire, WI; Monday to Thursday 8–8, Friday 8–5, Saturday 9–5

Joseph Bacon began his business after discovering that surplus patio door panes doubled perfectly as passive solar panels in the greenhouse he was building—and cost up to 50% less. Since founding Arctic Glass in 1979, he's watched it outgrow several facilities and increase revenues 2,000%. In fact, Mr. Bacon has shipped to 49 of the 50 states—he's just waiting for that order from Hawaii!

Arctic Glass sells surplus patio door panels from two of the best-known manufacturers in the business. Different types of double panes are available (some with low E coating), most of the glass is ³/₁₆″ thick, and all of the panes are double-sealed. The many suitable applications and uses for those panels are listed in the literature. Arctic also stocks Velux skylights and the complete line of Kolbe & Kolbe doors and windows—wood-framed casements, tilts, slider, direct-set, eyebrow, and fanlight windows and a variety of doors. Weather Shield wood and vinyl windows and doors, Therma-Tru doors, and Velux skylights are also available.

Prices average 10% to 50% below list, and all of the panels are guaranteed against leakage or failure for ten years. The warranty terms and installation instructions, including retrofitting, are detailed in the literature. If you have any questions, you can talk them over with Mr. Bacon himself.

Special Factors: Quantity discounts are available; minimum crating charge is $50 for mail orders; returns are accepted within 30 days for exchange, refund, or credit; minimum order is $50.

ARSCO MANUFACTUR-ING COMPANY, INC.

3564 BLUE ROCK RD.
CINCINNATI, OH 45247
800–543–7040
513–385–0555
FAX: 513–741–6292

Catalog: free
Pay: check, MO, MC, V, Discover
Sells: radiator enclosures
Store: same address; Monday to Friday 8–4

"Once you own ACE Radiator Enclosures, you won't ever catch yourself staring at those naked radiators." So reads the brochure from ARSCO Manufacturing, which makes enclosures for conventional steam radiators, fan coil units, and fin tube (baseboard) heaters. If you live within 500 miles of Cincinnati, ARSCO will send someone to measure your radiator; farther afield, you can use the guide ARSCO provides and do it yourself.

Standard sizes run up to 42" high and 96" long (larger sizes can be made), and there are 14 stock colors of paint enamel, although custom color matches can be provided for a fee. Other options include special notches, doors, or cutouts for valve access, a built-in humidifier pan, insulated tops, and adjustable legs for uneven floors. Prices are a solid 35% below those charged by local sources for the same kinds of enclosures, and if your unit is measured by ARSCO's personnel, the fit is guaranteed. If you're measuring it yourself, do it twice and then again, since the enclosures are all made to order, and are *not* returnable.

Special Factors: Enclosures are not returnable.

BATHS FROM THE PAST, INC.

**83 EAST WATER ST.
ROCKLAND, MA 02370
800–697–3871
617–335–2445
FAX: 617–871–8533**

Catalog: free (see text)
Pay: check, MO, MC, V, Discover
Sells: bathroom and kitchen hardware
Store: same address; Monday to Friday 10–5

Nothing completes a period bathroom like authentic-looking hardware—brass spigots, porcelain shower roses, and telephone-style tub fillers—but nothing breaks a budget faster. Baths from the Past makes it more affordable to buy these, as well as kitchen faucets, shower curtain rods, Victorian porcelain bathroom sinks, and bathroom accessories, at prices up to 30% below other sources (for comparable quality and finish—chrome, polished brass, and polished lacquered brass). Baths from the Past has been in business since 1981, and guarantees the finishes for three years, and the fixtures themselves for life (against failure or defective workmanship).

Special Factors: Satisfaction is guaranteed; minimum order is $50; C.O.D. orders are accepted.

CISCO

**CHANUTE IRON &
SUPPLY CO.
P.O. DRAWER E
1502 W. CHERRY ST.
CHANUTE, KS 66720–1005
316–431–9289
FAX: 316–431–7354**

Information: price quote
Pay: check, MO, MC, V, AE, Discover
Sells: plumbing supplies and fixtures
Store: same address; Monday to Friday 8–5, Saturday 8–12 noon
E-mail: m_becker@computer-services.com

CISCO stocks a full range of fixtures and equipment for plumbing, heating, and air conditioning. CISCO has been selling plumbing supplies, fixtures, and tools since 1941 and offers a portion of the inventory by mail at savings of 25% to 40%. Delta and Moen faucets, In-Sink-Erator garbage disposers, Burnham boilers, NuTone medicine chests and accessories, and whirlpools and fixtures by American Standard, Aqua Glass, Aquatic, Grohe, Jason, and Kohler are available. There are Elkay, Moen, and Swanstone sinks, Crane fixtures, Cal-Spas and saunas, spa and swimming pool accessories and parts (no chemicals), tools by Rigid, and the professional line of tools by Makita. Replacement parts for all types of faucets are also stocked.

Please note: No catalog is available.

Special Factors: Price quote by phone, fax, or letter with SASE; minimum order is $25; CISCO pays freight on UPS-shippable items over $100.

THE CLEANING CENTER

DEPT. WC
P.O. BOX 39
POCATELLO, ID 83204
208–232–6212

Catalog: free
Pay: check, MO, MC, V, AE, Discover
Sells: cleaning tools and products
Store: 311 S. 5th Ave., Pocatello, ID; Monday to Saturday 9–6

When you've been in the cleaning business for a quarter of a century, you develop some strong opinions on the best way to do a job. Don Aslett, "America's #1 Cleaning Expert," used his expertise in speed-cleaning techniques to create *Is There Life After Housework?*, the first of many books on how to do more cleaning in less time and "plan" the dirt out of your house. He brings both the books and his tools of choice to market through the informative "Cleaning Report" catalog, 48 pages of concentrated solutions for general cleaning and windows, wood, bathroom fixtures, waxed floors, and carpets, plus deodorizers, disinfectants, protective acrylic sealer, spot removers, and wax stripper. Mr. Aslett's favorite tools are available—scrub brushes, commercial spray bottles, cleaning cloths, Ettore window scrubbers and squeegees, the "Scrubbee Doo" mop system, professional mop buckets and push brooms, carpet rakes, and walk-off mats. He also sells the Sanitaire upright vacuum cleaner and Eureka's Mighty Mite II, and replacement bags (standard and super-filter) for both models.

The Cleaning Center products represent excellent value on a per-use basis, compared to supermarket brands. In addition, price checks showed good savings compared to other specialty sources: The X-O

Odor Neutralizer that pros use to combat serious smells cost 20% to 50% less from the Cleaning Center than from another discounter; the "dry sponge," used to clean unwashable surfaces, cost $3.75 from a popular tool and gadget catalog but just over $2 here, or as little as $1.75 when bought by the dozen. Check the back of the catalog for the seasonal specials—mats and window-cleaning tools seem to go on sale once a year.

Please note: The cleaning solutions are concentrated and must be diluted and used according to directions. Any spray bottles you fill should be clearly labeled and used for refills of the same product only.

Canadian readers, please note: Only U.S. funds are accepted.

Special Factors: Satisfaction is guaranteed; returns are accepted for exchange, refund, or credit; C.O.D. orders are accepted.

COPPA WOOD-WORKING INC.

1231 PARAISO AVE.
SAN PEDRO, CA 90731
310–548–4142
FAX: 310–548–6740

Catalog: $1
Pay: check, MO, MC, V
Sells: Adirondack furniture, screen doors, windows, etc.
Store: same address; Monday to Friday 8–5

¡Sí!

Coppa Woodworking is a small firm that manufactures Adirondack-style furniture, screen doors, and window screens in a variety of finishes, woods, and other options, at prices up to 40% below those charged elsewhere for comparable products. (You know you're dealing directly with the craftsmen when the catalog itself smells of fresh lumber!) Classic low-slung, slat-back Adirondack chair styles are featured, from the children's model for about $30 to the "fanback" for under $70 to a 51-inch-wide love seat for about $100. All of the seating and complementing footrests and side tables are made of unfinished pine that can be stained (white, blue, or green) for a small fee. Old-fashioned butcher block tables with 2½" red-oak tops begin at $126, and other woods and custom-painted bases are available.

The other side of Coppa's business is screen doors, window screens, and sidelights (panels); the doors can be produced in over 100 styles to suit every decor. A number of options are available, including wood choice (Douglas fir, sugar pine, red oak, mahogany), stain and varnish, single or double-door fixtures, custom sizes, built-in pet doors, and a choice of fiberglass screening materials (including heavy-duty cat-proof mesh). Prices begin at just $42 for the plainest style in pine, and custom charges are quite reasonable. And if you'd like a feature or detail not mentioned, be sure to ask, since Coppa may be able to provide.

Special Factors: Satisfaction is guaranteed; returns are accepted.

DESIGNER'S HARD-WAREHOUSE

P.O. BOX 484, DEPT. WB
WICKLIFFE, OH 44092
216–944–8800
FAX: 216–944–6130

Catalog: free
Pay: check, MO, MC, V
Sells: builders' hardware and accessories
Store: mail order only

There are few things sadder than a houseful of custom-milled, six-panel solid oak connecting doors installed with cheap hinges and flimsy locksets, especially when good-quality components can be bought at great discounts. That's the business of Designer's HardWareHouse, which sells hardware by Baldwin and Hansgrohe and about 50 other manufacturers. The catalog shows clear drawings of drawer pulls, privacy sets, door knockers, towel racks, door and cabinet hinges, doorbells, window hardware, house numbers, and even switch plates—and that's just a sampler of what's available. You can call for a price quote if you know the manufacturer's name and style or code number of what you want, and the finish and any other options. Savings of a third to half the suggested list prices apply to both stock and special-order items (special orders may not be canceled once placed). See the catalog for terms of the sales policy, and a roundup of well-priced useful hardware, including some products exclusive to Designer's HardWareHouse.

Special Factors: Price quote by phone or letter; returns (except special orders) are accepted within 45 days for exchange, refund, or credit.

THE FAUCET OUTLET

P.O. BOX 547
MIDDLETOWN, NY 10940
800–444–5783
FAX: 914–343–1617

Catalog: $4 (see text)
Pay: check, MO, MC, V
Sells: bathroom and kitchen fixtures
Store: mail order only; phone hours Monday to Friday 8–6 ET
E-mail: faucet@faucet.com
Online: http://www.faucet.com

We don't spend much time thinking about those things that deliver water from the pipes into the shower, tub, or sink, so when they need replacing it's a shock to discover how many there are, and how much they cost. Thank goodness for The Faucet Outlet.

This mail-order concern specializes in spigots, spouts, knobs, connections, hot water dispensers, and related items by Alsons, American Standard, Chicago Faucets, Delta, Elkay, Grohe, Jado, Kohler, Moen, Price Pfister, St. Thomas Creations, Speakman (shower heads), Swanstone, and other firms. A selection of bathroom accessories for the disabled—elevated toilet seats, grab bars and rails, benches, and flush levers—are also available. The 32-page catalog features a sampling of products from a number of manufacturers, as well as valuable service information and The Faucet Outlet's sales policy. NuTone chimes, fans, intercoms, security videos, and medicine cabinets are also available. You can order the catalog, or if you know exactly what you want or don't see the model you're looking for, call with the stock or item number for a price quote. (Check before ordering to make sure your fixtures comply with local codes and are compatible with existing plumbing.) Discounts run up to 50% on manufacturers' list prices at this writing, but are subject to change and may vary from line to line.

Please note: The catalog fee, usually $4, is $2 to readers of this book, so be sure to mention WBMC when you send for it.

Special Factors: Authorized returns are accepted; price quote by phone or letter.

MONARCH RADIATOR ENCLOSURES

DEPT. WBMC
2744 ARKANSAS DR.
BROOKLYN, NY 11234
201–796–4117
FAX: 201–796–7717

Brochure: $1, refundable with order
Pay: check, MO, MC, V
Sells: all-steel radiator enclosures
Store: mail order only
Online: http://www.quikpage.com/ M/monarchrad

If you're tired of looking at the exposed ribs of the radiators in your home, consider enclosures. They not only render the unsightly heating fixtures more decorative, but also help to direct the heat into the room.

Monarch sells radiator enclosures in two dozen styles, from a basic grillwork design to an elaborate enclosure that includes shelves. Monarch's enclosures are constructed of heavy steel, and price comparisons show savings of up to 35%. There is a choice of colors in baked enamel, including wood-grain finishes. Monarch's literature includes a guide to measuring your radiator prior to ordering.

Special Factors: Most enclosures can be shipped by UPS; larger enclosures are shipped via common carrier.

OREGON WOODEN SCREEN DOOR

2767 HARRIS ST.,
* DEPT. WBMC*
EUGENE, OR 97405
541–485–0279
FAX: 541–484–0353

Brochure and Price List: $3
Pay: check, MO, MC, V
Sells: wooden screen and storm doors
Store: same address

The satisfying "thock" of a wooden screen door closing is one of the many small sounds of a great summer day. Revive this lovely component of a well-tailored home with the help of Oregon Wooden Screen Doors, which sells 30 door styles, but allows you to amend the designs with your choice of spandrels, brackets, and other embellishments. The categories break down into "Ornamental," "Classic," "Muscular," and the

"Designers Collection." They range in complexity from "Settler," a straightforward, two-panel door, to "Wright's Delight," a tribute to the master architect. Each door is constructed of 1¼" thick, vertical-grain fir, with mortise-and-tenon and dowel joinery, for strength and warp resistance. Wood-framed screen and storm inserts are available, and all of the wood is primed with wood preservative—you provide the final finish. Solid brass hardware can be ordered with your door, or you can obtain it locally.

Prices begin at under $200 for the kit versions of the simplest styles, to several hundred for the most elaborate. Since the doors are made to measure, this approximates a custom job—at a prefab price! If you have questions about any aspect of design or construction, or want a fully customized design, the staff will be pleased to help.

Special Factors: Authorized returns are accepted.

SHUTTERCRAFT, INC.

DEPT. WBM
282 STEPSTONE HILL RD.
GUILFORD, CT 06437
203–453–1973
FAX: 203–245–5969

Brochures and Price Lists: free
Pay: check, MO, MC, V
Sells: interior and exterior house shutters and hardware
Store: same address; Monday to Friday 9–5

Authentic, "historic" exterior wood shutters with movable louvers are sold here at prices well below those charged for custom-milled shutters. An added advantage: They look more substantial than the vinyl versions, and the firm's literature points out that "real wood shutters are naturally ventilating and do not cause the wood siding behind them to rot." Shuttercraft's cedar shutters can be bought in widths up to 36", in lengths to 144", and in shapes that include half-circle tops, Gothic arches, and cutouts in the raised panels. (A pine tree and 24 other styles are shown, and Shuttercraft will execute your pattern for $15 per pair of shutters.) Also available are fixed-louver shutters, exterior raised-panel shutters in Western cedar, interior plantation styles, S-shaped holdbacks, and shutter hinges. Shuttercraft will prime, paint, trim, and rabbet your shutters for a fee; details are given in the brochures.

Special Factors: Shipping is not charged on orders totaling $500 or more.

SEE ALSO

AAA-All Factory Vacuum Cleaners • *floor-care machines and supplies* • *APPLIANCES*

ABC Vacuum Cleaner Warehouse • *floor-care machines and supplies* • *APPLIANCES*

AVAC Corporation • *floor-care machines, supplies, and parts* • *APPLIANCES*

Clothcrafters, Inc. • *mosquito netting and flannel polishing cloths* • *GENERAL MERCHANDISE*

EDGE Distributing, Inc. • *name-brand home cleaning products in case lots* • *GENERAL MERCHANDISE*

King's Chandelier Co. • *replacement parts for chandeliers* • *HOME: DECOR: LIGHTING*

Manufacturer's Supply • *wood-burning furnaces and heaters* • *TOOLS*

Marshall Domestics • *janitorial cleaning tools and supplies, cloths, etc.* • *GENERAL MERCHANDISE*

Percy's, Inc. • *garbage disposals* • *APPLIANCES*

Safe Specialties, Inc. • *safes for home, office, and business* • *OFFICE*

Sew Vac City • *floor-care machines* • *APPLIANCES*

Staples, Inc. • *cleaning products, janitorial supplies, paper towels, brooms, trash bags, etc.* • *OFFICE*

Value-tique, Inc. • *safes for home, office, and business* • *OFFICE*

Water Warehouse • *swimming pool maintenance equipment and supplies* • *SPORTS*

Woodworker's Hardware • *hardware and fittings for cabinets, doors, cupboards, etc.* • *TOOLS*

Kitchen

Cookware, bakeware, restaurant equipment, and food storage

These firms sell everything from measuring spoons to commercial ranges, frequently at discounts of 30% to 50% on the regular retail prices. For other kitchen electronics, see "Appliances"; for kitchen tools and linens, see the next section, "Linen"; and look in "Books" for cookbooks. A number of firms selling specialty ingredients and cookware are listed in the "Food and Drink" chapter—including several that offer stupendous buys on herbs, spices, and other flavorings.

FIND IT FAST

CAMP COOKWARE, CAST IRON • **ChuckWagon Outfitters**
CHEESE-MAKING EQUIPMENT • **New England Cheesemaking Supply**
COMMERCIAL FIXTURES • **Kaplan Bros., Peerless, Thomas**
GOURMET COOKWARE • **Broadway Panhandler, Open House, Professional Cutlery, Zabar's**

BROADWAY PANHANDLER

477 BROOME ST.
NEW YORK, NY 10013
212–966–3434
FAX: 212–966–9017

Information: price quote (see text)
Pay: check, MO, MC, V, AE
Sells: cookware, cutlery, kitchenware, bakeware, and tabletop accessories
Store: same address; Monday to Friday 10:30–7, Saturday 11–7, Sunday 11–6

Broadway Panhandler is located just blocks from the Bowery, New York City's commercial kitchenware district, but it draws a steady stream of trade from those who like the firm's mix of high-end home cookware and well-chosen professional equipment. Broadway Panhandler doesn't publish a catalog, but you can call or write for prices on appliances and equipment by All-Clad, Bodum, Bourgeat, Braun, Calphalon, Chicago Metallic, Le Creuset, Cuisinart (machines), Kaiser, KitchenAid, Krups, Omega, Pavoni, Pelouze, and Vollrath. Broadway Panhandler's knife department includes Global, Lamson & Goodnow, Sabatier, and Wüsthof-Trident (price lists and manufacturers' brochures may be available for the cutlery). If you're able to visit the store, you'll also find cookbooks, serving pieces, kitchen linens, candy molds, baking supplies, and lots of baskets, and gadgets. Savings vary by brand and season, but open-stock cutlery is about 30% off at this writing, and selected cookware lines are discounted up to 35% off list.

Special Factors: Price quote by phone or letter.

CHUCKWAGON OUTFITTERS

Catalog: free (see text)
Pay: check, MO, MC, V, AE, Discover
Sells: cast-iron cookware, accessories
Store: same address

250 AVILA BEACH DR.
SAN LUIS OBISPO, CA
  93405
800–543–2359
805–595–2434
FAX: 805–595–7914

E-mail: cwo@fix.net

Whether you like cast-iron cookware for its down-home good looks or its serviceability, you'll appreciate ChuckWagon Outfitters for bringing so much of it your way. This family-run firm, established in 1992, features the Lodge brand of ironware that includes the Dutch oven that's the "official cookware of the Boy Scouts of America," as well as other lines. True to its affiliations, ChuckWagon's 20-page catalog shows a wide range of fryers, skillets, kettles, muffin tins, trivets and stands, and related camp gear, all at savings of up to 40% on comparable retail. The Dutch ovens that inspired the business itself are available in flat-bottomed styles for stovetop use, and footed for campfires. The MACA extra-deep ovens can accommodate whole turkeys, and you can order them with lids that are personalized with "your name or your ranch name." (Considering the fact that they look as if they could double for manhole covers with handles, it's hard to imagine them walking away, but al fresco dining makes its own rules.) Those who are unfamiliar with the Dutch oven culture and cooking methods should see the dozens of histories and cookbooks in the catalog for help. (Hint: The Dutch oven appears to be a precursor of the Crock-Pot.)

If you've been searching for square skillets, cast-iron woks, flat griddles, perch-shaped muffin tins, or a cast-iron teakettle or bundt pan, you've found the source. There are a number of classic "catalog curiosities," including ranch chimes (triangles), sad irons (replicas of the non-electric irons that were heated on top of a woodstove), cast-iron trout andirons, enamelware chamber pots, and Volcano cookers, among others. The catalog, regularly $2, is free to readers of this book, so be sure to mention WBMC when you call or write for it.

Wholesale buyers, please note: The minimum opening order is $300, subsequent order minimum is $75. For a price list and terms of sale, call 805–595–2434.

Special Factors: Satisfaction is guaranteed; returns are accepted for exchange, refund, or credit.

COLONIAL GARDEN KITCHENS

▬▬▬▬▬▬

DEPT. CGZ4182
HANOVER, PA 17333–0066
800–323–6000

Catalog: $2
Pay: check, MO, MC, V, AE, CB, DC, Discover
Sells: kitchen equipment and household helps
Store: mail order only

Colonial Garden Kitchens is one of the Hanover Direct, Inc. companies offering moderately priced gadgets, as well as name-brand appliances, at a discount. A third or more of the goods in the color catalog are usually on "sale" at 20% to 40% below their regular prices. And every catalog features the latest in kitchen appliances, specialty cookware and utensils, work units and food storage containers, serving and entertaining equipment, hard-to-find cleaners, bed and bath organizers, and lots of other things that are handy to have around the house. Bread makers, tabletop grills, deep fryers, commercial oven mitts, microwave bacon crispers, and cast-iron muffin tins are among the popular products that have appeared in past catalogs. Everything is backed by the CGK's guarantee of satisfaction.

Special Factors: Satisfaction is guaranteed; returns in new or like-new condition are accepted for exchange, refund, or credit.

KAPLAN BROS. BLUE FLAME CORP.

523 W. 125TH ST.
NEW YORK, NY
10027–3498
800–528–6913
212–662–6990
FAX: 212–663–2026

Brochure: free with SASE
Pay: certified check or MO
Sells: commercial restaurant equipment
Store: same address; Monday to Friday 8–4:30

Kaplan Bros. Blue Flame Corp., established in 1953, sells commercial restaurant equipment at discounts of 50% on list prices and will send you manufacturers' brochures on request for a self-addressed, stamped envelope. Blue Flame is best known as a source for Garland commercial stoves and the Dynamic Cooking System.

Please note: Goods are shipped to "mainland U.S.A." only—no orders can be shipped to Alaska, Hawaii, Canada, or APO/FPO addresses.

Special Factors: Request brochures by name of manufacturer; if purchasing a stove for residential installation, have kitchen flooring, wall insulation, and exhaust system evaluated before ordering and upgrade if necessary.

KITCHEN ETC.

DEPT. WBM98
32 INDUSTRIAL DR.
EXETER, NH 03833
603–773–0020
FAX: 603–778–9328

Catalog: free
Pay: check, MO, MC, V, Discover
Sells: tableware and kitchenware
Store: West Hartford, CT; Burlington, Dedham, Natick, and Peabody, MA; Nashua and North Hampton, NH; and South Burlington, VT (see the catalog for locations)

Kitchen Etc. has put together a great catalog of fine and everyday china, cookware, cutlery, and serving pieces that brings you helpful buying information, as well as prices that usually run from 20% to 40% below regular retail. The firm has been doing business since 1983, and has eight stores throughout New England.

Kitchen Etc. features fine and casual dinnerware patterns from Franciscan, Johnson Brothers, Lenox, Mikasa, Nikko, Noritake, Pfaltzgraff, Royal Doulton, Royal Worcester, Studio Nova, Wedgwood, and many more. The available patterns are listed, as well as a guide to the shape of each piece, present and future availability (if known), and suggested retail and discount prices. Stemware from Gorham, Lenox, Marquis by Waterford, Mikasa, Miller Rogaska, Noritake, and Royal Doulton is sold. Stainless steel and silverplate flatware is available from Gorham, Mikasa, Oneida, Pfaltzgraff, Reed & Barton, Wallace, and Yamazaki.

The catalog offers cookware and serving pieces from All-Clad, Calphalon, Circulon, Le Creuset, Revere, and T-Fal. If you're looking for cutlery, check the prices on knives from Chicago Cutlery, J.A. Henckels, and Wüsthof-Trident. Selected small kitchen appliances are also available, as well as pasta bowl sets, woks, pizza stones, glassware, and other hard-to-find items. Special orders are accepted on some goods, so if you don't see what you're looking for in the catalog, call to see whether the firm can get it. Kitchen Etc. also maintains a bridal registry service.

Special Factors: Satisfaction is guaranteed; price quote by phone, fax, or letter.

NEW ENGLAND CHEESEMAKING SUPPLY COMPANY, INC.

DEPT. WBM
P.O. BOX 85
ASHFIELD, MA 01330–0085
413–628–3808
FAX: 413–628–4061

Catalog: $1
Pay: check, MO, MC, V
Sells: cheese-making supplies and equipment
Store: same address; Monday to Friday 8–4 (call first)
E-mail: info@cheesemaking.com
Online: http://www.cheesemaking.com

Making cheese at home is one of the few do-it-yourself endeavors with a nominal price tag that doesn't require significant skills or time investment. New England Cheesemaking Supply, in business since 1978, can provide you with all the tools and materials you'll need to produce hard, soft, and semi-soft cheeses, at savings of up to 80% on the prices charged by supermarkets and specialty stores for the same kinds of cheeses.

Soft cheese is the easiest to make, and may be the cheapest, since you can get as much as two pounds of cheese from a gallon of milk. Milk sells for $1.30 a half gallon in some parts of the country, and flavored soft cheeses often cost $4.50 to $7.00 per pound, or as much as $2.80 for packaged, four-ounce varieties. So, by using the "Gourmet Soft Cheese Kit," you can recoup the $16.95 cost, plus the price of the milk, after making as little as two pounds of soft cheese. This kit is designed for the beginner and comes with cheese starter, cheesecloth, a dairy thermometer, and recipes. It can be used to make *crème fraiche* as well as *fromage blan*—generic soft cheese—in as little as ten minutes. (If you use skim milk, you can produce low-calorie, low-cholesterol cheese, and omit the salt for sodium-restricted diets.)

New England Cheesemaking Supply also sells a "basic" cheese kit (for ricotta, Gouda, Monterey Jack, cheddar, etc.), and others for making mozzarella and goat cheese. Rennet (animal and vegetable), a large selection of starter and direct-set cultures, lipase powders, mold powder, cheese wax, cheesecloth, thermometers, molds for shaping hard and soft cheese, and several books on cheese production are offered. Experienced cheese producers should see the 16-page catalog for the machinery as well: a home milk pasteurizer and Wheeler's hard cheese press are available. The woman who runs this firm is an experienced cheese producer and can answer your questions by phone or letter.

Special Factors: Price quote by phone, e-mail, or letter (with SASE); minimum order is $20 with credit cards; C.O.D. orders are accepted.

OPEN HOUSE

206 BALA AVE.
BALA-CYNWYD, PA 19004
610–664–1488

Information: price quote
Pay: check, MO, AE
Sells: flatware, stemware, cookware, etc.
Store: same address; Monday to Saturday 10–5

Open House has been doing business since 1960, and prices its collection of tableware, cookware, cutlery, and linens at up to 40% below list or usual retail prices. There is no catalog, but you can call for a price quote on goods from All-Clad, Arabia, Calphalon, Copco, J.G. Durand, Fitz & Floyd, Guzzini, Libbey, Mikasa, Nikko, Retroneau, Schott-Zwiesel, Tri-Chef, and other makers. If you're trying to find the best price on name-brand cookware or table settings, give this firm a call—it may be available.

Special Factors: Minimum order is $25.

PEERLESS RESTAURANT SUPPLIES

DEPT. WBMC
1124 S. GRAND BLVD.
ST. LOUIS, MO 63104
800–255–3663
314–664–0400
FAX: 314–664–8102

Catalog: $10
Pay: check, MO, MC, V
Sells: commercial cookware and restaurant equipment
Store: same address; Monday to Friday 8–5
E-mail: peerless@prls.com
Online: http://www.prls.com

The hefty Peerless catalog—yours for $10—has everything you need to set up a professional kitchen or restaurant dining room, except the food. Since so many of the appliances and utensils can do double duty in home kitchens, the catalog makes a good investment if you're planning any significant kitchenware purchases.

Peerless represents over 2,000 manufacturers of everything from diner sugar shakers to walk-in refrigerators: tableware, trays and carts, bar accessories, restaurant seating, table linens and kitchen textiles, cookware, ranges and ovens, refrigerators, sinks, worktables, cleaning supplies and equipment, ice machines, dishwashers, and much more. Sample offerings include Libbey glassware, Hall and Buffalo china, cutlery by Dexter Russell, WearEver pots and pans, Vollrath stainless steel stock pots and chafing dishes, Rubbermaid's professional line of janitorial storage and food-service containers, Pelouze food scales, Waring professional bar appliances, Peerless' own commercial cleaners and polishes, Metro wire shelves, Market Forge steamers, and Robot Coupe food processors. Peerless also sells cooking equipment by Castle, Dean, Frymaster, Montague, Southbend, and Vulcan; commercial microwave ovens from MenuMaster and Panasonic; refrigeration from Delfield, Ice-O-Matic, Kelvinator, Raetone, Scotsman, Traulsen, and True; Eagle sinks, In-Sink-Erator commercial disposers, ventilation equipment, and much more. Peerless offers UL-approved zero-clearance ranges for home kitchens, from Garland, Imperial, Viking, and Wolf.

If you know what you want by manufacturer and model number, you can call or write for a price quote—but the catalog is worth the $10 fee if you're buying more than a couple of items. Food-service professionals should note the services Peerless can provide, including facility design, installation, construction supervision, concept development, and equipment leasing. Used kitchenware is available at big savings, and if you get to St. Louis, stop in and check out the "Bargain Room," which features closeouts.

Special Factors: Quantity discounts are available; authorized returns are accepted within 30 days for exchange, refund, or credit (a 10% restocking fee may be charged, or 20% on special orders); minimum order is $50.

PROFESSIONAL CUTLERY DIRECT

DEPT. WBM8
170 BOSTON POST RD.,
  SUITE 135
MADISON, CT 06443
800–859–6994
203–458–5015
FAX: 203–458–5019

Catalog: $3, refundable
Pay: check, MO, MC, V
Sells: kitchen cutlery, cookware, cookbooks, etc.
Store: mail order only
E-mail: wbm8@p-c-d.com
Online: http://www.p-c-d.com

Serious cooks require commercial-quality equipment, which is what you'll find in the 64-page catalog from Professional Cutlery Direct. It's geared to cooks who know the merits of high-carbon stainless steel (it resists corrosion and can be sharpened), or why wood cutting boards are better than plastic (the latter actually promote the breeding of bacteria!). No matter what your experience level, you'll warm to everyday discounts of 20% to 30%, with specials reaching as much as 45% off list.

PCD's stock includes several lines by Cuisine de France Sabatier, F. Dick, Forschner/Victorinox, Global, Kyocera Ceramics, Lamson Sharp, and Wüsthof-Trident: boxed sets, sharpeners and steels, blocks with and without knife sets, wall-mounted knife holders and magnetic strips, professional roll-packs (used by teachers and caterers), and knife attaché cases from a variety of manufacturers, filled with "any professional dream of knives." Hardwood cutting boards are available in several sizes and styles, as well as the entire All-Clad line, Sitrum, and Chaudier cookware, whisks, pastry tools, mandolines, mortar-and-pestle sets, Bourgeat professional copper cookware, Enclume pot racks, professional cookbooks, and even chef's attire.

The PCD catalog includes product information to help you choose the cutlery that's best for your needs, as well as details on special offers, and the volume discount plan for commercial cookware. And there's a cap on shipping—$13.50 at this writing, no matter how much you buy!

Special Factors: Price quote by phone or letter; quantity discounts are available on selected items; returns of most items are accepted within 30 days for exchange, refund, or credit; minimum order is $10.

THOMAS FOOD EQUIPMENT, INC.

1767 BARLOW
TRAVERSE CITY, MI 49686
616–946–7760
FAX: 616–946–7126

Catalog: $3
Pay: check, MO, MC, V
Sells: food and beverage equipment and furnishings for restaurant, bar, camp, club, church, concession, office, etc.
Store: same address; Monday to Friday 9–5
E-mail: tfe@gtii.com

Thomas Food Equipment, formerly known as Fivenson, has been selling restaurant, concession, pizza, ice cream, bakery, institutional, bar, grocery, and ventilation equipment and furniture to the food-service industry since 1937 and offers consumers the same products at prices up to 60% below list. The catalog features just a sampling of the hundreds of manufacturers and thousands of products available here: ranges, ovens, steamers, fryers, and toasters by Dean, Frymaster, Garland, Savory, Toastmaster, U.S. Range, and Vollrath; Amana microwave ovens, Regal coffee urns, commercial blenders from Hamilton Beach, dishwashers, cooling units of every description from Delfield, Traulson, True, Ultra, and Victory; Pelouze scales; and sinks, lunchroom furniture, bakery racks, equipment for popcorn, hot dog, and concession stands. Thomas also sells office coffee service equipment, smoke-reduction equipment, air doors, ice makers, cleaning tools, chafing dishes, restaurant china, and other supplies. (The china and glassware are sold by the case only.) Since the $3 catalog is a brief 16 pages, you'll save money if you can decide what you want and then call, fax, or write Thomas for a price quote. Note that special orders are taken for goods from a number of manufacturers—Wüsthof-Trident, Westmark, Dexter-Russell—and for products as varied as meat grinders for hunters and battery-powered lamps. If you don't see what you're looking for, ask!

Special Factors: Price quote by phone or letter with SASE; commercial (not residential) kitchen layout and design services are available; minimum order is $25 (some products are sold by the case only).

ZABAR'S & CO., INC.

**2245 BROADWAY
NEW YORK, NY 10024
212–496–1234
FAX: 212–580–4477**

Catalog: free
Pay: check, MO, MC, V, AE
Sells: gourmet food, cookware, and house-wares
Store: same address; Monday to Friday 8–7:30, Saturday 8 a.m.–8 p.m., Sunday 9–6; housewares mezzanine daily 9–6
E-mail: info@Zabars.com

¡Si!

Zabar's, thought of by many as New York City's ultimate deli, offers the better part of North America a sampling from its famed counters and housewares mezzanine via a 62-page catalog. Zabar's has been around since 1934, and offers savings of up to 50% on name-brand kitchen-ware, and competitive prices on foodstuffs.

Past catalogs have offered smoked Scottish, Norwegian, and Irish salmon, plum pudding, peppercorns, Bahlsen cookies and confections, pâtés, mustards, crackers, escargot, Lindt and Droste chocolate, Tiptree preserves, Dresden stollen, olive oil, prosciutto and other deli meats, and similar gourmet fare. The cookware selections include Mauviel hotel-weight copper pots and pans (send a postcard for a price list); Calphalon, Cuisinart Commercial, Le Creuset, Magnalite, and Spring of Switzerland equipment; Krups and Simac machines, DeLonghi, Krups and Melitta coffee makers, KitchenAid food processors, Mouli kitchen tools, and products by Henckels, T-Fal, Wagner, Wüsthof-Trident, and other firms. Zabar's distinguishes itself among kitchenware vendors for the enormous selection of goods and the substantial discounts. The cat-alog features a representative selection from the store, and price quotes are given over the phone—if you don't see it in the catalog, just call.

Special Factors: Minimum order is $15; minimum shipping fee is $5.50; no orders are shipped to Alaska, Hawaii, APO/FPO addresses, Canada, or Puerto Rico; phone orders are accepted Monday to Saturday 9–5.

SEE ALSO

Bernie's Discount Center, Inc. • *microwave ovens and kitchen appliances* • **APPLIANCES**
Bruce Medical Supply • *food preparation equipment for those with limited strength and mobility* • **MEDICINE: SPECIAL NEEDS**

Cabela's Inc. • *camping cookware, stoves, implements* • **SPORTS**

CISCO • *garbage disposals, sinks, etc.* • **HOME: IMPROVEMENT**

Clothcrafters, Inc. • *kitchen textiles and kitchen utensils* • **GENERAL MERCHANDISE**

Coppa Woodworking Inc. • *butcher block tables* • **HOME: IMPROVEMENT**

The CMC Company • *cookware for Mexican and Asian specialties* • **FOOD: BEVERAGES AND FLAVORINGS**

Current, Inc. • *canning labels, recipe boxes, etc.* • **GENERAL: CARDS**

Cutlery Shoppe • *fine kitchen cutlery, sharpeners, etc.* • **SPORTS**

Eastern Butcher Block • *custom-cut butcher block counters, chopping blocks, etc.* • **HOME: FURNISHINGS**

Grandma's Spice Shop • *spice racks, wine racks, mortar and pestle sets, teapots, etc.* • **FOOD: BEVERAGES AND FLAVORINGS**

Jessica's Biscuit • *cookbooks* • **BOOKS**

Johnny's Selected Seeds Inc. • *food mills, dehydrators, canning supplies, etc.* • **FARM**

E.C. Kraus Wine & Beermaking Supplies • *bottle washers, cherry pitters, funnels, corkscrews* • **FOOD: BEVERAGES AND FLAVORINGS**

Lanac Sales • *select cutlery, cookware, and serving pieces* • **HOME: TABLE SETTINGS**

LVT Price Quote Hotline, Inc. • *microwave ovens, major appliances, etc.* • **APPLIANCES**

Marshall Domestics • *kitchen textiles, clothing for food-service workers, potholders, etc.* • **GENERAL MERCHANDISE**

The Paper Wholesaler • *disposable bakeware and cake-decorating supplies* • **TOYS**

Penzeys' Spice House • *pepper mills and spice jars* • **FOOD: BEVERAGES AND FLAVORINGS**

Percy's, Inc. • *major appliances* • **APPLIANCES**

Plastic BagMart • *garbage can liners* • **OFFICE: SMALL BUSINESS**

Rafal Spice Company • *kitchen gadgets, cookbooks* • **FOOD: BEVERAGES AND FLAVORINGS**

S & S Sound City • *microwave ovens* • **APPLIANCES**

Sultan's Delight • *Turkish coffee pots and cups, mamoul and falafel molds, mortars and pestles* • **FOOD**

Walnut Acres Organic Farms • *cookware, bakeware, serving pieces, etc.* • **FOOD**

West Marine • *galley gear* • **AUTO**

Weston Bowl Mill • *woodenware, knives, and kitchen helpers* • **GENERAL MERCHANDISE**

Linen

Bed, bath, and table textiles, accessories, and services

Retailing tradition honors January as white-sale month, but there's no reason to wait. You can buy your sheets, towels, pillows, and table linens from discounters who sell at savings of up to 60% every day, year-round. In addition to goods from the major mills, several of the firms can provide sheets to fit water beds, sofa beds, and oddly shaped mattresses, will rejuvenate down pillows and comforters, and make shower curtains, pillows, bed skirts, and coordinating lamp shades to match your sheets or bedroom fabric.

You can coax extra years of wear from bed, bath, and table textiles by treating them right, so follow the manufacturers' care instructions— avoid chlorine bleach and overdrying. Protect down-filled bedding with duvets or slipcases, and when it must be washed, use mild detergent, warm water, the machine's gentle settings, and be sure to dry it thoroughly. Use fabric bags for storage instead of plastic, which will hold humidity, and don't store down-filled goods in cedar or camphor since the down will pick up those odors permanently.

DOMESTICATIONS

DEPT. DOM8779
P.O. BOX 41
HANOVER, PA 17333–0041
800–962–2211, EXT.
  DOM8779

Catalog: free
Pay: check, MO, MC, V, AE, CB, DC, Discover, NOVUS
Sells: bed, bath, and table linens, dinnerware, gifts, etc.
Store: mail order only

Domestications, Hanover Direct's home style catalog, offers a colorful selection of goods for bed, bath, and table, plus well-priced home decorating accents. The full-color catalog emphasizes sheets and bedding, with traditional florals, a spectrum of solids, classic contemporary designs, and an assortment of the latest juvenile patterns. In addition to Domestications' private-label designs, there are selections from the best names in the business, including Bill Blass, Fieldcrest/Cannon, Martex, Louis Nichole, Dan River, Springmaid, J.P. Stevens, and Wamsutta. Choose from a full selection of all-cotton and cotton-blend sheets, blankets, bedspreads, and comforters, as well as down comforters, pillows, mattress pads, and hard-to-find items like sofa-bed sheets. The rest of the catalog features a variety of fashion-forward home accessories—tablecloths, window treatments, lamps, carpets, tableware, and even occasional furniture. Prices run from market rate to bargain basement.

Special Factors: Satisfaction is guaranteed; returns are accepted; minimum order is $20 with credit cards.

ELDRIDGE TEXTILE CO.

277 GRAND ST., DEPT. L
NEW YORK, NY 10002
212–925–1523
FAX: 212–219–9542

Catalog: $3, refundable
Pay: check, MO, MC, V, Discover
Sells: bed, bath, and window textiles
Store: same address; Sunday to Friday 9–5:30

 ¡Si!

Eldridge has been selling soft goods and housewares since 1940, and offers mail-order customers savings of up to 40% on bed, bath, and window treatments. Fully coordinated ensembles are available from Laura Ashley, Bay Linens, Cameo, Collier Campbell, Croscill, Crown Crafts,

Echo, Faribo, Fieldcrest/Cannon, Martex, Pacific Designs, Phoenix (down products), Revman, Richloom, Royal Sateen, Thomasville, Utica, Wamsutta, and other firms. Some of the best-selling sheet and towel lines are featured in the 32-page color catalog, as well as upholstered headboards, ottomans, and footstools.

Special Factors: Price quote by phone or letter with SASE; returns of unused goods are accepted within 30 days for refund or credit.

HARRIS LEVY, INC.

DEPT. WBM
278 GRAND ST.
NEW YORK, NY 10002
800–221–7750
212–226–3102
FAX: 212–334–9360

Catalog: $2, refundable
Pay: check, MO, MC, V, AE
Sells: bed, bath, and table linens; kitchen and closet accessories
Store: same address; Monday to Thursday 9–5, Friday 9–4, Sunday 9–4:30
E-mail: HarrisLevy@aol.com

Harris Levy, established in 1894, is one of the plums of New York City's Lower East Side—a firm that sells the crème de la crème of bed, bath, and table linens at savings of up to 60%. One-of-a-kind and imported items are available in the store, and *none* of the stock is seconds or discontinued merchandise. What makes Levy special are things like heavy Matelassé blanket covers at about half the price charged by luxury linens catalogs, a sleep connoisseur's choice of pillows, and even mundane items like bath mats in fresh designs, all-cotton mattress pads, and heavy wooden coat hangers.

Harris Levy's imports include Egyptian cotton percale and linen sheets, English kitchen towels, Irish damask tablecloths, and bedding from Switzerland, England, France, and Italy—all worth a trip to the store. Mail-order shoppers can send $2 for the catalog (refundable on purchases made within one year), or call for price quotes on bed and bath linens from the major names: Cannon, Croscill, Crown Crafts, Fieldcrest, Frette, Martex, Palais Royal, Revman, Sheridan, and Wamsutta. The catalog also gives a sampling of Harris Levy's large selection of imported sheets, fine blankets, down comforters, rugs, towels, closet organizers, and hangers. Levy specializes in custom services and can provide monogramming and sheets in special sizes and shapes, tablecloths, dust ruffles, curtains, pillowcases, and other products from stock sheets or your own fabric.

Special Factors: Price quote by phone, fax, or letter with SASE; store is closed Saturdays.

THE LINEN SOURCE

5401 HANGAR CT.
P.O. BOX 31151
TAMPA, FL 33631–3151
813–243–6170
FAX: 813–882–4605

Catalog: free
Pay: check, MO, MC, V, AE, Discover
Sells: bed linens, home accessories
Store: mail order only; phone hours Monday to Friday 8:30–6 ET

 ¡Si!

Why wait for a white sale when you can restyle your bedroom at a discount any day of the year? The 60-page catalog from The Linen Source features the latest fashions in bed dressing, with an emphasis on bold colors and strong graphics, and rich, romantic ensembles. You'll find current designs in sheets, comforters, and accessories by Laura Ashley, Burlington House, Crown Crafts, Dakotah, Fieldcrest/Cannon (Court of Versailles, Adrienne Vittadini), Gear, Martex, Dan River (Alexander Julian), Utica, Wamsutta, and other names. Patchwork quilts and window treatments are shown, as well as vases, statuary, framed prints, rugs, lamps, tableware, and other accents. The best savings are on sheet sets, but most of the other products are competitively priced—usually 20% to 35% off regular retail.

Special Factors: Satisfaction is guaranteed; returns are accepted.

J. SCHACHTER CORP.

5 COOK ST.
BROOKLYN, NY
  11206–4003
800–INTO–BED
718–384–2732, 2754
FAX: 718–384–7634

Catalog: $1, refundable
Pay: check, MO, MC, V, Discover
Sells: down-filled bedding, linens, and custom services
Store: same address; Monday to Thursday 9–5, Friday 9–1:30

 ¡Si! ★

Schachter has been making comforters and pillows for the bedding industry and recovering old comforters for private customers since 1919.

Custom work is featured in the firm's-12-page catalog, but stock goods are also available. Schachter specializes in custom jobs: Comforters, coverlets, bed ruffles, pillow shams, duvets, and shower curtains are popular requests, and Schachter will take your sheets and create quilted blanket covers, or lightweight summer quilts, with them. Filling choices for the comforters include lamb's wool, polyester, white goose down, and a nonallergenic synthetic down alternative. Schachter carries bed and bath linens by the major mills—Cannon, Croscill, Fieldcrest, Martex, Springs Industries, J.P. Stevens, and Wamsutta—and labels from France, Germany, England, Switzerland, Italy, and Belgium—Bruna, Palais Royal, Peter Reed, Sferra, and Sufolla. Carter cotton bath rugs, and blankets by Atkinson, Chatham, Early's of Whitney, Faribo, and Hudson Bay are offered, as well as pillows in down, feather/down blend, latex rubber, and poly fill. Schachter's own stock comforters and accessories are all available, and the firm can recover and sterilize old down pillows and comforters.

Special Factors: Store is closed Saturdays and Sundays.

SEE ALSO

Baby Bunz & Co. • crib bedding • **CLOTHING: MOTHER AND CHILD**
BMI Home Decorating • custom-made bedspreads and pillows • **HOME: DECOR**
Campmor • sleeping bags, sleeping bag liners • **SPORTS**
Chock Catalog Corp. • crib and bassinet bedding • **CLOTHING**
Clothcrafters, Inc. • plain cotton sheets, towels, table linens, etc. • **GENERAL MERCHANDISE**
Designer's HardWareHouse • bath mirrors and hardware • **HOME: IMPROVEMENT**
Gettinger Feather Corp. • pillow feathers • **CRAFTS**
Gohn Bros. Mfg. Co. • sheets and blankets • **CLOTHING**
Kitchen Etc. • table linens • **HOME: KITCHEN**
Marshall Domestics • institutional-quality bed and bath linen, bedding, tablecloths, kitchen textiles, etc. • **GENERAL MERCHANDISE**
Plexi-Craft Quality Products Corp. • acrylic bathroom accessories • **HOME: FURNISHINGS**
Retired Persons Services, Inc. • waffle foam bed pads • **MEDICINE**
Rubens & Marble, Inc. • bassinet and crib sheets • **CLOTHING: MOTHER AND CHILD**
Shama Imports, Inc. • crewel-embroidered bedspreads • **HOME: DECOR**

Table Settings

China, crystal, glass, flatware, woodenware, and related goods

Buying active patterns of tableware is as easy as picking up the phone and calling one of the discounters listed here. But if your china, crystal, or silver pattern is discontinued, you'll need a replacement specialist. Two firms listed here—Beverly Bremer and Buschemeyer—sell discontinued silver flatware (also called "estate" silver). If you're missing pieces of a china or crystal pattern, write to Replacements, Ltd., 302 Gallimore Dairy Rd., Greensboro, NC 27400–9723, or call 910–275–7224. Replacements has over 250,000 pieces in stock, and can help you identify your pattern if you're not sure of the name. The China Connection is another source for discontinued china patterns, by such manufacturers as Castleton, Haviland, Lenox, and Noritake. Send details on the maker, pattern, and piece you're trying to match to The China Connection, 329 Main St., P.O. Box 972, Pineville, NC 28134.

ALBERENE ROYAL MAIL

P.O. BOX 902, CENTER
VILLAGE
HARRISVILLE, NH 03450
800–843–9078
603–827–5512

Price List: free with long, stamped, self-addressed envelope
Pay: check, MO, MC, V
Sells: creamware and Edinburgh crystal
Store: mail order only

Alberene Royal Mail is a terrific source for creamware, that ivory-colored earthenware that was popularized by Wedgwood a century ago. Alberene carries the Hartley Greens brand, which has become easier to find in recent years, but usually at a price. Alberene pares up to 35% off the going rate, making these pretty pieces affordable. The flyers from Alberene show photographs (photocopied) of vases with bas-relief decoration, bowls with cutwork edges, plates, bombés, openwork fruit baskets, napkin rings, and other delightful tableware, home accents, and gifts. Alberene also sells crystal (Edinburgh's "Thistle" and "Star of Edinburgh" patterns) and Buchan Pottery's heavy "Thistle" tableware, which is embellished with handpainted thistles and flowers. You can send a self-addressed envelope for the price lists, or if you know the name of the Hartley Greens, Edinburgh Crystal, or Buchan Pottery piece you want, you can call for availability and pricing. And note that Alberene doesn't charge shipping to addresses within the U.S., which saves you even more!

Special Factors: Satisfaction is guaranteed; returns are accepted for exchange, refund, or credit.

BARRONS

P.O. BOX 994
NOVI, MI 48376–0994
800–538–6340
FAX: 800–523–4456

Catalog: free
Pay: check, MO, MC, V, Discover, NOVUS
Sells: dinnerware, giftware, and home accessories
Store: mail order only
E-mail: barronsdw@aol.com

Barrons has been selling fine tableware since 1975 and offers savings of up to 65% on the list prices of china, crystal, flatware, and gifts, and stocks over 1,500 patterns. Past catalogs have showcased popular lines of china from Block, Fitz & Floyd, Franciscan, Gorham, Hutschenreuther, Johnson Brothers, Lenox, Mikasa, Minton, Nikko, Noritake, Royal Albert, Royal Doulton, Royal Worcester, Spode, Waterford, and Wedgwood. Crystal from Atlantis, Gorham, Lenox, and Mikasa is offered, and you can save on stainless steel, silverplate, and sterling flatware from Dansk, Gorham, International, Kirk-Stieff, Lunt, Mikasa, Oneida, Reed & Barton, Towle, Wallace, and Yamazaki. Royal Doulton figurines, Gorham crystal gifts, Towle silver serving pieces, and other collectibles and accessories are also sold at a discount.

Special Factors: Satisfaction is guaranteed; returns are accepted within 30 days for exchange, refund, or credit.

BEVERLY BREMER SILVER SHOP

Information: inquire (see text)
Pay: check, MO, MC, V, AE, Discover
Sells: new and estate silver flatware, hollowware, gifts, etc.
Store: same address; Monday to Saturday 10–5

DEPT. WBMC
3164 PEACHTREE RD., NE
ATLANTA, GA 30305
800–270–4009
404–261–4009

Beverly Bremer herself presides over this shop, which has an astounding inventory of American and Continental sterling, from new flatware to old loving cups. "The store with the silver lining," which opened in 1975, is worth a detour if you're traveling anywhere around Atlanta. But if you can't get there, call or write with your needs—Beverly Bremer does nearly half her business by mail, and is now completely computerized (request a current list of your flatware pattern).

The briskest trade here is done in supplying missing pieces of sterling silverware in new, discontinued, and hard-to-find patterns. The brands represented include Buccellati, Gorham, International, Jensen, Kirk-Stieff, Lunt, Odiot, Old Newbury Crafters, Oneida, Reed & Barton, Schofield, Frank Smith, State House, Tiffany, Towle, Tuttle, Wallace, Westmoreland, and other firms. If you know the pattern name, call to see whether the piece you want is in stock; you can also send a photocopy of both sides of a sample piece if you're unsure of the pattern. Beverly Bremer will send you a printout of the available pieces in your pattern, and a brochure profiling the company.

Although the shop's specialty is flatware, the shelves and cases sparkle with vases, epergnes, picture frames, candlesticks, jewelry, christening cups, thimbles, and other treasures. Silver collectors should note that over 1,000 patterns are carried in stock here, "beautiful as new," and Ms. Bremer says that, unless noted, there are no monograms on the old silver. (She doesn't sell silver on which monograms have been *removed,* either.) She recommends against resilvering old silverplate as "not a wise use of your money," and notes that sterling holds its value over time. How many other investments can do that—and enhance your dinner table as well!

Special Factors: Sterling silver pieces are bought; appraisals are performed.

BUSCHEMEYER SILVER EXCHANGE

515 S. FOURTH AVE.
LOUISVILLE, KY 40202
800–626–4555
FAX: 502–589–9628

Information: price quote (see text)
Pay: check, MO, MC, V, AE, Discover
Sells: new and discontinued flatware and hollowware
Store: same address; Monday to Friday 10–5, Saturday 10–4

Buschemeyer, in business since 1865, can help you save on purchases of new flatware—sterling, silverplate, and hollowware. But if you're looking for a discontinued pattern, Buschemeyer also may have what you need. The firm stocks "all active and inactive sterling and silverplate flatware," including current American-made sterling patterns, and will hold your want list if what you're looking for isn't currently available. You can call, write, or fax for a price quote on active silver lines, and call (if you know the pattern) about discontinued pieces, or send a photocopy of the front of a teaspoon or fork if you're not sure of the name. Please remember to include your name, address, phone number, and any other information you have about the piece with your query.

Special Factors: Orders are shipped worldwide.

THE CHINA WAREHOUSE

P.O. BOX 21807
CLEVELAND, OH 44121
800–321–3212
216–831–2557

Brochure: free
Pay: check, MO, MC, V
Sells: tableware and gifts
Store: mail order only

The China Warehouse has been in business since 1983 and offers "all major china and crystal lines," as well as flatware, decorative accessories, giftware, and collectible figurines. The brands include Armetale, Block, Gorham, Lenox, Noritake, Orrefors, Reed & Barton, Riedel, Royal Doulton, Sasaki, Spode, Towle, Wallace, Waterford, Wedgwood, and dozens of others, in china, crystal, and stainless and sterling flatware. A catalog is available, but you can also call or write for a price quote.

Special Factors: Orders are shipped worldwide.

COINWAYS/ANTIQUES LTD.

475 CENTRAL AVE.
CEDARHURST, NY 11516
800–645–2102
516–374–1970
FAX: 516–374–3218

Information: price quote
Pay: check, MO, MC, V, AE, DC, Discover
Sells: new and used sterling flatware
Store: same address; Monday to Friday 10:30–5:30, Wednesday 10:30–7:30, Saturday 11–5

Coinways/Antiques Ltd. should be on your list of firms to call when the garbage disposal claims one of your good teaspoons—especially if it's one from an old set, or a discontinued pattern. Coinways, which has been in business since 1979, sells both new and used ("estate") sterling flatware, by the piece or in full sets.

You'll save up to 75% on the suggested retail or market prices of silver manufactured by Alvin, Amston, Dominick & Haff, Durgin, Easterling, Gorham, International, Kirk-Stieff, Lunt, Manchester, National, Oneida, Reed & Barton, Royal Crest, State House, Tiffany, Towle, Tuttle, Wallace, Westmoreland, F.M. Whiting, and other firms. If you're replacing a piece in an old pattern that's still active, try to find a piece of the same vintage. (Over the years, some manufacturers have reduced the amount of silver they use in each piece, so that a fork made today will be lighter and feel less substantial than the same piece, circa 1930.) If you write to Coinways for a quote, note the name of the piece, its length and shape, and include a photocopy of the design if you don't know the pattern name.

Special Factors: Orders are shipped worldwide.

MICHAEL C. FINA CO.

UNTIL NOVEMBER 1997:

580 FIFTH AVE.

NEW YORK, NY 10036

AS OF NOVEMBER 1997:

545 FIFTH AVE.

NEW YORK, NY 10017

800-BUY-FINA

718–937–8484

FAX: 718–937–7193

Catalog: free
Pay: check, MO, MC, V, AE, Discover
Sells: jewelry, tableware, and giftware
Store: 3 W. 47th St., New York, NY; Monday to Friday 9:30–6, Thursday 9:30–7, Saturday 10:30–6

 ¡Si!

Fina, which has been in business since 1935, is known to New Yorkers for great prices on jewelry. Fina also offers an impressive line of tableware, including china by Aynsley, Ceralene Raynaud Limoges, Lynn Chase, Christofle, Dansk, Denby, Phillippe Deshoulieres, Franciscan, Richard Ginori, Gorham, Haviland Limoges, Johnson Brothers, Lalique, Lenox, Mikasa, Minton, Mottahedeh, Noritake, Pickard, Portmeirion, Rosenthal, Royal Copenhagen, Royal Crown Derby, Royal Doulton, Royal Worcester, Sasaki, Spode, Thomas, Versace, Villeroy & Boch, and Wedgwood. Crystal stemware from Atlantis, Baccarat, Christofle, Gorham, Kosta Boda, Lalique, Lenox, Miller Rogaska, Noritake, Orrefors, Riedel, Royal Doulton, St. Louis, Sasaki, Stuart, and Waterford (including Marquis) is available. Fina also sells flatware from Christofle, Jean Couzon, Cuisinart, Dansk, Gorham, International, Georg Jensen, Kirk-Stieff, Ralph Lauren, Lunt, Mikasa, Oneida, Puiforcat, Reed & Barton, Retroneau, Towle, Wallace, and Yamazaki. Sterling silver baby gifts, picture frames, stainless steel and silverplate giftware, and estate pieces are usually available. Fina maintains a bridal registry, and employs sales reps fluent in French, Italian, and Russian, as well as Spanish.

Special Factors: Satisfaction is guaranteed; returns (except engraved or personalized items) are accepted within three weeks for exchange, refund, or credit.

FORTUNOFF FINE JEWELRY & SILVER-WARE, INC.

P.O. BOX 1550
WESTBURY, NY 11590
516–294–3300
FAX: 516–873–6984

Catalog: $2
Pay: check, MO, MC, V, AE, DC
Sells: jewelry, tableware, and giftware
Store: 681 Fifth Ave., New York, and 1300 Old Country Rd., Westbury, NY; also Paramus Park Mall, Paramus, West Belt Mall, Wayne, and 441 Woodbridge Center Dr., Woodbridge, NJ

In addition to spectacular buys on fine jewelry and watches, Fortunoff is a top source for place settings in stainless, silverplate, and sterling silver. Attractive groups of silver giftware—chafing dishes, tea and coffee services, candlesticks, ice buckets, picture frames, and antique vanity accessories—appear frequently in the catalogs. Flatware from Empire Silver, International, Kirk-Stieff, Lauffer, Mikasa, Oneida, Reed & Barton, Retroneau, Roberts & Belk, Supreme, Towle, C.J. Vander, and Yamazaki is available—call for prices on specific patterns. Some of the Fortunoff stores carry a broader variety of products, including outdoor furniture, leather goods, decorative accents for the home, linens for bed and bath, organizers, and similar items.

Special Factors: Price quote on flatware by letter with self-addressed, stamped envelope; minimum order is $25; orders are not shipped outside the United States.

JAMAR SILVERWARE AND CHINA

Information: price quote
Pay: check, MO, MC, V
Sells: tableware
Store: same address; Monday to Saturday 11–5:30

1714 SHEEPSHEAD BAY
RD.
BROOKLYN, NY 11235
888–722–2238
718–615–2222
FAX: 718–615–2224

Jamar has been in business since 1952, and offers the best names in china, crystal, and silver, as well as gifts and collectibles. If you know the patterns and pieces you're looking for, you can call for a quote; Jamar doesn't have a catalog, but will beat any other advertised price.

Special Factors: Price quote by phone or letter; store is closed Mondays during the summer.

KAISER CROW INC.

Brochure: free
Pay: check, MO, MC, V, AE, Discover
Sells: Oneida stainless flatware
Store: mail order only

14998 W. SIXTH AVE., #500
GOLDEN, CO 80401
800–468–2769
303–215–1111
FAX: 303–215–1115

Kaiser Crow has been in business since 1985 and sells Oneida stainless-steel flatware at discounts of up to 57%. The brochure illustrates the choices, and all of the goods are first-quality. Call or write for a price quote if you don't see what you're looking for. Details of the Oneida warranty are available upon request.

Special Factors: Satisfaction is guaranteed; returns are accepted within 60 days.

LANAC SALES COMPANY

73 CANAL ST.
NEW YORK, NY 10002
800–522–0047
212–925–6422
FAX: 212–925–8175

Catalog: free
Pay: check, MO, MC, V, AE, Discover
Sells: fine tableware, home accents, and jewelry
Store: same address; Monday to Thursday 9–6, Friday 9–2, Sunday 10–5, closed Saturdays

You can send for the 40-page catalog from Lanac Sales to see the selection of gifts and home accents: Limoges hinged boxes, MontBlanc pens, art-glass perfume bottles, fine jewelry, and figurines and collectibles by Guiseppe Armani, Belleek, Fitz & Floyd, Lenox, Lladró, and Royal Doulton, among others. There's a nice collection of home accents and entertaining accessories in the current issue—barware, snifters, decanters, vases, crystal giftware, silver tea services—and even select kitchen equipment, such as Cuisinart coffee makers and food processors, Omega juicers, Henckels knives, cappuccino machines, and more—all sold at a discount.

But Lanac Sales has built four decades of business on the fundamentals of the formal dining table: china, crystal, and silver. Lanac offers everything from stoneware to porcelain by Aynsley, Bernardaud Limoges, Ceralene Limoges, Fitz & Floyd, Richard Ginori, Gorham, Haviland Limoges, Hutschenreuther, Ralph Lauren, Lenox, Mikasa, Muirfield, Nikko, Noritake, Packard, Swid Powell, Rosenthal, Royal Albert, Royal Doulton, Royal Worcester, Spode, Villeroy & Boch, and Wedgwood. Browse the catalog or call for prices on stainless, plate, and sterling silver from Jean Couzon, Cuisinarts, Dansk, W.M. Fraser, Gorham, International, Kirk-Stieff, Lenox, Lunt, Reed & Barton, Retroneau, Sasaki, Towle, Tuttle, and Wallace. And crystal stemware is available from Atlantis, Baccarat, Ceska, Edinburgh, Gorham, Kosta Boda, Ralph Lauren, Lenox, Mikasa, Miller Rogaska, Orrefors, Swid Powell, Rosenthal, Royal Doulton, St. Louis, Stuart, Villeroy & Boch, and Waterford. Savings run up to 65% on suggested retail, and Lanac provides bridal registry services and sells a full line of storage cases to protect your service when it's not in use.

Special Factors: Satisfaction is guaranteed; price quote by phone or letter.

MARKS CHINA AND GLASS

**315 FRANKLIN AVE.
WYCKOFF, NJ 07481–2053
800–862–7578
201–891–0422**

Information: price quote
Pay: check, MO, MC, V, Discover
Sells: tableware and giftware
Store: same address; Monday to Thursday 11–8, Friday 10–4, Sunday 11–5, closed Saturday

Set your table for less at Marks, where open stock china is sold at good prices, and "satisfaction is a must." Marks carries the major names, including Aynsley, Bernardaud Limoges, Block Gorham, Hutschenreuther, Lenox, Mikasa, Noritake, Oneida, Pickard, Reed & Barton, Royal Doulton, Sasaki, Spode, Towle, Villeroy & Boch, Wallace, Wedgwood, and Yamazaki, among others. Call the store during business hours with the name of the pattern and the piece you need for a price quote. Marks maintains a bridal registry and can special order settings not in stock, so inquire if you need these services.

Special Factors: Satisfaction is guaranteed; price quote by phone or letter with SASE only; returns (except special orders) are accepted within 14 days for exchange, refund, or credit.

MEIEROTTO'S MIDWESTERLING

**DEPT. WBMC
4311 NE VIVION RD.
KANSAS CITY, MO
   64119–2890
816–454–1990
FAX: 816–454–1605**

Information: inquire
Pay: check, MO, MC, V
Sells: replacement sterling flatware
Store: same address; Monday to Saturday 10–6 (closed Wednesday and Sunday)
E-mail: sterling@kcnet.com
Online: http://www.kcnet.com/sterling

Meierotto's MidweSterling is home to over half a million pieces of sterling flatware, in both discontinued and current patterns. (Dirilyte, new silverplate and stainless flatware, china, crystal, and giftware are also sold.) Meierotto's offers a lowest-price guarantee on the flatware, maintains a bridal registry, and accepts layaways (20% down). Send a long, stamped, self-addressed envelope for a price-quote form, which includes a guide to standard flatware shapes and sizes. If what you want isn't in stock, Meierotto's will search for it. The firm also buys used silver (inquire for information), and performs silverware repairs and knife reblading. And if you're in the Kansas City vicinity, be sure to drop in— Meierotto's runs "the busiest jewelry store" in the city, doing a big trade in everything from diamonds to watches (Bertolucci, Charriol, Concord, Movado, Omega, Patek Philippe, Piaget, Rado, Sector, Tissot, Raymond Weil, etc.).

Please note: Meierotto's is closed on Wednesdays and Sundays.

Special Factors: Satisfaction is guaranteed; price quote by phone, fax, or letter; layaway orders are accepted (20% deposit).

MIKASA OUTLET STORE

25 ENTERPRISE AVE.
SECAUCUS, NJ 07096
201–867–3517

Information: inquire (see text)
Pay: check, MO, MC, V, AE, Discover
Sells: Mikasa tableware and gifts
Store: same address; Monday to Saturday 10–6, Thursday 10–9, Sunday 11–6

¡Si!

Mikasa strikes the balance between fashion-forward style and affordability in china, crystal, flatware, and gifts. Although some of Mikasa's most popular china patterns feature flowers and abstract geometrics rimming the plates and banding the cups, the full range includes much more sedate, traditional designs. The flatware and crystal patterns complement the selection, and are also mid-priced for upper-end table settings.

The Mikasa store sells both first-quality Mikasa tableware at a discount, and has a clearance room with seconds and discontinued patterns. If you can't visit, call with the pattern name, name of the piece (white wine goblet, dinner knife, dessert plate, etc.), and the quantity you'd like to buy. If it's in stock or can be obtained, you'll receive a price quote and shipping estimate. Don't delay in ordering, especially if the pattern or piece has been discontinued, because stock moves quickly here.

Special Factors: Authorized returns are accepted for exchange, refund, or credit.

ROGERS & ROSENTHAL, INC.

**2337 LEMOINE AVE.,
   SUITE 101
FORT LEE, NJ 07024–0212
201–346–1862
FAX: 201–947–5812**

Information: price quote
Pay: check or MO
Sells: tableware
Store: mail order only

  (see text)

Rogers and Rosenthal, two old names in the silver and china trade, represent the business of this firm: the best in table settings at up to 60% below list prices. Rogers & Rosenthal has been in business since 1930, selling flatware (stainless, plate, and sterling) by top manufacturers. The brands include Fraser, Gerber, Gorham, International, Jensen, Kirk-Stieff, Lauffer, Lunt, Oneida, Reed & Barton, Sasaki, Frank Smith, Supreme, Towle, Tuttle, Wallace, and Yamazaki. There are china and crystal lines by Aynsley, Bernardaud Limoges, Block, Coalport, Franciscan, Gorham, Hutschenreuther, Lauffer, Lenox, Mikasa, Noritake, Pickard, Portmeirion, Rosenthal, Royal Copenhagen, Royal Doulton, Royal Worcester, Spode, and Wedgwood. Silver baby gifts, Lladró and other figurines, and pewter hollowware are also stocked. Please write or call for a price quote—*there is no catalog.*

Canadian readers, please note: Only special orders are shipped to Canada.

Special Factors: Price quote by phone or letter with SASE; returns are accepted for exchange.

RUDI'S POTTERY, SILVER & CHINA

180 RTE. 17 NORTH
PARAMUS, NJ 07652
800–631–2526
IN NJ 201–265–6096
FAX: 201–265–2086

Information: price quote
Pay: check, MO, MC, V, Discover
Sells: tableware
Store: same address and 357 Rte. 9 S., Manalapan, NJ; Monday to Saturday 10–5:30

Rudi's has been in business since 1968, and in the intervening years has expanded the firm's stock to include some of the finest goods available at savings of up to 60% on list. China, crystal, and flatware are stocked here; the silverware brands include Gorham, International, Kirk-Stieff, Lunt, Reed & Barton, Towle, Tuttle, and Wallace. Rudi's china dinnerware and crystal stemware lines include Arzberg, Baccarat, Belleek, Bernardaud Limoges, Coalport, Fitz and Floyd, Galway, Gorham, Kosta Boda, Lalique, Lenox, Mikasa, Minton, Noritake, Orrefors, Rosenthal, Royal Copenhagen, Royal Doulton, Royal Worcester, Sasaki, Spode, Stuart, Wedgwood, and Yamazaki. Rudi's also offers limited-edition Christmas ornaments and collectibles issued by a number of the same manufacturers. Call or write for a price quote on your pattern, suite, or limited-issue collectible.

Special Factor: Price quote by phone or letter with SASE.

NAT SCHWARTZ & CO., INC.

DEPT. LIBI8
549 BROADWAY
BAYONNE, NJ 07002
800–526–1440
FAX: 201–437–4903

Catalog: free
Pay: check, MO, MC, V, AE, NOVUS
Sells: tableware, giftware, and housewares
Store: same address; Monday to Friday 9:30–6, Thursday 9:30–8, Saturday 10–5

Nat Schwartz & Co., established in 1967, publishes a 32-page catalog filled with fine china, crystal, flatware, housewares, and gifts that represent just a fraction of the firm's inventory. Schwartz's china and giftware department offers Arzberg, Aynsley, Belleek, Bernardaud, Bing & Grøndahl, Block, Edward Marshall Boehm, A. Raynaud (Ceralene) Limoges, Lynn Chase Designs, Dansk, Denby, Philippe Deshoulieres, Christian Dior, Fabergé, Fitz and Floyd, Franciscan, Gien Limoges, Ginori, Haviland Limoges, Hermes, Hummel, Hutschenreuther, Johnson Brothers, Ralph Lauren, Lenox, Lladró, Mikasa, Minton, Mottahedah, Muirfield, Nao by Lladró, Nikko, Noritake, Pickard, Poole Pottery, Portmeirion, Swid Powell, Rosenthal, Royal Copenhagen, Royal Crown Derby, Royal Doulton, Royal Worcester, Sasaki, Spode, Thomas, Villeroy & Boch, Vista Alegre, Wedgwood, and other firms. Crystal suites and gifts by Atlantis, Baccarat, Ceska, Daum, Da Vinci, Christian Dior, Fabergé, Galway, Gorham, Ralph Lauren, Lenox, Miller/Rogaska, Noritake, Swid Powell, Rosenthal, Royal Doulton, St. Louis, Sasaki, Stuart, Tipperary, Val. St. Lambert, and Waterford are available, among others. Also featured are flatware and hollowware by Baldwin Brass, Boda Nova, Buccellati, Jean Couzon, Cuisinart, Dansk, Empire, W.M.F. Fraser, Gorham, International, Kirk-Stieff, Ralph Lauren, Lunt, Nambé & Nambé Studio, Oneida, Swid Powell, Reed & Barton, Retroneau, Ricci, Sambonet, Sheffield, Towle, Tuttle, Wallace, Wilton Armetale, and Yamazaki. Among the housewares lines are Braun, Calphalon, Le Creuset, Cuisinart, J.A. Henckels, KitchenAid, Krups, Sabatier, Waring Professional, and Wüsthof-Trident. Schwartz provides a number of valuable services, including coordination of silver, crystal, and china patterns, gift and bridal registry, and a corporate gift program. Gift wrapping is offered at no extra charge, and hand engraving is now available. You can send for the catalog, or call for a price quote.

Special Factors: Satisfaction is guaranteed; price quote by phone, fax, or letter; special orders are accepted with a nonrefundable 20% deposit (unless the order is canceled while still on back order); undamaged returns (except engraved items) are accepted within 30 days (a restocking fee may be charged).

THE SILVER QUEEN INC.

**730 N. INDIAN ROCKS RD.
BELLEAIR BLUFFS, FL
  33770
813–581–6827
FAX: 813–586–0822**

Brochure: free
Pay: check, MO, MC, V, Discover
Sells: new and estate silver flatware
Store: same address; Monday to Friday 9–5,
Saturday 10–4
Online: http://varbbs.com/sq

The Silver Queen publishes a brochure with clear color photos of scores of popular sterling flatware patterns, from manufacturers that include Alvin, Buccellati, Frank Smith, Gorham, International, Georg Jensen, Kirk-Stieff, Lunt, Oneida, Reed & Barton, Towle, Tuttle, Wallace, and Westmoreland. The Silver Queen has been in business since 1972, and will quote prices on the pieces of your choice, at an average of 30%-plus off list. You can call without getting the brochure if you're shopping for a pattern still in production, or an exact replacement for an old design (estate silver is available). But do get the brochure if you don't have a guide to your pattern: It has six pages of pictures of specialty pieces—mustard ladles, lemon forks, berry spoons, etc.—and provides an excellent visual guide to the relative shapes and sizes.

    Special Factors: Price quote by phone or letter.

ALBERT S. SMYTH CO., INC.

**DEPT. WM98
29 GREENMEADOW DR.
TIMONIUM, MD 21093
800–638–3333
410–252–6666
FAX: 410–252–2355**

Catalog: free
Pay: check, MO, MC, V, AE, Discover
Sells: tableware, giftware, and jewelry
Store: same address; Monday to Saturday
9–5, Thursday 9–9

All that gleams and glitters can be found at Smyth, at savings of up to 50% on comparable retail and list prices. Smyth has been doing business since 1914, and publishes a 24-page color catalog that features a wide range of jewelry. Diamonds, strands of semiprecious beads, colored stone jewelry, and pearls are shown, as well as watches by Concord, Movado, Omega, Seiko, Tag Heuer, and Tissot. Pens by MontBlanc, Parker, Visconti, and Waterman are available, as well as things like mahogany jewelry chests. Tableware and home decorative accents are sold here at impressive savings, including such items as British carriage clocks, Baldwin brassware, Waterford giftware, fine picture frames, and gifts from Kirk-Stieff and Virginia Metalcrafters. You'll find pewter candlesticks, coffee sets, punch bowls, and place settings by Aynsley, Gorham, Kirk-Stieff, Lenox, Noritake, Reed & Barton, Royal Doulton, Spode, Towle, Villeroy & Boch, Wallace, Waterford, and Wedgwood among the offerings.

Smyth maintains a bridal registry and provides gift consultations and a gift-forwarding service. The catalog shows a fraction of the inventory, so write or call for a price quote if you don't see what you're looking for.

Special Factors: Satisfaction is guaranteed; returns (except personalized and custom-ordered goods) are accepted within 30 days.

THURBER'S

2256-C DABNEY RD.
RICHMOND, VA 23230
800–848–7237
804–278–9080
FAX: 804–278–9480

Catalog: $1
Pay: check, MO, MC, V, AE, Discover
Sells: tableware, giftware, and Christmas ornaments
Store: same address; Monday to Saturday 9–5

The 24-page color catalog from Thurber's showcases both fine tableware and gifts, but you can call or write year-round for quotes on specific items. Thurber's has been in business since 1985, selling gifts and the accoutrements of gracious living at up to 60% off list prices. Place settings and other tableware by Ceralene Limoges, Dansk, Denby, Gorham, International, Kirk-Stieff, Lenox, Lunt, Miller Rogaska, Noritake, Oneida, Portmeirion, Reed & Barton, Royal Doulton, Royal Worcester, Spode, Tirschenreuth, Towle, Villeroy & Boch, Wallace, Wedgwood, and Yamazaki are available as well, at savings of up to 60%. The holiday catalog features a lovely selection of limited-edition Christmas ornaments, and plates. Thurber's maintains a bridal registry, and provides a Bridal Registry Kit to make it easy to inform friends and relatives of your selections.

Special Factors: Satisfaction is guaranteed; returns are accepted within 30 days for exchange, refund, or credit.

SEE ALSO

Bruce Medical Supply • *dining aids and cutlery for those with limited strength or muscle control* • **MEDICINE: SPECIAL NEEDS**

Kitchen Etc. • *tableware* • **HOME: KITCHEN**

Harris Levy, Inc. • *table linens* • **HOME: LINEN**

M & N International, Inc. • *party and catering supplies, disposables, etc.* • **TOYS**

Marshall Domestics • *institutional-quality tablecloths and napkins* • **GENERAL MERCHANDISE**

The Paper Wholesaler • *party and catering supplies, disposables, etc.* • **TOYS**

Paradise Products, Inc. • *party supplies, disposables, etc.* • **TOYS**

Pendery's Inc. • *Mexican glassware* • **FOOD: BEVERAGES AND FLAVORINGS**

Weston Bowl Mill • *wooden plates, trays, and tableware* • **GENERAL MERCHANDISE**

INSURANCE AND CREDIT

Consumer insurance and
credit information sources

Insurance is the price of protecting yourself or others from absorbing the entire cost of misfortune and disaster. As no one's favorite topic, it's rivaled by "credit," the business of borrowing money. They're two of life's necessary expenses, but they're amazingly variable in cost. Since it's possible to save a considerable sum on car, health, home, and life insurance and consumer credit, it repays investing a few evenings studying some consumer literature on the subject (see the sources listed below). If you don't turn up new savings, it means you've already made the best choices possible!

Whether you're buying insurance or borrowing credit, the same money-saving strategies apply, overall: Determine the type of product that best fits your needs and situation, then shop price and terms among reliable providers.

Before consulting books that deal exclusively with insurance or credit, get a grounding in finance basics. You can begin with the government publication offered from the Consumer Information Center and the Superintendent of Documents (see the listings in "Books.") The following books are excellent primers on consumer finance, including insurance and credit. If you don't really understand how bonds work, or how to calculate your net worth and set a retirement savings plan, these books will help show you.

1. *Making the Most of Your Money,* by the eminently reliable Jane Bryant Quinn (Simon & Schuster, 1991), takes you from assessing your financial situation to choosing a bank, writing a will, creating a budget, buying insurance, owning a home, paying for education, investing, and retirement planning. Because the topics naturally flow into one another, you can use it as a workbook, as well as a general reference.

2. *Personal Finance for Dummies,* by Eric Tyson (IDG Books, 1994), is another in the "Dummies" series of books that use a forgiving approach with pop overtones and lots of cartoons and graphics to teach—in this volume—about savings and interest, consumer credit and debt issues, financial planning and budgets, mortgages, insurance, investments, retirement planning, and related money issues that stymie many of us. There are cute icons in the margins that highlight "technical stuff," tips, warnings, points to keep in mind, special caveats, and related products and services that are "Dummies Approved." Despite the friendly face, this book packs lots of information wallop and may appeal to those looking for a hip, humorous approach to finance. Investment novices should check the "Dummies" volume on mutual funds for the same kind of guidance.

3. *The Wall Street Journal Guide to Understanding Personal Finance,* by Kenneth M. Morris and Alan M. Siegel (Lightbulb Press, Inc., 1992) takes the graphical approach further with full-color photographs of *everything,* from the front and back of a canceled check to the anatomy of a mutual-funds index. This approach is very helpful to those who are phobic about forms and charts; it breaks things down into their comprehensible elements and explains how they work. Banking, credit and interest, financing a home, insurance, financial planning, investing, and taxes are covered.

In addition to these sources, see *Cut Your Spending in Half,* which is described in the introduction to "General Merchandise."

INSURANCE

Where once we depended on an insurance agent for our education, we now have Ralph Nader, *Consumer Reports,* and personal-finance writers to explain the mechanics of insurance and how to make good choices. Use their resources, and you may profit: The editor of this book was able to save over $800 on her home insurance (with no loss in necessary coverage) with the help of a few good tips and reference works:

1. The books on general consumer-finance topics, above, all cover insurance basics and are a good way to get acquainted.

2. *Winning the Insurance Game: The Complete Consumer's Guide to Saving Money* (Knightsbridge Publishing Co., 1990) teams consumer advocates Ralph Nader and Wesley J. Smith in 538 pages on the general mechanics of insurance, and in-depth sections on auto, health, home, and life insurance, summaries of government benefits, and notes on how to document and file claims and resolve disputes. Appendices of bad bets, government insurance agencies, information organizations, and sample policy terms cover all the bases.

3. *The Guide to Buying Insurance: How to Secure the Coverage You*

Need at an Affordable Price, by David L. Scott (Globe Pequot Press, 1994) covers life, health, car, home, and liability insurance, with lots of commonsense advice.

4. The National Insurance Consumer Helpline can answer questions on all aspects of insurance, from car to COBRA. Call 800–942–4242 or 703–549–8050, Monday to Friday 8 a.m. to 8 p.m. ET.

5. Get a package deal: Ask the insurer about discounts for handling more than one policy—homeowner and auto, for example—and you may save up to 15%.

6. Raise the deductibles: Home and auto policies make you pay more if the insurer has to cover the first $500 to $1000 of loss or damage. If you can afford to cover a high deductible yourself, you'll save significantly on your premiums.

7. Lengthen the waiting/coverage period: Disability coverage is cheaper if you're willing to defer the date when coverage begins, or limit the duration of payout.

When it comes to understanding *health and life insurance,* you *must* do your homework. Where there were once "whole" and "term" life insurance policies are now a variety of complex investment and estate-planning tools. The resources listed above evaluate the forms of life insurance; for more information, see the resources below:

1. The *Consumer Reports Life Insurance Handbook,* by Jersey Gilbert (Consumer Reports Books, 1994), explains the differences among insurance products and teaches you how to find the one that's right for your needs.

2. Price shop: When you've decided on the kind of life or health insurance you need, you can hire Quotesmith Corp. to feed your request to its computers for a printout of 25 to 50 policies meeting your requirements. You can also get all of the ratings on a single insurance carrier ($15 extra). Quotesmith has over 300 insurance companies on file, and covers Medigap and long-term care policies, as well as life and standard health insurance. You can still work with a broker after running a quote, but the printout should help you to negotiate the best price.

3. Check the ratings: In addition to Quotesmith's ratings check, Insurance Forum, an industry newsletter, compiles a yearly master listing of the ratings of about 1,700 insurance providers (life and health). The issue is updated in the spring; send a $10 check or money order to Insurance Forum, Inc., P.O. Box 245, Ellettsville, IN 47429, and request the "annual ratings issue."

4. Skip the broker: Save on fees and sales commissions by buying life insurance directly from the insurer. Term and cash-value insurance policies are sold directly to consumers by USAA Life Insurance Co. (800–531–8000), or Ameritas Life Insurance Corp. (800–552–3553).

The time to think about saving on your *auto insurance* is before you buy your next vehicle. If you're in the market for a new car, be sure that you account for typical insurance costs for any vehicle you consider. Even an old clunker can have high rates if it's prone to needing repairs or is on the list of cars thieves target for parts. The books on general insurance topics (listed previously) all cover cars, and the following information can help as well:

1. The Chartered Property Casualty Underwriters Society publishes "Understand Your Auto Insurance Policy and Get the Most for Your Money" and "Team Up with Your Insurance Adjuster When You File a Claim" (home or auto). They're free on request; send a long, stamped, self-addressed envelope for each pamphlet to Chartered Property Casualty Underwriters Society, Box 3009, Malvern, PA 19355.

2. The Equifax Insurance Consumer Center can provide you with a copy of your insurance report, if you've received a notice from your home or auto insurance carrier. The service requires the 14-digit reference number that should be included on the correspondence, as well as the carrier name, your driver's license number, date of birth, and Social Security number. Call 800–456–6004 for more information or to order a report.

Home, or property insurance, may cover aspects of auto-related problems—the theft of personal property from your car, for example—so make sure you understand the provisions of both. In addition to consulting the general references on insurance listed earlier in this section, study the actual policy you receive. Make a list of questions as they occur to you, then work through them with your broker. Make sure you understand the limitations of your coverage, and adjust or change it to cover your needs.

Buying the right amount of insurance coverage requires knowing how much it would cost to rebuild your home and replace the contents. Local contractors can help you determine the cost of rebuilding, or your insurance broker may have a formula that does the math.

"Taking Inventory" is the name of a very helpful form from the Insurance Information Institute. It's an inventory work sheet, broken down room by room, with lists of typical items and furnishings, and a blank for their purchase date and cost. This is for a *general* inventory and wouldn't cover fine-arts or antiques scheduling, but will give you the foundation for finding replacement values. Request the brochure by name from Insurance Information Institute, 110 William St., New York, NY 10038; include a long, stamped, self-addressed envelope.

See the mention of the Chartered Property Casualty Underwriters Society, and National Insurance Consumer Helpline for more assistance in filing claims and understanding your policy.

CREDIT

"Credit" is the right to borrow on the strength of your promise to pay, and "interest" is the cost of exercising that right. The most commonly used forms of credit are the revolving charge account, followed by car loans. Together, they accounted for $1.2 *trillion* in American consumer debt in 1996. The average outstanding balance is $1,700, and at an average card rate still around 18%, that's a hefty contribution to the issuer's profit margin.

The following resources offer credit-shopping tips, comparison results, and techniques to help you maximize card value, not cost:

1. *The Ultimate Credit Handbook: How to Double Your Credit, Cut Your Debt, and Have a Lifetime of Great Credit,* by Gerri Dettweiler (Plume/Penguin Books, 1993) has garnered endorsements by congressional representatives and the president of the National Consumer League. Ms. Dettweiler was long the Executive Director of Bankcard Holders of America, and covers everything from "the secrets of a great credit rating" to "a lifetime strategy for great credit." No matter how badly you've managed credit in the past, this book will help you figure out where you stand and what you need to do to improve your situation. The explanation of how the credit industry works equations for computing your "safe" debt load can help you spot your best credit buy and shoulder debt responsibly.

2. Bankcard Holders of America (BHA), a membership organization, performs quarterly reviews of credit-card offerings to find those offering the lowest rates and best terms. The most recent list costs $4; it's a big help in figuring out whether to jump, consolidate, or "churn" (transfer balances to new cards offered at low introductory rates, from cards that are raising their rates). BHA also offers a computer-based "Debt Zapper" service: Complete the form BHA sends you, providing current credit-card debt information and the $15 fee, and you'll receive a printout detailing how much to pay on each debt to minimize interest. The Zapper showed BHA members who participated in the trial of the service how to save an average of 25% on their credit costs. Send a long, stamped, self-addressed envelope for membership information and a list of current publications and services, to BHA, Customer Service, 524 Branch Dr., Salem, VA 24153.

3. RAM Research compiles monthly lists of the best credit-card offers; copies are available for $5 each. Request RAM's CardTrack from RAM Research, Box 1700, Frederick, MD 21702.

4. Consumer Credit Counseling Services (CCCS) has over 1,000 offices nationwide to help the troubled credit consumer. If you're having problems, get in touch; this private foundation will work with you to craft the best plan of action credit-wise, for a nominal fee, or free. For the location of the CCCS office nearest you, call 800–388–2227.

JEWELRY, GEMS, AND WATCHES

Fine, fashion, and costume jewelry; loose stones, watches, and services

You'll find everything from inexpensive neck chains to investment-grade gems here, at savings of 20% to 75%, from firms that sell to amateur and professional jewelry makers, and sometimes supply pieces in finished form.

Before making a financial commitment of any magnitude, make sure you know what you're buying. *Beyond the Glitter: Everything You Need to Know to Buy, Sell, Care For, and Wear Gems and Jewelry Wisely* by Gerald L. Wykoff (Adamas Publications, 1989), and *Jewelry & Gems: The Buying Guide: How to Buy Diamonds, Colored Gemstones, Pearls, Gold & Jewelry With Confidence and Knowledge* covers precious and semi-precious stones, pearls, metals, and other materials used in jewelry. For an inside look at the business, try *Modern Jeweler's Consumer Guide to Colored Gemstones,* by David Federman (Modern Jeweler Magazine, 1990), which has dazzling color photographs by Tino Hammid. A gem-like production in its own right, it reveals the intrigue and chicanery that shape each stone's market, and discusses irradiation and heat treatment of gems. Write to Modern Jeweler, Vance Publishing Corporation, P.O. Box 1416, Lincolnshire, IL 60069–9958, for availability, price, and ordering information.

The Federal Trade Commission (FTC) has established guidelines for the jewelry trade and publishes pamphlets for consumers that discuss the meanings of terms, stamps and quality marks, and related matters. Request "Gold Jewelry," "Bargain Jewelry," and "Guidelines for the Jewelry Industry" from the Federal Trade Commission, Public Reference Office, Washington, DC 20580.

If you need help in finding an appraiser, contact the American Society of Appraisers at 212–687–6305. The Society will locate an appraiser in your area and have that person contact you, at no charge. (The Society's senior members have at least five years of experience and are required to pass an exam; they handle all "appraisables," not just jewelry.)

The Gemological Institute of America (GIA) can tell you what should appear on a GIA report and confirm whether an appraiser has been trained by the organization. For more information, write to the Gemological Institute of America, Inc., 1180 Avenue of the Americas, New York, NY 10036. There is also a GIA office in California, at P.O. Box 2110, 1660 Stewart St., Santa Monica, CA 90406.

The Jewelers' Vigilance Committee can tell you whether your dealer is among the good, the bad, or the ugly. This trade association monitors the industry and promotes ethical business practices. For more information write to the Jewelers' Vigilance Committee, 1180 Avenue of the Americas, 8th Fl., New York, NY 10036.

DIAMONDS BY RENNIE ELLEN

15 W. 47TH ST., RM. 401
NEW YORK, NY 10036
212–869–5525

Catalog: $2
Pay: check, MO, teller's check, bank draft
Sells: stock and custom-made jewelry
Factory: visits by appointment only

It's hard to believe that you can buy diamond engagement rings wholesale, but that's Rennie Ellen's business. You can save up to 75% on the price of similar jewelry sold elsewhere by buying here. Rennie Ellen is honest, reputable, and personable, and she's been cutting gems since 1966.

Rennie Ellen sells diamonds of all shapes, sizes, and qualities, set to order in platinum or gold. The color catalog shows samples of Ms. Ellen's design work, including rings, pendants, and earrings set with diamonds. Engagement and wedding rings are a specialty, and the cards and notes from grateful young marrieds that line her office walls testify to her success. The factory is open to customers by appointment only.

Special Factors: Price quote by phone or letter; a detailed bill of sale is included with each purchase; returns are accepted within five working days; minimum shipping, handling, and insurance charge is $15 (sent by registered mail).

ELOXITE CORPORATION

DEPT. 4

P.O. BOX 729

WHEATLAND, WY 82201

307–322–3050

FAX: 307–322–3055

Catalog: $1

Pay: check, MO, MC, V

Sells: jewelry findings

Store: 806 Tenth St., Wheatland, WY; Monday to Friday 8:30–4, Saturday 8:30–3

Eloxite has been selling jewelry findings, cabochons, beads, and other lapidary supplies since 1955. Prices here are up to 75% below those charged by other crafts sources for findings and jewelry components. Jewelry findings with a Western flair are featured: bola ties and slide medallions, belt buckles and inserts, and coin jewelry are prominent offerings. Also shown are pendants, rings, earrings, lockets, tie tacks, and pins made to be set with cabochons or cut stones, as well as jump rings, chains, pillboxes, screw eyes, and ear wires. The stones themselves are sold—cut cubic zirconia and synthetic gemstones and oval cabochons of abalone, agate, black onyx, garnet, opal, obsidian, jasper, and malachite. A recent catalog included loosely strung gemstone bead necklaces and jewelers' tools and supplies.

Sandwiched between the pages of jewelry components are quartz clock movements and blanks for clock faces, clock hands, and ballpoint pens and letter openers for desk sets. Discounts are available on most items, and specials are usually offered with orders of specified amounts.

Special Factors: Quantity discounts are available; undamaged returns are accepted within 15 days for exchange or refund (a $2 restocking fee may be charged); minimum order is $15; C.O.D. orders are accepted.

HONG KONG LAPIDARIES, INC.

2801 UNIVERSITY DR.
CORAL SPRINGS, FL 33065
954–755–8777
FAX: 954–755–8780

Catalog: $3, $5 outside the U.S.
Pay: check, MO, MC, V
Sells: jewelry supplies, beads, cabochons, and loose stones
Store: mail order only

  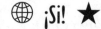

Hong Kong Lapidaries, established in 1979, sells a wide range of precious and semiprecious stones in a variety of forms. The 60-page catalog lists items of interest to hobbyists as well, and the prices run as much as 70% below comparable retail.

Thousands of cabochons, beads, loose-faceted and cut stones, and strung chips of pearl, garnet, amethyst, onyx, abalone, and other kinds of semiprecious stones are offered through the catalog, which comes with a separate 12-page color brochure that shows representative pieces. Egyptian clay scarabs, coral, cameos, cubic zirconia, yellow jade, cloisonné jewelry and objets d'art, 14K gold-filled and sterling silver beads, and ball earrings are available. Hobbyists should note the necklace thread—100% silk or nylon—in a score of colors and 16 *sizes*—plus stringing needles.

Special Factors: Satisfaction is guaranteed; price quote by fax; quantity discounts are available; returns are accepted within 12 days; minimum order is $50; C.O.D. orders are accepted.

HOUSE OF ONYX, INC.

THE AARON BUILDING
GREENVILLE, KY
    42345–0261
800–844–3100
502–338–2363
FAX: 502–338–9605

Catalog: free
Pay: check, MO, MC, V, Discover
Sells: investment-grade stones, jewelry, and gifts
Store: 120 Main St., Greenville, KY; Monday to Friday 9–4 CT

The House of Onyx publishes a large tabloid catalog filled with reports on the gem industry and listings of diamonds and other precious stones, as well as specials on gifts and jewelry. Imported gifts and jewelry from Mexico, China, and India have been offered in the past, including Aztec onyx chess sets, ashtrays, bookends, vases, statuettes (including dinosaurs), and candlesticks. Cloisonné and vermeil beads, jewelry, and artware, and carvings of soapstone, rose quartz, tiger's eye, Burmese jadeite, lapis lazuli, carnelian, turquoise, and agate are usually available. The jewelry includes semiprecious bead necklaces, freshwater and cultured pearls, cameos, and diamond and gemstone rings, earrings, and pendants, from department-store grade to fine one-of-a-kind pieces. Collectors of crystals and mineral specimens should check here for amethyst, fluorite, quartz, pyrite, and other geodes and samples. House of Onyx also offers Jim Kaufmann's unusual semiprecious intarsia, and can supply solid-gold mountings as well.

House of Onyx has been in business since 1967, and offers a wide range of investment-quality stones, with discounts of 50% and 60% offered on parcels of $1,000 and up. The investment stones account for much of the business here, and the catalog is packed with useful information and commentary on gems and investing.

Special Factors: Satisfaction is guaranteed; investment gemstones are sold with an unlimited time return guarantee and a "100% purchase price refund" pledge; other returns are accepted within 30 days; minimum order is $25.

NATURE'S JEWELRY

**27 INDUSTRIAL AVE.,
DEPT. NJ–106E
CHELMSFORD, MA
01824–3692
800–333–3235
FAX: 800–866–3235**

Catalog: free
Pay: check, MO, MC, V, AE, Discover
Sells: fashion and novelty jewelry
Store: mail order only

No matter what your personal style, taste, or budget, you'll find a bauble to suit your fancy in the Nature's Jewelry catalog. Each issue has nearly 100 pages of classic, theme, and holiday jewelry and accessories, including strands of semiprecious stones, preserved wildflower jewelry, pins and watches with environmental themes, jewelry for the season—from "star" bow earrings in red and green for Christmas to a cuff of enameled hearts for Valentine's Day—and much more, at very affordable prices. Many of the designs are exclusives, so they're hard to compare to other jewelry, but prices on items at Nature's Jewelry are up to 50% lower than those charged elsewhere for similar pieces. Many of the pierced earrings are priced under $10, and a large number of the other pieces cost under $20.

If you'd like to be able to wear fresh flowers every day, you'll love the collection of handmade, hand-painted stone-and-resin buds and blossoms. Past catalogs have shown lilacs, roses, irises, pansies, poppies, and other flowers, and there's even a line of *preserved* blossoms in earrings, pins, and pendants. Love pigs? They've shown up here, as adornments for dress or person, as have cows, sheep, lots of cats, horses, dinosaurs, dolphins, whales, pandas, fish, birds, dragonflies, coyotes, frogs, and many other animals. Inexpensive tennis bracelets, golf-motif jewelry, "pieces of nature" (real parsley, four-leaf clovers, maple leaves, etc.) dipped in 24K gold, and chunks of "beach glass" made into beautiful, jewel-like necklaces and earrings have also appeared. Every catalog features with lots of new offerings in each issue, as well as sale pages with dozens of pieces at 50% off.

Special Factors: Satisfaction is guaranteed; returns are accepted for exchange, refund, or credit.

SIMPLY DIAMONDS

DEPT. A
P.O. BOX 682
ARDSLEY, NY 10502–0682
800–552–2728
914–693–2370
FAX: 914–693–2446

Information: inquire (see text)
Pay: check, MO, MC, V, AE, Discover
Sells: diamond jewelry
Store: mail order only
E-mail: 75224.1032@compuserve.com

Thanks to family affiliations with merchants who've been doing business in New York City's diamond district for decades, Simply Diamonds can offer both stock and custom jewelry at excellent prices. Simply Diamonds features a lovely line of jewelry, including diamond name bracelets and charms—wonderful gifts for birthdays, Mother's Day, graduations, anniversaries. . . Simply Diamonds has access to thousands of settings for rings, pendants, men's rings, and other pieces, and can provide color pictures on request. The firm also executes individual commissions—including engagement rings—at a discount. The custom division will work with you from concept to execution, or you may send ad photos or other depictions of the piece you want replicated. (Color postcards and brochures of some of the custom pieces are available.)

Simply Diamonds wants its customers to understand what they're buying, and would be pleased to discuss grade, size, color, and clarity—all factors that affect the price and value of the stones. As the proprietors themselves say, "Buying diamond products is a very confusing and mysterious subject to most. Anyone is welcome to call, and we will be glad to answer any diamond-related question." Pieces are backed by GIA, EGL, and IGI certificates (available on request), and satisfaction is guaranteed on every purchase.

Special Factors: Satisfaction is guaranteed; returns are accepted within seven days for exchange, refund, or credit; C.O.D. orders are *not* accepted.

WATCH DEPOT
SHOP-AT-HOME

━━━━━━━━━

WORLD TIME CORP. OF
  AMERICA
2227 NORTH FEDERAL
  HWY., SUITE 508
HOLLYWOOD, FL
  33020–9863
800–469–2824
954–921–2445
FAX: 800–932–9928
FAX: 954–921–2508

Flyer: free
Pay: check, MO, MC, V, AE, Discover
Sells: watches and pens
Store: mail order only
E-mail: invicta@worldnet.att.net

 ¡Si!

The Watch Depot catalog is a glossy, colorful poster of sport and fashion wristwatches, priced up to 50% below regular retail. The brands include Carriage, Casio, Citizen, Invicta, Lorus, Miracle, Movado, Pulsar, Q & Q, Seiko, Swatch, Victorinox, Wenger, and Zioba Design. Each watch is photographed and listed with the price, but not the model name or manufacturer's code number. If you're shopping for a specific model, you can call for a price quote, or to confirm that a pictured model is the one you're looking for. If you're a reseller, you'll find collections of watches—8, 12, 15, and even 100 pieces—at extra savings. And Watch Depot also sells pens by Parker, Waterman, and other firms, at a discount—see the models in the flyer, or call for a price quote if you know the manufacturer's model number.

Special Factors: Satisfaction is guaranteed; returns are accepted for exchange, refund, or credit.

WEDDING RING HOTLINE

━━━━━━━━━━

172 RTE. 9
ENGLISHTOWN, NJ 07726
732–972–7777
FAX: 732–972–0720

Brochure: free
Pay: check, MO, MC, V, AE, Discover
Sells: wedding bands, diamonds, and engagement rings
Store: same address (by appointment)
E-mail: diamondmjs@aol.com
Online: http://www.weddingcircle.com/wedring

Why pay a fortune for your wedding rings, when you can save from 30% to 70% through Wedding Ring Hotline. This firm, a division of Bride & Groom's West, manufactures its own line of classic styles in solid white, pink, and yellow 14K gold. All sizes are available, in 2 mm to 12 mm widths, with plain and milgrain (tiny beading) edges. Wedding Ring Hotline can also produce the rings in 10K and 18K gold, and platinum. Engraving services are available, and the firm also sells diamond wedding and engagement rings, nationally advertised lines of wedding rings, and can make other jewelry to order; inquire for information, or call for a price quote on any name-brand engagement or wedding ring.

Special Factors: Satisfaction is guaranteed; price quote by phone or letter; returns are accepted within 30 days for exchange, refund, or credit; engraving is free on all orders over $200.

SEE ALSO

Bennett Brothers, Inc. • *costume and fine jewelry and watches* • **GENERAL MERCHANDISE**
Berry Scuba Co. • *underwater timepieces* • **SPORTS**
Central Skindivers • *underwater timepieces* • **SPORTS**

Ceramic Supply of New York & New Jersey, Inc. • *jewelry findings* • **ART MATERIALS**

Michael C. Fina Co. • *fine jewelry and watches* • **HOME: TABLE SETTINGS**

Fortunoff Fine Jewelry & Silverware, Inc. • *fine jewelry and watches* • **HOME: TABLE SETTINGS**

Manny's Millinery Supply Co. • *hat pins* • **CLOTHING**

Professional Cutlery Direct • *Swiss Army watches* • **HOME: KITCHEN**

Nat Schwartz & Co., Inc. • *fine jewelry* • **HOME: TABLE SETTINGS**

Albert S. Smyth Co., Inc. • *fine jewelry and watches* • **HOME: TABLE SETTINGS**

Weaver Leather, Inc. • *Montana Silversmiths belt buckles, conchos, and saddle decorations* • **CRAFTS**

LUGGAGE AND LEATHER GOODS

Small leather goods, handbags, briefcases, attaché cases, luggage, trunks, and services

The firms listed here stock everything you should need to tote your effects around town, to the office, and farther afield. In addition to handbags, briefcases, suitcases, trunks, and small leather goods, some of the firms also sell cases for musical instruments and portfolios for models and artists.

If you're buying luggage, consider the pros and cons of different luggage materials: waterproof, puncture-proof materials and lockable closures are good considerations. Wheeled suitcases help bridge the distances in mammoth hub airports, and built-in, partly recessed wheels that are designed to avoid jamming in conveyor belts are the best bets. Whatever style suitcase you use, make it as thief-proof as possible: Use small combination locks, since pros who work airports have masters to popular keyed models; bind your luggage with webbed belting, which will keep clamshell suitcases from springing open if their locks fail, and prevents easy access by anyone rifling the luggage while it's in transit. Keep a list of the contents of the suitcase with you in case your luggage is lost, since the list will help to identify the suitcase, and can be used for insurance valuation. For more buying tips, consult the most recent review of luggage and briefcases in *Consumer Reports* and *Consumers Digest*.

Companies that sell small leather goods and handbags are also listed in "Clothing," portfolios and display cases and binders are available from some of the companies listed in "Art Materials," and companies selling travel accessories are listed in "Travel."

ACE LUGGAGE AND GIFTS

2122 AVE. U
BROOKLYN, NY 11229
800-DIAL ACE
718–891–9713
FAX: 718–891–3878

Catalog: $2, refundable (see text)
Pay: check, MO, MC, V, AE, Discover
Sells: luggage and leather goods, fine pens, etc.
Store: 2122 Ave. U, Brooklyn, NY; Monday to Saturday 10–6, Thursday 10–7 (extended hours in December), Sunday 12–5
E-mail: lugage@aol.com

Ace, which was established in 1961, sells luggage by Andiamo, Esq., French, Lark, Lexi, Lucas, Metro Dakota, Samsonite, LeSport Sac, Travelpro (Rollaboard), and Zero Halliburton, at discounts of up to 40%. Briefcases and attaché cases by Eagle Creek, Jack Georges, Jansport, Lodis, National, and Sacoche are available, as well as handbags and small leather goods by Etienne Aigner, Bosca, Filofax, Garys, and Rolfs. You'll find leather desk accessories, travel alarms, Victorinox Swiss Army knives and watches, lighters, pens, and other small luxuries. The 36-page catalog that's published during the holiday season features gift merchandise, but catalogs and price quotes on the luggage and leather goods are available throughout the year, and special discounts are available for corporate and quantity orders.

Readers in Canada, please note: Orders are shipped via UPS.

Special Factors: Price quote by phone (please have brand and model number before calling).

AIRLINE INTERNATIONAL LUGGAGE & GIFTS, INC.

8701 MONTANA AVE.
EL PASO, TX 79925
800–592–1234
915–778–1234
FAX: 915–778–1533

Catalog: free
Pay: check, MO, MC, V, AE, Discover
Sells: luggage and leather goods, gifts, etc.
Store: same address; Monday to Saturday 9:30–6, Thursday 9:30–7, Sunday 11–5; also Sunland Park Mall (upper level), El Paso, TX; Monday to Saturday 10–9, Sunday 12–6
E-mail: airint@whc.net
Online: http://www.airint.com

Airline International began its life in 1978 as a luggage-repair business serving airlines in the El Paso area, and began selling new luggage when the airlines needed replacements for suitcases too badly damaged to be fixed. The firm has expanded over the years to offer luggage from every major manufacturer, as well as other small leather goods and gifts. The 36-page color catalog shows attaché cases, briefcases, overnighters and suitcases, laptop cases, backpacks, and other pieces by Andiamo, Atlantic, Hugo Bosca, Kenneth Cole, Dakota, Dilana, Dopp, Jack Georges, Hartmann, High Sierra, Kipling, Mundi, Outta Here, Rolfs, St. Thomas, Travelpro (Rollaboard), and other firms. Airline International also sells leather desk sets and agendas, travel accessories, and a broad selection of well-chosen executive gifts, such as Seth Thomas weather stations, Howard Miller clocks, calculators, globes, jewelry boxes, collapsible umbrellas, Swiss watches, Cross and Waterman pens, banks, puzzles, and games. Savings on the luggage shown in the review catalog averaged 25% on list prices, but Airline International says that some prices are as low as 50% off suggested retail. And if your suitcase was mauled on your last business trip, you'll appreciate the fact that you can still get your luggage or handbag fixed here.

Special Factors: Price quote by phone or letter; returns are accepted for exchange, refund, or credit.

AL'S LUGGAGE

**2134 LARIMER ST.
DENVER, CO 80205
303–295–9009
303–294–9045
FAX: 303–296–8769**

Catalog: $2, refundable
Pay: check, MO, MC, V, AE, Discover
Sells: leather goods and luggage
Store: same address; Monday to Friday
9–5:30; Saturday 9–5

 ¡Si! ★

The $2 catalog fee (refundable with purchase) brings you a sheaf of photocopied materials from Samsonite, including price lists, brochures, ordering instructions, and shipping rate charts. Al's Luggage has been selling leather goods and luggage since 1948, and carries Diane Von Furstenberg, Jordache, Lion Leather, London Fog Luggage, Members Only, Platt, Stebco, Winn, and WK. In addition to current lines of suitcases, overnight bags, cosmetics cases, totes, wardrobes, duffels, and garment bags, Al's offers business cases, portfolios, and even camcorder carrying cases. The catalog shows only Samsonite models, which are sold here for 30% to 50% below list prices. If you're shopping for an item by another manufacturer, call or write for a price quote.

Special Factors: Price quote by phone or letter with SASE; C.O.D. orders are accepted.

JOBSON'S LUGGAGE WAREHOUSE

**666 LEXINGTON AVE.
NEW YORK, NY 10022
800–221–5238
212–355–6846
FAX: 212–753–3295**

Catalog: free
Pay: check, MO, MC, V, AE, DC, Discover
Sells: luggage, leather goods, and accessories
Store: same address; Monday to Saturday
9–6, Sunday 11–5

   ¡Si!

Jobson's Luggage Warehouse has served New York City since 1949, and makes its "warehouse-priced" inventory available to customers worldwide through a very clear, 32-page catalog. Jobson's sells luggage, attaché cases, backpacks, laptop cases, and accessories by Air Express, American Tourister, Atlas, Boyt, Delsey, Eastpack, Eiffel, Perry Ellis,

Hartmann, Jansport, Lark, Lion, Lucas, Paolo Marino, Samsonite, Schlesinger, Skyway, Travelpro, Zero Halliburton, and other manufacturers. Jobson's has a great selection of business cases, choice small leather goods, desk and travel accessories, manicure sets, pens by Cross and MontBlanc, and gifts. You can send for the catalog, which shows just a fifth of Jobson's inventory, or if you have the model and color information for anything from any of the firms mentioned, call or write for a price quote.

Special Factors: Satisfaction is guaranteed; price quote by phone or letter; unused returns are accepted within 30 days for exchange, refund, or credit.

LEATHER UNLIMITED CORP.

DEPT. WBMC98
7155 CTY. HWY. B
BELGIUM, WI 53004–9990
414–994–9464
FAX: 414–994–4099

Catalog: $2, refundable
Pay: check, MO, MC, V, AE, Discover
Sells: leather-crafting supplies and equipment and finished products
Store: same address; Monday to Friday 7–3:30

Here's a catalog for the beginner, the seasoned leather worker, and the rest of us. It offers all sorts of leather-crafting supplies, from kits to raw materials, as well as leather cleaners and conditioners, a line of bags, business cases, small leather goods, and even black-powder (shooting) supplies. Leather Unlimited has been in business since 1970, and offers substantial savings on crafts supplies, beginning with leather—sold by the hide, or in pieces. The weights run from fine lining grade to heavy belting leather, in a variety of finishes and colors. There are laces, belt blanks, key tabs, and dozens of undyed embossed belt strips; these are matched by hundreds of belt buckles, which run from embossed leather buckles to a line with organization logos and sporting themes. The 92-page catalog features dozens of kits for making all sorts of finished goods, plus stamping tools, punches, carvers, rivets, screws, snaps, zippers, lacing needles, sundry findings, leather-care products and dyes by Fiebing's, and Missouri River patterns for making authentic Native American and frontier-style clothing.

Among the finished products available here are sheepskin rugs, slippers, mittens, hats, and purses made of sheepskin and deerskin, duffels and sports bags, leather totes, and wineskins. Leather Unlimited also manufactures leather motorcycle accessories and sells top-grain belt leather business cases, portfolios, wallets, and other small leather goods. And the firm recently added a line of books on Indian lore, crafts, and related topics. The prices are outstandingly low—up to 50% below comparable retail on some items—and extra discounts are given on quantity or volume purchases.

Special Factors: Satisfaction is guaranteed; authorized returns are accepted within 30 days; minimum order is $40.

THE LUGGAGE CENTER

960 REMILLARD CT.
SAN JOSE, CA 95122
800–450–2400
408–288–5363
FAX: 408–998–2536

Information: price quote
Pay: MO, MC, V, AE, Discover
Sells: luggage, business cases, and travel accessories
Store: locations in Bakersfield, Berkeley, Burlingame, Dublin, Emeryville, Fresno, Los Gatos, Mountain View, Pleasant Hill, Redwood City, Sacramento, San Francisco, San Jose (four), San Rafael, Vacaville, and Walnut Creek, CA

The Luggage Center can save you up to 50% off the manufacturers' suggested list prices on the top names in luggage, and even more when the firm is running a sale. The latest lines from well-known makers are available, including Andiamo, Briggs & Riley, Delsey, Eagle Creek, Lark, Lifestyles International, Ricardo, Samsonite, and Skyway. Business cases, garment bags, and travel accessories are carried as well; call or write for a price quote.

Canadian readers, please note: Orders to Canada are shipped via UPS.

Special Factors: Returns are accepted within 30 days.

LUGGAGE UNLIMITED

**FOX VALLEY
AURORA, IL 60504
800–314–2247
630–851–9070
FAX: 630–851–7999**

Information: price quote
Pay: check, MO, MC, V, AE, Discover, JCB
Sells: luggage and travel accessories
Store: same address; also Bloomingdale and Orland Park, IL
E-mail: traveler@synet.net
Online: http://worldtraveler.com/

Luggage Unlimited, better known on the Internet as WorldTraveler, can supply top-quality luggage and travel accessories at discounts of up to 50%. The brands available here include American Tourister, Delsey, Hartmann, Jansport, Samsonite, Travelpro (Rollaboard), and Zero Halliburton. If you have the model number of the piece you want, you can call for a price quote. Or you can visit the website, which has a complete online catalog with product photos, dimensions, list and discount prices, and ordering information. You'll find luggage of all descriptions, garment bags, briefcases and attachés, computer cases, duffels, and even backpacks. Luggage Unlimited also sells travel accessories—voltage converters, luggage straps and locks, money belts, and hanging toiletry bags—also value priced.

Special Factors: Satisfaction is guaranteed; returns are accepted for exchange, refund, or credit; minimum shipping charge is $10 for luggage.

NEW ENGLAND LEATHER ACCESSORIES, INC.

**187 GONIC RD.
ROCHESTER, NH 03866
603–332–0707
FAX: 603–332–4526**

Catalog and Samples: $5, refundable
Pay: check, MO, MC, V, Discover
Sells: leather handbags and accessories
Store: same address; Monday to Saturday 9–5

The 12-page catalog from New England Leather is illustrated with line drawings and photographs of its handsome leather bags and accessories, which are priced up to 30% below comparable leather goods. The $5 catalog fee also brings you a handful of butter-soft leather samples that show you the color range—tobacco, mallard green, brown, wine, and black.

Dozens of handbags and small leather items are available, mainly classic envelopes, hobo bags, knapsacks, and variations on simple pouch designs. The bags are lined, constructed with brass hardware, and treated to repel rain. Prices run from under $30 for a clutch purse to about $200 for an enormous "mailbag." New England Leather has been in business since 1976, continuing on in the tradition of the region, which was once the leather-working capital of the country. Everything produced by the firm is 100% American made.

Special Factors: Returns are accepted.

SANTA MARIA DISCOUNT LUGGAGE

125-F E. BETTERAVIA
SANTA MARIA, CA 93454
805–928–2252
FAX: 805–928–2252

Information: price quote
Pay: check, MO, MC, V, AE, Discover
Sells: luggage and travel accessories
Store: same address; Tuesday to Friday 10–6, Saturday 10–5; also San Luis Luggage, 1135 Chorro St., San Luis Obispo, CA
Online: http://www.luggageman.com

Santa Maria Discount Luggage offers everything from backpacks to three-suiters, at discounts of up to 60% on list. This family-run firm has been in business since 1971, and sells only first-quality goods. The available brands include American Valise, Atlantic, Briggs & Riley, Eagle Creek, Jansport, Samsonite, Travelpro (Rollaboard), Zero Halliburton, and other manufacturers. You can call or write with a model name and number for prices on suitcases, business cases, garment bags, backpacks, duffels, and anything else made by these firms. Or you can visit the Discount Luggage website, which has an online catalog and ordering information. If you're in the Santa Maria area or are near the San Luis Obispo store, drop in—and bring any luggage that needs fixing, because both shops do repairs.

Special Factors: Satisfaction is guaranteed; returns are accepted within 30 days for exchange, refund, or credit.

J. TIRAS CLASSIC HANDBAGS, INC.

6101 ROYALTON, #106
HOUSTON, TX 77081
800–460–1999
713–660–0090
FAX: 713–660–0095

Brochure: free with long, stamped, self-addressed envelope
Pay: check, MO, MC, V, AE
Sells: designer handbag look-alikes
Store: The Centre at Post Oak, 5000 Westheimer, Houston, TX; Monday to Saturday 10–7, Sunday 12–5

Great design, fine workmanship, and top-notch materials are what justify paying hundreds of dollars for bags by Bottega Venetta, Louis Vuitton, Salvatore Ferragamo, Bally, Donna Karan, Judith Leiber, and other designers. But if you had the chance to buy a look-alike for up to 80% less, would *you* insist on the real thing?

Jerome and Jeannie Tiras have been building their business since 1989 on the obvious answer, with a great lineup of copies of handbags by well-known designers, *sans* trademarks, logos, etc. If you know the originals, you'll recognize the copies—but not the prices, which average $80 to $160 for the leather copies, and begin at $75 for a gold evening bag and run to $750 for a leopard-patterned mini-audiere done completely in rhinestones and crystals. (The inspirations for many of the evening bags are Judith Leiber's creations, which routinely fetch $950 to thousands of dollars for jewel-encrusted specimens. The "everyday" bags are copies of designer originals selling for $300 to $2,000.) Tiras' color brochure shows a selection of handbags, totes, change purses, wallets, purse accessories, and other little luxuries, as well as a collection of fashion jewelry.

Special Factors: Unused returns (except sale items) are accepted within 10 days for exchange, refund, or credit; minimum order is $50.

SEE ALSO

Bennett Brothers, Inc. • small leather goods, luggage, and luggage carts • **GENERAL MERCHANDISE**
Dairy Association Co., Inc. • Tackmaster leather balm • **ANIMAL**
The Deerskin Place • deerskin leather goods • **CLOTHING**
A. Feibusch Corporation • replacement luggage-weight zippers • **CRAFTS: TEXTILE ARTS**

Holabird Sports • *racquet-sports bags* • **SPORTS**

IMPCO, Inc. • *leather conditioner* • **AUTO**

Justin Discount Boots & Cowboy Outfitters • *leather-care preparations* • **CLOTHING: FOOTWEAR**

M.C. Limited Fine Leathers • *steer hides and hide pillows* • **HOME: DECOR**

United Pharmacal Company, Inc. • *leather-care products* • **ANIMAL**

Weaver Leather, Inc. • *leather, leather-working tools, dyes, and leather-care products* • **CRAFTS**

MEDICINE

Prescription and over-the-counter drugs,

hearing aids, contact lenses, eyeglasses, etc.

Buying medication by mail is convenient, and it *can* be less expensive than having prescriptions filled at the local drugstore. Even generic drugs may be cheaper by mail, affording you savings of up to 60% on some commonly prescribed remedies. But not all medications are discounted, so price out each prescription you have filled. Always try local sources, since savings vary and sometimes they'll have a "meet-or-beat" pricing policy.

If you take medications regularly, and especially if you take more than one, consider getting a copy of *Worst Pills Best Pills II,* by Dr. Sidney Wolfe. It's nearly 700 pages of information on drugs commonly prescribed to older Americans with a list of scores of others to avoid. The same activist spirit informs *Getting the Best from Your Doctor,* by Wesley J. Smith, which can help you choose a practitioner, understand your rights and the role of medical insurance, and use the medical system to your benefit. *Getting the Best from Your Doctor* is available for $10 (check or money order, shipping included, U.S. deliveries only) from the Center for Study of Responsive Law, P.O. Box 19367, Washington, DC 20036. *Worst Pills Best Pills II* is also reasonably priced; it may be ordered from Public Citizen Publications, 2000 P. St. NW, Suite 600, Washington, DC 20036 (inquire for the current price and shipping costs). You can check a doctor's credentials through the American Board of Medical Specialties; call 800–733–2267 Monday to Friday 9–6 ET, to find out whether the doctor in question is board certified, and when he or she received certification and in what field of practice. And if you or someone you care for is going to be hospitalized, Karen Keating McCann's *Taking Charge of Your Hospital Stay* (Plenum Publishers,

$25) can guide you through the process, with checklists, resources, definitions, and advice on avoiding billing problems.

Drugs, dietary supplements, medical devices, and related products can have unintended, and sometimes harmful, side effects. The Food and Drug Administration (FDA), which is responsible for tracking such problems, has consolidated its forms and reporting procedures so that adverse reactions can be identified more quickly—which means solutions can be found, warnings issued, and products removed from the market sooner. The voluntary medical products reporting program, *MedWatch,* uses a 10-page form to document the complaint. If you're under a physician's care when you experience such a problem, you can have your doctor contact the MedWatch hotline at 800–FDA–1088, or you can call the consumer information line at 800–532–4440 or 301–827–5006 (Monday to Friday 10–4 ET) to request a copy of the form to file yourself. For more information, you can see the FDA's Internet site, http://www.fda.gov/

Contact lenses, eyeglasses, and other commonly used aids are featured in this chapter as well. Please let your doctor know if you're using mail-order suppliers for glasses or lenses, so that he or she can make sure the fit and the prescription are correct.

For savings on breast forms, and products for persons with limited mobility, chronic conditions, and convalescent and post-op patients, see "Special Needs," immediately following this section.

For nutritional supplements, toiletries, and over-the-counter preparations, see the listings in "Health, Fitness, and Beauty."

FIND IT FAST

CONTACT LENSES AND SUPPLIES • **Contact Lens Replacement Center, National Contact Lens Center**
EYEGLASSES AND FRAMES • **Hidalgo, Prism Optical**
PRESCRIPTION DRUGS • **Medi-Mail, Retired Persons Services**

CONTACT LENS REPLACEMENT CENTER, INC.

P.O. BOX 1489, DEPT. 98
MELVILLE, NY 11747
800–779–2654
516–491–7763
FAX: 516–643–4009

Price List: free with long, stamped, self-addressed envelope
Pay: check, MO, MC, V, AE, Discover
Sells: contact lenses and sunglasses
Store: mail order only

Contact Lens Replacement Center, in business since 1986, sells contact lenses of every type at savings of up to 50%. The replacement lenses include hard, soft, planned-replacement, disposable, and gas-permeable types. Toric, bifocal, and aphakic lenses are also available. The brands include Barnes Hind/Hydrocurve, Bausch & Lomb, Boston, Ciba, Coopervision, CSI, Fluorex, Fluoroperm, Hydron/Ocular Sciences, Johnson & Johnson, Paraperm, Sunsoft, and Wesley-Jessen. All soft, planned-replacement, and disposable lenses are shipped in factory-sealed containers. Hard and gas-permeable lenses are made to order. Please note: This is a *replacement* service—not for first-time lens wearers—and you must supply a current prescription for the lenses you are now wearing. The prices are so low that it may make sense to discontinue lens insurance and rely on this service if you lose or damage your contacts—the Center's staff can help you determine the least expensive way to replace your prescribed lenses. And there are *no* membership fees of any kind. Sunglasses by Bollé, Randolph Engineering, Ray-Ban, Revo, Serengeti, Liz Claiborne, Sun Cloud, and Vuarnet are also available, at discount prices. Call with the specific model name and number for a price quote.

Special Factors: Price quote by phone or letter with a long, stamped, self-addressed envelope.

HIDALGO, INC.

DEPT. WM
45 LA BUENA VISTA
WIMBERLEY, TX 78676
512–847–5571
FAX: 512–847–2393

Catalog: free
Pay: check, MO, MC, V, AE, Discover
Sells: prescription eyeglasses, sunglasses, binoculars, watches, knives, etc.
Store: Wimberley North Too Shopping Center, Wimberley, TX; Monday to Friday 10–6, closed Saturdays

Hidalgo's 48-page catalog makes ordering your eyeglasses by mail seem so easy, you'll wonder why you haven't tried it before. Hidalgo has been in business since 1967 and understands the concerns of the person who's buying glasses by mail. The catalog includes detailed descriptions of the frames, lenses, and special coatings, and includes a "Consumers' Guide to Sunglasses" that answers just about every question you can think of. There are instructions on taking your "pupil distance" measurements, and a chart that shows the light transmission data on the lenses sold by Hidalgo. The "try-on program" allows you to order up to three frames and try them out *before* ordering your glasses—a great feature for people who have a hard time finding frames that fit or flatter.

Hidalgo's own frames dominate the selection, and the lens options include a choice of materials (glass, plastic, etc.), colors, coatings, and UV protection. Terms of Hidalgo's warranty are stated clearly in the catalog, as well as details of the "try-on" program. The prices are as much as 40% less than regular retail on the nonprescription eyewear, and 50% or more below customary charges for prescription glasses.

Special Factors: Returns in new, unused condition are accepted within 30 days for exchange, refund, or credit.

MEDI-MAIL, INC.

P.O. BOX 98520
LAS VEGAS, NV 89193–8520
800–793–3548
FAX: 800–323–1028
TDD: 800–423–3724

Brochure: free
Pay: check, MO, MC, V
Sells: prescription drugs and health-care products
Store: mail order only
Online: http://www.metnetmpc.com/

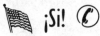 ¡Si!

Medi-Mail is a national pharmacy-by-mail that offers name-brand and generic prescription medications and over-the-counter health products at competitive prices. You may request the firm's brochure, which answers general questions, as well as a catalog of over-the-counter items. Medi-Mail can provide an itemized receipt with each order, which may be submitted to your insurance carrier or kept for your records—be sure to ask for the receipt when you order.

Special Factors: Price quote by phone; minimum order is $10.

NATIONAL CONTACT LENS CENTER

4930 PINECROFT WAY
SANTA ROSA, CA
95404–1311
800–326–6352
707–538–4444
FAX: 707–538–7766, 7799

Brochure: free
Pay: check, MO, MC, V, Discover, JCB
Sells: soft and gas-permeable contact lenses
Store: same address; Monday to Friday 8–5
Online: mtalmadg@interserv.com

  ⊕

National Contact Lens Center, established in 1974, can save you up to 75% on your next pair of contact lenses. You must be an experienced lens wearer to buy here, since the firm can't provide, through the mail, the fitting and monitoring services needed by first-time wearers. No membership fees are ever charged.

National Contact Lens Center sells all the major soft contact lens brands, including lines by American Hydron, Bausch & Lomb, Boston, Ciba, Coopervision, Johnson & Johnson (Acuvue), Ocular Science, Pilk-ington/Barnes Hind, and Wesley-Jessen. Colored, standard, extended-wear, disposable, planned-replacement, and opaque lenses are offered, as well as toric (for astigmatism) lenses. Hard and gas-permeable lenses are also available. Savings can reach 75%, depending on the lens and manufacturer, and every lens is backed by National Contact Lens Center's 30-day replacement guarantee—honored even if the vials are opened.

Please note: A Japanese-language edition of the price list and order form are available upon request.

Special Factors: Satisfaction is guaranteed; price quote by phone; returns are accepted within 30 days for replacement, exchange, refund, or credit.

PRISM OPTICAL, INC.

10992 NW 7TH AVE.,
DEPT. WC98
NORTH MIAMI, FL 33168
305–754–5894
FAX: 305–754–7352

Catalog: $2, $5 outside the U.S.
Pay: check, MO, MC, V, AE, Discover
Sells: prescription eyeglasses, contact lenses, and sunglasses
Store: same address; Monday to Friday 8:30–5

Prism Optical has been selling prescription eyeglasses by mail since 1959, and publishes a 24-page color catalog that shows over 100 eyeglass frames for men, women, and children, discounted an average of 30% to 50%. Frames (and designer sunglasses) from Armani, Bollé, Carrera, Cazal, Christian Dior, Gucci, Anne Klein, Neostyle, Polo, Ray-Ban, Revo, and Serengeti are available. One of the benefits of ordering from Prism is being able to choose from a number of lens options, including photochromic lenses, polycarbonate (ultra-thin) lenses, permanently tinted lenses, lenses with gray mirror-finish, and UV-filtering coating and scratch-resistant coating. The lens styles include single-vision and bifocal lenses, trifocals, and "invisible" bifocals, among others. Prism guarantees that the glasses will fit correctly, and the catalog provides guides to gauging the correct size of the temple and bridge pieces.

Prism Optical also sells prescription contact lenses at prices up to 70% below those charged elsewhere. The firm sells "all brands," factory-sealed and guaranteed against defects. Call Prism with your prescription information for availability and price information.

Special Factors: Satisfaction is guaranteed; returns are accepted within 30 days for refund or credit; C.O.D. orders are accepted.

RETIRED PERSONS SERVICES, INC.

Catalog: free
Pay: check, MO, MC, V, Discover
Sells: prescription drugs and OTC products
Store: mail order only

DEPT. 493000
500 MONTGOMERY ST.
ALEXANDRIA, VA
22314-1563
ORDERS AND INFO:
800-456-2277
FAX: 800-456-7631
TDD: 800-933-4327

Retired Persons Services, Inc. is the mail-order pharmacy of the American Association of Retired Persons (AARP). Ordering from the AARP Pharmacy is a benefit of membership in the AARP, which may be the smartest $8 you ever spend (see the listing for the AARP in "General Merchandise")—but you don't have to be an AARP member to buy here. The 112-page Retired Persons Services catalog offers nutritional supplements, over-the-counter remedies, analgesics, supplies for diabetics, nail clippers and scissors, support hosiery and foot-care products, dental-care items, hearing aid batteries, and much more. Prices of generic and branded prescription drugs are given by phone (800-456-2226) Monday through Friday, 7 a.m. to 7 p.m. and Saturday, 9 a.m. to 1 p.m. You may also speak directly with a pharmacist (800-456-2277) if you have questions. If you're an ostomy patient, call 800-284-4788 for the separate Ostomy Care Catalog. Medical information leaflets for seniors are provided with most prescriptions, and computerized prescription histories are available for tax and insurance purposes. RPS will call your doctor for you on prescription drug refills, and the AARP Pharmacy also participates in major prescription drug insurance plans. Orders are filled on an invoice basis—you'll be billed, instead of paying when you place the order.

Special Factors: Satisfaction is guaranteed; returns (except prescription drugs) are accepted for exchange, refund, or credit.

Special Needs

---

*Products and services for persons with
limited mobility, chronic medical conditions,
and convalescent and post-op patients*

When the Americans with Disabilities Act was passed in 1990, it was lauded as long-overdue legislation that would eliminate discrimination and barriers for persons with disabilities. What's emerging as the law is invoked and enforced is the story of how the law is applied, and a shaping of the very understanding of what constitutes a disability. To begin learning about the terms and titles, read the act itself. It's available from the Department of Justice's ADA helpline, 800–514–0301. John Wiley & Sons has published the *Pocket Guide to the ADA* ($19.95), and AARP will send "Accessibility: It's Yours for the Asking" if you send a postcard requesting Publication D15520 from AARP Fulfillment, P.O. Box 22796, Long Beach, CA 90801–5796.

Purchasing home health-care equipment can prove a great challenge, especially if you're uninsured, or insurance doesn't cover the cost of some items. Wheelchairs can be quite costly, and it may be difficult for first-time buyers to know what to look for in features and performance. The National Association for Medical Equipment Services (NAMES), a lobbying group for the home-medical equipment (HME) industry, publishes a brochure, *Health Care in Your Home: A Shopper's Guide to Home Medical Equipment.* The pamphlet has general buying guidelines and caveats, and is available from your local HME distributor or from NAMES at 703–836–6263. In addition, each year *Sports 'N Spokes* publishes a review of wheelchairs; contact the magazine for information at 2111 E. Highland Avenue, Suite 180, Phoenix, AZ 85016–4702, or call 602–224–0500.

For purposes of categorization, and not constituting any definition, firms selling aids to general vision correction and hearing aids are listed in the preceding section, "Medicine." The firms listed here serve more specialized needs—for diabetics, ostomates, persons with incontinence problems, post-surgical requirements, etc.

When meeting the challenge of a long-term illness or a change in motor or sensor ability, you often need information—on coping, on care, on different therapies—as much as specialized products. The not-for-profit groups founded around fund-raising and education functions for individual diseases and conditions—arthritis, cancer, diabetes mellitus, multiple sclerosis, cystic fibrosis, spina bifida, and AIDS are a few of the best known—can often help to refer you to local support groups and networks, specialists, related groups, and other information sources. (Your medical specialist should be able to give you the name of the biggest groups or foundations.) You can also search *Books in Print* for titles on the subject, read related medical journals, and find facts and support through the Internet. The major online services have disabilities fora that unite users with diverse disabilities for discussions on practical and philosophical issues. Newsgroups and chat rooms have been established for just about every disability or chronic condition imaginable—a search on the Internet should yield a number of leads. The database at the University of Michigan is a good example (http://mel.lib.mi.us/social/SOC-disable.html); it yields links to everything from the ABLEDATA of The National Institute on Disability and Rehabilitation Research, to "United Cerebral Palsy Associations." For a listing of the online organizations, BBS's, and other resources available, you can also see the current edition of *The Internet Yellow Pages,* by Harley Hahn and Rick Stout (Osborne McGraw-Hill), or a similar directory of Internet resources.

FIND IT FAST

BREAST FORMS • **Bosom Buddy**
GADGETS • **Comfort House**
INCONTINENCE PRODUCTS • **Medical Supply**
NURSING HOME CLOTHING • **Senior's Needs**
OSTOMY AND TRACHEOSTOMY SUPPLIES • **Bruce Medical**
SUPPORT HOSIERY AND GARMENTS • **Bruce Medical, Support Plus**

BOSOM BUDDY BREAST FORMS

B & B LINGERIE COMPANY, INC.
DEPT. WC01
2417 BANK DR.
P.O. BOX 5731
BOISE, ID 83705–0731
800–262–2789
208–343–9696
FAX: 208–343–9266

Brochure: free
Pay: check, MO, MC, V, Discover
Sells: breast prostheses
Store: mail order only

B & B has been producing the "Bosom Buddy Breast Form," a comfortable, reasonably priced external breast prosthesis, since 1976. The form is weighted and shaped to ideal dimensions with cushioned pillows, each of which contains 1½ ounces of tiny glass beads. (The weight may be adjusted by adding or removing pillows.) The form itself is all-fabric (no silicone or plastic is used), made of nylon softened with fiberfill, with an all-cotton backing that rests next to your skin. Bosom Buddy is interchangeable (fits both left and right sides), available in sizes from 32AAA to 46DDD, and it costs $60 for sizes AAA and AA, $65 for sizes A through D, and $70 for sizes DD and DDD. These prices are about 50% below silicone models. The brochure gives complete details, and B & B's staff can answer any questions you may have by phone.

Wholesale customers, the minimum order is three breast forms, or $100.

Special Factors: Satisfaction is guaranteed; returns are accepted.

BRUCE MEDICAL SUPPLY

DEPT. 10736
411 WAVERLY OAKS RD.
WALTHAM, MA 02154
800–225–8446
FAX: 617–894–9519

Catalog: free
Pay: check, MO, MC, V, AE, Discover
Sells: ostomy, tracheostomy, diabetic, and general medical products
Store: mail order only

  ¡Si!

The Bruce Medical Supply catalog is a valuable aid to persons who are in need of home health products, including those needing goods for laryngectomies, colostomies, ileostomies, urostomies, or mastectomies, as well as diabetes, arthritis, incontinence, or special dietary restrictions. Bruce Medical Supply, which has been in business since 1978, also stocks products designed to make all sorts of routine tasks easier.

The 64-page catalog offers a comprehensive range of ostomy supplies, diabetes monitoring supplies and equipment, bathtub safety benches, tub grips, wheelchairs, walkers, canes, crutches, magnifying glasses, reading glasses, blood pressure kits, stethoscopes, compresses, and similar products. Most of the goods are from well-known firms, including Ames, Amoena, Convatec, Hollister, Johnson & Johnson, Kimberly Clark, Mentor, Procter & Gamble, and 3M. Books on related topics, and general nursing and caretaker supplies are available. The catalog also features a good selection of dining, food preparation, dressing, grooming, and bathing aids for persons whose range of movement or strength is limited. Bruce Medical Supply stresses prompt shipment and delivery.

Special Factors: Satisfaction is guaranteed; price quote by phone or letter; goods are shipped in unmarked boxes; C.O.D. orders are accepted.

COMFORT HOUSE

189-WM FRELINGHUYSEN
AVE.
NEWARK, NJ 07114–1595
973–242–8080
FAX: 973–242–0131

Catalog: $2, refundable
Pay: check, MO, MC, V, AE, Discover
Sells: all-around helpful tools and gadgets
Store: mail order only
E-mail: comforthse@aol.com
Online: http://www.comforthouse.com

Here are 28 pages of products designed to make the little things easier for everyone, beginning with the catalog itself, which is printed in a big, clear typeface. Comfort House, in business since 1991, sells things like cleaning tools with extension poles, that anyone might find useful, as well as electric vegetable peelers and power-seat lifters, designed specifically for those with limited strength and mobility. There are door-knob turners, dressing aids, various gripping devices, exercisers, sleeping and bathing aids, travel accessories, gardening tools, and much more. Comfort House is not a *discount* catalog, although a couple of price-checks showed savings of over 30% on some of the body-care products; this is simply a great collection of products that can help people perform everyday tasks more easily and more safely, as well as coping with changed conditions.

In addition to what's shown in the catalog, Comfort House accepts special orders for any of thousands of products for general personal care, incontinence, mobility assistance, or needs associated with orthopedics, ostomy, laryngectomy, mobility, and urology.

Wholesale terms are available to drug, medical, and surgical-supply stores only. Inquire on company letterhead for terms and pricing.

Special Factors: Satisfaction is guaranteed; returns in unused condition are accepted within 30 days.

MEDICAL SUPPLY CO., INC.

P.O. BOX 250
HAMBURG, NJ 07419–0250
800–323–9664
201–209–8448
FAX: 201–209–4799

Price List: free with SASE
Pay: check or MO
Sells: diapers, underpads, disposable briefs
Store: mail order only

Coping with incontinence is easier now that Attends, Depends, and similar products have come onto the market. But these products aren't cheap, so it's great to find a source for incontinence products at a discount. Medical Supply Co. has been in business since 1977, selling Depends briefs and Chux underpads at savings of up to 50%. For example, Depends selling for 90¢ each in a local drugstore are sold here as "Incontinence Pants" at 50¢ each (in cases of 50). The Chux underpads run from 13¢ to 41¢ each (sold in cases), depending on the size. Medical Supply accepts Medicaid (in Delaware and New Jersey only) and does not charge shipping on orders delivered in Connecticut, New Jersey, New York, and Pennsylvania. (Customers in other states pay UPS charges collect.)

Special Factors: Shipping is not charged on deliveries to CT, NJ, NY, and PA; inquire about Medicaid acceptance (if applicable); minimum order is one case.

SENIOR'S NEEDS, INC.

THE BASIC APPAREL CO.
875 PAGE ST.
MANCHESTER, NH 03109
800-777-2006
(WEEKDAYS)
603-644-8398
FAX: 800-875-1405

Catalog: free
Pay: check, MO, MC, V, AE
Sells: adaptive apparel
Store: mail order only

Senior's Needs was founded to create a source for attractive, well-priced clothing for nursing home residents. The 32-page catalog shows a broad selection of "adaptive apparel" for men and women, in easy-fitting styles and easy-care fabrics. There are a number of dusters and house-dresses, most in back-snap style, and shirts and pants for men. Jackets, nightwear, jogging suits, sweaters, footwear, hosiery, and accessories are offered in both men's and women's styles. Some of the convention-ally styled underwear is offered in large sizes—bras to 52DD and panties to 15 for women, and men's undershirts and shorts to size 4X.

The catalog is geared to people who take care of the clothing needs of nursing home residents and the prices are great—under $28 for dresses, back-snap slips for less than $8, and men's cutaway slacks for $23 are a few examples. Extra-low prices are offered on the Senior's Needs "budget" specials, but there's no choice of color or style.

Special Factors: Satisfaction is guaranteed; authorized returns are accepted.

SUPPORT PLUS

━━━━━━━━

99 WEST ST., DEPT.
  WBM98
BOX 500
MEDFIELD, MA 02052
800–229–2910
508–359–2910
FAX: 508–359–0139

Catalog: free
Pay: check, MO, MC, V, AE, Discover
Sells: support hosiery, therapeutic apparel, foot products, comfort footwear
Store: same address; Tuesday, Thursday, Saturday 10–1

Support Plus has been in business since 1972, and offers an extensive selection of supportive hosiery and undergarments for men and women, as well as comfortable leather footwear. Discounts average about 15%, but some items are priced 30% less than regular retail.

If your physician recommends or prescribes support (elastic) hosiery, you'll find this catalog a helpful guide to what's available. Support Plus offers panty hose, stockings, knee-highs, and men's dress socks in different support strengths. (The compression rating for each style is given in the catalog descriptions.) Among the brands sold here are Bauer & Black, Berkshire, Futuro, Hanes, T.E.D., and Support Plus' own line. Maternity, cotton-soled, control-top, open-toe, and irregular styles are available.

Support Plus also sells posture pads for chairs and beds, joint "wraps" for applications of heat and cold, Dale abdominal and lumbrosacral supports, Futuro braces and joint supports, and personal-care products and bathing aids—eating and dressing implements, bedding, underpads and disposable pants, bath seats and rails, and toilet guard rails. The catalog also features a collection of comfort-styled shoes and slippers for women by Barefoot Freedom, Clinic Shoe, Foot Saver, Daniel Green, Munro, and Soft Spots, in standard and hard-to-fit sizes, and a line of women's underwear and foundation garments.

Special Factors: Price quote by phone for quantities in excess of 12 pairs; unworn returns are accepted.

SEE ALSO

Bailey's, Inc. • *first-aid kits* • **TOOLS**
Campmor • *snake bite kits, variety of first-aid kits* • **SPORTS**
Chock Catalog Corp. • *snap-back women's clothing* • **CLOTHING**

Creative Health Products • *fitness equipment, blood pressure kits, skinfold calipers, etc.* • **HEALTH**

Dallas Midwest • *office work tables with wheelchair access* • **OFFICE**

Defender Industries, Inc. • *first-aid kits, marine safety gear* • **AUTO**

The Faucet Outlet • *bathroom fixture aids for disabled persons* • **HOME: IMPROVEMENT**

Freeda Vitamins, Inc. • *dietary supplements* • **HEALTH**

Goldbergs' Marine Distributors • *first-aid kits, marine safety gear* • **AUTO**

Hillestad International, Inc. • *dietary supplements* • **HEALTH**

K-Log, Inc. • *wheelchair-access computer workstations* • **OFFICE**

Lady Grace Stores, Inc. • *mastectomy underwear and breast prostheses* • **CLOTHING**

Marshall Domestics • *incontinence supplies, latex exam gloves, scrubs, patient gowns, hospital sheets, etc.* • **GENERAL MERCHANDISE**

No Nonsense Direct • *nurses' hosiery* • **CLOTHING**

Omaha Vaccine Company, Inc. • *biologicals and pharmaceuticals for livestock* • **ANIMAL**

Orion Telescopes & Binoculars • *telescopes* • **CAMERAS**

Plastic BagMart • *zip-top plastic bags* • **OFFICE: SMALL BUSINESS**

S & S Sound City • *closed-caption decoders* • **APPLIANCES**

Scope City Inc. • *telescopes* • **CAMERAS**

Tafford Manufacturing, Inc. • *uniforms, footwear, and medical equipment for health-care professionals* • **CLOTHING**

Uniform Connection • *uniforms and footwear for health-care professionals* • **CLOTHING**

United Pharmacal Company, Inc. • *animal biologicals and vet instruments* • **ANIMAL**

World Wide Aquatics • *post-mastectomy swimsuits* • **SPORTS**

MUSIC

Instruments, supplies, and services

Professional musicians rarely pay full price for their instruments, and if you buy from the same sources they use, neither will you. The firms listed here sell top-quality instruments—everything from school band recorders to grand pianos—and electronics, and supplies, and while they usually serve the knowledgeable, they can assist you even if you're a musical neophyte. If you catch the clerks during a lull in store trade, you can usually get the same kind of help over the phone—but please understand that they're usually very busy. Some of the stores take trade-ins, some rent instruments, and most sell used equipment. In fact, the resale market for quality pieces is good. Buy wisely today and you may be selling your "vintage" ax to Elderly Instruments or Mandolin Brothers 20 years down the road for several times what you paid!

If you're looking for one all-purpose site for music information, check CDnow (http://www.cdnow.com/), which sells music—from classical to world beat—on CD, tape, laser disc, and vinyl—as well as movies on video. The listings are annotated with biographical information and rated. Not only can you buy your music here at good prices (shipping is under $5 per order for U.S. deliveries at this writing), but CDnow has one of the best collections of music-related links to other Internet sites on the WWW. There is no print catalog, but you can reach the company to place an order for an in-print music or movie title at CDnow, 401 Old Penllyn Pike, Suite 5, Penllyn, PA 19422, or call 215–654–8076, or fax 215–283–4965 (checks and money orders in U.S. funds, MasterCard, Visa, and American Express are accepted). If you don't live within the U.S., please see the schedule of shipping charges and the delivery timetable posted on the website (see the "Policies" section).

FIND IT FAST

ACCORDIONS • **Accordion-O-Rama**
DRUMS • **American Musical, Sam Ash, Lone Star, Swords, Thoroughbred Music, Wray's**
FRETTED INSTRUMENTS • **American Musical, Metropolitan Music, Shar, Swords, Thoroughbred Music, Weinkrantz, Wray's**
GENERAL, SCHOOL, AND MARCHING BAND INSTRUMENTS • **Giardinelli, Interstate Music, Kennelly Keys, National Educational Music, West Manor**
GUITARS AND ELECTRONICS • **American Musical, Sam Ash, Carvin, Kennelly Keys, Manny's, Musician's Friend, Swords, Thoroughbred Music, Wray's**
PIANOS AND ORGANS • **Altenburg**
REEDS • **Discount Reed**
SHEET MUSIC • **Patti Music**
STRINGS • **Thoroughbred Music**
VINTAGE INSTRUMENTS • **Elderly Instruments, Mandolin Brothers, Wray's**

ACCORDION-O-RAMA, INC.

━━━━━━━━

DEPT. WBMC
307 SEVENTH AVE.,
20TH FL.
NEW YORK, NY 10001
212–675–9089
212–206–8344

Catalog: $1
Pay: check, MO, MC, V
Sells: accordions, accessories, and services
Store: same address (20th Floor); Tuesday to Friday 10–5, Saturday 11–3 (may be open longer; call)

Accordion-O-Rama, in business since 1950, has an extensive inventory of new and rebuilt accordions and concertinas that are all sold at a discount. Accordion-O-Rama is an authorized dealer and factory-service center for several leading brands, and can customize your instrument to meet your requirements—including MIDI. Concertinas and accordions—electronic, chromatic, diatonic, and piano—are offered here at considerable savings. Accordion-O-Rama carries its own line, as well as instruments by Arpeggio, Avanti, Cordovox, Crumar, Dallape, Elka, Excelsior, Farfisa, Ferrari, Gabbanelli, Galanti, Guerrini, Hohner, Polytone, Sano, Scandalli, Solton, Sonola, Paolo Soprani, Vox, and other firms. The catalog features color photos of individual models with specifications. New and reconditioned models are stocked, and accordion synthesizers, amps, speakers, generators, organ-accordions, and accordion stands are available.

When you write for information, be sure to describe the type of accordion that interests you. In addition to the color catalog ($1), you can request the black-and-white catalog, which is free, or order a video: The "Demonstration" video provides a tour of Accordion-O-Rama and the "Basics of MIDI" tape gives an introduction to MIDI. Either tape can be purchased for $25 or both for $45 (postpaid in the United States).

Special Factors: Trade-ins are welcomed; wholesale prices are based on volume.

ALTENBURG PIANO HOUSE, INC.

1150 EAST JERSEY ST.
ELIZABETH, NJ 07201
908–351–2000
FAX: 908–527–9210

Brochure: free
Pay: check, MO, MC, V, AE, Discover
Sells: pianos and organs
Store: same address; Monday to Friday 8–7, Saturday 8–5, Sunday 12–5; also Asbury Park and Trenton, NJ

The Altenburg Piano House has been doing business since 1847, and is run today by a descendant of the founder. Altenburg sells pianos and organs by "almost all" manufacturers, including lines by Baldwin, Hammond, Petrof, and Mason, and Altenburg's own models. Prices are at least 35% below list or suggested retail, and if you call for literature, you'll receive information on Altenburg's line of pianos—upright, grand, and console models. Complete specifications are listed for each, including details on the encasing, keys, pin block, bridges, soundboard, action, strings, hammer felt, and warranty. If you're in the area of Elizabeth, New Jersey, drop by the Art Deco showroom and hear an Altenburg—they've been recommended by no less than Franz Liszt! And if you're pricing a branded model, call or write with the name of the piano or organ for price and shipping details.

Special Factors: Inquire for information.

AMERICAN MUSICAL SUPPLY

**600 INDUSTRIAL AVE.
PARAMUS, NJ 07652–3607
800–458–4076
FAX: 201–262–3332**

Catalog: free
Pay: check, MO, MC, V, AE, Discover
Sells: musical instruments and recording equipment
Store: Victor's House of Music, 235 Franklin Ave., Ridgewood, NJ; Monday to Thursday 9–8, Friday 9–6, Saturday 10–6
E-mail: victorshom@aol.com
Online: http://www.victors.com (store)
Online: http://www.americanmusical.com (catalog)

Forget the brass and woodwinds—American Musical Supply is rock and roll all the way. The 124-page catalog opens with Shure and Audio-Technica mics, and ends with Roland keyboards and MIDI peripherals. Recorders, speakers, amps, headsets, signal processors, monitors, digital audio tape and CD players and recorders, equalizers, mastering decks, pedals and effects boxes, cables, pickups, tuners, and other accessories are offered. Guitars are featured as well—the latest acoustic and electric models from Charvel, Fender, Gibson, Ibanez, Martin, and Washburn. The percussion section includes drums by Pearl and Tama, as well as cymbals, chimes, cowbells, and other esoteric instruments. American Musical Supply sells electronic keyboards and accessories, books, manuals, and videos on technique, making music with MIDI, Recorded Versions Guitar transcriptions, and much more. Prices run up to 70% below list, although discounts vary from item to item. AMS is the mail-order division of Victor's House of Music, a third-generation family business. If you need advice on the best equipment for your music, they should be able to help.

Special Factors: Minimum order is $10; C.O.D. orders are accepted.

SAM ASH MUSIC CORP.

DEPT. WBMC
P.O. BOX 9047
HICKSVILLE, NY 11802
800–472–6274
908–572–0263
FAX: 908–572–7138

Information: inquire
Pay: check, MC, V, AE, Discover
Sells: instruments and electronics
Store: 160 W. 48th St., New York, NY; Monday to Saturday 10–9; also New Haven, CT; Margate and Miami Lakes, FL; Brooklyn, Carle Place, Forrest Hills, Huntington Station, and White Plains, NY; Cherry Hill, Edison, and Paramus, NJ; Cleveland and Columbus, OH; and King of Prussia, PA

In 1924, violinist and bandleader Sam Ash opened a musical-instrument shop in Brooklyn. The company is still family-run, but now boasts 16 stores and patronage by superstars, schools and institutions, and recording studios, as well as the music-making general public. Regular half-off specials are a feature here, so don't buy anywhere else until you've given Sam Ash a call.

Musical instruments, musical electronics, karaoke, music software, sound systems, electronic keyboards, recording equipment, disk jockey equipment, digital home pianos, specialized lighting, and accessories are available from hundreds of manufacturers, including Akai, AKG, Audio-Technica, Bach, Bose, Buffet, Bundy, Casio, Cerwin-Vega, Charvel, dbx, DigiTech, DOD, Electro-Voice, E-Mu, Ensoniq, Epiphone, Fender, Gemeinhardt, Fostex, Gibson, Guild, Ibanez, Jackson, JBL, JVC, Karaoke (sing-along machines), Kawai, Klipsch, Kurzweil, Leblanc, Ludwig, Mackie, Marshall, Martin, Mesa-Boogie, Noble & Cooley, Ovation, Paiste, Pearl, Rickenbacker, Roland, Sabian, Schilke, Selmer, Sennheiser, Shure, Paul Reed Smith, Sony, Suzuki, SWR, Tama, Takamine, Tascam, Technics, Toa, Yamaha, and Zildjian. Sheet music is stocked, repairs and service are performed, and trade-ins are accepted at the stores.

Please note: For a Spanish-speaking sales representative, call 212–719–2299 (NY) or 305–628–3510 (FL).

Special Factors: Minimum order is $25.

CARVIN CORP.

**12340 WORLD TRADE DR.
SAN DIEGO, CA 92128
800–854–2235
760–487–1600
FAX: 760–487–8160**

Catalog: free
Pay: check, MO, MC, V, AE, Discover
Sells: Carvin instruments and accessories
Store: same address; Monday to Friday
9:30–6; also 7414 Sunset Blvd., Hollywood,
and 1907 N. Main St., Santa Ana, CA; Monday to Friday 10–7, Saturday 10–6, both locations
Online: http://www.carvinguitars.com

Carvin "Guitars & Pro Sound" manufactures its own line of instruments
and equipment to exacting standards. You'll find the specifications, features, and individual guarantees of each instrument noted in the 48-
page color catalog; prices are up to 50% less than those of comparable
models. You'll also find luminaries of the music world shown throughout the catalog, alongside Carvin equipment—Chet Atkins, David Roe,
Seal, Wayne Newton, Greg Allman, and Stanley Clarke are a few who've
appeared in past catalogs.

Mixers, amps, mikes, monitor systems, and electric guitars are offered
here, as well as professional-quality guitars designed for the requirements of professional musicians. All of Carvin's instruments and equipment are sold under a 30-day free trial arrangement. Servicing and
performance testing is done free of charge during the warranty period,
and warranties range from one to five years, depending on the item.

Please note: The toll-free line is staffed Monday to Friday 7–6 and Saturday 10–4 PT.

Special Factors: Satisfaction is guaranteed; returns are accepted for
refund; minimum order is $25 with credit cards.

DISCOUNT REED COMPANY

24307 MAGIC MOUNTAIN
  PKWY., #181
VALENCIA, CA 91355
800–428–5993
805–294–9437
FAX: 805–294–9762

Price List: free
Pay: check, MO, MC, V, Discover
Sells: reeds for musical instruments
Store: mail order only

Discount Reed sells just that—"mail order reeds at fantastic savings"—through the eight-page price list. The firm, which began business in 1980, sells woodwind reeds by the box, priced up to 50% less than the list prices—which represents really big savings if you're used to buying reeds one at a time. Both natural and synthetic reeds for all types of clarinets and saxophones are stocked, as well as reeds for oboes and bassoons, in strengths from 1 to $5\frac{1}{2}$ (soft to hard). The names include Bari, Fibracell, Grand Concert, Dave Guardala, Fred Hemke, Java, Jones (double reeds), Marca, Mitchell Lurie, Olivieri, Peter Ponzol, Queen, Rico, RKM, Eugene Rosseau, V–12, V–16, Vandoren, La Voz, and Zonda. (If you're looking for a reed not listed in the flyer, call or write, since it may be available.) In addition, Discount Reed sells Harrison and Vandoren reed cases, reed trimmers, La Voz reed guards, Blue Note sax straps, swabs, and other accessories.

Special Factors: Satisfaction is guaranteed; institutional accounts are available (purchase orders from schools accepted, 30 days net); minimum order is $20 with credit cards.

ELDERLY INSTRUMENTS

P.O. BOX 14249-WM98
LANSING, MI 48901
517–372–7890, EXT. 123
FAX: 517–372–5155

Catalog: free (see text)
Pay: check, MO, MC, V, Discover
Sells: new and vintage musical instruments, books, videotapes, and recordings
Store: 1100 North Washington, Lansing, MI; Monday to Wednesday 11–7, Thursday 11–9, Friday and Saturday 10–6; mail-order hours: Monday to Saturday 9–5
E-mail: web@elderly.com
Online: http://www.elderly.com

 ¡Si!

Elderly Instruments has an extraordinary selection of in-print, hard-to-find recordings of all types of music, from folk and bluegrass to jazz and classical, listed in the closely printed 106-page "Recordings" catalog. (For a sample of Elderly's picks, call "Dial-a-Ditty-a-Day," several minutes of an Elderly selection: 517–372–1212, Touch-Tone required.) Elderly Instruments also sells books on dance, repair and construction of instruments, music history, folklore, and even songbooks and videotapes (request the "Books, Videos, and Instructional Tapes" catalog).

Despite the impressive publication department, this firm has built 25 years of business on vintage instruments. Epiphones, Fenders, Martins, Dobros, Gibsons, Rickenbackers, and other electric and acoustic guitars have been offered in the past, as well as banjos, violins, mandolins, and other fretted instruments. (There are two additional catalogs—"Electric" and "Acoustic," for new guitars and effects of each type. Request the catalog that better answers your needs.) Elderly Instruments also sells new instruments, lays claim to the title of world's largest dealer of new Martin guitars, and is among the top 20 Gibson dealers. You'll find a good selection of equipment here by Alvarez-Yairi, Boss, Collings, Crate, DiMarzio, Dobro, DOD, E.S.P., Fender, Gibson, Guild, Martin, Sigma, Steinberger, Stelling, Taylor, and Yamaha, among other names. The monthly "vintage used instruments list" is sent free with catalog orders or on request ($2 if sent outside the U.S.), or you may subscribe for $15 ($30 outside the U.S. and Canada). Prices are as low as 50% off list, and everything is covered by the Elderly Instruments guarantee of satisfaction (see the catalog for details).

Please note: Mail-order hours are Monday to Saturday, 9–5.

Special Factors: Satisfaction is guaranteed; unused, authorized returns are accepted within five days for exchange, refund, or credit; minimum order is $10.

GIARDINELLI BAND INSTRUMENT CO., INC.

7845 MALTLAGE DR.
LIVERPOOL, NY 13090
800–288–2334
315–652–4792
FAX: 800–652–4535
FAX: 315–652–4534

Catalog: free, $7 outside the U.S.
Pay: check, MO, MC, V, AE, Discover
Sells: brasses, woodwinds, string, percussion, and accessories
Store: same address; Monday to Friday 8:30–5, Saturday 9–1
E-mail: music@giardinelli.com
Online: http://www.giardinelli.com

Giardinelli has been selling fine brasses and woodwinds since 1947, and publishes a 188-page catalog with an exhaustive listing of brass, woodwinds, percussion, and string instruments. Trumpets, flugelhorns, trombones, French horns, euphoniums, tubas, clarinets, flutes, piccolos, saxophones, oboes, bassoons, violins, violas, cellos, drum sets, and keyboard percussion are all available, as well as a full line of accessories. The brands include Bach, Besson, Buffet, Bundy, Courtois, DEG, Emerson, Farkas, Gemeinhardt, Getzen, Glaesel Strings, Holton, Humes & Berg, Leblanc, Ross Percussion, Schilke, K. Schiller Strings, Selmer, Signet, Denis Wick, Yamaha, Yanigasawa, and others. Mouthpieces, mutes, reeds, metronomes, tuners, cases, stands, cleaning supplies, and books round out the catalog, and Giardinelli features its own line of fine stock and custom mouthpieces for brasses. Savings run up to 50%, and the customer service department can assist you if you have questions or need advice.

Please note: If you're contacting Giardinelli online, please use the e-mail address given above.

Special Factors: Satisfaction is guaranteed; returns are accepted for exchange, refund, or credit; institutional accounts are available.

INTERSTATE MUSIC SUPPLY

P.O. BOX 510865
NEW BERLIN, WI 53151
800–982–BAND
FAX: 414–786–6840

Catalog: free (see text)
Pay: check, MO, MC, V, Discover
Sells: instruments, electronics, and accessories
Store: Cascio Music Co., 13819 W. National Ave., New Berlin, and 11010 North Port Washington Rd., Mequon, WI; Monday to Thursday 10–8, Friday 10–5:30, Saturday 10–4
E-mail: ims@execpc.com
Online: http://www.execpc.com/~interstate

Interstate Music Supply is a division of Cascio Music Company, which has been in business since 1946. IMS serves everyone's musical needs, beginning with schools and music teachers. The 370-page *School Discount Catalog* lists a wide range of equipment, at savings of up to 60%. Everything from woodwind reeds and corks to full lines of brass, woodwind, percussion, and stringed instruments is available, including repair kits and parts, cleaning supplies, neckstraps, cases, storage units, music stands, stage lighting, sound systems, piano labs, and even riser setups for bands and orchestras. There are great buys on goods from Anvil, Bach, Blessing, Buffet, Bundy, Dynamic, Emerson, Engelhardt, Fender, Fostex, Franz, Gemeinhardt, Gibson, Holton, Korg, Kramer, Leblanc, Ludwig, Mesa-Boogie, Orff, Ovation, Pearl, Roland, Sansui, Schilke, Seiko, Selmer, Trace-Elliot, Vandoren, Vito, Yamaha, and Zildjian.

Interstate Music also produces three other 132-page catalogs: *Guitars* (guitar/bass instruments), *Keyboards* (including keyboards and computer software), and *Drums,* percussion instruments and accessories. But if you don't see what you want, call or write—it may be available.

Special Factors: Satisfaction is guaranteed; price quote by phone or letter with SASE; returns are accepted within 10 days for exchange, refund, or credit; institutional accounts are available; minimum order is $25.

KENNELLY KEYS MUSIC, INC.

20505 HWY. 99
LYNNWOOD, WA 98036
800–426–6409
206–771–7020
FAX: 206–670–6713

Information: price quote
Pay: check, MO, MC, V, AE, Discover
Sells: musical instruments and accessories
Store: same address
E-mail: kennelly@seanet.com
Online: http://www.musicconnect.com/

Kennelly Keys Music, in business since 1960, offers discounts of up to 40% on the retail prices of instruments and accessories. The brass and woodwind names represented here include Altus, Blessing, Buffet, Burbank, Canadian Brass, Getzen, Holton, Keilworth, LeBlanc, Powell, Schilke, and Yanagisawa. The guitar, keyboard, percussion, and combo departments carry EV, Gibson, Godin, Hamer, Heritage, LP, Mackie, Marshall, Martin, Ovation, Pearl, Seagull, Sonor, Soundtech, and Takamine. Kennelly Keys Music offers a full-line service department for repairs, tune-ups, and questions, and provides "dealer prep" on all instruments it sells. There is no catalog, so see the website, or call or fax with inquiries and for price quotes; product literature is available on specific models or lines.

Special Factors: Institutional accounts are available; authorized returns are accepted; minimum order is $25.

LONE STAR PERCUSSION

10611 CONTROL PLACE
    DR.
DALLAS, TX 75238
214–340–0835
FAX: 214–340–0861

Catalog: free with a long, self-addressed, stamped envelope
Pay: check, MO, MC, V, Discover
Sells: percussion instruments
Store: same address; Tuesday to Friday 9:30–5:30, Saturday 9:30–2
Online: http://www.lonestarpercussion.com

Concert, marching, jazz, and rock percussion—Lone Star stocks it all. This firm has been doing business with individuals and institutions worldwide since 1978, and publishes a 48-page catalog that lists drums and heads, cases, drumsticks, keyboard mallets, cymbals, castanets, gongs, tambourines, triangles, wood blocks, bells, percussion for Latin music, and much more. The brands include Abel, Adams, Afro, American Drum, Balter, Blocks, Deagan, Deschler, Vic Firth, Gambal, Tom Gauger, Gross, Grover, Hinger, R. Holmes, Impact, Innovative, J.B., Latin Percussion, Lone Star, Ludwig, Malletech, Musser (Ludwig), Payson, Pearl, Premier, Pro-Mark, Remo, Rock-N-Soc, Sabian, Seiko, Silverfox, Spectrasound, Tama, Wuhan, Yamaha, Zildjian, etc. In the unlikely event you don't see what you're looking for among the thousands of items listed, call or write—it's probably available.

Special Factors: Satisfaction is guaranteed; authorized returns are accepted within two weeks (a restocking fee of up to 20% may be charged); institutional accounts are available.

MANDOLIN BROTHERS, LTD.

629 FOREST AVE.
STATEN ISLAND, NY
10310–2576
718–981–3226, 981–8585
FAX: 718–816–4416

Catalog: free
Pay: check, MO, MC, V, AE, Discover
Sells: new and vintage fretted instruments and accessories
Store: same address; Monday to Saturday 10–6
E-mail: mandolin@mandoweb.com
Online: http://www.mandoweb.com

Mandolin Brothers has been selling vintage fretted instruments at good prices since 1971, and offers select new instruments at a standard discount of 35% from list prices. The 75-page catalog is packed with listings of vintage guitars, mandolins, mandolas, banjos, electric basses, ukeleles, and other stringed instruments. Part of the catalog is devoted to new equipment—guitars, mandolins, banjos, electronics, and accessories. The instruments carried include Benedetto, Bourgeois, Breedlove, Buscarino, Campellone, Collings, D'Angelico, D'Aquisto, Deering, Dobro, Everett, Flatiron, Gibson, James Goodall, Guild, Heritage, Hofner Basses, Kentucky, Larrivee, Lowden, Martin, National Reso-Phonic, Ovation, Parker Fly, Jose Ramirez, Bart Reiter, Rich & Taylor (banjos), Rickenbacker, Santa Cruz, Paul Reed Smith, Steinberger, Stelling, Taylor, Ted Thompson, Trace (acoustic amps), Trinity College, and Wildwood. There are pickups by DiMarzio, EMG, and Seymour Duncan, travel guitars, acoustic basses, cables, strings, straps, frets, mutes, capos, books, videos, and more. Written instrument appraisals and repairs are available, and if you're a collector or vintage instrument enthusiast, be sure to visit the website: Mandolin Brothers publishes its comprehensive listing of instruments in *Vintage News,* which may be read online, or you can subscribe (see the catalog or website for current rates). The site also has an excellent collection of links. Mandolin Brothers ships in-stock instruments on a three-day approval basis—and that includes vintage equipment. If you're in the Staten Island area, be sure to visit the well-stocked showroom, an official site on the "New York Music Trail," and try out the instruments.

Special Factors: Satisfaction is guaranteed; returns are accepted within three days.

MANNY'S MUSIC MAILBOX

▬▬▬▬▬▬▬

ATTN: MAILBOX MUSIC
156 W. 48TH ST.
NEW YORK, NY 10036
212–869–5172
FAX: 212–382–1446

Catalog: free
Pay: check, MO, MC, V, AE, DC, Discover
Sells: instruments, electronics, and accessories
Store: same address; Monday to Saturday 10–6; also Audio Technique, 1600 Broadway, New York, NY

Manny's has been selling musical instruments since 1935, and it's rare that this store on New York City's "Music Row" doesn't have a rock luminary or two checking out the equipment. The 104-page Manny's Music Mailbox catalog (call for a copy) testifies to the firm's illustrious history as a purveyor to the stars, and showcases the breadth of its inventory. All major brands are carried, and live sound, studio recording, computer software, keyboards, and MIDI products are available, as well as drums, guitars, amps, and accessories. Manny's also offers a complete line of band instruments. When you're in New York City, you're invited to stop in and see the photos of hundreds of musical celebrities lining the walls of the store.

Special Factors: Price quote by phone, fax, or letter with SASE.

METROPOLITAN MUSIC CO.

P.O. BOX 1415
STOWE, VT 05672
802–253–4814
FAX: 802–253–9834

Catalog: $1.25
Pay: check or MO
Sells: stringed instruments and accessories
Store: mail order only

Metropolitan Music Co., in business since 1928, sells stringed instruments and accessories through the 40-page catalog and maintains a workshop for repairs and adjustments. There are some "student" quality instruments here, but most of the models are chosen for professional musicians. Metropolitan carries John Juzek violins, violas, cellos, and basses, and bows by F.N. Voirin, Glasser, and Emile Dupree. Bridges, pegs by Taperfit and other firms, bow hair and parts, fingerboards, necks, chin rests, Resonans shoulder rests, Ibex tools, strings, cases, and bags are all stocked. This is an excellent source for the experienced musician who is familiar with the instruments and accessories. Books on instrument repair and construction are available, as well as a fine selection of wood, parts, and tools. The prices listed in the catalog are subject to discounts of 30% to 50%.

International readers, please note: Metropolitan Music can supply a list of worldwide distributors upon request, but does not handle overseas shipments.

Special Factors: Price quote by phone or letter with SASE; minimum order is $15.

MUSICIAN'S FRIEND

P.O. BOX 4520
MEDFORD, OR 97501
800–776–5173
FAX: 541–776–1370

Catalog: free
Pay: check, MO, MC, V, Discover
Sells: guitar, bass, and keyboard electronics, stage and studio gear, etc.
Store: 2570 Crater Lake Hwy., Medford, and 65J Division, Eugene, OR; also Totem Lake Mall, 12608 120th Ave. N.E., Kirkland, WA; Monday to Friday 10–8
Online: http://www.musiciansfriend.com

 ¡Si!

Musician's Friend garnered a ringing endorsement from a New York City performer who found the firm's service and selection preferable to the music emporiums of the city. Musician's Friend has been supplying the pros with recording equipment and electronics, including keyboards, guitars, bass, and recording gear, since 1981. (The catalogs are customized to your interest, so specify the instrument you play when you call or write.)

The catalog copy includes specs, list and discount prices, and equipment features; the brands include Alesis, ART, Boss, Charvel, DigiTech, DiMarzio, Epiphone, Fatar, Gibson, Ibanez, Jackson, Kawai, Korg, Kurzweil, Marantz, Marshall, Martin, Pignose, QSC, Rocktron, Roland, SansAmp, SKB, Sony, VOX, Washburn, Zoom, and others. You can send for the catalog, which details the terms of sale and returns policy and the "45-day price-protection plan," or call the toll-free line with the manufacturer's name and the model number of the equipment you want for a price quote. And don't miss the books and videos, which include guides to home recording, writing better lyrics, good stuff like Stevie Ray Vaughan's signature licks, and dozens of teaching tapes and method studies.

If you can get to the website, you'll find the catalog, and then some: product reviews, music software downloads, a free electronic newsletter, a directory of manufacturers' support numbers, a great page of links, and even a page for tracking your order.

Special Factors: Satisfaction is guaranteed; price quote by phone; authorized returns are accepted within 45 days for exchange, refund, or credit.

NATIONAL EDUCA-TIONAL MUSIC CO.

DEPT. WBMC
1181 RTE. 22
MOUNTAINSIDE, NJ 07092
908–232–6700
FAX: 908–789–3025

Catalog: free
Pay: check, MO, MC, V, AE
Sells: instruments and accessories
Store: mail order only

NEMC has been supplying schools with new band and orchestra instruments since 1957, at savings of up to 60% off the manufacturers' suggested list prices. NEMC sells brass, woodwind, stringed, and percussion instruments by Alpine, Amati, Blessing, Buffet, Decatur, DEG, F.E. Olds, Fox, Gemeinhardt, Getzen, Holton, International Strings, John Juzek, Korg, Larilee, Leblanc, Lewis, Ludwig, Meisel, Mirafone, Pearl, F.A. Reynolds, Ross, Schreiber, Vito, Zildjian, and other makers. The 64-page catalog also offers imported master violins and violas, as well as cases, stands, strings, bows, and other accessories. NEMC provides "the longest warranty in the industry" on woodwinds, drums, and brass and stringed (except fretted) instruments.

Please note: Only U.S. funds are accepted.

Special Factors: Returns (of instruments) are accepted within seven days (a restocking fee may be charged); minimum order is $50.

PATTI MUSIC COMPANY

DEPT. 39
P.O. BOX 1514
MADISON, WI 53701–1514
800–777–2884
FAX: 608–257–5847

Catalog: $2
Pay: check, MO, MC, V, Discover, JCB
Sells: sheet music, music books, teaching methods and aids, metronomes, etc.
Store: 414 State St., Madison WI; Monday to Friday 9:30–5:30, Saturday 9:30–5
E-mail: ajsmadsn@aol.com
Online: http://www.pattimusic.com

One of the hardest items to find at a discount is sheet music, but that's the raison d'être of Patti Music Company's mail-order department. Patti Music has been in business since 1936, and publishes a 192-page catalog of sheet music and books and teaching methods for piano and organ, including 10 pages of metronomes, tuners, and related products. Savings on the sheet music run around 15%, and the other goods are discounted up to 33%.

Piano methods, teaching solos, and ensembles are among the 17,000 titles featured in the catalog, representing music publishers from Alfred to Zimmermann. The catalog also lists repertoire and methods for organ, books and dictionaries for musicians and teachers, Christmas music, New Age music, music from movies and Broadway shows, plus manuscript paper, theory books, flash cards, and other teaching aids. The proficiency levels of the music and instructional material run from beginner to advanced. In addition to sheet music, there are metronomes from Franz, Matrix, Seiko, and Wittner, tuners from Korg and Seiko, piano and music furniture, music stands, and musical award and gift ideas.

Please note: The $2 catalog fee is waived for teachers or music professionals.

Special Factors: Discounts are available through the catalog only, not in the store.

SHAR PRODUCTS COMPANY

P.O. BOX 1411
ANN ARBOR, MI 48106
800–248–7427
800–793–4334
   (CUSTOMER SERVICE)
800–438–4538 (FINE
   INSTRUMENTS)
FAX: 313–665–0829

Catalog: free
Pay: check, MO, MC, V, Discover
Sells: sheet music, stringed instruments, videos, accessories
Store: 2465 S. Industrial Hwy., Ann Arbor, MI; Tuesday to Friday 9–6, Saturday 9–5

"Shar is managed by knowledgeable string players and teachers, who are sympathetic to the needs of the string community," states the firm, which has been in business since 1962 and sets prices up to 50% below list or full retail. The 64-page general catalog gives equal time to stringed instruments and to the firm's extensive collection of classical music videos and accessories. If you play violin, viola, cello, or bass, see the catalog for the cases, bows, chin and shoulder rests, strings, bridges, tailpieces, pegs, music stands, humidifying tubes, endpins, and other supplies and equipment. Student violins by Fischer, Hoffman, Schneider, and Suzuki are available, as well as a large collection of new, old, and rare violins by master violin makers.

The accessories catalog features hundreds of books of sheet music, manuals, videotapes, and audiocassettes. (The separate sheet music catalog, with thousands of titles, is available for $2.) Shar sells the Suzuki books and records line, videotapes of master artists (Casals, Segovia, Pavarotti, Heifetz, and others) in performance, classical recordings on CD, and sheet music for a wide range of instruments. Not all goods are discounted, but savings overall average 30%, and selected lines are offered at further savings periodically.

Canadian readers, please note: Personal checks are not accepted at the Ann Arbor location. Most of the products available in the U.S. store are also offered at Shar of Toronto, at 26 Cumberland St., Toronto, Ontario M4W 1J5, Canada; for current hours and stock availability, call 416–960–8494.

Special Factors: Satisfaction is guaranteed; C.O.D. orders are accepted.

SWORDS MUSIC COMPANIES INC.

4300 E. LANCASTER AVE.
FORT WORTH, TX
  76103–3225
800–522–3028
817–536–8742
FAX: 817–536–8745

Information: price quote
Pay: check, MO, MC, V
Sells: electronic and band instruments
Store: same address; Monday to Saturday 10:30–7, CT

Swords Music Companies has been selling music equipment and accessories since 1969 and offers savings of up to 50% on suggested list. You can call or write for availability and prices on guitars, drums, keyboards, amps, and band equipment from Akai, Alesis, Crate, DigiTech, DOD, E-MU, Fender, Fostex, Gibson, Hamer, Ibanez, Jackson, Korg, Leblanc, Ludwig, Marshall, Martin, Pearl, RCA, Roland, Shure, Sigma, Takamine, Tama, Watson, and Yorkville, among others. When you call for a quote, ask about Swords' "meet-or-beat" pricing, and details on the returns policy.

Special Factors Price quote by phone or letter with SASE; returns are accepted within 14 days for exchange, refund, or credit; minimum order is $50.

THOROUGHBRED MUSIC INC.

5511 PIONEER PARK BLVD.
TAMPA, FL 33634
800–800–4654
INTERNATIONAL:
813–889–3874
FAX: 813–881–1896

Catalog: free, $5 outside the U.S.
Pay: check, MO, MC, V, AE, Discover, NOVUS
Sells: music electronics and accessories
Store: stores in Clearwater, Sarasota, and Tampa, FL
E-mail: jarata@ix.netcom.com
Online: http://www.tbred-music.com/network/

Serious rock musicians and studio engineers should see the catalog from Thoroughbred Music, which showcases amps, CD and digital audiotape players and recorders, drum machines and effects boxes, MIDI equipment, special-effect lighting, matador timbales, and hundreds of other electronics and instruments (guitars and bass, banjos, mandolins, drums, etc.). The manufacturers represented include Akai, Audio Technica, dbx, Fostex, Gibson, Guild, Hartke, Ibanez, Jackson, Klipsch, Lexicon, Mackie, Marshall, Ovation, Pearl, Rickenbacker, Roland, Shure, Takamine, Tama, Tascam, Yamaha, and Zildjian. The catalog includes a number of pages of instructional books, tapes, and videos.

If you're in the Clearwater area, stop in to see who's playing at Thoroughbred's Kapok Pavilion. Catalog customers enjoy the same "guaranteed low prices" enjoyed in the store, and if you don't see what you're looking for, call—it may be available. And be sure to visit the website, which offers an online catalog, nearly 200 webpages of material at this writing, over 600 links, and lots of other goodies for the musician.

Special Factors: Satisfaction is guaranteed; price quote by phone or letter.

WEINKRANTZ MUSICAL SUPPLY CO., INC.

870 MARKET ST., SUITE 1265
SAN FRANCISCO, CA 94102–2907
800–736–8742
FAX: 415–399–1705

Catalog: free
Pay: check, MO, MC, V
Sells: stringed instruments and accessories
Store: same address; Monday to Friday 9–5, PST

Stringed instruments are the whole of Weinkrantz's business—violins, violas, cellos, and basses. Weinkrantz, founded in 1975, prices the instruments and accessories 30% to 50% below suggested retail. The 40-page catalog lists the available instruments and outfits, cases, music stands, metronomes, bows, strings, and other supplies. There are several pages of strings alone, including Jargar, Larsen, Pirastro, Prim, and Thomastik. Weinkrantz carries violins and violas by T.G. Pfretzschner, Roma, Ernst Heinrich Roth, and Roman Teller. Cellos by these firms and Karl Hauser, Wenzel Kohler, Lothar Semmlinger, and Anton Stohr are cataloged, as well as basses from Roth and Emanuel Wilfer. Instruments from well-known smaller workshops are also in stock, but not cataloged because of limited production. Call or write with specific requests.

If you don't want to buy an outfit, you can order the bow, case or bag, rosin, string adjusters, and other equipment à la carte. Strings, bow hair, chin rests, bridges, metronomes, and tuners are all sold at a discount. Instrument bags and cases by Gewa, Gordge, Jaeger, Reunion Blues, and Winter are also available.

Special Factors: Satisfaction guaranteed (see the catalog for the policy on strings).

WEST MANOR MUSIC

831 EAST GUN HILL RD.
BRONX, NY 10467-6109
718-655-5400
FAX: 718-655-1115

Price List: free
Pay: check, MO, MC, V
Sells: musical instruments
Store: same address; call for hours

West Manor Music has been supplying schools and institutions with musical instruments since 1956, and offers a wide range of equipment at average discounts of 45%. The 16-page catalog lists clarinets, flutes, piccolos, saxophones, oboes, trumpets, trombones, French horns, cornets, flugelhorns, euphoniums, Sousaphones, violas, violins, cellos, guitars, pianos, drums, cymbals, xylophones, glockenspiels, and other instruments. Drum stands and heads, strings, reeds, cases, music stands, metronomes, mouthpieces, and other accessories are sold. The brands represented include Alpine, Amati, Armstrong, Artley, Benge, Besson, Blessing, Buffet, Bundy, Conn, DEG, Fender, Fox, Gemeinhardt, Holton, King, Leblanc, Ludwig, Meisel, Noblet, Olds, Premier, Sabian, Selmer, Signet, Vito, and Zildjian, among others. All of the instruments sold are new, guaranteed for one year. West Manor also offers an "overhaul" service for popular woodwinds and brasses, and can perform repairs as well.

Special Factors: Quantity discounts are available; minimum order is $25, $100 with credit cards.

WRAY'S MUSIC HOUSE

326 MARKET ST.
LEMOYNE, PA 17043
888–761–8222
717–761–8222
FAX: 717–731–0568

Information: price quote
Pay: check, MO, MC, V, AE, Discover
Sells: musical instruments and electronics
Store: same address; Monday to Friday 10–7,
Saturday 10–5
Online: http://www.wrays.com

Wray's has brought the sound of music to Central Pennsylvania since 1955, and runs a very busy showroom serving area musicians. You can enjoy the store's selection, if not the ambiance, by visiting Wray's website, where you'll find both lists and pictures of the new and vintage equipment sold here—new and used guitars, amps, effects, synths, keyboards and pianos, percussion, MIDI, pro-audio gear, digital audiotape, and recording equipment. The names include AKG, Alesis, Ashly, Audio Technica, Behringer, Beyer, Crest, Crown, dbx, Drum, Digitech, Seymour Duncan, Electro-Voice, Epiphone, E.T.A., Fatar, Fender, Gibson, Guild, Hafler, Hart Dynamics, Kawai, Korg, Kurzweil, Latin Percussion, Lexicon, Mackie, Marshall, Mesa Boogie, Ness, Numark, Ovation, Peavey, Premier, PRS, Roland, Rolls, Sabian, Shure, Slingerland, Paul Reed Smith, Studio Master, Takamine, Tascam, Taylor, Telex, Toca, Yamaha, Zildjian, and Zoom. Wray's also offers an extensive selection of sheet music and lighting equipment—call with your needs.

Savings at Wray's can reach 50% on list, and the firm is run by seasoned musicians who know the equipment. If you can't get to the store or the website, you can call or write for prices on new equipment. And if you live in the greater Harrisburg area, you can visit both Wray's Music House and Do Wray Mi Pianos, which offers both acoustic and electronic models.

Special Factors: Satisfaction is guaranteed; returns are accepted for exchange, refund, or credit.

SEE ALSO

Audio House • used CDs • **BOOKS: RECORDINGS**
Berkshire Record Outlet, Inc. • classical recordings • **BOOKS: RECORDINGS**
Cherry Tree Toys, Inc. • music box parts • **CRAFTS: WOODCRAFT**
Dover Publications, Inc. • classical music scores • **BOOKS**
Wholesale Tape and Supply Company • tape duplicating machines and equipment • **APPLIANCES**

OFFICE AND BUSINESS

Office machines, furniture, and supplies; printing and related services

If you're still using a single source for your office needs, send for catalogs from a few of the vendors listed here, then pull your last few supply invoices. Compare prices—especially on items your firm uses in bulk. You're probably paying more than you should, and the perks you get from a dedicated supplier are also available from the discounters: open accounts, quick shipment, special orders, and custom services are now routine. The firms listed here sell supplies, printing services, office and institutional furnishings, and the countless products needed to run a business.

Several also sell computer hardware, software, and supplies, but you'll find firms specializing in systems and software listed in the next section, "Computing." Look there for computers and peripherals, software, ergonomic furniture, computer-related paper goods, maintenance supplies, and computer-related services.

Some of the firms in this section offer bulk pricing on garbage bags, mailroom supplies, and other packaging materials, but see the listings in "Office: Small Business," following "Computing," for the specialists.

For other sources of office furnishings (especially for the home office), see the "Find it Fast" section in the introduction to "Home: Furnishings."

FIND IT FAST

BUSINESS CARDS, STATIONERY, FORMS • *Brown Print, Iroquois, Lighthouse, Moore, Pennywise, Rapidforms, Sunrise*

CASH REGISTERS • **Business Technologies, Quill**
GENERAL OFFICE SUPPLIES • **Fidelity, OfficeMax, Pennywise, Quill, Reliable, Staples, Sunrise, Viking**
OFFICE FURNITURE • **Alfax, Business & Institutional Furniture, Dallas Midwest, Factory Direct Furniture, Frank Eastern, K-Log, National Business Furniture, OfficeMax, Pennywise, Quill, Reliable, Staples, Sunrise, Viking**
OFFICE MACHINES • **OfficeMax, Quill, Reliable, Staples, Sunrise, Viking**
PENS AND PEN REPAIRS • **Artlite, Fountain Pen Hospital**
POSTAL SCALES • **Triner Scale**
RECYCLED GOODS AND RECYCLING CONTAINERS • **Business & Institutional Furniture, Factory Direct Furniture, Quill, Reliable, Staples, Viking**
SAFES • **Quill, Safe Specialties, Staples, Value-tique, Viking**

ALFAX WHOLESALE FURNITURE

DEPT. C–1501
370 SEVENTH AVE., SUITE
1101
NEW YORK, NY
10001–3981
800–221–5710
212–947–9560
FAX: 800–638–6445
FAX: 212–947–4734

Catalog: free
Pay: check, MO, MC, V, AE
Sells: office and institutional furniture
Store: mail order only

 ¡Si!

Alfax has been selling office furnishings since 1946 and does a brisk business with institutional and commercial buyers, especially schools and churches. The best discounts are given on quantity purchases, but even individual items are reasonably priced.

The 100-page color catalog shows furnishings for offices, cafeterias, libraries, conference rooms, and even religious institutions. Tables and chairs are offered in several styles, as well as a range of files and literature storage systems. There are several pages of institutional nursery and child-care furnishings, play centers, cots, and accessories. Pulpits and lecterns, stackable padded pews, PA systems, trophy cases, carpet mats, lockers, hat racks, park benches, heavy steel shelving, prefabricated office and computer stations and workstations are just a few of the institutional furnishings and fixtures available. Representative brands include Abco, Bevis, BPI, Bretford, D.M.I., Globe, Harvard, High Point, Krueger, Lee, Luxor, Lyon Metal, Safco, Samsonite, Sauder, and Signor. Many products have home applications, and all of the equipment is designed for years of heavy use.

Special Factors: Satisfaction is guaranteed; institutional accounts and leasing are available.

ARTLITE OFFICE SUPPLY COMPANY

1851 PIEDMONT RD., NE
ATLANTA, GA 30324
800–327–7367
404–875–7271
FAX: 404–875–2623

Catalog: free
Pay: check, MO, MC, V, AE
Sells: writing instruments, briefcases, etc.
Store: same address; Monday to Friday 8–6, Saturday 9–5

 ¡Si!

Artlite has been supplying Atlanta with fine writing instruments and office supplies since 1964. The 48-page color catalog shows fountain pens, ballpoints, and mechanical pencils by Aurora, Cartier, Cross, MontBlanc, Montegrappa, Namiki, OMAS, Parker, Pelikan, Sheaffer, Tombow, Waterford, and Waterman. Artlite also sells briefcases, portfolios, organizers and agendas, albums, desk sets, clocks, pen cases, and other executive accessories by Bosca, Kenneth Cole, Filofax, Scully, Charles Underwood, and other manufacturers.

Savings average 20%, but reach over 30% on certain brands and models. Artlite's superb selection and services—pen monogramming and engraving, corporate gifts, and expert advice—make this a great source for pen neophytes as well as the collector.

Special Factors: Returns in original packaging are accepted within 60 days for exchange, refund, or credit.

BROWN PRINT & CO.

P.O. BOX 935
TEMPLE CITY, CA 91780
818–286–2106
FAX: 818–287–7307

Price List and Samples: $2
Pay: check or MO
Sells: custom-designed business cards
Store: mail order only

Brown Print & Co. has been designing and printing business cards and stationery since 1966 and offers the person looking for something different just that. Mr. Brown, the proprietor, will send you a generous assortment of actual samples, ranging from black glossy stock and gold foil with iridescent metallic colors to standard black and white cards with raised inks and artwork. Fold-overs and other unusual formats are also available. Mr. Brown's talents would be wasted on someone who wanted a conventional card; his specialty is unusual design, and he enjoys working with his customers to create "the amusing, the novel, and other effective visual concepts."

Special Factors: Quantity discounts are available; minimum order is 250 or 500 cards.

BUSINESS & INSTITUTIONAL FURNITURE COMPANY, INC.

BOX 92039
MILWAUKEE, WI
   53202–0039
800–558–8662
414–272–6080
FAX: 800–468–1526
FAX: 414–272–0248

Catalog: free
Pay: check, MO, MC, V, AE, Discover
Sells: office and institutional furnishings
Store: mail order only; phone hours Monday to Friday 7–7, Saturday 8–2, CT
E-mail: bi@bi-furniture.com
Online: http://www.bi-furniture.com

Although the best prices at B & I are found on quantity purchases, even individual pieces of furniture and office equipment are competitively priced. The 84-page "business" catalog is devoted to office furnishing basics, and includes a range of items appropriate for waiting and reception rooms, home offices, and studies. B & I has been in business since 1960, and offers a lowest-price guarantee (see the catalog for terms).

The office furniture includes desks, files, bookcases, credenzas, and panels and panel systems (for office partitioning). The seating runs from stacking lunchroom chairs to leather-upholstered ergonomic executive thrones—reception, clerical, specialty, folding—they're all here. There are data- and literature-storage units, computer workstations, waste cans, mats, announcement boards, outdoor furniture, energy-saving devices, and much more. Over 250 brands are represented, and B & I can provide space planning and design services, free of charge. B & I also publishes a "school" catalog of everything from auditorium seating to overhead projectors, all at a discount. You can call for a free copy of either catalog, or order them online from the website.

Special Factors: "15-year, no-risk guarantee"; volume discounts are available.

BUSINESS
TECHNOLOGIES

3350 CENTER GROVE DR.
DUBUQUE, IA 52003–5225
800–451–0399
319–556–7994
FAX: 319–556–2512

Catalog: free
Pay: company check, MO, MC, V
Sells: cash registers and related supplies
Store: same address; Monday to Friday 8:30–5

Business Technologies sells Sharp cash registers and supplies for just about every other cash register brand. Upon inquiry, you'll receive manufacturers' brochures, a selection guide, and a roster of optional accessories that can customize the register to the needs of your business. Even the "simple" machines have programmable tax and percentage capabilities, and the top-of-the-line models are built-in bookkeepers and gofers: One system allows a restaurant to track employees' tips, guests' balances, and even transmit orders to a printer in the kitchen. Other features include management reports, credit authorization, currency conversion, and scanner functions, among others (depending on the model). Prices at Business Technologies average 30% below list, and the firm provides technical support, a one-year warranty, and free programming.

Special Factors: Price quote by phone, fax, or letter; minimum order is $25.

DALLAS MIDWEST

4100 ALPHA RD.,
SUITE 111
DALLAS, TX 75244
972–866–0101
FAX: 972–866–9433

Catalog: free
Pay: check, MO, MC, V, AE
Sells: office and institutional furniture
Store: mail order only

  ⊕ ¡Si!

The Dallas Midwest catalog runs fewer than 100 pages, but showcases furnishings and fixtures for hospitals, schools, nurseries, and churches, as well as offices. In addition to executive desks and chairs, Dallas Midwest sells conference furniture, partitions and dividers for cubicles, computer and AV carts and workstations, wooden and metal files, and all sorts of folding and adjustable work tables. There's a good selection of stacking chairs—padded, molded, and wooden—and heavy-duty folding chairs in metal and wood. Many of these items can be used in institutional settings, as well as the indoor and outdoor sign boards, crowd-control post and rope systems, mobile stages and risers, lecterns, and shelving.

If you're purchasing for a school or day care center or need sturdy, child-sized equipment, see the pages of classroom desks and chairs, stools, maple plywood storage units for toys and books, canvas sling cots and map mats, easels, play sinks and stoves made of birch, activity tables in various shapes, oak tables and chairs, and even a sandbox, slide, seesaws, and a wooden playground set. The church furnishings include pulpits, kneelers, credence tables, communion tables, and stands, and include a well-priced line of unfinished pieces in solid oak. (A separate catalog devoted to unfinished furnishings for school and church is available upon request.)

Dallas Midwest also sells heavy-duty library shelving and book carts, park benches, picnic tables, bike racks, and such useful things as folding lecterns and the "Lightning" boards that can be used with markers, chalk, crayons, slides, and magnetic and adhesive products. The brands include ABCO, Allied, Balt, Bevis, Car Stone, ChairWorld, DMI Furniture, Durham, Fixture World, Globe, High Point, Howell, Imperial, KFI, KI, La-Z-Boy, Luxor, Meilink, MicroCentre, RAM, Samsonite, Screenflex, Signore, Sirco, Stoway, UltraPlay, and Virco. Dallas Midwest discounts 30% to 50% on list prices and offers special savings on orders over $1,000. All products carry a 15-year warranty against defects in material and workmanship.

Institutions, please note: Terms are net 30 days for qualifying institutions, and a 2% discount is given for orders paid by check.

Special Factors: Price quote by phone; quantity discounts are available; authorized returns are accepted for exchange, refund, or credit; institutional accounts are available.

FACTORY DIRECT FURNITURE

P.O. BOX 92967
MILWAUKEE, WI 53202
800–972–6570
414–289–9770
FAX: 414–289–9946

Catalog: free
Pay: check, MO, MC, V, AE
Sells: office furniture and institutional equipment
Store: mail order only

The 80-page catalog from Factory Direct Furniture features some of the best buys around on office furniture, filing cabinets, bookcases, seating, workstations, storage units, office panel systems, and institutional furnishings. Factory Direct Furniture has been in business since 1974, and carries ergonomic seating for the executive as well as support staff, a full range of files, panel systems, computer workstations and work centers, bulletin and announcement boards, reception furniture, lockers, stacking chairs, and conference furniture. The manufacturers represented include Allied, Balt, Bevis, BPI (office panels), Diversified, DMI, Edsal, Excel, FireKing, Ghent, Global Furniture, Globe, Hale, Harvard, High Point, Integra, Jefsteel, Krueger, La-Z-Boy, Lee, MLP, National, Planto, SafCo, Samsonite, Sauder, Signore, Sirco, Stylex, and Virco, among others. Savings of 40% are routine, and a number of items are tagged 70% below manufacturers' list prices.

Please note: Factory Direct Furniture offers a 10-year guarantee on everything it sells, normal wear and tear excepted. See the catalog for details on the warranty and the firm's "meet or beat" pricing policy.

Special Factors: Satisfaction is guaranteed; quantity discounts are available.

FIDELITY PRODUCTS CO.

5601 INTERNATIONAL
  PARKWAY
P.O. BOX 155
MINNEAPOLIS, MN
  55440–0155
800–328–3034
FAX: 800–842–2725

Catalog: free
Pay: check, MO, MC, V, AE, Discover
Sells: office supplies, shipping supplies, graphics products, etc.
Store: mail order only
E-mail: Bwagner@libertydifersified.com
Online: http://www.fidelityproducts.com

Fidelity, established in 1961, is one of the country's biggest suppliers of corrugated storage and general business products. The 68-page catalog features a broad selection of heavy-duty file units, as well as shipping supplies, scales, parts bins, industrial shelving, ladders, dollies, hand trucks, lockers, and more. The prices represent average savings of 40% on list prices, and quantity discounts are offered on many items.

Fidelity also publishes a 68-page graphics catalog of tools and supplies for architects, engineers, contractors, and anyone doing desktop publishing and computer-aided design. Here are drawing boards and tables, computer furniture, light boxes and projection equipment, studio furniture, lighting, Pantone color charts, Brother and Kroy lettering equipment, a wide range of writing instruments and markers, paper and production supplies, portfolios, plotter media, flat files and roll storage, and much more. Spot checks showed that prices are an average 30% below list, and quantity pricing is offered as well.

Please note: Specify your area of interest (office supplies, shipping items, graphics products) when calling or writing for the catalog.

Special Factors: Satisfaction is guaranteed; price quote by phone; quantity discounts are available; returns (in original packing) are accepted within 30 days for exchange, refund, or credit.

FOUNTAIN PEN HOSPITAL

10 WARREN ST.
NEW YORK, NY 10007
800–253–PENS
212–964–0580
FAX: 212–227–5916

Catalog: free (see text)
Pay: check, MO, MC, V, AE, Discover
Sells: fountain pens, writing instruments, and repair services
Store: same address; Monday to Friday 8–5:45
E-mail: fountainpenhospital@worldnet.att.net
Online: http://www.fountainpenhospital.com

The Fountain Pen Hospital has been restoring fine fountain pens to health since 1946, and does a brisk business in vintage pens and new models—at a routine 20% off list, to 40% on some lines and models. The 64-page pen catalog shows writing instruments from Aurora, Bexley, Bossert & Erhard, Caran d'Ache, Colibri, Cross, Delta, Ecobra, Élyseé, Eversharp, Lamy, Le Boeuf, Marlen, MontBlanc, Montegrappa, Namiki, OMAS, Parker, Pelikan, Michel Perchin, Platinum, Quill, Reform, Retro 51, Rotring, Sensa, Sheaffer, S.T. Dupont, Stipula, Tombow, Visconti, Waterman, and Yafa. There are handsome leather pen cases, satin-lined chests that can accommodate up to 52 pens and pencils, refills (ink cartridges, leads, erasers, etc.), Filofax agendas, books on pen collecting, and desk accessories.

In addition to the yearly catalog, Fountain Pen Hospital publishes a quarterly catalog featuring new arrivals and best buys. "Vintage Pen Quarterly," a roundup of the current selection of rare and vintage pens and pencils is also available—over 170 were shown in the review copy of the catalog (a stapled sheaf of photocopied pages, $10 for a year's subscription). You can also call or write to inquire about the availability of specific old or new models, or ask about the procedure for sending in a pen for repair.

Special Factors: Satisfaction is guaranteed; price quote by phone or letter; returns are accepted within seven days for exchange, refund, or credit; minimum order is $10.

FRANK EASTERN CO.

599 BROADWAY
NEW YORK, NY
10012–3258
212–219–0007, EXT. 311
FAX: 212–219–0722

Catalog: $1
Pay: check, MO, MC, V
Sells: office, institutional, and computer furniture
Showroom: same address; Monday to Friday 9–5

 ¡Si!

Frank Eastern, in business since 1946, offers furnishings and equipment for business and home offices at discounts of up to 60% on list and comparable retail. Specials are run in every 72-page catalog. Frank Eastern's offerings include desks, chairs, filing cabinets, bookcases, storage units, computer workstations, and wall systems and panels. Seating is especially well represented: ergonomic, executive, clerical, drafting, waiting room, conference, folding, and stacking models in wood, leather, chrome, and plastic are shown in the catalog. Ergonomic seating is a Frank Eastern specialty, and the prices here are a good 25% less than those listed in two comparable office-supply catalogs. Manufacturers represented include Allied, BPI, Global Furniture, Globe Business, Jefsteel, Sauder, and Sirco. Don't overlook good buys on solid oak bookcases, wall organizers, lateral filing cabinets, and mobile computer workstations.

Special Factors: Satisfaction is guaranteed; quantity discounts are available; minimum order is $75 with credit cards.

IROQUOIS PRODUCTS CO.

2220 W. 56TH ST.
CHICAGO, IL 60636–1099
800–453–3355
773–436–3900
FAX: 773–436–4908

Catalog: free
Pay: check, MO, MC, V, AE
Sells: packing and shipping supplies
Store: mail order only; phone hours Monday to Friday 8–5 CT

 ¡Si!

Iroquois Products bills itself as "Packaging and Shipping Supplies Specialists," and offers more kinds of polypropylene and PVC tape alone than most office-supply firms. (The "no chatter" PVC tape promises to "come off the roll silently.") There's a choice of other types—kraft-gummed, filament reinforced, strapping, duct, masking, and conventional office tape—and dispensers are available as well. Cartons and mailers are stocked in hundreds of sizes, from a 4" cube to 36" by 35" by 40", as well as multidepth mailers, crush-proof boxes, book boxes, floppy disk and printout mailers, and padded envelopes, foam and bubble sheeting, packing peanuts, cellulose wadding, poly bags, and poly and steel strapping and related tools. The box of 6,500 feet of heavy-duty poly twine represents savings of at least 60% compared to buying it locally in 250-foot coils—just one example of the easy savings Iroquois offers on everyday needs. Poly bags, antifatigue mats, shop towels, "bags-of-rags," and other shipping room and janitorial supplies are available.

Iroquois also produces custom-printed labels in a range of sizes, shapes, and colors for shipping and mailing (including tractor-fed and laser-compatible formats), as well as for warnings, instructions, inventory-control, advertising, etc. Prices on all of the goods are competitive in small amounts, and quantity discounts push savings to 50% and more.

Special Factors: Satisfaction is guaranteed; price quote by phone; quantity discounts are available; authorized returns are accepted within 90 days for exchange, refund, or credit; institutional accounts are available (net 30 days).

K-LOG, INC.

P.O. BOX 5
ZION, IL 60099–0005
800–872–6611
847–872–6611
FAX: 847–872–3728

Catalog: free
Pay: check, MO, MC, V
Sells: office, A/V, and computer furniture and equipment
Store: mail order only

K-Log can outfit every department in the company, from the executive suite to the shipping room. The office furniture, much of which is suitable for schools, includes desks and tables, a wide range of seating, filing cabinets, literature racks, shelving, wall-panel systems, easels, bulletin boards, and display systems. The AV section includes projectors and screens, PA systems, electronic presentation systems and components, and equipment carts and tables. And over a third of the catalog shows computer furniture—components and space-saving workstations, including models that position the monitor below the desktop (it's viewed through a glare-shielded cutout), computer workstations, carrels, and computer-study units designed for wheelchair access. K-Log pledges to "sell lower than any competitor's published price" for identical products.

Please note: Unless the catalog copy states otherwise, all goods are shipped unassembled.

Special Factors: Price quote by phone or letter; quantity discounts are available; authorized returns are accepted (a restocking fee may be charged) for exchange, refund, or credit; institutional accounts are available.

LIGHTHOUSE COLORPRINT

DEPT. WBMC
P.O. BOX 465
SAINT JOSEPH, MI
 49085–0465
616–428–7062, EXT. 2
FAX: 616–428–0847

Order Kit and Samples: $5, refundable (see text)
Pay: check or MO
Sells: color printing services
Store: mail order only

   ★

If you're looking for an understated business card on engraved stock, keep dialing. Lighthouse Colorprint produces calling cards that won't disappear in anyone's wallet—they feature a full-color photograph of you, or your building, your delivery van, your product line—in short, whatever image you want clients to associate with your firm. Lighthouse cites its own marketing studies that show full-color business cards are held longer and generate more sales than any other medium. The pricing includes typesetting, layout, photo scanning, color separations, and full color proofs. The resolution of 200 lines per inch—up to 50% higher than the industry standard—helps to preserve the quality of the image.

Lighthouse Colorprint believes that it can meet your best price, if not beat it, and "the larger the order, the lower the price per piece." For example, a standard photographic business card job goes from 22¢ each for 1,000 to 7¢ on orders of 3,750 or more; 4" by 6" postcards drop from

33¢ each at 1,000 to 6¢ at 15,000. (Making fair comparisons can be difficult, since no two jobs are identical—from the prep to the specs to the time frame—but customers have reported savings of up to 75%.) The $5 fee Lighthouse charges for the "Custom Order Kit" brings you price lists, order forms, samples of business cards, postcards, and brochures, and a $25 certificate that "may be redeemed on any order," says the firm. The samples demonstrate the print quality, typography, and paper stock and finish, and the price lists detail extra options and charges. Anticipate some back-and-forth on type specs and color, options, proofs, and other details—just as you would with a walk-in print house.

Wholesale buyers, please note: A resale number is required for the wholesale discount of 20% on regular rates.

Special Factors: Price quote by phone or letter; quantity discounts are available; minimum order is 1,000 pieces.

MOORE BUSINESS PRODUCTS

P.O. BOX 5000
701 WOODLANDS
  PARKWAY
VERNON HILLS, IL
  60061–9926
800–323–6230
847–367–3000
FAX: 800–329–6667

Catalog: free
Pay: check, MO, MC, V, AE, Discover
Sells: business forms, desktop publishing and presentation forms
Store: mail order only
Online: http://www.moorebsd.com/

The Moore Business Products catalog features continuous forms (single and multiple) and checks, preprinted and ready to run through your accounting, payroll, or other software program. The list of compatible software covers hundreds of titles, the forms can be produced for manual or typewriter use, and other customizing options allow you to tailor the forms to your needs and have a logo imprinted. The prices are lower than those charged by local print shops even on small orders of 250 pieces, and 50%-plus on quantities of 2,000 or more. Invoices, statements, payroll vouchers, checks, self-mailers, letterhead, envelopes, labels, and related forms are offered, as well as blank and lined printout paper, postcards, business cards, and rotary cards.

Moore's separate "Image Street" catalog shows laser stationery suites—coordinated sets of letterhead, envelopes, mailing labels, business cards, announcement cards, brochure forms, and other items—designed to reflect different business personalities. Image Street also sells formatted newsletters, heavy-coated laser papers, bordered cards and invitations, certificates and awards forms, presentation folders, placards, die-cut tent cards, and place cards. The bookshelf includes desktop publishing classics, primers on writing copy, publicity handbooks, and even label-formatting and forms software. Image Street can also provide printing services in conjunction with selected software programs (also available), which can reportedly cut your printing costs by half, and reduce the turnaround time by as much as two-thirds. It's a great way to upgrade your business image without breaking the budget. Moore also publishes a catalog for the health-care professional, with forms and other office needs created expressly for the needs of a medical practice.

Special Factors: Satisfaction is guaranteed; request catalog by type or order from the website; quantity discounts are available; returns are accepted for exchange, refund, or credit; institutional accounts are available; minimum order is $30.

NATIONAL BUSINESS FURNITURE, INC.

735 N. WATER ST.
P.O. BOX 92952
MILWAUKEE, WI 53202
414–276–8511
FAX: 414–276–8371

Catalog: free
Pay: check, MO, MC, V, AE
Sells: office and computer furnishings
Store: mail order only

 ¡Si!

You can furnish your office for less through the 164-page catalog from National Business Furniture, which offers everything from announcement boards to portable offices at savings of up to 64%. NBF has been in business since 1975 and sells office systems, desks and tables for every purpose, credenzas, bookcases, shelving, computer workstations, desk organizers, literature racks, service carts, lockers, floor mats, reception furniture, and much more. The selection is super: There's a range of filing cabinets, and an extensive line of seating, including executive, clerical, luxury, ergonomic, conference, folding, stacking, and reception chairs. The manufacturers include DMI, Fire King, Global, Harvard,

High Point Furniture, KI, La-Z-Boy Chair, Miller Desk, National Office Furniture, Safco, Samsonite, Sauder, Signore, Stylex, and Workspace, among others.

Special Factors: Price quote by phone or letter with SASE; quantity discounts are available.

OFFICEMAX, INC.

3605 WARRENSVILLE
CENTER RD.
SHAKER HEIGHTS, OH
44122–5203
800–788–8080

Catalog: free
Pay: check, MO, MC, V, AE, Discover, OfficeMax account
Sells: office supplies and equipment
Store: stores nationwide (call for nearest location)
Online: http://www.officemax.com

OfficeMax, with over 575 locations, is one of the country's largest office products superstore chains. The stores themselves offer discounts of up to 70% on thousands of office and computer products, while the color catalog showcases the best-selling items—from paper clips to computers—and includes list prices, the OfficeMax discount prices, and your savings. You'll recognize the brands: Acco, Avery, Compaq, Cross, Dennison, Digital, Eldon, Epson, Global, Hewlett-Packard, IBM, Lotus, Macintosh, MontBlanc, O'Sullivan, Rolodex, Sentry, Smead, Texas Instruments, and Xerox are a few. If you don't see what you want in the catalog, it can probably be special-ordered from the master catalog at all OfficeMax stores. Shipping is free on orders of $50 or more if you're within the trading area of an OfficeMax store. Call for locations, and the current catalog.

OfficeMax has a website at http://www.officemax.com/ and is also online with America Online (Keyword: OfficeMax).

Special Factors: Satisfaction is guaranteed; shipping is free on orders of $50 or more within designated store areas.

PENNYWISE OFFICE PRODUCTS

Catalog: free
Pay: check, MO, MC, V, AE, Discover
Sells: office supplies, equipment, and furniture
Store: mail order only

6911 LAUREL BOWIE RD.,
SUITE 209
BOWIE, MD 20715
800–942–3311
301–699–1000
FAX: 301–277–6700

Pennywise has been in the discount office supply arena for over a decade, and uses a time-honored formula: low prices on everyday office needs, and free shipping on qualifying orders. Place an order from the 64-page catalog of specials, and you'll receive the "big book" that showcases over 18,000 products. Both list and the Pennywise discount prices are listed, and a number of items that are usually sold by the box are available here by the piece—helpful if your pens keep drying up before you can use them. In addition to supplies, Pennywise sells office furniture, electronics, some peripherals, and business services—rubber stamps, business cards and stationery, printed envelopes and binders, embossing stamps, imprinted pens and gifts, and more. Orders of $25 or more (with some exceptions) are delivered free within the United States, and open accounts are available.

Wholesale buyers, please note: Pennywise *does not* sell goods for resale.

Special Factors: Satisfaction is guaranteed; shipping is not charged.

QUILL CORPORATION

Catalog: free (see text)
Pay: check, MO, MC, V, AE
Sells: office supplies and equipment
Store: mail order only
Online: http://www.quillcorp.com

100 SCHELTER RD.
LINCOLNSHIRE, IL
60069–3621
800–789–1331
FAX: 800–789–8955

Quill, founded in 1956, offers businesses, institutions, and professionals savings of up to 80% on a wide range of office supplies and equipment.

There are real buys on Quill's house brand of office and computer supplies, which are comparable in performance and quality to name brands costing much more. Quill's semiannual 600-plus-page "big book" is augmented with monthly 72-page catalogs featuring specials and general office supplies and equipment, including files, envelopes, mailers, supplies for typewriters, word processors, and printers. In addition to everyday needs—labels, scissors, paper trimmers, pens and pencils, etc.—Quill sells copiers and supplies, word processors, telephones, fax machines, binders and machines, dictating machines, accounting supplies, office furnishings, and much more. Quill's custom department offers competitive prices on custom-imprinted letterhead, labels, mailers, forms, cards, signs, and stamps.

In addition to the general editions, Quill publishes specialty catalogs of shipping supplies, computer products, desktop publishing (laser and inkjet supplies), presentation equipment and supplies, business furniture, school supplies, calendars, and holiday cards and stationery. You can order any of the specialty catalogs (as well as products) from the website, and learn about special offers and promotions.

Please note: Quill does business with companies and professionals. Terms (30 days net) are available to qualified businesses. Goods are *not* shipped outside the U.S.

Special Factors: Satisfaction is guaranteed; institutional accounts are available; returns are accepted; minimum order is $25.

RAPIDFORMS, INC.

301 GROVE RD.
THOROFARE, NJ 08086
800–257–8354
FAX: 800–422–8113

Catalog: free (see text)
Pay: check, MO, MC, V, AE
Sells: business forms and products
Store: mail order only

Rapidforms offers five different specialty catalogs featuring a wide range of business forms designed for every commercial purpose, which are formatted to expedite routine transactions. The firm has been doing business since 1939, and emphasizes commitment to service and quality products.

The "Manufacturing and Wholesale" catalog features invoices, purchase orders, bills of lading, export forms, shipping products, checks, stationery, and labels in various sizes, shapes, and designs. In the "Retail" catalog, you'll find a complete line of sales slips, plastic and paper bags, gift certificates, pricing guns and labels, garment tags, security systems, and other retail merchandising products. The "Contractor" catalog offers specialty forms and products, such as proposals, job invoices, work orders, estimating forms, change orders, and subcontractor agreements. The "Holiday Card" catalog, published in late summer, showcases a variety of seasonal greetings. And the "Omni," or full-line catalog, is a collection of forms and products from each of the specialty catalogs, as well as forms for the repair service and automotive trades. Each forms catalog also includes a line of continuous computer forms, with a compatibility index for numerous software programs.

Special Factors: Request the catalog desired *by title;* shipping is not charged on prepaid orders; C.O.D. orders are accepted.

RELIABLE CORP.

P.O. BOX 1502
OTTAWA, IL 61350-9914
800-359-5000
FAX: 800-326-3233

Catalog: free
Pay: check, MO, MC, V, AE, Discover
Sells: office supplies and equipment
Store: mail order only
E-mail: CustomerService@reliable.com
Online: http://www.reliable.com

Reliable's commitment to giving deep discounts to small businesses has been its strong suit since 1918. The firm's big catalog, published twice a year, features thousands of products from nationally known manufacturers—from Ampad legal tablets to Xerox copier cartridges. Discounts run to 80% on list prices, and you *don't* have to buy in huge quantities to save. Reliable augments the general book with a slew of specialty catalogs: business furniture, computer supplies and accessories, home office, desktop printing, shipping and warehouse supplies, and seasonal items. You'll receive separate catalogs based on what you order from the big book and general sales catalogs, or you can request them—by phone or the website. And Reliable backs everything it sells with an unconditional assurance of satisfaction.

Special Factors: Satisfaction is guaranteed; institutional accounts are available; minimum order is $25.

SAFE SPECIALTIES, INC.

10932 MURDOCK RD.,
SUITE 104–05A
KNOXVILLE, TN 37932
800–695–2815
423–675–2815
FAX: 423–675–2850

Catalog: $2
Pay: check, MO, MC, V, AE, Discover
Sells: home and office safes
Store: same address (Exit 374, off I–40);
Monday to Friday 10–6, Saturday 10–2
E-mail: sspecial.vic.com

Safe Specialties, Inc., has been selling home and office safes since 1989, and offers popular home and office models at an average of 30% off list prices. If you're shopping for a depository safe, pistol box, gun safe, secured box for your RV or truck, a data or diskette safe, in-wall or in-floor safe, fire-resistant file cabinet, or hotel safe, try Safe Specialties: Models from Amsec, Cannon, Crystal Vault, DeCoy, FireKing, Ft. Knox, Hayman, Homak, Liberty, Meilink, Star, and other firms are available, at competitive prices. Money-handling equipment—cash drawers, coin counters, money bags, and related products—are also offered, as well as mailroom supplies and mailboxes.

Special Factors: Inquire for information on shipping rates and methods.

STAPLES, INC.

ATTN: STAPLES DIRECT
8 TECHNOLOGY DR.
WESTBOROUGH, MA
01581–1727
800–333–3330
FAX: 800–333–3199

Catalog: free
Pay: check, MO, MC, V, AE, Discover, Staples Charge
Sells: office supplies, furniture, and business machines
Store: 550 stores in the U.S. and Canada
Online: http://www.staples.com

Staples delivers "The Price Revolution in Office Products," an office superstore with deep discounts on every item. Staples was founded in 1986 and has earned a loyal following among buyers for small and home offices, as well as larger firms. Staples publishes a 280-page catalog of products with the "catalog list" prices and the Staples price.

These are first-quality products from Acco, Adams (forms), Alvin, Apple Computer, AT&T, Bates, Brother, Canon, Casio, Cross, Curtis, Dell, Dennison Carter's, Eldon, Esselte, Faber Castell, GBC, Globe-Weis, Hammermill, Hewlett-Packard, IBM, Maxell, MontBlanc, Murata, Olympus (recorders), Panasonic, Parker, Phone-Mate, Ricoh, Rolodex, Rubbermaid, SCM, Sentry (safes), Sharp, Sony, Southworth (paper), Texas Instruments, 3M, Vanguard, Velobind, Verbatim, Waterman (pens), and Wilson Jones, among others. You can order office furniture, computers and supplies, paper and forms, filing supplies, business cases, calendars, pens and pencils, adhesives, mailing room supplies, janitorial products, fax machines, copiers, phones and phone machines, and much more through the catalog or by phone. If there's a trade-off for the savings and product choice, it's in *options,* like color or odd sizes.

One of the features that's endeared Staples to legions of firms and home-office buyers nationwide is free next-day delivery on orders over $50 (within the store trading area, with some exceptions for furniture). Staples also offers a 150% price protection plan (see the catalog for details), and can provide furniture assembly services within the local trading area.

Canadian readers, please note: Business Depot Direct is the catalog delivery division of Staples within Canada.

Special Factors: Returns in original packaging are accepted within 90 days (30 days for software, unopened) for exchange, refund, or credit.

SUNRISE BUSINESS PRODUCTS

43 ROYALSTON LN.
CENTEREACH, NY
 11720–1414
800–222-PENS
516–698–0700
FAX: 516–698–0837,
 718–937–3171

Catalog: free (see text)
Pay: check, MO, MC, V, AE, Discover
Sells: office supplies and equipment
Store: mail order only
E-mail: sunrise1@mail.idt.net
Online: http://www.sun-rise.com

When you send for a catalog from Sunrise you'll receive the 36-page roundup of best-selling office supplies; order from that, and you'll receive the mammoth office supply catalog. Sunrise is using the techniques of the superstores but going them better on price on some items, and on product selection and delivery ($35 is the floor for free delivery, not the $75 customarily set). The stock is what you'd expect from a firm that can offer over 60,000 items, deliver furniture free and set it up (with some limits), perform document printing and binding, check printing, and "print-on-demand" services (no prepress or Veloxing required). Sunrise has been in business since 1953, and commits to next-day delivery on orders placed by 5 p.m. ET. If you don't see what you're looking for in the catalog you receive, just call for availability and pricing—it may be in the warehouse.

Special Factors: Satisfaction is guaranteed; price quote by phone or letter; shipping is included on orders over $35; quantity discounts are available; returns in original packaging are accepted within one week of delivery for exchange, refund, or credit (a restocking fee of 20% applies after 7 days, and no returns are accepted after 30 days).

TRINER SCALE

2842 SANDERWOOD
MEMPHIS, TN 38118
901–363–7040
FAX: 901–363–3114

Flyer: free
Pay: check, MO, MC, V, Discover
Sells: manual and electronic scales
Store: same address; Monday to Friday
8–4:30

Triner Scale, which was founded in 1897, sells a full line of mechanical and electronic scales. Triner also sells a pocket scale, a precision instrument that weighs things (up to four ounces). A finger ring permits the scale to hang while measurements are taken; the thing to be weighed is secured with an alligator clip. Suggested uses include postage determination (a rate chart is included), food measurement, lab use, craft and hobby use, and weighing herbs. It's a useful item to have on hand, and it can give you accurate readings of postage costs. The pocket scale costs under $10, and the electronic miniscales, $125; inquire for information.

Wholesale buyers: Quantity pricing begins at $6.50 for 1 to 20 units.
Special Factors: Shipping is not charged.

20TH CENTURY PLASTICS, INC.

P.O. BOX 2376
BREA, CA 92622–2376
714–441–4500
FAX: 714–441–4550

Catalog: free
Pay: check, MO, MC, V, AE, Discover
Sells: photo albums and accessories, binders, organizers, etc.
Store: mail order only

¡Si!

20th Century Plastics helps you save your memories with a wide selection of archival photo and slide storage sheets and albums, as well as safekeepers for your collections of stamps, baseball cards, recipes, and periodicals. The 60-page, color catalog also features a variety of binders and report covers, as well as photo albums, video- and audiocassette portfolios, static-proof floppy disk storage, CD storage, and business-card files. The prices of the archival quality photo storage products are excellent, and there are especially good prices on the albums. Whether you're organizing snapshots at home or creating a storage and filing system for a large office, you'll find solutions at 20th Century Plastics.

Please note: Specify the "photo" or "business" catalog when you call or write.

Special Factors: Satisfaction is guaranteed; returns are accepted within 30 days for exchange, refund, or credit.

VALUE-TIQUE, INC.

P.O. BOX 67, DEPT. WBM
LEONIA, NJ 07605
201–461–6500

Catalog: $1 (in cash, see text)
Pay: check, MO, MC, V, AE, DC, Discover
Sells: Sentry safes, fireproof files, media safes and storage chests
Store: Discount Safe Outlet, 117 Grand Ave., Palisades Park, NJ; Monday to Friday 9–5, Saturday 9–1
Online: http://www.cwn.com/discountsafe

Value-tique has been selling home and office safes since 1968, and offers a range of well-known brands at discounts of 25% and more. Your savings are actually greater because Value-tique also pays for shipping. And the $1 catalog fee (cash is requested) buys a $5 credit certificate, good on any purchase. Value-tique sells Sentry Safes, the EDP Media-Safe and media chests for computer disk storage, a standard home and office safe, and different wall safes. Elsafe, Gardall, Knight, Meilink, and Star safes are also available, as well as Pro-Steel gun safes. Models include wall and in-floor safes, cash-drop safes, styles with digital keypad push-button locks, and many others for home and business use. If you're not sure of the best type for your security purposes, call Value-tique to discuss your needs. Before ordering, *measure* to be sure the safe will fit the intended location.

Special Factors: Shipping is free in the contiguous 48 United States.

VIKING OFFICE PRODUCTS

13809 SO. FIGUEROA ST.
LOS ANGELES, CA 90061
213–321–4493
FAX: 310–327–2376

Catalog: free (see text)
Pay: check, MO, MC, V, AE
Sells: office supplies, furniture, computer supplies, stationery
Store: mail order only

   ¡Si!

Viking Office Products began business in 1960, and sells office supplies, furnishings, and computer supplies at discounts of up to 60%. The semi-annual, 550-page general catalog features daily office needs, from pens and markers to ergonomic seating and filing cabinets, all of which are sold at a discount. The brands represented include Avery, BIC, Boston, Canon, Eaton, Faber Castell, IBM, La-Z-Boy, Pendaflex, Pentel, Rubbermaid, Smead, Sony, 3M, Toshiba, and Wilson Jones, as well as Viking's own label. Once you place an order, you'll receive the monthly sale catalogs, with extra-deep discounts on everyday office needs. Viking covers every purchase with a 30-day free trial and a one-year unconditional guarantee of satisfaction, and expedited delivery service is routine.

Special Factors: Satisfaction is guaranteed; institutional accounts are available; shipping is free on orders over $25 within the 48 contiguous United States.

VULCAN BINDER & COVER

Catalog: free
Pay: check, MO, MC, V, AE
Sells: binders and supplies
Store: mail order only

KEY WBM

BOX 29

VINCENT, AL 35178

800–633–4526

205–672–2241

FAX: 205–672–7159

Three-ring binders can be pricey at the stationery store, so if you need more than a couple, it makes sense to buy from the manufacturer. Vulcan can save you up to 40% on all of your binder needs, from light-duty models with flexible covers to heavy-duty binders with 3" D-rings. The 48-page catalog also shows magazine files, zippered binders, catalog binders, 19-ring styles, pocket sizes, tabbed inserts, notepad holders, report covers, page protectors, cassette cases, and business cases and leather luggage. Custom imprinting is available on the binders and tabbed dividers.

Special Factors: Satisfaction is guaranteed; quantity discounts are available; returns are accepted within 15 days for exchange, refund, or credit; minimum order is $25.

SEE ALSO

Ace Luggage and Gifts • *attaché cases and briefcases* • **LUGGAGE**
Airline International Luggage & Gifts, Inc. • *organizers, attaché cases, and business gifts* • **LUGGAGE**
The American Stationery Co., Inc. • *custom-printed stationery, notepads, and envelopes* • **GENERAL: CARDS**
Bernie's Discount Center, Inc. • *phones, phone machines, fax machines, copiers, calculators, etc.* • **APPLIANCES**
Delta Publishing Group, Ltd. • *wholesale magazine subscriptions* • **BOOKS**
Jerry's Artarama, Inc. • *ergonomic chairs and flat files* • **ART MATERIALS**
Don Lamor Inc. • *office furnishings* • **HOME: FURNISHINGS**
Leather Unlimited Corp. • *leather attaché cases, card cases, portfolios, etc.* • **LUGGAGE**
Loftin-Black Furniture Company • *office furnishings* • **HOME: FURNISHINGS**

The Luggage Center • business cases • **LUGGAGE**

LVT Price Quote Hotline, Inc. • calculators, typewriters, phones, fax machines, pens, etc. • **APPLIANCES**

Phoneco, Inc. • vintage telephones and repair supplies • **ART & ANTIQUES**

Plastic BagMart • trash can liners • **OFFICE: SMALL BUSINESS**

Plexi-Craft Quality Products Corp. • acrylic racks, desk accessories, etc. • **HOME: FURNISHINGS**

S & S Sound City • phones and phone machines • **APPLIANCES**

Sobol House of Furnishings • contract furnishings • **HOME: FURNISHINGS**

Stuckey Brothers Furniture Co., Inc. • office furnishings • **HOME: FUR-NISHINGS**

Think Ink • inexpensive thermographic color hand printers • **CRAFTS**

Turnkey Material Handling Co • parts bins, office and institutional furnishings, and fixtures • **TOOLS**

U.S. Box Corp. • product packaging for resale • **OFFICE: SMALL BUSINESS**

University Products, Inc. • archival-quality storage supplies for microfiche and microfilm; library supplies and equipment • **OFFICE: SMALL BUSINESS**

Wholesale Tape and Supply Company • mailing supplies for tapes • **APPLI-ANCES**

Computing

Computers, peripherals, software, supplies, furniture, and accessories

If you're a first-time computer buyer or want to upgrade your current system, do your homework before you buy anything. Learn as much as you can from as many sources as possible: demonstrations of new products, trial and demo versions of software, hardware and software evaluations in magazines and on websites, discussion in online fora and newsgroups, and from colleagues who work with different systems and programs. Ask questions. Don't assume that any software will perform as promised, no matter who's vouching for it. Evaluate your current and anticipated requirements as carefully as possible, so you can maximize the use without outgrowing it too soon. Try to envision what you'll be doing with the computer and what you might like to do in six months, and a year. How much RAM will the software and operating system require? If gaming is important to you, what's the ideal operating system, and which components will optimize performance? Will the computer be used for business, family, or recreational purposes—or all three? If travel is in the future, should the computer be a laptop with a docking station? Is a combination of separate notebooks and desktop systems practical, or would docking stations work best? Consult the repair shop of a large computer outlet to get an idea of how much repairs run on different types of equipment, and evaluate manufacturers' warranties and service contracts offered by the resellers *before* committing yourself to added expense. (Check the manufacturers' websites, too, for "firmware fixes," patches, and other corrections to problems discovered after the equipment has been released. A large number of fixes may indicate quality-control problems with a hardware manufacturer.) Be sure to visit the online fora of the major computer vendors to see what's going on in their customer-service sections—high levels of distress from the users may indicate transitory problems, or more serious concerns. Be especially wary if problems seem long-standing, and the company does not seem to be resolving them. Use your credit card to pay for *every* purchase, and open, install, and test the hardware or software you order as soon as you get it. Notifying the vendor or manufacturer of problems within the first 30 to 60 days may be vital to getting a replacement product, free upgrade or other "fix," full refund, or making a legitimate request for a chargeback, if that becomes necessary. When you get your system, make sure you use a good-quality surge suppressor or UPS, and make recovery and system disks as soon as you get it up and running. Use virus-detection software that you keep up to date, and a trusted system-maintenance and diagnosis program. Last but most critical, make regular backups, and *verify* that they're usable—there are few things worse than suffering a hard-drive crash, and discovering *then* that your tape backup is worthless.

COMPUTER DISCOUNT WAREHOUSE

CDW COMPUTER CENTERS, INC.
200 NORTH MILWAUKEE
VERNON HILLS, IL 60061
847–465–6000
FAX: 847–465–6800

Catalog: free
Pay: check, MO, MC, V, Discover
Sells: computers, peripherals, software, etc.
Store: same address; Monday to Friday 9–8, Saturday 9–5; also 315 W. Grand Ave., Chicago, IL; Monday to Friday 9–7, Saturday 10–5
Online: http://www.cdw.com

CDW is a major discounter of computers, components, software, and related accessories. The firm sells products by Adaptec, AST, Borland, Canon, Cheyenne, Corel, Epson, Hewlett-Packard, IBM, Intel, Iomega, Lexmark, Logitech, Lotus, Magnavox, Maxtor, Microsoft, Motorola, NEC, Norton, Pacific Data, Sony, Targus, Toshiba, and USR, among many others. CDW has been in business since 1982 and publishes a 40-page catalog, but you can call for price quotes on desktops, towers, notebooks, hard drives, memory, coprocessors, monitors, printers, scanners, UPS systems, and popular software—utilities, spreadsheets, graphics, DTP, data management, communications, and networking programs. You can also visit the website, which includes an online catalog. Both the print version and the website detail the sales and returns policy.

Please note: A $25 handling fee is charged on orders shipped outside the United States.

Special Factors: Price quote by phone or letter; C.O.D. orders are accepted.

DARTEK COMPUTER SUPPLY CORP.

DEPT. WBMC

175 AMBASSADOR DRIVE

NAPERVILLE, IL 60540

800–832–7835

630–355–3000

FAX: 800–808–1106

Catalog: free

Pay: check, MO, MC, V, AE, Discover

Sells: PC and Macintosh supplies and equipment

Store: mail order only

E-mail: info@dartek.com

Online: http://www.dartek.com

Dartek and MacWholesale (800–531–4MAC) can save you up to 60% on the equipment you need to make the most of your PC or Mac. Dartek has been serving the industry since 1978, and offers everything from software to workstations through its catalogs, and a selection is shown on the website. Both the Dartek (PC) and MacWarehouse catalogs show a full range of hardware, components, software, and accessories, by Adobe, Brother, Hayes, Hewlett-Packard, IBM, Iomega, Magnavox, Maxell, Microsoft, Novell, O'Sullivan, Seagate, Sony, Syquest, 3M, and Verbatim, among others. Dartek sells a wide range of software, including desktop publishing, word processing, PIMs and contact management, accounting and spreadsheet, legal, mailing list management and databases, virus detection and other utilities, disk management, communication, information/reference, programming, tutorials. And you'll find the supplies you'll need to stay productive—cables, power conditioners, data storage, toner cartridges, ribbons, paper, labels, binding equipment, computer care and maintenance supplies, security devices, and telephony devices, also at savings.

Special Factors: Satisfaction is guaranteed; quantity discounts are available; authorized returns are accepted (a restocking fee may be charged) within 45 days for exchange, refund, or credit; institutional accounts are available; minimum order is $25; C.O.D. orders are accepted.

DCS

6501 STATE RTE. 123 N.
FRANKLIN, OH 45005
800–735–3272
513–743–4060
FAX: 513–743–4056

Catalog: $3, refundable
Pay: MC, V, Discover
Sells: toner cartridges, diskettes, cables, printer ribbons, etc.
Store: same address; Monday to Friday 8–5

DCS, formerly known as Dayton Computer Supply, offers a comprehensive selection of supplies for computers, printers, copiers, and other office machines. If you're looking for buys on magnetic media, see the firm's own bulk-pack computer disks, which meet or exceed ANSI standards and are backed by the DCS guarantee. DCS also sells diskettes and other data storage media by BASF, Dysan, KAO, Maxell, Sony, 3M, and Verbatim. There's a full line of cabling supplies and various accessories, including switch boxes, gender changers and adapters, surge protection devices, mice and mouse supplies, printer stands, and disk storage boxes.

In business since 1979, DCS is one of the top 50 toner cartridge remanufacturers in the nation, producing cartridges for hundreds of laser printers and copiers. (New cartridges from the original manufacturers—Apple, Canon, Epson, Hewlett-Packard, IBM, Okidata, Panasonic, Toshiba, and Xerox—are also available.) And DCS is a major ribbon distributor, so if you're having trouble locating replacements, try here. "If we can't find it. . . it probably cannot be found," say the management.

Please note: Orders are shipped to Canada via UPS only, and shipped to APO/FPO addresses by U.S. mail.

Special Factors: Satisfaction is guaranteed; price quote by phone; quantity discounts are available; C.O.D. orders are accepted; institutional accounts are available.

EDUCALC CORPORATION

27953 CABOT RD.
LAGUNA NIGUEL, CA
92677
800–713–6519
714–582–2637
FAX: 714–582–1445

Catalog: free
Pay: check, MO, MC, V, AE, Discover
Sells: calculators, palmtops, PDAs, notebooks, peripherals, books, software, etc.
Store: same address; Monday to Friday 8–5:30
E-mail: info-educalc@educalc.com
Online: http://www.educalc.com

EduCALC, in business since 1976, specializes in calculators, palmtops, and laptops. The firm is strong on Hewlett-Packard, and offers peripherals and accessories for the HP 48G calculator series, HP95/100/200/300LX palmtop computers, handheld units, and Psion and OmniBook notebook computers. Canon, HP, Sharp, and Texas Instruments calculators are available—graphic, scientific, business, and school models are offered, as well as batteries, carrying cases, and even used calculators are sold. The savings average 25%, but some items are discounted up to 40%; trade-ins are available for some calculator/palmtops—inquire for information.

When hooked up to the appropriate peripherals, the HP calculators can be linked to PCs, receive messages by satellite, edit programs, save data on RAM cards, develop programs, perform language translations, and analyze mathematical, scientific, engineering, and business data with the aid of software cards. The equipment currently available includes printers and plotters, modules, interface units, RAM/ROM cards, disk drives, adapters, and personal (portable) diaries. Stands, covers, keyboard overlay systems, ribbons, printing paper, disks, plotter pens, and other supplies are offered as well. The 72-page catalog should be noted for its comprehensive bookshelf—both general and calculator-related reference texts on astronomy, navigation, engineering, programming, and computer systems and languages are listed. The catalog descriptions are comprehensive, easy to understand, and include product specifications. For more information, an automated calculator/palmtop news line is available 24 hours a day at 714–582–3976. You can also visit the website, which includes an extensive database of technical notes on the HP palmtops and handheld units, as well as information on currently available products and accessories.

Special Factors: Satisfaction is guaranteed; returns are accepted within 30 days.

EDUCORP DIRECT

7434 TRADE ST.
SAN DIEGO, CA
92121–2410
800–843–9497
619–536–9999
FAX: 619–536–2345

Catalog: free
Pay: check, MO, MC, V, AE, Discover
Sells: CD-ROM software and Macintosh shareware
Store: mail order only and "by chance"

EDUCORP Direct offers thousands of CD-ROM software titles for Macintosh, Windows, and DOS platforms—games, entertainment, general interest, education, multimedia tools, and desktop publishing clip art, fonts, and photos. EDUCORP also carries hard-to-find titles, so check here if you can't locate a program elsewhere.

Special Factors: Quantity discounts are available *for dealers*; authorized returns are accepted within 30 days (a 25% restocking fee may be charged); institutional discounts are available.

EGGHEAD COMPUTER

P.O. BOX 177
LIBERTY LAKE, WA
99019–8553
800-EGGHEAD
TDD: 800–949–3447

Catalog: free
Pay: check, MO, MC, V, AE
Sells: software and computer accessories
Store: 86 stores in AZ, CA, CT, DC, IL, MA, MD, MI, NC, NJ, NM, NY, OR, PA, TN, UT, VA, and WA; locations are listed on the website
Online: http://www.egghead.com

Egghead offers a broad selection of software, hardware, and accessories featured in frequent sale catalogs and fliers. The electronic catalog on the website offers over 5,000 items at this writing. Becoming a "CUE" member entitles you to an extra 5% discount on everything you buy—and membership is free.

Special Factors: See the catalog or website for sales terms and details of the returns policy.

GLOBAL COMPUTER SUPPLIES

Catalog: free
Pay: check, MO, MC, V, AE
Sells: hardware, software, networking equipment, etc.
Store: mail order only
Online: http://www.globalcomputer.com

11 HARBOR PARK DR.
PORT WASHINGTON, NY
  11050
800–227–1246
516–625–6200
FAX: 516–625–6683

Global publishes three catalogs to serve computing needs: "Computer Supplies," heavy on hardware and accessories; "Hardware and Software," over 200 pages of programs and equipment for PC and Mac platforms; and "Datacom," networking and data communications for both platforms. Global, which also sells office supplies and furniture, safety products, and industrial equipment, offers the winning combination of the latest releases, a selection that includes hard-to-find equipment as well as best-sellers, low prices, and a 30-day guarantee of satisfaction backing the manufacturers' warranties. The brands run from AST to Xerox, and Global sells some goods under its own name at extra savings. The catalog copy is brief, so do your homework before ordering. Should you go wrong—and compatibility problems can make even sure things not—you're covered by the 30-day return window (except on hardware, networking equipment, or software, unless it's defective).

Special Factors: Satisfaction is guaranteed; price quote by phone or letter; quantity discounts are available; returns (except used, nondefective hardware, networking equipment, or software) are accepted within 30 days for exchange, refund, or credit; business leasing is available.

LYBEN COMPUTER SYSTEMS, INC.

5545 BRIDGEWOOD
STERLING HEIGHTS, MI
  48310
800–493–5777
810–268–8100
FAX: 810–268–8899

Catalog: free
Pay: check, MO, MC, V, AE
Sells: computers and hardware, software, and accessories
Store: mail order only
Online: http://www.lyben.com

Lyben Computer Systems, Inc. has been in business since 1982 and offers a full range of computer accessories, supplies, and peripherals. Lyben can save you up to 70% on the suggested retail price on goods from such companies as American Power, GVC, Panasonic, Sony, and 3M, to name a few. Lyben's 242-page full-line catalog runs from batteries to workstations and wrist pads, with all of your computer needs in between—magnetic media, storage units, cleaning tools and products, shredders, binding systems, memory upgrades, cables, switches, game cards, modems, buffers, network products, software and CD-ROM, printers, and much more. The promotional, 48-page catalogs give you a sample of the 7,000-plus items Lyben sells—if you don't see what you're looking for, call for the big book. If you're online, visit the website—you'll find a sample of the products there, as well as the "Internet Specials."

Special Factors: Minimum order is $15; C.O.D. orders are accepted.

THE MAC ZONE

707 S. GRADY WAY, #3
RENTON, WA 98055–3233
800–248–0800
425–430–3000
FAX: 425–430–3500

Catalog: free
Pay: check, MO, MC, V, AE, Discover
Sells: Mac-compatible hardware, software, accessories, and peripherals
Store: mail order only
Online: http://www.zones.com

Like its counterpart for PCs, the Mac Zone catalog delivers 140 pages of hardware and software for your system. Look here for the most recent releases in communications, productivity, databases, word processing, desktop publishing, graphics, multimedia, voice-recognition software, spreadsheets and financial programs, system tools and utilities, entertainment, games, reference works, training software and tapes, and much more. The hardware runs from memory to monitors—scanners, digital cameras, printers, video and sound cards, drives (hard, optical, CD-ROM, removable, etc.), input devices, modems, power managers, and entire systems are all available. Prices run up to 50% below manufacturers' suggested list or comparable retail, and if you don't see what you're looking for in the catalog, call—chances are it's available.

Please note: The Zone has separate, dedicated phone lines for international sales (by country), and corporate, education, and government buyers—see the catalog for information.

Special Factors: Authorized returns are accepted; corporate and business accounts are available.

MACWAREHOUSE

DEPT. WBM98

1720 OAK ST.

P.O. BOX 3013

LAKEWOOD, NJ

   08701–3013

800–255–6227

FAX: 908–905–9279

Catalog: free

Pay: check, MO, MC, V, AE, Discover

Sells: Macintosh software and peripherals

Store: mail order only

Online: http://www.warehouse.com

Whether you're a dedicated Macintosh user or are toying with making a cross-platform leap, you'll want to see the 204-page catalog from MacWarehouse. More than a roundup of current releases and enhancements, MacWarehouse offers upgrades for a wide range of programs, an extensive line of enhancements and memory upgrades, network media, monitors, video cards, online service packages, and a broad range of accessories, tools, cables, hardware, and little things to make your Mac sing—including MIDI connections, video imaging kits, and sound-recording systems. MacWarehouse has an equally impressive selection of software and programs: word processing, databases, utilities, accounting, graphics, desktop publishing, project managers and PIMs, spreadsheets, multimedia packages, security systems, and much more. The products run from Access PC to Zephyr, and the discounts are a satisfying 25% to 50%—and even more on specials and bundled software.

    Special Factors: Price quote by phone or letter; authorized returns are accepted; institutional accounts are available; C.O.D. orders are accepted.

MEI/MICRO CENTER

1100 STEELWOOD RD.
COLUMBUS, OH
  43212–9972
800–634–3478
614–481–4417
FAX: 614–486–6417

Catalog: free
Pay: check, MO, MC, V, AE, Discover
Sells: CD-ROM and data storage, ribbons, paper, etc.
Store: mail order only; phone hours Monday to Friday 8–11, Saturday 9–7, ET
Online: http://www.mei-microcenter.com

MEI/Micro Center founded its business in 1986 on great buys on magnetic media, which are still here, in the 96-page catalogs—diskettes, data cartridges, optical disks, data cartridges, and accessories. The brands include Dysan, Iomega, Precision, Syquest, 3M, Verbatim, and MEI's own label—all offered at excellent discounts. You'll also find media storage units, backup units, sound cards, surge suppressors, printer supplies (ribbons, toner cartridges, inkjet modules, etc.), CD-ROM software and hardware—printers, scanners, memory, modems, input devices, and more. Check the pricing on the paper: laser stock, certificates and brochure papers, business cards, parchment, labels, and transparencies are all offered at good prices.

Please note: MEI/Micro Center doesn't ship goods outside the United States and Canada.

Special Factors: Satisfaction is assured; returns are accepted.

MICRO WAREHOUSE, INC.

DEPT. WBM98
1720 OAK ST.
P.O. BOX 3014
LAKEWOOD, NJ 08701–3014
800–367–6808
FAX: 908–370–2432

Catalog: free
Pay: check, MO, MC, V, Discover
Sells: computers, components, software, and accessories
Store: mail order only
Online: http://www.warehouse.com

   ¡Si!

There's one way to keep up with the new releases, upgrades, innovations in peripherals, and other developments in computing—find a source to do it for you. MicroWarehouse not only leads with the latest releases, it also gives you great prices on everything it sells. The 164-page catalog is packed with software for current operating systems, as well as modems, fax machines, scanners, disk drives, expansion devices, printers, monitors, memory upgrades, and much more. The software runs the gamut from word processing and integrated communications to databases, utilities, graphics, and contact management. The Upgrade Warehouse division can handle both live and competitive upgrades, and detailed product information is available through a fax-back service. All of this, and savings of up to 50%, have helped establish MicroWarehouse as a leading supplier. The MicroSystems Warehouse catalog gives you another 78 pages of hardware—systems from makers that run from AST to Zenith. The Data Comm Warehouse catalog provides networking solutions specialties, and MacWarehouse handles the needs of Macintosh users. Be sure to request the catalog that best serves your needs.

Special Factors: Authorized returns of defective items are accepted within 120 days for exchange, refund, or credit; institutional accounts are available; C.O.D. orders are accepted.

MISCO
■■■■■■■■■

ONE MISCO PLAZA
HOLMDEL, NJ 07733
800–333–5640
908–264–1000
FAX: 908–264–5955

Catalog: $4
Pay: check, MO, MC, V, AE
Sells: computers software, peripherals, and accessories
Store: mail order only

MISCO's "In-Stock Guarantee" helps assure you that the warehouse will have what you want, when you need it. The 164-page catalog is strong on computer accessories—keyboard drawers, wrist rests, laptop bags, etc.—and ergonomically designed chairs and workstations. MISCO also offers a good selection of media and storage, toner cartridges and paper, software, peripherals for stand-alone and networked PCs, input devices, modems, monitors, memory boards, SCSIs and hard drives, scanners, printers, fax machines, telephones, line drives, cables and connectors, and much more. This is a great source for anyone running a home office, and bigger businesses can contact MISCO's Bid Department for volume discounts.

Special Factors: Quantity discounts are available; returns are accepted; minimum order is $30; C.O.D. orders are accepted.

NEW MMI CORP.

DEPT. WBMC01
2400 REACH RD.
WILLIAMSPORT, PA 17701
800–221–4283
FAX: 717–327–1217

Catalog: free
Pay: check, MO, MC, V, Discover
Sells: computers, peripherals, and software
Store: New MMI Corp., 2400 Reach Rd.,
Williamsport, PA; Monday to Friday 9–6, Saturday 10–3

New MMI Corp. has been in business since 1981, selling computer systems, disk drives, boards, monitors, printers, modems, software, and accessories by a number of manufacturers, at savings of up to 40%. New MMI provides technical assistance before and after the sale, is an authorized dealer for everything it sells, and an authorized repair center for a number of major brands. The catalog shows a wide selection of current releases and includes specifications; if you don't see what you're looking for in the catalog, call, fax, or write for a price quote—it may be available. The firm's website includes an online catalog, weekly specials, and details on the firm's custom-built desktops and laptops.

Special Factors: Authorization is required for returns (a restocking fee may be charged); C.O.D. orders are accepted.

PC CONNECTION, INC.

P.O. BOX 19
528 RTE. 13
MILFORD, NH 03055
800–800–0011
603–446–1111
FAX: 603–446–7791

Catalog: free
Pay: check, MO, MC, V, AE, Discover, NOVUS
Sells: hardware, software, and supplies
Store: mail order only
Online: http://www.pcconnection.com/

PC Connection, Inc. is one of the country's leading mail-order companies selling systems, software, and accessories for both PC and Macintosh platforms. In business since 1982, it's run with a dedication to selection and service that makes it a standout in the field. PC Connection offers the latest versions of products from hundreds of manufacturers, often bundled with valuable extras. The catalogs feature products for both platforms, and the Systems Connection division of the firm will configure a Mac or PC system to order (see the catalog for details). PC Connection provides warranty backup and toll-free technical support for everything it sells, and is a factory-authorized repair center for Acer, Apple, Canon, Compaq, Epson, IBM, Iomega, Okidata, and Texas Instruments products. Orders are taken until 3:00 a.m. ET for next-day delivery (for a nominal fee). Call for a current catalog, or see the ads in major computer magazines. If you don't see what you're looking for, call—at this writing, PC Connection has over 10,000 items and will probably have what you want. And be sure to check the full-featured website for product specials, links to manufacturers and computer-related sites, and much more.

Special Factors: Price quote by phone; volume discounts are available; returns are accepted for exchange, refund, or credit; licensing and leasing options for software and hardware; corporate and institutional accounts are available.

THE PC ZONE

RENTON, WA 98055–3233
800–248–9948
206–430–3000
FAX: 206–430–3420

Catalog: free
Pay: check, MO, MC, V, AE, Discover
Sells: PC and Mac components, software, hardware, and accessories
Store: mail order only
Online: http://www.zones.com

The Zone catalogs—PC and Mac—give you 140 pages of software and hardware for your system and platform. You'll find the latest releases in personal productivity, communications, databases, desktop publishing, utilities, spreadsheets, word processing, graphics, multimedia, and more. PC and Mac Zone also offer entertainment and games packages, reference works, training tapes and tutorials, and laptop luggage, and the catalogs list memory upgrades, CD-ROM drives, OCR devices and scanners, bar-coding equipment, monitors, mice, modems, UPS's and power managers, voice-recognition software and equipment, backup devices, printers, other peripherals and accessories, and much more. Request the PC or Mac catalog, and if you don't see what you're looking for, call—it may be available, just not listed. You can also search the website's online catalog for specific products and check for current specials.

Please note: The Zone has separate, dedicated phone lines for international sales (by country), and corporate, education, and government buyers—see the catalog for information.

Special Factors: Authorized returns are accepted; institutional accounts are available; C.O.D. orders are accepted.

RECYCLED SOFTWARE, INC.

P.O. BOX 33999
LAS VEGAS, NV 89133
800–851–2425
702–655–5666
FAX: 702–655–5662

Price List: free
Pay: check, MO, MC, V, AE, Discover
Sells: used computer software
Store: mail order only; phone hours Monday to Friday 7–4 PT
E-mail: recycledsw@aol.com
Online: http://members.aol.com/recycledsw/

Recycled Software markets complete, original, pre-owned software for IBM-compatible systems (DOS, Windows 3.1 and 95, OS/2, etc.), at prices 50% and more off original list. The software comes from individuals and firms, and may be resold legally (if a manufacturer prohibits resale, Recycled Software won't offer that software). Both current and earlier versions of programs are available, including popular titles of all kinds—games, entertainment, reference, education, PIMS, organizers, calendars, flow charts, project planners, data bases, word processors, spreadsheets and financial programs, fonts and font managers, print utilities, graphics, clip-art and 3D, presentation programs, OCR and scanning software, disk maintenance utilities and memory managers, integrated packages, operating systems, compilers, etc. The earlier versions are a great way to take advantage of a version or competitive upgrade discount, or for use on older machines that can't handle 32-bit programs.

Recycled Software sells only fully documented, non-OEM software, English-version as sold in the United States, guaranteed free of viruses or defects (checked with two virus-detection programs). At this writing, the price list includes the version number, list price, media size (CD or disk sizes), the date (for games), and the Recycled Software price—one if the materials include a blank registration form, a lower one if the form is not included. The price list from Recycled Software includes complete ordering instructions and answers to several FAQs. The price list is updated weekly on the website.

Wholesale buyers, please note: Purchases of $1,000 or more are discounted 10%.

Readers outside the United States, please note: Recycled Software honors publisher prohibitions on sale of programs outside the United States when such restrictions are imposed.

Special Factors: Satisfaction is guaranteed; price quote by phone; returns are accepted within 30 days for exchange, refund, or credit.

SEE ALSO

The Astronomical Society of the Pacific • *astronomy-related computer programs* • **BOOKS**

B & H Photo-Video • *computer imaging components and equipment* • **CAMERAS**

Business & Institutional Furniture Company, Inc. • *computer workstations* • **OFFICE**

C & T Bridge Supplies • *bridge computer programs* • **TOYS**

Clothcrafters, Inc. • *cotton computer covers* • **GENERAL MERCHANDISE**

Frank Eastern Co. • *computer workstations* • **OFFICE**

Genada Imports • *computer workstations* • **HOME: FURNISHINGS**

Jobson's Luggage Warehouse • *laptop cases* • **LUGGAGE**

Luggage Unlimited • *laptop cases* • **LUGGAGE**

National Business Furniture, Inc. • *computer workstations* • **OFFICE**

Plexi-Craft Quality Products Corp. • *acrylic computer stands* • **HOME: FURNISHINGS**

Quill Corporation • *computers, peripherals, software, etc.* • **OFFICE**

Rapidforms, Inc. • *formatted continuous forms* • **OFFICE**

Reliable Corp. • *computer supplies, printer cartridges, etc.* • **OFFICE**

Safe Specialties, Inc. • *data and diskette safes, lockboxes, etc.* • **OFFICE**

Staples, Inc. • *computer disks, data binders, workstations, software, etc.* • **OFFICE**

20th Century Plastics, Inc. • *static-proof disk storage* • **OFFICE**

Viking Office Products • *computer supplies, peripherals, and furniture* • **OFFICE**

Small Business

Products and services for businesses

Whether you're running a small office or just drafting the plans for your first venture, maximize every dollar you spend by buying from firms that will sell to you at "bulk" discounts, or wholesale. The companies listed here can help you hold down costs even if you can't compete with the buying power of the Fortune 500. None of the firms requires a resale certificate—at most, they ask you to send your catalog request on letterhead, or enclose your business card. But many impose minimum orders and have less generous return policies than those offered by consumer-oriented mail-order firms, so order accordingly.

Over the past few years, there's been enormous growth in "alternative" purchasing—buying clubs, members-only warehouses, barter organizations, and co-ops. Explore the options available to you and find the right combination of vendors and services for your needs; there's usually no single "right" source, and it's up to you to determine the balance between paying list price and pushing for the deepest discounts on *everything*. Case in point: premiums and incentives. The firms listed here offer everything from giveaway key rings and wood pencils to golf balls, mantel clocks, polo shirts, and portfolios. Because the discounts vary so widely, get several catalogs, calculate delivered costs, and compare carefully for the best buys.

ASSOCIATED BAG COMPANY

400 W. BODEN ST.
MILWAUKEE, WI
53207–7120
800–926–6100
FAX: 800–926–4610
TDD: 800–926–4611

Catalog: free
Pay: check, MO, MC, V, AE
Sells: poly bags, shipping and packaging supplies
Store: mail order only

 ¡Si! Ⓒ

Bags, boxes, bubble pack—that's just the beginning of what's available from Associated Bag Company, a container specialist that's been in business since 1938. The well-designed catalog features over 100 pages of plastic bags and packaging materials for a range of purposes: zipper-lock bags, flat poly bags, rolls and envelopes of bubble material, foam sheeting, corrugated boxes and rolls, cloth drawstring bags, mailing tubes and envelopes, sealing tape, stretch wrap, shrink wrap, packing peanuts, antistatic bags, giant covers and liners, and much more. Recycled products are noted throughout the book, and dispensers for tape and paper, shrink guns, and other equipment are also available. Prices are good, and savings are greater on quantity buys.

In addition to the customary commercial uses, these products are suited to a number of household tasks, including one very costly undertaking—moving. Get the containers locally, but handle the packing yourself with wrapping materials from Associated Bag, and you can save several hundreds of dollars in materials and labor. Just make sure your homeowner policy, or the moving company, will still provide coverage if there's breakage.

Special Factors: Satisfaction is guaranteed; price quotes on custom orders; competitive bidding; quantity discounts are available; free test samples available; returns are accepted; minimum order is $25.

THE BEST IMPRESSIONS CATALOG COMPANY

Catalog: free
Pay: check, MO, MC, V, AE
Sells: business-promotion products
Store: mail order only

P.O. BOX 802
LASALLE, IL 61301
800–635–2378
FAX: 815–883–8346

The Best Impressions catalog of promotional goods won't overwhelm you with choices. Instead, it features the most popular items currently appearing at seminars and conventions and—hopefully—your clients' desks in the near future. Most of the products are in the $1 to $5 price range—pens, pocket calculators, rulers, wipe-off boards, mouse pads, memo cubes, key rings, and similar items lead the 32-page catalog. There are novelties (stress balloons, stuffed toys, etc.), "giveaways" (sunglasses, playing cards, fortune cookies, lapel pins, magnets, buttons, etc.), and the classics—ceramic mugs and sports bottles, measuring tapes, flashlights, golf balls, fanny packs, caps, tote bags, and calendars. The small collection of executive gifts includes travel alarms, desk clocks, portfolios, and mugs with matching tile coasters. Savings can run up to 50%, depending on the item and quantity ordered, and prices include execution of your design in one color in one imprint area. Camera-ready artwork is required, or it can be produced by the firm's art department for $30 per item. Each product has a minimum order—250 Bic Clics, 100 mouse pads, and 1,000 balsa gliders are typical examples—but many minimums can be lowered (surcharges apply). And selected products are available for accelerated shipment, at no extra charge—see the catalog for details.

Special Factors: Price quote by phone; quantity discounts are available; institutional accounts are available; minimum orders vary by item.

NELSON MARKETING

P.O. BOX 320
OSHKOSH, WI 54902–0320
800–722–5203
FAX: 800–355–5043
TDD: 800–642–2076

Catalog: free
Pay: check, MO, MC, V, AE, Discover
Sells: business-promotion products
Store: mail order only
Online: http://www.nelmark.com

Nelson Marketing offers businesses 56 pages of 450 proven imprinted promotional products—pens and pencils, plaques and awards, folios, totes and duffels, sport towels, hats, golf accessories, sweatshirts, printed note cubes and "stickies," mouse pads, magnets, first-aid kits and safety devices, flying disks and novelties, flashlights and tools, clocks, mugs, squeeze bottles, and more. Compared to several other catalogs of business-incentive merchandise, Nelson Marketing had some of the lowest prices on quantity buys of a popular pen, while prices were higher on other items (such as wipe-off memo boards). The catalog descriptions include notes on surcharges for setup, dies, screens, cuts, logos, etc., making it easy to calculate the delivered price. Items that can be expedited through production are flagged with a "quick-ship" symbol, and product samples are available. And everything is backed by a "Double the Difference" guarantee—see the catalog or the customer-service section of the website for details.

Special Factors: Goods are guaranteed to be delivered exactly as ordered, or the order will be rerun, refunded, or credited; quantity discounts are available; institutional accounts are available.

PLASTIC BAGMART

904 OLD COUNTRY RD.
WESTBURY, NY 11590
516–997–3355
FAX: 516–997–1836

Catalog: free with SASE
Pay: check, MO, MC, V
Sells: plastic bags
Store: same address; Monday to Friday 9–5, Saturday 9–3

 ¡Si! ★

Plastic BagMart, established in 1980, offers plastic bags in sizes most frequently used in homes, offices, and industry. Prices are up to 60% lower than those charged by supermarkets and variety stores for smaller lots. The BagMart stocks plastic bags in sizes from 2" square to 50" by 48", one to four mils thick. Garbage and trash cleanup bags, kitchen and office waste-can bags, food-storage bags, recycling bags, large industrial-type bags, zip-top styles, plastic shopping bags, compactor, garment, and other types are available. The bags are sold in case lots only (100 to 1,000 bags per case, depending on the size). The little 12-page catalog features the most popular lines, but if you don't see what you need, write with particulars.

Canadian readers, please note: Orders are shipped by UPS only.

Special Factors: Satisfaction is guaranteed; price quote by letter with SASE; returns are accepted within 10 days; minimum order is one case.

UNIVERSITY PRODUCTS, INC.

517 MAIN ST.
HOLYOKE, MA 01041–0101
800–628–1912
FAX: 800–532–9281

Catalog: free (see text)
Pay: check, MO, MC, V, AE, DC, Discover
Sells: archival-quality materials
Store: mail order only
Online: http://www.universityproducts.com/upi/

You may not know it, but anarchy reigns on your bookshelves, in the pages of your photo albums, and among the works of art on your walls. It's sad, but true: most of us store and display our precious belongings in materials and under conditions that damage them, sometimes irreparably.

Help is available from University Products, which publishes the comprehensive *Archival Quality Materials Catalog*. University Products has been selling conservation and library supplies to institutions since 1968 and does business with preservation-minded individuals and institutions who want to protect their collectibles and other treasures. Both the materials used in display and storage, and the conditions under which we keep them affect the long-term "health" of many collectibles. Problems with spotting, discoloration, and damage may be seen in stamps, antique textiles, comic books, baseball trading cards, postcards, scrapbooks, photographs, sheet music, and even currency. To meet the need for safe storage of these goods, University Products sells acid-free manuscript boxes and interleaving pages, files, photo albums and Mylar page protectors, archival storage tubes, slide and microfiche storage materials, mounting materials and adhesives, an extensive selection of acid-free papers of all types, storage cases and cabinets, dry-mount and framing equipment, and related tools and supplies. The catalog includes valuable information on conservation basics for a range of materials and collectibles. Since a "basic retouching" of an old photograph can cost over $100, each dollar spent in preservation can save a hundred in restoration—*if* restoration is possible. You can also check the website to view the products.

Special Factors: Satisfaction is guaranteed; quantity discounts are available; institutional accounts are available.

U.S. BOX CORP.

1296 MCCARTER HWY.
NEWARK, NJ 07104
800–221–0999
201–481–2000
FAX: 201–481–2002

Catalog: free
Pay: check, MO, MC, V, AE
Sells: resale packaging
Store: mail order only
E-mail: sales@usbox.com
Online: http://www.usbox.com

 ¡Si!

U.S. Box Corp. has been selling packaging—boxes, bags, canisters, and displays—since 1948. This is primarily a business-to-business firm, but it offers products that consumers use routinely: wrapping paper, tape, gift boxes, ribbon, and mailing bags, for example. Prices are as much as 60% lower here than those charged for comparable items in variety and stationery stores. Volume discounts run from 5% on orders over $500 up to 15% on totals of $2,500 plus. Samples of the goods may be purchased at unit cost plus $2 shipping; this is recommended, since returns are not accepted.

U.S. Box Corp.'s 100-page color catalog shows an extensive selection of plain and decorated corrugated cardboard mailers, boxes, shopping bags, gift and presentation boxes, poly bags, rigid plastic boxes, plastic display cases, showcase and window displays, and a full line of velvet boxes, inserts, and stands for jewelry sale and display. Both consumers and businesses should see the selection—and prices—of U.S. Box Corp.'s colorful excelsior, cellophane, gift wrap and gift tins, bows and package decorations, ribbons, and tissue paper. The selection here includes all the basics, as well as the latest packaging and wrapping concepts, designs, and materials. Consolidate your packaging needs and you'll easily meet the $150 minimum order—the current catalog includes computer disk mailers, all-purpose gift stickers, gold and silver cord-handled bags, folding gift and candy boxes, hatbox sets, hinged partitioned plastic boxes (perfect for notions, hardware, and small parts), jewelry display pieces (many of which could double as jewelry collection organizers), and even leopard-print bags and boxes!

Special Factors: Returns are not accepted; minimum order is $150.

SEE ALSO

Business Technologies • cash registers • **OFFICE**
Current, Inc. • gift wrapping paper and ribbon • **GENERAL: CARDS**
Hunt Galleries, Inc. • custom-upholstered furnishings for institutions, designers, etc. • **HOME: FURNISHINGS**
Iroquois Products Co. • packaging and shipping supplies • **OFFICE**
M & N International, Inc. • promotional items, display materials, etc. • **TOYS**
Oriental Trading Company, Inc. • fund-raising and promotional items • **TOYS**
Rapidforms, Inc. • gift boxes, packing and shipping supplies, etc. • **OFFICE**
Reliable Corp. • packing, shipping, and mailroom supplies, etc. • **OFFICE**
Sunrise Stationers • business printing and binding services • **OFFICE**
Turnkey Material Handling Co. • parts bins, office and institutional furnishings, and fixtures • **TOOLS**
U.S. Toy Company, Inc. • gifts, premiums, fund-raising items • **TOYS**
Yazoo Mills, Inc. • shipping tubes • **ART MATERIALS**

SPORTS AND RECREATION

Equipment, clothing, supplies, and services
for recreational activities

Organized sports and outdoor athletic pursuits—from fishing to golf to volleyball—are supplied here, and discounts of 30% are routine. These suppliers sell clothing and equipment for cycling, running, golfing, skiing, aerobics, racquet sports, skin and scuba diving, camping, hunting, hiking, basketball, triathlon, soccer, and other endeavors. Custom services, such as racquet stringing and club repairs, are usually priced competitively as well. Buying your gear by mail may be the only sport that repays a nominal expenditure of energy with such an enhanced sense of well-being.

If you've been sedentary for some time, have a complete physical before beginning any workout program or sport. Stop and cool down if you're in pain, but don't give up. You can make running, aerobics, and racquet sports easier on your joints by wearing properly fitted shoes, learning correct foot placement, and working out on a resilient surface. Low-impact aerobics, fast-paced walking, and swimming are less stressful than running, calisthenics, and traditional sports. Getting fit should be a pleasure, and if you take the time to find an enjoyable, challenging sport or workout routine, cardiovascular health and vigor will be more easily won.

FIND IT FAST

CAMPING • **Campmor, Herter's, Sportsman's Guide, Survival Supply**
CYCLING • **Bike Nashbar, Performance Bicycle Shop**
EXERCISE EQUIPMENT • **Better Health, Fitness Factory**
GOLF • **Golf Haus, Golfsmith, Telepro**

HUNTING • **Bowhunters Warehouse, Cabela's, Cheap Shot, Deer Shack, Herter's, Sportsman's Guide, Wiley**
KITING • **BFK Sports**
KNIVES • **Cutlery Shoppe**
INLINE SKATES • **The House**
RACQUET SPORTS • **Holabird**
SNOWBOARDING • **The House**
SOCCER • **Soccer International**
SWIMWEAR AND POOL SUPPLIES • **Water Warehouse, World Wide Aquatics**
VOLLEYBALL • **Spike Nashbar**
WATER SPORTS • **Bart's, Berry Scuba, Central Skindivers, The House, Overton's, Performance Diver**

BART'S WATER-SPORTS

▬▬▬▬▬▬▬▬

P.O. BOX 294-WBM
NORTH WEBSTER, IN
46555
800–348–5016
219–834–7666
FAX: 219–834–4246

Catalog: free, $5 outside the U.S.
Pay: check, MO, MC, V, AE, Discover
Sells: water sports, marine/boating, and personal watercraft goods
Store: Hwy. 13, North Webster, IN; Monday to Saturday 9–6
E-mail: bartsports@kconline.com
Online: http://www.bartsports.com

The thrills of water sports are cheaper at Bart's, where wet suits, skis, and marine products cost up to 40% below list, and clearance items are offered at even greater savings. Bart's has been in business since 1972, and backs every sale with a guarantee of satisfaction. The 64-page color catalog features name-brand water skis, personal watercraft accessories, and marine equipment for boats. Wakeboarders can choose from pages of boards and accessories, and there's a large selection of floats, tubes, and other inflatables. Ski vests and wet suits for men, women, and children are offered, in addition to wet-suit accessories, swimwear for men and women, T-shirts, sunglasses, gloves, boat lifts, and boat/PWC covers. Brands include Body Glove, Body Guard, Connelly, Eagle, Intensity, O'Brien, Skiwarm, Slippery When Wet, and others.

Special Factors: Satisfaction is guaranteed; quantity discounts are available; returns are accepted within 60 days; minimum order is $250 on shipments overseas.

BERRY SCUBA CO.

DEPT. W–98
6674 N. NORTHWEST
  HWY.
CHICAGO, IL 60631
800–621–6019
773–763–1626
FAX: 773–775–1815

Catalog: free
Pay: check, MO, MC, V, AE, Discover
Sells: scuba-diving gear
Store: same address; also Lombard and Palatine, IL; and Atlanta, GA

Berry Scuba, "the oldest, largest, and best-known direct-mail scuba firm in the country," carries a wide range of equipment and accessories for diving and related activities. Shop here for regulators, masks, wet suits, fins, tanks, diving lights, strobes, underwater cameras and housings, diving watches, pole spears, and other gear and accessories for underwater use. Berry has been in business since 1960 and sells on a price-quote basis, but will send you the free catalog, on request.

Special Factors: Orders are shipped worldwide.

BETTER HEALTH FITNESS

5302 NEW UTRECHT AVE.
BROOKLYN, NY 11219
718–436–4693, 4801
FAX: 718–854–3381

Information: inquire
Pay: check, MO, MC, V, AE
Sells: exercise and playground equipment
Store: same address; Monday to Wednesday 10–6, Thursday 10–8, Sunday 12–5 (closed Friday and Saturday)

Whether you're buying a stationary bicycle for rainy-day workouts or outfitting an entire gym, you'll get it for less at Better Health. The firm has been selling top-of-the-line equipment and gear since 1977, including Alva (ballet barres), Apex Mats, Barracuda (swim gear), Century, Everlast, Fitness Master, Healthometer, Healthrider, Impex, K-Swiss (footwear), Landice, Life Fitness, Massage, Monark (cycles), Pacemaster (treadmills), Parabody, Park Structures (commercial playground equipment), Pro-Form, Sacro Ease (car seat supports), Schwinn, Trek Fitness, Trimline, Trotter (treadmills), Tuff Stuff, and Tunturi. You can save up to

20% on the regular prices of equipment by these and other manufacturers. Call or write for quotes on treadmills, ski machines, dual-action exercise cycles, multistation units, free-weights, benches, aerobic and tumbling mats, dance studio equipment, saunas, locker room equipment, boxing equipment, indoor/outdoor resilient flooring, and related goods. If you're within the New York/New Jersey/Connecticut area, Better Health can design and install a wooden, metal, or Plastisol-coated steel home or commercial playground set, or provide you with gym layout and related design services. Treadmills and weights are available on a regional basis.

Special Factors: Satisfaction is guaranteed; price quote by phone or letter with SASE; authorized returns are accepted within 15 days for exchange, refund, or credit; minimum order is $50.

BFK SPORTS, INC.

2500 E. IMPERIAL HWY.
#122
BREA, CA 92821
714–529–6589
FAX: 714–529–6152

Catalog: free
Pay: check, MO, MC, V, AE, Discover, JCB
Sells: kites and kiting supplies
Store: same address; Monday to Saturday
11–6, Sunday 12–5
E-mail: bfk@gte.net
Online: http://www.kitestore.com

If the last kite you flew was cut from a surplus shopping bag and sported a tail made from strips of an old sheet, you'll find BFK Sports a revelation. Here are "sport" kites, used for recreation and in kiting competitions, which are flown using two, three, or even four lines. Beyond sport kiting lies the world of stunt flying and "buggy" kiting, in which operator navigates a "high traction" kite from a three-wheeled buggy platform on the ground. BFK carries the kites and equipment for all levels of kiting, from Aerie Kiteworks, Air Masters, Benson, Cobra, HQ, Laser Pro, MEFM, Prism, Shanti, Sky Burner, and other names. You'll find all types of kite line, winders, carbon spars, kite bags, windsocks and wind meters, and books, magazines, and videos. BFK also offers other "flying toys"— boomerangs, rubber-band gliders, rockets, and yo-yos. Even custom-made land sailers are available—no kiting experience required.

BFK's website and catalog showcase the current stock, and include details on the firm's "lowest price" policy. And you can visit the website or the stores to find discontinued and closeout items at up to 50% off list price.

Special Factors: Satisfaction is guaranteed; new, unused returns (with some exceptions) are accepted within 15 days for exchange, refund, or credit; C.O.D. orders are accepted.

BIKE NASHBAR

DEPT. WBM8

4111 SIMON RD.

YOUNGSTOWN, OH

44512–1343

800-NASHBAR

FAX: 800–456–1223

Catalog: free

Pay: check, MO, MC, V, Discover

Sells: bicycles, accessories, apparel, and equipment

Store: same address, call for hours

Online: http://www.nashbar.com/

Bike Nashbar, one of the country's top sources for casual and serious cyclists, publishes a 70-plus-page catalog that runs from rain parkas to panniers, sold at "guaranteed lowest prices." Bike Nashbar has been in business since 1973 and sells its own line of road, touring, and ATB bikes, which have features usually found on more expensive models. There are full lines of parts and accessories, including saddles from Avocet, San Marco, Selle Italia, TRICO, and Vetta, gears, brakes, chain wheels, hubs, pedals, derailleurs, handlebars, and other parts by Campagnolo, Control Tech, Shimano, and other firms. Panniers and bags, racks, helmets, protective eyewear, gloves, tires and tubes, wheels, toe clips, locks (Nashbar, Kryptonite, and Specialized), handlebar tape, grips, tire pumps, lights, and other accessories are offered. Bike Nashbar also features a large selection of cycling clothing, both its own label, and Cannondale, Inmotion, and Insport, as well as shoes by Duegi, Look, Reebok, Scott, Sidi, Specialized, Time, and Vittoria. The catalog includes a good bit of technical information, and if you need more assistance, just call.

Special Factors: Satisfaction is guaranteed; technical advice is available.

BOWHUNTERS WAREHOUSE, INC.

1045 ZIEGLER RD.
P.O. BOX 158
WELLSVILLE, PA 17365
800–735–2697
717–432–8611
FAX: 717–432–2683

Catalog: free
Pay: check, MO, MC, V, Discover
Sells: equipment for bow hunting, hunting, and archery
Store: same address; Monday, Wednesday, and Friday 10–8, Tuesday and Thursday 10–6, Saturday 10–4

You can save up to 40% on a complete range of supplies for bow hunting, bow fishing, archery, and hunting through the 144-page catalog from Bowhunters Warehouse, which has been in business since 1974. The catalog features a large selection of bows and arrows, as well as points, feathers, bow sights, rests, quivers, targets, bow-hunting books and videotapes, game calls, camouflage clothing and supplies, shooting equipment, and other gear for outdoor sports. Accra, Bear, Beman, Browning, Darton, Delta, Easton, Golden Eagle, Hoyt, Martin, PSE, Saunders, and other manufacturers are represented. Bowhunters Discount Warehouse also builds arrows to order, and the catalog includes a complete description of the features and available options for custom arrows. Specifications are included with the information on the hunting equipment, making this a good reference as well as a source for real savings.

Special Factors: Authorized returns are accepted; minimum order is $15; C.O.D. orders are accepted.

CABELA'S INC.

812 13TH AVE.
SIDNEY, NE 69160
800–223–9155
FAX: 308–254–6102
TDD: 800–695–5000

Catalog: free
Pay: check, MO, MC, V, AE, Discover
Sells: hunting, fishing, and camping gear
Store: I–80, Exit #59, Sidney, NE; also E. Hwy. 30, Kearney, NE; Monday to Saturday 8–8, Sunday 12 noon–5:30, both locations
Online: http://www.cabelas.com

Cabela's, the "world's foremost outfitter" of fishing, hunting, and outdoor enthusiasts, has been praised by several readers. Cabela's catalog pricing represents savings of up to 40% on regular retail on some goods, but *do not ask for discounts.*

Cabela's sells rods, reels, and tackle from well-known manufacturers, including Berkley, Blue Fox, Daiwa, Fenwick, Abu Garcia, G. Loomis, Mitchell, Shakespeare, and Shimano. There's an extensive selection of lures, line, tackle boxes, hooks, nets, and other fishing gear, and pages of Minn Kota electric boat motors, electronics by Eagle, Humminbird, Interphase, and Seacom, boat covers, boat seats, Sea Eagle dinghies, Starcraft fishing boats, down riggers, winches, batteries, and trailer parts. Fishing is the strong suit in the spring and summer catalogs, but a comparable range of hunting equipment is offered in other issues.

General outdoor needs are served by the camping department: Eureka tents, sleeping bags and mats, gear bags, backpacks, cookware and kitchen equipment, heavy-duty flashlights, Pentax and Tasco binoculars, Hobie and Ray-Ban sunglasses, hunting knives, and related products are offered. And there's a good selection of outdoor clothing, including waders, camouflage wear, fishing vests and hunting jackets, snakeproof boots, moccasins, bush jackets, parkas, jeans, and more. The 296-page color catalog includes complete product descriptions and specifications, but if you need help with your selection or are buying for someone else, the customer service department can assist you.

Special Factors: Satisfaction is guaranteed; price quote by phone; returns are accepted for exchange, refund, or credit.

CAMPMOR

P.O. BOX 700
SADDLE RIVER, NJ
07458–0700
800–230–2151
201–445–5000

Catalog: free
Pay: check, MO, MC, V, AE, Discover
Sells: camping gear and supplies
Store: 810 Rte. 17 N., Paramus, NJ; Monday to Friday 9:30–9:30, Saturday 9:30–6, closed Sunday
E-mail: catalog-request@campmor.com
Online: http://www.campmor.com/

Campmor's 144-page catalog is full of great buys on camping goods, bike touring accessories, and clothing. You'll save up to 50% on clothing by Borglite Pile, Columbia Interchange System, Sierra Designs, Thinsulate, and Woolrich, as well as duofold and Polypro underwear, Sorel and Timberland boots, and other outerwear. Swiss Victorinox knives are offered at 30% off list, and Buck knives, Coleman cooking equipment, Sherpa snowshoes, Silva compasses, Edelrid climbing ropes, and books and manuals on camping and survival are available. You'll also find tents and sleeping bags by Coleman, Eureka, Moonstone, The North Face, Sierra Designs, Slumberjack, Wenzel, and Campmor's own lines, as well as backpacks by JanSport, Kelly Camp Trails, and Peak. Campmor has been in business since 1946, and is worth a trip if you're in the Paramus area—or check the website, which includes complete ordering information and numbers, shipping rates, and other details for overseas customers.

Special Factors: Returns are accepted for exchange, refund, or credit; minimum order is $20 on phone orders.

CENTRAL SKINDIVERS

160–09 JAMAICA AVE.
JAMAICA, NY 11432–6111
718–739–5772
FAX: 718–739–3679

Catalog: free
Pay: check, MO, MC, V, AE, Discover
Sells: SCUBA-diving equipment
Store: same address; Monday to Saturday 10–6:30

 ¡Sí!

Central Skindivers, in business since 1952, sells diving gear at savings of up to 40%, including tanks from Dacor, Sherwood, and U.S. Divers, and a full range of regulators, masks, fins, gauges, computers, suits, and other gear. There are buoyancy jackets from Dacor, Seaquest, Sherwood, U.S. Divers, and Zeagle, and watches and timers from Chronosport, Citizen, Heuer, and Seiko. Call for the catalog or a price quote.

Special Factors: Shipping is not charged; minimum order is $50.

CHEAP SHOT, INC.

━━━━━━━━━━

1797 RTE. 920
CANONSBURG, PA 15317
412–745–2658
FAX: 412–745–4265

Catalog: free
Pay: check or MO
Sells: ammunition
Store: Gun Runner, 950 S. Central Ave., Canonsburg, PA; Monday to Friday 8–8, Saturday 8–5, Sunday 10–4

Cheap Shot, "shooters serving shooters since 1978," offers savings of 33% and more on the usual prices of ammo and reloading components from CCI, Federal, Hornady, Remington, and Winchester. The 16-page catalog also offers a "reloading library," with several manuals on the subject. Because Cheap Shot specializes in ammo and buys in volume, the discounts are better than those offered by many hunting catalogs.

Please note: Federal regulations on age and identification requirements are stated in the catalog, and you must provide signature and drivers' license number in order to purchase ammunition.

Special Factors: Authorized returns are accepted (a 20% restocking fee may be charged); C.O.D. orders are accepted (a 25% deposit is required).

CUTLERY SHOPPE

━━━━━━━━━━

390 E. CORPORATE DR.
P.O. BOX 610
MERIDIAN, ID 83706–0610
800–231–1272
208–884–7500
FAX: 208–884–7575

Catalog: free
Pay: check, MO, MC, V, AE, Discover
Sells: cutlery, knives, sharpeners, etc.
Store: same address

The Cutlery Shoppe was established in 1984 by a supermarket meat manager who'd been a self-avowed knife nut since the age of eight. He's turned his passion into a great source for the collector, survivalist, hunter, camper, fisher, knife thrower, and even medievalist—there are 2 pages of daggers and swords among the 76 pages of knives, axes, sheathes, scabbards, whetstones, and related goods. The manufacturers include Benchmade, BK&T, Blackjack, Boker, Buck, Gerber, Gryphon, Leatherman, Al Mar, Normark (skinning axes), Puma, Russell Belt, SOG, Spec Plus, Spyderco, Timberline, and Victorinox. The catalog devotes a number of pages to knives used by the military and enforcement personnel—the SOG blade chosen by the Navy Seals, Ka-Bar USMC combat knives and Vietnam Tomahawks, and Aitor's "Jungle King" are among the current offerings. Telescoping batons, pepper spray, high-intensity flashlights, handgun portfolios, holsters, Kevlar body panels, and training devices are available.

Cutlery Shoppe also sells survival gear, including Katadyn water filters, folding shovels, cutlery kits, trail saws, camp axes, and knife-tool combinations by Leatherman and Victorinox. The catalog concludes with an extensive selection of Gerber and Henckels kitchen cutlery and implements, Kyocera knives with ceramic blades (reportedly harder than steel), and chef steels, bench stones, diamond hones, metal polishes, books and videos on knife use and collecting, and custom services—sheathes and blade engraving. None of the knives are cheap, even with discounts averaging 30% on list, but the collectors and connoisseurs who've helped establish the firm aren't complaining.

Please note: Consult your local ordinances regarding the purchase, possession, and use of weaponry and personal-protection devices.

Special Factors: Satisfaction is guaranteed; volume discounts are available; returns are accepted within 30 days for exchange, refund, or credit.

DEER SHACK

DEPT. WBMC-98
P.O. BOX E
977155 CTY. HWY. B
BELGIUM, WI 53004–0905
800–443–3337
414–994–9818
FAX: 414–994–4099

Catalog: $2
Pay: check, MO, MC, V, Discover
Sells: deer-related and hunting products
Store: mail order only

This catalog is devoted to the culture of the deer hunter, where a camo gun sock is listed under "Great Stocking Stuffers," and the audiotapes include *Vocabulary of Deer.* Much of the 64-page color catalog shows handsome gifts—limited edition prints of hunting scenes, handpainted bronzes, mirrors and home accents adorned with shed antlers, and signs, mats, plaques, desk accessories, belt buckles, mugs, and humorous literature. The hunting gear includes bow and gun accessories, decoy and scent supplies, game transport and processing supplies, Hatchbag vehicle liners, camo wear and blinds, tree stands, maps, and books and tapes covering everything from locating game to tanning the hides.

Special Factors: Satisfaction is guaranteed; returns (except personalized goods) are accepted for exchange, refund, or credit.

FITNESS FACTORY OUTLET

2875 S. 25TH AVE.
BROADVIEW, IL 60153
800–383–9300
708–345–9000
FAX: 708–345–9772

Catalog: free
Pay: check, MO, MC, V, AE, Discover
Sells: fitness and exercise equipment
Store: same address; Monday to Friday 11–7, Saturday 10–5 CT
Online: http://www.fitnessfactory.com

Fitness Factory Outlet has been supplying homes, schools, and gyms with fitness equipment since 1988, and offers a full range of machines and accessories at discounts averaging 40%. The biggest savings are on professional-quality, institutional-grade machines that run about $1,300. Home-use equipment and gyms begin at under $100, and the featured "Body-Solid" line offers a lifetime warranty on frames, pads, pulleys, cables, hardware, and all of the parts. The 48-page color catalog also shows rubber flooring, dumbbells, cable attachment bars, boxing and aerobic-conditioning equipment (treadmills, steppers, stationary bicycles, etc.), at good savings. You can call or write for the catalog, or request one from the website, which showcases most of the current product offerings.

Special Factors: Satisfaction is guaranteed; authorized returns in like-new condition are accepted for return within 31 days for exchange, refund, or credit (shipping and handling charges are not refundable).

DON GLEASON'S CAMPERS SUPPLY, INC.

9 PEARL ST.
P.O. BOX 87
NORTHAMPTON, MA
01061–0087
413–584–4895
FAX: 413–586–8770

Catalog: free
Pay: check, MO, MC, V, Discover
Sells: camping supplies and equipment
Store: same address; Monday to Friday
9–5:30, Thursday til 8:30, Saturday 9–5

Don Gleason has been helping America hit the trail since 1957, with everything from tents to trowels. The firm's 64-page catalog is packed with good buys on equipment—tents and screen houses by Eureka, The North Face, and Sierra Designs, sleeping bags by The North Face and Slumberjack, air mattresses, tarps, blankets, primus stoves and cookware, Coleman and Gott coolers, first aid kits, Buck knives, duffles, and backpacks and rucksacks by Camp Trails, Eagle Creek, JanSport, and The North Face. Don Gleason has an excellent selection of tent stakes and grommet kits, seals and other tent-mending supplies, hook-and-loop fastening, bungee cords and bungee-by-the-yard, camp toilets, cots, compasses, flashlights, insect repellents, axes, picks, and even gold-panning equipment. Savings run up to 50%, and there are volume discounts of 10% and 15% on the freeze-dried food from Mountain House. See the catalog for details of the no-hassle warranty.

Special Factors: Satisfaction is guaranteed; quantity discounts are available; returns are accepted for exchange, refund, or credit; minimum order is $10 with credit cards.

GOLF HAUS

700 N. PENNSYLVANIA
LANSING, MI 48906
517–482–8842
FAX: 517–482–8843

Price List: free
Pay: check, MO, MC, V
Sells: golf clubs, apparel, and accessories
Store: same address; Monday to Saturday
9–5:30

Golf Haus has "the absolute lowest prices on pro golf clubs" any-where—up to 70% below list—and stocks goods by every major manu-facturer. All of the models sold here are available nationwide, which means that, unlike the "exclusive models" offered by a number of dis-counters, the goods at Golf Haus can be price-shopped fairly. There are clubs, bags, putters, balls, and other golf equipment and supplies by Cobra (including the "King Cobra" line), Hogan, Lynx, MacGregor, Maxfli, Ping, PowerBilt, Ram, Spalding, Taylormade, Tiger Shark, Titleist, Wilson, and other firms. There are shoes by Dexter, Etonic, Footjoy, and Reebok, as well as Bag Boy carts, gloves, umbrellas, spikes, scorekeep-ers, visors, rain suits, tote bags, socks, and much more.

Please note: Golf Haus is offering a free set of headcovers with an order of a complete set of clubs (woods and irons) to readers who mention WBMC.

Special Factors: Free shipping and insurance on orders shipped within the continental United States; minimum order is $50.

GOLFSMITH
INTERNATIONAL, INC.

11000 N. IH35
AUSTIN, TX 78753
800–456–3344
512–837–4810
FAX: 512–837–1245

Price List: free
Pay: check, MO, MC, V, Discover
Sells: golf clubs, components, accessories
and repair equipment
Store: same address; Monday to Friday 7–7,
Saturday 8–7, Sunday 9–7
Online: http://www.golfsmith.com

Golfsmith International's accessories catalog, *The Golf Store*, features the top names in golf equipment as well as the firm's own line of Golfsmith clubs. Golfsmith can make woods and irons in any flex, length, weight, or grip size. The Golf Store catalog brings you 60 pages of putters, specialty clubs, bags, balls, clothing, footwear, gloves, pull carts, and other accessories, including instructional videos and books. Golfsmith, which opened its doors in 1967, offers savings of up to 50% on the cost of comparable name-brand products.

The 228-page *Clubhead and Components* catalog offers a complete selection of golf club heads for woods, irons, and putters, as well as grips, shafts, refinishing supplies and tools, and instruction manuals. Golfsmith conducts the Harvey Penick Golf Academy (and codesigned the line of Harvey Penick clubs), and also offers four different training programs in making, repairing, and fitting clubs, for every level of experience. All of the courses are conducted at Golfsmith's complex in Austin, Texas.

Non-U.S. readers, please note: Orders must be paid in U.S. funds.

Special Factors: Request each catalog desired by name; C.O.D. orders are accepted.

HERTER'S

DEPT. 24626
P.O. BOX 1819
BURNSVILLE, MN
 55337–0819
800–654–3825
FAX: 612–894–0083

Catalog: free
Pay: check, MO, MC, V, AE, Discover
Sells: waterfowl-hunting, trapping, and related equipment
Store: 111 E. Burnet St., Beaver Dam, WI
Online: http://www.northernonline.com

 ¡Si!

Herter's, "The Waterfowling & Outdoor Specialists," serves hunters, guides, gunsmiths, forest rangers, and explorers with 48 color pages of everything from camouflage clothing to a cast-iron kit for turning a 55-gallon drum into a barrel stove. There are several pages of hunting decoys and duck and goose calls, and tree stands, snowshoes, optics, ATV accessories and truck items, gun cases and cabinets, rifles (air and pellet), and hunting-related books and videos are all available. A number of the products sold here—unbreakable Thermoses, illuminated watches, folding stools, etc.—would be useful to campers and outdoors enthusiasts generally, as well as to hunters. The prices are competitive, but since list prices aren't given and some of the products are hard to comparison-shop, check to make sure you're getting the best deal before ordering.

Please note: Herter's reminds you that compliance with legal requirements and restrictions on the purchase of hunting-related equipment is your responsibility.

Special Factors: Authorized returns are accepted within 30 days for exchange, refund, or credit (see the catalog for details).

HOLABIRD SPORTS

9220 PULASKI HWY.
BALTIMORE, MD 21220
410–687–6400
FAX: 410–687–7311

Brochure: free
Pay: check, MO, MC, V, AE, Discover
Sells: racquet sports equipment and athletic footwear
Store: same address; Monday to Friday 9–5, Saturday 9–3
Online: http://www.holabirdsports.com

  ⊕ ¡Si!

Buy here and get the "Holabird Advantage": equipment and footwear for racquet sports at up to 40% below list prices, service on manufacturers' warranties, and free stringing with tournament nylon on all racquets. If you're in the Baltimore area, drop by and try out a racquet on Holabird's indoor court.

Holabird has been in business since 1981, and carries tennis racquets by scores of firms, including Donnay, Dunlop, Estusa, Fischer, Fox, Head, Kneissl, Mizuno, Prince, Pro-Kennex, Rossignol, Slazenger, Spalding, Volkl, Wavex, Wilson, Wimbledon, Yamaha, and Yonex. There are tennis balls by Dunlop, Penn, and Wilson, ball machines by Lobster, and footwear by Adidas, Asics, Avia, Converse, Diadora, Fila, Head, K-Swiss, New Balance, Nike, Prince, Prince, Reebok, Wilson, and others.

Racquetball players should check the prices on racquets by E-Force, Ektelon, Head, Pro-Kennex, Spalding, and Wilson. The squash department features racquets by Black Knight, Dunlop, Ektelon, Fox, Head, Pro-Kennex, Prince, Slazenger, Spalding, and Wilson, and eye guards by Black Knight, Ektelon, Leader, and Pro-Kennex. Pros can save their clubs sizable sums on court equipment and maintenance supplies, such as court dryers, tennis nets, ball hoppers, and stringing machines.

Holabird also stocks a full line of basketball, cross-training, aerobic, running, walking, and hiking shoes, as well as sandals, T-shirts, socks, caps, sunglasses from Ray-Ban, and Timex sport watches. See the monthly eight-page catalog for specials, or call or write for a price quote.

Special Factors: Authorized returns (except used items) are accepted within seven days.

THE HOUSE

**300 S. OWASSO BLVD.,
DEPT. WBMC
ST. PAUL, MN 55117
612–482–9995
FAX: 612–482–1353**

Catalog: free
Pay: check, MO, MC, V, AE, Discover
Sells: windsurfing, snowboarding, in-line skating, and kayaking equipment
Store: same address; Monday to Friday 10–8, Saturday 9–2
Online: http://www.the-house.com

Put wind and water together, and you have the prime ingredients for the thrilling sport of windsurfing, also known as sailboarding. The right equipment helps, which is what you'll find at The House—at discounts that average 25%, but run much deeper on sale items and special purchases. The House has been in business since 1982, selling light to heavy wind sailboards, sails, masts, harnesses, fins, and a broad selection of windsurfing apparel. The 40-plus-page catalogs feature equipment by BIC, Chinook, DaKine, Fanatic, Fiberspar, Maui Magic, Mistral, NeilPryde, O'Brien, SeaTrend, Simmer, Tiga, Topsails, Windsurfing Hawaii, and other manufacturers. The boards run from entry-level to custom models for pros, and the catalog includes numerous informative sidebars on choosing equipment and evaluating construction and materials. Car racks by Automaxi, Barrecrafters, and Thule are offered, as well as windsurfing books and videos, and wet suits, drysuits, harnesses and other accessories by Bare, Body Glove, O'Neill, and Ronny.

The House also answers your winter sports needs with a full line of snowboards from Aggression, Apocalypse, H-Ride, Heavy Tools, Joyride, Kemper, Kingpin, Limited, Liquid, Original Sin, Pyramid, and Rad Air; boots by Alpina, Airwalk, Grunge, and Vans; and related equipment. And if the day brings neither wind nor snow, strap on a pair of Kinetic or Rollerblade in-line skates (sold here at a discount), and take on the pavement instead!

Please note: Phone hours are Monday to Friday 8–7, Saturday 9–1 CT.

Special Factors: Satisfaction is guaranteed; authorized returns are accepted within 20 days for exchange, refund, or credit.

MUELLER SPORTING GOODS, INC.

DEPT. 60
4825 SO. 16TH ST.
LINCOLN, NE 68512
800–627–8888
402–423–8888
FAX: 402–423–5964

Catalog: free
Pay: check, MO, MC, V, Discover
Sells: billiards, table tennis, and darts equipment
Store: 2019 Hwy. 2, Lincoln, NE; also 5705 Hickman Rd., Des Moines, IA; Monday to Saturday 9–6, Sunday 1–5
E-mail: msginfo@inetnebr.com
Online: http://www.mueller-sporting-goods.com

"Billiards," opines Funk & Wagnalls, is a "family of games played on rectangular tables twice as long as they are wide, with balls propelled by tapered, leather-tipped rods called cues." What began as an outdoor game played on the ground has moved inside and is now played on a field of green felt. Mueller Sporting Goods serves the serious enthusiast and billiards parlor manager with a full selection of cues and accessories for pool (the American version of billiards). The 164-page catalog shows an extensive selection of cues from Mali, McDermott, and Meucci, including limited editions and collectors' models, as well as more modestly priced "house cues" by Valley. Carrying cases, racks, bridges, balls, chalk, replacement felt and table bumpers, and a complete selection of cue-repair materials are offered. (Repair services are available; prices for replacing tips, ferrules, shafts, collars and joints, and rewrapping the staff are listed.) Mueller also sells products designed to give you an edge—wood conditioners, tip shavers, burnishers, and waxers—and books and videos on every aspect of the game.

Mueller serves two other interests—table tennis and the British pub favorite, darts. There are tournament-grade dart boards and page after page of darts, annotated with copy that reads more like Defense Department announcements of stealth weapons than descriptions of equipment for a bar game. The darts can be customized with a choice of shafts and "flights"—the feather element—and bar stools, posters, and dart-related gifts are also available. Both list and discount prices are given, and savings average 40% but reach 55% on some items.

Special Factors: Price quote by phone or letter; quantity discounts are available; returns (except personalized and custom-made goods) are accepted within 30 days for exchange, refund, or credit.

OVERTON'S SPORTS CENTER, INC.

DEPT. 57612

P.O. BOX 8228

GREENVILLE, NC 27835

800–334–6541

919–355–7600

FAX: 919–355–2923

Catalog: free
Pay: check, MO, MC, V, AE, Discover
Sells: boating accessories and water sports goods
Store: 5343 South Boulevard, Charlotte; 111 Red Banks Rd., Greenville; and 3062 Wakeforest Rd., Raleigh, NC
E-mail: custserv@overtonsonline.com
Online: http://www.overtonsonline.com/

Overton's lays claim to title of "World's Largest Water Sports Dealer," selling a wide range of equipment for boating, water skiing, snorkeling, and other avocations at up to 40% off list. Overton's was established in 1975, and publishes three catalogs. The 132-page, color *Water Sports* catalog features skis and accessories ranging from junior trainers to experts' tricks, jumpers and slaloms by Connelly, EP, Jobe, Kidder, O'Brien, and other firms. Wet suits, apparel, knee boards, water toys, inflatables, snorkeling accessories, boating accessories, books, videotapes, and personal watercraft accessories are also offered. The 48-page swimwear and apparel catalog, "Kristi's," features such names as De La Mer, Bendigo, Venus, Solar Tan Thru, Point Conception, OP, O'Neill, Take Cover, Club Sportwear, and many more. The look is California young, with eye-popping prints dominating the collection.

The 200-page Discount Boating Accessories answers your boating needs with a wide range of products: boat seats and covers, safety equipment, instruments, electronics, hardware, cleaners, fishing equipment, clothing, fuel tanks, and performance accessories. The brands include Apelco, Aqua Meter, Brinkman, Eagle, Humminbird, Interphase, Ray Jefferson, Maxxima, Newmar, PowerWinch, Shakespeare, and Si-Tex, among others. The equipment catalogs give both the list or comparable retail, and Overton's discount prices. If you're online, don't miss the terrific website—products, sports information, special buys, and much more.

Canadian readers, please note: Only U.S. funds are accepted.

Special Factors: Satisfaction is guaranteed; quantity discounts are available; unused returns are accepted within 30 days for exchange, refund, or credit; C.O.D. orders are accepted.

PERFORMANCE BICYCLE SHOP

P.O. BOX 2741
CHAPEL HILL, NC
   27515–2741
800–727–2453
FAX: 800–727–3291

Catalog: free
Pay: check, MO, MC, V, Discover
Sells: bicycle parts and cycling apparel
Store: 35 stores in CA, CO, IL, MD, NC, OR, PA, VA, and WA
Online: http://www.performancebike.com

Serious cyclists are familiar with Performance Bicycle Shop for the company's line of bicycling parts, accessories, and clothing. The firm's parts department is well stocked with components by Campagnolo, Look, Mavic, Shimano, Time, and other firms. Performance has been in business since 1981 and offers a large selection of cycling clothing, as well as helmets, cycling shoes, gloves, panniers, and hundreds of products to enhance performance. The brands represented in the 80-page color catalog include Avocet, Bell, Blackburn, Giro, Nike, Profile, Scott USA, Shimano, Specialized, Thule, and Vetta, among others. In-line skates (Rollerblades) and camping gear are also available.

Special Factors: Satisfaction is guaranteed.

PERFORMANCE DIVER

DEPT. WBMC
P.O. BOX 2741
CHAPEL HILL, NC
   27514–2714
800–933–2299
FAX: 800–727–3291

Catalog: free
Pay: check, MO, MC, V, Discover
Sells: scuba equipment and apparel
Store: Raleigh, NC
E-mail: catalog@performancediver.com

Performance Diver, established in 1990, sells a full line of scuba equipment, accessories, apparel regulators, gauges, BDCs, wet suits, and a wide variety of accessories. Although many of the items are manufactured by the same companies that sell under well-known labels in dive shops, they're available here under the Performance name at savings of up to 50% on comparable retail. The catalog emphasizes technologically advanced design, with the latest construction methods used to maximize performance, comfort, and safety. You don't have to dive to appreciate the good selection of Citizen watches, T-shirts, Supplex trunks and Lycra tanks, or duffel bags—but any recreational activity that features "treasure recovery bags" in multiple sizes is definitely worth a look.

Special Factors: Satisfaction is guaranteed; returns are accepted for exchange, refund, or credit.

SIERRA TRADING POST

DEPT. WBMC–98
5025 CAMPSTOOL RD.
CHEYENNE, WY
82007–1802
U.S.: 800–713–4534
307–775–8000
FAX (U.S.): 800–378–8946
FAX: 307–775–8088

Catalog: free
Pay: check, MO, MC, V, Discover
Sells: outdoor clothing and equipment
Store: same address; Monday to Saturday 9–6, Sunday 12–6; also 2000 Harvard Way, Reno, NV; Monday to Saturday 10–7, Sunday 11–5

Sierra Trading Post, established in 1986, offers casual and outdoor clothing and camping gear in a charming, 48-page catalog. Sierra is essentially a mail-order outlet store that sells closeouts, overruns, and special purchases at savings of up to 70%. Rugged clothing and outerwear, shoes for hiking and running, great pants and shorts, socks, sweaters, underwear, and even comfortable dresses are among the offerings. Name brands pepper the catalog—Acorn, Calida, Columbia, Descente, Duofold, Fenwick, Hanes, Hind, Kelty, Lowe, Marmot, Merrell, New Balance, Nike, Pearl Izumi, Sierra Designs, Sportif USA, and Teva are among the manufacturers represented in past mailings. Sleeping bags, backpacks, and tents are also available.

Non-U.S. readers, please note: Orders are shipped outside the United States (via USPS) to APO/FPO destinations, Canada, and Japan only.

Special Factors: Satisfaction is guaranteed; returns are accepted for exchange, refund, or credit.

SOCCER INTERNATIONAL, INC.

P.O. BOX 7222,
DEPT. WBM–98
ARLINGTON, VA
22207–7222
703–524–4333

Catalog: $2
Pay: check or MO
Sells: soccer gear, accessories, and gifts
Store: mail order only
E-mail: sdobson@cais.com
Online: http://www.soccerinternational.com/soccerintl

 (see text)

Soccer International, founded in 1976 by a rabid soccer buff, publishes an 18-page color catalog of game-related items ranging from professional equipment to novelties. The savings run up to 30% on some goods, compared to the prices charged by other firms, but generally average about 20% less. The catalog is a must-see for any soccer enthusiast or friend of one, since it's a great resource for gifts as well as gear.

You'll find a number of balls here from Adidas, Brine, Mikasa, and Umbro, plus a variety of jerseys and T-shirts. PVC leg shields and ankle guards, a ball inflator, nets and goals, practice aids, and a great selection of books and videotapes on coaching, game strategy, and soccer rules are available. If you're stuck on the sidelines, you'll want Lava Buns, the stadium cushion. Pop it in the microwave for a few minutes, and it will keep your bottom warm for hours. Soccer International also sells soccer-theme games, radios, door mats, mugs, ties, cloisonné pins, bumper stickers, doorknobs, and lamps. This is where you'll find the World Cup 1994 video highlights (of most of the games), poster, tie, and playing cards, as well as replica team jerseys of four of the top soccer-playing countries. Soccer-loving puzzle buffs will enjoy the challenge of Mordillo jigsaw puzzles from Germany, which run from 500 to 2,000 pieces.

Canadian readers, please note: Orders must be paid in U.S. funds, drawn on the Canadian postal service, or on a U.S. bank.

APO/FPO readers, please note: Orders are not shipped to APO/FPO addresses during November or December.

Institutional buyers, please note: Catalog prices are mainly for single items, but Soccer International's specialty is sales to teams, leagues, clubs, and schools. If you're buying in multiples for a group, let the company know when you request the catalog.

Special Factors: Minimum order is $15; shipping is not charged on orders over $35 sent within the contiguous United States.

SPIKE NASHBAR, INC.

DEPT. WBM8
4111 SIMON RD.
YOUNGSTOWN, OH 44512
800-SPIKE-IT
FAX: 800-456-1223

Catalog: free
Pay: check, MO, MC, V, Discover
Sells: volleyball gear and apparel
Store: same address (Nashbar Outlet Store);
call 330-782-2244 for hours
E-mail: mail@spike.nashbar.com
Online: http://www.nashbar.com/

Spike Nashbar, established in 1990, offers competition volleyball gear, clothing, and accessories. The 40-page color catalog offers over two dozen balls for indoor and outdoor play, from Brine, Mikasa, Molten, Sideout, Spalding, Tachikara, and Wilson. Over two dozen lines of clothing are offered, and several nets and net systems are available, including one from Park and Sun for under $90 and "the best portable net system available," the Spectrum series, which costs about $226. There are volleyball shoes for men and women by Asics, Kaepa, Mizuno, Power, and Reebok. Sport bras, socks, T-shirts, shorts, duffels, sport watches, and sunglasses from Bausch & Lomb are also sold, as well as vital knee protection from Asics and Body Glove. If you've ever watched or played serious volleyball, you'll know why they're part of the standard uniform of the game. Spike Nashbar has a "guaranteed lowest price" policy; see the catalog for details. And don't miss the website—you can order a print catalog, look at the online catalog, or check the closeouts and bargains while you're there.

Canadian readers, please note: Only U.S. funds are accepted.

Special Factors: Satisfaction is guaranteed; quantity discounts are available; returns are accepted for exchange, refund, or credit.

THE SPORTSMAN'S GUIDE, INC.

DEPT. WBM 8
411 FARWELL AVE.
ST. PAUL, MN 55075–0239
800–888–3006, DEPT. WBM 8
FAX: 800–333–6933

Catalog: free
Pay: check, MO, MC, V, AE, Discover
Sells: outdoor clothing and footwear, hunting and camping gear, military surplus, etc.
Store: mail order only
Online: http://www.sportsmansguide.com

The Sportsman's Guide is a potpourri of gear and goodies for the rough-and-ready set, over 200 pages that begin with thermal underwear and end with insulated gloves. In between are work boots and athletic footwear, parkas and Australian-style dusters, flannel shirts, work jackets, and much more, from well-known manufacturers. The catalog shows gear for camping (tents and sleeping bags) and hunting (rifle optics and ammo), as well as auto accessories, watches, power tools, and hunting-related gifts. Prices run from reasonable to great, and devotees of The Sportsman's Guide can join the firm's Buyer's Club (about $30 annually at this writing) for a 10% discount on regular catalog prices and "Members Only" specials. Even if you're not the hunting type, you may find that membership pays off—any catalog that offers lava lamps, snowshoes, and abdominal exercisers is aiming for the broadest possible appeal!

Special Factors: Satisfaction is guaranteed; see catalog order form for information and shipping restrictions on certain goods; returns are accepted for exchange, refund, or credit.

SURVIVAL SUPPLY CO.

P.O. BOX 4582-WM
COEUR D'ALENE, ID
83814–1960
208–765–6201

Catalog: $2
Pay: check, MO, MC, V, AE
Sells: camping and outdoor gear, survival supplies, etc.
Store: mail order only
E-mail: bob541@directcon.net

Survival Supply began business in 1988 and serves two distinct but overlapping markets: outdoors enthusiasts and survivalists. The 44-page catalog is heavy on emergency food and gear, and lists books on everything from combat ammunition to Caribbean tax havens. There's an extensive selection of dehydrated foods, including goods from Back-packers Pantry and Ready Reserve. Survival Supply's survival kits can keep one or two persons going for 3 to 30 days, or a party of four sustained for up to a year. A seven-day food kit for four costs about $250 at this writing, and includes water purification tablets, stoves and fuel, a cooking kit, 30 candles and waterproof matches, and much more, besides the food. In addition, Survival Supply offers a small selection of camp stoves and lanterns, mess kits, flashlights, camp saws and shovels, gas masks, knives, first-aid kits, duffels, camouflage BDUs, and survival guides—from genuine military manuals to handbooks on poaching. Everything is offered at prices that average 25% below regular retail, and quantity discounts are available on food items.

If you do the purchasing for an institution, corporation, city, or county with an emergency preparedness program, you can call, fax, or write for the corporate price list. It features a number of kits for large-scale emergencies—the "five member search and rescue" and "25 person disaster and trauma first aid" kits are examples. Water pouches and drums and nitrogen-packed dehydrated foods are available, as well as MRE (Meals Ready to Eat) rations. Please note that you must be from a *qualifying group* to receive the price list.

Special Factors: Quantity discounts are available.

TELEPRO GOLF SHOP

1425 N. MAIN ST.
SANTA ANA, CA 92701
800–835–8473
FAX: 714–542–4141

Brochure: free
Pay: check, MO, MC, V, Discover
Sells: golf clubs
Store: Shamrock Golf Shops in Lakewood, Los Angeles, Newport, Palos Verdes, Pasadena, and Santa Ana, CA; addresses are listed in the brochure

Telepro, a division of Shamrock Golf Shops, sells first-quality golf clubs and accessories at savings of up to 40%. Telepro has been in business since 1973, and sells clubs by Callaway, Cobra, Hogan, Lynx, Mizuno, Ping, Pinnacle, Shamrock, Spalding, Taylormade, Titleist, Wilson, Yonex, and other manufacturers. Bags and other accessories are sold at varying discounts. The brochure includes a questionnaire on your golfing style, which helps Telepro determine the best clubs for your game.

Special Factors: Satisfaction is guaranteed; returns (except special orders) are accepted within 30 days (a 10% restocking fee may be charged).

WATER WAREHOUSE

6950 51ST ST.
KENOSHA, WI 53144–1740
800–574–7665
FAX: 414–605–1065

Catalog: $2
Pay: check, MO, MC, V, Discover
Sells: swimming pool supplies and equipment
Store: mail order only

Swimming pools have two lives—summer and winter—and Water Ware-house sells supplies and equipment for both seasons, at savings of up to 50% on list or comparable retail. Here are all the chemicals you need to keep the water safe, and cut down on maintenance: Monarc chlorinating tabs, oxidizers (shocks), rust and scale preventers, algaecides, pH bal-ancers, and other agents. You'll also find water-testing kits, pool skim-mers, vacuums, thermometers, filters, and brushes, and the tools for enjoying the fruits of your labor—inflatable loungers, sport tubes, kiddie "riders," flippers, water balls, and diving games. When the weather turns cool, Water Warehouse helps out with high-speed pool pumps (for quick draining), repair kits for vinyl liners, winterizing plugs (to save the skim-mer), covers for all pool shapes and sizes, and water sleeves to hold the covers down. The 52-page color catalog features these products and more, from names like Arneson, Jacuzzi, Polaris, and Teledyne, and there are seasonable sales that lower the discount prices even further.

Special Factors: Satisfaction is guaranteed; returns are accepted within 30 days for exchange, refund, or credit.

WILEY OUTDOOR SPORTS, INC.

DEPT. WBMC
P.O. BOX 99
DECATUR, AL 35602
800–494–5397
FAX: 205–351–8743

Catalog: free (see text)
Pay: check, MO, MC, V, Discover
Sells: hunting, camping, and outdoor gear and equipment
Store: 1808 Sportsman Lane, Huntsville, AL; Monday to Friday 9–6, Saturday 9–4:30
Online: http://www.fyeo.com

This family-run business has been outfitting hunters with a full range of equipment and gear since 1953, and offers savings that average 30%, but can run as high as 50% on certain items and lines. Wiley specializes in hunting, reloading, camping, and optical equipment, and serves the dedicated outdoors enthusiast. The catalog includes a good selection of tents, backpacks, knives, binoculars, and clothing, as well as the hunting equipment. The firm prides itself on its commitment to good service and lifelong customer relationships, and invites serious inquiries only about its goods.

Special Factors: Satisfaction is guaranteed; unused returns are accepted within 10 days for exchange, refund, or credit; minimum order is $25; C.O.D. orders (via UPS only) are accepted.

WORLD WIDE AQUATICS

Catalog: free, $2 outside the U.S.
Pay: check, MO, MC, V, AE, Discover
Sells: swimwear and accessories
Store: mail order only

DEPT. WBMC
10500 UNIVERSITY CEN-
   TER DR., SUITE 250
TAMPA, FL 33612–6462
800–726–1530
813–972–0818
FAX: 813–972–0905

Buying a swimsuit is one of the top ten Most Dreaded Shopping Activities, in part because of the convergence of large expanses of skin, fluorescent lights, and endless mirrors. Swimsuit styles are also problematical —they're often cut to reveal more than comfort and reputation allow. World Wide Aquatics solves all of these problems, and offers savings of up to 50% on selected suits as well.

The firm's 48-page color catalogs show swimsuits, trunks, shorts, and coverups for men, women, and children from Arena, Hind, Hydro-Fit, Ocean, Quintana Roo, Speedo, and Tyr. The styles run from racing-sleek to skirted, full-coverage models, including a line designed for post-mastectomy wear. The sizes run from children's 4 to women's size 24, men's to a 40-inch waist. "Aqueous" shoes for use in the pool and water-exercise equipment are also available. World Wide Aquatics sells workout wear by Dolphin and Speedo (including triathlon clothing that goes from bike to beach), wet suits, swimming goggles, bathing caps, and competition equipment and books.

World Wide Aquatics has been in business since 1972, and offers deep discounts on multiples of 12 of selected suits—ideal for schools and swim clubs. See the catalog for details, or if you know the style you want from one of the manufacturers listed here, call for availability and a quote.

Special Factors: Satisfaction is guaranteed; new, unused returns (except books and videos) with hangtags and labels are accepted in the original packaging for exchange, refund, or credit.

SEE ALSO

Bruce Medical Supply • small selection of fitness equipment • **MEDICINE: SPECIAL NEEDS**

The Button Shop • zippers for tents and sleeping bags • **CRAFTS: TEXTILE ARTS**

Car Racks Direct • car racks for sports equipment, boats, etc. • **AUTO**

ChuckWagon Outfitters • camp cookware, cookbooks, etc. • **HOME: KITCHEN**

CISCO • swimming pool accessories and parts • **HOME: IMPROVEMENT**

Clothcrafters, Inc. • flannel gun-cleaning patches, mosquito netting, sleeping bag liners • **GENERAL MERCHANDISE**

Creative Health Products • exercise equipment • **HEALTH**

Dance Distributors • dancewear, gymnastics shoes, etc. • **CLOTHING**

Defender Industries, Inc. • water sports accessories • **AUTO**

E & B Marine Supply, Inc. • water skis • **AUTO**

Ewald-Clark • binoculars • **CAMERAS**

A. Feibusch Corporation • replacement tent zippers • **CRAFTS: TEXTILE ARTS**

Leather Unlimited Corp. • black-powder supplies, suede duffel bags • **LUGGAGE**

Mardiron Optics • binoculars and spotting scopes • **CAMERAS**

Mass. Army & Navy Store • government surplus camping and survival gear • **CLOTHING**

Newark Dressmaker Supply, Inc. • replacement zippers for sleeping bags and tents • **CRAFTS: TEXTILE ARTS**

Orion Telescopes & Binoculars • binoculars • **CAMERAS**

Racer Wholesale • auto-racing safety equipment and accessories • **AUTO**

Ruvel & Company, Inc. • government surplus camping supplies and survival goods • **TOOLS**

RV Direct • folding bicycles, bike racks, RV equipment, etc. • **AUTO**

Safe Specialties, Inc. • gun safes and pistol boxes • **OFFICE**

Scope City Inc. • field binoculars, spotting scopes • **CAMERAS**

Sport Europa • swimwear and workout clothing for men and women • **CLOTHING**

Sportswear Clearinghouse • athletic apparel • **CLOTHING**

State Line Tack, Inc. • saddle and tack, riding clothing, etc. • **ANIMAL**

TOOLS, HARDWARE, ELECTRONICS, ENERGY, SAFETY, SECURITY, SURPLUS, AND INDUSTRIAL GOODS

Materials, supplies, equipment, and services

This chapter offers the do-it-yourselfer, woodworker, hobbyist, woodcutter, and small-time mechanic a wealth of tools and hardware, some of it at rock-bottom prices. Replacement parts for lawn mowers, trimmers, garden tractors, snowmobiles, snow throwers, blowers, go-carts, minibikes, and even plumbing and electrical systems are available from these companies. The tools run from hex wrenches and fine wood chisels to complete work benches and professional machinery, and the hardware includes hard-to-find specialty items as well as nuts and bolts.

Observing safety precautions is as important as selecting the right tool for the job. When you're working, use goggles, dust masks, respirators, earplugs, gloves, and other protective gear as appropriate. (A number of the firms listed here sell safety equipment.) Keep your blades sharpened, and make sure your tools, hardware, and chemicals are kept out of the reach of children and pets. If you're using a chain saw, make sure it's fitted with an approved antikickback device (contact the manufacturer for recommendations). Make sure your work area is equipped with a fire extinguisher and first-aid kit for emergencies, and make sure you'd be able to get help if you had an accident.

For more tools and related products, see "Crafts and Hobbies," "General Merchandise," and the "Improvement" section of "Home."

ABRASIVES • **Econ-Abrasives, Red Hill, Woodworker's Hardware**
LOGGING EQUIPMENT • **Bailey's, H & H, Zip Power Parts**
MINIATURE TOOLS • **Micro-Mark**
SAFETY GEAR • **Bailey's, Econ-Abrasives**
SURPLUS GOODS • **H & R, Ruvel, Surplus Center**
TOOLS AND HARDWARE • **William Alden, Camelot, Clegg's, Coastal, H & R, Harbor Freight, Holz, Northern Hydraulics, Tool Crib, Tools on Sale, Wholesale Tool, Woodworker's Hardware**

WILLIAM ALDEN COMPANY

27 STUART ST.
BOSTON, MA 02116
800–249–8665
617–426–3430
FAX: 800–249–8665
FAX: 617–426–3430

Catalog: free
Pay: check, MO, MC, V, AE, Discover
Sells: tools for contractors, woodworkers, general handy work
Store: mail order only; phone hours Monday to Friday 8 a.m.–9 p.m., Saturday 9–5 ET

The 152-page color catalog from William Alden Company showcases the hand and power tools most in demand from do-it-yourselfers, contractors, and woodworkers. Equipment from Bosch, DeWalt, Freud, Hitachi, Irwin, Jet, Makita, Milwaukee, Porter-Cable, and Ryobi is available, as well as clamps and vises from American Tool, Gross Stabil, Jorgensen, Pony, Stanley, and Vise-Grip; Fuller countersinks; Lenox hole saws; and Stanley measuring tapes and hand tools. You'll find gauges, gouges, levels, chisels, saws, nippers, snips, hammers, mallets, cabinet hardware and drawer slides from Amerock and Knape & Vogt, and a good basic selection of furniture pulls and knobs. The discounts run up to 50%, and there are excellent prices on items that are often sold closer to list price—like the Goldblatt tool bags, face masks and breathing filters, and Maglite flashlights. Past catalogs have included a "Bulk Buy Page" with extra savings on things you may use regularly: multiples of sanding belts, wood glue, dust masks, paint rollers, drill bits, and masking tape. Everything is covered by the William Alden pledge that "We sell only NEW, FIRST QUALITY products. . . NO SECONDS!"

Special Factors: Satisfaction is guaranteed; price quote by phone or letter; returns are accepted within 30 days for exchange, refund, or credit.

ALL ELECTRONICS CORP.

DEPT. WBMC
P.O. BOX 567
VAN NUYS, CA 91408–0567
800–826–5432
818–904–0524
FAX: 818–781–2653

Catalog: free, $5 outside the U.S.
Pay: check, MO, MC, V, AE, Discover
Sells: surplus electronics and tools
Store: 905 S. Vermont Ave., Los Angeles, CA; Monday to Friday 9–5, Saturday 9–4; also 14928 Oxnard St., Van Nuys, CA; Monday to Friday 9–6:30, Saturday 9–5
Online: http://www.allcorp.com

 ¡Si!

Electronics hobbyists will appreciate the 96-page catalog from All Electronics, which has been in business since 1967. Every issue features a huge number of surplus parts, hardware items, and tools: semiconductors, transducers, heat sinks, sockets, cables and adapters, fans, plugs, switches, solenoids, relays, capacitors, piezoelectric elements, fuses, resistors, transformers, potentiometers, keyboards, computer fans, PC boards, and hard-to-find and one-of-a-kind items are typical offerings. While much of the stock is for electronics hobbyists, the catalogs usually offer such items as telephone cords and jacks, TV and video accessories, screwdrivers, soldering irons, hemostats, and rechargeable batteries.

Special Factors: All parts are guaranteed to be in working order; returns are accepted within 30 days.

BAILEY'S

44650 HWY. 101
P.O. BOX 550
LAYTONVILLE, CA 95454
800–322–4539
FAX: 707–984–8115

Catalog: free, $6 outside the U.S.
Pay: check, MO, MC, V, AE, Discover
Sells: "woodsman" supplies
Store: same address; Monday to Friday 7–6, Saturday 8–1; also 196 Edwards Dr., Jackson, TN; Monday to Friday 7–6, Saturday 8–1 (TN)
E-mail: baileys@bbaileys.com
Online: http://www.bbaileys.com

Bailey's, one of the country's best sources for "mail-order woodsman supplies, at discount prices," stocks a large number of goods everyone will find useful—specialty boots, leather conditioners, outdoor clothing, and safety gear. Campers and even urbanites will appreciate the well-priced outerwear (Filson jackets and pants, flannel shirts, rain slickers, etc.), and the first-aid kits and portable fire extinguishers. In addition, there are boot dryers, E.A.R. plugs and headset noise mufflers, and work gloves.

The 92-page color catalog (free on request, $6 if sent to addresses outside the U.S.) features woodcutting equipment (including chain saws), and lists Oregon and Bailey brand chain reels and bars for saws by Echo, Homelite, Husqvarna, McCulloch, Pioneer, and Stihl. Silvey chain grinders, spark plugs, automatic measuring tapes, guide bars, bar and chain oil, bar wrenches and files, and other tools are available. Bailey's stocks a full line of heavy-duty calked leather, rubber, and PAK-insulated boots, as well as Vibram and Air Bob boots, all available with and without steel toes. There are log splitters, Alaskan saw mills, Wood-bug and the new Lucas portable small-log sawmills, chain-saw-powered winches, firefighting equipment, climbing gear, and reforestation supplies (including seedlings). Bailey's is the place to call if you have questions about your chain saw. Savings run as high as 60% on goods in the general catalog, and even more on items offered in the sales flyers.

Special Factors: Bailey's NRI number is 23079956.

CAMELOT ENTERPRISES

P.O. BOX 65, DEPT. W
BRISTOL, WI 53104–0065
414–857–2695

Catalog: $2, refundable
Pay: check, MO, MC, V
Sells: fasteners, tools, and hardware
Store: 8234 199 Ave. (facing 83rd St.), Bristol, WI; Tuesday to Friday 8–6, Saturday 8–12; other hours by appointment only

Camelot, founded in 1983, sells "quality fasteners, hardware, and tools direct to the craftsman" at savings of up to 60%, through a 32-page catalog that's jam-packed with garage and workshop necessities. Camelot carries a full range of nuts (hex, K-lock, wing, stop, etc.), bolts (hex-head, machine, carriage), screws (wood, lag, drywall, machine), washers, grease fittings, turn buckles, eyebolts, solderless electrical terminals, cotter pins, anchors, and other hardware. And you don't have to buy by the pound to get wholesale prices—Camelot packages the hardware in counts of 10, 25, 50, 100, etc. Camelot's tools include screwdrivers, punches, air tools, pliers, snips, rasps, and other hand and power tools for hobbyist and machinist by Astro, Best Tool, Cal-Van, Camelot, Chicago Pneumatic, Excalibur, General, Ingersoll Rand, Lisle, Milton, Milwaukee, and Truecraft, among others. Shop equipment, Excalibur fastener sets, Marson pop rivets, and Camelot's own twist drills and fasteners are also sold at competitive prices.

Wholesale buyers, please note: If your business is in Illinois, Indiana, or Wisconsin, you must provide a copy of your resale certificate to buy wholesale from Camelot.

Special Factors: Satisfaction is guaranteed; price quote by letter only; returns are accepted within 10 days for replacement, refund, or credit; no collect calls are accepted.

CLEGG'S HANDYMAN SUPPLY

DEPT. W98
P.O. BOX 732
OREM, UT 84059–0732
801–221–1772

Information: inquire (see text)
Pay: check or MO
Sells: hardware, home fixtures, etc.
Store: mail order only

Clegg's, a family-run firm dedicated to the "frugal home handyperson," discontinued its catalog in favor of total customer service—special orders. Clegg's has provided readers with products they couldn't find locally, like the motel owner who bought a number of special deadbolt locks unavailable at his hardware store. Customers who haven't been able to find a certain item at a discount have found it here for less, and those looking for bulk discounts—a houseful of light switches and outlets, for example—have been pleased.

Clegg's says it best: "We carry, or can get, almost anything a typical hardware or home-improvement center has, and more. We don't normally ship anything that can't be sent via UPS or regular U.S. mail, such as a bathtub or snow blower. However, on a hard-to-find item where cost is not such a factor, special arrangements may be made."

Among the products available are plumbing supplies (faucets, faucet repair parts, sinks, drain parts, valves, toilet parts, shower heads, tub spouts, etc.), bathroom accessories (towel racks, vanity kits, medicine cabinets, etc.), electrical accessories (extension cords, lightbulbs, switches, outlets, boxes, light fixtures, ballasts, wire, etc.), appliance parts (thermostats and range elements, dryer vents and door switches, etc.), window and glass components (screening, latches, rollers, storm-door closers), general hardware (hinges, screws, weatherstripping, saw blades, screwdriver bits, etc.), hand and power tools, sundries (paint brushes and roller sleeves, sandpaper, drop cloths, masking tape, caulking, etc.), and much more. Some of the brands represented are C.R. Laurence, Chromalox, DAP, Delta, Douglas, Duracell, Eagle, Eveready, General Electric, Honeywell, Jensen, Kwikset, Legend, Lenox, Leviton, MagnaTek, Makita, Milwaukee, Moen, Nibco, Price-Pfister, Robertshaw, Stanley, Weiser Lock, and Watts. Prices average 30% to 50% or more below suggested or regular retail, depending on the item and quantity ordered. Clegg's has been in business since 1992, and prides itself on responding to the needs of its customers. Clegg's has published *How and Where to Buy Handyman Supplies at The Best Possible Price*—a guide to mail-order sources, strategies for getting the best prices locally, and sources of help for business owners. Clegg's doesn't have a catalog, but has prepared a free flyer describing the publication—and be sure to mention WBMC when calling or writing for it, since Clegg's is extending a special discount on *their* report to readers of *this* book!

Special Factors: Satisfaction is guaranteed; quantity discounts are available; returns are accepted.

COASTAL TOOL & SUPPLY

248 SISSON AVE.
HARTFORD, CT 06105
860–233–8213
FAX: 860–233–6295

Catalog: free
Pay: check, MO, MC, V, AE, Discover
Sells: hand, power, and air tools
Store: same address (Exit 46 off I–84); Monday to Friday 8–5, Saturday 8–4
E-mail: sales@coastaltool.com
Online: http://www.coastaltool.com

Coastal Tool offers the top names in tools at discounts of up to 50% on list price. Neither the catalog nor the website shows all of the thousands of products Coastal offers, but you can call or write if you don't see what you're looking for. The brands include Bosch, Delta, DeWalt, Dremel, Eklind, Emglo, Fein, Hitachi, Klein, Leatherman, Makita, Milton, Milwaukee, Porter-Cable, Roto-Zip, Senco, Skil, Stanley, Vise-Grip, Wilton, and Wiss, among others. Coastal's customers run from Saturday do-it-yourselfers to contracting firms and institutions, so the sales staff is used to fielding a wide range of questions and requests. If you can't visit, you can tap their collective wisdom through the website. Log on and send the "Tool Doctor" your toughest questions about power tools, or subscribe to Coastal's tip-filled e-mail newsletter. If you're not handy but know someone who is, see the "Gift List"—it's a great source for ideas when you're shopping for your favorite fix-it person.

Special Factors: Satisfaction is guaranteed; returns (in condition received) are accepted for exchange, refund, or credit.

ECON-ABRASIVES

DEPT. WBMC

P.O. BOX 1628

FRISCO, TX 75034

800–367–4101

972–335–9234

FAX: 972–377–2248

Catalog: free

Pay: check, MO, MC, V, Discover

Sells: abrasives and related products

Store: mail order only

Econ-Abrasives has been in the business for over 30 years, and began selling sandpaper by mail in 1987. As a manufacturer of industrial-grade abrasives, Econ-Abrasives applies the same high standards to the products it makes for the home shop hobbyist and professional woodworker: The belts are resin-bonded, aluminum-oxide grit, seamed with a butt joint that allows them to be run bi-directionally, offered in open or closed coat. (Silicon carbide and aluminum zirconia grits are available as well.) The grits run from 24 to 400, sizes from 1" by 30" to 6" by 200" to 53" by 103"—and if yours isn't on the list, Econ-Abrasives can make it up.

And that's what's on just 3 of the 32 pages of the catalog. Econ-Abrasives offers comparably diverse options in sanding sheets, adhesive-backed discs and rolls, sanding blocks and disc bases, flap wheels and sanding drums, and specially shaped forms for difficult sanding jobs (crevices, recesses, turnings, etc.). Other sanding-related goods are available, including sanding mitts, steel wool, rigid steel hand scrapers, belt-cleaning tools, glues and fillers, router and drill bits, wood chisels, buffing wheels, grinding wheels, and safety gear.

Prices are competitive with discount tools stores on small quantities, but volume purchases are where you'll really save. The catalog includes a glossary of abrasives terms and recommendations for different jobs, so you don't have to be a pro to shop here.

Special Factors: Price quote by phone or letter; minimum order is $25 with credit cards.

ENCO MANUFAC-
TURING COMPANY

DEPT. WBMC

5000 W. BLOOMINGDALE
  AVE.

CHICAGO, IL 60639

800–860–3400

773–745–1500

FAX: 800–860–3500

FAX: 773–645–1118

Catalog: free

Pay: check, MO, MC, V, Discover

Sells: machining tools and hardware

Store: same address; also 12 locations in AZ, CA, FL, GA, IL, MN, NH, OH, TX, and WA (see catalog for locations or call 800–873–3626)

E-mail: encomfg@aol.com

   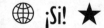

If the notion of saving big on lathes and mills has you riveted, read on. Enco, in business since 1940, is one of the country's biggest suppliers of machine shop equipment. The 500-page catalog lists lathes, mills, grinders, cutting tools, woodworking equipment, fabricating equipment, hand tools, air compressors, measuring tools, and more, including 10 pages of books, manuals, and software. You'll also find abrasives, safety equipment, tool storage units and chests, and even janitorial supplies here. The brands include Akro Mills, Baldor, Brown & Sharpe, Cobalt, Delta, Diamond, Dremel, Hanson, Huot, Jepson, Kurt, Mitutoyo, Rubbermaid, Stanley, Unibit, Wiha, and Xcelite, among many others. Prices are routinely 30% to 50% below list or comparable retail, and volume discounts are available. The catalog includes full terms of sale, and the locations and hours of Enco's 13 branches around the country.

Special Factors: Quantity discounts are available; institutional accounts are available; minimum order is $25; C.O.D. orders are accepted.

H & H MANUFAC-TURING & SUPPLY CO.

P.O. BOX 692
SELMA, AL 36701–0692
334–872–6067
FAX: 334–872–0813

Catalog: free
Pay: check or MO
Sells: chain-saw parts and logging equipment
Store: 111 Hwy. 80 E., Selma, AL; Monday to Friday 7–5, Wednesday 8–12 noon

H & H Manufacturing runs a mail-order firm known as "Saw Chain" that's been offering savings of up to 60% on saw chain and other logging needs since 1964. You can buy the chain, guide bars, and sprockets here for chain saws by Craftsman, John Deere, Echo, Homelite, Husqvarna, Jonsered, Lombard, McCulloch, Olympic, Pioneer, Poulan, Remington, Stihl, and other firms. The chain is sold in a range of pitches and gauges, and both gear-drive and direct-drive sprockets to fit all models are stocked. Swedish double-cut files, Esco rigging products, Windsor and Tilton saw chain and bars, wire rope, logging chokers, slings, and other logging equipment is also available. Remember to include all requested information when ordering chain and sprockets—make and model, chain pitch, gauge, number of drive links, type of bar, and length.

Special Factors: Chains, bars, files, and sprockets are guaranteed to last as long as or longer than any other make; returns are accepted for replacement; C.O.D. orders are accepted.

H & R COMPANY

16 ROLAND AVE.
MOUNT LAUREL, NJ
08054–1012
609–802–0422
FAX: 609–802–0465

Catalog: $5, year's subscription, refundable
Pay: check, MO, MC, V, Discover
Sells: new and surplus electromechanical, robotic, and optical components
Store: mail order only
E-mail: sale@herbach.com
Online: http://www.herbach.com

H & R Company, formerly known as Herbach & Rademan, was established in 1934 and offers surplus bargains—chiefly electronics, robotics, optics, and intriguing mechanical devices. The 108-page catalogs feature capacitors, lasers, motors, power supplies, compressors, fans, test equipment, relays, resistors, air and hydraulic cylinders, solenoids, transformers, and similar equipment. Computer components, including monitors, keyboards, cables, and power line filters, are usually available. H & R also sells goods that nearly anyone, electromechanically inclined or not, can use: security equipment, educational kits, phone accessories, digital scales, heavy-duty outlet strips and surge suppressors, model trains and cars, closed-circuit TV components, goggles, robotics components, compasses, cabinet slides, parts bins, tool cases and cabinets, magnets, weather balloons, and reference books on technical topics. Product specifications are given in the catalog.

Special Factors: Satisfaction is guaranteed; price quote by phone, fax, or letter; returns with original packing materials are accepted within 30 days; minimum order is $25, $50 on open account, $100 on orders outside the United States and Canada.

HARBOR FREIGHT TOOLS

3491 MISSION OAKS BLVD.
P.O. BOX 6010
CAMARILLO, CA 93011
800–423–2567
FAX: 805–388–0760

Catalog: free
Pay: check, MO, MC, V, AE, Discover
Sells: tools, hardware, industrial equipment, machinery
Store: same address; also Bakersfield, El Cajon, Carmichael, Chula Vista, Escondido, Fresno, Hemet, Hesperia, Lancaster, Modesto, Redding, Reseda, Riverside, Sacramento, Salinas, Santa Maria, Santa Rosa, Sparks, Stockton, Vallejo, and Visalia, CA; Lexington, KY; and Las Vegas, NV

You'll find great prices on everything from air compressors to woodworking equipment in the 60-page catalog from Harbor Freight Tools, which offers workshop necessities at savings of up to 80% on list and comparable retail. Specials are run frequently, making this a valuable source for the hobbyist and do-it-yourselfer.

The typical catalog offers air tools, compressors, hand tools for all kinds of work, automotive repair and maintenance equipment, shop equipment, power tools and supplies, metalworking, welding and plasma cutting tools, woodworking machines and tools, generators, engines, pumps, and even a roundup of useful things for home and garden—posthole diggers, stud sensors, push brooms, ladders, paint sprayers, and more. AEG, Black & Decker, Bosch, Campbell Hausfeld, Central Forge, Central Pneumatic, Chicago Electric, Chicago Pneumatic, Cummins, Delta, Dewalt, Homelite, Honda, Makita, Milwaukee, Pittsburgh, Porter-Cable, Quincy, Ryobi, Sentry, Skil, Stack-On, Stanley, Wayne, and WEN are among the brands represented.

Special Factors: Shipping is free on orders over $50 delivered within the continental United States.

HOLZ TOOL SUPPLY, INC.

DEPT. WBMC
819 BROADWAY
MT. VERNON, IL 62864
800–233–4676
618–242–4676
FAX: 618–242–4679

Catalog: $1, refundable
Pay: check, MO, MC, V, AE, Discover
Sells: professional-quality tools
Store: same address; Monday to Friday 7:30–5, Saturday 8–12
E-mail: holztool@accessus.net

Contractors, woodworkers, and serious do-it-yourselfers have been buying better for less from Holz Tool since 1985. Among the most popular lines are the Porter-Cable nailers and staplers, Amana router bits, Compass drywall and tek screws, Delta woodworking machinery, Bessey clamps, Elco tapcon concrete screws, Knaack jobsite tool chests, fiberglass ladders and equipment from Blue Ribbon Ladder, Performax power drum sanders, Sait grinding wheels and abrasives, Weather Guard truck boxes and van equipment, Western States concrete anchors, David White surveying equipment, and power tools by Makita, Milwaukee, Porter Cable, Skil, and other firms. The current 30-page catalog offers a wide selection of shop tools and blades and bits, but you can also send for manufacturers' catalogs, or call directly with model information for a price quote. Holz is an authorized service center for Delta and Milwaukee power tools, and assures us that "courteous people answer the phones and will help you find the proper tool for the job." If what you want is not in stock, Holz will be happy to order it.

Special Factors: Price quote by phone or letter; authorized returns are accepted for exchange, refund, or credit (a 15% restocking fee may be charged).

MANUFACTURER'S SUPPLY

DEPT. WBMC–98
P.O. BOX 167
DORCHESTER, WI
 54425–0167
800–826–8563
FAX: 800–294–4144

Catalog: free
Pay: check, MO, MC, V, Discover
Sells: replacement parts for chain saws, lawn mowers, snowmobiles, ATVs, etc.
Store: mail order only
Online: http://www.mfgsupply.com

Manufacturer's Supply is the source for the parts you'll need to get all kinds of things functioning again, at prices up to 50% below list or comparable retail. Consult the 216-page catalog for original replacement parts for equipment by Arctic Cat, Briggs & Stratton, Comet, Dayco, Hahn, Hoffco, Oregon, Tecumseh, and other makers, for chain saws, lawn mowers, motorcycles, snowmobiles, ATVs, snow throwers, trimmers, trailers, and Rototillers™. Logging safety equipment (hard hats, chaps, and boots), as well as sprockets and nose assemblies, chains, grinders, files, air filters, T-wrenches, starter springs, carburetor parts, and guide bars (for dozens of saw brands) are available.

In addition, Manufacturer's sells parts for standard and riding lawn mowers, as well as semi-pneumatic tires for mowers and shopping carts, wheelbarrows, and hand trucks. The firm stocks wheels, hubs, bearing kits, roller chains, sprockets, clutches, belts, and other goods for trailers, minibikes, go-carts, riding mowers, snow throwers, rototillers, garden tractors, and ATVs. The snowmobile parts include everything from lubricants to windshields—carburetors, fuel filters, cleats, tracks, studs, pistons, gaskets, drive belts, wear rods, slides, suspension springs, and engines, among other items. Also available are wood-chopping tools, Woodchuck wood-burning furnaces, and Magic Heat air circulators and chimney-cleaning brushes. Manufacturer's Supply has been in business since 1960, and welcomes inquiries on products not shown in the catalog. You can order a copy on the website, or view everything Manufacturer's stocks in the online version.

Special Factors: Authorized, unused returns are accepted within 30 days (a 20% restocking fee may be charged); shipping is $4.99 per order to destinations in the contiguous United States; minimum order is $10; C.O.D. orders are accepted.

MICRO-MARK

340–2314 SNYDER AVE.
BERKELEY HEIGHTS, NJ
07922–1595
908–464–6764
FAX: 908–665–9383

Catalog: $1
Pay: check, MO, MC, V, AE, Discover
Sells: model-building tools and supplies
Store: mail order only
E-mail: micromark@worldnet.att.net

Micro-Mark, "The Small Tool Specialists," offers a full line of hobby-sized hand and power tools and materials for working wood and metal, miniatures, and building models. Micro-Mark sells Dremel's rotary tools, attachments, bits, and blades, as well as Microlux's hobby-sized table saw, tiny power planes, drills, saws and sanders, miniature power lathes by Carba-Tec and Sherline, and a full range of measuring, cutting, gluing, filing, and sanding tools. The 80-page catalog lists scores of adhesives, casting supplies, paints, polishes, and other model supplies, and even has a "miniature lumber yard" with dollhouse molding, dowels, micro-cut balsa sheets, and hardwood pieces. You'll also find equipment and supplies for specific hobbies—model ships, railroads, cars, and dollhouses, as well as kits for the models themselves—and dozens of books and videos on related topics. Selected items are discounted about 20% off list price, but Micro-Mark is listed here as a great source for hard-to-find hobby tools and supplies.

Special Factors: Satisfaction is guaranteed; returns are accepted within 30 days for exchange, refund, or credit; institutional accounts; C.O.D. orders are accepted.

NORTHERN HYDRAULICS, INC.

DEPT. 24619
P.O. BOX 1499
BURNSVILLE, MN
55337–1499
800–533–5545
FAX: 612–894–0083

Catalog: free
Pay: check, MO, MC, V, Discover
Sells: do-it-yourself items, power tools, etc.
Store:same address and 31 other outlets in FL, GA, IA, MN, NC, SC, TN, TX, VA, and WI
Online: http://www.northern-online.com

  ¡Sí!

Northern Hydraulics makes it easy to save up to 50% on gas engines, pressure washers, generators, trailer parts, painting and welding equipment, tarps, air tools and compressors, winches, power tools, farm and garden and RV equipment, and much more. The 148-page catalog—and the smaller sale catalogs—offer a good selection of tools and equipment for home and commercial workshop, for farm, garage, rental store, construction firms, warehouses, and light industrial operations. You'll find tow hoes, shop hoists and presses, parts washers, log splitters, Homelite and McCulloch chain saws, hydraulic pumps and parts by J.S. Barnes and Parker. Vertical- and horizontal-shaft replacement gas engines from Briggs & Stratton, Honda, Kohler, and Tecumseh are offered, for tillers, mowers, and lawn tractors. Air compressors by American IMC and Campbell-Hausfeld are offered, as well as air tools from Chicago Pneumatic, Ingersoll-Rand, and Northern Hydraulics' own line.

Northern also sells go-carts and parts, tires, casters and wheels, RV equipment, tractor lamps and seats, sandblasting and painting equipment, trailer parts, hand and power tools by Black & Decker, Bosch, Makita, Skil, and others. The lawn and garden equipment includes gas trimmers, cultivators, garden carts, ag pumps, mower tires, blowers, sprayers, tillers, and much more. Georgia Boots, gloves, and other protective items are also available. And you'll find boating accessories, personal security devices such as lights and alarms, cordless phones, solar fences, and electronic fences, all at discount prices.

Special Factors: Authorized returns are accepted for exchange, refund, or credit.

RED HILL CORPORATION

P.O. BOX 4234
GETTYSBURG, PA 17325
800–822–4003
717–337–3038
FAX: 717–337–3936

Catalog: free
Pay: check, MO, MC, V
Sells: abrasives and hot-melt adhesives
Store: Supergrit® Abrasives, 1540 Biglerville Rd., Gettysburg, PA
E-mail: Redhill@mail.cvn.net

Red Hill's business is the rough stuff that gets things smooth—abrasives. The company was founded in 1978 and offers a wide range of abrasives and refinishing products at prices up to 50% below regular retail. The 28-page catalog includes belts (aluminum oxide, silicone carbide, and zirconia on cloth backing) in 19 sizes, plain-back, hook-and-loop, and pressure-sensitive sanding disks, paper disks for orbital sanders, sheets, sleeve and drums, sanding screens, rolls, graphite cloth to reduce friction between the sanding belt and the sander, and foam-core sanding blocks. In addition, the catalog offers abrasives for vibrating hand sanders, RAKSO's paper-backed steel wool sheets (to mount on sanders, for finishing work), felt-backed sanding disks that work with a hook-and-loop fastening system, abrasive cords and tapes (for getting into crevices). Triangles for Bosch, Fein, and Ryobi triangular sanders are sold in bags of 25 for 20¢ to 35¢ each, respectively, about half the price of regular retail. The catalog also lists auto-body refinishing products, masking tape, tack cloths, and a stick for cleaning sanding belts when the grit gets clogged—a money saver in itself.

Red Hill has introduced NicSand Sanding Gel in grits 3,000, 5,000, and 10,000, which is sold in a kit with a pad that attaches to electric drills (under $10). The gel is great for polishing marble or glass tabletops or your car, or for deglossing surfaces between finishes. And you'll find glue guns and glue sticks here—and at $5 a pound for five pounds of sticks (white clear, amber clear, and super amber), they cost just a third of the going rate at the typical hardware store, and the savings increase on larger quantities.

Special Factors: Price quote by phone or letter on special order sizes; quantity discounts are available; minimum order is $25; C.O.D. orders are accepted.

RUVEL & COMPANY, INC.

DEPT. WBMC
4128–30 W. BELMONT
   AVE.
CHICAGO, IL 60641
773–286–9494
FAX: 773–286–9323

Catalog: $2, $3 outside the U.S.
Pay: check, MO, MC, V
Sells: government surplus
Store: same address; Monday to Friday 10–4,
Saturday 10–2

Ruvel, established in 1965, is the source to check for good buys on government-surplus camping and field goods. U.S. Army and Navy surplus goods are featured in the 64-page catalog, including G.I. duffel bags, high-powered binoculars, leather flying jackets, mosquito netting, M65 field jackets, U.S. Marine Corps shooting jackets, dummy grenades, U.S. Army technical manuals, and similar items. Past catalogs have offered Israeli and M9 gas masks, Kevlar helmets, hammocks, snowshoes, strobe lights, mess kits, dinghies, nightsticks, snowshoes, U.S. Army blankets, parade gloves, first-aid kits, packboards, and duffel bags. Ruvel is noteworthy for its low prices and extensive stock of real surplus—there are hundreds of genuine government-issue items available here, and many intriguing, useful surplus things that are increasingly hard to find these days.

Special Factors: Order promptly, since stock moves quickly.

SURPLUS CENTER

P.O. BOX 82209
LINCOLN, NE 68501–2209
800–488–3407
FAX: 402–474–5198

Catalog: free
Pay: check, MO, MC, V, AE, Discover
Sells: new and surplus industrial goods, hardware, etc.
Store: 1015 W. "O" St., Lincoln, NE; Monday to Friday 8–5, Saturday 8–12

Surplus Center, established in 1933, publishes a 180-page catalog that's a treasury of parts for the "build-it-yourselfer." One-third of the catalog features hydraulic equipment of all types, including cylinders, valves, pumps, and motors, as well as hoses, filters, and tanks. Also featured are pressure washers, blowers, winches, electrical motors of all kinds, electrical generators, air compressors, surveying equipment, spray pumps, vacuum pumps, gearboxes, gas engines, and more. Heavy-duty 400-amp DC welders are available, as well as sandblasters, inverters, multimeters, battery chargers, and a full line of residential and commercial burglar alarms. Some of the goods are real government surplus, but most are brand new bargains. If you have any questions about an item, you can call Surplus Center's staff technicians for information.

Special Factors: Authorized returns are accepted (a restocking fee may be charged); C.O.D. orders are accepted.

TOOL CRIB OF THE NORTH

P.O. BOX 14040
GRAND FORKS, ND 58208
800–358–3096
FAX: 800–343–4205

Catalog: free
Pay: check, MO, MC, V, Discover
Sells: tools and hardware
Store: Duluth, MN; and Bismarck, Fargo, Grand Forks, and Minot, ND; locations listed in the catalog
Online: http://www.toolcribofthenorth.com

Do-it-yourselfers, hobbyists, contractors, and industrial buyers are among the numerous customers of Tool Crib, which has been in business since 1948. The firm offers a broad range of tools, industrial and shop equipment, and supplies—ladders, pumps, generators, motors, woodworking equipment, saws, compressors, abrasives, concrete-handling equipment, trailers, and much more. You can send for the 96-page, quarterly catalog, or call or write for price quotes on items by Black & Decker, Bosch, Delta, DeWalt, Emglo, Freud, Hitachi, Jet, Kawasaki, Makita, Milwaukee, Porter-Cable, Powermatic, Ryobi, Senco, Skil, Stanley, Target, David White, and other major manufacturers. Whether you're shopping for a circular saw or an adjustable scaffold system, you'll find it at Tool Crib—at up to 50% off list price. The catalog includes line drawings, products specifications, and both list and discount prices for most items, which makes it a good reference as well as a buying tool.

Canadian readers, please note: Only U.S. funds are accepted.

Special Factors: Satisfaction is guaranteed; shipping is not charged (with some exceptions) on orders over $75.

TOOL HAUZ INC.

**122 E. GROVE ST.
MIDDLEBORO, MA
02346–1288
800–533–6135
508–946–4800
FAX: 508–947–7050**

Brochure: free
Pay: check, MO, MC, V
Sells: tools and hardware
Store: same address and 57 Crawford St.,
Needham, MA

The "bargain list" from Tool Hauz Inc. features the best names in wood-working and power tools, at discounts that sometimes beat even those of the "wholesale" sources. You'll find everything from Barco Rocket hammers and Stabila levels to Bauer ladders and RMC saw stands—routers, drills, screw guns, disc sanders, and power saws; all types, by Black & Decker, Bosch, Hitachi, Homelite, Makita, Metabo, Milwaukee, Porter-Cable, Sioux, and Skil. Supplies and hardware, including abrasives, saw blades, hole saws, Jet and Tek screws, drill bits, tarps, tool aprons, glue, and related goods, are stocked as well. Call for the price list, or a price quote if you know the model you're looking for.

Special Factors: C.O.D. orders are accepted.

TOOLS ON SALE

**SEVEN CORNERS
HARDWARE, INC.
216 W. SEVENTH ST.
ST. PAUL, MN 55102
800–328–0457
FAX: 612–224–8263**

Catalog: free
Pay: check, MO, MC, V, AE, Discover
Sells: tools for contractors, masons, and woodworkers
Store: same address; Monday to Friday 7–5:30, Saturday 8–3 CT

If you can't get to St. Paul to visit Seven Corners Hardware, where there are "over 40,000 items on the floor," you can do business with the firm's mail-order division, Tools on Sale. The parent company was founded in 1933, and specializes in tools for contractors and woodworkers.

The Tools on Sale catalog is one of the last great freebies in America—496 pages of name-brand tools, at discounts of up to 50%. You'll find everything from air compressors to workbenches here, from manufacturers that include Black & Decker, Bosch, Delta, Dewalt, Dremel, Elu, Freud, Hitachi, Jorgensen, Maglite, Makita, Milwaukee, Porter-Cable, Rigid, Ryobi, Senco, Skil, Stanley (including contractor-grade tools), 3M, and David White, among others. If you're looking for carpet-installing tools, professional vacuum cleaners, laser levels, stair templets, Werner ladders and scaffolding, demolition hammers, moisture meters, water stones, or mechanics' cabinets, or just want to *see* 18 pages of construction aprons and nail bags, look no farther. And there are a dozen pages of books, videos, and manuals on everything from making a hobbyhorse to building a home. Free freight on orders shipped to the United States (except Alaska and Hawaii) is an added bonus.

Special Factors: Shipping is not charged on orders shipped within the 48 contiguous United States; authorized returns are accepted for exchange, refund, or credit.

TREND-LINES, INC.

135 AMERICAN LEGION HWY.

P.O. BOX 9117

REVERE, MA 02151–9117

617–853–0225

FAX: 617–853–0226

Catalog: $1
Pay: check, MO, MC, V, Discover, NOVUS
Sells: woodworking tools and hardware
Store: 63 stores in CT, MA, ME, NH, NY, RI, and VT; locations are listed in the catalog

Trend-Lines has been in business since 1981, selling complete lines of tools and hardware to professional woodworkers, at savings of up to 30%. The 68-page color catalog shows a wide range of woodworking tools and parts, including saws (jig, miter, band, reciprocating, scroll, radial-arm, and chain), drills, routers, trimmers, planers, jointers, sanders, nibblers, polishers, grinders, bits, blades, and other accessories. Bosch, Delta, DeWalt, Forstner, Freud, Hitachi, Makita, Milwaukee, Porter-Cable, Reliant, Ryobi, Shopcraft, Skil, Wagner, and other popular names are represented. The catalog also shows full lines of supplies such as abrasives (sheets, belts, and disks), lubricants, adhesives, paste stains and varnishes, wood plugs and buttons, toy wheels, dollhouse kits, and hand tools and cabinet hardware. Woodworking manuals and plans are also sold.

Special Factors: Satisfaction is guaranteed; returns of unused goods in the original packaging are accepted within 30 days for exchange, refund, or credit; C.O.D. orders are accepted.

TURNKEY MATERIAL HANDLING CO.

500 FILLMORE AVE.
P.O. BOX 1050
TONAWANDA, NY
14151–1050
800–828–7540
FAX: 800–222–1934

Catalog: free
Pay: check, MO, MC, V, AE, Discover, NOVUS
Sells: commercial and industrial furnishings, storage units, etc.
Store: mail order only
E-mail: cdcorp@usa.net

Turnkey's line is geared for industrial and commercial applications, but the sturdy storage units and other equipment sold here have home applications as well. Turnkey has been doing business since 1946, and publishes a 120-page catalog that features shelving and storage bins in a huge selection of sizes and styles. You'll find everything from small parts bins, ideal for hardware storage, to steel wall cabinets, plus plastic bin-and-frame arrangements. The catalog also shows mats and runners, workbenches, rolling carts, suspension files, lockers, flat and roll files, moving pads, canvas tarps, security gates, hand trucks, rolling ladders, trash cans, stretch wrap, zip-type resealable bags, power-failure lights, recycling centers, and many other products. Turnkey has expanded its line of shipping products, which include a wide range of padded mailers, bubble-pack, kraft paper, packing labels and envelopes, strapping tape, and other needs.

Special Factors: Satisfaction is guaranteed; authorized returns (except custom-made items) are accepted (a 20% restocking fee may be charged).

WHOLESALE TOOL CO., INC.

DEPT. WBMC

P.O. BOX 68

12155 STEPHENS DR.

WARREN, MI 48089–3962

800–521–3420

810–754–9270

FAX: 810–754–8652

FAX: 800–521–3661

Catalog: free
Pay: check, MO, MC, V, Discover
Sells: tools, hardware, and machinery
Store: same address; also Tampa, FL; Indianapolis, IN; Stoughton, MA; Charlotte, NC; Tulsa, OK; and Houston, TX (see catalog for locations)
E-mail: wtmich@aol.com

Wholesale Tool has been bringing good prices and a great tool selection to hobbyists and industry since 1960, through the 790-page "Full-Line Catalog." This hefty tome runs from Toyota forklifts to Crescent wrenches, and is a treasury for do-it-yourselfers as well as woodworkers, machinists, contractors, and surveyors. Wholesale Tool is geared to the professional, as you can see from the collection of reference works—no Sunset guides to building decks, but *Die Design Fundamentals,* the 25th edition of *The Machinery Handbook*, a guide to world screw threads, and *Creep Feed Grinding* are here, among others. Wholesale Tool represents both popular commercial brands and industrial suppliers: Black & Decker, Brown & Sharpe, Brubaker Tool, Chicago Pneumatic, Desmond, Dorian Tool, Dremel, Florida Pneumatic, Fowler, General, General Electric, Hanson, Heinrich, Jorgensen, Lufkin, Master Lock, Merit, Milwaukee, Minute Man, Mitutoyo, Norton, Porter-Cable, Rigid, Ryobi, Shop-Vac, Starrett, 3M, Vise-Grip, Wesco, and Yuasa, among others. The comprehensive product descriptions include model number, technical specifications, Wholesale Tool's price, and sometimes the list price. Savings average 30%, and the catalog features several pages of clearance and odd-lot items, which are sold below cost.

Special Factors: Authorized returns are accepted within 30 days (a 10% restocking fee may be charged); minimum order is $25.

WOODWORKER'S HARDWARE

Catalog: $3, refundable (see text)
Pay: check, MO, MC, V, Discover
Sells: cabinet and furniture hardware
Store: mail order only; phone hours Monday to Friday 8–8 (Sept. to April), Monday to Friday 8–5 (May to Aug.), Saturday 8–12 (Sept. to April) CT

P.O. BOX 180
SAUK RAPIDS, MN 56379
800–383–0130
FAX: 800–207–0180

Cupboards, drawers, cabinets, doors—they all require hardware, which is what you'll find at Woodworker's Hardware: 216 pages of hinges, knobs, pulls, slides, catches, latches, supports, and a variety of bits and other woodworking supplies. The current edition of the catalog showcases over 4,500 items, and you can order the catalog over the phone—the $3 is offset by a $5 coupon that can be applied to your first order.

The collection of specialty hinges, slides, mounts, and fixtures will be appreciated by anyone who's designing an entertainment center, curio or display cabinet, computer work station, bookcase, or built-ins. The catalog features an extensive selection of specialty shelving and bins for kitchen cabinets—"white wire" and plastic lazy Susans that make use of inaccessible space in corner cabinets, trays that conceal the steel wool and sponge behind the fixed panel in front of the sink, and heavy-duty drawer and cupboard organizers and caddies for all kinds of storage. Several models of the built-in ironing closets are offered, as well as folding step-stools designed to be fitted in behind a pull-out carcase side panel or fascia, and things like breadboards, swing-up shelves for heavy appliances, tambour doors, brass rail fittings and brackets, oak moldings, and TV and video mounts for wall or ceiling. Look here for cord grommets and paper slots for printer stands, mini-halogen cans and strip lighting, keyboard trays and slides, and more. Fasteners, drive screws, bits, levelers and glides, abrasives, respirators, glue, putties, and lubricants are all available. The brands include Amerock, Blum, DAP, Feeny, Franklin, National Cabinet Lock, Soss, Specialty Lighting, Stanley, 3M, Washington, and Waterloo. If you're looking for hardware from one of these firms, you can call for a price quote, or see the catalog.

Special Factors: Satisfaction is guaranteed; price quote by phone or letter; quantity discounts are available; authorized returns of unused, undamaged goods are accepted within 30 days for exchange, refund, or credit.

ZIP POWER PARTS, INC.

DEPT. WBM
P.O. BOX 10308
ERIE, PA 16514–0308
800–824–8521
FAX: 800–983–7278

Catalog: free
Pay: check, MO, MC, V, Discover
Sells: parts for chain saws, lawn mowers, trimmers, small engines, etc.
Store: 2008 E. 33rd St., Erie, PA; Monday to Friday 8–5, Saturday 9–1

If you own a chain saw, Zip Power Parts may be an old friend. In business since 1962, Zip Power Parts is one of the country's best sources for chain-saw parts, with a 28-page catalog of saw chains, bars, bar guards, and sprockets to fit all makes and models of chain saws. Saw-chain grinders, chain-saw repair parts, and small engine parts are all available, and there are shop tools for filing and grinding, wedges, lubricants, "mini-mills," hand tools, manuals, safety clothing and equipment, and woodcutting accessories. Additional parts for lawn mowers—mufflers, air filters, blades, starter rope and handles, fuel lines and filters, points, condensers, electronic ignitions, etc.—are listed in the catalog.

Special Factors: All products are guaranteed against defects in materials and workmanship; returns are accepted; minimum order is $25; C.O.D. orders are accepted.

SEE ALSO

Alfax Wholesale Furniture • *institutional furnishings and fixtures* • **OFFICE**
American Science & Surplus • *surplus tools, electronics, etc.* • **GENERAL MERCHANDISE**
Arctic Glass & Window Outlet • *replacement patio door panes and passive solar panels* • **HOME: IMPROVEMENT**
Cahall's Brown Duck Catalog • *work clothing and rugged footwear* • **CLOTHING**
Cherry Tree Toys, Inc. • *wooden toy parts, hardware, etc.* • **CRAFTS: WOODCRAFT**
CISCO • *professional power tools* • **HOME: IMPROVEMENT**
Clothcrafters, Inc. • *shop aprons, woodpile covers, tool holders* • **GENERAL MERCHANDISE**
Crutchfield Corporation • *car security systems* • **APPLIANCES**

Defender Industries, Inc. • *wood treatment products, marine hardware* • **AUTO**

Fidelity Products Co. • *storage equipment and safety and security products* • **OFFICE**

Frank Eastern Co. • *industrial and institutional supplies and furnishings* • **OFFICE**

Goldbergs' Marine Distributors • *wood treatment products, marine hardware* • **AUTO**

Knapp Shoes Inc. • *work shoes and boots* • **CLOTHING: FOOTWEAR**

Meisel Hardware Specialties • *wooden craft parts and brass hardware, woodworking plans* • **CRAFTS: WOODCRAFT**

Metropolitan Music Co. • *tools and supplies for making musical instruments* • **MUSIC**

Northwest Treasure Supply • *metal detectors and prospecting equipment* • **CRAFTS**

S & S Sound City • *surveillance equipment* • **APPLIANCES**

Shuttercraft, Inc. • *shutter-hanging hardware* • **HOME: IMPROVEMENT**

Staples, Inc. • *fire extinguishers* • **OFFICE**

Todd Uniform, Inc. • *work clothing and footwear* • **CLOTHING**

Woodworkers' Discount Books • *books and videos on woodworking and related topics* • **BOOKS**

Woodworker's Supply, Inc. • *wooden craft parts and brass hardware, woodworking plans and tools* • **CRAFTS: WOODCRAFT**

TOYS, GAMES, AND PARTY SUPPLIES

Juvenile and adult diversions

One of the greatest challenges for many budget-conscious parents is spending a "reasonable" amount of money on toys. The Power Rangers generation is well-informed on the features of the latest diversions, so gaining the upper hand takes work. You might begin to limit the number of ads your children see by reducing their exposure to commercial television. Replacing passive pastimes with activities built around challenges and the exercise of imagination is a good start. If you want to add toys to your child's life without adding much expense to your budget, join or start a toy library. The USA Toy Library Association, established a decade ago, helps individuals and communities start and support their own collections. Toy libraries often benefit children with special needs or disabilities, and may be brought to children by van— but they also can be established in the corner of the local public library. For more information about support materials and joining the USA-TLA, send a long, stamped, self-addressed envelope to USA Toy Library Association, 2530 Crawford St., Suite 111, Evanston, IL 60201.

One of your best defenses against crass materialism is to replace watching TV with reading. You can expand on your efforts by making *Zillions,* published by Consumers Union, part of their literary diet. This "Consumer Reports for Kids" is an ad-free guide to products, money management, and smart buying for shoppers from 8 to 13 years old. Help educate the next generation—buy a young friend a subscription. Write to Zillions, Subscription Dept., Box 51777, Boulder, CO 80322–0777, for rate information, or see the current issue of *Consumer Reports.* You might also try *365 TV-Free Activities You Can Do with Your Child,* by Steve and Ruth Bennett, another resource in the battle of the box.

In addition to toy and game supplies, party specialists are listed in this chapter. Many of them sell stuffed toys and other novelties that would appeal to children, and nearly all offer party decorations with juvenile themes. Please note that some of the products are not suitable for young children, so be sure to inquire before ordering if you're not sure whether they're age-appropriate.

FIND IT FAST

BRIDGE SUPPLIES • **Baron/Barclay, C & T Bridge**
CHILDREN'S TOYS • **Constructive Playthings, Oriental Trading, Stickers 'n' Stuff, U.S. Toy**
ORNAMENTS • **Kaye's Holiday**
PARTY GOODS • **M & N, Oriental Trading, Paper Wholesaler, Paradise Products, La Piñata, Sally, Stickers 'n' Stuff, Stumps, U.S. Toy**
STICKERS • **Stickers 'n' Stuff**

BARON/BARCLAY
BRIDGE SUPPLIES

**3600 CHAMBERLAIN
LANE, SUITE 230
LOUISVILLE, KY
40241–1989**
800–274–2221
502–426–0410
FAX: 502–426–2044

Catalog: free
Pay: check, MO, MC, V
Sells: bridge playing and teaching materials
Store: mail order only

Baron/Barclay Bridge Supplies carries materials and equipment for every kind of bridge player, from novice to old hand. Baron/Barclay was established in 1946, and stocks hundreds of books on bridge, and sells them at quantity discounts of up to 50%. Over half of the 64-page color catalog is devoted to teaching manuals and texts, books on strategy and bidding, bridge history and reference texts, and complete courses in bridge. Videotapes and instructional software are also available, as well as a great choice of playing cards, scoring cards and club forms, recap sheets, and a variety of gifts and equipment—bridge-motif china, scarves, jackets, magnetic card sets, games, jewelry, watches, pens and pencils, and even electronic bridge games.

Special Factors: Satisfaction is guaranteed; quantity discounts are available; returns are accepted within 30 days for exchange, refund, or credit (videotapes and software for exchange only).

C & T BRIDGE SUPPLIES

3838 CATALINA ST.
LOS ALAMITOS, CA 90720
800–525–4718
310–598–7010
FAX: 310–430–8309

Catalog: free
Pay: check, MO, MC, V, AE, ACBL scrip, Discover
Sells: bridge supplies
Store: same address; Monday to Friday 8–5
E-mail: tedinlosal@aol.com

The card game of bridge originated from the English game of whist about a century ago, but is often associated with the leisure pursuits of Eisenhower-era suburbanites. In reality, bridge is a demanding engagement whose challenge has survived fad and fashion. There are several variations on the game, each of which alter the ratio of luck to skilled bidding in the player's success. C & T Bridge offers the serious hand a great source for books on strategies, theory, play, bidding, self-tests and aids to mastering inner bridge, and even that great equalizer, playing bridge with your spouse. Several series of pamphlets are available, most on strategy and bidding methods. Bridge videos, computer programs, and hand-held games are available, as well as playing cards (by the single and dozen decks), timers, guide cards, boards, score slips, recap sheets, and card holders and shufflers. Pricing is competitive, and quantity discounts of up to 25% apply to the books and autobridge practice sets, and bridge teachers are extended an extra 10% off multiples of selected titles.

Special Factors: Quantity discounts are available.

CONSTRUCTIVE PLAYTHINGS

U.S. TOY COMPANY, INC.
1227 E. 119TH ST.
GRANDVIEW, MO
64030–1117
816–761–5900
FAX: 816–761–9295

Catalog: free (see text)
Pay: check, MO, MC, V
Sells: toys and educational products
Store: Garden Grove, CA; Englewood, CO; Apopka, FL; Skokie, IL; Leawood, KS; North Wales, PA; and Carrollton, TX
E-mail: ustoy@ustoyco.com
Online: http://www.ustoyco.com/

🍁 🏴 🌐 ¡Si!

Constructive Playthings sells wholesome, growth-oriented diversions for children, and makes a "lowest price guarantee" on everything it carries (see the catalog for details). Constructive Playthings has been in business since 1953, and features brightly colored, washable, durable toys, from activity centers and baby's first music box to teepees for backyard fun and a scaled-down kitchen, complete with sink. The toys are made to withstand lots of play; in fact, Constructive Playthings also sells directly to schools and child-care institutions (the school edition of the catalog costs $3). Before giving in to this year's movie character, see if you can't get your children interested in these games and diversions instead—they'll outlast seasonal fads and are easier on your budget.

Please note: If you represent an educational institution, write on letterhead and request the school edition of the catalog (minimum order, $25).

Special Factors: Satisfaction is guaranteed; returns are accepted for exchange, refund, or credit; institutional accounts are available.

KAYE'S HOLIDAY

DEPT. WBMC98
6N021 MEREDITH RD.
MAPLE PARK, IL 60151
630–365–2224
FAX: 630–365–2223

Catalog: $1 for 2 issues (see text)
Pay: check, MO, MC, V
Sells: holiday ornaments
Store: mail order only

Tired of missing those post-Christmas clearances with the half-price buys on ornaments? Here's a sale that never stops: Kaye's Holiday, where decorations for Christmas, Easter, Halloween, and other holidays are priced from 20% to 75% below regular retail (and sometimes well below *wholesale*) every day. Kaye has been in business since 1982, and sends out a little eight-page, black-and-white catalog showing hand-made ornaments of blown glass, fabric, straw, and wood, tagged at $1 to $5 each. These are the same ornaments—from Poland, Germany, Czechoslovakia, and all over the globe—that can be found in import shops and gift catalogs selling for three times as much. Ornaments make wonderful gifts and keepsakes, and they're great to give when you're dropping in on people during the holidays.

Wholesale buyers, please note: The minimum order for wholesale pricing is $500.

Special Factors: Order as early as possible for the best choice.

M & N INTER-
NATIONAL, INC.

DEPT. WBMC98
13860 W. LAUREL DR.
LAKE FOREST, IL
  60045–4531
847–680–4700
FAX: 800–PARTYON
FAX: 847–816–1200

Catalog: free, $6 outside the U.S.
Pay: check, MO, MC, V, Discover
Sells: party supplies
Store: same address; Monday to Friday 9–4

You can turn your next get-together into an event with a little help from M & N International, where it's *always* time to party. The firm's 160-page color catalog is published in spring and fall, and each edition features seasonal themes as well as year-round party staples. The spring/summer catalog includes St. Valentine's Day, Easter, St. Patrick's Day, Mardi Gras, the Chinese New Year, Mother's Day, Father's Day, Bastille Day, graduation themes, Independence Day, and weddings, anniversaries, and showers. M & N sells the streamers, balloons, banners, cutouts and posters, table props, and hats and favors for the holidays, as well as classic themes like Casino Night, the playoffs (football, baseball, basketball, and hockey), Hawaiian luaus, rock and nostalgia, Oktoberfest, and "Western Chuckwagon Roundup," to name a few. The depth of the stock is impressive—there are six pages of props for Mardi Gras events alone—and parents, office managers, and teachers will appreciate the great selection of basics for all kinds of celebrations, promotional events, and entertaining. For example, the "Caterer's Corner" features a number of large-capacity crystal-cut acrylic trays and bowls—perfect for serving crowds at home or at the office—as well as table cloths and skirts, ice molds, cutlery and tableware, candles, disposable buffet-warming pans, specialty carryout and meal service containers (including several styles perfect for catering children's parties), doilies, tissue paper and curling ribbon, confetti and streamers, party hats of all types, message banners, backdrop paper, and more. If you're planning a promotional event, you can also order a number of items imprinted with your logo and message, including paper shopping bags, sport bottles and insulated mugs, flying disks, pens and pencils, lollipops, key rings, magnets, sun visors, buttons, napkins, wrapped mints, buckets, balloons, and even "wrist ticket" armbands used for admission management at concerts and sports events. M & N International has been in business since 1961, will meet or beat the competition's prices, and charges a reasonable 6% shipping on orders over $200 (at this writing).

Special Factors: Satisfaction is guaranteed; quantity discounts are available; authorized returns are accepted for exchange, refund, or credit; institutional accounts are available; C.O.D. orders are accepted.

ORIENTAL TRADING COMPANY, INC.

DEPT. 868
P.O. BOX 3407
OMAHA, NE 68103
800–327–9678
402–331–6800
FAX: 800–327–8904
TDD: 800–833–7352

Catalog: free
Pay: check, MO, MC, V, AE, Discover
Sells: party goods, novelties, etc.
Store: mail order only
Online: http://www.oriental.com

Before you throw another party or plan a single fund-raising event, consult "The World's Biggest Toy Box," from Oriental Trading. It's a novelty shop in 156 pages, crammed with everything from balloons and stickers to spun glass bridal favors, resin animals and figurines, party favors, tickets, bingo supplies, penny candies, ribbon, inflatables, stuffed toys, masks, glow-in-the-dark jewelry, tropical drink stirrers, costumes, and lots more. Most of the products are sold by the dozen, gross, pound, or other multiple, at prices that are easily 50% below what individual items cost in party goods stores—and often even cheaper. Oriental Trading has been in business since 1932, and releases seasonal catalogs with special holiday selections regularly.

Special Factors: Quantity discounts are available; authorized returns (except food, candy, and costumes) are accepted after contacting customer service within five days of receipt of goods.

THE PAPER WHOLESALER

17800 NE FIFTH AVE.

NORTH MIAMI, FL 33162

305–651–6900

FAX: 305–651–6300

Catalog: $3
Pay: check, MO, MC, V, AE, Discover
Sells: party supplies, restaurant disposables
Store: (warehouses) same address; also 2638 SW 28th Lane, Coconut Grove; 410 W. 49th St., Hialeah; 8259 W. Flagler, Miami; and 10151 Pines Blvd., Pembroke Pines, FL

 ¡Si! ★

The Paper Wholesaler, in business since 1983, sells restaurant and party and entertaining supplies and related goods in case lots and "retail packs," at discounts of up to 40% on the regular prices. The 32-page color catalog is full of table goods, decorations, and the little things that add fun to festive occasions: paper plates and napkins in vibrant colors and snappy designs, including ensembles for children's birthdays, wedding parties, and showers; plastic cutlery and cups, tablecloths, doilies, balloons, crepe paper, party hats, streamers and pennants, favors, and other novelties. Guest towels and toilet paper are sold here, as well as a good selection of candles, hors d'oeuvre picks and drink stirrers, cocktail napkins with amusing slogans, wrapping paper, gift bags, bows and ribbon, and invitations in upbeat designs and colors.

The Paper Wholesaler has a "serious" section for restaurateurs and caterers, which includes a selection of cake-decorating supplies, cake pans, deli and bakery containers, commercial-sized rolls of foil and poly film, ice scoops and bar tools, carafes, syrup pitchers, ashtrays, and even the brooms, mops, and buckets you'll need when the guests are gone. And there's food—restaurant-sized containers of Pepperidge Farm Goldfish, Hellmann's mayonnaise, Orville Redenbacher popcorn, Planter's peanuts, and other condiments and snacks. The catalog includes tips on party planning, and the order form even features shopping lists so you don't overlook anything.

Special Factors: Satisfaction is guaranteed; returns of unopened, unused goods are accepted within 30 days for exchange, refund, or credit.

PARADISE PRODUCTS, INC.

DEPT. WBMC
P.O. BOX 568
EL CERRITO, CA
  94530–0568
510–524–8300
FAX: 510–524–8165

Catalog: $2 bulk mail, $3 sent first-class
Pay: check, MO, MC, V
Sells: party paraphernalia
Store: mail order only
E-mail: paradise-party@worldnet.att.net

Paradise Products has been sponsoring bashes, wingdings, and festive events since 1952, when it began selling party products by mail. The 104-page catalog is a must-see for anyone throwing a theme event. The firm sells materials and supplies for over 100 different kinds of events, including celebrations of Oktoberfest, the 50s, the Gold Rush, Presidents' Day, St. Patrick's Day, fiestas, "Las Vegas Night," Hawaiian luaus, pirate parties, Super Bowl celebrations, weddings, graduations, Fourth of July parties, baby showers, and back-to-school festivities. Balloons, streamers, tissue balls and bells, party hats, banquet table coverings, crepe paper by the roll, pennants, garlands, and novelties are among the items available. Paradise's prices are as much as 50% below those charged by other party-supply stores, depending on the item and the quantity ordered.

Canadian readers, please note: Paradise requires payment for the catalog and orders in U.S. funds drawn on U.S. banks only, or by MasterCard or VISA.

Special Factors: Goods are guaranteed to be as represented in the catalog; shipments are guaranteed to arrive in time for the party date specified (terms are stated in catalog); minimum order is $30 or a $4 service charge applies.

LA PIÑATA

NO. 2 PATIO MARKET,
OLD TOWN
ALBUQUERQUE, NM 87104
505–242–2400
FAX: 505–242–2400

Brochure: $2, refundable
Pay: check, MO, MC, V, Discover
Sells: piñatas, paper flowers, and porcelain dolls
Store: same address; Monday to Saturday 10–5:30, Sunday 11–5:30

La Piñata, established in 1955, is a marvelous source for piñatas—the hollow papier-mâché animals and characters that are traditionally filled with candy and broken by a blindfolded party guest. Prices here are low, most between $2.50 and $12. The stock includes superheroes like Batman, Superman, Spiderman, and Sesame Street characters, pumpkins, Santa, snowmen, witches, stars, reindeer, footballs, and other seasonal themes. And there are all sorts of animals, including bears, burros, bulls, elephants, unicorns, tigers, pigs, kangaroos, and cows—as well as a piñata bat your guests can use to smash your selection to bits. La Piñata also offers a spectacular but inexpensive line of brilliantly colored paper flowers, dozens of handsome porcelain collector dolls in Native American costume, and both papier-mâché and genuine chile wreaths and ristras (ropes). The highlight is a large cluster of real chiles wired so that each pepper actually lights up—a singular decoration, and just $25!

Special Factors: Price quote by phone or letter; C.O.D. orders are accepted.

SALLY DISTRIBUTORS, INC.

4100 QUEBEC AVE. N.
MINNEAPOLIS, MN 55427
800–472–5597
612–533–7100
FAX: 800–575–1453
FAX: 612–533–0141

Catalog: free, $5 outside the U.S.
Pay: check, MO, MC, V, Discover
Sells: party goods, toys, etc.
Store: Monday to Friday 8–5, Saturday 8–12
E-mail: sallydist@sallydist.com

Sally Distributors can help your church, organization, or school make merry on a budget, or serve as your own personal source for well-priced decorations for holidays and celebrations. The 86-page color catalogs feature the season's strong sellers—Fourth of July themes, Valentines Day, Easter, St. Patrick's Day, Halloween, etc.—with table and room decorations, favors, games, banners, novelties, and a wide selection of stuffed toys. Every edition shows latex and Mylar balloons and inflation equipment (custom printing services are available, minimum 1,000 balloons), garlands and streamers, decorative light sets, greeting cards, gift wrap and ribbon, flags and pennants, toys and novelties, and all sorts of prizes and treats—feather masks, party classics like woven finger traps and kazoos, "wedding bubbles" (a fun alternative to rice), and even piñatas and the candy to go in them are a few examples.

Most of the products are packed in multiples—balloons are sold by the dozen (30" metallics) or gross (11" latex in 42 colors), bandannas by the dozen, and things like plastic bird warblers and bead necklaces by the gross. Prices are easily 40% less than usual retail, and savings are even greater on quantities of certain items. Sally Distributors passes on the actual shipping costs only, a welcome departure from the inflated fees asked by many vendors. It's that kind of thinking that's kept the company going since 1921!

Please note: The products are not intended for use by children under three years of age.

Special Factors: Quantity discounts are available; only authorized returns are accepted for exchange, refund, or credit; institutional accounts are available; a $2 surcharge is imposed on orders under $30.

STICKERS 'N' STUFF INC.

Catalog and Samples: $2
Pay: check, MO, MC, V, AE
Sells: novelty stickers
Store: mail order only

DEPT. WBM
P.O. BOX 430
LOUISVILLE, CO
 80027–0430
303–604–0422
FAX: 303–665–8779

Stickers 'n' Stuff, founded in 1980, sells a wide variety of adorable stickers: prism (rainbow effect), chrome (foil background), hologram (like the emblem on your credit card), fuzzies, and neon stickers. The designs include lots of bears, cats, unicorns, balloons, rainbows, wild animals, sports figures, holiday themes (Christmas, Thanksgiving, Valentine's Day, etc.), and the American flag. In addition, Stickers 'n' Stuff sells striped adhesive bandages in heart shapes, sticker collecting books, "liquid crystal" jewelry, sticker "earrings," endangered species stickers, and even scratch-and-sniff stickers. Parents, teachers, and daycare workers may derive the most benefit from a stash of assorted stickers, skillfully deployed on a rainy day. Thanks to this firm, stickers that cost 25¢ in the toy store cost as little as 6¢ here, or an average of 8¢ for the Sampler Assortment of 366 stickers. You can save even more on half or full cases, which are usually bought for resale. And you can try them out before you order: $2 brings you the catalog and a generous batch of stickers, enough to last a couple of Saturday afternoons!

Special Factors: Satisfaction is guaranteed; quantity discounts are available; returns are accepted for exchange, refund, or credit.

STUMPS

ONE PARTY PLACE
P.O. BOX 305
SOUTH WHITLEY, IN
   46787–0305
800–348–5084
219–723–5171
FAX: 219–723–6976

Catalog: free
Pay: check, MO, MC, V, AE, Discover
Sells: party goods, display items, etc.
Store: mail order only; phone hours Monday to Friday 7 a.m.–9 p.m., Saturday 8–3 CT
Online: http://www.stumpsparty.com

Stumps, in business since 1926, specializes in "the latest and the most innovative ways to make any event glamorous and fun." According to the company, schools and theaters are partial to Stumps' "celestial" and Hollywood theme kits, which include magnificent lighted archways, shooting stars, gigantic moons and suns, and larger-than-life movie cameras and awards.

Stumps also offers everything required to brighten a room for a holiday or a wedding, including 150 different balloons, thousands of holiday decorations, gossamer, streamers, parade materials, and a variety of tableware—much of which is priced up to 50% below retail. And if you're looking for real savings, check the quantity pricing on imprinted favors—glassware, frames, key rings, invitations, noisemakers, and even clothing are available. You'll find most of the imprintables in the 376-page Prom catalog, and other festive imprinted items and decorations in the other specialty catalogs.

Special Factors: Satisfaction is guaranteed; price quote by phone or letter; quantity discounts are available; authorized returns (except worn clothing and personalized/customized products) are accepted within 15 days for exchange, refund, or credit (a 15% restocking fee may apply); institutional accounts are available; minimum order is $15.

U.S. TOY CO., INC.

1227 E. 119TH ST.
GRANDVIEW, MO
64030–1117
816–761–5900
FAX: 816–761–9295

Catalog: $3
Pay: check, MO, MC, V
Sells: novelties and fund-raising items
Store: Garden Grove, CA; Englewood, CO; Apoka, FL; Skokie, IL; Leawood, KS; North Wales, PA; and Carrollton, TX (see catalog for locations)
Online: http://www.ustoyco.com/

It's always party time at the U.S. Toy Company, where masks, costumes, favors, festive tableware, streamers and decorations, games, grab-bag prizes, little toys and novelties, penny candy, jewelry, stuffed animals, inflatables, balloons, hats, crowns, and other fun things are available at discounts of up to 70% on regular retail. In addition to party goods grouped by theme—Halloween, St. Patrick's Day, Easter, Mardi Gras, etc.—the 144-page U.S. Toy catalog has everything you need for your fund-raiser. (In addition to everything short of the rides themselves, U.S. Toy also offers a carnival-planning guide.) Some products are sold in cases or large lots, but much is available in small quantities—making this a great source for parents, teachers, camp directors, and anyone else looking for inexpensive party materials.

Special Factors: Institutional accounts are available; minimum order is $25.

SEE ALSO

American Science & Surplus • educational materials for elementary-grade sciences • **GENERAL MERCHANDISE**
Better Health Fitness • custom-designed playground equipment • **SPORTS**
BFK Sports • kites and kite-building supplies • **SPORTS**
Cherry Tree Toys, Inc. • wooden toy kits, parts, and plans • **CRAFTS: WOODCRAFT**

Christian Book Distributors, Inc. • *Christian-oriented games* • **BOOKS**

CR's Crafts • *doll- and toy-making supplies and parts* • **CRAFTS**

Dover Publications, Inc. • *cut-and-assemble projects, stickers, dioramas, etc.* • **BOOKS**

A. Feibusch Corporation • *zippers for doll clothing* • **CRAFTS: TEXTILE ARTS**

The Fiber Studio • *doll-making fibers* • **CRAFTS: TEXTILE ARTS**

Gohn Bros. Mfg. Co. • *dominos, "Dutch blitz," and other games* • **CLOTHING**

Home-Sew • *doll and stuffed animal parts* • **CRAFTS: TEXTILE ARTS**

Meisel Hardware Specialties • *wooden wheels and other toy parts, toy plans* • **CRAFTS: WOODCRAFT**

Monterey, Inc. • *fun fur yardage and remnants for toys* • **CRAFTS: TEXTILE ARTS**

The Natural Baby Co., Inc. • *wooden toys* • **CLOTHING: MOTHER AND CHILD**

Newark Dressmaker Supply, Inc. • *supplies for making dolls and toys* • **CRAFTS: TEXTILE ARTS**

RV Direct • *sleds, toboggans, go-carts, panel wagons, etc.* • **AUTO**

R.C. Steele Co. • *dog trivia, dog-breed playing cards, etc.* • **ANIMAL**

Taylor's Cutaways and Stuff • *kits and patterns for making dolls and toys* • **CRAFTS: TEXTILE ARTS**

Wicker Warehouse Inc. • *wicker doll buggies, reproduction miniatures* • **HOME: FURNISHINGS**

Woodworker's Supply, Inc. • *wooden toy parts, plans, and dollhouse plans* • **CRAFTS: WOODCRAFT**

TRAVEL

This section includes listings of information sources, discount travel brokers, money-saving accommodations, and travel-related services. In addition, membership in professional organizations, unions, buying clubs, and other groups may entitle you to travel discounts and services—check your benefits package to find out before purchasing other services elsewhere.

CONSOLIDATORS/BUCKET SHOPS

Consolidators, also known as bucket shops, are travel wholesalers who buy cruise slots, blocks of rooms, and plane seats from airlines, hotels, and charter agents, and resell them for less than the hotels, airlines, or often the charter operators themselves are willing to accept for individual tickets or rooms. Travel agents are big customers of consolidators, but individuals may buy from them, too, which will often save them 20% to 30% on APEX fares and much more on full economy tickets.

Unitravel III Corporation, one of the oldest consolidators in the business, books flights in the United States and Europe and sells directly to individuals. Contact Unitravel about a month before you anticipate traveling, and allow for some uncertainty since tickets might not be available until shortly before the day of departure. Call 800–325–2222 or for more information, or write to 1177 North Warson Rd., St. Louis, MO 63132–1810.

Council Charter, another consolidator, has been in business for over 40 years and is affiliated with the Council on International Educational Exchange, a not-for-profit travel concern. Council specializes in low-cost fare to Europe. For information on Council Charter's current offerings, call 800–223–7402 or 212–882–2800.

Council Travel, a leader in student, youth, and low-priced fares, has offices in over 20 states and districts. For more information and the location nearest you, contact the New York office (212–822–2700) or the San Francisco branch (415–421–3473, fax 415–421–5603); there is no toll-free line at this writing.

STA Travel has a number of offices in major California cities, as well as in the District of Columbia, Chicago, Boston and Cambridge, New York City, Philadelphia, and Seattle; call 800–777–0112 for the location nearest you.

Nouvelle Frontiers is an off-price travel broker that sells to consumers as well as to travel agencies. For information, call 212–779–0600, or 800–366–6387. You can also try *Travac Tours and Charters,* at 212–563–3303, or 800–872–8800.

DISCOUNT TRAVEL AGENTS

Common sense tells you that commissions pegged to the selling price of a ticket may not inspire a travel agent to find you the lowest fare. Compounding the problem is the real difficulty in getting "hard" information in a market that literally changes overnight, every night. Inexperienced and undermotivated travel agents can be compromised on both counts, for which you pay the price.

You can improve the odds of getting the lowest rate by pricing your trip with at least three travel agents and asking for the cheapest fare. Make sure you know just what you're buying *before* you buy it. Ask for a statement of the agency's cancellation policy, and get it in writing if the travel agent is booking your trip through a tour operator.

The problems with agents make *Travel World* (also known as *Fare-finders*) worth checking before your next trip. This travel agency is run by Annette Forest, who's been in the business for over a decade and uses a wide range of information sources to find the lowest fares. Travel World will search for the best rates on travel by air, train, or ship, as well as cruises and tours to any destination worldwide. You can buy your tickets and book reservations through Travel World, but it's optional—there's no obligation for the fare-finding services. Ms. Forest also teaches hands-on college classes for aspiring travel agents at Travel Smart, and invites inquiries on her course. Write to Travel World, 11899 West Pico Blvd., West Los Angeles, CA 90064, or call 310–479–6093 for information.

If you're just interested in a good price on a cruise, give *Cruises Worldwide* a call. This travel agency will send you a printout of last-minute opportunities (from 3-day getaways to 14 days on the high seas), as well as cruises scheduled up to a year from now. Discounts run from 5% to 50% on the published rates, and major lines are well represented. For information or the current printout, call 800–6-CRUISE, fax 714–975–1849, or write to Cruises Worldwide, 16585 Von Karman, Irvine, CA 92714 (there is a $1 fee for the information).

Other cruise discounters include *Cruise Time,* which has two offices: 1 Hallidie Plaza, Suite 406, San Francisco, CA 94102; 800–338–0818, fax

415–391–1856, and 9864 Main St., Fairfax, VA 22031; 800–627–6131. *World Wide Cruises* also books at a discount: 8059 W. McNab Rd., Ft. Lauderdale, FL 33321; 800–882–9000, or 954–720–9000, fax 954–720–9112. And you can request a catalog of cruises from *Cruises of Distinction,* 93 Dorsa Ave., Livingston, NJ 07039; 800–634–3445, 201–716–0088; fax 201–716–9893.

STANDBY TRAVEL

If you can be flexible in your plans, consider the world of standby travel. It really is a last-minute affair, but it can be one of the cheapest ways to fly.

Airhitch is an old friend among travelers who favor 11th-hour departures. The firm has offices in several large cities, but does most of its business by mail. You first phone for information, have a registration form sent to you, apply for the desired dates or range (which must be at least five days long), and call for availability on the Wednesday before your desired departure dates. The procedure is involved, but it works. Airhitch also runs Sunhitch and Airhitch USA, companion services providing discount runs to Caribbean/Mexican locations and domestic U.S. routes, respectively. The friendly phone system at Airhitch has been programmed to dispense all the details of the standby program. Make sure you have pen and paper at hand before calling 800–326–2009, or 212–864–2000.

LODGING AND DINING DISCOUNTS

Entertainment Publications runs very successful programs featuring accommodations and meals at discounts, in the United States and abroad. To join, purchase the directory suited to your travel and entertainment needs; the directory comes with a membership card, which is presented to validate the offer. At this writing, *National Hotel and Dining Directory,* covering over 3,500 hotels in the United States and Canada, costs about $38; and there are over 130 other guides for individual cities and different regions of the country and Canada, priced from about $30 to about $55. The potential savings are enough to justify getting a directory if you travel at all, since the big guide covers over 4,000 lodging sources in the United States, Canada, Mexico, and the Caribbean and entitles you to price breaks of 20% to 25% on meals in over 1,000 restaurants around the country. And *Entertainment Europe* features coupon offers on dining and hotels in nearly 150 cities. For more information and prices, write to Entertainment Publications, Inc., 2125 Butterfield Rd., Troy, MI 48084, or call 800–445–4137 (810–637–8400 in MI).

Taste Publications International runs another popular program that nets savings on dining, entertainment, and accommodations. *America at*

50% Discount, $19.95 yearly, offers savings of up to 30% on rack rates at participating hotels (chiefly budget to mid-priced), discounted meals at selected locations, plus reduced-price movie passes (offered by mail for United Artists, Loews, and other major chains), and RV- and car-rental discounts. For more information, call 800–248–2783 or 410–825–3463 (Monday to Friday 9 to 5), or write to Taste Publications International, 1031 Cromwell Bridge Rd., Baltimore, MD 21286.

Great American Traveler offers discounts at about 2,000 hotels nationwide and over 200 in Canada; membership costs $49.95, but you can upgrade to the "Golf Access" membership for $40 more, netting you 50% discounts on courses in North America, among other benefits. The "Travel Portfolio" includes both programs and a package of discounts on cruises, airfare, RV rental, tours, and more, and costs about $150. Call 800–548–2812 for more information.

Encore has excellent coverage in the United States, with over 3,000 participants, as well as over 300 in Canada, and some sites in Mexico and the Caribbean. In addition to accommodations, the Encore program offers discounts on car rentals, restaurants, cruises, and tours. Call 800–638–0930 for membership information; live customer service is available Monday to Friday 8 a.m. to 10 p.m., Saturday 8 to 1 ET.

Carte Royale provides largely first-class accommodations in about 800 hotels and resorts worldwide (about 600 in the United States), as well as corporate rates at over 3,000 other hotels affiliated with the program. Call 800–847–7002 for current rates and specials, or write to The Carte Royale, Inc., 131 N. State St., Lake Oswego, OR 97034.

And as a general tip on saving money when booking hotel accommodations, always ask whether a special rate is available. You can often take advantage of promotions as nebulous as a "shopper's special" that one Chicago hotel holds regularly; anyone who claims to be in Chicago to shop is entitled to 50% off—but you have to know about the program to claim the discount!

HOTEL BROKERS

Another way to save on your hotel stays is to book through a broker, who may work like a consolidator or an independent agent, providing reservations and confirmations, often at a discount, but sometimes when space is otherwise unavailable. Many of these services require prepayment to the service for the room and stay, for which you'll receive a voucher that can be used when you check in. The services listed below act as agents and allow you to pay the hotel in the customary way:

Quikbook has connections with good mid-priced hotels in 20 major U.S. cities and in Montreal and can be reached at 800–789–9887,

212–532–1660, or by fax at 212–532–1556; or write to Quikbook, 381 Park Ave. South, New York, NY 10016.

Central Reservation Service handles reservations in major metropolitan areas that are strong vacation destinations: New York City, Boston, Atlanta, New Orleans, San Francisco, Miami, and Orlando. The staff speaks both Spanish and English, and other travel services are offered as well. Call 800–548–3311 or 407–339–4116, fax 407–339–4736; by mail, Central Reservation Service, 505 Maitland Ave., Altamonte Springs, FL 32701.

HOME EXCHANGES

One of the cheapest ways to save on hotel bills, especially if you're quartering a family, is to billet in someone else's home. *International Home Exchange Service/Intervac* is an organization that compiles three directories a year listing over 9,000 homes worldwide (most are outside the United States). A year's subscription costs $44 ($35 plus $9 for postage), and entitles you to one free listing. The apartments and houses in this directory are available for exchange *and* rent, so you don't necessarily have to exchange your own home to take advantage of a good deal. For more information, write to International Home Exchange Service/Intervac, 30 Corte San Ferrando, Belvedere Tiburón, CA 94920, or call 415–435–3497.

CONNECTIONS

Most travelers insist on the lowest possible prices for airline tickets, but squander comparatively large sums on the last leg of the journey—the trip from the airport to the hotel. Avoid this pitfall with the help of *Crampton's International Airport Transit Guide,* which lists schedules and rates of taxis, car services, trains, buses, car-rental agencies, and other connections from airports worldwide to nearby cities. The pocket-sized guide costs under $5, is updated yearly.

EDUCATIONAL TRAVEL

Combining education with travel isn't a new concept, but *Elderhostel* brings it to a specific group—those 60 and over—and does it so successfully that it's created a loyal group of followers who plan their travel around Elderhostel programs. The organization was founded in 1981 and currently offers programs in hundreds of colleges in the United States, Canada, and overseas—from Australia to Germany. There are study cruises, "RV" programs for hostelers who are bringing their own accommodations (tent or RV), and "Intensive Studies" programs that offer more in-depth courses, as well as the popular courses held on campuses around the country. Previous catalogs have offered programs as diverse as "Christmas Around the World" at Lakeland Community College, "The Role of the U.S. Intelligence in a Democracy" at Southern Utah University, "The Magic of Opera" at Eckerd College in St. Petersburg, Florida, and "Cults in America" at the Cape May Institute in New Jersey. The price is right, and programs include everything except transportation—classes, meals, lodging, and even entertainment. (The overseas programs are more expensive than the U.S. programs, since they include round-trip airfare, sightseeing, transfers, and all other costs.) Even the RV hostelers are bused to the campus or course site, where they receive all their meals. Please note that you, or your spouse, must be at least 60 to participate, but there is no membership fee. Elderhostel's programs provide a wonderful avenue to new interests, friends, and travels, at a very reasonable price. For information, write to Elderhostel, 75 Federal St., 3rd Fl., Boston, MA 02110.

Imagine taking up painting on the coast of Cornwall, or embarking on a safari by jeep in New Mexico. These are two of hundreds of educational opportunities that have been enjoyed through *Learning Vacations* (Peterson's Guides, 1986), by Gerson G. Eisenberg. Although some of the programs are limited to enrolled students, most are extension courses taught on campuses in the United States, Canada, Europe, and as far afield as Tanzania. Prices for the courses vary considerably from program to program, usually depending on the type of accommodations.

STUDENT TRAVEL

Like seniors, students can benefit from a variety of travel opportunities and savings. One of the best-known names in this field is the *Council on International Educational Exchange (CIEE),* which also runs Council Charter (see the previous section, "Consolidators/Bucket Shops"). If you're a high school or college student working toward a degree, CIEE can issue you an International Student Identity Card (ISIC), which you'll need to qualify for discounts on train and plane travel, admission to cultural and entertainment centers, and CIEE's own travel programs. The card costs $16, and other cards for teachers and those 25 or under ("GO 25") are also available. For an application and details on the program, write to Council on International Educational Exchange, 205 E. 42nd St., New York, NY 10017, or call 212–822–2700.

THE TRAVELER WITH DISABILITIES

Travel can be especially trying for persons with disabilities, which is why *Access to the World* (Henry Holt and Company, 1986), by Louise Weiss, is such an important book. It lists hotels with accommodations for the handicapped, covers all aspects of travel by plane, bus, train, ship, car, and RV, and gives hundreds of references to *other* access guides, travel services for the disabled, and travel tips. *Access to the World* may be available from Amazon.com, listed in "Books."

Whole Person Tours, an enterprise providing tours for the disabled in Europe and the United States, also publishes *The Itinerary,* a bimonthly magazine for the disabled traveler. Inquire for current rates from The Itinerary, P.O. Box 1084, Bayonne, NJ 07002.

DEALING WITH PROBLEMS ABROAD

No one plans to fall ill while traveling, but it happens. If you go abroad frequently or want to play it safe on your vacation, consider becoming a member of the *International Association for Medical Assistance to Travelers (IAMAT).* Your $25 contribution to this not-for-profit organization nets you membership and a roster of 850 English-speaking doctors in 125 foreign cities, a guide to immunization requirements around the world, a climate chart, and tips on staying healthy during your trip. For more information, write to IAMAT, 417 Center St., Lewiston, NY 14092, or call 716–754–4883.

The State Department "assists Americans in distress abroad," and may be able to provide information about the arrest, welfare, or whereabouts of a traveler through its Overseas Citizens Emergency Center. The State Department also issues travel advisories for countries afflicted by civil unrest, natural disasters, or outbreaks of serious diseases. All of this information, as well as visa requirements for travel to specific countries, may be obtained by calling 202–647–5225.

Planning the problems *out* of your trip is the best way to avoid them. Here are some pamphlets that can help ensure a pleasant experience: "Your Trip Abroad," "Travel Tips for Senior Citizens," "A Safe Trip Abroad," and "Tips for Americans Residing Abroad." Each booklet costs $1; request them by title from The Superintendent of Documents, U.S. Government Printing Office, Washington, DC 20402.

NEWSLETTERS

If you travel frequently or would like to be able to afford to, you'll find the following newsletters of interest:

Consumer Reports Travel Letter, produced by Consumers Union, is a well-regarded "consumerist" publication for both business and recreational travelers. *CRTL* conducts in-depth comparisons of accommodations and prices in the United States and abroad, scrutinizes airline food, investigates travel scams, recommends methods of screening travel agents, and has probed the mare's nest of airline booking systems. Each monthly issue of *CRTL* runs around 24 pages; a year's subscription costs $39 at this writing, or $59 for two years. See the current *Consumer Reports* for an order form, call 800–234–1970, or write to Circulation Department, Consumer Reports Travel Letter, 256 Washington St., Mount Vernon, NY 10553, for information. Single copies of back issues are available for $5 each. For a summary of current information, see *Best Travel Deals: How to Get Big Discounts on Airfares, Hotels, Car Rentals, and More*. Published by Consumer Reports Books, it summarizes recent newsletter articles of note, and is the best $9 you'll spend on travel this year.

Travel Smart is another newsletter that stays current with travel opportunities of all types, including discount fares and rates (including specials for seniors). Subscribers are offered deals on car rentals, cruises, accommodations, and air travel. And Travel Smart is full of great tips especially valuable to frequent travelers: A recent issue offered tips on how to see Israel on the cheap, listed a number of airline price drops, recommended restaurants in several cities for their moderately priced meals, and featured a guide to taking a break in the Caribbean at "affordable prices." A year of monthly issues costs $44; for more information, write to Travel Smart, 40 Beechdale Rd., Dobbs Ferry, NY 10522–9989.

OTHER RESOURCES

Whether your travels are confined to your armchair or you actually get up and go, you'll find travel guides a great help in planning your trip. The best-known series are *Fodor's, Fielding's, Frommer's, Baedeker's,* and *Birnbaum's*. These are reliable, general-purpose guide books to whole countries and major cities. The Frommer "$-A-Day" series is especially helpful if you're pinching pennies, but don't overlook the other books. If you're traveling abroad and want an informed guide to culturally and historically significant sites, see the *Blue Guide* series, which is highly recommended. Zagats offers *Zagat's United States Hotel Survey,* a directory of accommodations nationwide that have been rated by the Zagats' corps of paying guests and diners; it's widely available in bookstores across the country.

Many of the firms listed in "Books" sell travel guides and related literature, but specialty bookstores have far better stock and selection, and the staff can usually provide personal assistance in selecting the right book for your needs, even by mail.

The Complete Traveller Bookstore does a brisk mail-order trade through its 48-page catalog, which lists all the major guides, as well as *Insider's Guides,* the *Michelin* green and red guides, *Crown Insider's Guides* (written by expatriate Americans), the fascinating *Lonely Planet* books, and scores of specialty guides that cover everything from Alaskan hideaways to shopping in Seoul. Maps, foreign language tapes, and travel accessories are sold through the catalog as well. Store shoppers can peruse the collection of antiquarian travel books, including some early Baedekers, which are perched at the tops of the bookcases. For a copy of the catalog, send $1 to The Complete Traveller Bookstore, 199 Madison Ave., New York, NY 10016. Please note: This is *not* a discount bookseller.

The Forsyth Travel Library has an extensive selection of popular guides, road maps to cities and countries around the world, Berlitz phrase books, Audio-Forum language tapes, and Thomas Cook surface transit timetables. Through Forsyth, you can order rail passes to Europe and Britain (including "The Britainshrinkers" sightseeing tours) and subscribe to over a dozen travel publications, including *Consumer Reports Travel Letter*. Voltage converters and plug adapters, money belts, and other travel accessories are also available. Send 50¢ for the current brochure to Forsyth Travel Library, Inc., 9154 W. 57th St., Shawnee Mission, KS 66201–1375. Forsyth does *not* sell at a discount.

Book Passage publishes a 44-page catalog full of tantalizing reads, including the major travel guides and several language courses on tape. Book Passage also offers titles on family travel, menu converters, railway timetables, shopping guides, maps, a number of guides to doing business abroad, and accessories—overnight bags, pocket-sized computer translators, fanny packs, etc. Request the catalog from Book Passage, 51 Tamal Vista Blvd., Corte Madera, CA 94925. Book Passage does *not* sell at a discount.

Traveler's Checklist specializes in travel accessories, including money converters, adaptors and plugs, personal-care items, and related goods. Request a catalog from Traveler's Checklist, Cornwall Bridge Rd., Sharon, CT 06069. Please note that Traveler's Checklist does *not* sell at a discount.

Magellan's, for "more comfortable, safe and rewarding travel," sells the latest luggage, totes, travel clothing, translators, electronic and telephonic converters, alarm clocks, travel appliances, first-aid and medical supplies, water purifiers, and much more. Magellan's is not a discount catalog, but may have just the product you need to make your trip hassle-free. Just *think* what you'd have given for a folding hand truck, disposable toothbrushes, or a portable insect tent on some of your previous travels! Call 800–962–4943, or write to Magellan's, Box 5485, Santa Barbara, CA 93150–5485.

Travel Accessories & Things has just that—those little items that can make life away from home a little easier. Inflatable pillows, personal "safes" of several types, eye masks, a folding cane, world-time alarm clocks, currency converters, and other useful travel aids have been offered in the past. Write to Travel Accessories & Things, P.O. Box 1178, Agoura Hills, CA 91301, for the current catalog.

SEE ALSO

Ace Luggage and Gifts • *travel clocks, gift items* • **LUGGAGE**
American Association of Retired Persons (AARP) • *car rental and lodging discounts* • **GENERAL MERCHANDISE**
Consumer Information Center • *travel tips and related information* • **BOOKS**
Grandma's Spice Shop • *Melitta coffee travel kit* • **FOOD: BEVERAGES AND FLAVORINGS**
Jobson's Luggage Warehouse • *travel accessories* • **LUGGAGE**
Kennel Vet Corp. • *airline animal carriers* • **ANIMAL**
The Luggage Center • *travel accessories* • **LUGGAGE**
Luggage Unlimited • *travel accessories* • **LUGGAGE**
Superintendent of Documents • *travel tips and related information* • **BOOKS**

THE COMPLETE GUIDE TO BUYING BY MAIL

CATALOGS AND PRICE QUOTES

CATALOGS

Most of the companies in this book publish catalogs, which usually cost between $1 and $5. Firms sometimes ask for a SASE, which is a long (#10), self-addressed envelope with one first-class stamp. If a SASE is requested and you don't send one, don't expect a response.

You can order the stamps to mail all those catalog requests directly from the U.S. Postal Service. Both stamps and stamped envelopes are available; ask your postmaster or carrier for PS Form 3227, "Stamps by Mail," or request it from the Consumer Advocate, U.S. Postal Service, Washington, DC 20260. You can also call 800-STAMP–24 (MasterCard and VISA are accepted). The stamps are usually delivered within a few days.

"Refundable" Catalogs. Catalog fees that are "refundable" can be recouped when you place an order. Please note: If you don't place an order, you won't get the refund. Procedures for reimbursement vary; some firms send a coupon with instructions to enclose it with your order and deduct the amount from the total. (The coupon may be dated, forcing you to order within a limited time to recoup the fee.) If there's no coupon in the catalog, deduct the amount from the order total after adding tax, shipping, and other surcharges, and note the reason for the deduction on the order form. If there's no time limit on deducting the fee, assume a six-month limit.

Sending for Catalogs. Unless the listing states otherwise, you can call first and make sure the catalog is available. Sometimes the customer service rep will process a request right then, saving you the time it takes to write a letter, and possibly the catalog fee as well. If you write for the catalog, you can send a postcard for any that are free, and a letter for any requiring payment. The correspondence should note the catalog you want (some firms have several), mention enclosures, include your return address, and refer to WBMC as your source. If the catalog costs up to $1, you can send a dollar bill or coins taped between thick pieces of cardboard. For catalogs costing over a dollar, send a check. (If the check is lost and never cashed, you're not out any money, but if you use a money order, you may have to pay a stop-payment fee in excess of the face value of the order to get reimbursed—a loss no matter what.) Tip: When writing the check, jot down the address and phone number of the firm in the memo field or in the endorsement area on the back of the check (in very small letters), and in your check register. This way, you're sure to be able to get in touch with the firm if you don't receive the catalog. (Do this if you order and pay by check, too, since you may inadvertently toss the catalog and later regret it.) Don't send stamps unless they're requested, and don't assume you can pay for a catalog by credit card—call and ask first.

Catalogs from Foreign Firms. When ordering a catalog from a foreign firm, use an international money order (IMO) or personal check if the catalog costs $5 or more, and cash or International Reply Coupons (see below) if it costs less than that. Money orders can be purchased at a bank or post office.

International Reply Coupons (IRCs) are certificates that can be exchanged for units of surface postage in foreign countries. They're available at the post office for 95¢ each and are recommended when the catalog costs 75¢ or less.

You can save handling charges if the catalog costs $5 or less by sending cash through the mail. (In fact, several firms have requested it.) Technically it's risky and should be used only when you're dealing with currency. To conceal money and enclosures and remain within the half-ounce weight limit of a 50¢ stamp, slip the currency inside a piece of lacquered wrapping paper, or other kind of lightweight, opaque paper. This will camouflage the enclosure completely. Remember to mention enclosures in your letter, and if your information source is over a year old, write or call first, before sending money.

Receiving Catalogs. Catalog publication schedules vary, and when firms run out of catalogs, are between printings, or issue catalogs seasonally, there can be a delay of weeks or months before you receive one. Some firms notify customers of delays; most don't. Consequently, please allow six to eight weeks to receive your catalog.

PRICE QUOTES

Some mail-order firms don't publish catalogs, but sell their goods on a price-quote basis. Their name-brand goods can be identified by manufacturer's name, stock or model number, and color or pattern name or code. Cameras, appliances, audio and TV/video components, tableware, furniture, and sporting goods are commonly sold by discounters on a price-quote basis.

A price quote is simply the statement of the cost of that item from that firm. The company may guarantee that price for a limited period of time, or until stock is depleted. Some firms include tax, shipping charges, insurance, and handling in their price quotes, giving you one figure for the final cost.

Finding the Information. Before writing or calling for a price quote, have the manufacturer's name, product code (model or style number or pattern name), and size and color information, if applicable. You'll find this information on the factory cartons or tags of goods in stores and in manufacturers' brochures. If you're pricing an item you found in a catalog, remember to look for the manufacturer's data, not the vendor's catalog code numbers. If you're using a buying guide or magazine as a source for information, verify the information before requesting a price quote—the reference may be out of date or contain typos.

Price Quotes by Letter. Most of the firms listed in this book will give quotes over the phone—in fact, many prefer it. When you write requesting price quotes, include all of the available information about the item or items. Leave blanks next to each item so the person giving the quote can enter the price, shipping cost or estimate, and related charges. Ask the firm to note how long it will honor the given prices, and ask for prices of no more than three items at a time. Note: You must include a SASE with your request if you want a response.

Price Quotes by Phone. Have all of the information in front of you when you call. Don't make collect calls, and to avoid problems later, ask to speak to the manager, take down his or her name, and make notes of the conversation.

HOW TO ORDER

Before ordering, make sure you're getting the best deal.

COST COMPARISONS

Your chief consideration is the delivered price of the product. Compute this from your price quotes and/or catalogs, then compare the figure to the delivered cost of the item if purchased from a local supplier. Consider mileage costs if you must drive to the local source, parking fees, sales and use tax, shipping and trucking, installation, etc. If you're buying a gift, compare the costs of having the mail-order firm wrap and send the item to the value of your own time, and materials and mailing costs. Finally, weigh the intangibles—return policies, the prospect of waiting for a mail delivery versus getting the item immediately, the guarantees offered by the retailer and mail-order firm, etc. After contemplating costs and variables, you'll reach the bottom line and best buying option.

Before ordering any large item, measure all of the doorways through which the article must pass, allowing for narrow hallways, stairs, and the like. Some savvy shoppers even construct a carton dummy of the item by taping boxes together, and maneuver that through a dry-run delivery before ordering.

ORDERING

If the catalog is more than six months old and unless it's an annual, verify stock availability and prices by phone, or request a new edition and order from that. (You may find yourself billed for the difference between the old price and the new if you order from an out-of-date catalog.) Use the catalog order form, along with the self-sticking address label on the catalog. If there's no order blank, use one from another catalog as a guide. Transcribe the code numbers, names of items, number of items ordered, units, prices, tax, and shipping charges onto a separate piece of paper. Include your name, address, and phone number, the firm's name and address, and appropriate information if you're having the order sent to another address. Note any minimum-order requirements. Make a copy of the order, and file it with the catalog.

Second Choices and Substitutions. When the firm advises it and you're willing to accept them, give second choices. These usually refer to differences in color, not product. If you'll accept substitutions, which may be different products that the firm considers comparable to what you ordered, you must give permission in writing on the order form. It's unlawful for a firm to make substitutions without written authorization from the buyer. If you don't want second choices and want to be sure the firm knows this, write "NO SECOND CHOICES OR SUBSTITUTIONS ACCEPTED" in red on the order form.

PHONE ORDERS

Phone orders have a number of advantages over mail orders. They're usually processed more quickly and, when the phone operator has stock information, you'll know right away whether an item is available.

ORDERING

Before picking up the phone to place your order, follow this procedure:
1. Have your credit card ready.
2. Make sure the card is one that's accepted by the firm, has not expired, and has a credit line sufficient for the purchase.

3. Have the delivery name, address, and ZIP code available.
4. Fill out the order form to use as a guide, and a record of the trans-action. Include the catalog code numbers, units, colors, sizes, etc.
5. Have the catalog from which you're ordering at hand—the opera-tor may ask for encoded information on the address label.

When you place the call, ask the operator the following:
1. What is your name or operator number?
2. What are the terms of the return policy (unless they're clearly stated in the catalog)?
3. Are any of the items you're ordering out of stock? If yes, when is new stock expected?
4. When will the order be shipped?
5. Will any of the items be shipped separately?
6. What is the total, including shipping and tax, that will be charged to my account?
7. What is my order number?

Many operators are required to ask for your home phone number, and sometimes your office number as well. This is done so they can verify that you are the person placing the order, not a criminal who's obtained your card information illegally. Since the firm may be stuck with the bill if the charge is fraudulent, it may refuse your order if you won't divulge your number, especially if you're buying certain types of goods and your order total is high.

While you're on the phone, the operator may try to "upsell" you, or get you to buy more goods. Beware of such unplanned purchases if you're trying to stick to a budget, but listen—you may be offered a real bargain on goods the firm wants to clear out. When this happens, the company's loss is your gain. Just make sure you really want the item, since a bargain you'll never use is no bargain at all.

Once the transaction is completed and you've noted the operator's name or number, recorded the order number, checked off the items you ordered, struck off those you didn't, entered the billing amount, and noted the date of the call, put this record in your file with the catalog. They may prove valuable later, if you have problems with your order.

ORDERING FROM FOREIGN FIRMS

Despite the fact that the world was supposed to be switching to the metric scale, many of the catalogs from Europe and elsewhere use the U.S. system—inches and pounds—in measurements. Converting metric measurements to U.S. equivalents is easy, though. Use the chart you'll find in any good dictionary.

There are confusing differences in sizing systems, color descriptions, and generic terms from one country to another. Sizes fall into three categories: U.S., British, and Continental, and the size chart on page 636 can be used as a general guide to equivalents. Always measure yourself before ordering clothing, and list the measurements on the order form if you're unsure of the proper size.

Color descriptions and terms are usually more poetic than precise, in both U.S. and foreign catalogs. Remember that color charts can resolve these questions, but you must allow for variations between photographic reproductions and the product itself. For a true match, write to the firm and ask for samples before you order, or at least make sure the firm will make refunds on returns.

The majority of foreign firms listed in this book give their prices in U.S. dollars. If they don't, you'll have to convert the firm's currency when you order. First, compute the total, including shipping, insurance, and other charges (but do not include duty). Next, convert this figure to dollars using the rate of exchange prevailing on the day you send the order. Get the rate from a bank, business newspaper, or the American Express office nearest you.

Before ordering, determine the rate of duty you'll be charged when the goods arrive and any shipping or transportation costs not included in the order total. See these sections for more information: "Paying for Goods from Foreign Firms," page 606; "Shipments from Foreign Countries," page 611; "Duty," page 613; and "Deliveries from Foreign Firms," page 619.

BUYING AT WHOLESALE

Buying at true wholesale assumes that you're operating as a business, which intends to resell what you're buying, whether in its purchased state or in another form. You can buy at wholesale from those firms listed in this book that have a star in the row of symbols—but only if you and/or your order qualify. At least one of the following special sales terms will apply to your order:

Letterhead or Business Card Required. This provides evidence that you're doing business as a company, not as an individual.

Resale Number or Business Certificate Required. This proves that you're registered with local authorities as a business entity. Resale numbers are usually required for sales tax exemption.

Bank and Credit References Required. These are not usually necessary unless you want to open an account or have the order invoiced instead of paying when you place it.

Limitation of Payment Methods. Some firms allow you to charge a wholesale order to a credit card, and some require a check or money order—especially with the first order.

Minimum Order Requirements. Minimums almost invariably apply to wholesale orders; they're usually stated in dollars, although they may be in number of items or multiples, and sometimes a combination of the two.

Many of the firms listed in this book that sell at wholesale will send you the same catalog that consumers receive, with a discount schedule or a separate price list. Some have completely separate retail and wholesale catalogs, with different product lines. Wholesale catalogs often have much less descriptive information than their consumer equivalents, making "sample orders" quite valuable. Because return policies are customarily strict—restocking fees of 10% to 25% are often charged—be sure you know what you're buying before you order. (It's not wise to buy anything that's marked "final sale, no returns accepted.") On the positive side, the shipping costs are usually charged as a fraction of the order value, or are the actual shipping costs, paid C.O.D. to the carrier. In several comparisons to the rates charged to consumers, they worked out to much less—which should surprise no one who's bought by mail recently.

Be sure to check the listing before contacting the company as a wholesale buyer, since wholesale sales terms may be noted in the text. And please don't ask the company to accept your order if you won't meet their terms.

PAYMENT

There are two basic ways to pay for your order: now or later. You can prepay, using a check, money order, or debit card, or buy on credit. The distinction between these types of payments is based on the rules that apply to refunds under the FTC Mail or Telephone Order Rule, but some methods have characteristics of both categories.

Prepaid Orders. Payments made by check or money order are sometimes called "cash" by catalogers, since the firm receives dollars instead of extending credit on the basis of a promise to pay.

Personal checks, accepted by most firms, are inexpensive and can be sent without going to the bank or post office. Since some firms wait until your check has cleared before sending your order, shipment may be delayed by as much as two weeks. Checks do provide you with a receipt (the canceled check), which is returned with your monthly statement. (If your bank is dropping this service, or charging extra for it, consider using another bank or paying by credit card.) Use the "memo" space on your checks to jot down the firm's address, so if you lose track of the company in the future, you'll have a way to find it again.

Certified checks are guaranteed personal checks. You bring your check to the bank on which it's drawn, and pay a fee of about $5 to $9. The bank marks the check "certified" and freezes that sum in your account. Every company that accepts personal checks will accept a certified check, and the guarantee of funds should obviate the delay for clearance. The canceled certified check is returned with the other canceled checks in your statement. Firms that request certified checks for payment will usually accept a bank check, a teller's check, or a cashier's check as well.

Bank money orders are issued by banks for a fee, usually $1 to $3. Ask the teller for a money order in the desired amount and fill in the firm's name and your name and address. If the order isn't dated mechanically, insert the date. Most come with a carbon receipt; some have stubs that should be filled in on the spot before you forget the information.

Bank money orders are generally treated as certified checks (i.e., no waiting for clearance). If necessary, you can have the order traced, payment stopped, and a refund issued. You'll find this vital if your order is lost in the mail, since there's always a chance it's been intercepted.

Postal money orders, sold at the post office, are available in amounts up to $700 and cost 75¢. They're self-receipting and dated, and can be replaced if the order is lost or stolen. Copies of the cashed money order can be obtained through the post office for up to two years after it's paid. This can prove helpful in settling disputes with firms that claim nonreceipt of payment. And, like stamped envelopes and stamps, money orders can be bought from postal carriers by customers who live on rural routes, or have limited access to the post office.

Bank international money orders, issued by banks, are used to pay foreign firms. You complete a form at the bank and, if the catalog prices are listed in foreign currency, the bank computes the amount in dollars based on the day's exchange rate. These orders cost a few dollars or more, and they are receipted. Like domestic money orders, you send them to the firm yourself with the order. They are usually treated as immediate payment.

Postal international money orders are used to pay foreign firms; their cost varies, depending on the amount of the order. (For example, the service charge on a $200 postal IMO sent to Britain is $3 at this writing.) They're not for every transaction: Ceilings on amounts to different nations vary from $200 to $500, they can't be sent to every country, and amounts of $400 or more must be registered. When you buy a postal IMO, you fill out a form with your name and address and the name and address of the firm, and you pay the order amount and surcharge. The post office forwards the information to the International Exchange Office in St. Louis, Missouri, which sends a receipt to you and forwards the money order, in native currency, directly to the firm (or to the post office nearest it, which sends it on). The entire procedure takes a few weeks; if you use postal IMOs, allow for this delay.

Bank drafts, or transfer checks, are the closest you can come to sending cash to a foreign firm through the mail. You pay the order amount, a mailing fee, and a service charge to your bank, then send one copy of the draft form to the firm and another to the firm's bank. You must have the name and address of the company's bank to do this. When the firm receives the form, it takes it to the bank, matches it to the other copy, and collects the funds. The forms will take five to ten days to reach the foreign country, provided they're sent airmail. Most banks charge $5 or more for bank drafts, depending on the amount of the check, but all foreign firms accept them.

Debit cards, which look like credit cards, are actually more like remote-control cash cards that are hooked into your checking account. See the following section for special caveats that apply to the use of debit cards when buying by mail.

Credit, Charge, and Debit Cards. Those wafers of plastic in your wallet have been important factors in the mail-order boom, and the pairing of 800 lines and credit cards has proven an irresistible combination for millions of consumers, creating phenomenal growth in phone orders.

Paying for an order with a credit card is simplicity itself—use a card accepted by the firm, make out the order form, and provide your account number, card expiration date, phone number, and signature in the blanks. If you're ordering from a catalog without a form, supply the same information on a sheet of paper. Using credit cards can make life easier if the shipping costs aren't given or are difficult to calculate—they'll be added to the order total, and the order won't be held up as it might be if you paid by check or with a money order. Always check the minimum-order requirements when using a card, since they're often higher than those imposed on prepaid orders.

If you're low on cash but determined to order from a firm that doesn't accept cards, you can have Western Union send the company a money order and charge it to your MasterCard or VISA account. The surcharge is high—$14 to $37, and higher if you call in the order instead of placing it in person at a Western Union office. But it can be worth the expense if you might otherwise miss the buy of a lifetime.

The card companies, banks, and financial institutions that issue credit cards consider your past credit history, your current salary, and the length of time you've been at your current job when reviewing your application for a card. Since there are thousands of card issuers and the market is considered saturated, the consumer is being wooed with reduced yearly fees and APRs, extended warranties, tie-ins with frequent-flyer programs, personal and auto insurance, discounts on lodging, charitable contributions, and other benefits. Beware that the terms of the deals that induce you to choose one card over another can be changed by the issuer at will, so it's important to read the notices occasionally inserted with your monthly statement. If you need help comparing cards, Bankcard Holders of America (BHA), a not-for-profit consumer advocacy organization, can help you find the one that best suits your buying habits. BHA publishes a list of banks with low APRs, and its bimonthly newsletters have useful information and updates on pending legislation that will affect bank card holders. For membership information and a publications list, write to Bankcard Holders of America, 560 Herndon Parkway, Suite 120, Herndon, VA 22070.

"Debit" cards deserve a special mention because they may *look* like regular credit cards, but when the issuing bank receives the invoices for purchases, it deducts those amounts from your checking, savings, or money management account. This makes the debit card an electronic, instantly debited check, not a credit card, and it's important to know that the FTC views debit-card payments as cash payments. See the discussion of the FTC Mail or Telephone Order Rule for more information on the debit-card issue.

Paying for Goods from Foreign Firms. You can usually pay for goods from foreign firms with a personal check, bank draft, or credit card. Using a credit card is advisable (see "The Fair Credit Billing Act," page 631, for an explanation), but keep the following caution in mind:

If you use a credit card, the card issuer will charge you for the currency-conversion expense—a surcharge of 0.25% to 1%. The methods used to determine the rate of exchange vary widely, and are subject to the regulations existing in each foreign country. Your credit card statement should tell you the date the conversion was made and the surcharge. Check it carefully; the foreign currency total should be the same as your original order total, unless there was a price increase, short shipment, or shipping costs were higher than originally calculated. Check the interbank rate of exchange valid on the day the money was converted or the invoice was processed by the card company (your bank should be able to quote this). If there's a significant discrepancy between the interbank rate and the one the card firm used, write or call the customer-service department for an explanation.

Please read "Ordering from Foreign Firms," page 601, before ordering.

RETURN POLICIES

Most catalog firms guarantee satisfaction and will accept returns within 10, 14, or 30 days after you've received the order. Firms selling on a price-quote basis usually accept returns only if the product is defective. There are companies that don't accept any returns under any circumstances, but they're not listed in this book.

Some goods—personalized or monogrammed, custom-made, surplus, and sale items—are routinely exempted from full return policies. (If a firm has to special-order an item for you, it may refuse to accept returns on that item—and may require you to buy a minimum number or amount.) Health regulations usually prohibit returns of intimate apparel and bathing suits, but some companies will accept them. For more information, see "Returns," page 621.

Check the company's return policy before ordering. If you're shopping for a big-ticket item that carries a manufacturer's warranty, ask the mail-order firm for a copy before you buy, and see "Evaluating Warranties," page 625, for determining its value.

For more information, see "Returns," page 621.

CANCELING YOUR ORDER

When you order goods or services from a firm, whether by phone or mail, you enter into a contract of sale. You don't have the right to call the firm and rescind an order, nor do you have the right to stop payment on a check or money order on the basis of what an FTC staffer described as "buyer's remorse." (This term seems almost poetic in an industry that thrives on impulse purchases.) State laws vary on matters of contract, but, strictly speaking, your second thoughts might give the firm cause to bring legal action against you. This is especially true if the company has undertaken action on an order, in what is termed "constructive acceptance of payment."

But if, after placing an order, you learn that the firm is in financial trouble or has a bad business record, stopping payment would seem worth the risk. If you're considering canceling an order, check the terms of the offer first. Magazine and book subscriptions are often sent on an approval basis, giving you a cancellation option anyway. Goods offered with an unconditional guarantee of satisfaction can be sent back when they arrive. If these terms aren't offered and you're determined to cancel, contact the firm to discuss the matter.

SHIPPING, HANDLING, INSURANCE, SALES TAX, DUTY, AND SHIPMENTS ABROAD

When comparison shopping, consider shipping, insurance, tax, and handling as part of the total. (See "Cost Comparisons," page 599, for more information.) If you're having goods sent to Canada, an APO or FPO address, or another country, see "Shipments Abroad," page 614, for more information.

SHIPPING

This section addresses the concerns of consumers buying from U.S. firms who are having goods delivered to addresses in the United States.

Shipping Computations. The largest ancillary cost of an order is usually shipping, which is calculated in a variety of methods described below.

Postpaid item prices, which include shipping charges, are popular because there's no math for customers to do. The shipping and packing costs are passed along in the item price, however.

Itemized shipping costs are often seen as amounts in parentheses after the product price or code number. If you compare the UPS or USPS tape on the delivered parcel, you may find that the shipping fee you paid the firm is higher than what it really cost. But your fee may include the cost of packing and materials, or it may be prorated. (A California firm might compute all shipping charges based on the price of sending goods to Kansas, midway across the country, making up on local deliveries what it loses on shipments to the East Coast.) And there are some firms that, quite simply, seem to be gouging the consumer with shipping charges that are far higher than their real costs. If you feel charges are exorbitant, contact the company and protest—or take your business elsewhere.

Numeric charges are based on the number of items you're ordering, as in "$2.50 for the first item; 75¢ each additional item." Companies often limit these kinds of charges, so additional purchases made after you reach a certain number of items are exempted from shipping charges entirely.

Flat order fees are simple dollar amounts charged on all orders, usually regardless of the number of items or weight. (Extra charges may apply if part of the order is shipped to another address.) A flat fee may represent a bargain if you're placing a large order, but note that some firms selling this way will charge extra for heavy, outsized, or fragile items. Check the catalog carefully before ordering.

Free shipping is offered, often by smaller companies, on large orders. Customarily, orders under a certain dollar or item amount are charged shipping on some basis, but if your order exceeds a certain amount, no shipping is charged. The fact is often noted on the order blank—"on orders $100 and over, WE pay postage," or "free shipping on three dozen pairs or more same size, style, and color"—usually with the proviso that the order must be sent to one address.

Sliding scales, tied to the cost of the order, are used by many companies. For example, if the goods total $15.00, you pay $2.75 for shipping; from $15.01 to $30.00, the charge is $3.50, etc. This is great if you're ordering many inexpensive, heavy items, but seems unfair when you're buying one, expensive thing. Some firms remedy this by using itemized shipping charges for small, high-ticket goods, and most limit the shipping charges to a maximum dollar amount, usually $7 to $12.

Tables, based on the weight and sometimes delivery distance of the order, require the most work on your part: You must tally the shipping weights given with the item prices, find your zone or area on the rate chart, and then compute the shipping charges. Outsized goods will have to be shipped by truck; their catalog code numbers often have a suffix letter indicating this. Some firms include in their catalogs all the rate charts you'll need to figure exact costs; others state at the bottom of the order form, "Add enough for postage and insurance. We will refund overpayment." In this case, the best solution is to pay by credit card, or call the firm itself and ask the shipping department to give you a quick calculation over the phone. If you're paying by check, you could send in the order without adding anything for shipping and ask the firm to bill you, but this may delay delivery.

Saving on Shipping Costs. When you have a chance to save on shipping by placing a large order, consult friends and coworkers to see if they want to combine orders with you. But count the time spent conferring, consolidating orders, and distributing the goods as part of the cost of the order.

Carriers. No matter which method a firm uses to calculate shipping, it will usually send your goods by USPS, UPS, truck, or an overnight delivery service.

United Parcel Service (UPS): UPS is the delivery system many businesses prefer for mail order. UPS is cheaper, all costs considered, than USPS; it automatically insures each package for up to $100; it also picks up the packages at the firm's office or warehouse.

Under its Common Carrier Service, UPS handles packages weighing up to 70 pounds with a combined girth and length measurement of up to 108", with some qualifications. (A 150-pound limit is being negotiated at this writing.) If your package exceeds the size/weight restrictions, it will be transported by a private trucking firm. UPS offers overnight delivery to certain states and zip codes through its Next Day Air service, and 2nd Day Air delivery to the contiguous United States and some parts of Hawaii. The delivery fee charged by UPS is determined by the delivery address, pickup location, the dimensions and weight of the package, and the service used.

United States Postal Service (USPS)—Parcel Post (PP): The costs for Parcel Post, or fourth-class mail, are somewhat higher than UPS charges, but Parcel Post offers one distinct advantage: only packages sent by the U.S. Postal Service can be delivered to a post-office box. (UPS must have a street address to deliver goods, although carriers will usually deliver to rural routes.) If you're having a package sent to a post-office box, write "DELIVERY BY PARCEL POST ONLY; UPS NOT ACCEPTABLE" in bold red letters on the order form, unless there's a box to check to indicate your preference. On the check, write "GOODS TO BE DELIVERED BY PARCEL POST ONLY." When the firm cashes the check, it's agreeing implicitly to this arrangement and should send the goods by Parcel Post.

While postal rates escalate by leaps and bounds, the size/weight restrictions remain relatively constant. USPS accepts parcels with a combined girth and length measurement of up to 84" that weigh up to 70 pounds. Packages weighing under 15 pounds, with a combined girth/length measurement over 84", are accepted at rates for 15-pound packages.

Truck: When the firm specifies that an item must be sent by truck, or if you've ordered both mailable and nonmailable (outsized) goods, the entire order may be sent by truck. Sometimes firms indicate that goods are to be trucked with the term "FOB" or "freight," followed by the word "warehouse," "manufacturer," or the name of the city from which the goods are trucked. "FOB" stands for "free on board," and it means that the trucking charges will be billed from that point. When "manufacturer" follows FOB in the catalog, it means that the mail-order firm is probably having that item "drop-shipped," or sent from the manufacturer, instead of maintaining its own warehouse inventories of the product. If you're ordering nonmailable goods that you think will be drop-shipped, ask for the location of the manufacturer's warehouse so you can estimate the trucking costs. If you want the item quickly, ask the mail-order company to verify that the manufacturer has the product in stock before placing the order, and whether the manufacturer can ship it by an overnight service.

Truck charges are usually collected in cash or certified check upon delivery, and the additional expense is a real factor to consider when ordering very heavy items from a firm that's located far away. Truckers usually make "dump deliveries," meaning they unload the goods on the sidewalk in front of your home or business. For an additional fee (usually $10 to $20), you can usually have the goods delivered inside your house or apartment. Additional fees may be incurred if your order happens to be the only one the trucker is picking up from the firm that day or if the driver has to notify you of delivery. Before ordering an item you know will have to be trucked, get the price plus trucking charges and compare it to the cost of the same item if bought locally and delivered.

SHIPMENTS FROM FOREIGN COUNTRIES

After your payment has been authorized or has cleared the bank, the firm should ship your order. Depending on the dimensions and weight of the package, it may be shipped by mail or sent by sea or air freight.

Mailable Orders. If the package weighs up to 20kg (about 44 pounds) and has a length of up to 1.5 meters (about 59") and a length/girth measurement of up to 3 meters (about 118") for surface mail or up to 2 meters (about 79") for airmail, it can be mailed. Almost everything you can buy from the non-U.S. firms listed in this book will be mailable, but you may have a choice of air or surface shipment. Mailed packages will be delivered by your postal carrier, regardless of the service used by the company, and duty will be collected on delivery.

Airmail is the most expensive service; airmailed packages generally take a week to 10 days to arrive after they're dispatched, although some firms ask you to allow three weeks for delivery.

Surface mail, which includes both overland and boat shipment, is the cheapest service, but orders can take up to two months.

Nonmailable Orders. In the unlikely event your order exceeds mail weight and/or size restrictions, it will have to be sent by an air or ship carrier.

Air freight is the best choice when the item or order just exceeds mail restrictions. Charges are based on the weight and size of the order, as well as the flight distance. The firm arranges to have the order sent to the airport with a U.S. Customs office that's closest to your delivery address. You pay the firm for air-freight charges, it sees the order to the airport and sends you a Customs declaration form and invoice. When the airport apprises you of arrival, get right over with the forms, since most airports will charge a holding fee on goods still unclaimed five to ten days after delivery. In addition, you should make arrangements to have the package trucked to your home if it's too large to transport yourself. Once you clear Customs, you can take the goods home or release them to the truckers you've hired and they'll make the delivery.

Sea freight is much less expensive than air, but it can take months for an order to reach you. If you live near a port, you may want to handle Customs clearance yourself and hire a trucker to deliver the goods to your home. You can also hire an agent (customs broker) to clear Customs and arrange inland trucking. This service will cost from $75 to $125, but it's the only practical way to deal with the process if you live far from the docking site and the foreign firm that sent the goods doesn't have arrangements with a U.S. agent who could take care of these details for you.

The procedure is similar to that of clearing an air shipment: You present the forms the firm has provided to the shipper and Customs officer, pay duty charges, and transport the goods home or release them to the truckers you've hired.

For information on duty rates, trademark regulations, and shipment of problematical or prohibited goods, see "Duty," page 613. For information on payment of duty on mailed goods, see "Deliveries from Foreign Firms," page 619.

HANDLING

Some firms charge an extra fee for processing or packing your order (usually $1 to $5), which is often waived on orders over a certain dollar amount. The handling fee helps to cover the costs of labor and materials used in processing your order, and it, like the shipping fee, may be taxed in certain states.

INSURANCE

Packages shipped by UPS are automatically insured for up to $100; you shouldn't have to pay extra insurance on those orders. (If you're buying from a firm that delivers via UPS but has a preprinted charge for insurance on the order form, don't pay it.) UPS charges an additional fee for each additional $100 in value on the same package, the cost of which is usually covered in the shipping charge. The USPS doesn't insure automatically, so if you're having your package delivered by mail, not UPS, be sure to request insurance. Charges for postal insurance range from 70¢ for goods worth up to $50, to $5.00 for package contents worth from $400.01 to $500.00. Goods valued at more than $500 but under $25,000 must be registered as well as insured, and some goods can't be insured. If the item you're buying is uninsurable, have the firm arrange shipping with a carrier that will insure it. If you're not sure whether the firm will insure your goods, ask—before you order. The small fee is a worthwhile expense, something you know if you've ever had an uninsured order go awry. (See "Accepting Deliveries" for more information.)

Most insurance claims arise as a result of damage to or loss of goods. Procedures for claiming and reimbursement vary according to the carrier's rules and the firm's policy, but contact the firm as soon as you discover any damage to your shipment and ask the customer service department what to do. If there is documentation (signature of receipt on the UPS carrier's log or USPS insurance receipt), the claim can be verified and processed, and eventually you should be reimbursed or receive replacement goods. If there is no documentation and the worst happens—the goods never arrive—the firm may absorb the loss and send a replacement order. (If you paid with a credit card, you should be able to get a charge-back. See "The Fair Credit Billing Act," page 631, for more information.) But if repeated entreaties for a refund or duplicate order meet resistance, state your case to the agencies listed in "Obtaining Help," page 629. And be sure to tell WBMC—see "Feedback," page 635, for more information.

SALES TAX

You're supposed to pay sales tax on an order if you're having goods delivered to an address in the same state in which the mail-order firm, a branch office, or representative is located, and when the goods ordered are taxable under the laws prevailing in the area. Most states require payment of sales tax on handling, packing, and shipping charges, as well as the goods.

Those are the general rules. The right of a state to create its own definition of "doing business" in that state, or "establishing nexus," rankles consumers who have to pay tax on what they perceive as out-of-state orders, and businesses that have to be tax collectors for 50 states. The issue of nexus is no stranger to the Supreme Court; one energetic individual took on both Sears and Montgomery Ward over 40 years ago and lost, and other mail-order firms have done battle with state governments and lost as well.

State governments are trying to collect tax on all mail-order purchases delivered to residents of their states, calling such a tax a "use" tax. Mail-order companies envision an accounting nightmare, and consumers stand to lose one of the traditional benefits of shopping out-of-state: not paying sales tax on their purchases (unless nexus exists). The court cases now being decided are running in favor of the tax department, which means we're seeing changes—more firms are collecting taxes from more customers. And regardless of the practices of the company, your personal obligations are never waived—if your state requires you to pay sales tax on purchases from out-of-state firms, you're required to do so. The common perception of actual compliance with such a law is "I'd have to have rocks in my head to pay tax if I don't *have* to." If you have questions, and especially if your purchases include business deductions and involve depreciation, you'd be smart to consult an accountant or the local tax authority for guidance.

DUTY

Orders from foreign firms are usually charged duty, which can't be prepaid. Duty is paid to the postal carrier who delivers your package or the Customs agent if the order is delivered by air or sea freight.

Assessment of Duty. U.S. duty is calculated on the transaction value, or actual price, of the goods being imported, on an ad valorem (percentage) or specific (per-unit) basis, and sometimes a combination of the two. Some goods—such as certified antiques, postage stamps, truffles, and original paintings—are imported duty-free. Check your local U.S. Customs office for current regulations, since rates and classifications are subject to change.

Prohibitions and Restrictions. Some goods can be imported only under certain conditions, and others are prohibited outright. You can't import narcotics, pornography, fireworks, switchblade knives, absinthe, poison, or dangerous toys. If you wish to import animals, animal products, biologicals, petroleum products, plants, or seeds, you must make prior arrangements with certain agencies for the necessary permits. And if you want to buy name-brand goods, be sure to check trademark restrictions. The manufacturers of certain goods register the trademarks with Customs, limiting the number of those items that an individual may import. Sometimes the manufacturer requires removal of the trademarked symbols or names, which is done by the Customs agent or the firm selling the goods. Goods that often fall under trademark restrictions include cameras, lenses, optics, tape recorders, perfumes, cosmetics, musical instruments, jewelry, flatware, and timepieces. Many foreign firms offer trademark-restricted goods in their catalogs, but don't inform you of U.S. regulations—find out before you buy.

Obtaining Information. If you want to know more about duty rates and classifications, import restrictions, permits, and prohibitions, request the free booklet "Rates of Duty for Popular Tourist Items" from the Office of Information and Publications, Bureau of Customs, 1301 Constitution Ave., NW, Rm. 6303, Washington, DC 20226. Use it as a general guide only—contact your local Customs office for the latest rates. Provide a description of the goods you're ordering (materials, composition, and decoration or ornamentation), since the classification of goods is more specific than is indicated by the brochure.

If you want to import fruits, vegetables, or plants from abroad, write to Quarantines, Department of Agriculture, Federal Center Building, Hyattsville, MD 20782, and ask for an import permit application.

For more information on related matters, see "Ordering from Foreign Firms," page 601; "Paying for Goods from Foreign Firms," page 606; "Shipments from Foreign Countries," page 611; and "Deliveries from Foreign Firms," page 619.

SHIPMENTS ABROAD

Shipments to and from Canada: The U.S.–Canada Free Trade Agreement. The Free Trade Agreement (FTA) is a pact between the United States and Canada intended to promote trade and expand and enhance markets in both countries by removing some restrictions. The linchpin of the FTA is the mutual elimination of duties by 1998. Duties are being reduced in three ways: Some were eliminated when the FTA went into effect January 1, 1989; others are being reduced 20% a year over five years; and all others are being phased out over 10 years. This tripartite formula allowed industries that were ready for the increased competition to benefit from the new policy immediately, while protecting others that might be destabilized by the rapid abatement of tariffs.

The FTA affects an enormous range of raw materials and consumer goods—from fish and computers to ferrous alloys and plywood—but only those goods that are produced in the United States or Canada are entitled to free-trade treatment. (Tariffs on products of other countries are unaffected by the FTA, which is intended to benefit the U.S.–Canadian market.) The pact permits restrictions and quotas on products of certain industries and includes provisions dealing with "dumping" of goods at below-market prices and special considerations for government-subsidized products of both countries.

Despite the scope of the Free Trade Agreement, it's worth noting that prior to its enactment, more than 75% of the goods traded between the United States and Canada were exempt from tariffs. It may take a number of years for the effects of economies of scale and specialization to be discerned in the marketplace. Since only domestically produced goods are covered and phase-in periods may apply, mail-order shoppers must consult the nearest office of U.S. Customs or the Customs and Excise Office in Canada for rates and current information.

Shipments to APO/FPO Addresses. Most of the firms listed in this book will send goods to APO and FPO addresses. Finding out which is easy: Look for the stars and stripes next to the maple leaf on the line with the dollar signs and phone symbol.

Mail-order firms generally ship orders via the USPS's PAL (parcel airlift) to the military mail dispatch center, where they are shipped overseas via SAM (space available mail). The size restrictions are 60" in combined girth and length, and 30 pounds in weight. Firms sometimes charge additional handling fees for shipping to APO/FPO addresses, so read the catalog carefully and write for a shipping estimate before ordering if instructions aren't clear. Please note that neither UPS nor Federal Express makes APO/FPO deliveries, and that the USPS does not offer C.O.D. service to APO/FPO addresses

Many of the companies that ship to Canada and U.S. military personnel also ship orders worldwide. (This is noted in the "Special Factors" section at the end of each listing.) If you're planning to have goods delivered to Japan, Israel, Europe, or any other address not in the United States or Canada, see the catalog (if available) for details on the firm's shipping policy. If it's not clear, or if the firm sells on a price-quote basis, write or call the company before sending any funds and request a shipping quote. Since the employees of firms listed in this book are unlikely to be familiar with import restrictions and duty rates in other countries, check before placing your order to avoid unpleasant surprises. Most firms request payment in U.S. funds; this may be most easily handled by charging your purchase to your credit card, but before ordering check with your issuing bank for rates and charges that may apply to converting funds. Note that "The Complete Guide to Buying by Mail" has been compiled for readers who are having goods delivered to U.S. addresses and will not apply in all parts to non-U.S. deliveries.

RECEIVING YOUR ORDER

What do you do when your order arrives? And if it doesn't? The following section details your basic rights and responsibilities.

ACCEPTING DELIVERIES

When the postal or UPS carrier or trucker delivers your order, inspect the carton, bag, or crate before signing for it. If you're having someone else accept the package, ask that person to do the same. If the packaging is extensively damaged, you can refuse to sign for or accept the goods. See "Returns," in this section, for caveats on this practice.

If the box, bag, or carton is in good condition, accept it and open it as soon as possible. Unpack the goods carefully, putting aside the packing materials and any inserts until you've examined the contents. Most firms include a copy of your order form or a computerized invoice itemizing the order. If it's a printout or there's no invoice at all, get your copy of the order and check to make sure you got what you requested. Check the outside of the box, since some firms insert the invoice with the packing slip in a plastic envelope affixed to the top or side of the carton.

Check your order for the following: damaged goods, short shipments, unauthorized substitutions, wrong sizes, colors, styles, or models; warranty forms if the products carry manufacturers' warranties; missing parts; and instruction sheets if a product requires assembly. Make sure ensembles are complete—that scarves, belts, hats, vests, ties, ascots, and other components have been included. Test electronic goods as soon as possible to make sure they function properly, and do not fill out the warranty card until you've tried the product and are satisfied that it's not defective. (Check the product itself for signs that it's been used. If you've been sold a demonstration model, reconditioned unit, or someone else's return as new and unused goods, you should seriously consider returning it—or negotiating a lower price.) Try on clothing and shoes to make sure they fit. Check printed, engraved, or monogrammed goods for accuracy. If you decide to return a product, see "Returns" for more information.

If the goods are damaged, contact the seller immediately. Describe the condition of the goods and what you'd like done to correct the problem. If the firm asks you to file a complaint with the delivery service, request shipping information from the seller (the seller's shipping address, day of shipment, seller's account number, applicable shipment codes, and other relevant data). File the complaint with the delivery service, documenting your claim with photographs, if it seems necessary, and send a copy of the complaint to the seller. If you charged the purchase on a card with an extended warranty program, contact the issuer about the matter. Be persistent but reasonable.

If you receive a short shipment (one or more items you ordered are not included in the package), the firm may have inserted a notice that the item is being shipped separately or an option notice if it's out of stock. (See "The Option Notice," page 618, for more information.) Some companies don't back order, and will include a refund check with the order or under separate cover when a product is out of stock, or bill your account with the adjusted total if you used a credit card. If your shipment is short and there's no explanation, first check the catalog from which you ordered to see whether that item is shipped from the manufacturer or shipped separately by the firm. If there's no mention of special shipping conditions or delays in shipment in the catalog, contact the firm immediately.

DELAYED SHIPMENTS

What constitutes a real delay in receiving an order? What should you expect from the company if it has to delay shipping your order? The following section details your basic rights and responsibilities in this event.

The FTC Mail or Telephone Order Rule. The Federal Trade Commission's "Mail or Telephone Order Rule" addresses one of the biggest problems in the mail-order industry: late delivery. Mail-order shoppers should understand the principles of the Rule, know what types of transactions are exempt from its protection, and understand what actions they're obliged to take to ensure protection under the regulations.

Please note: When a state or county has enacted laws similar in purpose to the functions of the FTC Mail or Telephone Order Rule, the law that gives the consumer the most protection takes precedence.

General terms of the Rule: The Rule specifies that a firm, or "seller," must ship goods within 30 days of receipt of a properly completed order, unless the firm asks for more time in its catalog, advertisement, or promotional literature. The operative term here is "ship"—the firm does not have to have delivered the goods within 30 days under the terms of the Rule. And it must have received a properly completed order: Your check or money order must be good, your credit must be good if you're charging the order, and the firm must have all the information necessary to process the order. The 30-day clock begins ticking when the firm gets your check or money order made out in the proper amount, but stops if it is dishonored. If you're paying with a credit card, it begins when the firm receives valid account data—*not* when it charges the card.

If your check or money order is insufficient to cover the order total or is dishonored by the bank, if your credit card payment is refused authorization, or if you neglect to include data necessary to the processing of your order (which could include size or color information, your address, etc.), the 30-day clock will not start until the problems are remedied— the firm receives complete payment, payment is honored by the bank, the credit card purchase is authorized, or you supply the missing data.

Exceptions to the Rule: The 30-day limit applies only when a firm does not ask you to allow more time for shipment. (Most qualifiers request extra time for delivery, which only confuses the issue.) Certain kinds of goods and purchases are not protected by the Rule. These include: seeds and growing plants; C.O.D. orders; purchases made under negative-option plans (such as book and record clubs); and magazine subscriptions and other "serial deliveries," except for the first issue. Genuinely "free" items don't fall under the Rule, but catalogs for which payment or compensation is requested are protected.

Assuming your order is covered under the Rule, the firm from which you're ordering must follow a specific procedure if it is unable to ship your order within 30 days. You must respond under the terms of the Rule if you want to retain all of your rights. Read on.

The Option Notice: If a firm is unable to ship within 30 days of receiving your properly completed order, or by the deadline given in its literature, it must send you an option notice. An option notice written in compliance with the Rule will tell you that there is a delay in shipping the item and may include a revised shipping date. If it does, and that date is up to 30 days later than the original deadline (either 30 days or a date specified by the firm), it should offer you the option of consenting to the delay or canceling the order and receiving a refund. The option notice must also state that lack of response on your part is implied consent to the delay. If you decide to cancel the order, the firm must receive the cancellation before it ships the order.

If the new shipping deadline is over 30 days after the original date, or the firm can't provide a revised shipping date, the option notice must say so. The notice should also state that your order will be automatically canceled unless the firm receives consent to the delay from you within 30 days of the original shipping date, and unless it is able to ship the order within 30 days after the original deadline and has not received an order cancellation from you as of the time of shipping.

The firm is required to send notices by first-class mail and to provide you with a cost-free means of response—a prepaid business-reply envelope or postcard. Accepting collect calls or cancellations over WATS lines is acceptable as long as the operators are trained to take them. If you want to cancel an order, get the response back to the firm as quickly as possible after you receive the option notice. Photocopy the card, form, or letter, and send it "return receipt requested" if you want absolute proof of the date it was received. (If the firm ships your order the day after it received your cancellation, and you can prove it, you have the right to refuse delivery, have the order returned to the firm at its expense, and claim a prompt refund or credit.)

The Renewed Option Notice: When a firm is unable to meet its revised shipping deadline, it must send you a renewed option notice in advance of the revised deadline. Unlike the first notice, second and subsequent notices must state that if you don't agree in writing to a new shipping date or indefinite delay, the order will be canceled. And the consent to a second delay must be received before the first delay period ends, or the order must be canceled, according to the Rule.

If you consent to an indefinite delay, you retain the right to cancel the order at any time before the goods are shipped. And the firm itself may cancel the order if it is unable to ship the goods within the delay period, and must cancel the order under a variety of circumstances.

The Rule and Refunds: Under the terms of the Rule, when you or the firm cancel the order, you're entitled to a prompt refund. If your order was prepaid, the firm must send you a refund check or money order by first-class mail within seven working days after the cancellation. If you paid with a debit card, inform the firm when you cancel or when it notifies you that it's canceling the order that it must treat the payment as if it were cash, a check, or a money order, and reimburse your account within seven working days or send you a refund check. If you used a credit card, the Rule states that refunds must be made within one billing cycle. (We assume that these "refunds" are credits to your account, which will void the charge made for the goods.) The firm is not permitted to substitute credit vouchers for its own goods instead of making a reimbursement.

DELIVERIES FROM FOREIGN FIRMS

The general guidelines outlined in "Accepting Deliveries," page 616, apply to deliveries from foreign firms. Please note that most FTC regulations do not apply to shipments from non-U.S. firms.

The delivery procedure for foreign orders is determined by the shipping method the firm has used. For a complete discussion of carriers, see "Shipments from Foreign Countries," page 611.

You usually pay duty, or Customs charges, when you receive your order. The amount you pay is based on the value, type, and origin of the goods. See "Duty," page 613, for more information.

Most orders from foreign firms are mailable and are delivered by your postal carrier. Before your order reaches you, it is sent through Customs. Orders processed with the least delay are those with goods designated as duty-free because they qualify under certain provisions of Customs laws, or those worth under $50 that are marked "unsolicited gift." Some firms mark orders as gifts to save you money; this is not in keeping with Customs regulations, unless the order originates outside the United States. Please don't ask a firm to send your order as an unsolicited gift, which can create problems.

The clearance procedure on dutiable goods includes entry, inspection, valuation, appraisal, and "liquidation," another term for determination of duty. Provided the necessary permits and entry papers have been filed with U.S. Customs and shipment of the goods violates no regulations, the Customs Department will attach an entry form listing a tariff item number, rate of duty, and the amount of duty owed on the goods to the package. It will be sent to the post office and delivered to you by your postal carrier. He or she will collect the amount of duty and a "Customs Clearance and Delivery Fee," currently $3.25, as "postage due." Some foreign firms are annoyed by this term, since customers assume that the charge is for insufficient postage and complain to the company. Postal authorities have told us that the handling fee is not charged unless the order is assessed duty. But even if your order has dutiable goods, you may not have to pay any Customs charges—a high proportion of small orders are delivered fee-free.

If your parcel is held at the post office and you don't collect it within 30 days, it will be returned to the firm. If you disagree with the duty charge, you can challenge it within 90 days of receiving the order by sending the yellow copy of the mail-entry form to the Customs office named on the form, along with a statement explaining your reasons for contesting the charge.

DELAYED SHIPMENTS FROM FOREIGN FIRMS

You can reasonably expect your goods to arrive within six to eight weeks, provided you sent the order by air, are having it shipped by airmail or air freight, didn't order custom-made goods, and paid the correct amount—and as long as the country concerned is not at war. If you sent the order via surface mail and/or are having the goods shipped that way, are having any custom work done, or the country is in turmoil, don't hold your breath. We've been told that the delay for orders sent by surface mail averages three to six months.

Transactions with foreign firms generally come under the jurisdiction of international law. If your order doesn't arrive, write to the company, including photocopies of your order and proof of payment, and send the letter by registered airmail. Allow at least one month for a response, then try again. Put a stop on your check, or a tracer and a stop on a money order, if you paid with one. If the check or money order has been cashed, go to the post office and fill out an "International Inquiry" form. It will be sent to the postal service in the country concerned, which should investigate the matter. Notify the firm of your actions, and keep copies of all correspondence related to the affair, since you may need them at a later date.

If you paid with a credit card and you have not received your order, follow the querying procedure outlined above. If you don't hear from the company, but find that your credit card has been charged for the order, dispute the charge immediately under the provisions of the Fair Credit Billing Act. You may do this only if you have not received the goods at all and if the bank issuing the credit card is a U.S. bank. For more information, see "The Fair Credit Billing Act," page 631.

For more information on resolving problems with foreign companies, see "Complaints About Foreign Firms," page 632.

RETURNS, GUARANTEES, AND WARRANTIES

Your right to return goods is determined by the policy of the firm, the problem with the order, the conditions under which you make the return, and state and federal laws. See "Return Policies" and "Accepting Deliveries" for general information. Product warranties, whether written or implied, apply to many goods bought by mail. "Guarantees and Warranties," following, provides a comprehensive discussion of all types of warranties.

RETURNS

Return policies are often extensions of a firm's pledge of satisfaction. The policy determines how quickly you must return the product after receipt (if there's a time limit), acceptable causes for return, and what the firm will do to remedy the problem. Some companies will take anything back, but most exclude custom-made goods, personalized items, special orders, intimate apparel, bathing suits, and hats. Some also exempt sale items. Even a no-frills policy usually makes provisions for exchanges when the firm has erred or if the product is defective. It's important to read "Implied Warranties" for information on laws concerning product performance and rights you may have that are not stated in the catalog.

Obtaining Authorization. Before returning a product for any reason, check the inserts that may have been packed with the order, as well as the catalog, for instructions on return procedures. If there are no instructions, contact the firm for authorization to return the item. This is easiest handled by phone; you'll usually receive an "RMA," or authorization number, which you must use on all correspondence concerning that return, and on the package when you send it back. The reverse side of the statement that was enclosed with your order may be printed as a return form; if so, complete it. If it's not, write a letter: State the reason for the return, the item price and order number, date of delivery, and what you'd like done. Depending on the firm's policy, you may request repairs or replacement of the item, an exchange, a refund check, credit to your charge account, or store credit for future purchases from the firm. Keep a photocopy of the letter for your files, or notes of your phone conversation.

Restocking Fees. Some firms impose a charge on returned goods, to offset the labor and incidental costs of returning the item to inventory. Restocking fees, usually 10% to 15% of the price of the item, are most commonly charged by firms selling furniture, appliances, and electronics. Restocking fees are not usually charged when you're returning defective goods, or if the item was shipped incorrectly.

Sending the Item. Follow the mailing procedure outlined in the catalog, order insert, or authorization notice from the firm. When you send the goods back, include the return form or a dated letter with your name and address, the order number, authorization number or name of the person approving the return (if applicable), and a statement of what you want—repair, exchange, refund, or credit. Keep file copies of your letter and invoices.

Pack the item in the original box and padding materials if requested, and insure it for the full value. Allow the firm at least 30 days to process the return or respond before writing or calling again, unless you were promised a more speedy resolution.

Refunds and Credits. If you want your charge account credited for the return, provide the relevant data. Not every firm will issue a refund check or credit your account; some offer replacement or repair of the product, an exchange, or catalog credit only.

Exchanges. If you're exchanging the product for something entirely different, state the catalog code number, size, color, price, unit, etc. of the item you want in the letter you enclose with the return or on the authorization form.

Postage Reimbursement. Some firms send UPS to pick up a return free, or accept returns sent postage-collect, or will reimburse you for the shipping and insurance charges on a return. Lots will not. Businesses are not required by federal law to refund the cost of returning goods, even when the return is a result of the firm's error. State and local laws, however, may make provisions for this; check to see whether they do.

GUARANTEES AND WARRANTIES

Although the terms "guarantee" and "warranty" are virtually synonymous, they're distinguished here for the sake of clarity. In this book, a "guarantee" is the general pledge of satisfaction or service a firm offers on the sales it makes. Guarantees and related matters are discussed in "Return Policies," "Returns," and "Implied Warranties." A "warranty" is used to mean the written policy covering the performance of a particular product. Both guarantees and warranties are free; paid policies (including "extended warranties") are service contracts.

Warranties are regulated by state and federal law. Understanding policy terms will help you shop for the best product/warranty value; knowing your rights may mean the difference between paying for repairs or a replacement and having the firm or manufacturer do it.

The Magnuson-Moss Warranty—Federal Trade Commission Improvement Act. Also known as the Warranty Act, this 1975 law regulates warranties that are in print. Oral "warranties"—the salesperson's assurance of product performance and pledge of satisfaction—are worthless unless they're in writing.

The Warranty Act requires that warranties be written in "simple and readily understood language" that states all terms and conditions. If the product costs more than $15, a copy of the warranty must be available before purchase. In a store, it should be posted on or near the product, or filed in a catalog of warranties kept on the premises with a notice posted concerning its location. Mail-order firms comply with the law by making copies of warranties available upon request.

The Warranty Act requires the warrantor to use the term "full" or "limited" in describing the policy. A single product can have several warranties covering different parts, and each can be labeled separately as "full" or "limited." For example, a TV set may have a full one-year policy on the set and a limited 90-day policy on the picture tube. Generally speaking, the conditions stated here apply to warranties on goods costing over $15.

Full warranties provide for repair or replacement of the product at no cost to you, including the removal and reinstallation of the item, if necessary. The warranty may be limited to a certain length of time, and must state the period of coverage. Full warranties can't be limited to the original purchaser—the warrantor must honor the policy for the full term even if the item has changed hands. Implied warranties (see page 624) may not be limited in duration by the terms of the full warranty, and in some states may last up to four years.

The item should be repaired within a "reasonable" length of time after you've notified the firm of the problem. If, after a "reasonable" number of attempts to repair, the product is still not functioning properly, you may invoke the "lemon provision." This entitles you to a replacement or refund for the product.

Registering your product with the warrantor under a full warranty is voluntary, a fact that must be stated clearly in the terms. You can send the registration card to the firm, but this is at your discretion and not necessary to maintain the protection of the warranty. You certainly have no obligation to provide any firm with the intimate details of your life—income, age, home-ownership status, purchasing and reading habits, dependents, pets, etc.—often solicited with such forms.

Limited warranties provide less coverage than full warranties. Under them, you can be required to remove, transport, and reinstall a product; to pay for labor if repairs are made; and to return the warranty card to the firm in order to validate the policy. The warrantor can also limit the warranty to the original purchaser and give you prorated refunds or credits for the product. (The "lemon provision" doesn't apply to a limited warranty.)

Warrantors may also limit implied warranties (see the following section) to the length of time their policies run, but no less. If they limit the implied-warranty time, they must also state: "Some states do not allow limitations on how long an implied warranty lasts, so the above limitation may not apply to you." The warrantor may not limit the extent of protection you have under implied warranties, however.

Other provisions of the Warranty Act include the following:

1. If you complain within the warranty period, the firm must act to remedy the problem within the terms of the warranty.
2. If a written warranty is provided with the product, the warrantor can't exclude it from protection under implied warranties.
3. A warrantor can exclude or limit consequential damages (see the following section) from coverage under both full and limited policies as long as the warranty states: "Some states do not allow the exclusion or limitation of incidental or consequential damages, so the above limitation or exclusion may not apply to you."
4. All warranties must include information on whom to contact, where to bring or mail the product, and the name, address, or toll-free phone number of the warrantor.
5. All warranties, full and limited, must state: "This warranty gives you specific legal rights, and you may have other rights that vary from state to state."

Implied Warranties. Implied warranties are state laws that offer protection against major hidden defects in products. Every state has these laws, which cover every sale unless the seller states that no warranties or guarantees are offered—that goods are sold "as is." But if a particular product sold by a firm with a no-guarantee policy carries a written warranty, the implied warranty of the state is also valid on that item. The terms of implied warranties differ from state to state, but many have similar sorts of provisions.

The warranty of merchantability is a common implied warranty. It means that the product must function properly for conventional use—a freezer must freeze, a knife must cut, etc. If the product does not function properly and your state has a warranty of merchantability, you're probably entitled to a refund for that item.

The warranty of fitness for a particular purpose covers cases in which the seller cites or recommends special uses for the product. For example, if a seller says that a coat is "all-weather," it should offer protection in rain and snow. If it claims that a glue will "bond any two materials together," the glue should be able to do that. When a salesperson makes these assurances, check the printed product information to verify the recommendation or call the manufacturer. While the salesperson may have a direct incentive—commissions—to inveigle you into buying a product, the manufacturer should be more committed to your satisfaction and return business.

Consequential Damages. Incidental or consequential damages occur when a product malfunction causes damage to or loss of other property. The FTC uses the example of an engine block cracking when the antifreeze is faulty. Less extreme is the food spoilage caused by a refrigerator breakdown or the damage resulting from a leaky waterbed mattress.

Written warranties usually entitle you to consequential damages, but warrantors are allowed to exempt this coverage under both full and limited warranties. If the warrantor excludes consequential damages from coverage, the warranty must state: "Some states do not allow exclusion or limitation of incidental or consequential damages, so the above limitation or exclusion may not apply to you."

Provisions for consequential damages entitle you to compensation for the property damage or loss, as well as repair or replacement of the defective product. In the engine block example, the exemption of damages must be considered as a definite disadvantage when evaluating the product/warranty value.

Evaluating Warranties. Appraise the written warranty as thoroughly as you do the product's other features before you buy. In reading the warranty, bear in mind past experiences with products and warranty service from that manufacturer or seller, experiences with similar products, and your actual needs. Don't rush to buy the first model of a new product if you can wait. Later models are sure to be cheaper and better—just consider VCRs, CD players, and computers.

In evaluating a warranty, ask yourself the following questions:

1. Is the warranty full or limited?
2. Does it cover the whole product, or specific parts?
3. How long is the warranty period?
4. Do you contact the manufacturer, seller, or a service center for repairs?
5. Will you have to remove, deliver, and reinstall the product yourself?
6. Do you have to have repairs done by an authorized service center or representative? If so, how close is the nearest facility?
7. Will the warrantor provide a temporary replacement for use while your product is being serviced?
8. Are consequential damages excluded? If the product turns out to be defective, could the consequential damages result in a significant loss?
9. If reimbursement is offered on a pro-rata basis, is it computed on a time, use, or price schedule?
10. Do you have the choice of a refund or replacement if the item can't be repaired?

Envision a worst-case scenario in which the product breaks down or malfunctions completely. What expenses could be incurred in consequential damages, supplying a substitute product or service, transporting the product to the service center or seller, and repair bills? Will returning the product be troublesome, and living without it while it's being repaired inconvenient? Your answers determine the value the warranty has for you. Consider that quotient along with the price and features of the product when comparison shopping to find your best buy.

Complying with Warranty Terms. Understanding and fulfilling the conditions of a warranty should be simple, but we've outlined a few tips that may make it easier:

1. Read the warranty card as requested.
2. Read the instructions or operations manual before using the product, and follow directions for use.
3. Keep the warranty and dated receipt or proof of payment in a designated place.
4. If the manufacturer offers a rebate on the product that requires sending the proof of payment, photocopy the receipt and keep the copy with the warranty.
5. Abuse, neglect, and mishandling usually void the warranty. Other practices that may invalidate the policy include improper installa-

tion, repair or service by an unauthorized person or agency, use of the product on the wrong voltage, and commercial use. If others will be using the product, be sure they know how to operate it.

6. Perform routine maintenance (cleaning, oiling, dusting, replacement of worn components, etc.) as required by the manual, but don't attempt repairs or maintenance that isn't required or permitted in the warranty or guide.

If you have a question about maintenance or use, contact the manufacturer or service center. If you void the warranty by violating its terms, you'll probably have to absorb the costs of repairs or replacement.

Obtaining Service. If the product breaks down or malfunctions, you'll find that you can expedite resolution if you follow these guidelines:

1. Read the operating manual or instructions. The problem may be covered in a troubleshooting section, or you may find that you expected the product to do something for which it wasn't designed.

2. Contact the warrantor, whose name, address, and/or phone number appear on the warranty, unless the seller offers service under warranty.

3. Call, write, or visit as appropriate. State the nature of the problem, the date it occurred, and whether you want a repair, replacement, refund, and/or consequential damages. Bring a copy of the warranty and proof of payment when you visit, and include copies if you write. (Remember that your rights in respect to the nature and extent of compensation depend upon the terms of the warranty and laws prevailing in your area.)

4. If you leave the product for repairs or have it picked up, get a signed receipt that includes the date on which it should be ready, an estimate of the bill if you have to pay for repairs, and the serial number of the product, if one is given.

5. If you send the product, insure it for the full value. Include a letter describing the problem, the date on which it occurred, and how you'd like it resolved.

6. After a call or visit, the FTC recommends sending a follow-up letter reiterating the conversation. Keep a photocopy, and send it by certified mail to the person or agency with which you spoke.

7. Keep a log of all actions you take in having the warranty honored, including dates on which actions, visits, and calls were made, and keep a record of the expenses you incur in the process.

8. If you've written to the seller or manufacturer concerning the problem and received no response after three to four weeks, write again. Include a photocopy of the first letter, ask for an answer within four weeks, and send the second letter by certified mail

(keep a photocopy). Direct the letter to the head of customer relations or the warranty department, unless you've been dealing with an individual.

9. If you've written to the manufacturer, it may help to contact the seller (or vice versa). A reputable firm doesn't want to merchandise through a seller who won't maintain good customer relations, and a responsible seller knows that marketing shoddy goods is bad for business. Bilateral appeals should be made after you've given the responsible party an opportunity to resolve the problem.

10. If you have repairs done, ask to see the product demonstrated before you accept it, especially if you're paying for repairs. If there are indications that the problem may recur (e.g., it exhibits the same "symptoms" it had before it broke or malfunctioned), tell the service representative—it may be due to something that wasn't noticed during the repair.

11. If you're paying for repairs, ask for a guarantee on parts and/or labor so you won't face another bill if the product breaks down shortly after you begin using it again.

12. If the product keeps malfunctioning after it is repaired and it is under full warranty, you can probably get a replacement or refund under the "lemon provision." Write to the manufacturer or seller, provide a history of the problems and repairs, plus a copy of the warranty, and ask for a replacement or refund. If the warranty is limited, the terms may entitle you to a replacement or refund. Write to the manufacturer or seller with the product history and a copy of the warranty, and ask for a new product or compensation.

13. Explore your rights under your state's implied-warranty and consequential-damages laws. They may offer you protections not given in the product warranty.

14. If you've been injured by a malfunctioning product, contact an attorney.

15. If, after acting in good faith and allowing the manufacturer or seller time to resolve the problem, you are still dissatisfied, contact your local consumer-protection agency for advice.

You may also report problems to other agencies and organizations. For more information, see "Obtaining Help," following.

COMPLAINTS

COMPLAINT PROCEDURES

A formal complaint is justified if you've notified the firm of a problem and asked for resolution, following procedures outlined in the catalog, warranty, or this guide, with unsatisfactory results. Give the firm one last chance to remedy the situation before asking for help from outside agencies. If your problem concerns nondelivery or dissatisfaction with a product and you paid with a credit card, you may be able to withhold payment or ask for a charge-back under the Fair Credit Billing Act. See "The Federal Trade Commission," following, for more information.

The Complaint Letter. State your complaint clearly and concisely with a history of the problem and all the appropriate documentation: photocopies of previous letters, proof of payment, the warranty, repair receipts, etc. Don't send original documents—use photocopies and keep the originals in your file. Make sure your letter includes your name and address, the order or product number or code and descriptive information about the product, and the method of payment you used. Type or print the letter, and please don't be abusive. Tell the firm exactly what you want done. Give a deadline of 30 days for a reply or resolution, and note that if you don't receive a response by that time, you'll report the firm to the U.S. Postal Service, Better Business Bureau, Direct Marketing Association, Federal Trade Commission, or other appropriate agency. (See "Obtaining Help," following, for information.)

If the firm doesn't acknowledge the request or you're not satisfied by the response, take action.

OBTAINING HELP

Several agencies and organizations can help you with different types of problems related to mail order. Some undertake investigations on a case-by-case basis, and others compile files on firms and act when the volume of complaints reaches a certain level.

When you seek help, provide a copy of your final complaint letter to the firm, as well as the documentation described in "The Complaint Letter."

Consumer Action Panels (CAPs). CAPs are third-party dispute resolution programs established by the industries they represent. They investigate consumer complaints, provide service information to consumers, and give their members suggestions on improving service to consumers.

@APX:MACAP helps with problems concerning major appliances. Write to Major Appliance Consumer Action Panel, 20 N. Wacker Dr., Chicago, IL 60606, or call 800–621–0477 for information.

Better Business Bureaus (BBBs). Better Business Bureaus are self-regulatory agencies, funded by businesses and professional firms, that monitor advertising and selling practices, maintain files on firms, help resolve consumer complaints, and disseminate service information to consumers. BBBs also perform the vital service of responding to inquiries about a firm's selling history, although they can't make recommendations. Most BBBs have mediation and arbitration programs, and are empowered to make awards (binding arbitration).

Whether you want to check a firm's record before ordering or file a complaint, you must contact the BBB nearest the company, not the office in your area. You can obtain a directory of BBB offices by sending your request and a SASE to the Council of Better Business Bureaus, Inc., 4200 Wilson Blvd., Suite 800, Arlington, VA 22203. Write to the appropriate office, and ask for a "consumer complaint" or "consumer inquiry" form, depending on your purpose.

Direct Marketing Association (DMA). The DMA is the largest and oldest trade organization of direct marketers and mail-order companies in existence. Over half of its members are non-U.S. firms; this gives it some clout in dealing with problematical foreign orders placed with member firms.

The DMA's Mail Order Action Line (MOAL) helps to resolve nondelivery problems with any direct-marketing firm, not just members. Upon receiving your written complaint, the DMA contacts the firm, attempts to resolve the problem, notifies you that it is involved, and asks you to allow 30 days for the firm to solve or act on the problem. To get help, send a copy of your complaint letter and documentation to Mail Order Action Line, DMA, 1101 17th St. NW, Washington, DC 20036.

Consumers may also use the DMA's "Telephone Preference Service" and "Mail Preference Service" to reduce the number of solicitation calls and/or mailings they receive. The DMA will keep your name on a list for five years; marketers who want to avoid mailing or calling unreceptive consumers can consult the list before launching a sales campaign. Remember: This is a service that's used by marketers, but unless every firm from which you're receiving solicitations consults it, it will not stop all contacts. To reduce mail, request an "MPS" form from Mail Preference Service, Direct Marketing Association, P.O. Box 9008, Farmingdale, NY 11735–9008. To reduce the number of solicitation calls you receive, request a "TPS" form from Telephone Preference Service, Direct Marketing Association, P.O. Box 9014, Farmingdale, NY 11735–9014. If, after a few months, you're still receiving calls and/or mail, try dealing with the marketer directly. And there is nothing wrong with politely saying "goodbye" to a complete stranger who intrudes in your home via the phone line, and hanging up. You have no obligation to have a conversation; moreover, you should be suspect of any person calling from one firm saying they "represent" another, like your phone company or credit-card firm. Request the person's name, phone number, and the name of the firm they work for, and hang up. Then contact the "referring" firm and make a complaint. Unscrupulous companies trying to induce you to switch phone service or otherwise garner your business may misrepresent themselves, and this helps to identify and stop such activity. And even if the referring firm authorized the contact, you can make it clear that you don't want your data shared with third parties.

The Federal Trade Commission (FTC). The FTC is a law-enforcement agency that protects the public against anticompetitive, unfair, and deceptive business practices. While it doesn't act on "individual" complaints, it does use your complaint letters to build files on firms. When the volume or nature of problems indicates an investigation is justified, the FTC will act. Several levels of action are possible, including court injunctions and fines of up to $10,000 for each day the violation is occurring. Report deviations from FTC regulations; your letter may be the one that prompts an investigation.

The Fair Credit Billing Act (FCBA). Passed in 1975 under the FTC's Consumer Credit Protection Act, this act offers mail-order shoppers who use credit cards as payment some real leverage if they have a problem with nondelivery. The Act established a settlement procedure for billing errors that include, among other discrepancies, charges for goods or services not accepted or not delivered as agreed. The procedure works as follows:

1. You must write to the creditor (phoning will not trigger FCBA protection) at the "billing error" address given on the bill.
2. The letter must include your name and account number, the dollar amount of the error, and a statement of why you believe the error exists.
3. The letter must be received by the creditor within 60 days after the first bill with the error was mailed to you. The FTC recommends sending it by certified mail, return receipt requested.
4. The creditor has to acknowledge your letter, in writing, within 30 days of receipt, unless the problem is resolved within that time.
5. You do not have to pay the disputed amount, the related portion of the minimum payment, or the related finance charges while it is being disputed.
6. If an error is found, the creditor must write to you, explaining the correction. The disputed amount must be credited to your account and related finance charges must be removed. If the creditor finds that you owe part of the amount, it must be explained in writing.
7. If the creditor finds that the bill is correct, the reasons must be explained in writing and the amount owed stated. You will be liable for finance charges accrued during the dispute and missed minimum payments.
8. You may continue to dispute at this point, but only if your state's laws give you the right to take action against the seller rather than the creditor. Write to the creditor within 10 days of receiving the justification of the charge and state that you still refuse to pay the

disputed amount. If you continue to challenge, contact your local consumer protection agency, since the creditor can begin collection proceedings against you and the agency may be able to recommend other means of handling the problem that don't jeopardize your credit rating.

Disputes over the quality of goods or services are covered under the FCBA if state law permits you to withhold payment from a seller. This applies to credit-card purchases over $50 that are made in your home state or within 100 miles of your mailing address. (The limits do not apply if the seller is also the card issuer, as is often the case with department stores.) Contact your local consumer protection agency for advice before taking action.

The United States Postal Service (USPS). The USPS takes action on complaints and resolves about 85% of the problems. This may be because, under provisions of the U.S. Code, it can go to court, get a restraining order, and withhold mail delivery to a company. (This is a very serious action and is never undertaken simply at a private citizen's request.) A number of readers have reported that the USPS acts more swiftly, with better results, than do any of the other agencies we've cited here. You can send a copy of your final complaint letter and documentation to the Chief Postal Inspector, U.S. Postal Service, Washington, DC 20260—but readers have told us that writing directly to the Postmaster of the post office nearest the firm is what does the trick.

Bankruptcy Courts. Bankruptcy courts may offer information, if no actual compensation, on errant orders and refunds. If you've written to the company and received no response and its phone has been disconnected, contact the U.S. Bankruptcy Court nearest the firm. Tell the clerk why you're calling, and ask whether the company has filed for reorganization under Chapter 11. If it has, get the case number and information on filing a claim. Chapter 11 protects a business against the claims of its creditors; all you can do is file as one of them, and hope. As a customer, your claim comes after those of the firm's suppliers, utilities, banks, etc. The "take a ticket" approach is no guarantee that you'll get anything back, but if it's your only shot, take the trouble to file.

COMPLAINTS ABOUT FOREIGN FIRMS

For general information on dealing with complaints about foreign firms, see "Delayed Shipments from Foreign Firms," page 620.

The DMA may be able to undertake an investigation on your behalf. See page 630 for more information on the organization and its address.

The Council of Better Business Bureaus has affiliates in Canada, Mexico, Israel, and Venezuela. If the firm is located in any of those countries, write to the Council for the address of the office nearest the company, and contact that office with the complaint. See page 630 for more information and the Council's address.

The foreign trade council representing the firm's country may be able to provide information that could prove helpful. Contact the council and briefly describe your problem. Ask whether the organization can supply the name of a regulatory agency or trade organization in that country that might be of help. The councils have offices in New York City, and directory assistance can provide you with their phone numbers.

The editor of WBMC will try to help resolve problems with firms listed in this book. See "Feedback," following, for more information.

FEEDBACK

Your suggestions, complaints, and comments help to shape each edition of *Buy Wholesale by Mail*. When you write, please use the guidelines that follow.

Firms: If you'd like your company considered for inclusion, have your marketing director send me a copy of your current catalog or literature with prices and background information on your firm. Companies are listed at the discretion of the editor and must meet the established criteria to qualify for inclusion.

Consumers: If you're writing a letter of complaint, please read the sections of "The Complete Guide to Buying by Mail" that may apply to your problem, and try to work it out yourself. If you can't remedy the situation on your own, write to me, and please include:

1. a brief history of the transaction
2. copies (not originals) of all letters and documents related to the problem
3. a list of the dates on which events occurred, if applicable (the date a phone order was placed, goods were received, account charged, etc.)
4. a description of what you want done (goods delivered, warranty honored, return accepted, money refunded or credited, etc.)

Include your name, address, and day phone number in your cover letter. Resolution cannot be assured, but an inquiry will be made.

If you wish to make suggestions for the next edition, send your postcard or letter to:

WBMC 1998
P.O. Box 150522
Brooklyn, NY 11215–0522
or e-mail WBMReader@aol.com

SIZE CHART

CLOTHING SIZES

Women's Garments

USA	6	8	10	12	14	16	18	20
Great Britain	8	10	12	14	16	18	20	22
Europe	36	38	40	42	44	46	48	50

Women's Sweaters

USA	XS	S	M	M	L	L
Great Britain	34	36	38	40	42	44
Europe	40	42	44	46	48	50

Women's Shoes

USA	5	5 $\frac{1}{2}$	6	6 $\frac{1}{2}$	7	7 $\frac{1}{2}$	8	8 $\frac{1}{2}$	9	9 $\frac{1}{2}$	10
Great Britain	3 $\frac{1}{2}$	4	4 $\frac{1}{2}$	5	5 $\frac{1}{2}$	6	6 $\frac{1}{2}$	7	7 $\frac{1}{2}$	8	8 $\frac{1}{2}$
Europe	36		37		38		39		40		41

Men's Suits and Sweaters

	S	S	M	M	L	XL
USA	34	36	38	40	42	44
Great Britain	34	36	38	40	42	44
Europe	44	46	48	50	52	54

Men's Shirts

USA/Great Britain	14	14 $\frac{1}{2}$	15	15 $\frac{1}{2}$	15 $\frac{3}{4}$	16	16 $\frac{1}{2}$	17	17 $\frac{1}{2}$	18
Europe	36	37	38	39	40	41	42	43	44	46

Men's Shoes

USA	7 $\frac{1}{2}$	8	8 $\frac{1}{2}$	9	9 $\frac{1}{2}$	10	10 $\frac{1}{2}$	11	11 $\frac{1}{2}$	12	12 $\frac{1}{2}$
Great Britain	6	6 $\frac{1}{2}$	7	7 $\frac{1}{2}$	8	8 $\frac{1}{2}$	9	9 $\frac{1}{2}$	10	10 $\frac{1}{2}$	11
Europe	39 $\frac{1}{2}$	40	40 $\frac{1}{2}$	41	42	42 $\frac{1}{2}$	43	44	44 $\frac{1}{2}$	45	45 $\frac{1}{2}$

COMPANY INDEX

Racer Wholesale, 83
Rafal Spice Company, 276
RAM Research, 416
Rapidforms, Inc., 490
Rare Earth Hardwoods, 342
Record-Rama Sound Archives, 124
Recycled Software, Inc., 513
Red Hill Corporation, 563
Red Hill Mushrooms, 263
Reliable Corp., 491
Replacements, Ltd., 395
Retired Persons Services, Inc., 442
Robinson's Wallcoverings, 327
Rogers & Rosenthal, Inc., 406
P.L. Rohrer & Bro., Inc., 243
Rubens & Marble Inc., 175
Rudi's Pottery, Silver & China, 407
Ruvel & Company, Inc., 564
RV Direct, 84

S & S Sound City, 35
Safe Specialties, Inc., 492
Sally Beauty Supply, 306
Sally Distributors, Inc., 581
Sam Ash Music Corp., 456
San Francisco Herb Co., 277
Santa Maria Discount Luggage, 433
San-Val Discount, Inc., 70, 85
J. Schachter Corp., 393
John Scheepers, Inc., 244
The Scholar's Bookshelf, 111
Nat Schwartz & Co., Inc., 407
Scope City Inc., 138
Seed Savers Exchange, 223
Senior's Needs, 449
Sew Vac City, 35
Sewin' in Vermont, 36
Sewing Machine Super Store, 37
Seymour's Selected Seeds, 245
Shama Imports, Inc., 328
Shar Products Company, 468
Sharp Bros. Seed Co., 246
Shaw Furniture Galleries, Inc., 361
R.H. Shumway Seedsman, 246
Shuttercraft, 376
Sierra Trading Post, 541
Silk Surplus, 329
The Silver Queen Inc., 408
Simply Diamonds, 422
Skrudland Photo, 139

Smiley's Yarns, 209
Daniel Smith, 61
Albert S. Smyth Co., Inc., 409
Snugglebundle Enterprises, 176
Sobol House of Furnishings, 361
Soccer International, Inc., 542
Solar Cine Products, Inc., 139
Solo Slide Fasteners, Inc., 210
Southland Furniture Galleries, 362
Spices, Etc., 278
Spike Nashbar, 543
Sport Europa, 157
The Sportsman's Guide, Inc., 544
Sportswear Clearinghouse, 158
STA Travel, 587
Staples, Inc., 492
Star Professional Pharmaceuticals,
    314
State Department, 592
State Line Tack, Inc., 14
R.C. Steele Company, 14
Stickers 'N' Stuff, Inc., 582
Storey Communications, Inc., 112,
    367
Strand Book Store, Inc., 113
Stu-Art Supplies, 62
Stuckey Brothers Furniture Co., Inc.,
    362
Stumps, 583
Suburban Sew 'N Sweep, Inc., 38
Sultan's Delight, 263
Sunglasses U.S.A., Inc., 315
Sunrise Stationers, 493
Superintendent of Documents, 114,
    412
Support Plus, 450
Surplus Center, 564
Survival Supply Co., 544
Swords Music Companies, Inc., 469

Tafford Manufacturing, Inc., 159
Tartan Book Sales, 115
Taste Publications International, 588
Taylor's Cutaways and Stuff, 211
Telepro Golf Shop, 545
Tender Heart Treasures, Ltd., 291
Terry's Village, 292
Texas Art Supply, 63
Thai Silks, 212
That Fish Place/That Pet Place, 15

PRODUCT INDEX

Editor's Note: To avoid duplication of information found elsewhere, this index has been designed as a *supplement* to other features of this book, including the organization of the company listings within chapters, the "Find It Fast" section (found right before the first company listing in most chapters), and the "*See Also*" cross-references at the end of each chapter. *See* "Using This Book," page vii, for more information.

car racks, 74, 537
catering supplies, 578, 579
caviar, 256
chandeliers, crystal, 334–336
cheese, 259, 264
cheese-making equipment, 383
chimney-cleaning equipment, 560
Christmas ornaments, 178, 180, 182, 292, 576
church audio equipment, 27
cider jelly and syrup, 266
cleaning tools and supplies, 288, 290, 371
climbing gear, 529
clock parts, 53, 178, 182, 216, 217, 218
closed-circuit TV systems, 35
clothing, auto racing, 83
club equipment, 125
combine parts, 74, 379, 382, 385, 387
computer stations, wheelchair-accessible, 485
concrete-handling equipment, 565
cookware, iron, 380
Corvair parts, 76
cruises, discount, 587–588
cutaways, 208, 211
cutlery, professional, 386

dance studio equipment, 525
dancewear, 148
darts, 538
decoupage supplies, 53
digital satellite systems, 29
dining, discount, 588
disk jockey equipment, 125, 455, 456
doll- and bear-making supplies, 183, 202, 205, 207, 211
dolls, collector, 229
doors, 368, 372, 375
drapery tapes, 195, 205
dry-mounting presses, 55
DVD, 35

embossing powder, 188
evergreens, seedling, 230, 239
exercise equipment, 308, 524

fabric
  crewel, 338

custom-laminated, 322
  extra-wide, 325
fat calipers, 308
feathers, 153, 185
ferret supplies, 6, 10, 11, 13, 17
fish supplies, 6, 10, 13, 14, 15, 16, 18
fitness clothing, 157
fitness equipment, 525, 532
flowers
  dried, 179, 189
  silk, 153
forklifts, 569
fountain pen repairs, 467, 82
framing, picture, 51, 52, 54, 56, 58, 64, 64
fruit crate labels, 45
fruitcake mix, 256

garbage disposals, 34
garden carts, 236, 241, 562
gas engines, 562
gas masks, 545, 564
gift wrap, 102, 299, 520, 578, 579
goat supplies, 10, 11
go-carts and parts, 562
gold-panning equipment, 533
gourd craft supplies, 181
gourds, 247
grasses, 236, 239, 243, 246, 247
"green" cotton baby clothing, 176
greenhouse supplies, 224, 227, 238, 248
ground cover plants, 242, 250
guinea pig supplies, 10, 13, 17
guitars, vintage, 459, 463, 473

hamster supplies, 10, 13, 17
handbags, designer copies, 434
hardwood flooring, 342
hat-making supplies, 153
heat sinks, 551
hemostats, 551
herb plants, 229
hermit crabs, 13
home exchanges, 590
homeopathic remedies, 175
horse supplies, 5, 10, 11, 12, 13, 14, 192
hosiery, 144

ikats, 203
incontinence products, 448, 450
Indian food ingredients, 269
inline skates, 537
ironing equipment, professional, 195, 210

jewelry
    diamond, 418, 422, 424
        custom made, 418
    fashion, 421
jewelry findings, 419, 420

kiting supplies, 525

labels, personalized, 299
lamp parts, 53, 62, 182, 191, 219
lawnmower parts, 560
leather balm, 5, 430
leather-working supplies, 192
light boxes, 52, 55
livestock supplies, 5, 10, 12
llama supplies, 11, 12
luggage repairs, 433

machine shop equipment, 556
magazine subscriptions, 93, 96, 101, 109
mailing and storage tubes, 65
mastectomy clothing and supplies, 152, 155, 445, 547
meats, organic, 257
mechanics' cabinets, 567
Mercedes-Benz auto parts, 81
mess kits, 154
metronomes, 460, 468, 471, 472
mica (wood stove glass), 219
microscopes, 135
Middle Eastern food ingredients, 264
military surplus, 47
models and supplies (car, ship, plane), 186
moisture meters, 567
mortar-and-pestle sets, 270, 278
mosquito netting, 151, 564
movie memorabilia, 42, 44
moving pads, 568
mushrooms, 263
music box parts, 53, 63, 216

nail aprons, 146
nurses' uniforms, 159, 161
nursing bras and supplies, 173
nutritional supplements, 311, 312, 313, 314, 442
nuts, 256, 258, 260, 261, 265

old advertising reproductions, 43
Oriental rugs, antique, 340

pet food, 13
pet supplies, 6, 7, 8, 9, 10, 11, 12, 13, 14, 15
petites, clothing for, 144, 145, 146, 147, 162
pews, 475
phone wiring supplies, 551, 558
phones, antique, 46
photo processing services, 132, 133, 135, 137, 139
photostat equipment, 55
pianos and keyboards, 454, 455, 456, 461, 466, 469
piezo electric elements, 551
pillow inserts, 196
pillow ticking, 151, 208
pillows, leather, 326
piñatas, 581
plant markers, 232
plasma-cutting tools, 558
plumbing fixtures, 370, 371, 373, 374
police scanners, 25
political memorabilia, 47
pond supplies, 10, 13, 15
posters, movie, 42, 44
posters, vintage, 42, 44
potentiometers, 551
potpourri ingredients, 179, 180, 189, 277
poultry supplies, 10
pro-audio equipment, 133, 473
pulpits, 475, 479

quilt batts, 196
quilting supplies, 196, 198, 199, 211

rabbit supplies, 10, 13, 17
radar detectors, 2, 32, 34
radio shows, old, 118
record-care products, 33

recording equipment, 33, 125, 455, 456, 464, 466
reforestation supplies, 552
religious literature, 98
reptile supplies, 10, 13, 17
riding clothing, 14
rugs, sheepskin, 143, 430
RV accessories, 84

safes, 492, 495
salad bowls, wooden, 293
scaffolding, 565, 567
scuba-diving equipment, 524, 537, 539, 540
seat-reweaving supplies, 181, 184, 219
security, personal, 154
seeds, open-pollinated, 228
sewing equipment, commercial, 195, 210
sewing machines, sergers, and accessories, 30, 35, 36, 37, 195, 198, 243
sheep supplies, 10, 11
sheet music, 456, 467, 469, 473
sheeting, 151, 208
shoe repairs by mail, 166
shoes, toe, 148
shower curtains, 287
shutters, 376
silver cloth, 208
silver, estate, 397, 398, 399, 404, 409
ski machines, 525
skylights, 368
snorkeling gear, 529, 537, 539
snowboarding gear, 537
snowmobile parts, 560
snowshoes, 535, 564
soap, 286, 290, 312
soccer gear, 542
souvenirs, 47
sphygmomanometers *see* blood pressure gauges
spinning supplies, 202, 204
stained glass supplies, 191
stair climbers, 308
stair rods, 339
stair templets, 567
stationary bicycles, 308, 532

stencils, 217
stethoscopes, 159, 308, 446
stickers, novelty, 102, 582
"Sun Print" paper, 186
sunglasses, 315, 438, 439, 523, 536
surplus goods, 282, 551, 557, 564, 565
survivalist products, 531, 544
suspenders, 152
swimming pool supplies and accessories, 371, 546
swimwear, 157

table pads, 351, 356, 364
tailoring equipment, 195, 210
tarps, 528, 529, 533
tents, 154, 528, 529, 533, 541, 547
Tex-Mex food ingredients, 273, 276
Thai food ingredients, 269
theater glasses, 135
tires, 78, 85
tools, miniature, 561
toys, educational, 576
tractor parts, 74
trail mix, 256
trailers, 565
transducers, 551
travel
    consolidators, 586
    disabilities, 591
    educational, 590
    medical care and, 592
    standby, 588
    student, 591
travel accessories, 594
travel advisories, State Dept., 592
travel agents, discount, 587
travel guides, 593
travel newsletters, 592
treadmills, 525, 532
treasure-hunting equipment, 187
turntable cartridges and styli, 33
tuxedos, 144

umbrellas, 147
uniforms, 159, 161, 162

vacuum cleaners, floor machines, and supplies, 23, 25, 30, 31, 35, 37, 567

veils, 153
ventilation equipment, 387
video duplicating, 39
volleyball gear, 543

watches, 423, 427
weather balloons, 558
weaving supplies, 202, 204, 214
wedding invitations, 296, 300
welding equipment, 562
Western boots, 167

wheelbarrows, 238, 239, 562
wheels, auto, 78, 85
wicker and rattan furnishings, 350, 351, 364
wildflowers, 241, 246
windows, 368
windsurfing gear, 537
wood-burning furnaces, 560
woodpile covers, 287

zippers, 195, 197, 201, 205, 207, 210